CULINARY
FOUNDATIONS

WAYNE GISSLEN

CULINARY
FOUNDATIONS

PHOTOGRAPHY BY J. GERARD SMITH

WILEY

This book was set in 9/12 Meta by Mauna Eichner and Lee Fukui and printed and bound by RR Donnelley & Sons Company. The cover was printed by RR Donnelley & Sons Company.

This book is printed on acid free paper.

For general information on our other products and services, or technical support, please contact our Customer Care Department within the United States at 800-762-2974, outside the United States at 317-572-3993 or fax 317-572-4002.

Wiley also publishes its books in a variety of electronic formats. Some content that appears in print may not be available in electronic books.

For more information about Wiley products, visit our website at http://www.wiley.com.

Library of Congress Cataloging in Publication Data:

ISBN 978-1-118-67373-7

Printed in the United States of America

10 9 8 7 6 5 4 3 2

This book is dedicated to the many
Chef-Instructors preparing a new generation of culinary professionals.

Contents

Recipe Contents

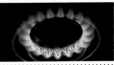

Welcome to Le Cordon Bleu!

In support of the Le Cordon Bleu initiative to ensure a quality culinary education, we have customized a book for you that specifically coincides with our curriculum and the teaching methodology of your chefs.

The contents of this book were selected by the curriculum committee and the academic team to support the educational goals of developing and graduating professional cooks and pastry cooks.

Stated more succinctly, learning the core competencies of cookery and pastry as shown in this textbook will focus and assist you in developing efficient skills needed in the kitchen while meeting your educational objectives.

Le Cordon Bleu College for Culinary Arts fosters a unique multi-cultural and educational environment, encouraging you to learn and grow in the lessons you undertake. It is our privilege to be able to help you overcome your toughest challenges and embrace your creative passion.

Working alongside our dedicated professional chefs, we are delighted to provide an environment that prepares and encourages you with unparalleled facilities and a focus on your ability to strive for your best, to follow your passion, and achieve whatever you set out to do.

All areas of your school and the Le Cordon Bleu program, along with your chef instructors, are expected to support the development of your skills as you progress through the program and build your education.

As you take pride going through the Le Cordon Bleu program, always remember to learn, cook, and engage every day with the passion that bought you here to Le Cordon Bleu.

My best and culinary regards,

Chef Edward G. Leonard, CMC
Vice President Culinary Education
Corporate Chef
Le Cordon Bleu North America

Preface

In preparing *Culinary Foundations*, I've been struck forcefully by two truths: culinary education has advanced greatly and evolved with the times, and, at the same time, the core curriculum has stayed focused on the essentials, the basic cooking techniques that are the foundation of success in the kitchen.

The changes seen through the years have been in many areas: advances in nutritional understanding; changes in diets, with greater emphasis on vegetables, grains, and other healthful ingredients; stronger sanitation and safety standards; increased understanding and appreciation of ingredients, techniques, and recipes from regional and international cuisines, and the adaptation of these ingredients and techniques to our own cooking; greater understanding of food science and its applications in the kitchen; and revolutionary new directions in cooking practices, such as sous vide techniques and molecular gastronomy.

Culinary Foundations has incorporated material reflecting these changes while retaining its focus on the center of a chef's training— the comprehensive understanding of ingredients and basic food preparation procedures, and the development of manual skills to apply this knowledge.

What's Important

Readers of *Culinary Foundations* will find a great deal of material reflecting advances in culinary practices and techniques. Among the most important features are those detailed below.

- Hundreds of photographs are included throughout the book, illustrating in even more detail the essential techniques and procedures of a chef's craft as well as finished dishes, key ingredients, and equipment.

- Hundreds of recipes are included, reflecting the increasing diversity of dishes in North American cuisine.

- International and regional cuisines receive increased attention. These recipes are indicated by a globe (see icon at right) in the text. Sidebars throughout the text give background information on these recipes and the cuisines and cultures they come from.

INTERNATIONAL RECIPES

- Core recipes are those specifically designed to illustrate and reinforce basic cooking techniques, and are indicated by a chef's hat (see icon at right). They are placed where appropriate throughout the book.

CORE RECIPES

- Important information devoted to vegetarianism and cooking for the various types of vegetarian diets is included. Recipes suitable for a vegetarian diet are indicated by the symbol shown here.

VEGETARIAN RECIPES

- Food science is highlighted in Chapter 4. Chefs are making ever more use of scientific principles to cook with greater precision.

- Culinary math is often a difficult subject for students and in Chapter 5, explanations of the calculations needed in the kitchen are included.

- Techniques of sous vide cooking are introduced, with emphasis on safety factors.

- An introduction to the avant-garde techniques of molecular gastronomy is included, with recipes to illustrate significant techniques. Of course it would take volumes to do justice to such a large and expanding subject, but the material here gives students a taste of an important new trend.

- To aid study and comprehension, "Key Points to Review" are included at strategic points in each chapter.

The Recipes

The recipes in this book are planned and organized to reinforce the basic skills being taught. In each case, specific recipes follow a discussion of theories, guidelines, and general procedures applicable to a defined category of foods and/or cooking methods. Students are encouraged, by means of recipe variations, to see how they can apply these procedures to other ingredients, and to see the similarities and differences among preparations.

Attention to the basics has always been the hallmark of this text. Because the purpose of the book is to teach fundamental cooking techniques, it is important to illustrate them—and to allow the student to experience them—with fundamental, straightforward recipes that reveal the connection between general theory and specific application in the most direct way. Many of the recipes included in this book provide updates and alternatives that will achieve these goals.

Certain recipes, usually those that directly follow an explanation of a procedure, are chosen because they are clear and direct applications of a fundamental technique. These core recipes give the student the opportunity to learn the technique by applying it in the most straightforward way, without the distraction of unusual techniques or unfamiliar ingredients. Of the hundreds of recipes in the book, some are designated as core recipes and are indicated by a special icon, as explained previously. Even if students produce no other recipes, practicing these core recipes, or comparable ones the instructor may wish to substitute, will give a basic foundation in food preparation.

While basic preparations illustrating fundamental principles are the core of the recipe collection, the book builds on these primary techniques to include more advanced styles of preparation. More challenging recipes, including many new to this edition, enable students to refine their techniques and to prepare dishes of increasing sophistication.

What makes a dish feel modern is as much a matter of presentation as it is of ingredients or recipe instructions. How an item, along with its garnish and sauce, is plated can make it look rustic or elegant, simple or elaborate, traditional or modern. Photographs accompanying the recipes illustrate a variety of preparations and plating styles. As the photographs show, a simple item such as a sautéed chicken breast can be as stylish as a complicated dish requiring exotic or expensive ingredients.

Readers are urged to study Chapter 5, "Menus, Recipes, and Cost Management," before proceeding with any of the recipes. This will ensure they know how to use the recipes in this book as well as understand the structure and limitations of the many recipes they will use in their careers.

While every culinary program has different requirements, the recipes in this book should be adaptable to any purpose. Most major recipes are written for 24 or 25 portions, a quantity that can be converted easily to higher or lower yields if necessary. Those recipes requiring more costly ingredients, those that are generally made to order, and those that are particularly complex are written for smaller yields, such as 8, 10, 12, or 16 portions. In addition, variations often indicate ingredient substitutions so the recipes will fit different budgetary requirements and different local or regional tastes.

Nutritional Information

Cooks and chefs are increasingly aware of the importance of preparing healthful foods. To support this effort, nutritional analyses are included for each main recipe. These analyses were done using the software program Genesis R&D 8.4.0, which calculates nutrients based on ingredients. It is important to realize that the actual nutrients in a prepared dish will vary depending on many factors, just as the taste, texture, and appearance of the dish will vary with the skill of the cook and the quality of the ingredients. The following factors should also be taken into account when reading the nutritional analyses:

- Where a portion size is indicated in the recipe, the analysis is per portion. Where there is no portion size, as for stock and sauce, the analysis is usually per ounce (28.35 g) or per fluid ounce (29.57 mL).

- The following ingredients are not included in the analyses: ingredients listed "to taste" or "as needed"; ingredients in sachets and bouquets garnis; optional ingredients; garnishes such as parsley sprigs.

- Stocks are adjusted for removal of bones, mirepoix, and other ingredients that are strained out.

- Ingredients in mirepoix are not included, except for a small amount of sodium.

- If a range is given for an ingredient quantity, the smaller number was used for analysis.

- Adjustments are made for recipes in which the food is degreased or the fat is skimmed off. The amount of fat remaining will vary depending on how thoroughly the item is degreased.

- Fat was calculated for pan-fried and deep-fried foods based on a percentage of the total weight. The amount of fat actually absorbed will vary depending on the temperature of the fat, the cooking time, and the surface area of the food.

- For marinated foods, 10 percent of the marinade is included in the analysis, unless the marinade is used to make a sauce, in which case all the marinade is, of course, included.

- The amount of fat used for sautéing was estimated for the analysis.

- The numbers for each nutrient are rounded off according to FDA rounding rules for food labeling.

- The "(% cal.)" information following the fat content in each analysis refers to percentage of calories from fat. It cannot be used to determine percentage of fat in the total diet.

To help you become more aware of the fat content of prepared foods, those dishes especially low in fat are designated by the heart symbol (see icon at right). *Low in fat* means, according to FDA labeling laws, that the food contains 3 grams of fat or less per reference amount (or serving size indicated in the analysis) if the reference amount is greater than 30 grams (about 1 ounce). This is to prevent making foods sound low in fat just by making the portion size smaller. Main-dish items and meals (weighing at least 6 ounces per serving and containing two or more from the four food groups—bread, cereal, rice and pasta; fruits and vegetables; milk, yogurt and cheese; or meat, poultry, fish, dry beans, eggs, and nuts) must contain 3 grams of fat or less per 100 grams and not more than 30 percent of calories from fat.

LOW IN FAT RECIPES

Goals and Organization of This Book

This book has a dual goal: *understanding*—that is, an understanding of cooking theory, of how to cook—and *performing*—that is, mastery of a set of manual skills and the ability to apply them to a wide range of cooking styles and products.

This book focuses on the development of flexible skills, which are essential for success in a cooking career. Modern food service is evolving rapidly. A tremendous variety of establishments is on the scene today, from executive dining rooms to school cafeterias, from simple short-order coffee shops to the most exclusive restaurants or clubs, from kitchens that make extensive use of convenience foods to those that use only fresh produce. The graduate who understands the workings of foods and the interplay of ingredients, cooking methods, cost factors, and other elements can function successfully in any type of food-service operation.

The Role of the Chef-Instructor

No textbook, of course, can substitute for practical kitchen experience. Furthermore, a book cannot replace an experienced chef-instructor who gives practical demonstrations, supervises students' work, answers questions, and gives advice and assistance as needed. Every instructor has unique experience and has developed special techniques and procedures. Many chefs, in fact, disagree on a number of points. Although this book presents methods and recipes that are widely used and accepted, many instructors will prefer procedures that differ from some explained in this text and may wish to supplement the recipes with their own. Throughout the book, the instructor's input is encouraged. Exposure to a variety of recipes and techniques can only enrich the students' education and deepen their experience.

Features

PRONUNCIATION GUIDES AND GLOSSARIES
Much kitchen terminology is taken from French. Phonetic guides are included for difficult words, giving the approximate pronunciation using English sounds. (Exact rendering is impossible in many cases because French and other foreign languages have sounds that don't exist in English.) Because food-service workers must be able to communicate with each other, definitions of terms introduced in the text are summarized in the glossary at the end of the book.

ILLUSTRATIONS
Hundreds of clear, concise, full-color photographs illustrate basic manual techniques *shown from the point of view of the person performing them*. Additional photographs illustrate ingredients and finished dishes. Numerous line drawings also enhance the text, illustrating hundreds of pieces of equipment you'll encounter in the professional kitchen.

FORMAT
This book is designed to be readable and useful. The format emphasizes and highlights key points in bold type, italics, and numbered sequences, so basic information can be located and reviewed at a glance.

REALISTIC PROCEDURES
Although supported by discussions of cooking theory, procedures given here are based on actual practices in the industry. Attention is given not just to quantity production but also to the special problems of cooking to order. Presentation and service of the finished product are considered in detail, as is pre-preparation, or mise en place—so essential to the organization of a working restaurant. At the same time, the major emphasis is on quality, too often neglected in the quest for convenience.

Even a book as large as this one cannot possibly contain all a cook needs to know. Other information is included if it has a direct bearing on kitchen and bakeshop work. More specialized information, such as stewarding and managerial skills, is necessarily omitted. Finally, although much of what we talk about is strongly influenced by the cooking of other nations, the practices discussed are primarily those of North American food service.

CulinarE-Companion™ Recipe Management Software

Recipes are the ultimate test of any culinary student's skills. Reinforcing these skills is the main goal of this upgraded version of **Wiley CulinarE-Companion™**. This easy-to-use software is no longer simply a recipe management resource with a complete database of recipes from *Culinary Foundations*. In addition to the recipes from the book, the software includes a range of useful features to make the recipes easy to adapt, learn from, and manipulate to suit individual needs. These additional features will not only help in your culinary education but also in managing and organizing your own recipes and related assets, such as photos and videos. The registration code included with each copy of *Culinary Foundations*, allows you to download and install this valuable software at no additional cost—and it's yours to keep!

Feature Highlights

- **Enhanced Recipe Management Tools:** In addition to being able to edit, scale, view nutritional information, convert from U.S. to metric measures and vice versa, and print and share recipes, users can add their own recipes:

  1. Directly into the database so you can use features such as scaling and metric conversion, create shopping lists, and get the nutritional analysis.

  2. Attach your existing recipe files (including Word, Excel, and .pdf) so they are easy to find and classify.

- **Skills:** Newly created and efficiently organized, this section contains relevant information organized around key skills for ease of use in reviewing important techniques.

Also included here are:

- **Videos:** To support students in building and enhancing their core skills and techniques, **CulinarE-Companion** features 25 targeted instructional technique videos and step-by-step procedures for essential culinary skills that are key to success in the kitchen.

- **Audio Pronunciations:** In addition to its extensive glossary of key terms and cooking vocabulary, **CulinarE-Companion** has over 1,000 vocabulary terms and recipe names with audio pronunciations to make learning to pronounce these terms a snap.

- **Tools:** Users can easily access the most important charts and conversion formulas at your fingertips, including can sizes and key conversion formulas.

- **My Files:** CulinarE-Companion allows you to easily organzie your recipes, images of your plated dishes, and your videos in one location. You can classify them so they are easy to find for future reference. And you can easily replace and update files as your skills progress.

Proven Features

- Add, edit, modify, and print recipes, portion sizes, and yields, and create shopping lists.

- Search recipes by main ingredient, primary cooking method, and cuisine type.

- Resize recipes in U.S. or metric measures.

- Perform metric conversions instantly.

- Calculate nutritional analyses of recipes in FDA format, and update nutritional analysis if an ingredient is changed.

Acknowledgments

Photographer Jim Smith has been my partner in these texts for nearly 30 years. His hundreds of photographs are an indispensable part of this book and valuable teaching tools. I can never thank him enough. Thanks also to Jeremy Grubard, Michael Vasiliauskas, and Vincent Cento for their work in Jim's studio.

During a long and productive session of planning, photography, and recipe testing for this edition, I was fortunate to have the expert assistance of Chef-Instructors Rick Forpahl, David Eisenreich, and Lynn Wolkerstorfer-Isakson of Hennepin Technical College. These chefs have been valuable collaborators on several editions of my books, and their suggestions and critiques have been significant in shaping each revision project. They have put in many long hours. In addition, their students, Zachary Colburn, Daniel Greer, Joe Howe, Michael Schroers, and Anthony E. Snooks, worked hard to help us complete the photography on schedule. Rick Elsenpeter of Lund's

market was untiring in his responses to innumerable special requests for meats and seafood. My wife, Meg, assisted our kitchen crew and helped with my research for many of the text revisions. I am grateful to one and all for their help. They were a pleasure to work with. In addition, I would like to thank Hennepin Technical College for the use of their kitchens.

Christin Loudon has again contributed her expertise and culinary understanding to provide nutritional analyses, for which I thank her most warmly. I would also like to thank Drew Appleby, whose expertly written test questions form an important part of the support materials for this text.

CulinarE-Companion™, the recipe management software that accompanies this book, is included because of a coordinated team effort. Thank you to Lydia Cheng and Thomas Kulesa for their consultation every step of the way in reviewing, conceptualizing, and coordinating the development of the new recipe management software. Thank you to project editor Michele Traeger for coordinating all of the editorial efforts for this project. I am also grateful to the many beta testers who took time to test **CulinarE-Companion**. Their testing and feedback were instrumental in the development and completion of this exciting new technology. Thanks also to Chef Jean Vendeville of Savannah Technical College for his review and input for the audio pronunciations that are included in CulinarE-Companion. Thank you to Chef William J. Easter of the Iowa Culinary Institute/Des Moines Area Community College for creating the PowerPoints for this book.

Finally, I would like to thank everyone at John Wiley & Sons who worked so hard on this project: Gabrielle Corrado, Michael Olivo, James Metzger, Jenni Lee, Jeff Rucker, Margaret Barrett, Susan Matulewicz, Barbara Russiello, Micheline Frederick, Carole Anson, and Harry Nolan. Thanks to Mauna Eichner and Lee Fukui who have designed and laid out the pages with care and to Madeline Perri who copyedited and coded the manuscript. Thanks to the John Wiley people in Indianapolis who have prepared the files for printing: Kristie Rees, project coordinator; Clint Lahnen, graphics supervisor; Brent Savage, color photos and imaging; Beth Brooks, senior page layout technician; and Cheryl Grubbs, illustrator. Special thanks are due to Julie Kerr, who has worked with me for so long and with such dedication, and to my editor and friend, Mary Cassells.

Reviewers

I would like to acknowledge the faculty and administrators at Le Cordon Bleu schools who have contributed to this book by suggesting revisions and additions and by answering survey questions.

Wiley CulinarE-Companion™ Recipe Management Software

Supporting chefs throughout their careers, *CulinarE-Companion* includes all recipes from *Professional Cooking, Seventh Edition* plus *90 bonus recipes*, *audio pronunciations*, *illustrated procedures*, and *technique videos*. Create shopping lists, resize recipes, perform metric conversions, and analyze nutritional content of ingredients and recipes. Add your own recipes, photos, and videos, and create your own cookbooks.

The software downloads and installs effortlessly on your computer's hard drive. It runs locally from your hard drive—so no need for an Internet connection. Once installed, *CulinarE-Companion* is yours to keep and never expires! At no additional cost, use the registration code and instructions included to install yours today.

The Homepage

◄ View recipes—click on "Professional Cooking" under "Cookbooks."

◄ With improved search functionality, search recipes by recipe name or even part of a name, and search by variation.

◄ View recipes, procedures, and technique videos—organized by kitchen skill: click on "Skills" tab.

◄ Click "Glossary" tab to access definitions from *Professional Cooking's* glossary plus hundreds of additional defined terms and audio pronunciations.

Recipe List

Refine your search by course, cuisine, main ingredient, primary cooking ► method, or dietary considerations.

Add recipes to your shopping list, as well as export and print recipes. ►

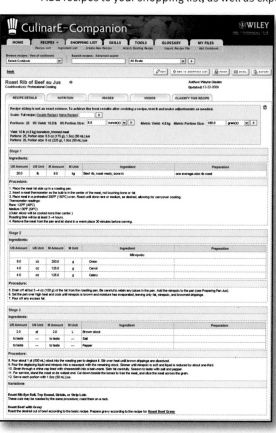

Recipe Screen

◄ Resize recipes, perform metric conversions, show recipe notes, variations, and more!

◄ Referenced procedures and recipes are easily accessible by simply clicking the relevant item.

◄ View photos of plated dishes: click the "Images" tab; view related technique videos: click the "Videos" tab; or add your own photos and videos.

Nutritional Information

View important nutritional information for ingredients and recipes. ►

Nutritional information calculates automatically for all recipes, even ► new recipes you add, by clicking "Create New Recipe."

CULINARY
FOUNDATIONS

Chapter 1

OD SERVICE INDUSTRY SANITATION AND SAFETY TOOLS AND EQUIPMENT BASIC PRINCIPLES OF FOOD
MANAGEMENT NUTRITION MISE EN PLACE STOCKS AND SAUCES SOUPS UN
AND GAME UNDERSTANDING POULTRY AND GAME BIRDS COOKING
Y AND GAME BIRDS UNDERSTANDING FISH AND SHELLFISH COOKING FISH AND SHELLFISH UNDERST

© Dan Lipow.

The Food-Service Industry

This is an exciting time to begin a career in food service. Interest in dining and curiosity about new foods are greater than ever. More new restaurants open every year. Many restaurants are busy every night, and restaurant chains number among the nation's largest corporations. The chef, once considered a domestic servant, is now respected as an artist and skilled craftsperson.

The growth of the food-service industry creates a demand for thousands of skilled people every year. Many people are attracted by a career that is challenging and exciting and, above all, provides the chance to find real satisfaction in doing a job well.

Unfortunately, many people see only the glamorous side of food service and fail to understand that this is a tiny part of the picture. The public does not often see the years of training, the long hours, and the tremendous pressures that lie behind every success.

Before you start your practical studies, covered in later chapters, it is good to know a little about the profession you are entering. This chapter gives you a brief overview of modern food service, including how it got to where it is today and where it is headed.

After reading this chapter, you should be able to

1. Name and describe four major developments that significantly changed the food-service industry in the twentieth century.
2. Identify seven major stations in a classical kitchen.
3. Explain how the size and type of an operation influence the organization of the modern kitchen.
4. Identify and describe three skill levels of food production personnel.
5. Identify eight behavioral characteristics food-service workers should develop and maintain to achieve the highest standards of professionalism.

A History of Modern Food Service

The value of history is that it helps us understand the present and the future. In food service, knowledge of our professional heritage helps us see why we do things as we do, how our cooking techniques have been developed and refined, and how we can continue to develop and innovate in the years ahead.

An important lesson of history is that the way we cook now is the result of the work done by countless chefs over hundreds of years. Cooking is as much science as it is art. Cooking techniques are not based on arbitrary rules some chefs made up long ago. Rather, they are based on an understanding of how different foods react when heated in various ways, when combined in various proportions, and so on. The chefs who have come before us have already done much of this work so we don't have to.

This doesn't mean there is no room for innovation and experimentation or that we should never challenge old ideas. But it does mean a lot of knowledge has been collected over the years, and we would be smart to take advantage of what has already been learned. Furthermore, how can we challenge old ideas unless we know what those old ideas are? Knowledge is the best starting point for innovation.

The Origins of Classical and Modern Cuisine

Quantity cookery has existed for thousands of years, as long as there have been large groups of people to feed, such as armies. But modern food service is said to have begun shortly after the middle of the eighteenth century. At this time, food production in France was controlled by guilds. Caterers, pastry makers, roasters, and pork butchers held licenses to prepare specific items. An innkeeper, in order to serve a meal to guests, had to buy the various menu items from those operations licensed to provide them. Guests had little or no choice and simply ate what was available for that meal.

In 1765, a Parisian named Boulanger began advertising on his shop sign that he served soups, which he called *restaurants* or *restoratives*. (Literally, the word means "fortifying.") According to the story, one of the dishes he served was sheep's feet in a cream sauce. The guild of stew makers challenged him in court, but Boulanger won by claiming he didn't stew the feet *in* the sauce but served them *with* the sauce. In challenging the rules of the guilds, Boulanger unwittingly changed the course of food-service history.

The new developments in food service received a great stimulus as a result of the French Revolution, beginning in 1789. Before this time, the great chefs were employed in the houses of the French nobility. With the revolution and the end of the monarchy, many chefs, suddenly out of work, opened restaurants in and around Paris to support themselves. Furthermore, the revolutionary government abolished the guilds. Restaurants and inns could serve dinners reflecting the talent and creativity of their own chefs rather than being forced to rely on licensed caterers to supply their food. At the start of the French Revolution, there were about 50 restaurants in Paris. Ten years later, there were about 500.

Another important invention that changed the organization of kitchens in the eighteenth century was the stove, or *potager*, which gave cooks a more practical and controllable heat source than an open fire. Soon commercial kitchens became divided into three departments: the rotisserie, under the control of the meat chef, or *rôtisseur*; the oven, under the control of the pastry chef, or *pâtissier*; and the stove, run by the cook, or *cuisinier*. The meat chef and pastry chef reported to the cuisinier, who was also known as *chef de cuisine*, which means "head of the kitchen."

Carême

All the changes that took place in the world of cooking during the 1700s led to, for the first time, a difference between home cooking and professional cooking. One way we can try to understand this difference is to look at the work of the greatest chef of the period following the French Revolution, *Marie-Antoine Carême* (1784–1833). As a young man, Carême learned all the branches of cooking quickly, and he dedicated his career to refining and organizing culinary techniques. His many books contain the first systematic account of cooking principles, recipes, and menu making.

At a time when the interesting advances in cooking were happening in restaurants, Carême worked as a chef to wealthy patrons, kings, and heads of state. He was perhaps the first real celebrity chef, and he became famous as the creator of elaborate, elegant display pieces and pastries, the ancestors of our modern wedding cakes, sugar sculptures, and ice and tallow carvings. But it was Carême's practical and theoretical work as an author and an inventor of recipes that was responsible, to a large extent, for bringing cooking out of the Middle Ages and into the modern period.

Carême emphasized procedure and order. His goal was to create more lightness and simplicity. The complex cuisine of the aristocracy—called *Grande Cuisine*—was still not much different from that of the Middle Ages and was anything but simple and light. Carême's efforts were a great step toward modern simplicity. The methods explained in his books were complex, but his aim was pure results. He added seasonings and other ingredients not so much to add new flavors but to highlight the flavors of the main ingredients. His sauces were designed to enhance, not cover up, the food being sauced. Carême was a thoughtful chef, and, whenever he changed a classic recipe, he was careful to explain his reasons for doing so.

Beginning with Carême, a style of cooking developed that can truly be called international, because the same principles are still used by professional cooks around the world. Older styles of cooking, as well as much of today's home cooking, are based on tradition. In other words, a cook makes a dish a certain way because that is how it always has been done. On the other hand, in Carême's *Grande Cuisine,* and in professional cooking ever since, a cook makes a dish a certain way because the principles and methods of cooking show it is the best way to get the desired results. For example, for hundreds of years, cooks boiled meats before roasting them on a rotisserie in front of the fire. But when chefs began thinking and experimenting rather than just accepting the tradition of boiling meat before roasting, they realized either braising the meat or roasting it from the raw state were better options.

Marie-Antoine Carême
L'Art de la Cuisine Française au Dix-Neuvième Siècle.
Paris: L'auteur, 1833–1844. Courtesy of the Rare
Manuscript Collections, Cornell University Library.

Escoffier

Georges-Auguste Escoffier (1847–1935), the greatest chef of his time, is still revered by chefs and gourmets as the father of twentieth-century cookery. His two main contributions were (1) the simplification of classical cuisine and the classical menu, and (2) the reorganization of the kitchen.

Escoffier rejected what he called the "general confusion" of the old menus, in which sheer quantity seemed to be the most important factor. Instead, he called for order and diversity and emphasized the careful selection of one or two dishes per course, dishes that followed one another harmoniously and delighted the taste with their delicacy and simplicity.

Escoffier's books and recipes are still important reference works for professional chefs. The basic cooking methods and preparations we study today are based on Escoffier's work. His book *Le Guide Culinaire*, which is still widely used, arranges recipes in a simple system based on main ingredient and cooking method, greatly simplifying the more complex system handed down from Carême. Learning classical cooking, according to Escoffier, begins with learning a relatively few basic procedures and understanding basic ingredients.

Escoffier's second major achievement, the reorganization of the kitchen, resulted in a streamlined workplace better suited to turning out the simplified dishes and menus he instituted. The system of organization he established is still in use, especially in large hotels and full-service restaurants, as we discuss later in this chapter.

Georges-Auguste Escoffier
Courtesy of Adjointe à la Conservation du Musée
Escoffier de l'Art Culinaire.

Modern Technology

Today's kitchens look much different from those of Escoffier's day, even though our basic cooking principles are the same. Also, the dishes we eat have gradually changed due to the innovations and creativity of modern chefs. The process of simplification and refinement, to which Carême and Escoffier made monumental contributions, is ongoing, adapting classical cooking to modern conditions and tastes.

Before we discuss the changes in cooking styles that took place in the twentieth century, let's look at some of the developments in technology that affected cooking.

DEVELOPMENT OF NEW EQUIPMENT

We take for granted such basic equipment as gas and electric ranges and ovens and electric refrigerators. But even these essential tools did not exist until fairly recently. The easily controlled heat of modern cooking equipment, as well as motorized food cutters, mixers, and other processing equipment, has greatly simplified food production.

Research and technology continue to produce sophisticated tools for the kitchen. Some of these products, such as tilting skillets and steam-jacketed kettles, can do many jobs and are popular in many kitchens. Others can perform specialized tasks rapidly and efficiently, but their usefulness depends on volume because they are designed to do only a few jobs.

Modern equipment has enabled many food-service operations to change their production methods. With sophisticated cooling, freezing, and heating equipment, it is possible to prepare some foods further in advance and in larger quantities. Some large multiunit operations prepare food for all their units in a central commissary. The food is prepared in quantity, packaged, chilled or frozen, and then heated or cooked to order in the individual units.

DEVELOPMENT AND AVAILABILITY OF NEW FOOD PRODUCTS

Modern refrigeration and rapid transportation caused revolutionary changes in eating habits. For the first time, fresh foods of all kinds—meats, fish, vegetables, and fruits—became available throughout the year. Exotic delicacies can now be shipped from anywhere in the world and arrive fresh and in peak condition.

The development of preservation techniques—not just refrigeration but also freezing, canning, freeze-drying, vacuum-packing, and irradiation—increased the availability of most foods and made affordable some that were once rare and expensive.

Techniques of food preservation have had another effect. It is now possible to do some or most of the preparation and processing of foods before shipping rather than in the food-service operation itself. Thus, convenience foods have come into being. Convenience foods continue to account for an increasing share of the total food market.

Some developments in food science and agriculture are controversial. Irradiation, mentioned above, caused much controversy when it was introduced because it exposes foods to radioactivity to rid them of organisms that cause spoilage and disease. Scientists say, however, that no traces of radioactivity remain in the foods, and the procedure is now used more widely.

A more controversial technique is genetic engineering, which involves artificially changing the gene structure of a food to give it some desirable trait, such as resistance to disease, drought, or insect damage.

FOOD SAFETY AND NUTRITIONAL AWARENESS

The development of the sciences of microbiology and nutrition had a great impact on food service. One hundred years ago, there was little understanding of the causes of food poisoning and food spoilage. Food-handling practices have come a long way since Escoffier's day.

Also, little knowledge of nutritional principles was available until fairly recently. Today, nutrition is an important part of a cook's training. Customers are also more knowledgeable and therefore more likely to demand healthful, well-balanced menus. Unfortunately, nutrition science is constantly shifting. Diets considered healthful one year become eating patterns to be avoided a few years later. Fad diets come and go, and chefs often struggle to keep their menus current. It is more important than ever for cooks to keep up to date with the latest nutritional understanding.

Complicating the work of food-service professionals is a growing awareness of food allergies and intolerances. Not only are chefs called upon to provide nutritious, low-fat, low-calorie meals, they must also adapt to the needs of customers who must eliminate certain foods from their diets, such as gluten, soy, dairy, or eggs.

TWO IMPORTANT COOKBOOKS

In the Middle Ages, cooking consisted mostly of roasting meats on spits in front of a fire and suspending pots from hooks over the fire. Ovens, which were used in ancient Rome, had disappeared, so there was no baking. Roasted meats and poultry were usually boiled before being placed on the spit, and most foods were heavily spiced. It wasn't until the thirteenth century that ovens were used again and that stews and sauces started to appear on the dining table.

Perhaps the first important cookbook to appear at the end of the Middle Ages was *Le Viandier* ("The Cook"), by Guillaume Tirel, usually known as Taillevent, born about 1310.

Taillevent invented many dishes, especially sauces and soups. He refined old recipes to depend less on heavy use of spices and more on the flavors of the foods themselves. He wrote his book before the invention of the printing press, and handwritten copies of it remained in use for more than a century, until 1490, when it became perhaps the first cookbook ever printed.

By the seventeenth century, cooking practices still had not advanced much beyond Taillevent's day. Perhaps the next most important cookbook after Taillevent's was *Le Cuisinier François* ("The French Chef"), by François-Pierre de La Varenne (1615–1678). This book, published in 1651, was a summary of the cooking practices in households of the aristocracy. It was one of the first books to present recipes and cooking techniques in an orderly fashion rather than as an unsystematic collection. *Le Cuisinier François* was one of the main reference works for cooks for more than 150 years.

These two chefs are memorialized in the names of two important culinary institutions. Taillevent is the name of a Paris restaurant that has long been one of the finest in France, and La Varenne is the name of a distinguished cooking school.

Cooking in the Twentieth and Twenty-first Centuries

All these developments have helped change cooking styles, menus, and eating habits. The evolution of cuisine that has been going on for hundreds of years continues. Changes occur not only because of technological developments, such as those just described, but also because of our reactions to culinary traditions.

Two opposing forces can be seen at work throughout the history of cooking. One is the urge to simplify, to eliminate complexity and ornamentation, and instead to emphasize the plain, natural tastes of basic, fresh ingredients. The other is the urge to invent, to highlight the creativity of the chef, with an accent on fancier, more complicated presentations and procedures. Both these forces are valid and healthy; they continually refresh and renew the art of cooking.

A generation after Escoffier, the most influential chef in the middle of the twentieth century was Fernand Point (1897–1955). Working quietly and steadily in his restaurant, La Pyramide, in Vienne, France, Point simplified and lightened classical cuisine. He was a perfectionist who sometimes worked on a dish for years before he felt it was good enough to put on his menu. "I am not hard to please," he said. "I'm satisfied with the very best." Point insisted every meal should be "a little marvel."

Point's influence extended well beyond his own life. Many of his apprentices, including Paul Bocuse, Jean and Pierre Troisgros, and Alain Chapel, later became some of the greatest stars of modern cooking. They, along with other chefs in their generation, became best known in the 1960s and early 1970s for a style of cooking called *nouvelle cuisine*. Reacting to what they saw as a heavy, stodgy, overly complicated classical cuisine, these chefs took Point's lighter approach even further. They rejected many traditional principles, such as the use of flour to thicken sauces, and instead urged simpler, more natural flavors and preparations, with lighter sauces and seasonings and shorter cooking times. In traditional classical cuisine, many dishes were plated in the dining room by waiters. Nouvelle cuisine, however, placed a great deal of emphasis on artful plating presentations done by the chef in the kitchen.

Very quickly, however, this "simpler" style became extravagant and complicated, famous for strange combinations of foods and fussy, ornate arrangements and designs. By the 1980s, nouvelle cuisine was the subject of jokes. Still, the best achievements of nouvelle cuisine have taken a permanent place in the classical tradition. Meanwhile, many of its excesses have been forgotten. It is probably fair to say that most of the best new ideas and the longest-lasting accomplishments are those of classically trained chefs with a solid grounding in the basics.

NEW EMPHASIS ON INGREDIENTS

Advances in agriculture and food preservation have had disadvantages as well as advantages. Everyone is familiar with hard, tasteless fruits and vegetables developed to ship well and last long, without regard for eating quality. Many people, including chefs, began to question not only the flavor but also the health value and the environmental effects of genetically engineered foods, of produce raised with chemical pesticides and fertilizers, and of animals raised with antibiotics and other drugs and hormones.

A prominent organization dedicated to improving food quality is Slow Food, begun in Italy in 1986 in reaction to the spread of fast-food restaurants. Slow Food has since become a global movement, with chapters in cities around the world. It emphasizes fostering locally grown food, using organic and sustainable farming practices, preserving heirloom varieties of plants and animals, and educating consumers about the food they eat.

A landmark event in the history of modern North American cooking was the opening of Alice Waters's restaurant, Chez Panisse, in Berkeley, California, in 1971. Waters's philosophy is that good food depends on good ingredients, so she set about finding dependable sources of the best-quality vegetables, fruits, and meats, and preparing them in the simplest ways. Over the next decades, many chefs and restaurateurs followed her lead, seeking out the best seasonal, locally grown, organically raised food products. A few years after Chez Panisse opened, Larry Forgione picked up the banner of local ingredients and local cuisine

SLOW FOOD TODAY

As with any movement, the growth of Slow Food has not been without controversy. For more than 20 years after its founding, Slow Food had little impact in North America, finding greater popularity in Europe. As recently as 2008, the organization had only 16,000 members in the United States out of more than 100,000 in all.

The movement has been criticized for elitism and snobbishness, for focusing primarily on pleasure, and for being against technology and globalization. Detractors say opposition to global food trade and rejection of industrial agricultural practices are unrealistic in today's world.

In recent years, however, Slow Food has expanded its focus and has addressed issues of race, poverty, and hunger as well as its more traditional concerns—the disappearance of local food traditions and people's dwindling interest in the food they eat, where it comes from, and how it tastes. A surge of interest in Slow Food has come at the same time as growing concerns about the environment and climate change. Members encourage sustainable, ecologically sound agriculture and stewardship of the land as part of their efforts to educate people about their food and their eating habits.

in his New York City restaurant, An American Place. Other chefs quickly followed suit, and soon chefs across the continent made names for themselves and their restaurants at least in part by emphasizing good-quality local ingredients. Half a century ago, nearly all the most respected chefs working in the United States and Canada were European-born. Today, the movement begun by the pioneering quality-oriented chefs of the 1970s and 1980s has fostered a great number of creative North American–born chefs who are among the most respected in the world.

The public has benefited greatly from these efforts. Today, in supermarkets as well as in restaurants, a much greater variety of high-quality foods is available than there was 40 or 50 years ago. Many chefs have modified their cooking styles to highlight the natural flavors and textures of their ingredients, and their menus are often simpler now for this reason.

INTERNATIONAL INFLUENCES

After the middle of the twentieth century, as travel became easier and as new waves of immigrants arrived in Europe and North America from around the world, awareness of and taste for regional dishes grew. Chefs became more knowledgeable not only about the traditional cuisines of other parts of Europe but about those of Asia, Latin America, and elsewhere. Many of the most creative chefs have been inspired by these cuisines and use some of their techniques and ingredients. For example, many North American and French chefs, looking for ways to make their cooking lighter and more elegant, have found ideas in the cuisine of Japan. In the southwestern United States, a number of chefs have transformed Mexican influences into an elegant and original cooking style. Throughout North America, traditional dishes and regional specialties combine the cooking traditions of immigrant settlers and the indigenous ingredients of a bountiful land. For many years, critics often argued that menus in most North American restaurants offered the same monotonous, mediocre food. In recent decades, however, American and Canadian cooks have rediscovered traditional North American dishes.

The use of ingredients and techniques from more than one regional, or international, cuisine in a single dish is known as *fusion cuisine*. Early attempts to prepare fusion cuisine often produced poor results because the dishes were not true to any one culture and were too mixed up. This was especially true in the 1980s, when the idea of fusion cuisine was new. Cooks often combined ingredients and techniques without a good feeling for how they would work together. The result was sometimes a jumbled mess. But chefs who have taken the time to study in depth the cuisines and cultures they borrow from have brought new excitement to cooking and to restaurant menus.

Today chefs make good use of all the ingredients and techniques available to them. It is almost second nature to give extra depth to the braising liquid for a beef pot roast by adding Mexican ancho chiles, for example, or to include Thai basil and lemongrass in a seafood salad. In the recipe sections of this book, classic dishes from many regions of the world are included among more familiar recipes from home. To help you understand these recipes and the cuisines they come from, background information accompanies many of them. The international recipes are identified in the Recipe Contents.

CATERINA DE MEDICI

The Medicis were a powerful Italian family that ruled Florence from the fourteenth to the sixteenth century and provided, in addition to the rulers of Florence, three popes and two queens of France.

Until recently, the accepted and often-told story is that when Caterina de Medici went to France in 1533 to marry the future King Henry II, she brought with her a staff of cooks as part of her household. This introduction of Italian cooking practices into France supposedly changed and modernized the cooking not only of France but of all of Western Europe. According to this story, Caterina and her Italian cooks should be credited with fostering modern cuisine.

When cookbooks and other culinary writings of the period are examined, however, it appears that French cooking didn't begin to modernize until at least a century later. During the hundred years after Caterina's arrival in France, no new, important cookbooks were written. There is no sign of a revolution in cooking. In fact, banquet menus that survive from the period are not much different from menus of the Middle Ages.

Banquets during the Middle Ages were like huge sit-down buffets. For each course, the table was loaded with large quantities of meats, poultry, and fish dishes, usually heavily spiced, and an assortment of side dishes and sweets. Diners generally ate only what they could reach. The course was then removed and another course, also meats and side dishes, was loaded onto the table. Again, each person ate only a fraction of the dishes present, depending on what was within reach.

The modern idea of a menu in which everyone at the table eats the same dishes in the same order did not appear until the 1700s.

So it is not historically accurate to give the Italian princess Caterina credit for modernizing French cuisine. On the other hand, it is fair to say she and her offspring brought more refined manners and elegance to European dining rooms. Italian innovations included the use of the fork as well as greater cleanliness in general. An additional Italian contribution was the invention of sophisticated pastries and desserts.

NEW TECHNOLOGIES

As described on page 4, new technologies, from transportation to food processing, had a profound effect on cooking in the twentieth century. Such changes continue today, with scientific developments that are only beginning to have an effect on how cooks think about food and menus.

One of these technologies is the practice of cooking *sous vide* (soo veed, French for "under vacuum"). Sous vide began simply as a method for packaging and storing foods in vacuum-sealed plastic bags. Modern chefs, however, are exploring ways to use this technology to control cooking temperatures and times with extreme precision. As a result, familiar foods have emerged with new textures and flavors. (Sous vide cooking is discussed further in Chapter 4.)

Another approach to cooking precision was pioneered by the Spanish chef Ferran Adrià in his acclaimed restaurant, El Bulli. Adrià explores new possibilities in gels, foams, powders, infusions, extracts, and other unexpected ways of presenting flavors, textures, and aromas. This approach to cooking is called *molecular gastronomy*, a name coined by the French chemist Hervé This, who has done much of the research in the field. Molecular gastronomy has been taken up by Heston Blumenthal in England, Wylie Dufresne, Grant Achatz, and Homaro Cantu in North America, and other chefs who continue to experiment and to explore what science and technology can contribute to food and food presentation. Many of the techniques make use of unfamiliar ingredients, such as natural gums, and put familiar ingredients, such as gelatin and pectin, to unfamiliar uses. Although this approach to cooking may be best known for its unusual ingredients and techniques, its finest chefs are focused on the food, treating the techniques primarily as new tools in the chef's repertoire.

Cooking and cooking styles continue to change. Men and women are needed who can adapt to these changes and respond to new challenges. Although automation and convenience foods will no doubt grow in importance, imaginative chefs who can create new dishes and develop new techniques and styles will always be needed, as will skilled cooks who can apply both old and new techniques to produce high-quality foods in all kinds of facilities, from restaurants and hotels to schools and hospitals.

> ### KEY POINTS TO REVIEW
>
> - How have the following developments changed the food-service industry: development of new equipment; availability of new food products; greater understanding of food safety and nutrition?
>
> - How have international cuisines influenced and changed cooking in North America?

The Organization of Modern Kitchens

The Basis of Kitchen Organization

The purpose of kitchen organization is to assign or allocate tasks so they can be done efficiently and properly and so all workers know what their responsibilities are.

The way a kitchen is organized depends on several factors.

1. **The menu.**
   The kinds of dishes to be produced obviously determine the jobs that must be done. The menu is, in fact, the basis of the entire operation. Because of its importance, we devote a whole chapter to a study of the menu (Chapter 5).

2. **The type of establishment.**
   The major types of food-service establishments are as follows:

   - Hotels

   - Institutional kitchens

        Schools

        Hospitals, nursing homes, and other health care institutions

        Employee lunchrooms and executive dining rooms

        Airline catering

        Military food service

        Correctional institutions

   - Private clubs

   - Catering and banquet services

   - Fast-food restaurants

- Carry-out or take-out food facilities, including supermarkets
- Full-service restaurants

3. The size of the operation (the number of customers and the volume of food served).

4. The physical facilities, including the equipment in use.

The Classical Brigade

As you learned earlier in this chapter, one of Escoffier's important achievements was the reorganization of the kitchen. This reorganization divided the kitchen into departments, or stations, based on the kinds of foods produced. A station chef was placed in charge of each department. In a small operation, the station chef might be the only worker in the department. But in a large kitchen, each station chef might have several assistants.

This system, with many variations, is still in use, especially in large hotels with traditional kinds of food service. The major positions are as follows:

1. The *chef* is the person in charge of the kitchen. In large establishments, this person has the title of *executive chef*. The executive chef is a manager who is responsible for all aspects of food production, including menu planning, purchasing, costing, planning work schedules, hiring, and training.

2. If a food-service operation is large, with many departments (for example, a formal dining room, a casual dining room, and a catering department), or if it has several units in different locations, each kitchen may have a *chef de cuisine*. The chef de cuisine reports to the executive chef.

3. The *sous chef* (soo shef) is directly in charge of production and works as the assistant to the executive chef or chef de cuisine. (The word *sous* is French for "under.") Because the executive chef's responsibilities may require a great deal of time in the office, the sous chef takes command of the actual production and the minute-by-minute supervision of the staff.

4. The *station chefs*, or *chefs de partie*, are in charge of particular areas of production. The following are the most important station chefs.

- The *sauce chef*, or *saucier* (so-see-*ay*), prepares sauces, stews, and hot hors d'oeuvres, and sautés foods to order. This is usually the highest position of all the stations.

- The *fish cook*, or *poissonier* (pwah-so-*nyay*), prepares fish dishes. In some kitchens, this station is handled by the saucier.

- The *vegetable cook*, or *entremetier* (awn-truh-met-*yay*), prepares vegetables, soups, starches, and eggs. Large kitchens may divide these duties among the vegetable cook, the fry cook, and the soup cook.

- The *roast cook*, or *rôtisseur* (ro-tee-*sur*), prepares roasted and braised meats and their gravies and broils meats and other items to order. A large kitchen may have a separate *broiler cook*, or *grillardin* (gree-ar-*dan*), to handle the broiled items. The broiler cook may also prepare deep-fried meats and fish.

- The *pantry chef*, or *garde manger* (gard mawn-*zhay*), is responsible for cold foods, including salads and dressings, pâtés, cold hors d'oeuvres, and buffet items.

- The *pastry chef*, or *pâtissier* (pa-tees-*syay*), prepares pastries and desserts.

- The *relief cook, swing cook,* or *tournant* (toor-*nawn*), replaces other station heads.

- The *expediter*, or *aboyeur* (ah-bwa-yer), accepts orders from waiters and passes them on to the cooks on the line. The expediter also calls for orders to be finished and plated at the proper time and inspects each plate before passing it to the dining room staff. In many restaurants, this position is taken by the head chef or the sous chef.

5. *Cooks* and *assistants* in each station or department help with the duties assigned to them. For example, the assistant vegetable cook may wash, peel, and trim vegetables. With experience, assistants may be promoted to station cooks and then to station chefs.

Modern Kitchen Organization

As you can see, only a large establishment needs a staff like the classical brigade just described. In fact, some large hotels have even larger staffs, with other positions such as separate day and night sous chefs, assistant chef, banquet chef, butcher, baker, and so on.

Most modern operations, on the other hand, are smaller than this. The size of the classical brigade may be reduced simply by combining two or more positions where the workload allows it. For example, the *second cook* may combine the duties of the sauce cook, fish cook, soup cook, and vegetable cook.

A typical medium-size operation may employ a chef, a second cook, a broiler cook, a pantry cook, and a few cooks' helpers.

A *working chef* is in charge of operations not large enough to have an executive chef. In addition to being in charge of the kitchen, the working chef also handles one of the production stations. For example, he or she may handle the sauté station, plate foods during service, and help on other stations when needed.

Small kitchens may have only a chef, one or two cooks, and perhaps one or two assistants to handle simple jobs such as washing and peeling vegetables. Cooks who prepare or finish hot à la carte items during service in a restaurant may be known as *line cooks*. Line cooks are said to be on the hot line, or simply on the line.

In many small operations, the *short-order cook* is the backbone of the kitchen during service time. This cook may handle the broiler, deep fryer, griddle, sandwich production, and even some sautéed items. In other words, the short-order cook's responsibility is the preparation of foods that are quickly prepared to order.

One special type of short-order cook is the *breakfast cook*. This worker is skilled at quickly and efficiently turning out egg dishes and other breakfast items to order.

By contrast, establishments such as school cafeterias may do no cooking to order at all. Stations and assignments are based on the requirements of quantity preparation rather than cooking to order.

Skill Levels

The preceding discussion is necessarily general because there are so many kinds of kitchen organizations. Titles vary also. The responsibilities of the worker called the *second cook*, for example, are not necessarily the same in every establishment. Escoffier's standardized system has evolved in many directions.

One title that is often misunderstood and much abused is *chef*. The general public tends to refer to anyone with a white hat as a chef, and people who like to cook for guests in their homes refer to themselves as amateur chefs.

Strictly speaking, the term *chef* is reserved for one who is *in charge of a kitchen* or a part of a kitchen. The word *chef* is French for "chief" or "head." Studying this book will not make you a chef. The title must be earned by experience not only in preparing food but also in managing a staff and in planning production. New cooks who want to advance in their careers know they must always use the word *chef* with respect.

Skills required of food production personnel vary not only with the job level but also with the establishment and the kind of food prepared. The director of a hospital kitchen and the head chef in a luxury restaurant need different skills. The skills needed by a short-order cook in a coffee shop are not exactly the same as those needed by a production worker in a school cafeteria. Nevertheless, we can group skills into three general categories.

1. **Supervisory.**
   The head of a food-service kitchen, whether called *executive chef, head chef, working chef,* or *dietary director,* must have management and supervisory skills as well as a thorough knowledge of food production. Leadership positions require an individual

who understands organizing and motivating people, planning menus and production procedures, controlling costs and managing budgets, and purchasing food supplies and equipment. Even if he or she does no cooking at all, the chef must be an experienced cook in order to schedule production, instruct workers, and control quality. Above all, the chef must be able to work well with people, even under extreme pressure.

2. **Skilled and technical.**
While the chef is the head of an establishment, the cooks are the backbone. These workers carry out the actual food production. Thus, they must have knowledge of and experience in cooking techniques, at least for the dishes made in their own department. In addition, they must be able to function well with their fellow workers and to coordinate with other departments. Food production is a team activity.

3. **Entry level.**
Entry-level jobs in food service usually require no particular skills or experience. Workers in these jobs are assigned such work as washing vegetables and preparing salad greens. As their knowledge and experience increase, they may be given more complex tasks and eventually become skilled cooks. Many executive chefs began their careers as pot washers who got a chance to peel potatoes when the pot sink was empty.

Beginning in an entry-level position and working one's way up with experience is the traditional method of advancing in a food-service career. Today, however, many cooks are graduates of culinary schools and programs. But even with such an education, many new graduates begin at entry-level positions. This is as it should be and certainly should not be seen as discouragement. Schools teach general cooking knowledge, while every food-service establishment requires specific skills according to its own menu and its own procedures. Experience as well as theoretical knowledge is needed to be able to adapt to real-life working situations. However, students who have studied and learned well should be able to work their way up more rapidly than beginners with no knowledge at all.

Other Professional Opportunities

Not all those who train to be professional culinarians end up in restaurant careers. Professional cooking expertise is valuable in many callings. The following are just a few of the employment opportunities available in addition to standard cooking positions. Most of these require advanced training in other fields in addition to food production.

- Hospitality management in hotels, restaurants, large catering companies, and other organizations with a food-service component.

- Product development and research for food manufacturers.

- Product sales representatives for food and beverage distributors.

- Product sales representatives for equipment companies.

- Restaurant design and consulting.

- Food styling for photography in books, magazines, and other publications, as well as for food packaging and marketing materials.

- Food writing for newspapers, magazines, food industry journals, and other publications—not only restaurant criticism but analysis and reporting on food-related topics such as nutrition and health, agriculture, and food supply.

- Training the next generation of chefs in culinary schools and in large hospitality companies with in-house training programs.

Standards of Professionalism

What does it take to be a good food-service worker?

The emphasis of a food-service education is on learning a set of skills. But in many ways, *attitudes* are more important than skills because a good attitude will help you not only learn skills but also persevere and overcome the many difficulties you will face.

The successful food-service worker follows an unwritten code of behavior and set of attitudes we call *professionalism*. Let's look at some of the qualities a professional must have.

Positive Attitude Toward the Job

To be a good professional cook, you have to like cooking and want to do it well. Being serious about your work doesn't mean you can't enjoy it. But the enjoyment comes from the satisfaction of doing your job well and making everything run smoothly.

Every experienced chef knows the stimulation of the rush. When it's the busiest time of the evening, the orders are coming in so fast you can hardly keep track of them, and every split second counts—then, when everyone digs in and works together and everything clicks, there's real excitement in the air. But this excitement comes only when you work for it.

A cook with a positive attitude works quickly, efficiently, neatly, and safely. Professionals have pride in their work and want to make sure it is something to be proud of.

Pride in your work and in your profession is important, but humility is important too, especially when you are starting out. Sometimes new culinary school graduates arrive on the job thinking they know everything. Remember that learning to cook and learning to manage a kitchen is a lifelong process and that you are not yet qualified to be executive chef.

The importance of a professional attitude begins even before you start your first job. The standard advice for a successful job interview applies to cooks as well as to office professionals: Dress and behave not for the group you belong to but for the group you want to join. Arrive neat, clean, appropriately dressed, and on time. Get noticed for the right reasons. Carry this attitude through every day on the job.

Staying Power

Food service requires physical and mental stamina, good health, and a willingness to work hard. It is hard work. The pressure can be intense and the hours long and grueling. You may be working evenings and weekends when everyone else is playing. And the work can be monotonous. You might think it's drudgery to hand-shape two or three dozen dinner rolls for your baking class, but wait until you get that great job in the big hotel and are told to make 3,000 canapés for a party.

Overcoming these difficulties requires a sense of responsibility and a dedication to your profession, to your coworkers, and to your customers or clients. Dedication also means staying with a job and not hopping from kitchen to kitchen every few months. Sticking with a job at least a year or two shows prospective employers you are serious about your work and can be relied on.

Ability to Work with People

Few of you will work in an establishment so small you are the only person on the staff. Food-service work is teamwork, and it's essential to be able to work well on a team and to cooperate with your fellow workers. You can't afford to let ego problems, petty jealousy, departmental rivalries, or feelings about other people get in the way of doing your job well. Today's kitchens hold people of many races, nationalities, and origins, some of whom speak languages different from yours. You have to be able to work on the same team as everyone. In the old days, many chefs were famous for their temper tantrums. Fortunately, self-control is more valued today.

Eagerness to Learn

There is more to learn about cooking than you will learn in a lifetime. The greatest chefs in the world are the first to admit they have more to learn, and they keep working, experimenting, and studying. The food-service industry is changing rapidly, so it is vital to be open to new ideas. No matter how good your techniques are, you might learn an even better way.

Continue to study and read. Seek extra work that gives you the opportunity to learn from people with more experience. For example, if you are working on the hot line in a restaurant, ask the pastry chef if you could come in early, on your own time, to help out and, in the process, gain new knowledge and experience.

Many culinary schools and programs have continuing education programs that can help you develop new skills. Professional associations such as the American Culinary Federation (ACF) and the International Association of Culinary Professionals (IACP) provide opportunities for learning as well as for making contacts with other professionals. The ACF, as well as other professional organizations such as the Retail Bakers of America (RBA) and the International Food Service Executives Association (IFSEA), sponsor certification programs that document a professional's skill level and encourage ongoing study.

A Full Range of Skills

Most people who become professional cooks do so because they like to cook. This is an important motivation, but it is also important to develop and maintain other skills necessary for the profession. To be successful, a cook must understand and manage food costs and other financial matters, manage and maintain proper inventories, deal with purveyors, and understand personnel management.

Experience

One of our most respected chefs said, "You don't really know how to cook a dish until you have done it a thousand times."

There is no substitute for years of experience. Studying cooking principles in books and in schools can get your career off to a running start. You may learn more about basic cooking theories from your chef instructors than you could in several years of working your way up from washing vegetables. But if you want to become an accomplished cook, you need practice, practice, and more practice. A diploma does not make you a chef.

Dedication to Quality

Many people think only a special category of food can be called *gourmet food*. It's hard to say exactly what that is. Apparently, the only thing so-called gourmet foods have in common is high price.

The only distinction worth making is between well-prepared food and poorly prepared food. There is good roast duckling à l'orange and there is bad roast duckling à l'orange. There are good hamburgers and French fries, and there are bad hamburgers and French fries.

Whether you work in a top restaurant, a fast-food restaurant, a college cafeteria, or a catering house, you can do your job well, or not. The choice is yours.

High quality doesn't necessarily mean high price. It costs no more to cook green beans properly than to overcook them. But in order to produce high-quality food, you must want to. It is not enough to simply know how.

Good Understanding of the Basics

Experimentation and innovation in cooking are the order of the day. Brilliant chefs are breaking old boundaries and inventing dishes that would have been unthinkable years ago. There is apparently no limit to what can be tried.

However, the chefs who seem to be most revolutionary are the first to insist on the importance of solid grounding in basic techniques and in the classic methods practiced since Escoffier's day. In order to innovate, you have to know where to begin.

As a beginner, knowing the basics will help you take better advantage of your experience. When you watch a practiced cook at work, you will understand better what you are seeing and will know what questions to ask. In order to play great music on the piano, you first must learn to play scales and exercises.

That's what this book is about. It's not a course in French cooking or American cooking or gourmet cooking or coffee shop cooking. It's a course in the basics. When you finish the book, you will not know everything. But you should be ready to take good advantage of the many rewarding years of food-service experience ahead of you.

KEY POINTS TO REVIEW

- What are the major stations in a classical kitchen? What are their responsibilities?
- How do the size and type of a food-service operation affect how the kitchen is organized?
- What are the three basic skill levels of modern kitchen personnel?
- What are eight personal characteristics that are important to the success of a food-service professional?

TERMS FOR REVIEW

Marie-Antoine Carême	executive chef	rôtisseur	working chef
Georges-Auguste Escoffier	chef de cuisine	grillardin	line cook
nouvelle cuisine	sous chef	garde manger	short-order cook
fusion cuisine	station chef	pâtissier	breakfast cook
sous vide	saucier	tournant	professionalism
molecular gastronomy	poissonier	expediter	
chef	entremetier	aboyeur	

QUESTIONS FOR DISCUSSION

1. Escoffier is sometimes called the father of modern food service. What were his most important accomplishments?
2. Discuss several ways in which modern technology has changed the food-service industry.
3. Discuss how an emphasis on high-quality ingredients beginning in the late twentieth century has influenced cooks and cooking styles.
4. What is fusion cuisine? Discuss how successful chefs make use of international influences.
5. What is the purpose of kitchen organization? Is the classical system of organization developed by Escoffier the best for all types of kitchens? Why or why not?
6. True or false: A cook in charge of the sauce and sauté station in a large hotel must have supervisory skills as well as cooking skills. Explain your answer.
7. True or false: If a culinary arts student in a professional school studies hard, works diligently, gets top grades, and shows real dedication, he or she will be qualified to be a chef upon graduation. Explain your answer.

Chapter 2

OOD SERVICE INDUSTRY SANITATION AND SAFETY TOOLS AND EQUIPMENT BASIC PRINCIPLES OF TOO
NAGEMENT NUTRITION MISE EN PLACE STOCKS AND SAUCES SOUPS U
AY AND GAME UNDERSTANDING POULTRY AND GAME BIRDS COOKING
RY AND GAME BIRDS UNDERSTANDING FISH AND SHELLFISH COOKING FISH AND SHELLFISH UNDERS

Part of the procedure for preparing pan jus.

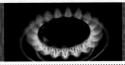
Tools and Equipment

Thorough knowledge of equipment is essential for success in the kitchen. Few food-service operations depend on nothing more than a range and an oven, an assortment of pots and pans, and knives and other hand tools. Modern technology continues to develop more and more specialized and technically advanced tools to reduce kitchen labor.

Much of this equipment is so complex or so sophisticated that only firsthand instruction and practice will teach you how to operate it effectively and safely. Other items, especially hand tools, are simple and need no explanation but require much practice to develop good manual skills.

A vast array of specialized equipment is available for today's kitchens. It would take a large book, not just a short chapter, to describe all of the many items you will encounter in your career—items such as pasta machines, crêpe machines, burger formers, breading machines, cookie droppers, beverage machines, Greek gyro broilers, doughnut glazers, conveyor fryers, and so on. In this technological age, nearly every year brings new tools to simplify various tasks.

This chapter introduces you to the most commonly used equipment in food-service kitchens. It cannot, in this short space, serve as an operating manual for every model of every machine you will use. It cannot take the place of demonstration by your instructor and of actual experience.

> **After reading this chapter, you should be able to**
>
> - Identify the do's and don'ts associated with the safe and efficient use of standard kitchen equipment; processing equipment; holding and storage equipment; measuring devices; and knives, hand tools, and small equipment.

Introduction to Quantity Food Equipment

Before we look at specific items, we must first consider points relating to the use of equipment in general.

Food Equipment Can Be Dangerous

Modern cooking and food processing equipment has an extraordinary capacity to burn, cut, smash, mangle, and amputate parts of the tender human body. This may sound like a harsh way to begin a chapter, but the intent is not to intimidate you or scare you but to inspire a healthy respect for the importance of proper safety and operating procedures.

Never use a piece of equipment until you are thoroughly familiar with its operation and all its features. You must also learn how to know when a machine is not operating correctly. When this happens, shut it down immediately and report the malfunction to a supervisor.

Not All Models Are Alike

Each manufacturer introduces slight variations on the basic equipment. While all convection ovens operate on the same basic principle, each model is slightly different, if only in the location of the switches. It is important to study the operating manual supplied with each item or to be taught by someone who already knows that item well and has operated it.

Cleaning Is Part of the Operating Procedure

Thorough, regular cleaning of all equipment is essential. Most large equipment can be partially disassembled for cleaning. Again, every model is slightly different. Operating manuals should describe these procedures in detail. If a manual is not available, you must get the information from someone who knows the equipment.

When purchasing equipment, look for models that have been tested and certified by recognized agencies that certify products and write standards for food, water, air, and consumer goods. Three prominent agencies are NSF International (www.nsf.org; formerly the National Sanitation Foundation), CSA International (www.csa-international.org; formerly Canadian Standards Association), and Underwriters Laboratory (www.ul.com). These three agencies are recognized internationally. Products meeting their testing requirements are labeled or marked accordingly (Figure 2.1). Criteria govern such factors as design and construction (for example, sealed joints and seams), materials used (for example, nontoxic materials, smooth and easily cleanable surfaces), and performance testing.

Conserve Energy

At one time, it was standard procedure for the chef to turn on the ovens and ranges first thing in the morning and keep them on all day. Today, high energy costs have made this practice expensive. Fortunately, modern equipment takes less time to heat.

Know the preheating time for all your cooking equipment so you don't need to turn it on before necessary. Plan production so equipment that requires a lot of energy is not on for long periods when not in use.

Your Hands Are Your Best Tools

Machines are intended to be laborsaving devices. However, the usefulness of specialized processing equipment often depends on the volume of food it handles. It takes less time for a cook to slice a few pounds of onions by hand than to set up a slicing attachment, pass the onions through it, and break down and clean the equipment. This is why it is important to develop good manual skills.

Figure 2.1

NSF International certification mark
Courtesy of NSF International.

The CSA International logo
Courtesy of the Canadian Standard Association.

The Underwriters Laboratory logo
Reproduced with permission of Underwriters Laboratory, Inc.

Cooking Equipment

Rangetops

The range is still the most important piece of cooking equipment in the kitchen, even though many of its functions have been taken over by other tools such as steamers, steam kettles, tilting skillets, and ovens.

TYPES OF COOKTOPS

1. **Open elements** (burners), either electric coils or gas flames. These tops are the fastest to heat and can be turned off after short use. However, cooktop space is limited to one pot per burner.

2. **Flattop** or **hot top** (lightweight). Burners covered with steel plate. More cook space is available. Top supports moderately heavy weights.

3. **Heavy-duty flattop.** Burners covered with heavy cast steel. The top supports many heavy pots. A thick top requires longer preheating. Set burners for different levels, and adjust cooking heat by moving pots to different spots on the top. A *ring-top range* is a type of flattop that has removable rings, allowing access to even more intense heat from the flames below.

Open-burner gas range with griddle
Courtesy of Vulcan Hart Company.

4. **Induction cooktops.** The top of an induction unit does not become hot. Rather, it works by magnetically agitating the molecules in steel or iron cookware so the cookware becomes hot. As a result, much less energy is used and the kitchen stays cooler, because only the pots and pans and their contents become hot. There are no hot surfaces or open flames. Also, no warm-up is required. The top can be turned instantly on or off. Small, easily portable induction burners are available. These are useful for off-premise catering operations, for buffet service, and even for tableside heating and cooking. The disadvantage of this cooktop is that only iron or steel pots can be used. Traditional aluminum or copper cookware will not work. Some manufacturers of cookware have responded to the new demand by producing pots and pans made of aluminum sandwiched between layers of stainless steel. In this way, the good heat-conducting qualities of aluminum are preserved as well as adapted to this new technology.

Flattop range
Courtesy of Vulcan Hart Company.

Ring-top range
Courtesy of Manitowoc Foodservice.

Portable induction cooktop
Courtesy of Fagor America, Inc.

DO'S AND DON'TS

1. Make sure gas pilots are lit before turning on burners. If burners do not light, turn off gas and allow the gas to ventilate before trying again to light pilots or burners.

2. For maximum heat, adjust air intake so gas flames are blue with a white tip.

3. Do not keep flattop ranges on high heat unless items are being cooked over them. Damage to tops could result.

Ovens

The oven and the rangetop are the two workhorses of the traditional kitchen, which is why they are so often found in the same unit. Ovens are enclosed spaces in which food is heated, usually by hot air or, in some newer kinds of ovens, by microwaves or infrared radiation.

In addition to roasting and baking, ovens can do many of the jobs normally done on the rangetop. Many foods can be simmered, stewed, braised, or poached in the oven, freeing the rangetop and the chef's attention for other tasks.

There are many kinds of ovens beyond those discussed here, but they are often for specialty or high-volume uses. These include **conveyor ovens**, which carry foods through the oven on a steel conveyor belt; **holding ovens** or warmers, which are designed to hold many types of foods at serving temperatures for extended periods without drying out or overcooking (this category includes ovens that also cook the food, then automatically switch to holding temperature); and high-volume **roll-in ovens**, with large doors into which one can roll carts loaded with trays of food.

CONVENTIONAL OVENS

Conventional ovens operate simply by heating air in an enclosed space. The most common ovens are part of the range unit, although separate oven units or ovens as part of a broiler unit are also available. **Stack ovens** are units that consist of individual shelves or decks arranged one above the other. Pans are placed directly on the oven deck rather than on wire shelves. Temperatures are adjustable for each deck.

DO'S AND DON'TS

Many of these points apply to other types of ovens as well.

1. Preheat ovens thoroughly, but no longer than necessary, to avoid excess energy use.

2. To avoid high energy loss and interruption of cooking, do not open the door more often than necessary.

3. Space items well to allow for heat circulation.

4. Be sure the pilot light is on before turning on gas ovens.

CONVECTION OVENS

Convection ovens contain fans that circulate the air and distribute the heat rapidly throughout the interior. Because of the forced air, foods cook more quickly at lower temperatures. Also, shelves can be placed closer together than in conventional ovens without blocking the heat flow.

DO'S AND DON'TS

1. For most products, set the temperature 25°–50°F (15°–30°C) lower than you would a conventional oven. Check the manufacturer's recommendations.

2. Watch cooking times closely. The forced heat cooks foods more quickly and tends to dry out some foods if they are overcooked. Roasts shrink more than they do in conventional ovens.

3. Many convection oven models should not be operated with the blower switch off, as the motor may burn out.

4. The forced air of a convection oven may deform soft items. Cake batters, for example, develop ripples. Check the manufacturer's recommendations.

REVOLVING OVENS

Revolving ovens, also called **reel ovens**, are large chambers containing many shelves or trays on an attachment like a Ferris wheel. This oven eliminates the problem of hot spots, or uneven baking, because the mechanism rotates the foods throughout the oven.

Revolving ovens are used in bakeshops and in high-volume operations.

Stack or deck ovens
Copyright Blodgett Corporation.

Convection oven
Courtesy of Vulcan Hart Company.

SLOW-COOK-AND-HOLD OVENS

The traditional oven is nothing more than a heated box equipped with a thermostat. Some modern ovens have more sophisticated features, such as computerized electronic controls and special probes that sense when a roast is done and tell the oven to switch from cooking temperature to holding temperature.

Many of these ovens are designed to be especially useful for low-temperature roasting. The sensitive controls make it possible to cook at steady, reliable temperatures of 200°F (95°C) or lower and to hold foods at 140°F (60°C) for long periods. Large cuts of meat take many hours to roast at a low temperature like 200°F (95°C). By setting the controls in advance, the operator can even let meats roast overnight, unattended.

These ovens are available as convection ovens and as regular stationary-air ovens.

COMBINATION STEAMER OVENS

The **combination steamer oven**, also called a *combi oven*, can be operated in three modes: as a convection oven, as a convection steamer (see p. 23), and, with both functions on at once, as a high-humidity oven. Injecting moisture into an oven while roasting meats can help reduce shrinkage and drying.

Combination steamer oven
Courtesy of Vulcan Hart Company.

BARBECUE OVENS OR SMOKE OVENS

Barbecue ovens are like conventional ovens, but with one important difference: They produce wood smoke, which surrounds the food and adds flavor while it bakes or roasts. Special woods such as hickory, mesquite, or fruitwoods such as apple or cherry must be added to the smoke-producing part of the oven according to the manufacturer's instructions. This device is usually nothing more complicated than an electric heating element that heats small blocks or chips of the wood so they are hot enough to smoke but not hot enough to burst into flame.

Depending on the model, various cooking features are available. Thus, ovens may have smokeless roast/bake cycles, cold-smoke cycles (with the smoke element on but the oven off), holding cycles, and broiling capabilities.

A barbecue oven that uses wood smoke should not be confused with a *smoker*, used for making hot-smoked and cold-smoked foods.

INFRARED OR RECONSTITUTING OVENS

Infrared units contain quartz tubes or plates that generate intense infrared heat. These ovens are used primarily for reconstituting frozen foods. They bring large quantities of foods to serving temperature in a short time. The heat is even and controllable.

Smoke oven
Courtesy of Cookshack, Inc.

WOOD-BURNING OVENS

Ancient ovens were made of heavy masonry, brick, or clay and heated by building a wood fire inside them. In this type of oven, the brick absorbs the intense heat of the fire and cooks foods long after the fire has gone out and the ashes removed. Items such as breads and pizzas are baked directly on the floor of the oven, just as in modern deck ovens. Wood-burning ovens have once again come into fairly wide use, mostly in specialty restaurants that feature roasted meats, pizzas, and similar items. The foods absorb some of the appealing wood-smoke flavors and aromas.

Because a traditional wood-burning oven lacks a temperature control knob, some experience is needed to produce baked goods of consistent quality. During the firing of the oven, a wood fire is built directly on the hearth inside the oven. The flue and the door are kept open to allow the smoke to escape. After the fire is stopped, the ashes and embers are swept out. The door and flue are closed to allow the heat to equalize inside the dome of the oven. Initial temperatures inside the oven at this point may be as high as 900°F (480°C). Pizza can be baked at this temperature. For meats and breads, the oven is left to stand until the temperature gradually drops to the desired range. Alternatively, a fire can be kept going in the back of the oven while foods are roasted toward the front, with the flue kept open.

Combination ovens, also available, are more controllable. These can be fired by gas alone, by wood alone, or by gas and wood together.

Modern wood-burning oven
Courtesy of Earthstone Ovens.

Microwave oven
Courtesy of Vulcan Hart Company.

MICROWAVE OVENS

In these ovens, special tubes generate microwave radiation, which creates heat inside the food. Microwave cooking is discussed in detail in Chapter 4.

Broilers and Salamanders

Broilers are sometimes called *overhead broilers* to avoid confusing them with grills. Overhead broilers generate heat from above, and food items are placed on a grate beneath the heat source. Broiling is a favorite way of preparing steaks, chops, chicken, and many other items.

Heavy-duty broilers produce very high heat and consume vast quantities of energy. Some broilers are said to go as high as 2,000°F (1,100°C) at the burner.

Heavy-duty broiler
Courtesy of Vulcan Hart Company.

Salamander (above range)
Courtesy of Vulcan Hart Company.

Foods must be watched closely to avoid burning. Cooking temperature is adjusted by raising or lowering the grate that holds the food.

Salamanders are small broilers used primarily for browning or glazing the tops of some items. They may also be used for broiling small quantities during off-peak hours. Salamanders are usually mounted above the range, as illustrated in the photo. In addition, the photo of an open-burner gas range on page 17 shows a salamander under the griddle.

Grills

Grills are used for the same cooking operations as broilers, except the heat source is below the grid that holds the food rather than above it. Many people like grilled foods because of their charcoal taste, which is created by smoke from meat fats that drip into the heat source.

Although smoke from meat fats creates the taste people associate with grilled foods, actual wood-smoke flavors such as hickory or mesquite can be added to foods if those woods are burned in the grill under the food. In order to do this, you must use a grill designed to burn such fuels.

Gas grill
Courtesy of Vulcan Hart Company.

TYPES

Many grill models are in use. The major differences in operation among them are due to the difference in heat source—gas, electricity, or charcoal.

To operate, set areas of the grill to different temperatures and place foods in the areas with the appropriate cooking temperature. Keep grills clean, as the high temperatures can easily start grease fires.

Griddles

Griddles are flat, smooth, heated surfaces on which food is cooked directly. Pancakes, French toast, hamburgers and other meats, eggs, and potato items are the foods most frequently cooked on a griddle. Griddles are available as separate units or as part of a rangetop (there is a griddle on the right side of the range pictured on page 17).

Clean griddle surfaces after every use so they will cook at peak efficiency. Polish with a griddle stone or griddle cloth until the surface shines. Follow the grain of the metal to avoid scratching.

Condition griddles after each cleaning or before each use to create a nonstick surface and to prevent rusting. Procedure: Spread a thin film of oil over the surface and heat to 400°F (200°C). Wipe clean and repeat until griddle has a smooth, nonstick finish.

Rotisseries

Rotisserie broilers cook meats and other foods by turning them slowly in front of electric- or gas-powered heating elements. Even though classical cooking theory categorizes spit-cooking as roasting, these cookers are more closely related to broilers in that the foods are cooked by the infrared heat of the elements.

Although they are especially suitable for chicken and other poultry, rotisseries can be used to cook any meat or other food that can be held on a spit or in any of various attachments or accessories.

Both enclosed (ovenlike) rotisseries and open or unclosed units are available. Small units hold about 8 chickens, and sizes range all the way to very large models that can hold as many as 70 chickens.

Because the heating elements are on the side (or sometimes above), the fats and juices don't drip into the flames as they do with grills. Drip pans catch juices, which can be used for basting or gravy making.

Deep Fryers

A deep fryer has only one use: to cook foods in hot fat. Yet because of the popularity of fried foods, this function is an important one.

Standard deep fryers are powered by either gas or electricity and have thermostatic controls that maintain fat at preset temperatures.

Automatic fryers remove food from the fat automatically after a preset time.

Pressure fryers are covered fry kettles that fry foods under pressure. Foods cook faster, even at a lower fat temperature.

DO'S AND DON'TS

Frying procedures and the care of frying fat are discussed in detail in Chapter 4. The following points relate to the operation of the equipment.

1. When filling kettles with solid fats, set the thermostat at 250°F (120°C) until the fat has melted enough to cover the heating elements.

2. Keep the kettles filled to the fill line.

3. Make sure the drain valve is shut before adding fat to the empty kettle.

4. Check the accuracy of the thermostat regularly by reading the fat temperature with a thermometer.

CLEANING

Cleaning procedures differ greatly depending on the model. Here is a general procedure.

1. Shut off the power.

2. Drain the fat through a filter into a dry container (unless you are discarding it). Be sure the container is large enough to hold all the fat before you start.

Deep fryers
Courtesy of Vulcan Hart Company.

3. Flush food particles from the sides and bottom of the kettle with some of the hot fat.

4. Wash the kettle with a mild detergent solution. If the kettle is not removable, turn on the fryer and bring the detergent solution almost to a boil (beware of foaming over). Scrub with a stiff brush.

5. Drain and rinse thoroughly with clean water.

6. Dry the kettle, heating elements, and baskets thoroughly.

7. Refill with strained or fresh fat.

Tilting Skillet

The tilting skillet, also known as the **tilting brazier** and **tilting fry pan**, is a versatile and efficient piece of equipment. It can be used as a griddle, fry pan, brazier, stewpot, stockpot, steamer, and bain-marie or steam table.

The tilting skillet is a large, shallow, flat-bottomed pot. To look at it another way, it is a griddle with sides 6 inches (24 cm) high, plus a cover. It has a tilting mechanism that enables liquids to be poured out of it. Power may be gas or electric.

Tilting skillet
Courtesy of Vulcan Hart Company.

Clean the skillet immediately after each use, before food has time to dry on. Add water, turn on the skillet to heat it, and scrub thoroughly.

Steam-Jacketed Kettles

Steam-jacketed kettles, or **steam kettles,** are sometimes thought of as stockpots heated not just on the bottom but on the sides as well. This comparison is only partly accurate. Steam kettles heat much more quickly and have more uniform and controllable heat than pots on the range.

Small tilt (trunnion) kettle
Courtesy of Vulcan Hart Company.

Large floor-model steam kettle
Courtesy of Vulcan Hart Company.

TYPES

Steam kettles range in capacity from 2 gallons (7.5 L) to over 100 gallons (378.5 L). Some large institutional kettles hold 4,000 gallons (15,142 L). **Tilt** or **trunnion kettles** can be tilted for emptying, either by turning a wheel or by pulling a lever. **Nontilt kettles** are emptied by a spigot and drain on the bottom. Heat is controlled by regulating the steam flow or by adjusting the thermostat. Steam may be from an outside source or self-generated. *Exercise caution when operating all steam equipment. Steam can cause serious burns.*

Clean immediately after use to avoid food drying on surfaces. Disassemble the spigot and drain, and clean with a bottle brush.

Steam Cookers

Steam cookers are ideal for cooking vegetables and many other foods rapidly and with minimum loss of nutrients and flavor. For this reason, they are becoming more common in both large and small kitchens.

TYPES

Pressure steamers cook foods under a pressure of 15 pounds per square inch (1.05 kg/cm) in high-pressure steamers or 4–6 pounds per square inch (0.28–0.42 kg/cm) in low-pressure steamers. They are operated by a timer, which shuts the equipment off after a preset time. The door cannot be opened until the pressure returns to zero.

Pressureless or **convection steamers** do not operate under pressure. Jets of steam are directed at the food to speed the heat transfer, just as the fan in a convection oven speeds cooking. The door can be opened any time during cooking.

Pressure steamer
Courtesy of Vulcan Hart Company.

Convection steamer
Courtesy of Vulcan Hart Company.

All steamers hold standard-size counter pans (12 × 20 inches or 325 × 530 mm) or fractions thereof. Their capacity varies from one to many pans.

Steamer operation varies greatly depending on the model. Check the operating manual and be sure you understand a particular model well before attempting to operate it.

Caution is important with all steam equipment because of the danger of severe burns.

> ### KEY POINTS TO REVIEW
> - What are the four basic types of cooktops?
> - What is the difference between a standard oven and a convection oven? List four guidelines for operating each type.
> - What is the difference between a broiler, a salamander, a grill, and a griddle?
> - What are four guidelines for operating a standard deep fryer? Describe the general procedure for cleaning a deep fryer.

Processing Equipment

Mixers

Vertical mixers are important and versatile tools for many kinds of food mixing and processing jobs, both in the bakeshop and in the kitchen.

TYPES

Bench-model mixers range in capacity from 5 to 20 quarts (5 to 20 L). Floor models are available as large as 140 quarts (133 L). Adaptor rings enable several bowl sizes to be used on one machine. Most mixers have three operating speeds.

Small table-model mixer
Courtesy of Hobart Corporation.

Large floor-model mixer
Courtesy of Hobart Corporation.

AGITATOR ATTACHMENTS

There are three main mixing attachments, plus some specialized ones. The *paddle* is a flat blade used for general mixing. The *wire whip* is used for such tasks as beating cream and eggs and making mayonnaise. The *dough arm* is used for mixing and kneading yeast doughs.

Mixer attachments: (left) whip, (center) paddle, (right) dough arm
Courtesy of Hobart Corporation.

DO'S AND DON'TS

1. Make sure the bowl and the mixing attachment are firmly in place before turning on the machine.

2. Make sure you are using the right size attachment for the bowl. Using a 40-quart paddle with a 30-quart bowl, for example, could cause serious damage. Sizes in quarts are marked on the sides of large bowls and on the tops of attachments.

3. Turn off the machine before scraping down the bowl or inserting a spoon, scraper, or hand into the bowl. Mixer motors are powerful and can cause serious injury.

4. Turn off the machine before changing speeds.

Rotation chopper
Courtesy of Hobart Corporation.

Food Cutter

The food cutter or rotation chopper, familiarly known as the **buffalo chopper,** is a common piece of equipment used for general food chopping. A variety of attachments (described in the next section) makes it a versatile tool.

GENERAL OPERATION

Food is placed in a rotating bowl, which carries the food to a pair of knives spinning rapidly under a cover. The fineness of the cut depends on how long the food is left in the machine.

DO'S AND DON'TS

1. Always make sure the machine is completely assembled before use.

2. Close the cover lock knob, or the machine will not turn on.

3. Never reach under the bowl cover while the machine is running.

4. For uniform chopping, place the food in the bowl all at one time.

5. Keep the knives sharp. Dull knives bruise food rather than cut it cleanly.

Grinder attachment (on separate motor)
Courtesy of Hobart Corporation.

Attachments for Mixers and Food Choppers

The following are the most common of the many attachments designed to fit both the food chopper and the vertical mixer.

1. The **food grinder** is used mostly for grinding meats, although other moist foods may be ground also. Food is forced through a feed tube into a screw, which pushes the food through holes in a plate, at which point it is cut by a rotating blade. The size of the holes regulates the fineness of the grind.

Make sure the rotating blade is attached properly, cutting edge out, when assembling the grinder.

2. The **slicer/shredder** consists of a hopper and a lever that feeds the food onto a rotating disk or plate. The plate cuts or shreds the food and drops it into a receiving container. The slicing plate may be adjusted to cut various thicknesses.

3. The **dicer** attachment forces foods through a grid-type blade that cuts them into perfect dice. Blades of different sizes may be used.

Slicer

The slicer is a valuable machine because it slices foods more evenly and uniformly than can be done by hand. This makes it valuable for portion control and for reducing cutting loss.

TYPES

Most modern slicers have blades set at an angle. Slices fall away from these blades with less breaking and folding than from vertical blades.

With manual machines, the operator must move the carriage back and forth to slice the food. Automatic machines move the carriage with an electric motor.

DO'S AND DON'TS

1. Be sure the machine is properly assembled before using.

2. Always use the end weight to press the food against the blade. This protects the hand from serious cuts and provides a more even pressure on the food, resulting in more uniform slices.

3. Set the thickness control knob to zero when the machine is not in use or is being cleaned.

4. Always unplug the machine before dismantling and cleaning.

5. Keep the blade sharp with the sharpening stones provided with the slicer.

Vertical Cutter/Mixer

The vertical cutter/mixer (VCM) is like a large, powerful, high-speed blender. It is used to chop and mix large quantities of foods rapidly. It can also be used for puréeing (soups, for example) and for mixing liquids.

TYPES

VCMs range in size from 15 to 80 quarts (14 to 75 liters). The small models have a hand-operated mixing baffle, which moves the foods into the blades. Larger machines have automatic baffles.

DO'S AND DON'TS

1. Watch processing times closely. Chopping times are so short that an extra second can make cabbage soup out of coleslaw.

2. Make sure the machine is properly assembled before use.

3. After turning off the machine, allow the blades to come to a full stop before opening the cover.

4. Keep the blades sharp. Dull blades bruise food.

Food Processor

Food processors were used in commercial kitchens long before home models were introduced. Professional models are 2–4 times larger than the largest home models. They consist of a motor in a heavy base topped by a cylindrical work bowl containing an *S*-shaped blade.

Slicer/shredder attachment
Courtesy of Hobart Corporation.

Slicer
Courtesy of Hobart Corporation.

Food processor
Courtesy of Robot Coupe USA.

Processors are used to chop or purée foods, including raw or cooked meats, and to mix or emulsify such items as sauces and flavored butters. With special disk attachments in place of the standard blade, they can also slice, shred, and julienne solid foods such as vegetables.

In basic design, a food processor is similar to a vertical cutter/mixer. The same do's and don'ts should be observed.

Blender

Like the VCM and the food processor, a blender consists of a motor in a base, topped by a container with a spinning blade. However, because the blender's container is tall and narrow, it is more suited for mixing and puréeing liquids than for chopping solid foods. In the commercial kitchen, the blender is used to mix, purée, and emulsify liquids such as soups, sauces, and batters. It is also used in bars and coffeehouses to prepare certain drinks.

Blender motors may have from 2 to 10 speeds, or even more. The containers are made of stainless steel, glass, or plastic. The blade assembly at the base of the container can be disassembled for thorough cleaning.

Immersion Blender

An immersion blender, also called a **stick blender** or **burr mixer**, consists of the blade of a blender, protected by a guard, at the bottom end of a long wand or shaft with a motor at the top. Using an immersion blender, the cook can purée or mix hot or cold foods in any container without transferring them to a blender jar. This makes it possible to blend hot foods in their cooking pots. The largest stick blenders are long enough to purée foods in large steam kettles.

Professional blender
Courtesy of Waring Products.

Sous Vide Equipment

Two types of equipment are essential for operations that use sous vide (see pages 7 and 65) cooking techniques: vacuum packaging equipment and cooking equipment.

The most commonly used packaging equipment in food service is a *chamber vacuum packer*. Food is placed in a specially designed plastic bag and inserted in the chamber. The chamber is then closed and the machine pulls the air from the bag and seals the bag. Vacuum pressure may be varied from low, for delicate, easily crushed foods, to high, for firmer foods.

Precise control of cooking temperature is at the heart of sous vide cooking, and for this, *immersion circulators* are used to heat the water in a hot-water bath. Immersion circulators have a heating element, a pump that constantly circulates the water, and a temperature control that can keep the water at a steady temperature to within a fraction of a degree.

Rapid cooling is also important in sous vide cooking. Larger operations may want to invest in a blast cooler. For smaller kitchens, a regular ice bath may be sufficient.

Chamber vacuum packer
Courtesy of PolyScience.

Immersion circulator
Courtesy of PolyScience.

Holding and Storage Equipment

Hot Food Holding Equipment

Several types of equipment are used to keep food hot for service. This equipment is designed to hold foods above 135°F (57°C) in order to prevent the growth of bacteria that can cause disease. Because food continues to cook at these temperatures, it should be held for as short a time as possible.

Steam table
Courtesy of Hobart Corporation.

1. **Steam tables** are standard holding equipment for serving lines. Standard-size counter pans or hotel pans are used as inserts to hold the foods. Flat or domed covers may be used to cover the foods.

    Check water levels in steam tables periodically to make sure they don't go dry. Electrically heated counters that operate dry—without steam—are also available.

2. A **bain-marie** is a hot-water bath. Containers of foods are set on a rack in a shallow container of water, which is heated by electricity, gas, or steam. The bain-marie is used more in the production area, while the steam table is used in the service area.

3. **Overhead infrared lamps** are used in service areas to keep plated food warm before it is picked up by the service staff. They are also used for keeping large roasts warm.

    Foods dry out quickly under holding lamps. This is a disadvantage for almost all foods except French fries and other deep-fried foods, which lose their crispness if they are kept moist.

Cold Food Storage Equipment

The quality of the food you serve depends to a great degree on refrigeration equipment. By keeping foods cold, usually below 41°F (5°C), the refrigerator (known in the trade as the *cooler* or the *box*) guards against spoilage and bacterial growth.

Several types of refrigerator are used in food service. The **walk-in** is a room-size refrigerator with built-in shelves on the walls. Walk-ins can be customized to fit nearly any available space.

The **reach-in** is a standard upright refrigerator similar in shape to a large home refrigerator, but without the freezer unit. It may have shelves or simply brackets for holding sheet pans.

Small reach-ins that fit under counters, as well as refrigerated drawers, are used in prep and service areas of the kitchen. Finally, refrigerated display cases are used in retail and the dining areas of delis, bakeries, diners, coffee shops, and some restaurants.

Freezers are used to hold foods for longer times, or to store foods purchased in frozen form. Like refrigerators, freezers are available as walk-ins, reach-ins, and smaller units.

To enable refrigerators and freezers to work at top efficiency, observe the following rules:

1. Place items far enough apart and away from the inside walls of refrigerators so cold air can circulate. Freezers, on the other hand, work most efficiently when they are full.

2. Keep the door closed as much as possible. When storing or removing an item, do it quickly and shut the door.

3. Keep stored foods well wrapped or covered to prevent drying and transfer of odors. Meats are an exception to this rule.

4. Keep refrigerators spotlessly clean.

KEY POINTS TO REVIEW

- What are four guidelines for the safe operation of a vertical mixer? What three types of beater attachment are used most often on a mixer, and what are they used for?

- What are five guidelines for the correct operation of a rotation chopper (buffalo chopper)?

- What are five guidelines for the safe operation of a slicing machine?

- What are five kinds of equipment used to keep foods out of the Food Danger Zone?

Pots, Pans, and Containers

Metals and Conductivity

A good cooking utensil distributes heat evenly and uniformly. A poor cooking utensil develops hot spots that are likely to burn or scorch the food being cooked. Two factors affect a pan's ability to cook evenly:

1. *Thickness of the metal.* A heavy-gauge pot cooks more evenly than one made of thin metal. Thickness is most important on the bottom.

2. *Kind of metal.* Different metals have different conductivity, or the speed at which they transfer or disperse heat. The following materials are used for cooking equipment:

   - *Aluminum* is used for most cooking utensils in food-service kitchens. It is a good conductor, and its light weight makes pots and pans easy to handle. Because it is a relatively soft metal, it should not be banged around or abused.

     Do not use aluminum for storage or for long cooking of strong acids because it reacts chemically with many foods. Also, it tends to discolor light-colored foods such as sauces, especially if they are stirred or beaten with a metal spoon or whip.

     Pans made of *anodized aluminum*, sold under such brand names as Calphalon, have surfaces that are harder and more corrosion-resistant than regular aluminum pans. Although this is not, strictly speaking, a nonstick finish, it is less porous than untreated aluminum, so foods are less likely to stick. Also, it is more resistant to acids than regular aluminum, and it will not discolor light-colored foods. Its disadvantages are that it is more expensive than and not quite as durable as standard aluminum.

   - *Copper*, the best heat conductor of all, was once widely used for cooking utensils. However, it is extremely expensive and requires a great deal of care. In addition, it is heavy. Today it is used mostly for show, although a few high-end restaurants use it for cooking as well.

     Copper reacts chemically with many foods to create poisonous compounds, so copper pans must be lined with another metal, such as tin or stainless steel.

   - *Stainless steel* is a poor heat conductor. Cooking pots and pans made of it tend to scorch foods easily because the heat does not disperse throughout the pan quickly and evenly. Stainless steel is ideal for storage containers because it does not react with foods as aluminum does. It is also used for low-temperature cooking or holding equipment, such as steamer pans and counter pans, where scorching or hot spots are not a problem.

     Stainless-steel pots and pans are available with a heavy layer of copper or aluminum bonded to the bottom. Heavy aluminum pans may also be lined with stainless steel on the inside, or on both the inside and outside. This feature gives the advantages of stainless steel (hardness, durability, nonreactivity with acid foods, and nondiscoloration of light sauces) with the heat-conducting qualities of copper or aluminum. These pans are usually expensive.

   - *Cast iron* is a favorite material with many chefs because of its ability to distribute heat evenly and to maintain high temperatures for long periods. It is used in griddles and heavy skillets. Cast iron cracks easily if dropped. It rusts quickly unless kept properly conditioned (see p. 227) and dry.

   - *Porcelain enamel-lined pans* should not be used. In fact, they are forbidden by some health departments. They scratch and chip easily, providing good hiding places for bacteria. Also, certain kinds of gray enamel can cause food poisoning if chipped.

   - *Nonstick plastic-type coatings*, known by brand names including Teflon and Silverstone, provide a slippery finish, but one that requires a lot of care because it is easily scratched. Do not use metal spoons or spatulas with this equipment. Instead, use tools made of plastic, silicone, or wood. Do not use abrasive materials to clean the nonstick surface.

Nonstick pans are best reserved for eggs and other items that are likely to be damaged if they stick. Many chefs keep a set of nonstick egg pans and use them for no other purpose. In addition, these pans are useful for dietary cooking because they enable cooks to sauté foods with little or no added fat.

Nonstick coatings should not be used for sautéing and braising procedures that involve deglazing to make a sauce (see page 154). Foods do not brown as well in nonstick pans as in traditional metal pans, and they do not form a fond (the flavorful browned bits that stick to the pan) that can be deglazed to make a sauce or braising liquid.

- *Glass* and *earthenware* have limited use in commercial kitchens because they break easily. They are poor conductors of heat but are resistant to corrosion and food acids.

Pots and Pans and Their Uses

Stockpot **Stockpot with spigot**

1. **Stockpot.**
   A large, deep, straight-sided pot for preparing stocks and simmering large quantities of liquids. Stockpots with spigots allow liquid to be drained off without disturbing the solid contents or lifting the pot. Sizes: 8–200 quarts (liters).

2. **Saucepot.**
   A round pot of medium depth. Similar to a stockpot but shallower, making stirring or mixing easier. Used for soups, sauces, and other liquids. Sizes: 6–60 quarts (liters).

Saucepot **Brazier**

3. **Brazier.**
   A round, broad, shallow, heavy-duty pot with straight sides. Also called a *rondeau*. Used for browning, braising, and stewing meats. Sizes: 11–30 quarts (liters).

Saucepan

4. **Saucepan.**
   Similar to a small, shallow, light saucepot, but with one long handle instead of two loop handles. May have straight or slanted sides. Used for general rangetop cooking. Sizes: 1½–15 quarts (liters).

5. **Sauté pan, straight-sided.**
   Also called a *sautoir*. Similar to a shallow, straight-sided saucepan, but heavier. Used for browning, sautéing, and frying. Because of its broad surface area, the sauté pan is used for cooking sauces and other liquids when rapid reduction is required. Sizes: 2½–5 inches (65–130 mm) deep; 6–16 inches (160–400 mm) in diameter.

Straight-sided sauté pan

6. **Sauté pan, slope-sided.**
   Also called a *sauteuse*. Used for general sautéing and frying of meats, fish, vegetables, and eggs. The sloping sides allow the cook to flip and toss items without using a spatula, and they make it easier to get at the food when a spatula is used. Sizes: 6–14 inches (160–360 mm) top diameter.

Slope-sided sauté pan

7. **Cast-iron skillet.**
   Very heavy, thick-bottomed fry pan. Used for pan-frying when steady, even heat is desired.

Cast-iron skillet

8. **Double boiler.**
   A pot with two sections. The lower section, similar to a stockpot, holds boiling water. The upper section holds foods that must be cooked at low temperatures and cannot be cooked over direct heat. Size of top section: 4–36 quarts (liters).

Double boiler

Sheet pan

Fish poacher
Courtesy of RSVP International, Inc.

Wok

Hotel pan

9. **Sheet pan or bun pan.**
A shallow rectangular pan (1 inch/25 mm deep) for baking cakes, rolls, and cookies, and for baking or broiling certain meats and fish. Sizes: full pan, 18 × 26 inches (46 × 66 cm); half-pan, 18 × 13 inches (46 × 33 cm).

10. **Bake pan.**
A rectangular pan about 2 inches (50 mm) deep. Used for general baking. Available in a variety of sizes.

Bake pan

11. **Roasting pan.**
A large rectangular pan, deeper and heavier than a bake pan. Used for roasting meats and poultry.

12. **Fish poacher.**
A long, narrow, straight-sided pan with a removable rack insert. Used for poaching whole fish.

Roasting pan

13. **Wok.**
A round-bottomed steel pan with two loop handles. Used for stir-frying, especially in Chinese cuisine. Woks are best used with special burner units that have a high heat output and a broad ring-shaped support that holds the wok steady during cooking.

14. **Hotel pan, also called** *counter pan*, *steam table pan*, or *service pan*.
A rectangular pan, usually made of stainless steel. Designed to hold foods in service counters. Also used for baking, steaming, and subsequent serving. Also used for storage. Standard size: 12 × 20 inches. Fractions of this size (½, ⅓, etc.) are also available. Standard depth: 2½ inches (65 mm). Deeper sizes are also available. (Standard metric pan is 325 × 530 mm.)

15. **Bain-marie insert, usually called simply** *bain-marie*.
A tall, cylindrical stainless-steel container. Used for storage and for holding foods in a bain-marie (water bath). Sizes: 1–36 quarts (liters).

16. **Stainless-steel bowl.**
A round-bottomed bowl. Used for mixing, whipping, and producing hollandaise, mayonnaise, whipped cream, and egg white foams. Round construction enables whip to reach all areas. Available in many sizes.

Bain-marie inserts

Measuring Devices

The following equipment is discussed in terms of U.S. measurements. Comparable items in metric units are also available.

Portion scale

Digital scale

1. **Scales.** Most recipe ingredients are measured by weight, so accurate scales are important. **Portion scales** are used for measuring ingredients as well as for portioning products for service. Traditional portion scales are spring-operated and usually have a dial to indicate weight. More accurate **digital scales** are electrically operated and provide a digital readout.

2. **Volume measures** used for liquids have lips for easy pouring. Sizes are pints, quarts, half-gallons, and gallons. Each size is marked off into fourths by ridges on the sides.

3. **Measuring cups** are available in 1-, ½-, ⅓-, and ¼-cup sizes. They can be used for both liquid and dry measures.

4. **Measuring spoons** are used for measuring very small volumes: 1 tablespoon, 1 teaspoon, ½ teaspoon, and ¼ teaspoon. They are used most often for spices and seasonings.

Liquid volume measure

Table 2.1 **Scoop Sizes**				
	U.S. MEASURE		**METRIC MEASURE**	
SCOOP NUMBER	**VOLUME**	**APPROXIMATE WEIGHT**	**VOLUME**	**APPROXIMATE WEIGHT**
6	⅔ cup	5 oz	160 mL	140 g
8	½ cup	4 oz	120 mL	110 g
10	3 fl oz	3–3½ oz	90 mL	85–100 g
12	⅓ cup	2½–3 oz	80 mL	70–85 g
16	¼ cup	2–2½ oz	60 mL	60–70 g
20	1½ fl oz	1¾ oz	45 mL	50 g
24	1⅓ fl oz	1⅓ oz	40 mL	40 g
30	1 fl oz	1 oz	30 mL	30 g
40	0.8 fl oz	0.8 oz	24 mL	23 g
60	½ fl oz	½ oz	15 mL	15 g

Note: Weights vary greatly with different foods, depending on how compact they are. Best practice is to weigh a scoopful of an item before proceeding with portioning.

5. **Ladles** are used for measuring and portioning liquids. The size, in ounces, is stamped on the handle.

Ladles

6. **Scoops** come in standard sizes and have a lever for mechanical release. They are used for portioning soft solid foods. Scoop sizes are listed in Table 3.1. The number of the scoop indicates the number of level scoopfuls per quart. In actual use, a rounded scoopful is often more practical than a level scoopful, so exact weights will vary.

Scoop

7. **Thermometers** measure temperature. There are many kinds for many purposes.

- A **meat thermometer** indicates internal temperature of meats. It is inserted before cooking and left in the product during cooking.

Meat thermometer

- An **instant-read thermometer** gives readings within a few seconds of being inserted in a food product. It reads from 0°F to 220°F. Many chefs carry these in their jacket pocket like a pen, ready whenever needed. Instant-read thermometers must not be left in meats during roasting, or they will be damaged.

- **Fat thermometers** and **candy thermometers** test temperatures of frying fats and sugar syrups. They read up to 400°F.

- Special thermometers are used to test the accuracy of oven, refrigerator, and freezer thermostats.

Instant-read thermometer with holder

Knives, Hand Tools, and Small Equipment

Knife Materials

The metal a knife blade is made of is an important consideration, as the metal must be able to take and hold a very fine edge.

1. **Carbon steel** was for many years the traditional favorite because it can be honed to an extremely sharp edge. Its disadvantages are that it corrodes and discolors easily, especially when used with acid foods and onions. Also, it discolors some foods (such

as hard-cooked eggs) and may leave a metallic taste. Because of these disadvantages, it has given way to high-carbon stainless steel (described below), which is now the preferred material for the best knives.

2. **Traditional stainless-steel alloys** will not rust or corrode, but they are much harder to sharpen than carbon steel. Stainless steel is used mostly for low-cost, lightweight knives.

3. **High-carbon stainless steel** is a relatively new alloy that combines the best aspects of carbon steel and stainless steel. It takes an edge almost as well as carbon steel, and it will not rust, corrode, or discolor. Knives made of this material are highly prized and relatively expensive. Most high-quality knives today are made of high-carbon stainless steel.

Knife Parts

Chef's knives and other knives have a number of parts, and you should be familiar with their names. These parts are illustrated in the diagram.

The **spine** is the back of the blade. It is the edge opposite the **cutting edge**. The **tip** is the pointed end of the blade, while the **heel** is the back end of the blade closest to the handle. On some knives, the blade has a raised part called a **bolster** at the heel end. The bolster is a sort of guard that helps protect the hand from slips and also helps balance the weight of the knife.

The **tang** is the portion of the metal blade inside the handle. The highest-quality, most durable knives have a **full tang**, which means the tang runs the full length of the handle. On knives with traditional wood handles, **rivets** hold the **handle** to the tang. The rivets should be perfectly smooth and flush with the handle. Composite molded handles are bonded to the tang without rivets.

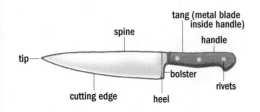

The parts of a chef's knife

Knives and Their Uses

1. **French knife or chef's knife.**
   Most frequently used knife in the kitchen, for general-purpose chopping, slicing, dicing, and so on. The blade is wide at the heel and tapers to a point. Blade length of 10 inches (260 mm) is most popular for general work. Larger knives are for heavy cutting and chopping. Smaller blades are for more delicate work.

   This is your most important tool, so you must learn to handle it and care for it well. Chapter 7 explains its use in detail.

French knife or chef's knife

2. **Santoku knife or Japanese cook's knife.**
   A wide-bladed knife that is becoming increasingly popular as a substitute for the traditional chef's knife. Blades are usually 5 inches (13 cm) or 7 inches (18 cm) long.

Santoku knife or Japanese cook's knife

3. **Utility knife or salad knife.**
   A narrow, pointed knife 6–8 inches (160–200 mm) long. Used mostly for pantry work, cutting and preparing lettuce, fruits, and so on. Also useful for carving roast chicken and duck.

Utility knife

4. **Paring knife.**
   A small pointed blade 2–4 inches (50–100 mm) long. Used for trimming and paring vegetables and fruits.

Paring knife

5. **Boning knife.**
   A thin, pointed blade about 6 inches (160 mm) long. Used for boning raw meats and poultry. Stiff blades are used for heavier work. Flexible blades are used for lighter work and for filleting fish.

Boning knife

6. **Slicer.**
   A long, slender, flexible blade up to 14 inches (360 mm) long. Used for carving and slicing cooked meats.

Slicer

7. **Serrated slicer.**
   Like a slicer, but with a serrated edge. Used for cutting breads, cakes, and similar items.

Serrated slicer

8. **Butcher knife.**
   A heavy, broad, slightly curved blade. Used for cutting, sectioning, and trimming raw meats in the butcher shop.

Butcher knife

9. **Scimitar or steak knife.**
   A curved, pointed blade. Used for accurate cutting of steaks.

Scimitar

10. **Cleaver.**
    A heavy, broad blade. Used for cutting through bones. Do not confuse a cleaver with a similarly shaped Chinese cook's knife, which is lighter in weight.

Cleaver

Chinese cook's knife

11. **Oyster knife.**
    A short, rigid, blunt knife with a dull edge. Used for opening oysters.

Oyster knife

12. **Clam knife.**
    A short, rigid, broad-bladed knife with a slight edge. Used for opening clams.

Clam knife

13. **Vegetable peeler.**
    A short tool with a slotted, swiveling blade. Used for peeling vegetables and fruits.

Vegetable peeler

Swiss-style vegetable peeler

14. **Steel.**
    Not a knife, but an essential part of the knife kit. Used for truing and maintaining knife edges (not for sharpening them—see Chapter 6).

15. **Cutting board.**
    An important partner to the knife. Hardwood boards are favored by many chefs. Hard rubber or plastic boards are thought to be more sanitary, but there is some evidence that bacteria actually survive longer on plastic and rubber than on wood. Cutting boards must be kept very clean, and they must be sanitized regularly. Color-coded composite boards are designed to help reduce cross-contamination, as each color is used for a different category of food (for example, green for vegetables, red for meats).
    Note: In some communities, wooden boards are prohibited by health regulations.

Steel

Hand Tools and Small Equipment

1. **Ball cutter, melon ball scoop, or parisienne knife.**
   The blade is a small, cup-shaped half-sphere. Used for cutting fruits and vegetables into small balls.

Parisienne melon baller

2. **Cook's fork.**
   A heavy, two-pronged fork with a long handle. Used for lifting and turning meats and other items. Must be strong enough to hold heavy loads.

Cook's fork

3. **Straight spatula or palette knife.**
   A long, flexible blade with a rounded end. Used mostly for spreading icing on cakes and for mixing and bowl scraping.

Straight spatula

4. **Sandwich spreader.**
   A short, stubby spatula. Used for spreading fillings and spreads on sandwiches.

Sandwich spreader

5. **Offset spatula.**
   A broad blade, bent to keep the hand off hot surfaces. Used for turning and lifting eggs, pancakes, and meats on griddles, grills, sheet pans, and so on. Also used as a scraper to clean benches and griddles.

Offset spatula

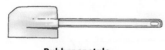

Rubber spatula

Bench scraper

Spoons: slotted, perforated, solid

Tongs

China cap

Strainer

Wire mesh strainer

6. **Rubber spatula or scraper.**
   A broad, flexible rubber or plastic tip on a long handle. Used to scrape bowls and pans. Also used for folding in egg foams and whipped cream.

7. **Pie server.**
   A wedge-shaped offset spatula. Used for lifting pie wedges from pan.

   Pie server

8. **Bench scraper or dough knife.**
   A broad, stiff piece of metal with a wooden handle on one edge. Used to cut pieces of dough and to scrape workbenches.

9. **Pastry wheel or wheel knife.**
   A round, rotating blade on a handle. Used for cutting rolled-out doughs and pastry and baked pizza.

   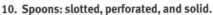

   Pastry wheel

10. **Spoons: slotted, perforated, and solid.**
    Large stainless-steel spoons that hold about 3 ounces (90 mL). Used for stirring, mixing, and serving. Slotted and perforated spoons are used when liquid must be drained from solids.

    Skimmer

11. **Skimmer.**
    A perforated disk, slightly cupped, on a long handle. Used for skimming froth from liquids and for removing solid pieces from soups, stocks, and other liquids.

12. **Tongs.**
    Spring-type or scissors-type tools used to pick up and handle foods.

13. **Wire whip.**
    Loops of stainless-steel wire fastened to a handle. There are two kinds of whips:

    - Heavy whips are straight, stiff, and have relatively few wires. Used for general mixing, stirring, and beating, especially heavy liquids.

      Wire mesh skimmer or spider

    - Balloon whips, or piano-wire whips, have many flexible wires. Used for whipping eggs, cream, and hollandaise, and for mixing thinner liquids.

14. **China cap.**
    A cone-shaped strainer. Used for straining stocks, soups, sauces, and other liquids. Pointed shape allows the cook to drain liquids through a relatively small opening.

    Wire whip

15. **Fine china cap or chinois (shee-nwah).**
    A china cap with very fine mesh. Used when great clarity or smoothness is required in a liquid.

    Chinois

16. **Strainer.**
    A round-bottomed, cup-shaped tool made of screen-type mesh or perforated metal. Used for straining pasta, vegetables, and so on.

17. **Drum sieve or tamis.**
    A screen-type mesh supported in a round metal frame. Used for sifting flour and other dry ingredients and for puréeing soft foods.

    Sieve

18. Colander.
A large perforated bowl made of stainless steel or aluminum. Used to drain washed or cooked vegetables, salad greens, pasta, and other foods.

19. Food mill.
A tool with a hand-turned blade that forces foods through a perforated disk. Interchangeable disks produce varying degrees of coarseness or fineness. Used for puréeing foods.

Colander

Food mill

Grater

20. Grater.
A four-sided metal box with grids of varying sizes. Used for shredding and grating vegetables, cheese, citrus rinds, and other foods.

21. Plane grater.
Usually known by the brand name Microplane. These graters shave off thin shreds of the item being grated, the way a carpenter's plane shaves wood. Available in varying degrees of fineness or coarseness.

Microplane

22. Zester.
A small hand tool used for removing the colored part of citrus peels in thin strips.

Zester

23. Channel knife.
A small hand tool used mostly in decorative work.

Channel knife

24. Mandoline.
A manual slicing implement consisting of blades fitted in a flat metal or wood framework. Folding legs position the mandoline on the worktable at a 45-degree angle for use. Levers allow the blades to be adjusted to control the thickness of the slices. A traditional mandoline has a flat blade and a serrated blade. Additional blades can be used in combination with the flat blade to cut julienne and bâtonnet. The serrated blade is used to cut gaufrette or waffle slices.

For safest use, a detachable guard is also supplied. The guard holds the food and allows it to be sliced without getting the fingers near the blades.

Mandoline

25. Pastry bag and tubes.
Cone-shaped cloths or plastic bags with an open end that can be fitted with metal tubes or tips of various shapes and sizes. Used for shaping and decorating with items such as cake icing, whipped cream, duchesse potatoes, and soft dough.

Pastry bag and tubes

26. Pastry brush.
Used to brush items with egg wash, glaze, etc.

Pastry brush

27. Can opener.
Heavy-duty can openers are mounted on the edge of the workbench. They must be carefully cleaned and sanitized every day to prevent contamination of foods. Replace worn blades, which can leave metal shavings in the food.

Can opener

KEY POINTS TO REVIEW

- How does the metal used to make a cooking pan affect its cooking qualities?
- What equipment is used to measure most recipe ingredients?
- What are five kinds of equipment used to measure foods by volume?
- What are the parts of a chef's knife? What metals are used to make high-quality knife blades?
- What knife is the most often used in the professional kitchen? Name and describe other important knives and their purposes.

Chapter 3

Baking and Pastry Equipment

Much of a baker's art and craft involves simple tools. Learning to become a successful baker requires developing a great deal of manual skill using these tools. For example, a pastry bag is nothing more than a cone-shaped piece of fabric or plastic, open at both ends. Although its construction is simple, and no operating manual is required to understand how it works, hours of practice are necessary to become skilled at using a pastry bag for decorative work.

At the other extreme are large machines such as floor-model mixers, ovens of many types, and dough-handling equipment such as molders, dividers, and sheeters. Of these, perhaps only ovens are essential to a baker's work. The other items are important labor-saving devices that enable workers to produce goods in large quantities with greater speed. Without this equipment, much of the output of a bakeshop would not be economically feasible.

This chapter is an outline of the most important pieces of equipment used by bakers and pastry chefs, from large equipment to containers and molds to hand tools. In addition to these tools, most bakeshops contain an array of equipment also found in most kitchens, including pots and pans, spoons, ladles, spatulas, knives, and so on. Learning to use these tools is the subject of much of this book.

After reading this chapter, you should be able to

1. Identify good safety and sanitation practices for purchasing and handling bakeshop equipment.
2. Identify the principal pieces of large equipment used in baking and pastry making and indicate their uses.
3. Identify the principal pans, container, and molds used in baking and pastry making and indicate their uses.
4. Identify the principal hand tools used in baking and pastry making and indicate their uses.
5. Identify other important pieces of equipment used in baking and pastry making and indicate their uses.

Equipment Sanitation and Safety

Before we look at specific items, we must first consider points related to the use of equipment in general.

Safety

Baking equipment can be dangerous. From large mixers to small hand tools such as knives, much of the equipment found in the bakeshop can inflict serious injuries if not used carefully and properly. Two guidelines are in order here:

* Never use a piece of equipment until you are thoroughly familiar with its operation and all its features. You must also learn to recognize when a machine is not operating correctly so you can shut it down immediately and report the malfunction to a supervisor.

* Be aware that not all models are alike. Each manufacturer introduces slight variations on the basic equipment. While all deck ovens or all vertical mixers, for example, operate on the same basic principles, each model is slightly different, if only in the location of the switches. It is important to study the operating manual supplied with each item, or be taught by someone who already knows the item well.

Sanitation

NSF International certification mark
Courtesy NSF International.

Thorough, regular cleaning of all equipment is essential. Most large equipment can be partially disassembled for cleaning. Read the operating manual, which should describe these procedures in detail, or get the information from someone who knows the equipment.

When purchasing equipment, look for models that have been tested and endorsed for food safety by recognized agencies that certify products and write standards for food, water, air, and consumer goods. Three prominent agencies are NSF International (www.nsf .org; formerly the National Sanitation Foundation), CSA International (www.csa-international. org), and Underwriters Laboratory (www.ul.com). These agencies are accredited by the American National Standards Institute (ANSI), as Standards Developing Organizations (SDOs). They are also accredited by ANSI to certify equipment (such as baking and other commercial food equipment) against the American National Standards that have been developed by each of these SDOs. The standards, and the certifications of these three agencies, are recognized internationally.

SANITATION
NSF/ANSI STD. NO.

The CSA sanitation mark
Courtesy of the Canadian Standard Association.

Products meeting the testing requirements of these agencies are labeled or marked accordingly, as shown in the illustration. Criteria govern such factors as design and construction (for example, sealed joints and seams, as well as accessible and component parts), materials used (for example, nontoxic materials, smooth and easily cleanable surfaces), and performance testing.

Large Equipment

The Underwriters Laboratory logo
Reproduced with permission of Underwriters Laboratory, Inc.

Mixers, ovens, and dough-handling equipment take up most of this category.

Mixers

Mixers of various types are essential tools in the bakeshop. While small quantities of doughs and batters can be mixed by hand, commercial baking in any quantity would be next to impossible without power mixers.

Two main types of mixer are used in small and medium-size bakeshops: vertical and spiral. Other types of specialized equipment are used in large industrial bakeries.

VERTICAL MIXER

Also called a *planetary mixer*, the vertical mixer is the most common type used in baking, as well as in cooking. The term *planetary* is descriptive of the motion of the beater attachment. Just as a planet spins on its axis while revolving around the sun, so too does the beater attachment spin on its axis while rotating in an orbit to reach all parts of the stationary bowl.

Tabletop mixers range in capacity from 5 to 20 quarts (4.75 to 19 L). Floor models are available as large as 140 quarts (132 L).

Vertical mixers have three main mixing attachments:

1. The *paddle* is a flat blade used for general mixing.

2. The *wire whip* is used for such tasks as beating egg foams and cream.

3. The *dough arm* or *hook* is used for mixing and kneading yeast doughs. Dough hooks may be standard *J*-hooks or spiral hooks.

Be sure to use the right-size attachment for the bowl. Using a 40-quart paddle with a 30-quart bowl could cause serious damage the equipment. Make sure both the bowl and the mixing attachment are firmly in place before turning on the machine. Always turn off the machine before scraping down the bowl or inserting a scraper, spoon, or hand into the bowl.

Additional special attachments are also available. These include the following:

- The *sweet dough arm* combines the actions of the dough arm and the flat paddle and is used for mixing sweet doughs.

- The *wing whip* is used for mixing materials too heavy for the standard wire whip.

- The *pastry blender* is used to blend fat and flour, as in making pie doughs.

Small table-model mixer
Courtesy of Hobart Corporation.

Large floor-model mixer
Courtesy of Hobart Corporation.

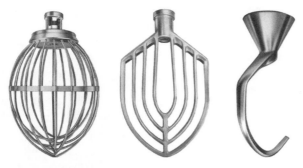

Mixer attachments (left to right): whip, paddle, dough arm
Courtesy of Hobart Corporation.

The availability of such a variety of attachments points up one of the main advantages of the planetary mixer: its versatility. With a single machine, the baker can produce a great variety of doughs, batters, creams, meringues, and other goods. In addition, vertical mixers have an attachment hub that can be used to power many other tools, such as grinders and slicers. This makes vertical mixers useful in the kitchen as well as the bakeshop.

SPIRAL MIXER

Spiral mixers are designed for doughs and heavy batters and are used primarily for making large quantities of yeast doughs for breads and bagels. Unlike vertical mixers, spiral mixers do not have interchangeable bowls and agitator arms. The agitator arm is in the shape of a spiral, and both the bowl and the spiral arm rotate to develop the dough quickly and efficiently. In a typical model, the bowl may be set to rotate in either direction.

Dough capacities range from 5 to 30 pounds (2.3 to 14 kg) for small machines to more than 500 pounds (230 kg) in large machines.

Because spiral mixers are used exclusively for mixing doughs, they do not have the versatility of vertical mixers, as just described. However, they do have several important features and advantages that make them the preferred mixers of bread bakers and pizza makers:

Spiral mixer
Courtesy of TMB Baking, Inc.

CONTINUOUS MIXER

Another type of mixer used in large bakeries is the *continuous mixer*. Here, small amounts of scaled ingredients enter the machine continuously at one end. The ingredients are blended and developed into a dough as they move through the machine. The finished dough emerges at the other end of the machine. These mixers are efficient because instead of having to blend, say, 200 pounds of flour into a dough all at once, they can take in the flour in 5-pound increments, making the blending much easier.

- Spiral mixers blend and develop dough more efficiently than planetary mixers. Because of their design, they develop dough more intensively and in less time, resulting in lower machine friction and dough warming.

- The design of the bowl and beater allows for a wide range of dough capacity for each machine. For example, a medium-size mixer may handle as little as 10 pounds (4.5 kg) of dough or as much as 200 pounds (90 kg). By contrast, a vertical mixer bowl handles only a narrow range of dough weights; too large or too small a quantity will not mix properly.

- Spiral mixers are sturdier and more rugged than vertical mixers. They handle more dough, last longer, and require less repair and maintenance.

Three main varieties of spiral mixer are available:

4. **Fixed-bowl mixers.** These have a nonremovable bowl. The dough must be lifted out by hand.

5. **Removable-bowl mixers.** These have a bowl that may be removed from the machine, usually on a wheeled trolley. They are useful for high-volume operations, because a new bowl of ingredients may be wheeled into place as soon as the earlier batch is removed.

6. **Tilt mixers.** On these machines, the entire machine tilts up to deposit the finished dough onto a tray or another container.

Most spiral mixers have two operating speeds, although some specialized machines for stiff doughs have only one speed. In a typical mixing procedure, the baker uses the first speed for the first phase of dough mixing, when the ingredients are blended, and switches to the second speed for the later phase of dough development. Machines with automated controls have timers to regulate each phase of mixing.

Similar to spiral mixers are *fork mixers*. Instead of a single spiral agitator or beater, these machines have a two-pronged fork-shaped beater that enters the bowl at about a 45-degree angle. Like spiral mixers, fork mixers are used specifically for bread doughs.

HORIZONTAL MIXER

Horizontal mixers are large, industrial size machines capable of handling as much as several thousand pounds of dough at a time. Each model is designed to work best with a specific range of products, such as bread doughs, pastry doughs, or soft doughs and batters. Beater or agitator designs differ for each of these specialized models.

Horizontal mixer
Courtesy of The Peerless Group.

Many horizontal mixers are equipped with water jackets that surround the mixing container. Water of the desired temperature is circulated through the jacket, enabling the operator to control the dough temperature with great precision.

Dough-Handling Equipment

DOUGH FERMENTATION TROUGH

This item is used to hold mixed yeast doughs during fermentation. Small operations might simply use large mixing bowls on stands instead.

Divider
Courtesy of American Baking Systems and S.A. Jac NV.

DIVIDER

Dividers cut scaled pieces of dough into equal portions by means of a die or cutter attached to a hydraulic or mechanical lever assembly. For example, a divider may cut a 3-pound piece of dough (called a *press*) into 36 pieces, 1⅓ ounces each, for making dinner rolls. After they are divided, the individual pieces must be rounded by hand.

DIVIDER-ROUNDER
This machine divides the dough, as does a simple divider, and it then automatically rounds the individual portions, greatly speeding makeup of the dough products.

DOUGH SHEETER
A sheeter rolls out portions of dough into sheets of uniform thickness. It consists of a canvas conveyor belt that feeds the dough through a pair of rollers. To make thin sheets, the dough usually must be passed through the rollers several times. The operator decreases the space between the rollers after each pass.

MOLDER
A molder rolls and forms pieces of bread dough for standard loaves, baguettes, and rolls, eliminating the need to perform these tasks by hand.

PROOFER
A proofer is a special box in which the ideal conditions for fermenting yeast doughs can be created. The box maintains a preset warm temperature and humidity level appropriate to the specific dough.

RETARDER
Chilling or refrigerating yeast dough slows or retards the rate of fermentation so the dough can be stored for later baking. A retarder is a refrigerator that maintains a high level of humidity to prevent the dough from drying out or crusting.

RETARDER-PROOFER
This machine is, as its name suggests, a combination retarder and proofer. A dough can be retarded for a preset time, after which the machine switches to proofing mode and warms up to a second preset temperature and humidity level. For example, breakfast breads can be made up the previous day, held, and be fully proofed and ready to bake when the shop opens the next morning.

Divider-rounder
Courtesy of TMB Baking, Inc.

Sheeter
Courtesy of American Baking Systems and S.A. Jac NV.

Molder
Courtesy of American Baking Systems and S.A. Jac NV.

Proofer
Courtesy of Bevles.

Retarder-proofer
Courtesy of TMB Baking, Inc.

Ovens

Ovens are, of course, the workhorses of the bakery and pastry shop. They are essential for producing breads, cakes, cookies, pastries, and other baked items. Ovens are enclosed spaces in which food is heated, usually by hot air (except in the case of microwave ovens, which are not especially useful in a bakeshop). Several kinds of oven are used in baking.

Steam is important in baking many kinds of breads. Ovens used in bakeshops, including deck ovens, rack ovens, and mechanical ovens, may have steam injected into them during part of the baking cycle.

DECK OVEN

Deck ovens are so called because the items to be baked—either on sheet pans or, in the case of some breads, freestanding—are placed directly on the bottom, or deck, of the oven. There are no racks for holding pans in deck ovens. Deck ovens are also called *stack ovens* because several may be stacked on top of one another. Breads baked directly on the floor of the oven rather than in pans are often called *hearth breads*, so another name for these ovens is *hearth ovens*. Deck ovens for baking bread are equipped with steam injectors.

Deck oven
Courtesy of Macadams Baking Systems (Pty) Ltd

RACK OVEN

A rack oven is a large oven into which entire racks full of sheet pans can be wheeled for baking. Normal baker's racks hold 8 to 24 full-size sheet pans, but racks made specifically to go into rack ovens usually hold 15 to 20 pans. Rack ovens hold 1 to 4 of these racks at once. The ovens are also equipped with steam injectors.

Although this usage is not strictly correct, you may hear the term *rack oven* used for conventional ovens, such as those found in restaurant ranges, because the pans are placed on racks rather than directly on the bottom, as in deck ovens.

Rack oven
Courtesy of Lang Manufacturing Company.

MECHANICAL OVEN

In a mechanical oven, the food is in motion while it bakes. The most common type is a revolving oven, in which the mechanism is like that of a Ferris wheel. This mechanical action eliminates the problem of hot spots, or uneven baking, because the mechanism rotates the foods throughout the oven. Because of their size, mechanical ovens are especially useful in high-volume operations. Revolving ovens can be equipped with steam injectors.

A typical revolving oven is shown in the illustration. Each of the multiple trays in such an oven holds one or more sheet pans. The operator loads one tray at a time through the narrow door in the front.

Revolving oven
Courtesy of Baxter/ITW Food Equipment Group, LLC.

CONVECTION OVEN

Convection ovens contain fans that circulate the air and distribute the heat rapidly throughout the interior. The forced air makes foods cook more quickly at lower temperatures. However, the strong forced air can distort the shape of items made with batters and soft doughs, and the airflow may be strong enough to blow baking parchment off sheet pans. Therefore, convection ovens are not as versatile for the baker as are the other kinds of ovens discussed here.

Convection oven
Courtesy of Vulcan-Hart Company.

Steam-Jacketed Kettle

Steam-jacketed kettles, or steam kettles, have double walls between which steam circulates. Liquids in the kettle itself are heated quickly and efficiently. Although restaurants may use large floor-mounted kettles for making stocks, smaller table models are more useful in the bakeshop for making custards, creams, and fillings.

Tilting kettles with a pouring lip are called *trunnion kettles*. Table models range in capacity from a few quarts or liters to 40 quarts (38 L).

Steam-jacketed kettle
Courtesy of Vulcan-Hart Company.

Fryer

Fryers are needed in the bakeshop for doughnuts and other fried items. Small operations often use standard deep fryers (or even stovetop kettles), but larger doughnut fryers are best if you make doughnuts in quantity. They should be used in conjunction with screens, for lowering the doughnuts into the fat and removing them when fried.

In the fryer in the illustration, the proofed doughnuts are arranged on the screen at the right side of the fry kettle. The operator then manually lowers the screen into the hot fat by means of the two raised handles. The illustration also shows, on the left side, a batter depositor for cake doughnuts.

Doughnut fryer
Courtesy of Belshaw, Bros., Inc.

Pans, Containers, and Molds

MANY OF THE pots and pans found in the hot kitchen are also used in the bakeshop. For example, saucepans are used to boil syrups and to cook creams and fillings. This section, however, concentrates on specialty containers and molds for the bakery. The following list gives a representative sample of the more important of these, in alphabetical order. Molds are of two types: those for baking dough or batter items, and those for giving shape to refrigerated items such as mousses and bombes. Other containers, such as mixing bowls, are included in the list.

Baba mold. A small thimble-shaped mold for making baba.

Banneton. A bentwood basket, available in various shapes, for holding and giving shape to certain hearth bread doughs as they proof. Similar canvas-lined baskets are also available.

Baba mold

Banneton

Barquette

Charlotte mold

Barquette. A small boat-shaped mold for petits fours and small tartlets.

Bombe mold. A dome-shaped mold for frozen desserts.

Brioche mold. A flared pan with fluted sides for making brioche.

Cake pans. Most cake pans are round, but other shapes, such as hearts, are available for specialty cakes. Cake pans come in many sizes.

Cake ring. See *Charlotte ring*.

Charlotte mold. The classic charlotte mold is round, tapered, and flat-bottomed, with two handles near the top rim. Except for the Apple Charlotte, which is baked in this mold, classic charlottes are made with a Bavarian cream filling and refrigerated until set, not baked.

Charlotte ring. Also called *cake rings*, these are stainless-steel rings in various diameters and heights, most often used for making molded desserts and for shaping and holding desserts made of layers of cake, pastry, and fillings. The rings are removed after the fillings have set and before serving or display.

Chocolate molds. Used for all sorts of chocolate work, from large display pieces to bite-size truffles.

Cornstick pan. Special baking pan with indentations shaped like small ears of corn. Used for baking cornbread items.

Flexipan. This is the brand name for a line of nonstick baking pans made of a flexible silicone material. Flexipans are available in dozens of shapes and sizes to make a wide range of products, from muffins and quick-bread loaves to petits fours.

Hotel pan. A rectangular pan, usually made of stainless steel. Designed to hold foods in service counters. Also used for baking and steaming, and often for baked items such as bread pudding. The standard size is 10 × 20 inches (325 × 530 mm). Fractions of this size (½, ⅓, and so on) are also available. Standard depth is 2½ inches (65 mm), but deeper pans are also available.

Full-size and half-size hotel pans

Loaf pan. A rectangular pan, usually with slightly flared sides, used for baking loaf breads. Loaf pans can also be used for molding refrigerated and frozen desserts. A special type of loaf pan is the Pullman pan, which has straight, not flared sides, and a removable lid, for baking Pullman loaves of bread.

Madeleine pan. A special baking pan with shell-shaped indentations, used for baking madeleines.

Loaf pan

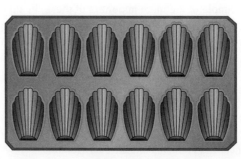

Pullman pan

Madeleine pan

Mixing bowls. The most useful mixing bowls are made of stainless steel and have round bottoms. They are used for general mixing and whipping. The round construction enables the whip to reach all areas, for thorough mixing or whipping.

Muffin pan. Metal baking pan with cup-shaped indentations for baking muffins. Pans are available for making muffins in several sizes.

Petit four molds. Tiny metal molds in a variety of shapes, used for baking an assortment of little tartlets, financiers, and other petits fours.

Pie pan. Shallow pan with sloping sides, used for baking pies. Disposable aluminum pie pans are usually used in retail bakeshops.

Savarin mold. Small ring-shaped or doughnut-shaped metal mold for baking savarins.

Savarin mold

Sheet pan. A shallow, rectangular pan (1 inch/25 mm deep) for baking sheet cakes, cookies, rolls, and other baked goods. A full sheet pan measures 18 × 26 inches (46 × 66 cm). Half-sheet pans are 13 × 18 inches (33 × 46 cm). Perforated sheet pans are the same size, but the bottom is full of tiny holes. These allow even baking and browning of breads and rolls because the holes let the oven's hot air circulate freely around the items as they bake.

Sheet pan

Pan extenders are metal or fiberglass frames that fit inside sheet pans. They give straight sides to sheet cakes and make the pan deeper. Extenders are usually 2 inches (5 cm) high.

Springform pan. A cake pan with a removable bottom. Used primarily for baking cheesecakes and other items too delicate to be easily and cleanly removed from standard cake pans.

Tart pan. A shallow (1 inch/2.5 cm deep) metal pan, usually with fluted sides, used for baking tarts. Stan-dard pans are round, but square and rectangular pans are also available. They may be made in one piece or with a removable bottom to make removal of the baked tart from the pan easier.

Tart pans make multiserving pastries, but smaller tartlet pans make single-portion tartlets. Like tart pans, these come in a variety of sizes. The smallest usually are in one piece and lack the removable bottom.

Tube pan. A deep cake pan with a tube in the center. The tube promotes even baking of angel food cakes and similar items.

Springform pan

Tart pan

Tube pan

Hand Tools

The category of hand tools is a broad one, encompassing large and small items, some more familiar than others. Those described here are considered indispensable to a bakeshop or commercial baking establishment.

Straight spatula

Blowtorch. A tool used for caramelizing and controlled browning of various pastry items, and for caramelizing the sugar topping of crème brûlée. Butane or propane is used as fuel, depending on the model.

Blowtorch

Bowl knife. Also called a *straight spatula* or *palette knife*, this tool has a long, flexible blade with a rounded end. Used mostly for spreading icing on cakes and for mixing and bowl scraping. A variant with an angled blade is called an *offset spatula*. The bent blade allows spreading and smoothing batters and fillings inside pans.

Bench brush

Brushes. Pastry brushes are used to brush items with egg wash, glaze, and so on. Larger bench brushes are used to brush flour from tabletops and from the surface of dough. Oven brushes are used to clean excess flour from deck ovens.

Chinois and china cap. A chinois is a conical strainer with a fine mesh, used mostly for straining sauces. A china cap is also a conical strainer, but it is made of perforated steel, so it doesn't strain as finely. A china cap is usually lined with several layers of cheesecloth if the liquid must be well strained.

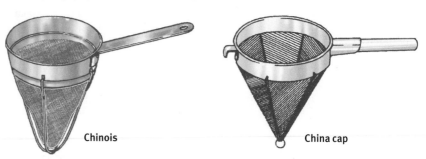

Chinois   **China cap**

Icing comb

Comb, icing. A small plastic tool, usually triangular, with serrated edges in various patterns, for decorating icings and other pastry and decorative items.

Cutters. Many types of cutters are used in the pastry department. Cookie cutters and pastry cutters, available in many shapes, cut decorative shapes by stamping them from rolled-out dough. Roller cutters have a handle on each end, like a rolling pin, and are rolled over rolled-out dough to cut repetitive shapes quickly and efficiently, with minimal loss of dough to trimmings and scraps. Roller cutters are often used for croissants.

Cookie cutters and pastry cutters

Pastry bag. A cone-shaped cloth or plastic bag with an open end that can be fitted with metal or plastic tubes or tips of various shapes and sizes. Used for shaping and decorating with items such as icing; for filling certain kinds of pastries and other items, such as éclairs; and for portioning creams, fillings, and doughs.

Peel. A thin, flat wooden board or steel sheet with a long handle, used for inserting and removing hearth breads from deck ovens. Because they are thinner than traditional wooden peels, steel peels are easier to slide under baked loaves.

Roller cutter

Peel

Roller docker. A tool that pierces holes in rolled-out dough to prevent bubbling during baking. It consists of a handle attached to a rotating tube fitted with rows of spikes.

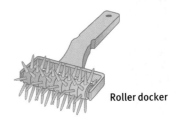
Roller docker

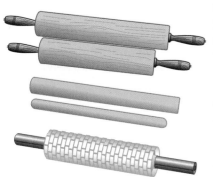
Ball-bearing rolling pins, straight wooden rolling pins, and textured rolling pin

Rolling pins. Many types of rolling pin are used in the bakeshop for rolling out doughs. Perhaps the most versatile pin, used for most general rolling tasks, is simply a solid hardwood rod, about 2 inches (5 cm) thick and 20 inches (50 cm) long. A French rolling pin is about 2 inches (5 cm) thick at the center and tapered toward the ends. It is useful for rolling pie doughs and other doughs that must be rolled to a circular shape. For large quantities or heavy work, a heavy ball-bearing pin may be used. This pin is 3 to 4 inches (8 to 10 cm) thick and has a swiveling rod inserted through the center, with a handle at each end. Textured rolling pins are used to emboss designs, such as a basketweave pattern, in sheets of marzipan and pastillage.

Scrapers. A bench scraper, also called a *dough scraper*, is a small rectangle of stainless steel with a handle along one of the long edges. It is used for cutting and portioning dough and for scraping tabletops. A bowl scraper is a piece of plastic about the same size, but with one curved edge and no handle. It is used for scraping out the contents of mixing bowls.

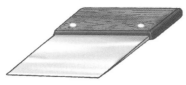
Bench scraper

Bowl scraper

Sieve. A round metal screen supported in a stainless-steel hoop frame. It is used for sifting flour and other dry ingredients. Also called a *drum sieve* or *tamis* (pronounced tah-mee).

Strainer. A round-bottomed, cup-shaped tool made of screen mesh or perforated metal, with a handle on one side. Used for separating solids from liquids, such as draining the juice from fruit. Screen-mesh strainers can also be used for sifting dry ingredients, like a sieve.

Sieve

Turntable. A round, flat disk that swivels freely on a pedestal base. Used for holding cakes for decorating.

Wire rack A wire grate used to hold baked goods as they are cooling, or to hold items such as cakes while liquid icings, such as fondant, are applied.

Whip. Loops of stainless-steel wire fastened to a handle. Whips with a few stiff wires are used for mixing and blending, and whips with many flexible wires are used for whipping foams, such as whipped cream and egg foams. Also called *whisk*.

Turntable

Whips

Miscellaneous Tools and Equipment

A number of other tools and equipment, which together may be categorized as miscellaneous, also should be considered essentials to the bakeshop or commercial bakery kitchen.

Acetate. A type of clear plastic. Acetate strips are used for lining charlotte molds (see above) in the production of certain cakes, pastries, and refrigerated desserts. For retail display, the strips can be left on after the charlotte rings are removed to support the dessert while displaying the layers.

Couche. A sheet of heavy linen or canvas, used for supporting certain breads, such as baguettes, as they are proofed. The cloth is placed on a sheet pan and pleated to form troughs to hold the loaves so they can proof without spreading.

Hydrometer. Also called a *sugar densimeter*, *saccharometer*, and *Baumé hydrometer*. Used to test the density of sugar syrups. (Sometimes called a *thermometer*, but this is inaccurate because it doesn't measure temperature.) It is a glass tube, weighted at one end, that is floated in the solution to be tested. Because it floats higher in denser solutions, the density can be read off the scale marked along the length of the tube at the point where the surface of the liquid meets the tube.

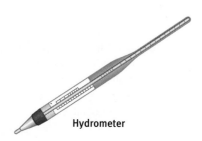

Hydrometer

Ice cream freezer. Machine for churning and freezing ice creams and sorbets. It consists of a large refrigerated canister or container with a paddle, called a *dasher*, that rotates inside. The ice cream or sorbet mix freezes against the walls of the canister and is continually scraped off and remixed to prevent the formation of ice crystals. Unlike home models, which depend on a salted ice water mixture to create freezing temperatures, commercial ice cream freezers contain a built-in electrically operated freezing unit.

Ice cream freezer

Marble. A stone material used for tabletop or work surfaces in pastry shops. The hard, cool surface of marble is ideal for working with pastry doughs, as well as for tempering chocolate and for some decorative work, such as pastillage. Marble slabs may be installed on top of under-the-counter refrigerated storage boxes. This keeps the marble cool even in warm weather.

Parchment paper. Also called *baking paper* or *silicone paper*, this is a sheet of treated nonstick paper sized to fit standard sheet pans. When used to line pans, parchment eliminates the need for greasing them. Also used to make piping cones for decorative work.

Rack, cooling. A wire rack used to hold baked goods while cooling. The rack allows air circulation around the items.

Silicone mat. Flexible fiberglass mat coated with nonstick silicone, used to line baking sheets. Available to fit full and half-size sheet pans. Also used in sugar work. The mats withstand temperatures up to about 480°F (250°C) and can be reused indefinitely if well cared for and not folded or creased. There are several manufacturers of silicone mats, but they are often known by one brand name, Silpat.

Thermometers. Thermometers have many uses in the bakery, and there are many types of specialized thermometers. The sugar thermometer, also called a *candy thermometer*, is one of the most important. It is used for measuring the temperature, and hence the concentration, of boiling sugar syrups. The chocolate thermometer is used for tempering chocolate. Other thermometers measure the temperature of bread doughs, frying fat, and the interiors of ovens, refrigerators, and freezers (to check the accuracy of the equipment's thermostat).

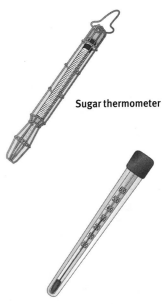

Sugar thermometer

Chocolate thermometer

KEY POINTS TO REVIEW

- What are the important safety and sanitation practices for purchasing and handling bakeshop equipment?

- What are the principal types of mixers and attachments?

- What are the principal types of dough-handling equipment used in the bakeshop?

- What are the four principal types of ovens used in the bakeshop?

Chapter 4

Part of procedure for preparing a purée soup, page 206.

Basic Principles of Cooking and Food Science

No written recipe can be 100 percent accurate. No matter how carefully a recipe is written, the judgment of the cook is still the most important factor in a preparation turning out well. A cook's judgment is based on experience, on an understanding of the raw materials available, and on knowledge of basic cooking principles and food science.

Ever since Carême began to define the principles and methods that lie behind the recipes we use (see p. 3), professional cooking has been based on procedures and methods rather than only on recipes. In the twenty-first century, chefs have improved their knowledge not just of cooking theory but also of the science behind it.

This chapter deals with basic principles. You will learn about what happens to food when it is heated, about how food is cooked by different methods, and about rules of seasoning and flavoring. It is important to understand the science of food and cooking so you can successfully use these principles in the kitchen.

After reading this chapter, you should be able to

1. Name the most important components of foods and describe what happens to them when they are cooked.

2. Name and describe three ways in which heat is transferred to food in order to cook it.

3. Describe the two factors or changes in cooked foods that determine doneness.

4. List three factors that affect cooking times.

5. Explain the advantage of boiling or simmering in a covered pot. Describe three situations in which a pot should not be covered during simmering or boiling.

6. Explain how cooking temperature affects the doneness characteristics of a food item.

7. Explain the differences between moist-heat cooking methods, dry-heat cooking methods, and dry-heat cooking methods using fat.

8. Describe each basic cooking method used in the commercial kitchen.

9. Identify the five properties that determine the quality of a deep-fried product.

10. Describe the two main steps in the process of cooking sous vide.

11. List six safety guidelines for cooking sous vide.

12. Explain the difference between a seasoning and a flavoring ingredient and give examples of each.

13. Identify appropriate times for adding seasoning ingredients to the cooking process in order to achieve optimal results.

14. Identify appropriate times for adding flavoring ingredients to the cooking process in order to achieve optimal results.

15. List eleven guidelines for using herbs and spices in cooking.

HEAT AND FOOD

To cook food means to heat it in order to make certain changes in it. Skillful cooks know exactly what changes they want to make and what they have to do to get them right. To learn these cooking skills, it is important for you to know why foods behave as they do when heated. For this, you have to study the theory.

Perhaps not all of this section will make sense to you at first. But the ideas should become clearer to you after you think about them in relation to specific techniques, as demonstrated by your instructor. Later in your studies, when you are learning about cooking meats, fish, vegetables, and other foods, review this section from time to time. Not only will you understand it better but also it should help you make more sense of the procedures you are learning and practicing.

What Is Heat?

Heat is a form of energy associated with the motion of atoms or molecules. When a substance absorbs heat, its molecules move faster. In liquids and gases, the molecules move more quickly from place to place and bounce off each other more frequently. In solids, the molecules stay mostly in place, but they vibrate with more energy. *Temperature* can be defined as a measure of this molecular activity. The higher the temperature, the faster the molecules are moving.

When fast-moving molecules in hot substances come in contact with slower molecules in cold substances, the fast molecules bump into the slower ones and transfer some of their energy, making the slower molecules move faster, or heat up. Thus, as heat is transferred, the hot substance loses energy and the colder substance gains energy.

The moving molecules in a liquid such as water sometimes move to the surface with enough energy to break through and escape to become a gas. This is called *evaporation*. When the molecules in the liquid move faster, more of them can escape in a shorter time. This is why hot water evaporates more quickly than cold water.

When we add enough heat to foods, the molecules may move so fast the structure of the food changes. For example, sucrose (regular sugar) may break apart and form new molecules that happen to have a brown color and the taste of caramel. Or protein molecules may break apart and reform with a different structure. Creating these molecular changes is called *cooking*.

Effects of Heat on Foods

Foods are composed of proteins, fats, carbohydrates, and water, plus small amounts of other compounds such as minerals (including salt), vitamins, pigments (coloring agents), and flavor elements. It is important to understand how these components react when heated or mixed with other foods. You will then be better equipped to correct cooking faults when they occur and to anticipate the effects of changing cooking methods, cooking temperatures, or ingredient proportions.

In other words, when you know why foods behave as they do, you can understand how to get them to behave as you want them to.

The following discussion is concerned with the physical and chemical reactions that affect the components of food. The nutritional aspects of these components are discussed in Chapter 6.

CARBOHYDRATES

1. Starches and sugars are carbohydrates. Both compounds are present in foods in many forms. They are found in fruits, vegetables, grains, beans, and nuts. Meats and fish also contain a small amount of carbohydrate.

2. For the cook, the two most important changes in carbohydrates caused by heat are caramelization and gelatinization.

- *Caramelization* is the browning of sugars. The browning of sautéed vegetables and the golden color of bread crust are forms of caramelization.
- *Gelatinization* occurs when starches absorb water and swell. This is a major principle in the thickening of sauces and in the production of breads and pastries.

Acids inhibit gelatinization. A sauce thickened with flour or starch will be thinner if it contains acid.

FRUIT AND VEGETABLE FIBER

1. *Fiber* is the name for a group of complex substances that give structure and firmness to plants. Fiber cannot be digested.

2. The softening of fruits and vegetables in cooking is, in part, the breaking down of fiber.

3. Sugar makes fiber firmer. Fruit cooked with sugar keeps its shape better than fruit cooked without sugar.

4. Baking soda (and other alkalis) makes fiber softer. Vegetables should not be cooked with baking soda because they become mushy and lose vitamins.

PROTEINS

1. Protein is a major component of meats, poultry, fish, eggs, milk, and milk products. It is present in smaller amounts in nuts, beans, and grains.

2. Proteins consist of long chains of components called *amino acids*. These chains normally form tight coils. As proteins are heated, the coils gradually unwind. At this point, the protein is said to be *denatured*.

   For the cook, the important fact about denaturing is that, when the protein coils unwind, they become attracted to each other and form bonds. This bonding is called *coagulation*. The coagulated proteins form a solid network of bonds and become firm. As the temperature increases, the proteins shrink, become firmer, and lose more moisture. Exposure of proteins to excessive heat toughens them and makes them dry. Most proteins complete coagulation or are cooked at 160°–185°F (71°–85°C).

3. Many protein foods, such as meats, contain small quantities of carbohydrate. When proteins are heated to about 310°F (154°C), the amino acids in the protein chains react with the carbohydrate molecules and undergo a complex chemical reaction. The result is that they turn brown and develop richer flavors. This reaction is called the *Maillard reaction*. It is what happens when meat browns. Because of the high temperature it requires, the Maillard reaction takes place only on the dry surface of the food. Because of its water content, the interior of the meat cannot get this hot.

4. *Connective tissues* are special proteins present in meats. Meats with a great deal of connective tissue are tough, but some connective tissues are dissolved when cooked slowly with moisture. Cooking tough meats properly, therefore, makes them more tender.

5. *Acids*, such as lemon juice, vinegar, and tomato products, have two effects on proteins:
   - They speed coagulation.
   - They help dissolve some connective tissues.

FATS

1. Fats are present in meats, poultry, fish, eggs, milk products, nuts, whole grains, and, to a lesser extent, vegetables and fruits. Fats are also important as cooking mediums, as for frying.

2. Fats can be either solid or liquid at room temperature. Liquid fats are called *oils*. When solid fats are heated, they melt, or change from solid to liquid. The melting point of solid fats varies.

3. When fats are heated, they begin to break down. When hot enough, they deteriorate rapidly and begin to smoke. The temperature at which this happens is called the *smoke point*, and it varies by type of fat. A stable fat—one with a high smoke point—is an important consideration in deep-fat frying.

4. Many flavor compounds dissolve in fat, so fats are important carriers of flavor. When fats melt and are lost from food, some flavors, as well as some vitamins, are lost with them.

MINERALS, VITAMINS, PIGMENTS, AND FLAVOR COMPONENTS

1. Minerals and vitamins are important to the nutritional quality of the food. Pigments and flavor components are important to a food's appearance and taste and may determine whether the food is appetizing enough to eat. So it is important to preserve all these elements.

2. Some of these components are soluble in water, and others are soluble in fats. All of these components may be leached out, or dissolved away, from foods during cooking.

3. Vitamins and pigments may also be destroyed by heat, by long cooking, and by other elements present during cooking.

4. It is important, then, to select cooking methods that preserve, as much as possible, a food's nutrients, taste, and appearance. This is addressed whenever cooking techniques are explained in the remainder of this book.

WATER

1. Nearly all foods contain water. Dried foods may contain as little as a fraction of 1 percent water, but fresh meats, fish, vegetables, and fruits consist mostly of water.

2. Water exists in three states: solid (ice), liquid, and gas (water vapor or steam). At sea level, pure liquid water becomes solid, or freezes, at 32°F (0°C) and turns to steam at 212°F (100°C). When water molecules turn to steam and energetically escape into the atmosphere, water is said to be *boiling*.

3. Water can also turn from liquid to gas at lower temperatures. When water turns to gas at any temperature, the process is called *evaporation*. Evaporation occurs more slowly the lower the temperature is. Evaporation is responsible for the drying of foods. The drying of food surfaces as they are cooked enables them to be browned.

4. Many minerals and other compounds dissolve in water, so water can be a carrier of flavor and of nutritional value.

5. When water carries dissolved compounds, such as salt or sugar, its freezing point is lowered and its boiling point is raised.

Heat Transfer

In order for food to be cooked, heat must be transferred from a heat source (such as a gas flame or an electric element) to and through the food. Understanding the ways in which heat is transferred and the speed at which it is transferred helps the cook control the cooking process.

Heat is transferred in three ways: conduction, convection, and radiation. It is important to remember that, during a cooking process, more than one of these methods of transfer may be happening at the same time. For example, food on a grill may be heated by conduction from the hot metal grill, by convection from hot air rising from the burner or charcoal, and by radiation from the glowing burner or coals.

Conduction

Conduction occurs in two ways:

1. When heat moves directly from one item to something touching it—for example, from the top of the range to a soup pot placed on it, from the pot to the broth inside, and from the broth to the solid food items in it.

2. When heat moves from one part of something to an adjacent part of the same item—for example, from the exterior of a roast to the interior, or from a sauté pan to its handle.

Different materials conduct heat at different speeds. Heat moves rapidly through copper and aluminum, more slowly in stainless steel, more slowly yet in glass and porcelain. Air is a poor conductor of heat.

Convection

Convection occurs when heat is spread by the movement of air, steam, or liquid (including hot fat). There are two kinds of convection:

1. **Natural.**

   Hot liquids and gases rise, while cooler ones sink. Thus, in any oven, kettle of liquid, or deep-fat fryer a constant, natural circulation distributes heat.

2. **Mechanical.**

   In convection ovens and convection steamers, fans speed the circulation of heat. Thus, heat is transferred more quickly to the food, and the food cooks faster.

Stirring is a form of mechanical convection. Thick liquids cannot circulate as quickly as thin ones, so the rate of natural convection is slower. This explains, in part, why it is so easy to scorch thick soups and sauces. The heat is not carried away from the bottom of the pan quickly enough, so it stays concentrated on the bottom and scorches the food. Stirring redistributes the heat and helps prevent this. (Using heavy pots made of a material that conducts heat well also helps prevent scorching because the pot conducts the heat more quickly and evenly across the bottom and up the sides.)

Convection is the process that carries the heat from the heat source to the food. Once the carrier of the heat (air or liquid) comes in contact with the food, the heat is transferred from the carrier to the food by conduction.

Radiation

Radiation occurs when energy is transferred by waves from a source to the food. The waves themselves are not actually heat energy but are changed into heat energy when they strike the food being cooked. (Light waves, radio waves, and X-rays are examples of radiation not used for cooking.)

Two kinds of radiation are used in the kitchen:

1. *Infrared.*

   Broiling is the most familiar example of infrared cooking. In a broiler, an electric element or a ceramic element heated by a gas flame becomes so hot it gives off infrared radiation, which cooks the food. High-intensity infrared ovens are designed to heat food rapidly.

2. *Microwave.*

   In microwave cooking, the radiation generated by the oven penetrates partway into the food, where it agitates the molecules of water. The friction this agitation causes creates heat, which cooks the food.

   - Because microwave radiation affects only water molecules, a completely waterless material will not heat in a microwave oven. Plates become hot only when heat is conducted to them by hot foods.

   - Because most microwaves penetrate no more than about 2 inches (50 mm) into foods, heat is transferred to the center of large pieces of food by conduction, just as in roasting.

   Cooking with microwaves is discussed in more detail later in this chapter.

Heat Management

The final temperature to which we cook a food ranges from about 120°F (49°C) for rare meats and fish to about 400°F (200°C) for the crisp exterior of such foods as breads and seared meats. The boiling point of water, 212°F (100°C), falls within this range. Notice, however, the heat sources we use in the kitchen, from electric elements to gas flames, are much hotter than this temperature. Managing the heat to cook foods to the desired degree is an important part of cooking.

In the discussion that follows, we first consider cooking time—that is, the time it takes to heat food until it changes to a condition that we call *done*. We then look at other problems with controlling heat in cooking.

Doneness and Cooking Times

We say a food is "done" when two things have happened:

1. **The interior temperature has risen to the desired degree.**
   Interior temperature is the most important factor when we are cooking tender meats. The difference between rare, medium, and well done is a difference in temperature, and we can measure this doneness with a thermometer. Interior temperature is also important for food safety.

2. **The desired changes have taken place in the food.**
   Earlier in this chapter, we discussed the changes that take place in foods as they are heated. These changes include gelatinization of starches, coagulation of proteins, breaking down of connective tissues, caramelization of sugars, and Maillard browning.
   In many foods, creating these changes is more important than simply heating the interior to a desired temperature. For example, the inside of a small piece of stew meat quickly becomes just as hot as the liquid in which it is simmering. However, we don't say it is "done" until enough connective tissue has broken down so it has a tender texture. It's not enough just to heat it to the desired degree.
   Similarly, the inside of a strand of spaghetti quickly rises to the temperature of boiling water, but it is not done until enough starch has absorbed water and gelatinized, so it has the desired texture.

Standards of doneness are different for every type of food and for every cooking method. As we discuss individual foods throughout the remainder of this book, we learn more about doneness in meats, poultry, fish, vegetables, starches, and other foods.

The time it takes to achieve doneness is affected by three factors:

1. **Cooking temperature.**
   This means the temperature of the air in the oven, the fat in the fryer, the surface of a griddle, or the liquid in which a food is cooking.

2. **The speed of heat transfer.**
   Different cooking methods transfer heat at different rates, as shown by these examples:
   Air is a poor conductor of heat, while steam is much more efficient. A jet of steam (212°F/100°C) will easily burn your hand, but you can safely reach into an oven at 500°F (260°C). This is why it takes longer to bake potatoes than to steam them.
   A convection oven cooks faster than a conventional oven, even if both are set at the same temperature. The forced air movement transfers heat more rapidly.

3. **Size, temperature, and individual characteristics of the food.**
   For example:

   A small beef roast cooks faster than a large one.

   A chilled steak takes longer to broil than one at room temperature.

   Fish items generally cook more quickly than meats.

   Beef shank, which has a lot of connective tissue, takes longer to cook than beef tenderloin.

Because there are so many variables, it is difficult or even impossible to determine exact cooking times in most recipes. Individual ovens, fryers, and steamers, for example, may transfer heat more or less efficiently or have different recovery times. Roasting charts that give cooking times for various cuts of meat can be used only as guidelines, and the cook must use his or her judgment to make the final determination of doneness. Cooking times are discussed again in the next chapter.

Controlling Heat

To control cooking, we must control how heat is transferred. The kitchen contains dozens of kinds of heat sources as well as a great array of pots, pans, and other cooking tools, Controlling cooking with so many options is a skill a cook gains with experience, by performing cooking tasks over and over.

In this section, we introduce the topic of heat management with a summary of two of the most common kinds of heat control problems.

HOW TO BOIL WATER

It's a common joke that boiling water is a cooking skill many noncooks have never learned. However, boiling water is a little more complex than such quips suggest. There is more to boiling water than just putting a pot on the stove.

Covering the Pot

To bring water to a boil on a cooktop, we apply heat to the bottom of a pot containing the water. The heat is transferred to the water, raising its temperature. Some of this heat energy quickly escapes from the top of the pot. If the pot is covered, much of the heat is trapped inside, and the water comes to a boil much more quickly. To raise the temperature of 1 gram of water 1 degree Celsius takes only 1 calorie of heat energy. But to turn 1 gram of boiling water to steam takes 539 calories. When the steam escapes, it takes this energy with it. A lot of energy is lost from an uncovered pot. By covering it, we save energy and shorten heating times.

After a liquid has come to a boil, keeping the pot covered can still be helpful. You have probably had the experience of removing the lid from a pot simmering over a low flame and seeing the bubbling slow down as soon as the lid is off. This is because so much heat escapes as soon as the cover is removed. By keeping the pot covered, you can maintain the desired cooking temperature using a lower burner setting.

Although covering pots is a more efficient use of energy, sometimes you must keep them uncovered:

- *When evaporation is desired.* In many cooking operations, one of the goals is to evaporate moisture to concentrate flavors or change textures. Keep the pot uncovered to speed evaporation.

- *When the contents must be visually monitored.* In some cases, you must keep an eye on the food as it simmers or boils, if only to make sure it continues to simmer at the proper rate, not too fast or too slow.

- *When green vegetables are cooked.* Plant acids that destroy green pigments must be allowed to escape, as explained on page 243.

Controlling the Heat

Water boils at 212°F (100°C) at sea level and at standard atmospheric pressure. When water is boiling, any additional heat is used to turn water to steam, which then carries the heat away. No matter how high you turn the heat, the water can never rise above 212°F (100°C). In other words, turning up the heat under a pot that is already boiling is a waste of energy and does not decrease cooking time. Furthermore, the increased agitation of rapidly boiling water does more damage to delicate foods. Remember, a rapid boil is no hotter than a slow boil.

COOKING TO THE CENTER

As we read earlier, heat is transferred from the outside of food to the inside by conduction. Conduction takes time, so cooking takes time.

Think of a steak cooking on a grill. Let's say we want to cook the steak to an interior temperature of 140°F (60°C), for medium doneness. When we first put the steak on to cook, the interior temperature is room temperature, or possibly refrigerator temperature. The outside,

> ### BOILING OIL
>
> The term *boiling oil* is commonly heard, but oil doesn't boil, at least in the way water does. The bubbling of boiling water, as the text explains, occurs when heated molecules of liquid water turn to gas—that is, steam—and rise to the surface. Oil that is free of water does not boil at normal cooking temperatures. The bubbling we see in cooking fat, such as that in deep fryers, is caused by water in submerged foods turning to steam. It's not the oil that is boiling.

however, rises to perhaps 400°F (200°C) very soon after we place it on the grill. Gradually, this heat moves to the center. By the time the center reaches the target temperature, the outside is much hotter. If we cut the steak through the center, we see a gradation from very well done at the outside to medium done in the middle.

Often this is just what we want. This is how people are used to eating steaks, so a person might be surprised to get a steak that was a uniform medium done all the way through.

By contrast, if we cook the steak at a low temperature, there is less temperature difference between the outside and inside, so the doneness of the meat is more uniform from outside to inside.

The same is true of large roasts. Roasting at a high temperature produces a strong gradation of doneness, from well done on the outside to less done in the center. Roasting at a low temperature gives more uniform doneness throughout. The roasting temperature we use depends on the results we want.

Of course, cooking at a low temperature doesn't create the well-browned crust most diners desire. We have two options to solve this problem:

- Brown the exterior with high heat, then cook to doneness at lower heat.
- Cook to doneness at low heat, then brown the exterior with a quick blast of high heat.

COOKING METHODS

Cooking methods are classified as moist heat or dry heat.

Moist-heat methods are those in which the heat is conducted to the food product by water or water-based liquids such as stock and sauces, or by steam.

Dry-heat methods are those in which the heat is conducted without moisture—that is, by hot air, hot metal, radiation, or hot fat. We usually divide dry-heat methods into two categories: without fat and with fat.

Different cooking methods are suited to different kinds of foods. For example, some meats are high in connective tissue and are tough unless this tissue is broken down slowly by moist heat. Other meats are low in connective tissue and naturally tender. They are at their best and juiciest when cooked with dry heat to a rare or medium-done stage.

Many other factors must be considered when choosing cooking methods for meats, fish, and vegetables, such as the flavor and appearance imparted by browning, the flavor imparted by fats, and the firmness or delicacy of the product. These factors are discussed in later chapters with respect to individual foods.

The basic cooking methods are summarized here. Their practical application to foods is discussed in detail in the remainder of the book and reinforced by your instructors' demonstrations and your own experience and practice.

Moist-Heat Methods

Poach, Simmer, and Boil

Poaching, *simmering*, and *boiling* all involve cooking a food in water or a seasoned or flavored liquid. The temperature of the liquid determines the method.

1. To *boil* means to cook in a liquid that is bubbling rapidly and greatly agitated. Water boils at 212°F (100°C) at sea level. No matter how high the burner is turned, the temperature of the liquid will go no higher.

   Boiling is generally reserved for vegetables and starches. The high temperature toughens the proteins of meats, fish, and eggs, and the rapid bubbling breaks up delicate foods.

2. To *simmer* means to cook in a liquid that is bubbling gently at a temperature of about 185°F to 205°F (85°C to 96°C).

   Most foods cooked in a liquid are simmered. The higher temperatures and intense agitation of boiling are detrimental to most foods. The word *boiled* is sometimes used as a menu term, as when simmered fresh beef is called "boiled beef."

3. To *poach* means to cook in a liquid, usually a small amount, that is hot but not actually bubbling. Temperature is 160°–180°F (71°–82°C).

   Poaching is used to cook delicate foods such as fish and eggs out of the shell. It is also used to partially cook foods such as variety meats in order to eliminate undesirable flavors and to firm the product before final cooking.

4. A rule of thumb: Whether a food is to be simmered or boiled, the liquid is often brought to a full boil at first. This compensates for the lowering of the temperature when the food items are added. The heat is then adjusted to maintain a steady temperature.

5. To *blanch* means to cook an item partially and briefly, usually in water but sometimes by other methods (as when French fries are blanched in deep fat).
   There are two ways of blanching in water:

   - Place the item in cold water, bring to a boil, and simmer briefly. Cool the item by plunging it into cold water.
     Purpose: to dissolve out blood, salt, or impurities from meats and bones.
   - Place the item in rapidly boiling water and return the water to the boil. Remove the item and cool in cold water.
     Purpose: to set the color and destroy harmful enzymes in vegetables, or to loosen the skins of tomatoes, peaches, and similar items for easier peeling.

6. Altitude note: The boiling point of water decreases as altitude above sea level is increased. At 5,000 feet (1,500 m) above sea level, water boils at about 203°F (95°C). Thus, it takes longer to boil foods to doneness at high altitudes because the temperature is lower.

Steam

To *steam* means to cook foods by exposing them directly to steam.

1. In quantity cooking, steaming is usually done in special steam cookers, which are designed to accept standard-size pans. Steaming can also be done on a rack above boiling water. This method is more cumbersome, however, and is used only occasionally in food service. Cooking in a steam-jacketed kettle is not steaming because the steam does not actually touch the food.

2. The term *steaming* also refers to cooking an item tightly wrapped or in a covered pan so it cooks in the steam formed by its own moisture. This method is used in cooking items *en papillote*, meaning "wrapped in parchment paper" (or foil). "Baked" potatoes wrapped in foil are actually steamed.

3. Steam at normal pressure is 212°F (100°C), the same as boiling water. However, it carries much more heat than boiling water and cooks foods very rapidly. Cooking times must be carefully controlled to avoid overcooking.

4. A *pressure steamer* is a steam cooker that holds in steam under pressure. The temperature of the steam then goes higher than 212°F (100°C), as the following chart shows:

Pressure	Steam Temperature
5 psi (pounds per square inch)	227°F (106°C)
10 psi	240°F (116°C)
15 psi	250°F (121°C)

   Because of these temperatures, pressure steaming is an extremely rapid method of cooking and must be carefully controlled and timed.

5. Steaming is widely used for vegetables. It cooks them rapidly, without agitation, and minimizes the dissolving away of nutrients that occurs when vegetables are boiled.

Note that steaming doesn't completely eliminate leaching. Some steam condenses on the vegetables and drips off, carrying some pigments and nutrients with it. This liquid can be collected in drip pans below the steamer pans and saved for later use.

Braise

To *braise* means to cook covered in a small amount of liquid, usually after preliminary browning. In almost all cases, the liquid is served with the product as a sauce.

Braising is sometimes referred to as a *combination cooking method* because the product is first browned, using dry heat, before it is cooked with a liquid. Nevertheless, in most cases, moist heat is responsible for most of the cooking process, and the browning may be thought of as a preliminary technique. The purpose of the browning step is not so much to cook the item as to develop color and flavor.

Some references describe braising and *stewing* as two different cooking methods. The term *braising* is used for large cuts of meat, and *stewing* is used for smaller items. In this book, however, we use the term *braising* for both methods because the basic procedure in both cases is the same—first browning with dry heat, then cooking with moist heat. (Note that the term *stewing* is also used for simmering in a small amount of liquid without preliminary browning.)

1. Braised meats are usually browned first using a dry-heat method such as pan-frying. This gives a desirable appearance and flavor to the product and sauce.

2. Braising also refers to cooking some vegetables, such as lettuce or cabbage, at low temperature in a small amount of liquid without first browning in fat, or with only a light preliminary sautéing.

3. Braises (see sidebar) are usually not completely covered by the cooking liquid. The top of the product is actually cooked by the steam held in the covered pot. Pot roasts, for example, are cooked in liquid that covers the item by one-third to two-thirds. The exact amount depends on how much sauce is needed for service. This method yields a flavorful, concentrated sauce.

   Stews are usually cooked in just enough liquid to cover them completely. Because the pieces of food in a stew are bite-sized, there is little space between them. Therefore, it doesn't take much cooking liquid to cover them, so this method also yields a flavorful, concentrated sauce.

4. In some preparations, especially of poultry and fish, no liquid is added. This is still considered braising because steam is trapped by the cover and the item cooks in its own moisture and in the moisture of other ingredients, such as vegetables.

5. Braising may be done on the range or in the oven. Oven-braising has three major advantages:
   - Uniform cooking. The heat strikes the braising pot on all sides, not just the bottom.
   - Less attention required. Foods braise at a low, steady temperature without having to be checked constantly.
   - Range space is free for other purposes.

Dry-Heat Methods

Roast and Bake

To *roast* and to *bake* both mean to cook foods by surrounding them with hot, dry air, usually in an oven. Cooking on a spit in front of an open fire may also be considered roasting.

The term *roasting* usually applies to meats and poultry. The term *baking* usually applies to breads, pastries, vegetables, and fish. It is a more general term than roasting, although, in practice, there is little or no difference in actual technique, and the terms are often interchangeable (except for breads and pastries).

Please note, however, that it has recently become fashionable on menus to apply the term *roasted* to a wide variety of foods, including meats, poultry, fish, and vegetables that

---

are not actually baked or roasted but rather sautéed, fried, or braised. One restaurant even labeled steamed vegetables as "roasted baby vegetables."

1. Cooking *uncovered* is essential to roasting. Covering holds in steam, changing the process from dry-heat to moist-heat cooking, such as braising or steaming.

2. Meat is usually roasted on a rack (or, if it is a rib roast, on its own natural rack of bones). The rack prevents the meat from simmering in its own juices and fat. It also allows hot air to circulate around the product.

3. When roasting in a conventional oven, the cook should allow for uneven temperatures by occasionally changing the position of the product. The back of the oven is often hotter because heat is lost at the door.

4. A roast may be browned by another cooking method, such as pan-frying or broiling, before being placed in the oven. This technique is most useful for small poultry and small cuts of meat, which may not brown sufficiently in the oven due to their short roasting times.

5. To *barbecue* means to cook with dry heat created by the burning of hardwood or by the hot coals of this wood. In other words, barbecuing is a roasting or grilling technique requiring a wood fire.

    Authentic, traditional barbecue is done in wood-burning ovens or pits, but these are not practical for the average restaurant that wants to add barbecued items to the menu. So today, most barbecuing is done in specially designed smoke ovens or cookers. In principle, these units work like regular ovens, except they also have a device that heats small pieces of hardwood to produce smoke. Foods should be suspended in the ovens or placed on racks so the smoke can contact all surfaces.

    Cooking temperatures in these ovens are kept low, 225°–250°F (107°–121°C). This is an ideal temperature range for cooking tougher cuts of meat, such as beef brisket and pork shoulder, to tenderness over a period of hours. (When tender meats are roasted with smoke at a higher temperature, the process is usually called *smoke-roasting* rather than *barbecuing*.)

6. *Rangetop smoke-roasting*, also called *pan-smoking*, is a procedure done in a closed container, using wood chips to make smoke. Use this procedure for small, tender, quick-cooking items such as fish fillets, tender meat and poultry pieces, and some vegetables.

    To smoke-roast, place a layer of fine hardwood chips or shavings on the bottom of a hotel pan (see Figure 4.1). Disposable pans may be used for light smoking. Place a rack in the pan over the chips and lay the seasoned food items on the rack. Cover tightly with a second hotel pan or with aluminum foil. Place on the cooktop (making sure the ventilating hood is on!) over moderate heat. Smoke will begin rising from the wood chips. After about 5 minutes, remove the food items from the smoke-roaster and, if necessary, complete the cooking in the oven. Leaving the food in the smoke too long results in a strong, bitter taste.

Broil

To *broil* means to cook with radiant heat from above.

Note: The terms *broiling, grilling,* and *griddling* are sometimes confused. Grilling (see following) is often called *broiling*, and griddling is called *grilling*. This book uses the terms that refer to the equipment involved. Thus, broiling is done in an overhead broiler, grilling on a grill, and griddling on a griddle.

1. Broiling is a rapid, high-heat cooking method used mainly for tender meats, poultry, fish, and a few vegetable items.

2. Note the following rules of broiling:
    - *Turn heat on full*. Cooking temperature is regulated by moving the rack nearer to or farther from the heat source.
    - *Use lower heat for larger, thicker items and for items to be cooked well done*. Use higher heat for thinner pieces and for items to be cooked rare. This is done so the inside and outside are cooked to the desired degree at the same time. It takes

Figure 4.1 Rangetop smoke-roasting:

(a) Place hardwood chips or sawdust in a disposable hotel pan. Place over moderately high heat and heat until the wood begins to smoke.

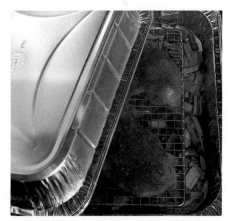

(b) Place the items to be cooked on a rack and set the rack over the chips so the food is not touching the chips. Cover tightly with another pan and cook for the desired time.

practice and experience to cook foods of different thickness to the right degree of doneness inside with the desired amount of surface browning.

- *Preheat the broiler.* This helps sear the product quickly, and the hot broiler makes the desired grill marks on the food.
- Foods may be dipped in oil to prevent sticking and to minimize drying. (This may not be necessary if the food is high in fat.) Care should be taken, as too much oil on a hot broiler grate may cause a fire.
- Turn foods over only once, to cook from both sides and to avoid unnecessary handling.

3. A low-intensity broiler called a *salamander* is used for browning or melting the top of some items before service.

Grill, Griddle, and Pan-Broil

Grilling, griddling, and pan-broiling are all dry-heat cooking methods that use heat from below.

1. *Grilling* is done on an open grid over a heat source, which may be charcoal, an electric element, or a gas-heated element. Cooking temperature is regulated by moving the items to hotter or cooler places on the grill. Grilled meats should be turned to achieve desired grill marks, just as in broiling.

2. *Griddling* is done on a solid cooking surface called a *griddle*, with or without small amounts of fat to prevent sticking. The temperature is adjustable and much lower (around 350°F/177°C) than on a grill. In addition to meats, items such as eggs and pancakes are cooked on a griddle.

   Grooved griddles have a solid top with raised ridges. They are designed to cook like grills but to create less smoke. Meats cooked on a grooved griddle do not have the charcoal-grilled flavor imparted by smoke from burning fats.

3. *Pan-broiling* is like griddling except it is done in a sauté pan or skillet instead of on a griddle surface. Fat must be poured off as it accumulates, or the process becomes pan-frying. No liquid is added, and the pan is not covered, or else the item would steam.

Dry-Heat Methods Using Fat

Sauté

To *sauté* means to cook quickly in a small amount of fat.

1. The French word *sauter* means "to jump," referring to the action of small pieces of food tossed in a sauté pan. However, larger foods, such as slices of meat and pieces of chicken, may be sautéed without actually being tossed in the pan.

2. Note these two important principles:
   - Preheat the pan before adding the food to be sautéed. The food must start cooking at high heat, or it will begin to simmer in its own juices.
   - Do not overcrowd the pan. Doing so lowers the temperature too much, and again the food begins to simmer in its own juices.

3. Meats to be sautéed are sometimes dusted with flour to prevent sticking and to help achieve uniform browning.

4. After a food is sautéed, a liquid such as wine or stock is often swirled in the pan to dissolve browned bits of food sticking to the bottom. This is called *deglazing*. The liquid becomes part of a sauce served with the sautéed items.

5. Stir-frying is a variation of sautéing. Stir-frying is especially popular for vegetables.

Pan-Fry

To *pan-fry* means to cook in a moderate amount of fat in a pan over moderate heat.

1. Pan-frying is similar to sautéing except more fat is used and the cooking time is longer. The method is used for larger pieces of food, such as chops and chicken pieces, and the items are not tossed by flipping the pan, as they often are in sautéing.

2. Pan-frying is usually done over lower heat than sautéing because of the larger size of the pieces being cooked.

3. The amount of fat depends on the food being cooked. Only a small amount is used for eggs, for example, while as much as 1 inch (2.5 cm) or more may be used for pan-fried chicken.

4. Most foods must be turned at least once for even cooking. Some larger foods may be removed from the pan and finished in the oven to prevent excessive surface browning. This method of finishing in the oven is also used to simplify production when large quantities of foods must be pan-fried.

Deep-Fry

To *deep-fry* means to cook a food submerged in hot fat. High quality in a deep-fried product is characterized by the following properties:

Minimal fat absorption

Minimal moisture loss (that is, not overcooked)

Attractive golden color

Crisp surface or coating

No off-flavors imparted by the frying fat

Many foods are dipped in a breading or batter before frying. This forms a protective coating between food and fat and helps give the product crispness, color, and flavor. Obviously, the quality of the breading or batter affects the quality of the finished product (see Chapter 6, pp. 128–130).

Guidelines for Deep-Frying

1. Fry at proper temperatures.
   Most foods are fried at 350°–375°F (175°–190°C). Excessive greasiness in fried foods is usually caused by frying at too low a temperature.

2. Don't overload the baskets.
   Doing so greatly lowers the fat temperature.

3. Use good-quality fat.
   The best fat for frying has a high smoke point (the temperature at which the fat begins to smoke and to break down rapidly).

4. Replace 15–20 percent of the fat with fresh fat after each daily use.
   This extends frying life.

5. Discard spent fat.
   Old fat loses frying ability, browns excessively, and imparts off-flavors.

6. Avoid frying strong- and mild-flavored foods in the same fat, if possible.
   French fries should not taste like fried fish.

7. Fry as close to service as possible.
   Do not leave foods in the basket above the fry kettle, and do not hold under heat lamps for more than a few minutes. The foods' moisture quickly makes the breading or coating soggy.

8. Protect fat from its enemies:
   Heat. Turn the fryer off or to a lower holding temperature (200°–250°F/95°–120°C) when not in use.
   Oxygen. Keep fat covered between services, and try to aerate the fat as little as possible when filtering.
   Water. Remove excess moisture from foods before frying. Dry baskets and kettle thoroughly after cleaning. Keep liquids away from the fryer to prevent accidental spills.
   Salt. Never salt foods over the fat.
   Food particles. Shake loose crumbs off breaded items before placing over the fat. Skim and strain the fat frequently.
   Detergent. Rinse baskets and kettle well after cleaning.

PRESSURE FRYING

Pressure frying means deep-frying in a special covered fryer that traps steam given off by the foods being cooked and increases the pressure inside the kettle.

In a standard fryer, even though the fat may be at 350°F (175°C), the temperature inside the food will not rise above 212°F (100°C), the boiling point of water. Just as in a pressure steamer, a pressure fryer raises this temperature and cooks the food more quickly without excessive surface browning. At the same time, the fat temperature can be lower, 325°F (165°C) or less.

Pressure frying requires accurate timing because the product cannot be seen while it is cooking.

Microwave Cooking

Microwave cooking refers to the use of a specific tool rather than to a basic dry-heat or moist-heat cooking method. The microwave oven is used mostly for heating prepared foods and for thawing raw or cooked items. However, it can be used for primary cooking as well.

Microwave oven models range in power from about 500 watts up to about 2,000 watts. The higher the wattage, the more intense the energy the oven puts out and the faster it heats foods. Most models have switches that allow you to cook at different power levels.

One of the most important advantages of the microwave oven in à la carte cooking is that it enables you to heat individual portions of many foods to order quickly and evenly. Instead of keeping such foods as stews hot in the steam table, where they gradually become overcooked, you can keep them refrigerated (either in bulk or in individual portions) and reheat each order as needed. This is perhaps the main reason why most restaurants have one or more microwave ovens, even though they may not use them for primary cooking.

Because the microwave oven is a unique tool in food service, the cook should observe the following special points regarding its use:

1. Small items will not brown in a standard microwave. Large roasts may brown somewhat from the heat generated in the item itself. Some models have browning elements that use conventional heat.

2. Watch timing carefully. Overcooking is the most common error in microwave use. High energy levels cook small items very rapidly.

3. Large items should be turned once or twice for even cooking.

4. An on/off cycle is often used for large items to allow time for heat to be conducted to the interior.

5. If your equipment has a defrost cycle (which switches the oven to lower power), use this cycle rather than full power to thaw frozen foods. Lower power enables the item to thaw more evenly, with less danger of partially cooking it. If your oven does not have this feature, use an on/off cycle.

6. Sliced, cooked meats and other items that are likely to dry out in the microwave should be protected either by wrapping them loosely in plastic or wax paper or by covering them with a sauce or gravy.

7. Because microwaves act only on water molecules, foods with high water content, such as vegetables, heat faster than denser, drier foods, such as cooked meats.

8. Foods at the edge of a dish or plate heat faster than foods in the center. This is because they are hit by rays bouncing off the walls of the oven as well as by rays directly from the energy source. Therefore:

   • Depress the center of casseroles so the food is not as thick there as at the edges. This will help it heat more evenly.

   • When you are heating several foods at once on a plate, put the moist, quick-heating items like vegetables in the center and the denser, slower-heating items at the edges.

9. Because microwaves do not penetrate metal, aluminum foil and other metals shield foods from the radiant energy. For example, a potato wrapped in foil will not cook in a microwave oven.

With older machines, it was a general rule not to put any metal in the oven, as the radiation could bounce off the metal and damage the magnetron (the oven's generator). With newer machines, it is possible to heat foods in foil pans and to shield certain parts of the food by covering them with pieces of foil so they do not overheat. Follow the procedures recommended by the manufacturer of the oven.

Because microwaves cook so rapidly, they will not break down the connective tissues of less tender meats. Slow, moist cooking is necessary for dissolving these connective tissues.

The more food placed in a microwave at once, the longer the cooking time. Thus, the primary advantage of microwave cooking—speed—is lost with large roasts and other large quantities.

Cooking Sous Vide

A new technology that has had a rapid growth in popularity among the world's top chefs is *sous vide* (soo veed) cooking. French for "under vacuum," the term is applied to cooking foods that have been vacuum-sealed in plastic bags.

In simplest terms, this food preparation technique is a two-step process:

1. Vacuum-pack the food item, plus any seasonings or marinades, in an appropriate plastic bag.

2. Cook the food item, while in the bag, at a constant low temperature, usually in a special water bath.

Precision Cooking

Although the name of the technique refers to the vacuum packing, the heart of sous vide cooking—and the reason many chefs are so excited about it—is the precise temperature control it permits.

As an example, think of roasting a boneless loin of lamb. We could place the meat in an oven at 400°F (200°C) and roast it until the center reaches a temperature of 140°F (60°C) for medium doneness. As we discussed on pages 57–58, however, the lamb will be medium done only in the center and more done everywhere else. In addition, we would have to monitor the cooking closely to make sure we remove it from the oven at the right time.

On the other hand, we could vacuum-pack the lamb loin in plastic and place it in a water bath heated to an exact 140°F (60°C). The temperature of the lamb would never go above that temperature, no matter how long we left it in the water bath. And it would be at exactly the same doneness from outside to center.

Because we like a browned exterior on the lamb, we could then remove it from the bag, brown it quickly in a hot sauté pan, and serve it immediately.

Sous Vide Applications

Sous vide cooking is such a new science that chefs are only beginning to explore its possibilities. Techniques will surely evolve and change in years to come.

Some of the main applications of sous vide cooking as it is practiced today are detailed below. Please note temperature ranges are approximate. Immersion circulators (p. 26) are extremely accurate, and chefs may specify temperatures to within a fraction of a degree to get the precise results they want.

TENDER MEATS AND POULTRY
Tender meats and poultry are usually cooked in a water bath heated to the exact doneness temperature desired. The lamb loin described above is a typical example. Cooking temperatures usually range from 140° to 149°F (60°–65°C), although higher or lower temperatures are also used, and cooking times may range from 20 to 60 minutes, or sometimes longer.

TOUGH MEATS

Tough meats can be cooked to tenderness while retaining more moisture than if they were braised or simmered. Cooking temperatures range from 149° to 158°F (65°–70°C). These temperatures are much lower than usual braising temperatures, but they are high enough to break down connective tissue. At the higher end of this range, meats become falling-apart tender, while at the lower end they retain more of their shape and have a firmer texture while still being tender and juicy.

Because it takes time to break down connective tissue, often 12–48 hours, tough meats are usually cooked to doneness, then immediately chilled and refrigerated for later use.

Because of the long cooking times, avoid cooking temperatures below 149°F (65°C). Higher temperatures provide more safety from bacterial growth.

FISH AND SEAFOOD

Fish are naturally tender and have even more delicate connective tissue than tender meats. Cooking procedures are similar to those for tender meats, but often with even lower temperatures and/or shorter cooking times. Typical cooking temperatures may range from 122° to 140°C (50°–60°C), or sometimes higher, with cooking times as short as 10–15 minutes. Use only the freshest, cleanest fish, and finish and serve it immediately after cooking.

Shellfish such as lobster and shrimp can be toughened by the higher heat of traditional cooking techniques, so sous vide cooking can be a benefit. Cooking temperature for these items is typically around 140°F (60°C).

VEGETABLES

Vegetables can benefit from sous vide techniques, especially those that discolor when exposed to air, such as artichokes. Vegetables are usually cooked at 185°F (85°C).

Safety Factors

Working with vacuum-packed foods increases the health dangers caused by anaerobic and facultative bacteria—that is, bacteria that can grow without oxygen. Because cooking temperatures are so low, there is danger that bacteria will not be killed if cooking is not carefully done. Salmonella, *E. coli*, listeria, and botulism bacteria are the most serious risks.

For these reasons, chefs and health officials are especially cautious about sous vide cooking and have instituted strict guidelines. The following steps summarize the most important aspects of these safety rules:

1. Know the rules for sous vide set up by your local health department, and follow them carefully. Health departments usually require that you establish a HACCP system for sous vide cooking.
2. Use only the freshest, most wholesome foods from reputable purveyors.
3. Chill all foods thoroughly before vacuum packing. If you sear a food item before packing, chill it after searing and before packing.
4. After packing, cook the food at once, or immediately refrigerate it at 38°F (3.3°C) or lower—or, even better, freeze it.
5. After cooking, serve the food immediately, or chill it as quickly as possible in an ice bath or a blast chiller.
6. Thaw cooked food frozen in its package in the refrigerator.

Sous vide cooking involves complex procedures, and the above summary is only a short introduction to its techniques and safety factors. Entire books have been written on the subject, some of which are listed in the Bibliography.

Finally, using the proper equipment, especially a chamber vacuum packager and an immersion circulator (described on p. 26), is important. Home-style vacuum packers might be useful for experimenting, but only a chamber packer can achieve the vacuum pressures chefs find they need. Furthermore, home machines are not able to pack liquids, so they can't pack meats with marinades. Most important, precise temperature control is critical when you are cooking at such low temperatures, and you need equipment with the capability of an immersion circulator for cooking sous vide.

Molecular Gastronomy

The approach to cooking known as *molecular gastronomy*, introduced on page 7, is the latest effort by creative chefs to find new ways of preparing and presenting food. The manipulation of food ingredients in new ways by the use of technology is known as *molecular gastronomy*. However, this description is misleading, because it suggests to many people that the technology is the most important part of this way of cooking. Even the name, molecular gastronomy, suggests scientists making artificial food in test tubes. Perhaps a better name might be *avant-garde cuisine* (see sidebar).

For the best chefs in the field, molecular gastronomy is not so much a culinary movement as a new collection of tools for their toolkit. Their focus is still the food and the dining experience, and they use all their judgment and skills, including their training in classical techniques, to put good food on the plate. In the hands of great chefs, what could be nothing more than clever stunts with food becomes a great dining experience.

With this in mind, we can offer a second definition of *molecular gastronomy*: the selective use of technology and nonstandard ingredients to help enhance the flavors, aromas, appearance, and textures of natural foods.

Avant-Garde Techniques and Ingredients

It is a challenge, in a short space, to describe molecular gastronomy because it consists of so many unrelated techniques. Also, every chef has his or her own style of cooking and uses a different set of favorite techniques and plating styles. Furthermore, it is important to understand that many or even most items on an avant-garde chef's menu are made with traditional techniques. The chef uses whatever cooking methods he or she feels are appropriate to the dish, whether a traditional technique or a molecular-gastronomy technique. You shouldn't think that such a menu is composed entirely of foams, bubbles, powders, and gels. In the definition in the preceding paragraph, the word *selective* is used to mean the chef selects a nonstandard technique when, and only when, it helps intensify a flavor or aroma or in another way to improve the dining experience.

The chef may use these techniques to change familiar foods into unfamiliar forms, to make unexpected combinations of foods, or to make one food look like another. Tricking the diner's expectations is another way the chef draws attention to flavors and aromas. One does not eat this food absentmindedly. Every bite is intended to be an exploration or an adventure.

In this style of cooking, using the best ingredients is necessary. Because the techniques are used to focus attention on flavors, colors, textures, and aromas, only the freshest foods have the quality to work in these dishes.

Chefs use countless individual techniques to create their versions of molecular gastronomy, and new ones are invented all the time. Just a few of the better-known and most talked-about of these techniques are described below. Following this list is a description of some of the ingredients used to achieve these effects.

- **Nontraditional thickeners.** In addition to the traditional starches, chefs have new ways to thicken sauces and to change the texture of liquids. Some of these thickening agents work without heating and are simply blended with the cold liquid. This allows the chef to create sauces and other liquids with a fresh, uncooked taste.

- **Foams, froths, and bubbles.** For many years, chefs have made foamy sauces by whipping or blending a sauce just before plating. These foams collapse quickly, however. Avant-garde chefs stabilize foams with gelatin, lecithin, and other ingredients. A well-made foam adds an additional flavor dimension to the plate without adding bulk.

- **Gels.** Turning a liquid, such as a vegetable juice, into a solid not only gives it a different texture but also enables the food to be cut into many shapes, allowing the chef to create different visual presentations. Chefs use regular gelatin as well as other jelling agents, such as agar-agar, which is derived from seaweed.

- **Drying and powdering.** Drying a food intensifies its flavor and, of course, changes its texture. Eating a cauliflower floret that was deep-fried and then dehydrated until crisp

AVANT-GARDE CUISINE

The term *avant garde* means "advance guard," and it was originally used to indicate the front ranks of an army advancing into battle. Today the term is used to describe any group that pushes the boundaries of a discipline beyond what is considered normal. The term is used most often in the arts and culture. Members of an avant-garde group experiment with and invent new techniques and new ways of applying new as well as old techniques.

is a much different experience than eating steamed, buttered cauliflower. If the dehydrated food is powdered, it becomes yet another flavor and texture experience.

- **Spherification.** This technique creates spheres of liquid contained inside a thin gel wall. In the standard method, the liquid is mixed with a hydrocolloid (see sidebar) called *sodium alginate*. In a separate container is a water bath containing calcium. When the liquid is dropped into the calcium bath, the alginate and the calcium react to form a thin wall of gel surrounding a liquid center. The chef can make tiny spheres by using an eye dropper or larger ones by freezing the liquid in a mold before dropping it into the calcium bath.

    The opposite method is to dissolve the calcium in the flavorful liquid and drop it in an alginate bath. This is called *reverse spherification*.

Below is an alphabetical list of some of the specialized ingredients used in molecular gastronomy. Many of these ingredients are used in tiny quantities. For this reason, avant-garde chefs are likely to be working in the metric system (see p. 95). It is easier to scale 2 grams of xanthan gum, for example, than 0.07 ounces. This need for precision carries over into every aspect of the chef's work, from scaling all ingredients and measuring temperatures to cutting ingredients and creating plate arrangements.

Agar-agar. A jelling agent derived from seaweed. Agar-agar is a traditional ingredient in Asian cuisines and has long been used in Western cooking as a vegetarian substitute for gelatin. To use, stir into a cold liquid and bring to a boil. The liquid sets to a gel when cooled to 95°F (35°C). Once jelled, it can be reheated to serve warm because it does not melt until heated to at least 185°F (85°C). To use as a thickener, jell the liquid and then blend in a blender.

Calcium lactate and **calcium choride.** Calcium compounds used in the process of spherification (see above).

Carageenan. A hydrocolloid or thickener derived from seaweed. Carageenans are mixed with cold liquids and then heated to thicken.

Guar gum. A hydrocolloid or thickener derived from the guar bean plant. This is a powerful stabilizer and thickener that has long been used in commercial ice creams.

Methylcellulose. A hydrocolloid derived from plant fiber. It has long been used as a dietary fiber supplement. It is an unusual thickener and jelling agent because it thickens as it is heated and thins out or melts when cooled. This allows the chef to create unusual effects. Methylcellulose is also used to stabilize foams.

Sodium alginate. A hydrocolloid derived from seaweed. This ingredient is used in the process of spherification. It does not have to be heated to make a gel, and the gel is *nonreversible*. This means once the gel formed, it stays solid even when heated.

Soy lecithin. A powerful emulsifier. Lecithin is the component of egg yolks that makes mayonnaise possible (see p. 386). Also extracted from soybeans, lecithin is used to stabilize many mixtures that would separate without it.

Tapioca maltodextrin. A modified food starch that, when mixed with fat, changes it to a powder. Because maltodextrin dissolves in water, an oil, such as olive oil, that has been powdered changes back to an oil in the mouth.

Ultra-Tex 3. A modified food starch extracted from tapioca. The name is a trademark of the National Starch Company, which makes it. Ultra-Tex 3 thickens cold liquids without heating. If the thickened liquid is poured into a thin layer, it dries to form a thin film or sheet.

Xanthan gum. A hydrocolloid or thickener made by fermenting sugar with a special bacterium. It has been used for years to give structure to gluten-free breads and other baked goods. Liquids thickened with xanthan gum have the same thickness whether hot or cold.

To give you a sense of how some of these ingredients and techniques are used, several recipes are included in Chapter 7 (pp. 133–187) and Chapter 8 (p. 197). Understand, however, this material gives you only a brief introduction to one aspect of molecular gastronomy. (When you consider that Chef Ferran Adrià closes his restaurant for six months a year in order to develop new recipes and techniques, you begin to realize how vast the subject is.) To get a fuller sense of the subject, you must do a lot more reading (see Bibliography).

HYDROCOLLOIDS

A *colloid* is a mixture in which one substance (called the *dispersed phase*) is evenly mixed throughout another substance (called the *continuous phase*). Many colloids are familiar to us. Milk, for example, is liquid water in which milk solids and tiny butterfat globules are evenly mixed. Foams are colloids in which air bubbles are evenly distributed throughout a liquid. Smoke is a colloid of soot particles mixed in air. Emulsions such as mayonnaise (p. 386) are familiar colloids from the kitchen.

A *hydrocolloid* is a colloid in which the continuous phase is water. The presence of particles mixed throughout the water changes the water's characteristics. For example, gelatin is a hydrocolloid familiar to all chefs. In this product, strands of proteins are mixed in water. Because these strands bind to each other, even a small amount of gelatin is enough to turn water from a liquid to a soft solid, called a *gel*. Another familiar example of a hydrocolloid is a sauce thickened with starch. The strands of starch change the water base from a thin liquid to a thicker one.

When chefs who practice molecular gastronomy use the word *hydrocolloid* to describe unusual thickeners and jelling agents, such as sodium alginate and other gums, it makes them sound especially scientific and mysterious. But remember, chefs have been using hydrocolloids their entire careers. They just haven't called them that.

Summary of Cooking Terms

The following is an alphabetical list of terms that describe ways of applying heat to foods. Basic cooking methods described earlier are included, as are more specific applications of these basic methods.

bake. To cook foods by surrounding them with hot, dry air. Similar to *roast*, but the term *bake* usually applies to breads, pastries, vegetables, and fish.

barbecue. (1) To cook with dry heat created by the burning of hardwood or by the hot coals of this wood. (2) Loosely, to cook over hot coals, such as on a grill or spit, often with a seasoned marinade or basting sauce.

blanch. To cook an item partially and very briefly in boiling water or in hot fat. Usually a pre-preparation technique, as to loosen peels of vegetables, fruits, and nuts, to partially cook French fries or other foods before service, to prepare for freezing, or to remove undesirable flavors.

boil. To cook in water or other liquid that is bubbling rapidly, about 212°F (100°C) at sea level and at normal pressure.

braise. (1) To cook covered in a small amount of liquid, usually after preliminary browning. (2) To cook certain vegetables slowly in a small amount of liquid without preliminary browning.

broil. To cook with radiant heat from above.

deep-fry. To cook submerged in hot fat.

deglaze. To swirl a liquid in a sauté pan, roast pan, or other pan to dissolve cooked particles of food remaining on the bottom.

dry-heat cooking methods. Methods in which heat is conducted to foods without the use of moisture.

fry. To cook in hot fat.

glaze. To give shine to the surface of a food by applying a sauce, aspic, sugar, or icing, and/or by browning or melting under a broiler or salamander or in an oven.

griddle. To cook on a flat, solid cooking surface called a *griddle*.

grill. To cook on an open grid over a heat source.

moist-heat cooking methods. Methods in which heat is conducted to foods by water or other liquid (except fat) or by steam.

pan-broil. To cook uncovered in a skillet or sauté pan without fat.

pan-fry. To cook in a moderate amount of fat in an uncovered pan.

(en) papillote. Wrapped in paper (or sometimes foil) for cooking so the enclosed food is steamed in its own moisture.

parboil. To cook partially in a boiling or simmering liquid.

parcook. To cook partially by any method.

poach. To cook gently in water or other liquid that is hot but not actually bubbling, 160°–180°F (71°–82°C).

reduce. To cook by simmering or boiling until the quantity of liquid is decreased, often to concentrate flavors.

roast. To cook foods by surrounding them with hot, dry air in an oven or on a spit in front of an open fire.

sauté. To cook quickly in a small amount of fat, usually while mixing or tossing the foods by occasionally flipping the pan.

sear. To brown the surface of a food quickly at a high temperature.

simmer. To cook in water or other liquid that is bubbling gently, 185°–205°F (85°–96°C).

smoke-roast. To cook with dry heat in the presence of smoke, as on a rack over wood chips in a covered pan.

sous vide. Vacuum-packed. Refers to techniques for cooking foods that are packaged under vacuum in plastic bags.

steam. To cook by direct contact with steam.

stew. To simmer or braise a food or foods in a small amount of liquid, which is usually served with the food as a sauce.

stir-fry. To cook quickly in a small amount of fat by tossing cut-up foods in a wok or pan with spatulas or similar implements. Similar to sauté, except the pan is stationary.

sweat. To cook slowly in fat without browning, sometimes under a cover.

KEY POINTS TO REVIEW

- What cooking methods are classified as dry-heat methods? What methods are dry-heat methods with fat? What methods are moist-heat methods? Describe each of these cooking methods.
- How do you determine quality in a deep-fried food?
- What are the two main steps in sous-vide cooking? List six safety guidelines to observe when cooking sous vide.

BUILDING FLAVOR

People eat because they enjoy the flavors of good food, not just because they must fill their stomachs to stay alive. Appearance, texture, and nutrition are important, too, but good taste is the first mark of good cooking. Enhancement and adjustment of flavors are among a cook's most critical tasks, one requiring experience and judgment.

The most important flavors of a given preparation are those of its main ingredients. A grilled beef tenderloin steak should taste like beef, green beans should taste like green beans, tomato soup should taste primarily of tomato. Plain, unseasoned foods, however, usually taste a little bland and one-dimensional, so it is the cook's job to add interest by combining ingredients to build depth of flavor. The harmony of ingredient flavors and aromas the cook creates by combining ingredients skillfully is sometimes called a *flavor profile*.

Building Flavor Profiles

Foods offer complex experiences for the senses. When composing a new dish, a cook must first of all understand that more than just taste should be considered. The senses of sight, smell, taste, and touch all come into play. The fifth sense, hearing, also plays a role, as when we react to the sizzle of a steak or the crunch of a potato chip, but this sense is less of a concern for the cook than the other four. Consider how we perceive these characteristics of a dish:

- Appearance (color and color contrast, shape, shine, arrangement on the plate)
- Aroma
- Taste
- Mouthfeel (texture, moistness or dryness, softness or crispness) and temperature

All of these factors are important to making a dish appealing to the diner. The discussion in this section, however, is concerned mostly with aroma and taste. Why not just taste? Taste buds on the tongue perceive only four basic sensations: salty, sweet, bitter, and sour (but see sidebar). What we think of as flavor is a combination of taste and aroma. When the sense of smell is lacking, such as when you have a cold, foods seem to have little flavor.

The flavors in a dish can be thought of as primary flavors and supporting, or secondary, flavors. The primary flavors are the flavors of the main ingredients. For example, in blanquette of veal the *primary flavor* is veal; the primary flavors in calf's liver lyonnaise are liver and onions; and the primary flavors in Irish lamb stew are lamb, onions, leeks, and potatoes. These are the flavors that predominate. When you taste each of these dishes, the first tastes you encounter are the main ingredients. Other flavors, which we can call *supporting flavors*, support and enhance the primary flavors of the main ingredients.

Examining how a flavor profile is built in a single classic and fairly simple recipe can help you begin to understand the general principles involved.

An Example of Flavor Building

Let's look more closely at the recipe for blanquette of veal mentioned above. Veal, by itself, does not have a strong or pronounced flavor. Unlike meats such as beef or venison, veal has a mild, subtle flavor. In this recipe, the veal is simmered, so the flavor is even milder than it would be if the meat were browned by roasting, sautéing, or braising. For this reason, when choosing seasonings and other supporting flavors, we want to avoid strong flavors that will mask the delicate flavor of the veal. Using white veal stock as a cooking medium reinforces and strengthens the primary flavor. We could use water, but the result would be a less flavorful dish. Brown stock would be too strong for our purpose and would completely change the character of the dish. White chicken stock might be an acceptable substitute, but it wouldn't reinforce the veal flavor as well. The onion and bouquet garni are added to the stock to give it more depth and fullness of flavor.

UMAMI

Although European and North American tradition recognizes four basic tastes—salty, sweet, bitter, and sour—food authorities have recently identified a fifth, called *umami*, which has long been recognized by Asian cultures. Sense receptors on the tongue react to certain amino acids. Because amino acids are components of proteins, this taste is strong in foods high in protein. In fact, *umami* is often translated as "meatiness." Beef, lamb, certain cheeses, and soy sauce are especially high in umami. The food additive monosodium glutamate (MSG), used as a seasoning or flavor enhancer in some Asian cuisines, produces strong umami.

Continuing to the finishing ingredients, we find roux, a cream-and-egg liaison, lemon juice, nutmeg, and white pepper. The roux functions as a thickener and contributes primarily to texture, although the butter in the roux also gives some richness to the flavor. The liaison is used for both texture and flavor, adding richness and creaminess. The cream and the simmered veal are a classic marriage of flavors that work well together in many dishes. However, too much richness, combined with the mildness of the veal, could make the dish cloying. The acidity of the lemon juice cuts through the richness of the cream and egg yolks, gives a more balanced flavor, and perks up the taste buds. Just enough lemon is used to balance the richness of the cream and egg, not so much as to make the dish taste lemony. Finally, the smallest amount of nutmeg and white pepper gives a pleasing complexity to the finished taste without adding identifiable flavors. If one of the first things you taste is nutmeg, then too much nutmeg has been used.

If the dish is well composed, all of these flavors, primary and supporting, combine to form a complex but unified whole we identify as the taste of veal blanquette.

General Concepts in Flavor Building

There are no fixed rules for combining flavors, but the example just discussed suggests some general principles. When you are developing or modifying a recipe, think about the following points.

Every ingredient should have a purpose. Start with the main ingredients, and then think about what will work with them. Continue to build the flavor, using just the ingredients you need.

Ingredients can work together by harmonizing or by contrasting. In the example above, the rich taste of the liaison and the mild taste of the veal harmonize. The tartness of the lemon, on the other hand, contrasts with the cream.

When two ingredients contrast, be sure they balance. For example, add just enough lemon juice to the blanquette to balance the cream, not too much or too little.

Consider not only the components of the single recipe but also the other items that will be served with it on the plate. For example, think of how we use lemon to balance the richness or fattiness of the cream in the blanquette. We can use the same idea to balance the fattiness of a pork pâté or sausage by serving it with a tart mustard or chutney on the side. In other words, think of building the flavor profile of the entire plate. Plan sauces, accompaniments, and garnishes to balance, enhance, and contrast with the main item and with each other, just as the flavors in an individual recipe do.

SIMPLICITY AND COMPLEXITY

Simpler is usually better. Some cooks mistakenly think that adding more ingredients is always preferable to adding fewer. But the more flavors you combine, the harder you have to work to balance them all. Further, the more competing flavors you have, the more you have to take care that the primary flavors of the main ingredients aren't lost.

This is true whether you are planning the ingredients in a single recipe or the components on a plate. Some cooks are tempted to put too many things on a plate. When you have a meat item perched on layers of three or four vegetables and starches, with additional garnishes and two or three sauces, the result is often a confused jumble.

It would be incorrect, however, to say that simpler is *always* better. Classic dishes from many of the world's regions have complex flavor profiles. Look through any collection of recipes from India, China, or Mexico, and you will find dishes that use a large number of spices and other flavoring ingredients. When these dishes work, all the ingredients blend well. In a good curry, for example, it is difficult, if not impossible, to taste each of the individual spices.

CLASSIC FLAVOR PROFILES

How do you know what flavors work together? Perhaps the best place to start is to study traditional recipes from around the world as well as from the classical cuisine passed down to us through Escoffier. These are dishes that have stood the test of time. We know the flavor combinations work because they have been used over and over for decades or even centuries.

We have already seen some classic flavor combinations in our discussion of veal blanquette. The combination of white meat, cream, lemon, and a hint of nutmeg is a quartet of flavors you will find repeatedly in classic and regional dishes.

International or ethnic dishes provide other examples. In northern India, many dishes are based on a mixture of onion, garlic, and fresh ginger puréed together and fried in a little oil. Studying these recipes suggests to us that these three flavors might be used together in new dishes as well. Similarly, the combination of ginger and soy sauce from Japan, paprika and cured ham from Spain, garlic, tomato, and parsley from Provence, and olives and anchovies from around the Mediterranean are all successful flavor mixtures we learn to use when we study classic dishes.

For chefs who want to create their own dishes, studying classic recipes is a good place to start.

Seasoning and Flavoring Ingredients

The preceding discussion of flavor building concerns all ingredients that add flavor to or change the flavor of a dish. These include the primary ingredients and the supporting or secondary ingredients. The remainder of this chapter is concerned primarily with herbs and spices as well as common flavoring ingredients such as onion, garlic, and mustard.

To repeat the most important concept of flavoring, the main ingredients are the primary sources of flavor. Use good-quality main ingredients, handle all foods with care, and employ correct cooking procedures. Remember that herbs and spices play only a supporting role. Badly prepared foods can't be rescued by a last-minute addition of herbs and spices.

Although chefs do not always use the terms this way, it might be said there is a difference between seasoning and flavoring. *Seasoning* means enhancing the natural flavor of a food without significantly changing its flavor. Salt is the most important seasoning ingredient. *Flavoring* means adding a new flavor to a food, thus changing or modifying the original flavor.

The difference between seasoning and flavoring is often one of degree. For example, salt is usually used only to season, not to flavor. But in the case of potato chips or pretzels, the salt is so predominant it can be considered an added flavoring. On the other hand, nutmeg is normally used for its distinctive flavor, but just a dash can perk up the flavor of a cream sauce without being detectable by most people.

Seasoning

1. The most important time for seasoning liquid foods is at the end of the cooking process.

   The last step in most recipes, whether written or not, is "adjust the seasoning." This means you have to first taste and evaluate the product. Then you must decide what should be done, if anything, to improve the taste. Often, a little salt in a stew or a dash of fresh lemon juice in a sauce is enough.

   The ability to evaluate and correct flavors takes experience, and it is one of the most important skills a cook can develop.

2. Salt and other seasonings are also added at the beginning of cooking, particularly for larger pieces of food, when seasonings added at the end would not be absorbed or blended in but just sit on the surface.

3. Adding some of the seasoning during the cooking process aids in evaluating the flavor along the way.

4. Do not add much seasoning if it will be concentrated during cooking, as when a liquid is reduced.

Flavoring

Flavoring ingredients can be added at the beginning, middle, or end, depending on the cooking time, the cooking process, and the flavoring ingredient.

CLASSIC FLAVORING COMBINATIONS

These are just a few of the many traditional flavoring combinations from around the world. Keep in mind that, although only one or two combinations are given for each country or region mentioned, they are not the only combinations used there. These are merely examples to stimulate your thinking.

Sour cream, paprika, caraway (Hungary)

Sour cream or mustard, dill (Scandinavia)

Caraway, onion, vinegar (Germany)

Apples, apple cider or apple brandy, cream (France—Normandy)

Shallot, garlic, parsley (France—Burgundy)

Tomato, basil, olive oil (Italy)

Olive oil, garlic, anchovy (Italy)

Lemon, oregano (Greece)

Cinnamon, nuts, honey (eastern and southern Mediterranean, Middle East)

Ginger, onion, garlic (India)

Fish sauce (nam pla), lemongrass, chiles (Thailand)

Ginger, soy sauce (Japan)

Soy sauce, sake or mirin, dried bonito (Japan)

Ginger, garlic, scallion (China)

1. Only a few flavorings can be added successfully at the end of cooking. These include fresh (not dried) herbs, sherry or flamed brandy, and condiments like prepared mustard and Worcestershire sauce.

2. Most flavorings need heat to release their flavors and time for the flavors to blend. Whole spices take longest. Ground spices release flavors more quickly and thus don't require as long a cooking time.

3. Too much cooking results in loss of flavor. Most flavors, whether in spices or in main ingredients, are *volatile*, which means they evaporate when heated. That is why you can smell food cooking.

We can conclude that herbs and spices should cook with the foods long enough to release their flavors but not so long that their flavors are lost. If cooking times are short, you can generally add spices and herbs at the beginning or middle of cooking time. If cooking times are long, it is usually better to add them in the middle or toward the end of cooking time.

Note: Food safety experts recommend adding dried spices and herbs at least 30 minutes before the end of cooking so any microorganisms they might carry are destroyed.

Common Seasoning and Flavoring Ingredients

Any food product can be used as a flavoring ingredient, even meat (as when crumbled bacon is added to sautéed potatoes or diced ham is included in a mirepoix). Sauces, which are complex preparations containing many flavoring ingredients, are themselves used as flavorings for meat, fish, vegetables, and desserts.

We obviously cannot treat all possible flavoring ingredients here, but we discuss some of the most important. A survey of herbs and spices is provided in Table 4.1.

Table 4.1 Herbs and Spices

PRODUCT	MARKET FORMS	DESCRIPTION	EXAMPLES OF USE
Allspice	Whole, ground	Small brown berry; flavor resembles blend of cinnamon, cloves, and nutmeg	Sausages and braised meats, poached fish, stewed fruits, pies, puddings
Anise seed	Whole, ground	Small seed; licorice flavor	Cookies, pastries, breads
Basil	Crushed leaves	Aromatic leaf; member of mint family	Tomatoes and tomato dishes, pesto (Italian basil sauce), egg dishes, lamb chops, eggplant, peas, squash
Bay leaf	Whole	Stiff, dark green, oblong leaves; pungent aroma	One of the most important herbs for stocks, sauces, stews, braised meats
Caraway seed	Whole	Dark brown, curved seeds; familiar rye bread seasoning	Rye bread, cabbage, sauerkraut, pork, cheese spreads, Eastern European dishes
Cardamom	Whole pod, ground seed	Tiny brown seeds inside white or green pod; sweet and aromatic; expensive	Pickling, Danish pastries, curries
Cayenne (red pepper)	Ground	Ground form of hot red chile; looks like paprika but is extremely hot	In small amounts in many sauces, soups, meat, fish, egg, and cheese dishes (see p. 76)
Celery seed	Whole, ground, ground mixed with salt	Tiny brown seeds with strong celery flavor	Salads, coleslaw, salad dressings, tomato products
Chervil	Crushed leaves	Herb with mild flavor of parsley and tarragon	Soups, salads, sauces, egg and cheese dishes
Chili powder	Ground blend	Blend of spices including cumin, chiles, oregano, garlic	Chili and other Mexican dishes, egg dishes, appetizers, ground meat
Chive	Fresh, dried, frozen	Grasslike herb with onion flavor	Salads, egg and cheese dishes, fish, soups
Cilantro (fresh coriander, Chinese parsley)	Fresh leaves	The plant that produces coriander seeds; delicate texture; assertive, herbaceous aroma and flavor; leaves resemble flat parsley	Widely used in Asian and Southwestern cooking and in dishes with various ethnic influences

Table 4.1 **Herbs and Spices** (continued)

PRODUCT	MARKET FORMS	DESCRIPTION	EXAMPLES OF USE
Cinnamon	Sticks, ground	Aromatic bark of cinnamon or cassia tree	Pastries, breads, desserts, cooked fruits, ham, sweet potatoes, hot beverages
Clove	Whole, ground	Dried flower buds of a tropical tree; pungent, sweet flavor	Whole: marinades, stocks, sauces, braised meats, ham, pickling; Ground: cakes, pastries, fruits
Coriander	Whole, ground	Round, light brown, hollow seed, slightly sweet, musty flavor	Pickling, sausage, pork, curried dishes, gingerbread
Cumin seed	Whole, ground	Small seed resembling caraway, but lighter in color	Ingredient of curry and chili powders, sausages and meats, egg and cheese dishes
Curry powder	Ground blend	A mixture of 16–20 spices, including chile, turmeric, cumin, coriander, ginger, cloves, cinnamon, black pepper; brands vary greatly in flavor and hotness	Curried dishes, eggs, vegetables, fish, soups, rice
Dill	Crushed leaves (called *dill weed*), whole seed	Herb and seed with familiar dill pickle flavor; seed is more pungent than the herb	Seed: pickling, sauerkraut, soups; herb: salads, cheese dishes, fish and shellfish, some vegetables
Epazote	Fresh and dried leaves	A pungent herb with coarse-textured leaves	Used in Mexican cooking; often cooked with beans
Fennel	Whole seed	Greenish-brown seeds similar in flavor to anise, but larger in size	Italian sausage, tomato sauce, fish
Garlic	Fresh: whole bulbs; dried: granulated, powder, and mixed with salt	Strong, aromatic member of onion family; fresh bulbs composed of many small cloves	Wide variety of foods
Ginger	Whole, ground (also fresh and candied or crystallized)	Light brown, knobby root of ginger plant	Baked goods and desserts, fruits, curried dishes, braised meats; fresh in Chinese and other Asian dishes
Juniper berry	Whole	Slightly soft, purple berries with piney flavor; principal flavoring of gin	Marinades, game dishes, sauerkraut
Lemongrass	Fresh stalks	A tropical grass with a slightly bulbous base and an aroma of lemon	Used in Southeast Asian dishes and in dishes influenced by Asian cuisine
Mace	Whole (blade), ground	Orange outer covering of nutmeg; similar flavor, but milder	Baked goods, desserts, fruits, sausages, pork, fish, spinach, squash, other vegetables
Marjoram	Crushed leaves	Gray-green herb with pleasant aroma and slightly minty flavor, similar to oregano, but much milder	Pâtés and ground meats, braised meats, sauces, roast lamb, poultry and poultry stuffings
Mint	Leaves	Aromatic herb with familiar cool flavor; two varieties: spearmint and peppermint	Lamb, fruits, tea and fruit beverages, peas, carrots, potatoes
Mustard seed	Whole, ground (also prepared mustard; see p. 88)	Very pungent seed in white or yellow and brown varieties—brown is stronger	Cheese and egg dishes, pickling, meats, sauces and gravies
Nutmeg	Whole, ground	Sweet, aromatic kernel of nutmeg fruit squash, potatoes), desserts, custards, breads, pastries	Soups, cream sauces, chicken, veal, many vegetables (spinach, mushrooms,
Oregano	Leaves, ground	Pungent herb known as the "pizza herb"	Italian and Mexican dishes, tomato products
Paprika	Ground	Ground form of a dried, sweet red chile. Spanish variety is brighter in color, mild in flavor; Hungarian is darker and more pungent	Spanish: used (or overused) primarily as garnish on light-colored foods; Hungarian: goulash, braised meats and poultry, sauces
Parsley	Fresh: whole sprigs, in bunches; dried: in flakes	Most widely used herb; dark green curly or flat leaves with delicate, sweet flavor	Almost all foods
Pepper, black and white	Whole (peppercorns); ground fine, medium, or coarse	Small black or creamy white hard berry; pungent flavor and aroma	Most widely used spice (see p. 75)

PRODUCT	MARKET FORMS	DESCRIPTION	EXAMPLES OF USE
Pepper, red	(see Cayenne)		
Peppercorn, pink	Whole	Bright pink dried seed or berry; pungent, floral taste; unrelated to black pepper	Limited uses in meat, poultry, and fish dishes; sauce garnish; used in peppercorn mixtures
Poppy seed	Whole	Tiny blue-black seeds with faint but distinctive flavor	Garnish for breads and rolls, buttered noodles; ground: in pastry fillings
Rosemary	Whole	Light green leaves resembling pine needles	Lamb, braised meats and poultry, soups, tomato and meat sauces
Saffron	Whole (thread)	Red stigma of saffron crocus; gives bright yellow color to foods; mild, distinctive flavor; very expensive	Steeped in hot liquid before use; rice dishes, poultry, seafood, bouillabaisse, baked goods
Sage	Whole, rubbed (finer consistency than whole leaves), ground	Pungent gray-green herb with fuzzy leaves	Pork, poultry, stuffings, sausage, beans, tomatoes
Savory	Crushed leaves	Fragrant herb of mint family; summer savory is preferred to winter	Many meat, poultry, fish, egg, and vegetable dishes
Sesame seed	Whole (hulled or unhulled)	Small yellowish seed with nutlike taste; familiar hamburger bun garnish; high oil content	Bread and roll garnish
Sichuan peppercorn	Whole	Brown seed pod, usually partially opened; spicy, peppery flavor, but unrelated to black peppercorns	Spicy meat and poultry dishes
Star anise	Whole or broken	Dried, star-shaped seed pod with an aniselike flavor (but unrelated to anise) but more aromatic	Braised Chinese dishes
Tarragon	Crushed leaves	Delicate green herb with flavor both minty and licoricelike	Béarnaise sauce, tarragon vinegar, chicken, fish, salads and dressings, eggs
Thyme	Crushed leaves, ground	Tiny brownish-green leaves; very aromatic	One of the most important and versatile of herbs; stocks, soups, sauces, meats, poultry, tomatoes
Turmeric	Ground	Intense yellow root of ginger family; mild but distinctive peppery flavor	A basic ingredient of curry powder; pickles, relishes, salads, eggs, rice

1. *Salt* is the most important seasoning ingredient. Don't use too much. You can always add more, but you can't take it out.

- Table salt has a fine granulation. It may contain iodine as a dietary additive. Table salt also may contain other additives to prevent caking.

- Kosher salt is prized in the kitchen because of its purity. Unlike table salt, it contains no additives. Because of its coarse or flaky granulation, it does not dissolve as quickly as table salt, but it is easier to use when added to foods by hand, so many chefs prefer it to table salt at their cooking stations.

- Sea salts of many origins and types are available. Many of them have colors ranging from gray to green to red, from various minerals and other impurities. These impurities also add subtle flavors to the salt. In addition, their coarse granulation gives them a pleasant mouthfeel. More expensive than other salts, sea salts are used primarily as garnishes for plated foods.

2. *Pepper* comes in three forms: white, black, and green. All three are actually the same berry, but processed differently. (Black pepper is picked unripe; white is ripened and the hull is removed; green peppercorns are picked unripe and preserved before their color darkens.)

- Whole and crushed *black pepper* are used primarily in seasoning and flavoring stocks and sauces and, sometimes, red meats. Ground black pepper is used in the dining room by the customer.

Basil

Chervil

Chives

Garlic chives

Cilantro

Dill

Epazote

Regular ginger and green ginger

Lemongrass

• Ground *white pepper* is more important as a seasoning in the food-service kitchen. Its flavor is slightly different from that of black pepper, and it blends well (in small quantities) with many foods. Its white color makes it visually undetectable in light-colored foods.

• *Green peppercorns* are fairly expensive and are used in special recipes, primarily in luxury restaurants. The types packed in water, brine, or vinegar (those in water and in brine have better flavor) are soft. Wet-pack peppercorns are perishable. Water-packed peppercorns keep only a few days in the refrigerator after they are opened, while the others keep longer. Dried green peppercorns are also available.

3. *Red pepper* or *cayenne* is completely unrelated to black and white pepper. It belongs to the same family as paprika and fresh sweet bell peppers. Used in tiny amounts, it gives a spicy hotness to sauces and soups without actually altering the flavor. In larger amounts, it gives both heat and flavor to many spicy foods, such as those of Mexico and India.

4. *Lemon juice* is an important seasoning, particularly for enlivening the flavor of sauces and soups.

5. *Fresh herbs* are almost always superior to dried herbs. They should be used whenever cost and availability permit. Not long ago, the only fresh herbs generally available in many areas of North America were parsley, chives, and sometimes mint and dill. Now, however, most herbs are available fresh. The accompanying photos illustrate the most commonly used fresh herbs as well as some unusual fresh flavoring ingredients.

6. *Onion, garlic, shallots,* and other members of the onion family, as well as carrots and celery, are used as flavorings in virtually all stations of the kitchen and even in the bakeshop. Try to avoid the use of dried onion and garlic products, except as a component of spice blends. They have less flavor, and the fresh product is always available.

7. *Wine, brandy,* and other alcoholic beverages are used to flavor sauces, soups, and many entrées. Brandy should be boiled or flamed to eliminate the high percentage of alcohol, which would be unpleasant in the finished dish. Table wines usually need some cooking or reduction (either separately or with other ingredients) to produce the desired flavors. Fortified wines like sherry and Madeira, on the other hand, may be added as flavorings at the end of cooking.

8. *Prepared mustard* is a blend of ground mustard seed, vinegar, and other spices. It is used to flavor meats, sauces, and salad dressings and as a table condiment. For most cooking purposes, European styles such as Dijon (French) or Dusseldorf (German) work best, while the bright yellow American ballpark style is more appropriate as a table condiment than as a cooking ingredient. A coarse, grainy style is sometimes called for in specialty recipes.

Marjoram

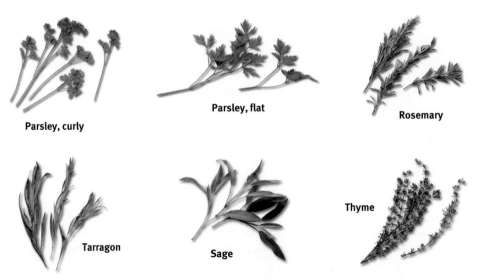

Mint

Parsley, curly

Parsley, flat

Rosemary

Oregano

Tarragon

Sage

Thyme

9. Grated *lemon* and *orange rind* is used in sauces, meats, and poultry (as in duckling à l'orange) as well as in the bakeshop. Only the colored outer portion, called the *zest*, which contains the flavorful oils, is used. The white pith is bitter.

10. *MSG*, or *monosodium glutamate*, is a flavor enhancer widely used in Asian cooking. MSG doesn't actually change the flavor of foods, but it acts on the taste buds. It has a reputation for causing chest pains and headaches in some individuals.

Using Herbs and Spices

Definitions

Herbs are the leaves of certain plants that usually grow in temperate climates.

Spices are the buds, fruits, flowers, bark, seeds, and roots of plants and trees, many of which grow in tropical climates.

The distinction is often confusing, but it is not as important to know which flavorings are spices and which are herbs as it is to use them skillfully.

Table 4.1 is not a substitute for familiarity with the actual products. Eventually, you should be able to identify any spice on your shelf by aroma, taste, and appearance without looking at the label. The accompanying photos illustrate a number of whole spices.

**Top row, left to right: black peppercorns, green peppercorns, pink peppercorns.
Bottom row, left to right: white peppercorns, Sichuan peppercorns**

**Top row, left to right: cloves, nutmeg, allspice, cinnamon sticks.
Bottom row, left to right: juniper berries, cardamom, saffron, star anise**

**Top row, left to right: celery seed, dill seed, coriander seed, caraway seed.
Bottom row, left to right: fennel seed, cumin seed, anise seed**

Guidelines for Using Herbs and Spices

1. Be familiar with each spice's aroma, flavor, and effect on food. Looking at a spice chart, including the one in this book, is no substitute for familiarity with the actual product.

2. Store dried herbs and spices in a cool place, tightly covered, in opaque containers. Heat, light, and moisture cause herbs and spices to deteriorate rapidly.

3. Don't use stale spices and herbs, and don't buy more than you can use in about 6 months. Whole spices keep longer than ground, but both lose much flavor after 6 months.

4. Be cautious after you have replaced old spices. The fresher products are more potent, so the amount you used before might now be too much.

5. Use good-quality spices and herbs. It doesn't pay to economize here. The difference in cost is only a fraction of a cent per portion.

6. Whole spices take longer to release flavors than ground spices, so allow for adequate cooking time.

7. Whole herbs and spices for flavoring a liquid are tied loosely in a piece of cheesecloth (called a *sachet*) for easy removal.

8. When in doubt, add less than you think you need. You can always add more, but it's hard to remove what you've already added.

9. Except in dishes like curry or chili, spices should not dominate. Often, they should not even be evident. If you can taste the nutmeg in the creamed spinach, there's probably too much nutmeg.

10. Herbs and spices added to uncooked foods such as salads and dressings need several hours for flavors to be released and blended.

11. Taste foods before serving whenever possible. How else can you adjust the seasoning?

KEY POINTS TO REVIEW

- How do chefs use the idea of flavor balance to combine a variety of ingredients into a single dish?

- What is the difference between seasoning and flavoring?

- What guidelines are used for correctly adding herbs and spices to foods?

TERMS FOR REVIEW

cooking	infrared	barbecue	molecular gastronomy
caramelization	microwave	rangetop smoke-roast	colloid
gelatinization	moist-heat methods	pan-smoke	hydrocolloid
fiber	dry-heat methods	broil	flavor profile
denature	boil	grill	umami
coagulation	simmer	griddle	primary flavor
Maillard reaction	poach	pan-broil	supporting flavor
connective tissues	blanch	sauté	seasoning
oils	steam	deglaze	flavoring
smoke point	en papillote	pan-fry	volatile
evaporation	braise	deep-fry	herb
conduction	stew	pressure fry	spice
convection	roast	sous vide	
radiation	bake		

QUESTIONS FOR DISCUSSION

1. Your broiler cook has just broiled a codfish fillet that turned out dry, rubbery, and shrunken. Explain what happened to it.
2. Why might adding some tomato product to a beef stew help make the meat more tender?
3. You are roasting a large quantity of ducklings and must use both your conventional ovens and your convection oven. You set all the ovens at the same temperature, but find the ducklings in the convection oven are done first. Why did this happen?
4. You are roasting two beef tenderloins of the same size, one in an oven set at 450°F (230°C), and the other in an oven at 250°F (120°C). You remove both of them from the oven when the temperature at the center is 135°F (57°C). Describe the doneness of each tenderloin from outside to inside.
5. Arrange the following cooking methods in three groups, depending on whether they are moist-heat methods, dry-heat methods without fat, or dry-heat methods with fat: braising, roasting, deep-frying, sautéing, poaching, steaming, broiling, pressure frying, grilling, simmering.
6. What are some advantages of braising a pan of Swiss steaks in the oven instead of on the range?
7. A cook in your restaurant is roasting several pans of chickens. He thinks they are browning too fast, and he covers the pans with foil to keep the chickens from browning much more. What is wrong with this?
8. You are sautéing beef tenderloin tips for stroganoff, and you suddenly find the meat is simmering in liquid rather than sautéing. What did you do wrong?
9. Your customers complain your French fries are too greasy and soggy. How can you correct the problem?
10. What food safety problems are posed by the vacuum packaging and the low cooking temperatures of sous vide cooking?
11. Describe the difference between *primary flavor* and *supporting flavor*. Select a favorite recipe and explain the function of each ingredient, indicating which are primary flavors and which are secondary flavors.
12. What is meant by the phrase "adjust the seasoning"?
13. What is wrong with adding whole caraway seed to a portion of goulash just before serving?

Chapter 5

French Onion Soup Gratineé, page 212.

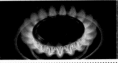
Menus, Recipes, and Cost Management

A menu is a list of dishes served or available to be served at a meal. But a menu is more than this. It is an important management tool. Nearly every aspect of the operation of a food-service business depends on the menu. In fact, it is fair to say the menu is the single most important document in the business. Purchasing, production, sales, cost accounting, labor management, even the kitchen layout and equipment selection of a new facility—all are based on the menu.

Recipes can be said to be the building blocks of the menu. Each item on the menu can be represented by the recipe or the procedure for preparing it. Therefore, recipes, like menus, are important management tools. They indicate ingredients to be purchased and stored, and they give measuring and preparation instructions to the kitchen staff.

In addition, recipes are important tools for the cook because they are a means of recording and passing along essential information. Learning to cook without being able to consult recipes would be like learning to play the piano without using written music.

This chapter discusses menus and recipes as they are used in commercial kitchens. How do we construct a menu that builds sales by offering the best choices to the customer and that also promotes efficiency and productivity? How do we read and understand recipes? How do we measure ingredients and portions, convert recipes to different yields, and calculate food cost with the aid of written recipes?

After reading this chapter, you should be able to

1. Explain how the makeup of a menu depends on the type of meal and on the institution using it.
2. Describe the differences between static and cycle menus, and between à la carte and table d'hôte menus.
3. List in order of their usual service the courses that might appear on modern menus.
4. Devise balanced menus that contain an adequate variety of foods and that can be efficiently and economically prepared.
5. Describe the problems and limitations of written recipes and the importance of using judgment when cooking.
6. Discuss the structure and functions of standardized recipes.
7. Use and understand the recipes in this book to practice basic cooking techniques.
8. Measure ingredients and portions.
9. Use metric measurements.
10. Convert recipes to higher or lower yields.
11. Perform yield-cost analysis.
12. Calculate raw food costs.

Menu Forms and Functions

Menus must be planned for the people eating the food. This sounds like a simple rule, but it is frequently forgotten. You must never forget the customer is the main reason for being in business.

This rule means that, in most operations, the taste and preferences of the cooks or chefs are of little importance when planning the menu. True, some of the most famous restaurants exist primarily as showcases for the chef's own artistry, but these are a small percentage of all food-service establishments. Instead, the taste and preferences of the clientele must be given top priority if the business is to succeed. The kind of clientele the business serves influences the form the menu takes.

The Clientele

TYPE OF INSTITUTION

Each kind of operation has a different menu because each serves the needs of a different clientele.

Hotels must provide a variety of services for their guests, from budget-minded tourists to businesspeople on expense accounts. Thus, their offerings may range from quick breakfast and sandwich counters to elegant dining rooms and banquet halls.

Hospitals must satisfy the dietary needs of the patients.

Schools must consider the ages of the students and their tastes and nutritional needs.

Employee food services need menus that offer substantial but quickly served and reasonably priced food for working customers.

Catering and banquet operations depend on menus that are easily prepared for large numbers but that are lavish enough for parties and special occasions.

Fast-food and take-out quick-service operations require limited menus featuring inexpensive, easily prepared, easily served foods for people in a hurry.

Full-service restaurants range from simple neighborhood diners to expensive, elegant restaurants. Menus, of course, must be planned according to the customers' needs. A menu of high-priced, luxurious foods in a café situated in a working-class neighborhood will probably not succeed.

CUSTOMER PREFERENCES

Even facilities with captive audiences, such as school cafeterias and hospital kitchens, must produce food that is appealing to their customers and in sufficient variety to keep those customers from getting bored with the same old things. Grumbling about the food is a favorite sport among students, but at least it can be kept to a minimum.

Restaurants have an even harder job because their customers don't just grumble if they don't like the selections. They don't come back. People are becoming more and more interested in trying unfamiliar foods, especially ethnic foods. Nevertheless, tastes vary by region, by neighborhood, by age group, and by social and ethnic background. Foods enjoyed by some people are completely rejected by others.

Prices must be kept in line with the customers' ability and willingness to pay. Prices, of course, place limits on what foods can be offered.

Kind of Meal

Menus vary not only by kind of operation but by meal as well.

BREAKFAST

Breakfast menus are fairly standard within any one country. In North America, for example, a restaurant has to offer the usual selection of fruits, juices, eggs, cereals, breads, pancakes, waffles, breakfast meats, and regional specialties because this is what customers want and expect. In addition, featuring one or two unusual items on the menu—such as an English muffin topped with creamed crabmeat and a poached egg, a special kind of country ham, or an assortment of freshly made fruit sauces or syrups for the pancakes and waffles—often attracts additional customers. Breakfast menus must feature foods that can be prepared quickly and be eaten in a hurry.

LUNCH

The following factors are important to consider when planning lunch menus.

1. **Speed.**
   Like breakfast customers, luncheon diners are usually in a hurry. They are generally working people who have limited time to eat. Foods must be prepared quickly and be easy to serve and eat. Sandwiches, soups, and salads are important items on many lunch menus.

2. **Simplicity.**
   Menu selections are fewer, and fewer courses are served. In many cases, customers select only one course. Luncheon specials—combinations of two or three items, such as soup and a sandwich or omelet and salad, offered at a single price—satisfy the need for simplicity and speed.

3. **Variety.**
   In spite of the shortness of the menu and the simplicity of the selections, luncheon menus must have variety. This is because many customers eat at the same restaurant several times a week or even every day. In order to keep the menu short, many operations offer several luncheon specials every day, so there is always something new on the menu.

DINNER

Dinner is usually the main meal and is eaten in a more leisurely fashion than either breakfast or lunch. Of course, some people are in a hurry in the evening, too, but, in general, people come to a restaurant to relax over a substantial meal. Dinner menus offer more selections and more courses. Not surprisingly, prices and check averages are also higher than at lunch.

Types of Menus

STATIC AND CYCLE MENUS

A *static menu* is one that offers the same dishes every day. These menus are used in restaurants and other establishments where the clientele changes daily or where enough items are listed on the menu to offer sufficient variety. A static menu may be in place indefinitely, or it may change at regular intervals, such as every season, every month, or even every week.

Some restaurants use a menu that is part static and part variable. This means they have a basic menu of foods prepared every day, plus daily specials to offer variety without putting too much strain on the kitchen. The daily specials may take advantage of seasonal produce and other occasionally available foods the chef or purchaser finds in the wholesale market.

A *cycle menu* is one that changes every day for a certain period; after this period, the daily menus repeat in the same order. For example, a seven-day cycle menu has a different menu every day for a week and repeats each week. This kind of menu is used in such operations as schools and hospitals, where the number of choices must be kept small. The cycle menu is a way of offering variety.

À LA CARTE AND TABLE D'HÔTE

An *à la carte* menu (Figure 5.1) is one in which each individual item is listed separately, with its own price. The customer makes selections from the various courses and side dishes to make up a meal. (*Note:* The term *à la carte* is also used to refer to cooking to order, as opposed to cooking ahead in large batches.)

Table d'hôte (tobbluh dote) originally meant a fixed menu with no choices—like a meal you would be served if you were invited to someone's home for dinner. Banquet menus are familiar examples of this kind of menu. The term has also come to mean a menu that offers a selection of complete meals at set prices. In other words, a customer may choose from among

Appetizers

SOUP OF THE DAY
MARKET

PIADINA SERVED WITH ROASTED FRUIT, SAGE HONEY AND ARTISAN BLUE CHEESE
$10.50

BISTRO HOUSE SALAD WITH BABY GREENS, BALSAMIC VINAIGRETTE AND MANCHEGO
$7.00

STAR PRAIRIE SMOKED TROUT SALAD WITH BIBB LETTUCE AND
WARM HORSERADISH/CREME FRAICHE DRESSING
$10.50

CLASSIC CAESAR SALAD WITH BABY ROMAINE, PARMESAN AND SEMOLINA CROUTONS
$8.50
WITH OIL-PACKED SPANISH ANCHOVIES ADD $2

SASHIMI OF TUNA SERVED ON BABY ARUGULA, PICKLED PINEAPPLE AND FRESH MINT
$12.50

BISTRO CALAMARI WITH THAI DIPPING SAUCE
$8.00

JP'S RUSTIC PIZZA WITH APPLEWOOD SMOKED BACON,
CASHEW/CURRANT PESTO AND PECORINO-ROMANO
$11.00

PIZZA WITH SAN MARZANO TOMATO SAUCE, BASIL AND HOUSE-MADE MOZZARELLA
$10.50

PIZZA OF THE DAY
MARKET

SEARED MINNESOTA FOIE GRAS SERVED WITH CARAMELIZED SHALLOTS AND QUINCE CONFIT
$15.00

SIDES

YUKON GOLD POTATO PURÉE $4.50 OR STEAMED JASMINE RICE $3.50

POMMES FRITES WITH SMOKED PAPRIKA OR VEGETABLE OF THE DAY
$4.50

BOWL OF OLIVES
$3.50

SPLIT PLATE CHARGE $1.00

Entrées

HOUSE-MADE FETTUCINI TOSSED WITH CHICKEN CONFIT,
ORGANIC BROCCOLI, HARISSA AND PARMESAN
$18.50

POTATO GNOCCHI WITH ORGANIC GREEN BEANS,
TOASTED HAZELNUT CREME FRAICHE, AND CHIVE OIL
$17.50

CARNAROLI RISOTTO WITH WILD MUSHROOMS, SWEET ONIONS AND GREMOLATA
$22.50

PAN-SEARED GROUPER SERVED ON YUKON GOLD POTATO PUREE WITH
BROWN BUTTER SPINACH AND BLOOD ORANGE RELISH
$27.50

WILD ACRES DUCK CONFIT RAVIOLI TOSSED WITH AN APPLE CIDER
DEMI-GLACE, SHAVED APPLE AND FRIED SAGE
$19.50

SEARED RIB-EYE RUBBED WITH GREEN THAI CURRY AND SERVED WITH
HOUSE-PICKLED PINEAPPLE, JICAMA AND RED ONION SALAD
$28.50

PAN-ROASTED VENISON STEAK ON YUKON GOLD POTATO PURÉE WITH
ROASTED BRUSSEL SPROUTS AND A CRANBERRY RED WINE REDUCTION
$32.50

BONE-IN PORK TENDERLOIN BRAISED WITH APPLE, ONION AND SWEET CURRY,
SERVED WITH GOLDEN RAISIN-RED BELL PEPPER RELISH
$24.50

SLOW-ROASTED DUCK BREAST AND CONFIT OF DUCK LEG WITH
SPINACH/MANGO SALAD AND ORANGE-MISO VINAIGRETTE
$28.50

ENTRÉE OF THE DAY
MARKET

Figure 5.1 An example of an à la carte menu from a fine-dining restaurant.
Courtesy of JP American Bistro, Minneapolis, MN

several selections, each of which includes an entrée and side dishes plus other courses, such as appetizer, salad, and dessert. Each full meal selection has a single package price.

Many restaurants use a combination of à la carte and table d'hôte selections. For example, a steak house may include salad, potato, vegetable, and beverage with the entrée choice, while additional dishes like appetizers and desserts may be offered at extra cost.

Closely related to the table d'hôte menu is the *prix fixe* (pree feex), meaning "fixed price," menu. On a pure prix fixe menu, only one price is given. Each guest may choose one selection from each course offered, and the total meal costs the single price indicated. Often, on such menus, a few items featuring costly ingredients carry an extra charge, called a *supplement*. The supplement is usually indicated in parentheses after the listing. It is best to limit the number of supplements as much as possible. Too many extra charges on a prix fixe menu can leave customers frustrated and angry.

A special variety of the prix fixe menu sometimes used in fine restaurants is the *tasting menu*, also known by its French name, *menu dégustation*. A tasting menu (Figure 5.2) is offered in addition to the regular menu and gives patrons a chance to try a larger number of the chef's creations. The menu may feature 5 or 6 or even as many as 10 or 12 individual courses served in small portions. Because of the complexity of service, a restaurant may require that the tasting menu can be served only if everyone at the table orders it. Tasting menus may change daily, depending on the chef's choices and the availability of ingredients.

Building the Menu

A *course* is a food or group of foods served at one time or intended to be eaten at the same time. In a restaurant, the courses are normally served in sequence, allowing enough time for each to be eaten before the next is served. In a cafeteria, the customers may select all their courses at once—appetizer, salad, main dish and vegetables, and dessert, for example—but eat them in a particular order.

In the following pages, we discuss the principles that apply to planning the courses that make up a menu. The main purpose of these principles is to lend variety and interest to a meal. They are not arbitrary rules you must follow for no reason.

The Classical Menu

Today's menus are descendants of elaborate banquet menus served in the nineteenth and early twentieth centuries. These menus had 12 or more courses, and the sequence in which they were served was well established by tradition.

The following sequence of courses is typical of one that may have been served at a great banquet early in the twentieth century.

1. **Cold hors d'oeuvres**
   small, savory appetizers

2. **Soup**
   clear soup, thick soup, or broth

3. **Hot hors d'oeuvres**
   small, hot appetizers

4. **Fish**
   any seafood item

5. **Main course, or pièce de resistance**
   a large cut of roasted or braised meat, usually beef, lamb, or venison, with elaborate vegetable garnishes

6. **Hot entrée**
   individual portions of meat or poultry, broiled, braised, or pan-fried, etc.

7. **Cold entrée**
   cold meats, poultry, fish, pâté, and so on

8. **Sorbet**
   a light ice or sherbet, sometimes made of wine, to refresh the appetite before the next course

9. **Roast**
   usually roasted poultry, accompanied by or followed by a salad

10. **Vegetable**
    usually a special vegetable preparation, such as artichokes or asparagus, or a more unusual vegetable such as cardoons

11. **Sweet**
    what we call *dessert*—cakes and tarts, pudding, soufflés, etc.

12. **Dessert**
    fruit and cheese and, sometimes, small cookies or petits fours

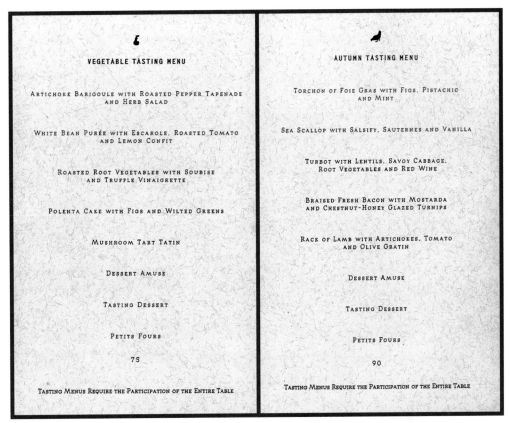

VEGETABLE TASTING MENU

ARTICHOKE BARIGOULE WITH ROASTED PEPPER TAPENADE AND HERB SALAD

WHITE BEAN PURÉE WITH ESCAROLE, ROASTED TOMATO AND LEMON CONFIT

ROASTED ROOT VEGETABLES WITH SOUBISE AND TRUFFLE VINAIGRETTE

POLENTA CAKE WITH FIGS AND WILTED GREENS

MUSHROOM TART TATIN

DESSERT AMUSE

TASTING DESSERT

PETITS FOURS

75

TASTING MENUS REQUIRE THE PARTICIPATION OF THE ENTIRE TABLE

AUTUMN TASTING MENU

TORCHON OF FOIE GRAS WITH FIGS, PISTACHIO AND MINT

SEA SCALLOP WITH SALSIFY, SAUTERNES AND VANILLA

TURBOT WITH LENTILS, SAVOY CABBAGE, ROOT VEGETABLES AND RED WINE

BRAISED FRESH BACON WITH MOSTARDA AND CHESTNUT-HONEY GLAZED TURNIPS

RACK OF LAMB WITH ARTICHOKES, TOMATO AND OLIVE GRATIN

DESSERT AMUSE

TASTING DESSERT

PETITS FOURS

90

TASTING MENUS REQUIRE THE PARTICIPATION OF THE ENTIRE TABLE

Figure 5.2 An example of two tasting menus from a fine-dining restaurant.
Courtesy of Gramercy Tavern, New York, NY.

Modern Menus: Courses and Arrangement

Such extensive classical menus are rarely served today. Even grand, elegant banquets comprising many courses are usually shorter than the menu we just described. However, if you study that menu, you will be able to see the basic pattern of modern menus hiding amid all those courses.

The main dish is the centerpiece of the modern meal. If the meal consists of only one dish, it is considered the main course, even if it is a salad or a bowl of soup. There is usually only one main course, although large banquets may still have more than one, such as a poultry dish followed by a meat dish.

One or more dishes may be served before the main dish. These are usually light in character so the customer is not satiated before the main course.

Study the following outline of the modern menu and compare it to the classical menu. The notes that follow explain several aspects that may be puzzling. Then, in the next sections, we discuss how to select specific dishes for each course to arrive at a balanced menu.

THE MODERN MENU

FIRST COURSES	Appetizer
	Soup
	(Fish)
	Salad
MAIN DISH	Meat, poultry, or fish
	Vegetable accompaniment
DESSERT DISHES	Salad
	Fruits and cheeses
	Sweets

NOTES

- Appetizer, soup, and salad are the three courses usually served before the main course. One, two, or all three of them may be served, and they are usually served in this order. Thus, meals may have the following courses:

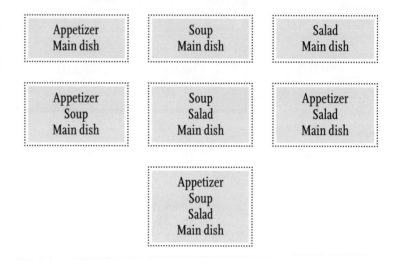

- A fish course is sometimes included in more formal dinners, after the appetizer and soup courses. It should be a relatively small portion, and the main dish should not also be fish.

- Salads may be served either before or after the main course (but not both). In more traditional meals, they are served after the main course to refresh the appetite before the cheese and sweet courses. Serving the salad before the main course is a comparatively recent development.

- Sometimes, one or more of the first courses are served at the same time as the main dish, possibly on the same plate. This is especially popular on luncheon menus, where quick service is desired. Thus, you will find soup and sandwich combinations, salad and omelet combinations, and so on.

- If both cheese and sweets are served for dessert, they may come in either order. English menus have cheese after the sweets, while French menus generally place the sweets last.

Variety and Balance

Balancing a menu means providing enough variety and contrast for the meal to hold interest from the first course to the last. To balance a menu, you must develop a feeling for which foods complement each other or provide pleasing contrasts. And you must avoid repeating flavors and textures as much as possible.

These principles apply whether you are planning a banquet menu, where the diners have no choices; a school cafeteria menu, where students have only a few choices; or a large à la carte menu, where customers have many choices.

Of course, with an à la carte menu, the customers' own choices determine how balanced their meals are. There's nothing wrong with listing a creamed dish among the appetizers and another creamed dish among the main dishes. But you should offer enough choices so customers can easily select balanced meals if they desire. In other words, if half the appetizers and half the entrée selections are served in a cream sauce, you're not offering enough variety.

The following factors must be considered in balancing a menu.

1. **Flavors.**
   Don't repeat foods with the same or similar tastes. This applies to any predominant flavor, whether of the main ingredient, of the spices, of the sauce, and so on. For example:

   - Don't serve broiled tomato halves with the main dish if the appetizer has a tomato sauce.

   - Don't serve both a spicy, garlicky appetizer and a spicy, garlicky main dish. On the other hand, don't make everything too bland.

   - Unless you operate a specialty restaurant like a steak house or a seafood restaurant, balance the menu among meats (beef, pork, lamb, veal), poultry, and fish.

   - Acid or tart foods are often served as accompaniments to fatty foods because they help cut the fatty taste. This is why applesauce and pork, mint sauce and lamb, and orange sauce and duckling are such classic combinations.

2. **Textures.**
   Texture refers to the softness or firmness of foods, their feel in the mouth, whether or not they are served with sauces, and so on. Don't repeat foods with the same or similar texture. For example:

   - Serve a clear soup instead of a thick soup if the main course is served with a cream sauce. On the other hand, a cream soup goes well before a simple sautéed or broiled item.

   - Don't serve too many mashed or puréed foods.

   - Don't serve too many heavy, starchy items.

3. **Appearance.**
   Serve foods with a variety of colors and shapes. Colorful vegetables are especially valuable for enlivening the appearance of meats, poultry, fish, and starches, which tend to be mostly white or brown.

4. **Nutrients.**
   The importance of a nutritionally balanced menu is obvious in the case of menus for hospitals and nursing homes, for example. But even à la carte menus in restaurants should provide enough nutritional variety to allow customers to select nutritionally balanced meals.

5. **Cooking method.**
   Cooking methods play an important role in determining the flavors, textures, and appearance of food. For the typical full-service restaurant, it is a good idea to offer a variety of roasted, braised, grilled, sautéed, and simmered foods. Obviously, this guideline doesn't apply to specialty operations such as a barbecue restaurant or a fish-and-chips shop. Using a variety of cooking methods also eases the pressure on each department in the kitchen, as discussed in the next section.

The possible combinations of foods are so many that it is impossible to give rules that cover all of them. Besides, creative chefs are continually experimenting with new combinations, breaking old rules, and coming up with exciting menus. Years of experience, however, are required to develop this kind of creativity and a feel for what makes certain combinations work. In the meantime, pay close attention to the principles discussed.

Kitchen Capabilities and Availability of Foods

Physical conditions place limitations on your menu. Depending on your equipment, your labor force, and the foods available to you, certain items will be inconvenient, difficult, or even impossible to serve.

EQUIPMENT LIMITATIONS

Know the capacities of your equipment and plan menus accordingly. If your broiler capacity is 200 steaks an hour and you plan a banquet menu for 400 people that features broiled shrimp as an appetizer and broiled steaks as a main course, you're in big trouble.

Spread the workload evenly among your equipment. If you have ovens, a broiler, and a fryer, balance the roasted and braised items, the broiled items, and the fried items. Don't let the broiler stand idle while orders are backed up at the deep fryer. Also, using a variety of cooking methods adds variety of taste and texture to the menu.

PERSONNEL LIMITATIONS

Spread the workload evenly among the workers. As with equipment, you don't want the fry cook to have more than he or she can handle, while the broiler cook has little to do.

Spread the workload throughout the day. Balance the cooked-to-order items against the cooked-ahead items so you don't have to do everything at the last minute.

Offer items the cooks are able to prepare. Don't put items on the menu that are above the skill level of the staff.

AVAILABILITY OF FOODS

Use foods in season. Foods out of season are expensive and often low in quality, and their supply is undependable. Don't put asparagus on the menu if you can't get good asparagus.

Use locally available foods. Fresh seafood is an obvious example of a food that is hard to get in some regions unless you—and your customers—are willing to pay premium prices.

Menus and Cost Control

Food costs are a major part of the expenses of any food-service operation. You can't afford to throw away food any more than you can afford to throw away money. Total utilization of foods must be planned into menus. Whether or not this is done can make or break an operation.

Cost control requires not only planning but also careful arithmetic. See pages 102–108 for a discussion of kitchen mathematics as well as other factors in cost control, including the role of the menu.

Menu Terminology and Accuracy

After you have selected the items you want to include on your menu, you face the problem of what to call them. Decades ago, when the classical cuisine of Escoffier was the normal offering in fine restaurants, a standard terminology existed. Everyone knew what was meant by Tournedos Chasseur, Suprême de Volaille Orly, and Sole Nantua, and these terms meant the same dish on any menu. Today, however, there is little standardization. Chefs feel obliged to give as much information on their menus as possible in order to describe their dishes adequately to their customers. As a result, one often sees menu descriptions that list almost every ingredient in a dish, including the farms the ingredients came from.

It is probably better to give too much information than too little. The important thing is to provide enough information so the customer will understand the basic character of the dish and not have any unpleasant surprises. An alternative to writing everything out on the menu is to educate the serving staff so they know the dishes well enough to fill in any missing details for the customer.

The menu is a sales tool, so it is understandable to try to make every dish sound as appealing as possible. Accurate and truthful descriptions, however, are required. Giving misleading names to menu items is not only dishonest and unfair to the customer, it is actually illegal in some localities that have adopted truth-in-menu laws, and you can be prosecuted for fraud for doing so. Furthermore, customers who feel confused or cheated may not come back.

Calling something chicken salad if it is made with turkey, veal cutlet if it is made with pork, or whipped cream if it is actually artificial whipped topping is such obvious mislabeling that it can hardly be accidental. However, some kinds of menu inaccuracies result not from intentional deception but from simple misunderstanding. In particular, look out for these types of labeling problems:

1. **Point of origin.**
   If your menu lists "Maine lobsters" or "New Brunswick lobsters," they must be from Maine or New Brunswick. Roquefort dressing must be made with Roquefort cheese from Roquefort, France. On the other hand, generally accepted names or names that indicate type rather than origin can be used. For example: Swiss cheese, French bread, Swedish meatballs.

2. **Grade or quality.**
   U.S. Choice and Canada A are names of grades, and you'd better be using those grades if you say you are. Incidentally, the word *prime* in "prime rib" indicates a cut, not a grade.

3. **Cooking method.**
   A menu item described as "grilled" or "roasted" should be cooked by the method indicated. Billing a pan-fried item as "roasted" because it sounds better on the menu misrepresents the item and risks disappointing the customer.

4. **"Fresh."**
   If you call something *fresh*, it must be fresh, not frozen, canned, or dried. There is no such thing as "fresh frozen."

5. **"Imported."**
   An item labeled *imported* must come from outside the country. Better and more specific than using the term *imported* is to indicate the country of origin.

6. **"Homemade."**
   The word *homemade* means the item was made on the premises. Adding a few fresh carrots to canned vegetable soup does not make it homemade.

7. **"Organic."**
   For a food to be labeled *organic*, it must be raised without the use of hormones, antibiotics, synthetic pesticides, irradiated components, genetically modified organisms, or reprocessed sewage. In some countries, including the United States, the use of the word *organic* on labels is defined by law (p. 247).

8. **Size or portion.**
   If you indicate a portion size on the menu, be sure you serve that size (within allowable tolerances). A "10-ounce steak" must weigh at least 10 ounces before cooking. "Jumbo shrimp" are not just big shrimp. They are a specific size.

9. **Appearance**
   Family-style restaurants that use illustrated menus should serve food that looks like the illustrations. If an illustration of a shrimp plate shows 6 shrimp, it would be a mistake to serve only 5.

Here are other examples of common violations:

Listing "maple syrup" and serving maple-flavored syrup.

Listing a product, such as a carbonated beverage, by brand name and serving another brand.

Listing "butter" and serving margarine.

Listing coffee or breakfast cereal "with cream" and serving milk or artificial cream.

Listing "ground round" and serving other ground beef.

Finally, please use a dictionary. Unfortunately, it is common to see menus full of misspellings. These errors reflect poorly on the restaurant. Customers may think that if you don't care enough even to spell words on the menu correctly, you may not care enough to cook the food correctly either. If you use terms from French, Italian, or another language, make sure the terms are spelled and used correctly.

KEY POINTS TO REVIEW

- How do the contents and design of a menu depend on the type of meal served and the type of food-service institution using it?

- What is a static menu? a cycle menu? an à la carte menu? a table d'hôte menu?

- What courses are usually listed on a modern dinner menu?

- What techniques can you use to create a menu that offers a good balance of choices for the customer?

- Why should the design and limitations of the kitchen and the skill level of the staff be considered when designing a menu?

The Written Recipe

A *recipe* is a set of instructions for producing a certain dish. In order to duplicate a desired preparation, it is necessary to have a precise record of the ingredients, their amounts, and the way in which they are combined and cooked. This is the purpose of a recipe.

In spite of their importance, written recipes have many limitations. No matter how detailed a recipe may be, it assumes you already have certain knowledge—that you understand the terminology it uses, for example, and that you know how to measure ingredients.

The Uses and Limitations of Recipes

Many people believe learning to cook means simply learning recipes. Knowledgeable cooks, in contrast, are able to prepare food without written recipes, if they have to, because they have a good understanding of basic principles and techniques. A recipe is a way of applying basic techniques to specific ingredients.

If you have read Chapter 4, or have even casually leafed through this book, you know it is not just a book of recipes. Although it contains hundreds of recipes, they take up a relatively small part of it. Your main concern is learning techniques and procedures you can apply to any recipe.

The main purpose of learning basic cooking principles is not to be able to cook without recipes, however, but to understand the recipes you use. As we said in the beginning of this section, every recipe assumes you have certain knowledge that enables you to understand the instructions and follow them correctly.

Some recipes supply very little information, and some supply a great deal. But no matter how detailed it is, a written recipe can't tell you everything, and some judgment by the cook is always required. There are several reasons for this:

1. **Food products are not uniform.**
   Food ingredients are natural products, so they are not uniform like machine bolts, ball-point pens, and printer paper. One tomato may be riper than another, one carrot more tender or sweeter than another, one oyster saltier than another. Such variations may affect how the ingredients are handled, how long they are cooked, what proportions are needed, and how much seasoning is required.

2. **Kitchens do not have the same equipment.**
   Different pans distribute heat at different rates. Different broilers heat to different temperatures. Liquid evaporates from wide pots faster than from tall, narrow ones, and so on.

3. **It is impossible to give exact instructions for many processes.**
   How do you set the burner if the instructions say "Cook over medium heat"? How thick is a "thick" sauce? How long do you broil a rare steak? Training and experience will help you learn to make accurate judgments about such questions.

The difference between an experienced cook and a beginning cook is the ability to make judgments about these variables.

Standardized Recipes

1. **Definition.**
   A *standardized recipe* is a set of instructions describing the way a particular establishment prepares a particular dish. In other words, it is a customized recipe developed by an operation for the use of its own cooks, using its own equipment, to be served to its own patrons.

2. **The structure of a standardized recipe.**
   Recipe formats differ from operation to operation, but nearly all of them try to include as much precise information as possible. The following details may be listed:

   • Name of the recipe.

   • Yield, including total yield, number of portions, and portion size.

- Ingredients and exact amounts, listed in order of use.

- Expected trim yields for any produce or other ingredients that must be fabricated.

- Equipment needed, including measuring equipment, pan sizes, portioning equipment, and so on.

- Directions for preparing the dish. Directions are kept as simple as possible.

- Preparation and cooking temperatures and times.

- Directions for portioning, plating, and garnishing.

- Directions for breaking down the station, cleaning up, and storing leftovers.

3. **The function of standardized recipes.**

   An operation's own recipes are used to control production. They do this in two ways:

   - *They control quality.* Standardized recipes are detailed and specific. This is to ensure the product is the same every time it is made and served, no matter who cooks it.

   - *They control quantity.* First, they indicate precise quantities for every ingredient and how they are to be measured. Second, they indicate exact yields and portion sizes, and how the portions are to be measured and served.

      By controlling quality and quantity, recipes are a key tool in controlling costs.

4. **The limitations of standardized recipes.**

   Standardized recipes have the same problems as all recipes—the problems we discussed earlier regarding variations in foods and equipment and vagueness of instructions. These problems can be reduced by writing the recipe carefully, but they cannot be eliminated. Even if an operation uses good standardized recipes, a new employee making a dish for the first time usually requires supervision to make sure he or she interprets the instructions the same way as the rest of the staff. These limitations don't invalidate standardized recipes. If anything, they make exact directions even more important. But they do mean that experience and knowledge are still very important.

Instructional Recipes

The recipes in this book are *not* standardized recipes. Remember that a standardized recipe is custom-made for a particular operation. The recipes in this book are obviously not.

The purpose of a standardized recipe is to direct and control the production of a particular food item. Directions must be as complete and exact as possible.

The purpose of the instructional recipes in this book is to teach basic cooking techniques. They provide an opportunity for you to practice, with specific ingredients, the general procedures you have learned.

If you glance at any of the recipes in this book, you will see they do not contain all the features of a standardized recipe, as described in the previous section. In particular, you will see the following differences:

1. **Instructions for preparation.**

   In most cases, recipes in this book follow a discussion of a basic procedure. The recipes are examples of the general procedure, and they give you experience in applying what you have learned. The information you are given in the recipe instructions is intended primarily to encourage you to think and to learn a technique, not just to turn out a product. You should consult your instructor when you have a question about a procedure.

2. **Variations and optional ingredients.**

   Many recipes are followed by variations. These are actually whole recipes given in abbreviated terms. It is possible to write them out as separate, full-length recipes. (You are encouraged to do this before preparing a variation, as a learning experience.)

      Giving recipes as variations rather than as separate recipes encourages you to see the patterns behind each. Again, you are learning techniques, not just recipes. You develop a lot more understanding of what you are doing if you see Spanish rice and Turkish pilaf, for example, or coconut cream pie and chocolate pudding as variations of the same basic techniques rather than as separate, unrelated recipes.

Table 5.1 Chicken Breasts Parmesan

PORTION SIZE: 1 CHICKEN BREAST, 4 OZ   TOTAL YIELD: 12 PORTIONS

QUANTITY	INGREDIENTS	EQUIPMENT
4 oz	Flour	2 half-size hotel pans
1¼ tsp	Salt	one 2-qt stainless-steel bowl
½ tsp	Ground white pepper	1 wire whip
5	Whole eggs, size large	1 meat mallet
3½ oz	Grated parmesan cheese	four 12-in. sauté pans
1½ oz	Whole milk	1-oz ladle
12	Boneless, skinless chicken breasts, 4 oz each	tongs
4 oz	Clarified butter	plastic wrap
		instant-read thermometer, sanitized

PROCEDURE

Advance Prep

CCP   1.   Collect and measure all ingredients. *Refrigerate eggs, cheese, milk, and chicken at 40°F or lower until needed.*

     2.   Collect all equipment.

     3.   Place the flour in the hotel pan. Season with the salt and white pepper.

     4.   Break the eggs into the stainless-steel bowl and discard the shells. Beat with the wire whip until foamy. Add the grated cheese and milk. Mix in with the whip.

CCP   5.   *Cover the bowl with plastic wrap and refrigerate at below 40°F until needed.*

     6.   Flatten the chicken breasts lightly with the meat mallet until ½ in. thick. Place the breasts in a hotel pan.

CCP   *Cover with plastic wrap. Refrigerate at below 40°F until ready to cook.*

CCP   7.   *Clean and sanitize the mallet and the work surface. Wash hands thoroughly.*

Cooking

     8.   Place one of the sauté pans over moderate heat. Allow to heat 2 minutes.

     9.   Measure 1 oz clarified butter into the pan.

    10.   One at a time, dip 3 chicken breasts in the seasoned flour until completely coated on both sides. Shake off excess. Dip in the egg
CCP   mixture. Coat both sides completely. *Return remaining chicken and egg mixture to refrigerator.*

CCP   11.   Place the 3 breasts in the sauté pan. *Wash hands after handling the raw chicken and before handling cooked food.*

    12.   Cook the chicken over moderate heat until golden brown on the bottom. Using the tongs, turn over and continue to cook
CCP   *until chicken reaches an internal temperature of 165°–170°F. Test internal temperature with sanitized instant-read thermometer.*

CCP   13.   Repeat with the remaining chicken breasts, using clean sauté pans. *If your work is interrupted before completion, cover and refrigerate chicken and egg mixture.*

CCP   14.   *If the chicken is not served immediately, hold in a heated holding cabinet to maintain internal temperature of 145°F.*

CCP   15.   *Discard leftover egg mixture and seasoned flour. Do not use for any other products. Clean and sanitize all equipment.*

Your instructors may have their own variations, or they may wish to make changes in the basic recipes in order to teach you certain points. Unlike standardized recipes, instructional recipes are not engraved in stone.

Cooking with Judgment

When you make a recipe for the first time, you should apply your knowledge and think about the recipe in relation to the skills you have. The first step in preparing a recipe is to read it carefully. Then read it again. Make sure you understand every ingredient and every instruction in the procedure. A common fault is to prepare a recipe according to what you think it says rather than what it actually says. You are especially likely to make this error if the procedure in the recipe is different from the way you usually prepare a similar dish.

Remember we said that some recipes supply very little information and depend largely on the cook's knowledge. With enough experience, you will even be able to cook from recipes like the following, a complete recipe for Filets of Sole Bercy, quoted in its entirety from *Le Répertoire de la Cuisine*, a favorite book used by chefs in classical French cooking: "Poached with shallots and chopped parsley, white wine and fish stock. Reduce the stock, add butter, and coat the fish, glaze."

KEY POINTS TO REVIEW

- Is this statement true? "If you have a good recipe, you don't need to know how to cook, because the recipe tells you what to do." Explain.

- What are standardized recipes? How are they used?

Measurement

Many restaurants budget a net profit of 10 percent or less. This means a sandwich selling for $5.00 makes a profit of only 50 cents. If the cook happens to put a half-ounce too much meat in the sandwich, the operation may be losing money on it. No wonder so many restaurants go out of business. (See the sidebar on page 103 for an explanation of net profit and gross profit.)

Careful measurement is one of the most important parts of food production. It is important for consistent quality each time a recipe is prepared and served. And it is important for cost controls.

There are two important kinds of measurement in the kitchen:

1. Ingredient measurement

2. Portion measurement, or portion control

Ingredient Measurement

WEIGHT

Weighing measures how heavy an item is. Weighing is the most accurate method of measuring ingredients. It is the method used for most solid ingredients.

Accurate scales are necessary for weighing. Small portion scales are often used in the kitchen because of their convenience. Balance scales are used in the bakeshop.

To be able to weigh ingredients, you must observe the difference between AP (as purchased) weight and EP (edible portion) weight.

AP weight is the weight of the item as purchased, before any trimming is done. Also known as *APQ* (as purchased quantity).

EP weight is the weight after all inedible or nonservable parts are trimmed off. Also known as *EPQ* (edible portion quantity).

Recipes sometimes specify which weight they are referring to. When they don't, you must judge from the instructions.

1. If a recipe calls for "2 lb potatoes" and the first instruction is "scrub, peel, and eye the potatoes," then you know AP weight is called for.

2. If the recipe calls for "2 lb peeled, diced potatoes," then you know EP weight is called for. You will need more than 2 lb AP.

> ### Procedure for Weighing Ingredients on a Portion Scale
>
> 1. Place the receiving container, if any, on the scale.
> 2. Set the scale so it reads zero.
> 3. Add the item being weighed to the container (or place on the scale, if no container is used) until the scale reads the desired weight.

VOLUME

Volume measures how much space an item fills. Volume measures are used for liquids. Measuring a liquid by volume is usually faster than weighing it, and accuracy is good.

Solid ingredients are usually not measured by volume because they cannot usually be measured accurately by this method. One pint of chopped onions will vary considerably in weight, depending on how large or small the onions are cut and whether the pint measure is filled loosely or packed.

Dry ingredients such as flour or sugar are usually weighed in the bakeshop. However, they are sometimes measured by volume in the kitchen, when speed is more important than accuracy. To measure dry ingredients by volume, fill a dry-volume measure until the ingredient is mounded over the top. Then level it off with a spatula or other straightedge.

Very small quantities, such as ¼ teaspoon salt, may be measured by volume when the amount is too small to weigh.

COUNT

Measuring ingredients by count is done in these circumstances:

1. When units are in fairly standard sizes. *Examples*: 6 large eggs for a pancake batter; 8 parsley stems for a stock.

2. When serving portions are determined by numbers of units. *Examples*: 1 baked apple per portion; 6 fried shrimp per portion.

Portion Control

Portion control is the measurement of portions to ensure the correct amount of an item is served. In order for portion control to be carried out, cooks and service personnel must be aware of proper portion sizes. These are usually indicated on the house recipes and on the working menu used in the kitchen and service areas.

PORTION CONTROL IN PREPARATION

Portion control actually begins with the measuring of ingredients. If this is not done correctly, then the yield of the recipe will be thrown off.

When portions are determined by count—1 hamburger patty, 2 tomato slices, 1 wedge of pie—then the units must be measured or cut according to instructions: 4 ounces meat per patty; ¼-inch slices of "5 × 6" tomatoes; 8 equal wedges per pie.

PORTION CONTROL IN PLATING AND SERVICE

Portioning for service may be done by the cook, as in a short-order restaurant, or by the service personnel, as in a cafeteria. The following tools and techniques are used.

1. **Count.**
   Examples: 1 slice of ham per order; 5 shrimp per order. This is accurate if cutting and other prep work have been done correctly.

2. **Weight.**
   Example: 4 ounces of sliced ham per order. A portion scale must be at the serving station for this method of portion control.

3. **Volume.**
   Ladles, scoops, and kitchen spoons come in standard volume sizes and are used for portioning. The exact size of the ladle or scoop needed for a portion must be determined in advance and indicated on service instructions.
   Kitchen spoons, either solid or perforated, are not as accurate for portioning but are often used for convenience and speed. You must be able to judge by eye how full to fill the spoon (rounded, heaped, etc.). Check a spoonful on a portion scale from time to time to make sure you are being consistent.

4. **Even division.**
   Examples: cutting a pie into 8 equal wedges; cutting a pan of lasagne 4 × 6 to make 24 equal portions.

5. **Standard fill.**
   Standard-size dishes, cups, or glasses are filled to a given level, as judged by eye. Example: a glass of orange juice. This is actually a form of volume measure.

Units of Measure

The system of measurement used in the United States is complicated. Even when people have used the system all their lives, they still sometimes have trouble remembering things like how many fluid ounces are in a quart or how many feet are in a mile.

Table 5.2 lists abbreviations used in this book. Table 5.3 lists equivalents among the units of measure used in the kitchen. You should memorize these thoroughly so you don't have to lose time making simple calculations.

Table 5.2 Abbreviations of U.S. Units in This Book

pound	lb
ounce	oz
gallon	gal
quart	qt
pint	pt
cup	cup (abbreviation not used)
fluid ounce	fl oz
tablespoon	tbsp
teaspoon	tsp
inch	in.

Table 5.3 Units of Measure—U.S. System

Weight		
1 pound	=	16 ounces
Volume		
1 gallon	=	4 quarts
1 quart	=	2 pints
		or
		4 cups
		or
		32 fluid ounces
1 pint	=	2 cups
		or
		16 fluid ounces
1 cup	=	8 fluid ounces
1 fluid ounce	=	2 tablespoons
1 tablespoon	=	3 teaspoons
Length		
1 foot	=	12 inches

Note: One fluid ounce (usually called simply ounce) of water weighs 1 ounce. One pint of water weighs 1 pound.

The Metric System

The United States is the only major country that uses almost exclusively the complex system of measurement we have just described. In Canada, this system is also used, at least part of the time, although the metric system has been introduced. Other countries use a much simpler system called the *metric system*. It is possible that someday the metric system may be used in U.S. kitchens. Even if this never happens, it is useful, in this age of international influences on cooking, to be able to read and use recipes from around the world. So it is a good idea to become familiar with the metric system.

BASIC UNITS

In the metric system, there is one basic unit for each type of measurement:

The *gram* is the basic unit of weight.

The *liter* is the basic unit of volume.

The *meter* is the basic unit of length.

The *degree Celsius* is the basic unit of temperature.

Larger or smaller units are made simply by multiplying or dividing by 10, 100, 1000, and so on. These divisions are expressed by *prefixes*. The ones you will need to know are:

kilo- (kill-o) = 1,000

deci- (dess-i) = 1/10

centi- (sent-i) = 1/100

milli- (mill-i) = 1/1,000

Once you know these basic units, there is no longer any need for complicated tables like Table 5.3. Table 5.4 summarizes the metric units you will need to know in the kitchen. (*Note*: The prefix deci- is rarely used in Canada, although the deciliter is a regularly used unit of volume in Europe.)

CONVERTING TO METRIC

Most people think the metric system is much harder to learn than it really is. This is because they think about metric units in terms of U.S. units. They read there are 28.35 grams in an ounce, and they are immediately convinced they will never be able to learn metrics.

Do not worry about being able to convert between U.S. and metric units. This is a very important point to remember, especially if you think the metric system might be hard to learn.

The reason for this is simple. You will usually be working in either one system or the other. You will rarely, if ever, have to convert from one to the other. (An exception might be if you have equipment based on one system but want to use a recipe written in the other.) If U.S. kitchens change to the metric system, everyone will use scales that measure in grams and kilograms, volume measures that measure in liters and deciliters, and thermometers that indicate degrees Celsius. And everyone will use recipes that indicate these units. No one will have to worry about how many grams are in an ounce. All one will have to remember is the information in Table 5.4.

To become accustomed to working in metric units, it is helpful to have a feel for how large the units are. The following equivalents may be used to help you visualize metric units. They are not exact conversion factors. (When you need exact conversion factors, see Appendix 1.)

A *kilogram* is slightly more than 2 pounds.

A *gram* is about 1/30 ounce. (1/2 teaspoon flour weighs a little less than 1 gram.)

A *liter* is slightly more than 1 quart.

Table 5.4 **Metric Units**		
BASIC UNITS		
QUANTITY	**UNIT**	**ABBREVIATION**
weight	gram	g
volume	liter	L
length	meter	m
temperature	degree Celsius	°C
DIVISIONS AND MULTIPLES		
PREFIX/EXAMPLE	**MEANING**	**ABBREVIATION**
kilo-	1,000	k
kilogram	1,000 grams	kg
deci-	1/10	d
deciliter	0.1 liter	dL
centi-	1/100	c
centimeter	0.01 meter	cm
milli-	1/1,000	m
millimeter	0.001 meter	mm

ROUNDING OFF NUMBERS

Rounding off means bumping a number up or down to the closest number that is "clean" and easiest to work with. For example, 197 is not a round number, but 200 is. In most cases, round numbers end in one or more zeros (such as 10, 300, 6000), although sometimes we use round numbers that end in 5.

The first step in rounding is find the "rounding digit." If you are rounding off to the nearest 10, your rounding digit is the tens' place (the second digit from the right). If you are rounding to the nearest hundred, the rounding digit is the hundreds' place.

Second, look to the place just to the right of the rounding digit. If that number is 1, 2, 3, or 4, the number is rounded down. Leave the rounding digit alone, and change all digits to the right to zero. But if the number to the right of the rounding digit is 5, 6, 7, 8, or 9, the number is rounded up. Change the rounding digit to the next higher number, and change all digits to the right to zero.

For example, 236, rounded off to the nearest ten, is 240. Thus, 240 is the closest "clean" number."

234, rounded off to the nearest ten, is 230.

3216, rounded off to the nearest hundred, is 3200, while 3278 rounded off to the nearest hundred is 3300.

A *meter* is slightly more than 3 feet.

A *centimeter* is about ⅜ inch.

0°C is the freezing point of water (32°F).

100°C is the boiling point of water (212°F).

An increase or decrease of *1 degree Celsius* is equivalent to about 2 degrees Fahrenheit.

METRIC RECIPES

Many recipe writers in the United States print exact metric equivalents in their recipes. As a result, you will see recipes calling for 454 grams potatoes, 28.35 grams butter, or a baking temperature of 191°C. No wonder many Americans are afraid of the metric system!

Kitchens in countries that use the metric system do not work with such impractical numbers, any more than cooks in the United States normally use figures like 1 lb 1¼ oz potatoes, 2.19 oz butter, or a baking temperature of 348°F. That would defeat the purpose of the metric system, which is to be simple and practi-cal. If you have a chance to look at a French cookbook, you will see nice, even numbers like 1 kg, 200 g, and 4 dL. (Note that the metric abbreviations used in this book are consistent with common usage in Canada. Abbreviations used in Europe are somewhat different, such as lowercase *l* instead of uppercase *L* for liter.)

The metric equivalents in the recipes in this book are rounded off. What's more, they are not always rounded off in the same way. In some places, you may see 1 pound rounded off to 500 grams, in other places to 450 grams. The object is to keep the recipe proportions and the total yield as close as possible to the original while arriving at practical measurements. Unfortunately, it is not always possible to keep the proportions exactly the same because the U.S. system is not decimal-based like the metric system. In some cases, the metric quantities may produce slightly different results due to these varying proportions, but these differences are small. If you have U.S. equipment, use the U.S. units, and if you have metric equipment, use the metric units. You should rarely have to worry about converting between the two.

KEY POINTS TO REVIEW

- How are most recipe ingredients measured?
- What tools are used for measuring in the kitchen?
- How are portion sizes measured?
- In the metric system, what are the units of measure for weight, volume, and length?

Converting Recipes

Unless you are working in an operation that uses only its own standardized recipes, you will frequently be required to increase or decrease recipes to different quantities. Each recipe is designed to make a specific amount of finishes product. This amount is called the *yield*. For example, you may have a recipe for 50 portions of Swiss steak but need only 25 portions. You need to change the yield of your recipe. This is called *converting the recipe*.

Converting recipes is an important technique. It is a skill you will probably need to use many times in this book. There is no "best" yield to write recipes for, as every operation, every school, and every individual has different needs.

Yields

Recipe yields are expressed in several ways. For example:

- As a total quantity. (A soup recipe that makes 3 qt; a pot roast recipe that makes 5 lb meat.)

- As a total number of portions. (A recipe for Eggs Benedict that makes 12 portions; a recipe for grilled breast of duck that makes 4 portions.)

- As a total number of portions of a specified size. (A recipe for beef stew that makes 8 portions of 6 oz each; a recipe for individual chocolate soufflés that makes 6 soufflés, 4 oz each.)

Most recipe conversions require changing the total quantity or the total number of portions. The math for doing both of these is the same. As long as the portion size stays the same, you can use either the *total quantity* or the *total number of portions* as the yield when you make your calculations.

A little later in the discussion, after you are familiar with solving these problems, we discuss how to change both the number of portions and the portion size when converting recipes.

Conversion Factors

Nearly everyone instinctively can double a recipe or cut it in half. It seems more complicated, though, to change a recipe from 10 to 18 portions, say, or from 50 to 35. Actually, the principle is exactly the same: You find a number called a *conversion factor*, and then multiply every quantity by this number.

The conversion factor can be defined as the number used to increase or decrease each ingredient when converting a recipe to a different yield. The first step in converting a recipe is to calculate the conversion factor (see Procedures for Calculating Conversion Factors and Converting Total Yields, p. 98).

In order to make these procedures clearer, let's work through the conversion of a full recipe to give you practice with the equations. The following examples are in the U.S. system of measures. For metric examples, see appendix.

In the sample recipe that follows are the ingredients and quantities for a sautéed beef dish. As you can see, the quantities indicated are enough to make 8 portions each.

CHANGING TO COMMON UNITS

Before we start converting recipe yields, we must deal with one more problem with our measuring system. As explained earlier, the U.S. system of measurement has many units that simply must be memorized: 16 ounces in a pound, 2 cups in a pint, 4 quarts in a gallon, and so on. When you are converting recipes, you often have to change back and forth between large and small units to get measurements you can work with. In most cases, the easiest way to make the calculations is to change larger units to smaller units.

- To change pounds to ounces, multiply by 16.
- To change cups to fluid ounces, multiply by 8.
- To change pints to fluid ounces, multiply by 16.
- To change quarts to fluid ounces, multiply by 32.

Note that these are the same numbers as found in Table 5.3.

After you have finished converting the recipe, you usually must convert the ounces and fluid ounces back to larger units in order to get units that are easy to work with. To do this, divide by the same numbers you used to multiply in the calculation above. For example, to change ounces back to pounds, divide by 16.

If you divide by hand, you often get a remainder. Leave this remainder in the smaller unit. For example:

Change 60 ounces to pounds.
$60 \div 16 = 3$, with a remainder of 12
60 ounces = 3 lb 12 ounces

If you are using a calculator, you often get a decimal. In order to change the numbers to the right of the decimal point to ounces, you have to again multiply this decimal portion by 16. Either way, you end up with the same answer.

$60 \div 16 = 3.75$
$0.75 \times 16 = 12$
60 ounces = 3 lb 12 ounces

Procedure for Calculating Conversion Factors

There is only one step in this procedure:

Divide the desired yield by the old yield stated on the recipe. This formula may be written like a mathematical calculation, as on a calculator, or as a fraction:

Mathematical Calculation: new yield ÷ old yield = conversion factor

$$\text{Fraction: } \frac{\text{new yield}}{\text{old yield}} = \text{conversion factor}$$

Example 1: You have a recipe with a yield of 8 portions, and you want to make 18 portions.

$$18 \div 8 = 2.25$$

Your conversion factor is 2.25. If you multiply each ingredient in your recipe by 2.25, you will prepare 18 portions, not the 8 of the original recipe.

Example 2: You have a recipe that makes 20 liters of soup, and you want to make 5 liters.

$$5 \div 20 = 0.25$$

Your conversion factor is 0.25. That is, if you multiply each ingredient by 0.25, you will prepare only 5 portions.

Notice in the second example the conversion factor is a number less than 1. This is because the recipe yield is decreased. You are making the recipe smaller. This is a good way to check your math. Decreasing the recipe yield will involve a conversion factor less than 1. Increasing the yield of a recipe will involve a conversion factor larger than 1.

Procedure for Converting Total Yield

1. Calculate the conversion factor as explained in the procedure given above:
2. Multiply each ingredient quantity by the conversion factor:

old quantity × conversion factor = new quantity

Note: In order to do this in the U.S. system, you may have to convert all weights to ounces and all volumes to fluid ounces. (This is not necessary in the metric system.) See page 107 for more explanation.

Example 1: You have a recipe for 10 portions of Broccoli Mornay requiring 3 lb AP broccoli and 2½ cups Mornay Sauce. Convert to 15 portions.

$$\frac{\text{new yield}}{\text{old yield}} = \frac{15}{10} = 1.5$$

Broccoli: 3 lb = 48 oz

$$48 \text{ oz} \times 1.5 = 72 \text{ oz} = 4 \text{ lb } 8 \text{ oz}$$

Sauce: 2½ cups = 20 fl oz

$$20 \text{ fl oz} \times 1.5 = 30 \text{ fl oz} = 3\tfrac{3}{4} \text{ cups}$$

Example 2: You have a recipe for 10 portions of Broccoli Mornay requiring 1,500 grams AP broccoli and 600 mL Mornay Sauce. Convert to 15 portions.

$$\frac{\text{new yield}}{\text{old yield}} = \frac{15}{10} = 1.5$$

Broccoli: 1500 g × 1.5 = 2250 g
Sauce: 600 mL × 1.5 = 900 mL

BEEF TENDERLOIN TIPS AND MUSHROOMS À LA CRÈME
PORTIONS: 8   PORTION SIZE: 8 OZ

Butter	2 oz	Prepared mustard	2 tsp
Onion	4 oz	Brown sauce	1½ pt
Flour	1 tbsp	Heavy cream	1 cup
Mushrooms	½ lb	Salt	to taste
Beef tenderloin	2½ lb	Pepper	to taste
White wine	½ cup		

Let's say we need 18 portions instead of 8. To find the conversion factor, we divide the new yield by the old yield:

$$\frac{\text{new yield}}{\text{old yield}} = \frac{18}{8} = 2.25$$

To convert the recipe to 18 portions, we simply multiply each ingredient quantity by the conversion factor of 2.25.

First, to make this easier, we should change pounds to ounces and cups, pints, and quarts to fluid ounces, using the figures in Table 5.2. This is called *converting to common units of measure*, as explained earlier. For example, to change the measurement for beef tenderloin to ounces, multiply 2½ (the weight in pounds) by 16 (the number of ounces in a pound) to get 40 ounces.

The equivalents we need for this recipe are as follows:

½ lb equals 8 ounces

2½ pounds equals 40 ounces

½ cup equals 4 fluid ounces

1½ pints equals 24 fluid ounces

In Example 1, we have substituted these equivalent quantities. Then we have multiplied all the ingredient quantities by the conversion factor to get the quantities we need for 18 portions. Check through all the calculations to make sure you follow them. The quantities for salt and pepper will still, of course, be indicated as "to taste."

Example 1

INGREDIENT	QUANTITY	TIMES	CONVERSION FACTOR	EQUALS	NEW QUANTITY
Butter	2 oz	×	2.25	=	4.5 oz
Onion	4 oz	×	2.25	=	9 oz
Flour	1 tbsp	×	2.25	=	2.25 tbsp or 2 tbsp plus ¾ tsp
Mushrooms	8 oz	×	2.25	=	18 oz or 1 lb 2 oz
Beef tenderloin	40 oz	×	2.25	=	90 oz or 5 lb 10 oz
White wine	4 fl oz	×	2.25	=	9 fl oz
Prepared mustard	2 tsp	×	2.25	=	4½ tsp or 1½ tbsp
Brown sauce	24 fl oz	×	2.25	=	54 fl oz or 3 pt plus 6 fl oz
Heavy cream	8 fl oz	×	2.25	=	18 fl oz or 2¼ cups

Now let's suppose we want to find the quantities needed to give us 40 portions, 6 ounces each. Because the portion size changes, we have to add extra steps to our procedure for calculating the conversion factor. The Procedure for Calculating Conversion Factors When Portion Size Changes (p. 100) explains these steps. Then we use this new conversion factor in the same way as we did in Example 1 above. For our Beef Tenderloin Tips recipe, we first calculate our new conversion factor:

$$8 \text{ (portions)} \times 8 \text{ oz} = 64 \text{ oz}$$

Do the same calculation for the desired yield:

$$40 \text{ (portions)} \times 6 \text{ oz} = 240 \text{ oz}$$

When we divide the new yield by the old yield (240 ÷ 64), we arrive at a conversion factor of 3.75. In Example 2, we have done the conversions using the new factor of 3.75.

The new calculations, using the conversion factor of 3.75, are shown in the Example 2 table.

Example 2

INGREDIENT	QUANTITY	TIMES	CONVERSION FACTOR	EQUALS	NEW QUANTITY
Butter	2 oz	×	3.75	=	7.5 oz
Onion	4 oz	×	3.75	=	15 oz
Flour	1 tbsp	×	3.75	=	3.75 tbsp or 3 tbsp plus 2¼ tsp
Mushrooms	8 oz	×	3.75	=	30 oz or 1 lb 14 oz
Beef tenderloin	40 oz	×	3.75	=	150 oz or 9 lb 6 oz
White wine	4 fl oz	×	3.75	=	15 fl oz
Prepared mustard	2 tsp	×	3.75	=	7½ tsp or 2½ tbsp
Brown sauce	24 fl oz	×	3.75	=	90 fl oz or 5 pt plus 10 fl oz
Heavy cream	8 fl oz	×	3.75	=	30 fl oz or 3¾ cups

Procedure for Calculating Conversion Factors When Portion Size Changes

1. Determine the total yield in the old recipe by multiplying the number of portions by the portion size:

old recipe number of portions × portion size = old yield

2. Determine the total yield desired (new yield) by multiplying the number of portions desired by the portion size desired.

desired number of portions × desired portion size = new yield

3. Divide the new yield by the old yield. This formula may be written like a mathematical calculation, as done on a calculator, or as a fraction:

Mathematical Calculation: new yield ÷ old yield = conversion factor

$$\text{Fraction: } \frac{\text{new yield}}{\text{old yield}} = \text{conversion factor}$$

Example: You have a recipe with a yield of 20 portions, 4 ounces each, and you want to make 30 portions, 5 ounces each.

1. Calculate the total yield of the original recipe.

20 portions × 4 ounces = 80 ounces

2. Calculate the total yield desired.

30 portions × 5 ounces = 150 ounces

3. Divide the new yield by the old yield.

150 ÷ 80 = 1.875

The calculation gives us a conversion factor of 1.875. We use this conversion factor the same way as explained above, using the Procedure for Converting Total Yield.

Problems in Converting Recipes

For the most part, these conversion procedures work well. But when you make some very large conversions—from 10 to 400 portions, for example, or from 500 to 6—you may encounter problems.

For example, you may have to make major equipment changes, like from a 2-quart saucepot to a large steam kettle. Consequently, you have to adjust your techniques and, sometimes, even ingredients. Evaporation rates may be different, thickening agents may need increasing or decreasing, seasonings and spices may have to be cut back. Sometimes quantities are too large or too small to mix properly.

This is one more example of the importance of cooking with judgment. Experienced chefs develop a feel for these problems over the years. When you make such adjustments on converted recipes, be sure to make a note of them for future reference.

Although there are no fixed rules you can learn for these adjustments, it is possible to list the most common types of problems encountered so you can be on the alert for them when making recipe conversions. In general, most of the pitfalls fall into one of the following categories.

MEASURING

This is most often a problem when you are expanding small recipes, such as when you want to take a consumer recipe for 4 portions and adapt it to a high-volume operation such as a large cafeteria. Many such recipes use volume measures for both solids and liquids. As we explained earlier, volume measurement of solids is inaccurate. Of course, small inaccuracies become large ones when a recipe is multiplied. Therefore, it is important to be cautious and to test carefully when you are converting a recipe that uses volume measures for solid ingredients.

Problems also occur in the opposite situation—when converting a large-quantity recipe to a much smaller yield. This is a typical problem when adapting a quantity recipe to single-portion size for à la carte service. Some quantities in the converted recipe may be so small as to be difficult to measure.

These problems usually can be avoided when all solids are measured by weight. But such items as spices and seasonings may be too small to be measured easily by weight, unless you use a scale that is accurate to a tiny fraction of an ounce. For this reason, it is usually a good idea to cut back on spices and salt in a converted recipe. You can always add more if you taste the product and decide it needs more seasoning.

SURFACE AND VOLUME

If you have studied geometry, you may remember that a cube with a volume of 1 cubic foot has a top surface area of 1 square foot. But if you double the volume of the cube, the top surface area is not doubled but is in fact only about 1½ times as large.

What in the world, you ask, does this have to do with cooking? Consider the following example.

Suppose you have a good recipe for 1½ gallons cream soup, which you normally make in a small soup pot. You want to make 16 gallons of the soup, so you multiply all ingredients by a conversion factor of 32 and make the soup in a steam kettle. To your surprise, not only do you end up with more soup than you expected but also it turns out rather thin and watery. What happened?

Your converted recipe has 32 times as much volume to start, but the amount of surface area has not increased nearly as much. Because the ratio of surface area to volume is less, there is less evaporation. This means there is less reduction and less thickening, and the flavors are not as concentrated. To correct this problem, you would have to use less stock, and preferably a stock that is more concentrated.

Suppose instead that you made the expanded recipe in a tilting skillet. In this case, there is so much surface area that the liquid would evaporate very quickly, resulting in an overly thickened and overly seasoned soup.

Differences in surface area and volume can cause other problems as well. Food-service operations must be more careful than home cooks do about food spoilage and the Food Danger Zone because large volumes of food cool and heat much more slowly than small volumes do.

For the same reason, a home baker worries about keeping a bread dough warm so it will ferment, but a commercial baker worries about keeping a dough cool enough so it doesn't ferment too fast. This is because a large batch of dough has so much volume in comparison with its surface area that it tends to retain heat rather than cool quickly to room temperature.

EQUIPMENT

When you change the size of a recipe, you must often change the equipment, too. This change often means the recipe does not work in the same way. Cooks must be able to use their judgment to anticipate these problems and to modify their procedures to avoid them. The example just given, of cooking a large batch of soup in a steam kettle or in a tilting skillet, is among the kinds of problems that can arise when you change cooking utensils.

Other problems develop because of mixers or other processing equipment. For example, if you break down a salad dressing recipe to make only a small quantity, you might find there is so little liquid in the mixing machine that the beaters don't blend the ingredients properly.

Or you might have a recipe for a muffin batter you usually make in small quantities and mix by hand. When you increase the recipe greatly, you find you have too much to do by hand. Therefore, you use a mixer but keep the mixing time the same. Because the mixer does the job so efficiently, you overmix the batter and end up with poor-quality muffins.

Many mixing and stirring jobs can be done only by hand. This is easy with small quantities but difficult with large batches. The result is often an inferior product. In contrast, some handmade products are better if they are done in large batches. It is hard, for example, to make a very small batch of puff pastry because the dough cannot be rolled and folded properly.

TIME

Some people make the mistake of thinking that if you double a recipe, you must also double the cooking time. That this is an error can be shown by a simple example. Assume it takes 15 minutes to cook a steak in a broiler. If you put two steaks in the broiler, it still takes 15 minutes to cook them, not 30 minutes.

If all other things are equal, cooking times stay the same when a recipe is converted. Problems arise, however, because all other things are not always equal. For example, a large pot of liquid takes longer to bring to a boil than a small pot. Therefore, the total cooking time is longer.

On the other hand, a big kettle of vegetable soup you are making ahead for tomorrow's lunch takes longer to cool than a small pot. Meanwhile, the vegetables continue to cook in the retained heat during the cooling. In order to avoid overcooking, you may need to undercook the large batch slightly.

In cases where the cooking time must be increased, you might find you must increase the amount of herbs and spices. This is because the flavors are volatile (see p. 71), and more flavor is lost because of the increased cooking time. (Another answer to this problem is to add the spices later.)

Changing recipe sizes can affect not only cooking times but also mixing times. The best way to avoid this problem is to rely not on printed cooking and mixing times but on your own judgment and skills to tell you when a product is properly cooked or properly blended.

RECIPE PROBLEMS

Many recipes have flaws, either in the quantities or types of ingredients or in the cooking procedures. When the item is made in small quantities, these flaws may not be noticeable, or the cook may almost unconsciously or automatically make adjustments during production. When the recipe is multiplied, however, the flaws may suddenly become apparent and the product quality lower. The only solution here is to carefully test recipes and to have a good understanding of basic cooking principles.

Food Cost Calculations

Food-service operations are businesses. This means someone in the operation must worry about budgets, cost accounting, bills, and profits. Usually this is the job of the manager, while the cook takes care of food production.

Cooks have a great deal of responsibility for food cost controls, however. They must always be conscious of accurate measurement, portion control, and careful processing, cooking, and handling of foods to avoid excess trimming loss, shrinkage, and waste.

The manager, on the other hand, is concerned with determining budgets, calculating profits and expenses, and so on. We cannot deal with these subjects here, as this is a book about food preparation. But you may encounter them later in your studies or in your career.

Regardless, every cook should understand three areas of cost accounting: doing yield analyses, calculating raw food cost or portion cost, and using food cost percentages.

Food Cost Percentages

An individual operation's food cost percentage is usually determined by the budget. The chef is interested in this figure because it tells him or her whether the menu prices and the costs for each item are in line.

The *food cost percentage* of a menu item equals the raw food cost or portion cost divided by the menu price:

$$\text{percentage} = \frac{\text{food cost}}{\text{menu price}}$$

You can use this figure in two ways:

1. If you know the menu price and want to see what your food cost should be in order to be within the budget, multiply the menu price by the percentage:

$$\text{food cost} = \text{menu price} \times \text{percentage}$$

   Example: Menu price is $6.75 and food cost percentage is 35 percent.

   $$35\% = 0.35$$

   $$6.75 \times 0.35 = \$2.36$$

2. If you know the food cost and want to determine what the menu price should be at a particular percentage, divide the cost by the percentage:

$$\text{menu price} = \frac{\text{food cost}}{\text{percentage}}$$

   Example: Food cost is $1.60 and food cost percentage is 40 percent.

   $$\frac{\$1.60}{40\%} = \frac{\$1.60}{0.40} = \$4.00$$

> ## GROSS PROFIT AND NET PROFIT
>
> When you are working with cost figures, it is important to understand the difference between *gross profit* and *net profit*. Gross profit for a food operation can be defined as 100 percent of sales minus food cost. Thus, if you have a food cost of 30 percent, your gross profit is 70 percent of sales. Net profit can be defined as gross profit minus overhead. Overhead includes labor costs, utility costs, real estate costs (rent or mortgage), interest on loans, and every other expense necessary to running the business. In our example, if you have a gross profit of 70 percent and overhead costs of 60 percent of sales, your net profit is 10 percent.

Yield Cost Analysis

In order to calculate portion costs of recipes, you must first determine the costs of your ingredients. For many ingredients, this is relatively easy. You just look at your invoices or at price lists from your purveyors.

Many recipes, however, specify trimmed weight rather than the weight you actually pay for. For example, a stew might call for 2 pounds sliced onion. Let's say you pay 24 cents a pound for onions, and to get 2 pounds sliced onions, you need 2¼ pounds untrimmed onions. In order to calculate the cost of the recipe correctly, you must figure out what you actually paid for the onions. In this case, the true cost is 54 cents (2¼ lb × $0.24 per lb), not 48 cents (2 lb × $0.24 per lb).

The following are two frequently used abbreviations you must understand:

- AP stands for *as purchased*. This means the untrimmed quantity, in the same form in which it is purchased. This is the amount you pay for.

- EP stands for *edible portion*. This means the raw, uncooked quantity after all trimming is done. This is the quantity you actually cook.

In the case of fruits and vegetables, the best way to determine AP quantities for use in costing recipes is to make a note of them when you are preparing the item. Tables of vegetable and fruit trimming yields in Chapters 10 and 14 will also help you. The next section explains how to use these numbers.

TRIMMING LOSS: CALCULATING YIELDS AND AMOUNTS NEEDED

The descriptions of vegetables and fruits in Chapters 10 and 14 include a number called *percentage yield*. The percentage yield of a vegetable or fruit indicates, on the average, how much of the AP weight is left after pre-prep to produce the ready-to-cook item, or EP weight. You can use this figure to perform two basic calculations.

1. **Calculating yield.**

   Example: You have 10 lb AP Brussels sprouts. Yield after trimming is 80 percent. What will your EP weight be?

   First, change the percentage to a decimal number by moving the decimal point two places to the left.

   $$80\% = 0.80$$

   Multiply the decimal by your AP weight to get EP yield.

   $$10\ lb \times 0.80 = 8\ lb$$

2. **Calculating amount needed.**

   Example: You need 10 lb EP Brussels sprouts. What amount of untrimmed vegetable do you need?

   Change the percentage to a decimal number.

   $$80\% = 0.80$$

   Divide the EP weight needed by this number to get the AP weight.

   $$\frac{10\ lb}{0.80} = 12\tfrac{1}{2}\ lb$$

In the case of ingredients such as meats and fish, figuring the cost can be a little more complicated. If you buy precut portion-controlled steaks or fish filets and use them just as you receive them, your AP and EP costs are the same. But if you buy whole loins of beef or whole fish and cut them yourself, you have to do a yield cost analysis in order to determine your actual costs.

The examples discussed in the remainder of this chapter use U.S. measures. For metric examples, see appendix.

RAW YIELD TEST

Suppose you work in a restaurant that serves veal scaloppine. The restaurant buys whole legs of veal. It is your job to bone out the veal, trim off all fat and connective tissue, separate the muscles at the seams, and cut the large pieces into scaloppine.

A typical whole leg of veal might weigh 30 pounds and cost $5 per pound for a total cost of $150. After finishing your trimming and cutting, you find you have 18 pounds of veal scaloppine. How do you figure the cost per pound of this meat?

The simplest example would be if you threw away all the trimmings, bones, and scrap meat. Then you would know your 18 pounds of veal cost you $150. Dividing $150 by 18 pounds gives you a cost per pound of $8.33.

But in your restaurant, you don't throw away the trimmings. You make stock with the bones, grind up the small trimmings for meatballs, use the larger trimmings for veal stew, and sell the fat to the fat collector who picks up all your waste fat once a week. Now you must do a *yield test* to figure your costs.

Table 5.5 shows a typical form you might use for a yield test. For simplification, the blanks in the form are of two types. The dotted lines are to be filled in by reading your invoices and by taking the weights from your actual yield test. The solid lines are to be filled in by doing calculations.

Note that in Table 5.6, the form has been filled in with the results of a yield test on a leg of veal. We go through the form step by step.

The executive chef in this restaurant fills out the first two lines based on the invoice, gives you the form, and requests you to do the test. You fill out the rest of the form, beginning with blank 1 on the third line. You proceed as follows:

1. Weigh the whole leg of veal and enter the weight in blank 1. Copy the price per pound and total cost from line 2 to blanks 2 and 3.

   Note that blank 3 can also be arrived at by multiplying the weight by the price per pound. However, suppose the veal were left in the cooler for several more days and dried out a bit. The weight then might be 29½ pounds. By multiplying 29.5 by $5.00, you would get a total cost of $147.50. But because the price you paid was actually $150, it is important to use that figure and not fill in the blank by multiplying.

2. Break down the veal into all its component parts and record the weights of the trim and waste, starting in blank 4. In this case, there are only six items: fat, bones, small meat scraps for grinding, meat for stew, unusable waste, and cutting loss.

Record the weight of the finished scaloppine in blank 13.

Table 5.5 Raw Yield Test Form

Item .... Test number .... Date ....

Purveyor .... Price per pound .... Total cost ....

AP weight **(1)** .... Lb price **(2)** .... Total cost **(3)** ....

Trim, salvage, and waste:

ITEM	WEIGHT	VALUE/LB	TOTAL VALUE (LB X VALUE)
(4)			
(5)			
(6)			
(7)			
(8)			
(9)			
(10)			

Total weight (4 thru 10) **(11)** _____ Total value (4 thru 10) **(12)** _____

Total yield of item **(13)** ....

Net cost (3 − 12) **(14)** _____

Cost per lb (14 ÷ 13) **(15)** _____

Percentage of increase (15 ÷ 2) **(16)** _____

Table 5.6 Completed Raw Yield Test Form

Item .... veal leg to scaloppine .... Test number .... 3 .... Date .... 6/5/10 ....

Purveyor .... ABC Meats .... Price per pound .... $5 .... Total cost .... $150 ....

AP weight **(1)** .... 30 lb .... Lb price **(2)** .... $5 .... Total cost **(3)** .... $150 ....

Trim, salvage, and waste:

ITEM	WEIGHT	VALUE/LB	TOTAL VALUE (LB X VALUE)
(4) fat	2½ lb	$0.12	$.30
(5) bone	3 lb 5 oz	$0.38	$1.26
(6) ground veal	2 lb 2 oz	$4.89	$10.39
(7) stew meat	3 lb	$5.29	$15.87
(8) unusable trim	14 oz	0	0
(9) cutting loss	3 oz	0	0
(10)			

Total weight (4 thru 10) **(11)** ___ 12 lb ___ Total value (4 thru 10) **(12)** ___ $27.82 ___

Total yield of item **(13)** .... 18 lb

Net cost (3 − 12) **(14)** ___ $122.18 ___

Cost per lb (14 ÷ 13) **(15)** ___ $6.79 ___

Percentage of increase (15 ÷ 2) **(16)** ___ 1.36 (136%) ___

What is *cutting loss*? This is not something you can actually weigh. However, there is always some loss of weight due to particles of meat and fat sticking to the cutting board, to drying, and to other factors. So when you add up all your weights, you find they total less than 30 pounds. To determine cutting loss, add up blanks 4 through 8 and blank 13. Subtract this total from line 1.

3. Enter the values per pound of the trim, salvage, and waste on lines 4 through 10. In this case, these numbers are given to you by the executive chef from the invoices.

   - The fat collector pays 12 cents per pound for waste fat.

   - When you have to buy extra bones for your stockpot, you pay 38 cents per pound for them, so this is their value to you. This is also the figure you use when you cost out your stock recipe. If you didn't make stock and threw out the bones, you'd enter 0 in this blank.

   - Similarly, the values entered for ground veal and stew meat are the prices you'd have to pay if you bought them.

   - Unusable trim and cutting loss have no value, so you enter 0.

4. Calculate the total value of each item on lines 4 through 10 by multiplying the weight by the value per pound. Note that this particular form tells you how to do all the calculations.

5. Add the weights in lines 4 through 10 and enter the total in blank 11. Add the total values in lines 4 through 10 and enter this figure in blank 12.

6. Subtract the total value of all the trim (blank 12) from the price you paid for the veal (blank 3). This gives you the net cost of your 18 pounds of scaloppine.

7. To find the cost per pound of the scaloppine, divide the net cost (blank 14) by the weight (blank 13). This is the figure you will use in costing recipes for veal scaloppine.

8. The percentage of increase in the last line is determined by dividing the net cost per pound (blank 15) by the price per pound of the whole leg (blank 2). This figure can be used as follows:

   Suppose next week you buy another leg of veal from the same purveyor, but the price has gone up to $5.29 per pound. Instead of doing another yield test, you can simply multiply this new price by the percentage of increase ($5.29 times 1.36) to get a new cost per pound of $7.19.

COOKED YIELD TEST

Earlier we introduced two important abbreviations: AP (as purchased) and EP (edible portion). A third expression sometimes used is *AS*, meaning *as served*. When foods such as fruits are served raw, AS may be the same as EP. But if the food is cooked, these weights are different.

In the case of the veal scaloppine, your recipe portions, and therefore your portion costs, are based on raw weight. For example, your scaloppine recipe might call for 5½ ounces raw meat per portion.

In some cases, on the other hand, your portions may be based on cooked weight. This is most often true of roasts. For example, let's say you buy whole fresh hams, bone and trim them, and serve them as roasts, allowing 6 ounces sliced, cooked meat per portion. To arrive at your cost, you will have to do a cooked yield test, as illustrated in Tables 5.7 and 5.8. (This form may be printed on the same sheet of paper as the raw yield test form so the operation can have a complete cost analysis on one form.)

This form has been filled in with the results of a cooked yield test done on a roast, boneless fresh ham. Let's assume this same ham has already had a raw yield test done on it.

The first half of the form, through blank 3, is filled in before the test starts. The numbers for blanks 1, 2, and 3 are taken from the raw yield test form, but you should double-check the net raw weight by weighing the item again before roasting.

Enter the total weight of cooked ham served in blank 4. You arrive at this figure by recording the total number of portions served and multiplying this number by the portion size. Let's say 22 portions are served at 6 ounces each. This gives us a total of 132 ounces (22 × 6), or 8¼ pounds.

You might be tempted to simply weigh the whole roast after cooking and trimming. Remember, though, that there will be some waste—crumbs on the slicer or cutting board, spillage of juices, and so on. It is more accurate to record the weight you actually sell.

Table 5.7 Cooked Yield Test Form

Item	Test number	Date	
AP price per lb			
Cooking temperature			
Net raw weight **(1)**	Net cost per lb **(2)**		
	Total net cost **(3)**		
Weight as served **(4)**			
Cooked cost per lb (3 ÷ 4) **(5)**			
Shrinkage (1 − 4) **(6)**			
Percentage of shrinkage (6 ÷ 1) **(7)**			
Total percentage of cost increase (5 ÷ AP price per lb) **(8)**			

Table 5.8 Completed Cooked Yield Test Form

Item .... roast fresh ham	Test number 2	Date 6/5/10	
AP price per lb $3.49			
Cooking temperature .... 325°			
Net raw weight **(1)** .... 12 lb	Net cost per lb **(2)** $3.93		
Total net cost **(3)** $47.16			
Weight as served **(4)** .... 8 lb 4 oz			
Cooked cost per lb (3 ÷ 4) **(5)** $5.72			
Shrinkage (1 − 4) **(6)** .... 3¾ lb			
Percentage of shrinkage (6 ÷ 1) **(7)** 31%			
Total percentage of cost increase (5 ÷ AP price per lb) **(8)** 164%			

If this had been a bone-in roast, you would have another reason to carve the meat before weighing, because you could not include the weight of the bone in your as-served figure.

The remaining blanks on the form are determined by doing the calculations, just as you would do the calculations for the raw yield test.

Portion Costs

Portion cost, or *raw food cost*, is the total cost of all the ingredients in a recipe divided by the number of portions served:

$$\text{portion cost} = \frac{\text{cost of ingredients}}{\text{number of portions}}$$

Here we cost out a sample recipe to show you how the procedure works. First, note the following points and keep them in mind when you are calculating portion costs. Many errors in costing are caused by forgetting one of these points.

1. Costs must be based on AP (as purchased) amounts, even though recipes often give EP (edible portion) quantities. These terms are explained in the preceding section.

2. Include *everything*. That means the lemon wedge and parsley garnish for the fish filet, the cream and sugar that go with the coffee, and the oil that used for pan-frying the eggplant. These are sometimes called *hidden costs*.

Seasonings and spices are a typical example of hidden costs that are difficult to calculate. Some operations add up the cost of all seasonings used in a year and divide that by the total food cost to get a percentage. This percentage is added to each item. For example, if the cost of an item is $2.00 and the seasoning cost percentage is 5 percent, the total cost is $2.00 plus 5 percent of $2.00, or $2.10.

Other hidden costs can be calculated in the same way. For example, you could figure out your cost percentage for frying fat and add the percentage to all deep-fried foods.

Some restaurants take an arbitrary figure for all hidden costs, usually 8 to 12 percent, and add this to all menu items.

3. Record the number of portions *actually served*, not just the number the recipe is intended to serve. If the roast shrank more than you expected during cooking, or if you dropped a piece of cake on the floor, those costs still have to be covered.

Procedure for Calculating Portion Cost

1. List ingredients and quantities of recipe as prepared.
2. Convert the recipe quantities to AP (as purchased) quantities.
3. Determine the price of each ingredient (from invoices, price lists, etc.). The units in this step and in step 2 must be the same in order for you to do the calculation.
4. Calculate the total cost of each ingredient by multiplying the price per unit by the number of units needed.
5. Add the ingredient costs to get the total recipe cost.
6. Divide the total cost by the number of portions served to get the cost per portion.

Example: Costing a Recipe   Item: Baked Rice

Ingredient	Amount	Recipe Quantity	Price	Total
Rice, long grain	4 lb	4 lb	$0.62/lb	$2.48
Butter	12 oz	0.75 lb	1.97/lb	1.48
Onions	1 lb	1.2 lb	0.36/lb	0.43
Chicken stock	4 qt	4 qt	0.25/qt	1.00
Salt	1 oz	¹⁄₁₆ lb	0.15/lb	0.01
			Total cost	$5.40
			Number of portions	50
			Cost per portion	$0.11

Note: Cost of chicken stock is determined by costing out the operation's recipe for chicken stock.

Controlling Food Costs

Calculating food costs is a critical part of the business of selling and serving food. The preceding section explains the basic mathematics of determining these costs. But cost control is much more than calculating costs based on written recipes. Cost control begins with menu planning and encompasses every phase of the operation, from purchasing to service.

Menu Planning

A well-planned menu takes care to utilize ingredients efficiently and in a way that avoids waste. When writing a menu, consider the following guidelines for total utilization of foods.

1. **Use all edible trim.**
   Unless you use only portion-controlled meats, poultry, and fish and only frozen and canned vegetables, you will have edible trim. You can either throw it away and call it a loss, or you can use it and make money on it.

   Plan recipes that utilize these trimmings and put them on the menu. For example:

- Use small meat scraps for soups, chopped meat, pâtés, creamed dishes, croquettes.
- Use larger meat trimmings for soups, stews, braised items.
- Use bones for stocks, soups.
- Use vegetable trimmings for purées, soups, stews, stocks, fillings for omelets and crêpes.
- Use day-old breads for stuffings, breading, French toast, croutons, meat extender.

2. **Don't add an item to the menu unless you can use the trimmings.**
   This is really the same as the preceding item, looking from the opposite angle. In other words, don't put rissolé potatoes on your menu unless you also plan to serve an item that uses the trimmings, such as whipped potatoes or croquettes.

3. **Plan production to avoid leftovers.**
   The best way to use leftovers is not to create them in the first place. Handling food twice—once as a fresh item and once as a leftover—is more expensive and time-consuming than handling it once, and it almost always results in loss of quality. Limited menus—that is, with fewer selections—decrease the likelihood of leftovers.

4. **Plan ahead for use of leftovers.**
   Careful planning of production can keep leftovers to a minimum. But some leftovers are almost inevitable, and it's better for your costs to use them than to throw them out. Whenever you put an item on the menu that could become a leftover, you should have a recipe ready that will use it. This is better than being surprised with leftovers you don't know what to do with.
   For example, if you served roast chicken for dinner one day, you might plan on chicken salad for a luncheon special the next day.
   Remember to handle all leftovers according to proper sanitary procedures.

5. **Avoid minimum-use perishable ingredients.**
   Minimum-use ingredients are those that are used in one or two items on your menu. For example, an operation might serve chicken breast topped with sautéed mushrooms but not use mushrooms in any other item. When the ingredient is perishable, the result is a high percentage of spoilage or waste.
   This situation can be remedied in any of three ways.

- Change the recipe to eliminate the minimum-use ingredient.
- Eliminate the item from the menu.
- Add other items to the menu using the ingredient.

   Be careful not to unbalance the menu, however, by using an ingredient in too many dishes. Try to avoid both extremes.

Purchasing

MANAGING INVENTORY

Par stock is the inventory of goods an operation must have on hand to continue operating between deliveries. It is important to maintain a proper par stock to avoid running out of essential items. On the other hand, it is costly to maintain a larger inventory than necessary. This is partly because part of your operating cash is tied up in unused inventory. Second, excessive inventory of perishable items can lead to spoilage and thus to loss. Accurate forecasting of future business, based on careful study of past business, is key to managing inventory and establishing par stock.

Carefully write specifications for each item purchased so the item is described accurately. Compare price and quality offered by several vendors in order to get the best quality for the best price. Order from up-to-date quotes and price lists.

Receiving

Pay careful attention to receiving procedures:

- Schedule receipts so an employee can devote full attention to checking the shipment without being rushed. Try to schedule deliveries so they don't arrive at the same time.

If the employee receiving the goods has kitchen duties as well, schedule deliveries during off hours so he or she has adequate time to check the shipments.

- Check the delivery immediately, while the driver is there. Don't allow the driver to unload the shipment and depart, leaving the order on the loading dock.

- Compare the delivery invoice to the order forms to make sure the right goods are delivered.

- Compare the delivery invoice to the actual goods received to make sure you have received everything you are paying for. Keep a scale at the receiving entrance so items can be checked for proper weight.

Check the delivery for quality:

- Check the temperature of refrigerated goods.

- Check the temperature of frozen goods, and check for signs of thawing and refreezing.

- Check all perishables for freshness.

- Check all containers and packaging for damage.

- Immediately transfer all goods to proper storage.

Storing

Proper storage is essential to avoid spoilage and loss of food items. Consult the index for further reference.

Measuring and Other Cooking Procedures

As discussed earlier in this chapter, the concept of measurement applies to two principal areas: measurement of ingredients in recipe preparation, and measurement of portions to be served, also known as portion control. The fundamentals of both types of measurement are explained earlier in this chapter (see pp. 93–95) and need not be repeated here.

Measurement is an indispensable part of good kitchen procedures. Think of measurement as part of your basic cooking procedures, not as something separate. All cooking procedures, including measuring, combine to help control food costs, because proper cooking procedures help avoid waste due to improperly prepared foods. For example, lack of attention at the grill station often results in meats returned by the customer for being overcooked. Having to discard and replace badly cooked foods greatly increases food cost.

Serving

All the cook's attention to measurement and portion control goes for nothing if a server drops the plate on the way to the dining room. A well-trained serving staff is an important part of controlling food costs. Serving staff must be trained in serving techniques and in portion control for those items, such as desserts or salads, they are responsible for plating. Servers must understand the menu well so they can explain each item to customers and avoid returned dishes. The chef often may wish to sell more of some items than others as part of inventory and cost control, so serving staff must also be trained to be effective but pleasant sales people. The demands made on the service personnel can best be met when the chef and the service manager cooperate in their training.

KEY POINTS TO REVIEW

- What is the procedure for converting a recipe to a different yield?

- Why do recipes sometimes not give the same results when converted to a different quantity? What kinds of adjustments might you have to make to avoid this problem?

- What are AP quantities and EP quantities? Explain how to perform yield calculations when you know the AP quantity and the percentage yield.

- What is the procedure for calculating food costs?

- What are some good ways to keep food costs as low as possible?

TERMS FOR REVIEW

static menu	homemade	liter	food cost percentage
cycle menu	organic	meter	yield test
à la carte	recipe	degree Celsius	cutting loss
table d'hôte	standardized recipe	kilo-	as served (AS)
prix fixe	AP (as purchased) weight	deci-	portion cost
tasting menu	EP (edible portion) weight	centi-	hidden cost
course	portion control	milli-	minimum-use ingredient
fresh	metric system	yield	par stock
imported	gram	conversion factor	

QUESTIONS FOR DISCUSSION

1. What role is played by the chef's favorite dishes when a menu is written?
2. What are the main differences among breakfast, lunch, and dinner menus?
3. Which of the following are most likely to have static menus?
   Fast-food restaurant   French restaurant   Army mess
   High school cafeteria   Employee lunchroom
4. The following menus are made up of dishes prepared from recipes in this book. Evaluate each for variety and balance.

Clear vegetable soup	Cream of mushroom soup
Green salad with French dressing	Waldorf salad
Chicken fricassée	Veal scaloppine à la crème
Cauliflower au gratin	Broccoli Mornay
	Rice pilaf

Scotch broth	Oxtail soup
Cucumber and tomato salad	Coleslaw
Roast rack of lamb with spring vegetables	Beef pot roast
	Braised green cabbage
	Bouillon potatoes

Oysters casino	Gazpacho
Vichyssoise	Tomato and avocado salad
Broiled steak	Chicken Pojarski
Baked potato	Baked acorn squash
Buttered green beans	Duchesse potatoes

5. What is the best solution to the problem of using up leftovers? What is the next best solution?
6. What are some reasons written recipes can't be 100 percent exact and must depend on the cook's judgment? Select two or three recipes (from this book or any other) and try to determine where they depend on the cook's judgment.
7. What is the purpose of a standardized recipe?
8. What are the three basic ways of measuring ingredients? Which method is used for most solid ingredients, and why?
9. What is the first step in portion control? List four other techniques of portion control.

10. Make the following conversions in the U.S. system of measurement:

    3½ pounds = _____ ounces

    6 cups = _____ pints

    8½ quarts = _____ fluid ounces

    ¾ cup = _____ tablespoons

    46 ounces = _____ pounds

    2¼ gallons = _____ fluid ounces

    5 pounds 5 ounces ÷ 2 = _____

    10 teaspoons = _____ fluid ounces

11. Make the following conversions in the metric system:

    1.4 kilograms = _____ grams

    53 deciliters = _____ liters

    15 centimeters = _____ millimeters

    2,590 grams = _____ kilograms

    4.6 liters = _____ deciliters

    220 centiliters = _____ deciliters

12. Turn to the recipe for Swedish Meatballs on page 367. Convert it to yield 35 portions.
13. Discuss the main types of problems you may face when converting recipe yields.
14. What is the difference between AP weight and EP weight? Explain how these terms are related to calculating costs per portion of menu items.
15. The following problems are calculations with food cost percentages, portion cost, and menu price. For each problem, two of the figures are given. Find the third.

Food Cost Percentage	Portion Cost	Menu Price
a. _____	$1.24	$4.95
b. 40%	_____	$2.50
c. 30%	$2.85	_____

Chapter 6

Chopping mirepoix, page 122

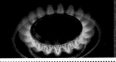
Mise en Place

To be successful in the food-service industry, cooks need more than the ability to prepare delicious, attractive, and nutritious foods. They also must have a talent for organization and efficiency. In every kitchen, a great many tasks must be completed over a given time and by a limited number of workers. No matter when these tasks are done, they all must come together at one crucial point: service time. Only if advance preparation is done thoroughly and systematically can service go smoothly.

Good chefs take pride in the thoroughness and quality of their advance preparation, or *mise en place* (meez-on-plahss). This French term, meaning "everything put in place," has become almost a professional password in North American kitchens because food-service professionals understand its importance to the success of the establishment.

This chapter deals with the basic concepts of mise en place as well as specific operations that are normally part of the mise en place.

After reading this chapter, you should be able to

1. Define *mise en place*, and explain why care must be taken in its planning.
2. Describe five general steps used in planning mise en place.
3. Explain the difference in preparation requirements for set meal service and extended meal service.
4. List five guidelines to observe when sharpening a chef's knife.
5. Demonstrate major cutting techniques required in food preparation.
6. Describe basic precooking and marinating procedures.
7. Set up and use a standard breading station.
8. Define *convenience foods* in the context of mise en place, and list eight guidelines for their use.

Planning and Organizing Production

Even on the simplest level, pre-preparation is necessary. If you prepare only one short recipe, you must first:

- Assemble your tools.
- Assemble your ingredients.
- Wash, trim, cut, prepare, and measure your raw materials.
- Prepare your equipment (preheat oven, line baking sheets, etc.).

Only then can you begin the actual preparation.

When many items are to be prepared in a commercial kitchen, the situation is much more complex. Dealing with this complexity is the basis of kitchen organization.

The Problem

Every food-service operation faces a basic conflict between two unavoidable facts:

1. There is far too much work to do in a kitchen to leave until the last minute, so some work must be done ahead.

2. Most foods are at their best quality immediately after preparation, and they deteriorate as they are held.

The Solution

To address this conflict, the chef must plan pre-preparation carefully. Planning generally follows these steps:

1. **Break down each menu item into its stages of production.**
   Turn to any recipe in this book. Note the procedures are divided into a sequence of steps that must be done in a certain order to make a finished product.

2. **Determine which stages may be done in advance.**

   - The first step of every recipe, written or not, is always part of advance preparation: *assembling and preparing the ingredients*. This includes cleaning and cutting produce, cutting and trimming meats, and preparing breadings and batters for frying.

   - Succeeding steps of a recipe may be done in advance *if the foods can then be held without loss of quality*.

   - Final cooking should be done as close as possible to service for maximum freshness.

     Frequently, separate parts of a recipe, such as a sauce or a stuffing, are prepared in advance, and the dish is assembled at the last minute.

     In general, items cooked by dry-heat methods, such as broiled steaks, sautéed fish, and French-fried potatoes, do not hold well. Large roasts are an important exception to this rule. Items cooked by moist heat, such as braised beef, soups, and stews, are usually better suited to reheating or holding in a steam table. Delicate items should always be freshly cooked.

3. **Determine the best way to hold each item at its final stage of pre-preparation.** *Holding temperature* **is the temperature at which a product is kept for service or for storage. Holding temperatures for all potentially hazardous foods must be outside the Food Danger Zone.**

   - Sauces and soups are frequently kept hot, above 135°F (57°C), for service in steam tables or other holding equipment. Foods such as vegetables, however, should be kept hot for short periods only because they quickly become overcooked.

- Refrigerator temperatures, below 41°F (5°C), are best for preserving the quality of most foods, especially perishable meats, fish, and vegetables, before final cooking or reheating.

4. **Determine how long it takes to prepare each stage of each recipe. Plan a production schedule beginning with the preparations that take the longest.**
   Many operations can be carried on at once because they don't all require your complete attention the full time. It may take 6 to 8 hours to make a stock, but you don't have to stand and watch it all that time.

5. **Examine recipes to see if they might be revised for better efficiency and quality as served.**
   For example:

   - Instead of preparing a full batch of green peas and holding them for service in the steam table, you might blanch and chill them, then heat portions to order in a sauté pan, steamer, or microwave oven.

   - Instead of holding a large batch of veal scaloppine in mushroom sauce in the steam table, you might prepare and hold the sauce, sauté the veal to order, combine the meat with a portion of the sauce, and serve fresh from the pan.

   Caution: Unless you are in charge of the kitchen, do not change a recipe without authorization from your supervisor.

The Goal

The goal of pre-preparation is to do as much work in advance as possible *without loss of quality*. Then, at service time, all energy can be used for finishing each item immediately before serving, with the utmost attention to quality and freshness.

Many preparation techniques in common use are designed for the convenience of the cooks at the expense of quality. Remember, quality should always take highest priority.

Adapting Preparation to Style of Service

The way you plan production and do your mise en place depends in large part on the style of meal service. The following discussion of *set meal service* and *extended meal service* illustrates the basic differences.

SET MEAL SERVICE

- All customers eat at one time.

- Often called *quantity cooking* because large batches are prepared in advance.

- Examples: school cafeterias, banquets, employee dining rooms.

The traditional method of set meal preparation, still widely used, is to prepare the entire quantity of each item in a single large batch and to keep it hot for the duration of the meal service. This method has two major disadvantages:

- Deterioration of quality due to long holding.

- Large quantities of leftovers.

Modern high-speed equipment, such as pressure steamers, convection ovens, infrared ovens, and microwave ovens, make possible a system called *small-batch cooking*. Required quantities are divided into smaller batches, placed in pans ready for final cooking or heating, and then cooked only as needed. The advantages of this system are

- Fresher food, because it is not held as long.

- Fewer leftovers, because servings not needed are not cooked.

Small-batch cooking also accommodates items prepared in advance and frozen or chilled for storage.

EXTENDED MEAL SERVICE

- Customers eat at different times.

- Often called *à la carte cooking* because customers usually select items from a written menu (*carte* in French).

- Examples: restaurants, short-order counters.

Individual items are cooked to order rather than cooked ahead, but pre-preparation is extensive, down to the final cooking stage.

The short-order cook, for example, must have everything ready to go: cold meats, tomatoes and other sandwich ingredients sliced and arranged, spreads prepared and ready, hamburger patties shaped, garnishes prepared, and so on. If the cook has to stop during service to do any of these things, orders will back up and service will fall behind.

A steak that takes 10 minutes to broil may be cut and trimmed in advance, but broiling should be started 10 minutes before it is to be served.

Obviously, if the last step in a recipe is to braise the item for 1½ hours, one cannot wait until an order comes in before beginning to braise. An experienced cook can estimate closely how many orders will be needed during the meal period and prepare a batch that, ideally, will finish braising just when service begins.

Note the differences in these two methods for Chicken Chasseur. In both cases, the final product is chicken in a brown sauce with mushrooms, shallots, white wine, and tomatoes.

1. **Quantity method—Chicken Chasseur:**

    Brown chicken in fat; remove.

    Sauté shallots and mushrooms in same fat.

    Add flour to make a roux.

    Add white wine, tomatoes, brown stock, seasonings; simmer until thickened.

    Add chicken; braise until done.

2. **À la carte method—Chicken Chasseur:**

    Prepare Sauce Chasseur in advance; hold in bain-marie.

    For each order:

    Brown chicken in sauté pan; finish cooking in oven.

    Deglaze pan with white wine; reduce.

    Add one portion of sauce; add chicken and simmer briefly; serve.

Mise en Place: The Required Tasks

Up to this point, we have discussed planning the production schedule. Our planning helps us determine the tasks we must do before beginning the final cooking during the meal service period. Chefs refer to performing these preliminary tasks as "doing the mise en place." In many restaurants, especially large ones, the mise en place is extensive. It includes the preparation of stocks, sauces, breadings, and batters as well as the cutting and trimming of all the meat, poultry, fish, and vegetables the chef expects will be needed during the meal service.

A large part of a cook's workday is spent doing mise en place. This means that a large part of learning how to cook is learning how to do mise en place. In fact, a large part of this book is devoted to these tasks of preparation. There are many more such tasks than can be included in a single chapter.

The remainder of this chapter discusses the most basic and general skills required for a mise en place. The most basic of these are knife skills. Fundamentals such as how to hold the chef's knife, how to maintain a sharp edge, and how to make basic cuts are illustrated. More specific techniques required for individual food products are explained in appropriate chapters later in the book. For example, vegetable trimming techniques are discussed in the first vegetable chapter, methods for cutting chicken in the first poultry chapter, and stock and sauce mise en place in Chapter 7.

KEY POINTS TO REVIEW

- What does *mise en place* mean? What kinds of tasks are included in this term?

- What are the five steps in planning mise en place?

- How does mise en place for à la carte service differ from mise en place for set meal service?

Using the Knife

Many laborsaving tools are available for cutting, chopping, and slicing fresh foods. Chapter 3 lists the basic kinds.

The chef's knife or French knife, however, is still the cook's most important and versatile cutting tool. The knife is more precise than a machine. Unless you are cutting a large quantity, the knife can even be faster. Cleaning a large machine takes time.

To get the best use out of your knife, *you must learn to keep it sharp and to handle it properly.*

Keeping a Sharp Edge

THE SHARPENING STONE

A stone is the traditional tool for sharpening a chef's knife. The best electric sharpeners do an excellent job of sharpening chef's knives, but many models wear away too much of your expensive knife without making a good edge. Modern professional knives are much harder than the old carbon steel knives, so they are more difficult to sharpen on a stone. Nevertheless, using a stone correctly is a valuable skill.

Follow these guidelines:

1. Hold the blade at a constant 20-degree angle to the stone, as shown in Figure 6.1.

2. Make light, even strokes, the same number on each side of the blade.

3. Sharpen in one direction only to get a regular, uniform edge.

4. Do not oversharpen.

5. Finish with a few strokes on the steel (see next page), and then wipe the blade clean.

Figure 6.2 illustrates one of several sharpening methods. There are other good ones, too, and your instructor may prefer a method not illustrated here.

Figure 6.3 To use a manual sharpener, draw the blade through the sharpener from the heel to the tip of the knife. Do not press down hard, but make several light strokes.

OTHER KNIFE SHARPENERS

As mentioned previously, today's professional knives are made of an especially hard material that is more difficult to sharpen by traditional methods. As a result, chefs often use other sharpeners to simplify the task. Such sharpeners typically have two stones set at the correct angle, so it is necessary only to draw the knife between them. Manual and power models of these sharpeners are available. Figure 6.3 shows a manual sharpener in use.

THE STEEL

This tool is used not to sharpen the edge but to *true the edge* (to perfect it, or to smooth out irregularities) and to *maintain the edge* (to keep it sharp as it is used).

Observe these guidelines for using the steel:

1. Hold the blade at a constant 20-degree angle to the steel, just as when using the stone (Figure 6.2). A smaller angle will be ineffective. A larger one will dull the edge.

2. Make light strokes. Do not grind the knife against the steel.

3. Make even, regular strokes. Alternate each stroke, first on one side of the blade, then on the other.

4. Use no more than five or six strokes on each side of the blade. Too much steeling can actually dull the blade.

5. Use the steel often. Then you will rarely have to sharpen the knife on the stone.

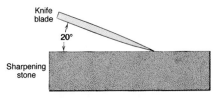

Figure 6.1 When sharpening a knife, hold the blade at a 20-degree angle to the stone.

Figure 6.2 Using a sharpening stone.

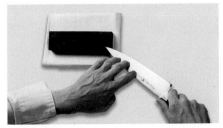

(a) Hold the knife firmly. Start with the tip of the knife against the stone as shown, and hold the edge against the stone at a 20-degree angle. Use the guiding hand to keep an even pressure on the blade.

(b) Start to draw the knife over the stone. Press very gently on the blade.

(c) Keep the motion smooth, using even, light pressure.

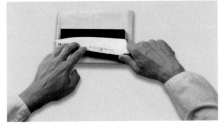

(d) Draw the knife across the stone all the way to the heel of the blade.

Figure 6.4 Using a steel.

(a) Hold the steel and the knife away from your body. With the knife in a vertical position and at a 20-degree angle to the steel, touch the steel with the heel of the blade.

(b) Pass the knife lightly along the steel, bringing the blade down in a smooth arc.

(c) Complete the movement. Do not strike the guard of the steel with the tip of the blade.

(d, e, f) Repeat the motion on the other side of the steel.

Figure 6.4 illustrates one of several steeling methods. This one is popular, but several others are equally correct. Carefully observe your instructors' demonstrations of their preferred methods.

Handling the Knife

THE GRIP

A proper grip gives you maximum control over the knife, increases your cutting accuracy and speed, prevents slipping, and lessens the chance of an accident. The type of grip you use depends, in part, on the job you are doing and the size of the knife.

The grip illustrated in Figure 6.5 is one of the most frequently used for general cutting and slicing. Many chefs feel that grasping the blade with the thumb and forefinger in this manner gives them greatest control.

Holding the knife may feel awkward at first, but practice will make it seem natural. Watch your instructors demonstrate the grips they use, and then practice under their supervision.

Figure 6.5 Grasping the blade of the knife between the thumb and forefinger gives the worker good control over the blade.

THE GUIDING HAND

While one hand controls the knife, the other hand controls the product being cut. Proper positioning of the hand achieves three goals:

1. **Hold the item being cut.**
   In Figure 6.6, the item is held firmly so it will not slip.

2. **Guide the knife.**
   Note the knife blade slides against the fingers. The position of the hand controls the cut.

3. **Protect the hand from cuts.**
   Fingertips are curled under, out of the way of the blade.

Basic Cuts and Shapes

Cutting food products into uniform shapes and sizes is important for two reasons:

1. It ensures even cooking.

2. It enhances the appearance of the product.

Figure 6.6 The position of the guiding hand, which holds the item being cut or sliced and also guides the blade, from two points of view.

Figure 6.7 shows common shapes, with their names and dimensions. The following terms describe other cutting techniques:

Chop: to cut into irregularly shaped pieces.

Concasser (con-cass-say): to chop coarsely.

Mince: to chop into very fine pieces.

Emincer (em-man-say): to cut into very thin slices (does not mean "to mince").

Shred: to cut into thin strips, either with the coarse blade of a grater (manual or power) or with a chef's knife.

Figure 6.7 Basic cuts and shapes.

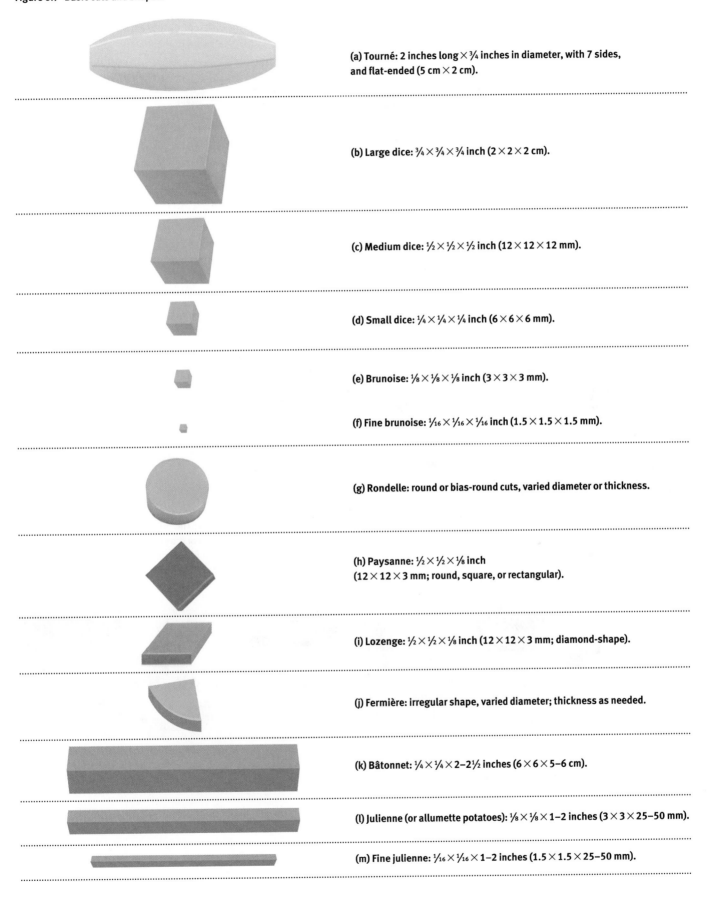

(a) **Tourné:** 2 inches long × ¾ inches in diameter, with 7 sides, and flat-ended (5 cm × 2 cm).

(b) **Large dice:** ¾ × ¾ × ¾ inch (2 × 2 × 2 cm).

(c) **Medium dice:** ½ × ½ × ½ inch (12 × 12 × 12 mm).

(d) **Small dice:** ¼ × ¼ × ¼ inch (6 × 6 × 6 mm).

(e) **Brunoise:** ⅛ × ⅛ × ⅛ inch (3 × 3 × 3 mm).

(f) **Fine brunoise:** ¹⁄₁₆ × ¹⁄₁₆ × ¹⁄₁₆ inch (1.5 × 1.5 × 1.5 mm).

(g) **Rondelle:** round or bias-round cuts, varied diameter or thickness.

(h) **Paysanne:** ½ × ½ × ⅛ inch (12 × 12 × 3 mm; round, square, or rectangular).

(i) **Lozenge:** ½ × ½ × ⅛ inch (12 × 12 × 3 mm; diamond-shape).

(j) **Fermière:** irregular shape, varied diameter; thickness as needed.

(k) **Bâtonnet:** ¼ × ¼ × 2–2½ inches (6 × 6 × 5–6 cm).

(l) **Julienne (or allumette potatoes):** ⅛ × ⅛ × 1–2 inches (3 × 3 × 25–50 mm).

(m) **Fine julienne:** ¹⁄₁₆ × ¹⁄₁₆ × 1–2 inches (1.5 × 1.5 × 25–50 mm).

Cutting Techniques

Different parts of the blade are appropriate for different purposes, as shown in Figure 6.8. (Note: Prying off bottle caps is not a function of any part of the knife.)

Figure 6.8 Using different parts of the knife blade.

(a) The tip of the knife, where the blade is thinnest and narrowest, is used for delicate work and small items.

(b) The center of the blade is used for most general work.

(c) The heel of the knife is used for heavy or coarse work, especially when greater force is required.

1. **Slicing.**

   Two basic slicing techniques are illustrated in Figures 6.9 and 6.10. When carrots and similar items are cut into round slices as shown, the cut is called *rondelle*.

Figure 6.9 Slicing technique 1.

(a) Start the knife at a sharp angle, with the tip of the knife on the cutting board.

(b) Move the knife forward and down to slice through the carrot.

(c) Finish the cut with the knife against the board. For the second slice, raise the heel of the knife and pull it backward, but be sure the tip stays on the board.

Figure 6.10 Slicing technique 2.

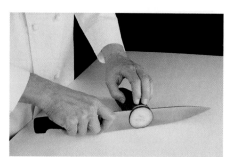

(a) Start the blade at a 45-degree angle, with the tip on the cucumber against the fingers of the guiding hand.

(b, c) Slice downward and forward through the item.

2. **Cutting dice, brunoise, bâtonnet, allumette, and julienne.**

   Figure 6.11 shows the steps in dicing a product, using a potato to illustrate. Note in Figure 6.11c that the process of cutting dice first requires you to cut stick shapes, such as bâtonnet. Thus, this illustration demonstrates the method used to cut not only *dice* and *brunoise* (broon wahz) but also *bâtonnet* (bah toh nay), *allumette* (ah lyoo met), and *julienne* (zhoo lee enn).

Figure 6.11 Slicing a potato.

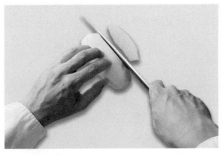

(a) Square off the peeled, eyed potato by cutting a slice from all sides. Use the trimmings for mashed potatoes or soup.

(b) Cut the potato into even slices of the desired thickness. Here we are making ¼-inch (6-mm) dice, so the slices are ¼-inch (6-mm) thick.

(c) Stack the slices and again slice across the stack in even ¼-inch (6-mm) slices. You now have bâtonnet potatoes, slightly smaller than regular French fries. Slices ⅛ inch (3 mm) thick would give you allumette potatoes.

(d) Looking from this angle shows how the slices have been stacked up.

(e) Pile the bâtonnets together and cut across in slices ¼ inch (6 mm) apart. You now have perfect ¼ inch (6 mm) dice.

Figure 6.12 Cut the vegetable into sticks ½ inch (12 mm) square. To cut the sticks into paysanne, cut them crosswise into thin slices.

3. **Cutting paysanne.**

   Paysanne are thin square, or roughly square, cuts. The procedure begins the same as for cutting medium dice. However, in the last step, cut the ½-inch (12-mm) -thick sticks into thin slices rather than into dice. Figure 6.12 illustrates.

4. **Cutting *lozenges*.**

   This is a diamond-shape cut, as illustrated in Figure 6.13.

5. **Cutting *fermière*.**

   Fermière is an irregular slice. Shapes may vary, depending on the item, but the pieces should be of uniform size. Thickness must also be uniform, usually around ⅛ inch (3 mm). Cut the item lengthwise into pieces of roughly uniform size and shape, and then slice as shown in Figure 6.14.

6. **Making *oblique cuts*.**

   Also called the *roll cut*, this cut is for long, cylindrical vegetables such as carrots. As illustrated in Figure 6.15, hold the knife at an angle, cut, roll the vegetable one quarter-turn, and make the next cut. For tapered vegetables, change the angle as you go to keep the pieces of approximately equal size.

Figure 6.13 To cut lozenges, first cut the vegetable into thin slices, and then cut these slices lengthwise into strips about ⅛ inch (3 mm) wide. Cut the strips at an angle to form diamond shapes.

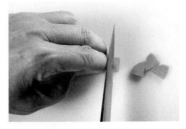

Figure 6.14 To cut fermière, cut the item lengthwise into roughly equal pieces, and then slice uniformly.

Figure 6.15 To make oblique cuts, cut the vegetable at a sharp angle, roll one quarter-turn, and make another cut.

7. Dicing an onion.

Dicing an onion presents a special problem for cutting because its form is in layers, not a solid piece. This technique is illustrated in Figure 6.16.

Figure 6.16 Dicing an onion.

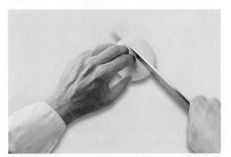

(a) Cut the peeled onion in half lengthwise, through the root end. Place one half on the cutting board, cut side down.

(b) With the root end away from you, make a series of vertical lengthwise cuts. Do not cut through the root end. The closer together you make the cuts, the smaller the dice will be.

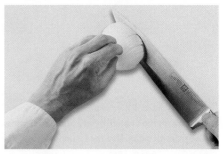

(c) Holding the onion carefully at the top, make a few horizontal cuts toward but not through the root end, which is holding the onion together.

(d) Finally, slice across the onion to separate it into dice. Again, the closer together the cuts, the smaller the dice.

(e) Continue making slices almost to the root end. The root end may be rough cut for mirepoix, to be used for stocks, sauces, and roasts.

Figure 6.17 To chop mirepoix, cut onions, celery, and carrots roughly into pieces of approximately equal size. The exact size depends on what the mirepoix is to be used for.

8. Chopping mirepoix.

Mirepoix is a mixture of coarsely chopped vegetables, primarily onions, carrots, and celery, used to flavor stocks, gravies, sauces, and other items, as explained in Chapter 7. Because mirepoix is not served—rather, it is almost always strained out of the product before finishing—neatness of cut is not important. The products are cut roughly into pieces of approximately uniform size—small pieces if cooking time will be short, larger pieces for longer cooking times. Figure 6.17 illustrates mirepoix ingredients being cut.

9. Chopping herbs.

This chopping technique is used to cut a product when no specific shape is needed. Figure 6.18 illustrates chopping parsley.

In the case of chives and scallions, a more regular cut is used, similar to the slicing cut used for larger items like carrots. Figure 6.19 illustrates this procedure.

Figure 6.18 Chopping with a French knife. Holding the tip of the knife against the cutting board, rock the knife rapidly up and down. At the same time, gradually move the knife sideways across the product on the board so the cuts pass through all parts of the pile of food. After several cuts, redistribute the pile and begin again. Continue until the product is chopped as fine as you want.

Figure 6.19 Stack chives and cut crosswise into very thin slices.

10. **Cutting parisienne.**

Cuts made with a ball cutter are perhaps most often used for potatoes. Potatoes cut into large balls, about 1⅓ inch (3 cm), are called *parisienne* (pah ree zee enn). When cut into smaller balls, about ⅞ inch (2.5 cm), they are called *noisette* (nwah zet). Of course, other solid vegetables, such as turnips, as well as many fruits, can be cut the same way. The procedure is illustrated in Figure 6.20.

Figure 6.20 Cutting parisienne potatoes.

(a) Place the ball cutter against the potato as shown.

(b) With the thumb, press the cutter firmly into the potato as far as it will go.

(c) Lift the handle of the cutter outward, twist the cutter around, and remove the ball.

11. **Cutting tournéed vegetables.**

To *tourné* (toor nay) a vegetable is to cut it into a neat seven-sided oval shape, as illustrated in Figure 6.21. Many root vegetables, such as carrots and turnips, are cut this way. When potatoes are tournéed, they are named according to their size. *Cocotte* potatoes are about 1½ inches (4 cm) long. *Château* potatoes are about 2 inches (5 cm) long.

Figure 6.21 Tournéing potatoes and other root vegetables.

(a) Cut the potatoes roughly into pieces slightly larger than the final size desired. Cut off the top and bottom of each piece so the top and bottom are flat and parallel.

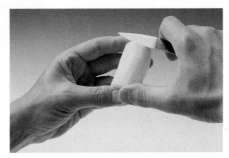

(b) Hold the potato between the thumb and forefinger. Place the paring knife against the top edge as shown and the thumb of the cutting hand firmly against the potato. Your hand should be far enough up on the blade to maintain steady control.

(c) Cut down toward your thumb with a curving movement of the blade.

(d) Turn the potato slightly (one-seventh of a full turn, to be exact) and repeat the motion.

(e) The finished product. If perfectly done, the potato has seven sides (but customers rarely count them).

12. Peeling grapefruit.

This technique, as shown in Figure 6.22, can also be used for peeling yellow turnips or other round vegetables and fruits with heavy peels.

Figure 6.22 Peeling a grapefruit.

(a) Cut off the ends of the grapefruit and turn it on a flat end so it is stable. Slice off a section of the peel, following the contour of the grapefruit.

(b) Make sure the cut is deep enough to remove the peel but not so deep as to waste the product.

(c) Continue making slices around the grapefruit until all the peel is removed.

(d) Slice or section the fruit. Squeeze the remaining pulp for juice. The membrane-free citrus section cut by this method are called *suprêmes*.

13. Chiffonade.

This term refers to cutting leaves into fine shreds. It is applied most often to lettuce and sorrel. To cut *chiffonade*, remove the heavy leaf ribs, roll the leaves into a tight cylinder, and then slice the cylinder crosswise into thin shreds, as shown in Figure 6.23.

Figure 6.23 Cutting a chiffonade of sorrel.

(a) Roll the leaves into a cylinder.

(b) Cut crosswise into thin strips or shreds.

14. **Cutting citrus zest.**

With a paring knife, cut strips from the citrus peel, removing only the colored part, not the white part below it. Then, with a chef's knife, cut the zest into thin strips or julienne, as shown in Figure 6.24b. An alternative method is to use a citrus zester, as shown in Figure 6.24c.

Figure 6.24 Cutting citrus zest.

(a) Use a paring knife to cut thin strips from the peel, being careful to cut only the outer colored part, not the inner white pith.

(b) Cut the strips of peel into julienne.

(c) Alternatively, draw a zesting tool over the fruit to cut thin strips of zest.

KEY POINTS TO REVIEW

- How do you sharpen a knife?

- When performing most cutting techniques, what is the correct and safe position of the guiding hand—that is, the hand not holding the knife?

- What are the dimensions of the following cuts: large dice, medium dice, small dice, brunoise, fine brunoise, bâtonnet, julienne, fine julienne, rondelle, paysanne, lozenge, tourné?

Preliminary Cooking and Flavoring

Advance preparation often requires precooking and flavoring of ingredients to make them ready for use in the finished recipe.

On the most obvious level, if a recipe for chicken salad calls for cooked, diced chicken, you must first cook the chicken before you can proceed with the recipe. A complete cooking procedure, in such a case, is part of the mise en place, or pre-preparation.

Blanching and Parcooking

Partial cooking is a significant part of advance preparation. It requires a degree of culinary skill and judgment to determine when and how much cooking is necessary or desirable.

Partial cooking may be done by any moist-heat or dry-heat method. Those commonly used are simmering or boiling (parboiling), steaming, and deep-frying (especially for potatoes). The term *blanching* may mean any of these methods, but it usually implies *very brief* cooking.

There are four main reasons for blanching or parcooking:

1. **To increase holding quality.**

   Heating helps preserve foods by:

   - Destroying bacteria that cause spoilage.

   - Destroying enzymes that discolor foods (as when potatoes turn brown) and cause them to deteriorate.

2. To save time.

It takes less time to finish parboiled vegetables for service than it does to finish raw vegetables. Large batches of foods may be blanched and chilled, and individual portions then finished to order.

Items, such as roast duck, that take too long to cook completely to order are often roasted half to three-quarters done and then finished as the orders are received.

3. To remove undesirable flavors.

Some variety meats and certain strong-flavored vegetables, such as rutabaga, are sometimes blanched to make them milder and more acceptable to the customer.

4. To enable the product to be processed further.

For example, vegetables and fruits such as tomatoes and peaches, as well as some nuts, are blanched to loosen the skins for peeling.

Sweetbreads are blanched so they are firm enough for slicing and breading or other kinds of handling.

Marinating

To *marinate* means to soak a food product in a seasoned liquid in order to:

1. Flavor the product.

2. Tenderize the product.

The tenderizing effect of the acids in the marinade is relatively small. It is still essential to match the proper cut of meat with the proper cooking techniques for greatest tenderness.

The marinade can also serve as the cooking medium and become part of the sauce. Vegetable marinades, called *vinaigrettes*, are served cold with the vegetables as salads or hors d'oeuvres without further cooking or processing.

Marinades have three categories of ingredients:

1. Oil.

Oil helps preserve the meat's moisture. Sometimes it is omitted, especially for long marinations, when the oil would only float on top, out of contact with the product being marinated.

Tasteless vegetable oils are used when a neutral flavor is required. Specialty oils, such as olive oil, are used to add flavor to the item being marinated.

2. Acid from vinegar, lemon juice, wine.

Acid helps tenderize protein foods.

It carries flavors (its own and dissolved flavors from spices and herbs).

Use caution when employing strong acids, such as vinegar and lemon juice. A marinade that is too acidic will partially coagulate the protein of the meat, making it seem partially cooked. When the meat is then cooked, its texture will not be as desirable. Strong acids can be used in marinades if they are used in small quantities or if the meat is marinated only a few hours.

3. Flavorings—spices, herbs, vegetables.

A wide choice is available, depending on the purpose.

Whole spices release flavors more slowly, so they are more suitable for long marination.

KINDS OF MARINADE

1. Cooked.

Used when long keeping quality is important. Modern refrigeration has made cooked marinades less widely used. An advantage of cooked marinades is that spices release more flavor into the marinade when it is cooked.

2. Raw.

Most widely used for long marination under refrigeration. Figure 6.25 shows meat in a raw marinade.

Figure 6.25 Beef chuck in a raw marinade of red wine, wine vinegar, spices, and aromatic vegetables.

3. **Instant.**

   The range of flavors and purposes is wide. Used for marinating a few minutes up to several hours or overnight.

4. **Dry.**

   A dry marinade, also called a dry rub or a spice rub, is a mixture of salt, spices, and herbs that is rubbed or patted onto the surface of a meat, poultry, or fish item. In some cases, a little oil or a moist ingredient, such as crushed garlic, is mixed with the spices to make a paste. The item is then refrigerated to allow it time to absorb the flavors. The rub may be left on the item or scraped off before cooking. This technique is widely used for barbecued meats. Figure 6.26 shows a dry rub being applied to a large cut of meat.

   Dry marinades are an effective way to flavor meats. Naturally, because they usually don't contain an acid, you can't expect dry marinades to produce the slight tenderizing effects of liquid marinades containing acids.

Figure 6.26 Applying a dry rub to a rack of spareribs.

Guidelines for Marinating

1. Marinate under refrigeration (unless product is to be cooked only a few minutes).
2. Remember: The thicker the product, the longer it takes for the marinade to penetrate.
3. Use an acid-resistant container, such as stainless steel, glass, crockery, or some plastics.
4. Tie spices in a cheesecloth bag (sachet) if easy removal is important.
5. Cover product completely with marinade. When marinating small items for a short time, you may use less liquid, but you must then turn the product frequently for even penetration.

BRINES

A *brine* may be considered a special kind of marinade. The primary use of brines is in curing. However, many chefs also use them for roast poultry and pork because of their tenderizing and moisturizing effects (see sidebar, p. 128). Brines are rarely used for red meats.

Procedure for Brining Meats and Poultry

1. Assemble the following ingredients:

Water	1 gal	4 L
Kosher salt	4 oz	125 g
Sugar	3 oz	90 g
Bay leaves	2	2
Dried thyme	2 tsp	10 mL
Whole cloves	4	4
Peppercorns	1 tbsp	15 mL

2. Combine the water, salt, and sugar in a stockpot. Make a sachet by tying the herbs and spices in a piece of cheesecloth. Add the sachet to the pot.
3. Bring the water to a boil, stirring to make sure the salt and sugar are dissolved.
4. Let cool, then refrigerate until completely cold. Remove the sachet.
5. Put the meat or poultry into the brine. Poultry must be weighted to keep it submerged. Refrigerate.
6. For large cuts, marinate at least 6 hours or as long as 2 days. For small pieces, such as chops and cutlets, marinate 2 to 6 hours.
7. Remove the meat from the brine, dry it, and proceed with the recipe. Treat the brined meat like fresh meat.
8. Discard the used brine.

A brine consists primarily of salt dissolved in water. Because of the harsh taste a high salt concentration can give to meats, chefs usually add sugar to the brine as well to counteract the strong salt flavor. In addition, herbs and aromatics may be added to the brine, although these have only a mild flavoring effect.

Salt concentration in brines ranges from 3 to 6 percent. The formula given in the procedure makes a concentration of 3 percent, so you could double the salt (and sugar) if desired.

Because of the salt and sugar concentration in the meat, pan drippings may not be usable for deglazing. Also, the sugar may burn to the bottom of the pan, so you may want to put a little water in the bottom of the roasting pan.

Preparation for Frying

Most foods to be deep-fried, with the major exception of potatoes, are first given a protective coating of breading or batter. This coating serves four purposes:

1. It helps retain moisture and flavor in the product.

2. It protects the fat against the moisture and salt in the food, which would speed the deterioration of the frying fat.

3. It protects the food from absorbing too much fat.

4. It gives crispness, flavor, and good appearance to the product.

Breading

Breading means coating a product with bread crumbs or other crumbs or meal before deep-frying, pan-frying, or sautéing. The most widely used method for applying these coatings is called the ***Standard Breading Procedure***.

THE THREE STAGES OF THE STANDARD BREADING PROCEDURE

1. **Flour.**
   Helps the breading stick to the product.

2. **Egg wash.**
   A mixture of eggs and a liquid, usually milk or water. More eggs give greater binding power but increase the cost. A small quantity of oil is occasionally added to the egg wash.

3. **Crumbs.**
   Combine with the egg wash to create a crisp, golden coating when fried. Fine, dry bread crumbs are most often used and give good results. Also popular are Japanese-style dry bread crumbs called *panko* (Japanese for "bread crumbs"). These coarser crumbs give a pleasing texture to fried items. Other products used are fresh bread crumbs, crushed corn flakes or other cereal, cracker meal, and cornmeal.

For small items like scallops and oysters, breading may be done with the aid of a series of wire baskets placed in the flour, egg wash, and crumbs, instead of by hand. The procedure is the same except the baskets are used to lift and shake small quantities of the product and to transfer them to the next basket.

To keep one hand dry during breading, use your right hand (if you are right-handed; if left-handed, reverse the procedure) only for handling the flour and crumbs. Use your other hand for handling the product when it is wet. In order to keep your dry hand dry, never handle a wet product with that hand. For example, to complete the breading of an item that has been dipped in egg wash, place it in the pan of crumbs and push more crumbs over the top of the item, as shown in Figure 6.27, and then pat them down, so all sides of the item are covered in dry crumbs before you pick it up.

Figure 6.27 To keep your dry hand dry, push crumbs over the top of egg-washed items in the crumb pan before touching them.

Procedure for Making Bread Crumbs

1. For fresh bread crumbs, use bread that is one or two days old. If the bread is fresh, its moisture content will make it difficult to process into crumbs without making gummy wads of bread. For dry bread crumbs, lightly toast the bread in a warm oven until the bread is dry but not browned. Do not use stale bread, which has an off flavor.

2. Trim off crusts to make crumbs of a uniform light color.

3. Cut or tear the bread into smaller pieces.

4. Depending on the quantity, place the pieces in a food processor or a vertical cutter/mixer. Process until the crumbs are of the desired fineness.

5. For dry bread crumbs of uniform size, pass the processed crumbs through a sieve (also called a *tamis*). See page 34.

Procedure for Proper Breading

Figure 6.28 illustrates a station setup for the Standard Breading Procedure.

1. Dry the product to get a thin, even coating of flour.

2. Season the product—or, for greater efficiency, season the flour (step 3). Do not season the crumbs. The presence of salt in contact with the frying fat breaks down the fat and shortens its life.

3. Dip the product in flour to coat evenly. Shake off excess.

4. Dip in egg wash to coat completely. Remove. Let excess drain off so the crumb coating will be even.

5. Dip in bread crumbs. Cover with crumbs and press them gently onto product. Make sure it is coated completely. Remove. Carefully shake off excess.

6. Fry immediately, or hold for service.

7. To hold for later service, place the breaded items in a single layer on a pan or rack and refrigerate. Do not hold very moist items, such as raw clams or oysters. The breading will quickly become soggy.

8. Strain the egg wash and sift the flour and crumbs as often as necessary to remove lumps.

Figure 6.28 Setup of station for Standard Breading Procedure. Right-handed cooks work from left to right. Left-handed cooks work from right to left, with order of pans reversed, as well.

Dredging with Flour

PURPOSE

The purpose of dredging is to give a thin, even coating of flour to a product.

Meats to be sautéed or pan-fried are often dredged with flour to give them an even, brown color and to prevent sticking.

Vegetables, such as sticks of zucchini, are sometimes coated only in flour before deep-frying to give them a light golden color and a very thin coating.

PROCEDURE

Follow steps 1 to 3 of the Standard Breading Procedure above.

Batters

Batters are semiliquid mixtures containing flour or other starch. They are used in deep-frying to give a crisp, flavorful, golden brown coating. There are many formulas and variations for batters.

1. Many liquids are used, including milk, water, and beer.

2. Eggs may or may not be used.

3. Thicker batters make thicker coatings. Too thick a batter makes a heavy, unpalatable coating.

4. Leavenings are frequently used to give a lighter product. These may be:
   - Baking powder
   - Beaten egg whites
   - Carbonation from beer or seltzer used in the batter

Handling Convenience Foods

Convenience foods play an increasingly prominent role in the food-service industry. Their use has become so important that no student of professional cooking can afford to be without knowledge of them.

Guidelines for Handling Convenience Foods

1. **Handle with the same care you give fresh, raw ingredients.**
   Most loss of quality in convenience foods comes from assuming they are damageproof and can be treated haphazardly.

2. **Examine as soon as received.**
   Particularly, check frozen foods—with a thermometer—to make sure they did not thaw in transit. Put away at once.

3. **Store properly.**
   Frozen foods must be held at 0°F (–18°C) or lower. Check your freezer with a thermometer regularly. Refrigerated foods must stay chilled, below 41°F (5°C), to slow spoilage. Shelf-stable foods (dry products, canned goods, etc.) are shelf-stable only when stored properly in a cool, dry place, tightly sealed.

4. **Know the shelf life of each product.**
   Nothing keeps forever, not even convenience foods. (Some, like peeled potatoes, are even more perishable than unprocessed ingredients.) Rotate stock according to the first in, first out principle. Don't stock more than necessary.

5. **Defrost frozen foods properly.**
   Ideally, defrost in a tempering box set at 28° to 30°F (–2° to –1°C) or, lacking that, in the refrigerator at 41°F (5°C) or lower. This takes planning and timing, because large items take several days to thaw.
   If you are short of time, the second-best way to defrost foods is under cold running water, in the original wrapper.
   Never defrost at room temperature or in warm water. The high temperatures encourage bacterial growth and spoilage.
   Do not refreeze thawed foods. Quality will greatly deteriorate.
   Certain foods, like frozen French fries and some individual-portion prepared entrées, are designed to be cooked without thawing.

6. **Know how and to what extent the product has been prepared.**
   Partially cooked foods need less heating in final preparation than do raw foods. Some cooks prepare frozen, cooked crab legs, for example, as though they were raw, but by the time the customer receives them, they are overcooked, dry, and tasteless. Frozen vegetables, for a second example, have been blanched and often need only to be heated briefly.
   Manufacturers are happy to give full directions and serving suggestions for their products. At least you should read the package directions.

7. **Use proper cooking methods.**
   Be flexible. Much modern equipment is designed especially for convenience foods. Don't restrict yourself to conventional ranges and ovens if compartment steamers, convection ovens, or microwave ovens might do a better job more efficiently.

8. **Treat convenience foods as though you, not the manufacturer, did the pre-preparation.**
   Make the most of your opportunity to use creativity and to serve the best quality you can. Your final preparation, plating, and garnish should be as careful as though you made the dish from scratch.

A *convenience food* may be defined as "any product that has been partially or completely prepared or processed by a manufacturer." In other words, when you buy a convenience product, you are having the manufacturer do some or all of your preparation for you.

Of course, you must pay for this service, as reflected in the price of the product. Although buying the convenience product will likely cost you more than buying the raw materials, you save in increased kitchen efficiency. As you remember from Chapter 5, labor costs as well as food costs must be figured into your menu prices.

Processed foods for restaurants and institutions range from partially prepared items that can be used as components in your recipes, such as frozen fish fillets, peeled potatoes, concentrated stock bases, and frozen puff pastry dough, to fully prepared items that need only be reconstituted or served as is, such as frozen prepared entrées and frozen pies and pastries. Some items, like frozen French fries, have wide acceptance, while other more fully prepared foods continue to be resisted by both customer and operator.

In general, the more completely a product is prepared by the manufacturer, the less it reflects the individuality of the food-service operator—and the less opportunity the cooks have to give it their own character and quality.

Is a stock made from scratch better than a product made from a convenience base? Most quality-conscious chefs would probably answer "Yes!" But the correct answer is, "Not if the homemade stock is poorly made." No matter what products you use, there is no substitute for quality and care. The fresh product is potentially the best, but not if it is badly stored or handled. Of course, convenience foods also require proper handling to maintain their quality.

The key to understanding and handling convenience foods is considering them as normal products with part of the pre-prep completed rather than as totally different kinds of products unlike your normal raw materials. *Convenience products are not a substitute for culinary knowledge and skill.* They should be a tool for the good cook rather than a crutch for the bad cook. It takes as much understanding of basic cooking principles to handle convenience products as it does fresh, raw ingredients, particularly if you want the convenience product to taste as much like the fresh as possible.

KEY POINTS TO REVIEW

- What is blanching? Why are foods blanched?
- What are the basic types of marinades?
- What are the three stages of the Standard Breading Procedure? Describe how to set up a breading station.
- What are convenience foods? Describe eight guidelines for handling and using convenience foods.

TERMS FOR REVIEW

mise en place	shred	lozenge	chiffonade
holding temperature	rondelle	fermière	blanching
set meal service	dice	oblique cut	marinate
extended meal service	brunoise	parisienne	brine
chop	bâtonnet	noisette	Standard Breading Procedure
concasser	allumette	tourné	panko
mince	julienne	cocotte	batter
emincer	paysanne	château	convenience food

QUESTIONS FOR DISCUSSION

1. How does preparation differ for set meal service and extended meal service?
2. It has been said that à la carte cooking, or cooking to order, is nothing more than small-batch cooking carried to its extreme. Based on what you know about pre-preparation, what do you think this statement means?
3. Why is it important to learn to cut foods accurately and uniformly?
4. Name six basic vegetable cuts, and give their dimensions.
5. Give six examples of foods that might be blanched or parcooked during pre-preparation, and give a reason for each.
6. Describe in detail how to set up a breading station and how to use it to bread veal cutlets.
7. The manager of the restaurant in which you are a cook has decided to try using frozen, breaded shrimp instead of having you bread shrimp by hand, but she is worried about customer acceptance and asks for your help. How will you handle the new product?

Chapter 7

From the procedure for adding a liaison to a sauce, page 153.

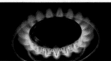

Stocks and Sauces

The importance of stocks in the kitchen is indicated by the French word for stock: *fond*, meaning "foundation" or "base." In classical cuisine, the ability to prepare good stocks is the most basic of all skills because so much of the work of the entire kitchen depends on them. A good stock is the foundation of soups, sauces, and most braised foods and stews.

In modern kitchens, stocks have lost much of the importance they once had. In the first place, increased reliance on portion-controlled meats has made bones for stock a rarity in most establishments. Second, making stocks requires extra labor, which most restaurants today aren't able to provide. Finally, more food today is served without sauces, so stocks aren't seen to be quite as necessary.

Nevertheless, the finest cuisine still depends on soups and sauces based on high-quality stocks, so stock-making remains an essential skill you should learn early in your training. Stocks and sauces are almost never served by themselves but are components of many other preparations. You will need to refer to this chapter in connection with many other subjects.

After reading this chapter, you should be able to

1. Prepare basic mirepoix.
2. Flavor liquids using a sachet d'épices, or spice bag.
3. Prepare white veal or beef stock, chicken stock, fish stock, and brown stock.
4. Cool and store stocks correctly.
5. Prepare meat, chicken, and fish glazes.
6. Evaluate the quality of convenience bases, and use convenience bases.
7. Explain the functions of sauces, and list five qualities a sauce adds to food.
8. Prepare white, blond, and brown roux, and use them to thicken liquids.
9. Prepare and use beurre manié.
10. Thicken liquids with cornstarch and other starches.
11. Prepare and use egg yolk and cream liaison.
12. Finish a sauce with raw butter (monter au beurre).
13. Prepare the five leading sauces: béchamel, velouté, brown sauce or espagnole, tomato, and hollandaise.
14. Prepare small sauces from leading sauces.
15. Identify and prepare five simple butter sauces.
16. Prepare compound butters and list their uses.
17. Prepare pan gravies.
18. Prepare miscellaneous hot and cold sauces.

STOCKS

The preparation of stocks has been simplified in many ways since the days of Escoffier, although this does not mean it demands less care or skill. Few chefs today bother to tie vegetables for a stock into a bundle, for example. They're going to be strained out anyway. The number and variety of ingredients is usually not as great as it once was. Nor is it common to cook stocks for as many hours as was once thought necessary. All these details are taken up one by one in this section.

A *stock* may be defined as a clear, thin—that is, unthickened—liquid flavored by soluble substances extracted from meat, poultry, and fish, and their bones, and from vegetables and seasonings. Our objective in preparing stocks is to select the proper ingredients and then to extract the flavors we want—in other words, to combine the correct ingredients with the correct procedure.

Ingredients

Bones

Bones are the major ingredient of stocks (except water, of course). Most of the flavor and body of stocks are derived from the bones of beef, veal, chicken, fish, and, occasionally, lamb, pork, ham, and game. (Vegetable stocks, an exception, draw their flavor entirely from vegetables; see p. 137.)

The kinds of bones used determine the kind of stock.

Chicken stock, of course, is made from chicken bones.

White stock is made from beef or veal bones, or a combination of the two. Chicken bones or even pork bones are sometimes added in small quantity.

Brown stock is made from beef or veal bones that have been browned in an oven.

Fish stock is made from fish bones and trimmings left over after filleting. Bones from lean white fish give the best stock. Fat fish are not normally used. The term *fumet* is often used for a flavorful fish stock, especially one made with wine. See the note at the beginning of the recipe for Fish Fumet (p. 143).

Lamb, game, turkey, and other stocks have specialized uses.

In Chapter 4, we discussed a group of proteins called *connective tissue*. Remember that some of these proteins are dissolved when cooked with slow, moist heat. You should learn and understand these two basic facts:

1. When certain connective tissues (called *collagen*) break down, they form *gelatin*. This gives body to a stock, an important feature of its quality. A well-made stock thickens or even solidifies when chilled.

2. *Cartilage* is the best source of gelatin in bones. Younger animals have lots of cartilage in their skeletons. As they become older, this hardens into solid bone, which is harder to dissolve into stocks. *Knuckle bones*, on the joints of major bones, have a lot of cartilage and are valued in stock-making. Neck bones and shankbones are also used a great deal.

Cut large bones into pieces about 3 inches (8 cm) long. This exposes more surface area and aids extraction. Also, the bones are easier to handle.

Meat

Because of its cost, meat is rarely used in stock-making anymore. (Exception: Chicken hearts and gizzards are often used in chicken stock.)

Occasionally, a broth is produced as a result of simmering meat or poultry, as when fowl is cooked for dishes like creamed chicken. This broth can then be used like a stock. However, the chicken is considered the object of the game in this case. The broth is just a byproduct.

In this book, we use the word *broth* to mean a flavorful liquid obtained from the simmering of meats and/or vegetables.

Mirepoix

Aromatic vegetables are the second most important contributors of flavor to stocks. (In the case of vegetable stocks, they are the most important.)

Mirepoix (meer-pwah) is a combination of onions, carrots, and celery. It is a basic flavoring preparation used in all areas of cooking—not only for flavoring stocks but also for sauces, soups, meats, poultry, fish, and vegetables. (The classical mirepoix of decades ago contained a wider variety of ingredients, sometimes including ham or bacon, leeks and other vegetables, and one or more fresh herbs. The modern version is considerably simplified.)

Learn the proportions in Table 7.1 well. Mirepoix is a basic preparation you will need throughout your career.

A *white mirepoix*, in which parsnips are substituted for carrots, is used when it is necessary to keep the stock as colorless as possible, usually for white beef or veal stock and fish stock. Celery root can be substituted for the stalk celery for an even whiter mirepoix. Mushroom trimmings may also be added. When cost permits, it is a good idea to include leeks in the mirepoix in place of part of the onions in a white mirepoix. They give an excellent flavor. (Note: Many chefs prefer to use a standard mirepoix rather than white mirepoix for all stocks.)

In vegetable stocks, a variety of vegetables is used in addition to or in place of the traditional mirepoix; see page 137 for a brief discussion.

Standard mirepoix (left) and white mirepoix (right)

CUTTING MIREPOIX

Chop the vegetables coarsely into pieces of relatively uniform size. As mirepoix is rarely served, it is not usually necessary to cut it neatly.

The size depends on how long the mirepoix will cook. If it will cook a long time, as for beef stock, cut the vegetables into large pieces (1 to 2 inches [3 to 5 cm]). Cutting into small pieces is necessary for releasing flavors in a short time, as when the mirepoix will be used for fish stock.

Table 7.1 **Mirepoix**		
TO MAKE:	**1 POUND**	**400 GRAMS**
Onions	8 oz	200 g
Celery	4 oz	100 g
Carrots	4 oz	100 g

Acid Products

Acids, as noted in Chapter 4 (p. 53), help dissolve connective tissues. Thus, they are sometimes used in stock-making to extract flavor and body from bones.

Tomato products contribute flavor and some acid to brown stocks. They are not used for white stocks because they would give an undesirable color. Similarly, when making brown stocks, be careful not to add too much tomato, which can make the stock cloudy.

Wine is occasionally used, especially for fish stocks. Its flavor contribution is probably more important than its acidity.

Scraps and Leftovers

In some kitchens, a stockpot is kept going all day, and scraps are constantly being thrown in. This may or may not be a good idea.

Scraps may be used in stocks if they are *clean, wholesome, and appropriate to the stock being made*. If done correctly, stock-making is a good way of utilizing trimmings that would otherwise be thrown out. It is better to save trimmings and use them in a planned way than to throw them into the stock randomly.

A stockpot is not a garbage disposal. The final product is only as good as the ingredients and the care that go into it.

Seasonings and Spices

Salt is usually not added when making stocks. Stocks are never used as is but are reduced, concentrated, and combined with other ingredients. If salt were added, it might become too concentrated. Some chefs salt stocks very lightly because they feel it aids in extracting flavor.

Herbs and spices should be used only lightly. They should never dominate a stock or have a pronounced flavor.

Herbs and spices are usually tied in a cheesecloth bag called a *sachet d'épices* (sa-shay day peace; French for "spice bag"), often called simply *sachet* for short. The sachet (Figure 7.1) is tied by a string to the handle of the stockpot so it can be removed easily at any time.

A *bouquet garni* is an assortment of fresh herbs and other aromatic ingredients tied in a bundle with string. A basic bouquet garni contains pieces of leek and celery, thyme sprigs, bay leaf, and parsley stems (see Figure 7.2). The ingredients can be changed to suit different recipes. Escoffier includes only parsley, thyme, and bay leaf in the classic bouquet garni.

The following seasonings, in varying quantities, are commonly used for stocks:

Thyme	Parsley stems
Bay leaves	Cloves, whole
Peppercorns	Garlic (optional)

ONIONS FOR FLAVORING

In addition to the onions in the mirepoix, an *oignon brûlé* (awn yohn broo lay; French for "burnt onion") is sometimes added to brown stock to give it color as well as flavor. To prepare, cut a large onion in half crosswise and place it, cut side down, on a flattop range or in a heavy skillet. Cook until the cut surface is dark brown. Add to the stock.

Another form of onion for flavoring is the *oignon piqué* (pee kay). This is used not so much for stocks but for soups and sauces. To prepare, stick a bay leaf to a whole, peeled onion with a whole clove. Adding the bay leaf and clove attached to the onion makes removing them easier when cooking is finished.

Figure 7.1 To make a sachet, place the spices and herbs in the center of a square of clean cheesecloth. Draw the corners together and tie with a length of twine. For making stock, use a piece of twine long enough to be tied to the handle of the stockpot for easy removal.

Figure 7.2 Tie the herbs and aromatic vegetables for a bouquet garni in a bundle. To tie small herbs securely, enclose them between the two halves of leek.

Oignon piqué (left) and oignon brûlé (right)

Ingredient Proportions

The proportions in Tables 7.2, 7.3, and 7.4 are basic, effective, and widely used, but using them is not an ironclad rule. Nearly every chef uses some variations.

Many cooks use ratios to help them remember the basic proportions, as follows:

Bones—80 percent

Mirepoix—10 percent

Water—100 percent

Guidelines for Canadian Stock Ingredient Ratios

As indicated in the text, not all chefs use the basic ingredient ratios outlined here. In Canada, the Interprovincial Standards Red Seal Program indicates the following ratios as a standard in its list of basic skills for cooks.

Bones—50 percent

Mirepoix—10 percent

Water—100 percent

Ingredients for Vegetable Stocks

Vegetable stocks, made without any animal products, play an important role in vegetarian cooking and are also used in more traditional kitchens in response to customers' requests for light, healthful dishes. The basic ingredients for vegetable stocks are vegetables, herbs and spices, water, and, sometimes, wine (see Figure 7.3).

Figure 7.3 Ingredients for vegetable stock

Ingredients and proportions can vary greatly. If you want a particular flavor to predominate, use a larger quantity of that vegetable. For example, if you want a broth tasting primarily of asparagus, use a large quantity of asparagus to make it, with smaller quantities of more neutral vegetables (like onion and celery) to round out the flavor. For a more neutral, all-purpose vegetable stock, avoid strong-flavored vegetables and use more balanced proportions of ingredients.

Here are a few additional guidelines for making vegetable stocks or broths:

1. Starchy vegetables, such as potatoes, sweet potatoes, and winter squash, make a stock cloudy. Use them only if clarity is not important.

2. Some vegetables, especially strong-flavored ones, are best avoided. Brussels sprouts, cauliflower, and artichokes can overwhelm a stock with a strong flavor or odor. Dark green leafy vegetables, especially spinach, develop an unpleasant flavor when cooked a long time. Beets turn a stock red.

3. Cook long enough to extract flavors but not so long that flavors are lost. Best cooking time is 30 to 45 minutes.

4. Sweating the vegetables in a small amount of oil before adding water gives them a mellower flavor, but this step can be omitted. Butter can be used if it is not necessary to avoid all animal products.

5. Ratios of vegetables to water may vary considerably, but the following proportions are a good starting point:

Vegetables:	4 lb	2 kg
Water:	1 gal	4 L
Sachet:	1	1

Table 7.2 White Stock (Chicken)

TO MAKE:	1 GALLON	4 LITERS
Bones	8 lb	4 kg
Mirepoix	1 lb	500 g
Water	5–6 qt	5–6 L
Sachet	1	1

Table 7.3 White Stock (Beef and Veal)

TO MAKE:	1 GALLON	4 LITERS
Bones	8 lb	4 kg
Mirepoix, white	1 lb	500 g
Water	5–6 qt	5–6 L
Sachet	1	1

Table 7.4 Brown Stock

TO MAKE:	1 GALLON	4 LITERS
Bones	8 lb	4 kg
Mirepoix	1 lb	500 g
Tomato product	8 oz	250 g
Water	5–6 qt	5–6 L
Sachet	1	1

Table 7.5 Fish Stock

TO MAKE:	1 GALLON	4 LITERS
Bones	10–12 lb	5–6 kg
Mirepoix, white	1 lb	500 g
Water	1 gal	4 L
White wine	24 fl oz	750 mL
Sachet	1	1

KEY POINTS TO REVIEW

• What is mirepoix? How is it prepared?

• What is a sachet d'épices? How is it prepared?

• What are the basic proportions of bones, mirepoix, and water to make a standard white stock or brown stock?

Procedures

Making stock may seem, at first glance, a simple procedure. However, many steps are involved, each with a rather complicated set of reasons. If you are to be successful at making consistently good stocks, you must understand not only what to do but also why you are doing it.

The following outlines give procedures for making basic stocks as well as the reasons for every step. After learning these procedures and checking with your instructors for any modifications or variations they may have, you will be able to turn to the individual recipes, where the steps are given again, but without explanations.

Blanching Bones

In Chapter 4, we discussed proteins coagulating when heated. Many proteins dissolve in cold water but solidify into small particles or into froth or scum when heated. It is these particles that make a stock cloudy. Much of the technique of stock-making involves avoiding cloudiness to produce a clear stock.

The purpose of blanching bones is to rid them of some of the impurities that cause cloudiness. The bones of young animals, especially veal and chicken, are highest in blood and other impurities that cloud and discolor stocks.

Chefs disagree on the importance of blanching. Many feel it is needed to produce clear white stocks. Others feel blanching causes valuable flavors to be lost. Fish bones, at any rate, are not blanched because of their short cooking time.

Procedure for Blanching Bones

1. **Rinse the bones in cold water.**
   This washes off blood and other impurities from the surface. It is especially important if the bones are not strictly fresh.

2. **Place the bones in a stockpot or steam-jacketed kettle and cover with cold water.**
   Impurities dissolve more readily in cold water. Hot water retards extraction.

3. **Bring the water to a boil.**
   As the water heats, impurities solidify (coagulate) and rise to the surface as scum.

4. **Drain the bones and rinse them well.**
   The bones are now ready for the stockpot.

Preparing White Stocks

A good white stock has rich, full flavor, good body, clarity, and little or no color. Chicken stocks may have a light yellow color.

Procedure for Preparing White Stocks

1. **Cut the bones into pieces, 3 to 4 inches (8 to 10 cm) long.**
   This exposes more surface area and helps extraction. A meat saw is used to cut heavy veal and beef bones. Fish and chicken bones don't need to be cut, but whole carcasses should be chopped for more convenient handling.

2. **Rinse the bones in cold water. (If desired, chicken, veal, or beef bones may be blanched.)**
   This removes some impurities that cloud the stock or, if the bones are old, give an off taste.

3. **Place the bones in a stockpot or steam-jacketed kettle and add cold water to cover.**
   Starting in cold water speeds extraction. Starting in hot water delays it because many proteins are soluble in cold water but not in hot.

4. **Bring water to a boil, and then reduce to a simmer. Skim the scum that comes to the surface, using a skimmer or perforated spoon.**
   Skimming is important for a clear stock because the scum (which is fat and coagulated protein) will cloud the stock if it is broken up and mixed back into the liquid.

5. **Add the chopped mirepoix and the herbs and spices.**
   Remember, the size to which you cut mirepoix depends on how long it is to be cooked.

6. **Do not let the stock boil. Keep it at a low simmer.**
   Boiling makes the stock cloudy because it breaks solids into tiny particles that get mixed into the liquid.

7. **Skim the surface as often as necessary during cooking.**

8. **Keep the water level above the bones. Add more water if the stock reduces below this level.**
   Bones cooked while exposed to air will turn dark and thus darken or discolor the stock. Also, they do not release flavor into the water if the water doesn't touch them.

9. **Simmer for the recommended length of time:**

Beef bones—8 to 10 hours	Chicken bones—3 to 4 hours
Veal bones—6 to 8 hours	Fish bones—30 to 45 minutes

   Most modern chefs do not simmer stocks as long as earlier generations of chefs did. It is true that longer cooking extracts more gelatin, but gelatin isn't the only factor in a good stock. Flavors begin to break down or degenerate over time. The above times are felt to be the best for obtaining full flavor while still getting a good portion of gelatin into the stock.

10. **Skim the surface and strain off the stock through a china cap lined with several layers of cheesecloth.**
    Adding a little cold water to the stock before skimming stops the cooking and brings more fat and impurities to the surface.

11. **Cool the stock as quickly as possible, as follows:**
    - Set the pot in a sink with blocks, a rack, or some other object under it. This is called *venting*. It allows cold water to flow under the pot as well as around it.
    - Run cold water into the sink, but not higher than the level of the stock, or the pot will become unsteady. An overflow pipe keeps the water level right and allows for constant circulation of cold water (see image on p. 140).
    - Stir the pot occasionally so all the stock cools evenly. Hang a ladle in the pot so you can give it a quick stir whenever you pass the sink without actually taking extra time to do it.

    Cooling stock quickly and properly is important. Improperly cooled stock can spoil in 6 to 8 hours because it is a good breeding ground for bacteria that cause food-borne disease and spoilage.

    Do not set the hot stock in the walk-in or, worse yet, the reach-in. All that heat and steam will overload the refrigerator and may damage other perishables as well as the equipment.

12. **When cool, refrigerate the stock in covered containers.** Stock will keep 2 to 3 days if properly refrigerated. Stock can also be frozen and will keep for several months.

Figure 7.4 Preparing white stock

(a) **Place the bones in a stock pot and cover with cold water.**

(b) **Skim the scum from the surface regularly.**

(c) **Add white mirepoix to the pot.**

(d) **Add a sachet d'épices. Tying the sachet to the pot handle enables it to be retrieved whenever necessary.**

Basic White Stock (Beef or Veal)

YIELD: 2 GAL (8 L)

U.S.	METRIC	INGREDIENTS
16 lb	8 kg	Beef or veal bones
10–12 qt	10–12 L	Water, cold
		Mirepoix, white (see Note):
1 lb	500 g	Onion, chopped
8 oz	250 g	Parsnip, chopped
8 oz	250 g	Celery, chopped
		Sachet:
1	1	Dried bay leaf
¼ tsp	1 mL	Dried thyme
¼ tsp	1 mL	Peppercorns
6–8	6–8	Parsley stems
2	2	Whole cloves

Per 1 fl oz (29.57 mL): Calories, 5; Protein, .6 g; Fat, .1 g (12% cal.); Cholesterol, 0 mg; Carbohydrates, 1 g; Fiber, 0 g; Sodium, 10 mg.

Note: If desired, use a standard mirepoix (with carrots) instead of white mirepoix. The stock will have slightly more color.

PROCEDURE

1. Review instructions for stock preparation (pp. 138–139).
2. If beef or veal bones are whole, cut into pieces 3–4 in. (8–10 cm) long with a meat saw. Rinse bones in cold water.
3. Blanch the bones: Place in a stockpot, cover with cold water, and bring to a boil. Drain and rinse.
4. Place the bones in the stockpot and cover with cold water. Bring to a boil, reduce heat to simmer, and skim the scum carefully.
5. Add mirepoix and sachet ingredients (tied in cheesecloth).
6. Simmer for required length of time, skimming the surface as often as necessary.
   Veal: 6–8 hours
   Beef: 8–10 hours
   Add water if necessary to keep bones covered.
7. Strain through a china cap lined with several layers of cheesecloth.
8. Cool the stock, vented, in a cold-water bath (see image below), and refrigerate.

VARIATIONS

Chicken Stock

Chicken stock is usually made with a standard mirepoix, substituting carrots for parsnips, although white mirepoix may also be used. Follow procedure in basic recipe, but reduce cooking time to 3–4 hours.

White Lamb Stock, Turkey Stock, Ham Stock

Prepare according to basic procedure, substituting appropriate bones.

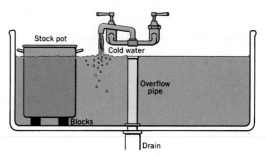

Setup for cooling stocks in a cold water bath.

Preparing Brown Stocks

The difference between brown stocks and white stocks is that the bones and mirepoix are browned for the brown stock. This causes a few complications, as you will see. Otherwise, the procedure is essentially the same.

A second method for browning the mirepoix is given in the alternative procedure.

Procedure for Preparing Brown Stocks

1. Cut the bones into pieces, 3 to 4 inches (8 to 10 cm) long, as for white stock. Veal and/or beef bones are used for brown stock.

2. Do not wash or blanch the bones. The moisture would hinder browning.

3. Place the bones in a roasting pan in one layer and brown in a hot oven at 375°F (190°C) or higher. The bones must be well browned to color the stock sufficiently. This takes over 1 hour. Some chefs prefer to oil the bones lightly before browning.

4. When the bones are well browned, remove them from the pan and place them in a stockpot. Cover with cold water and bring to a simmer.

5. Drain and reserve the fat from the roasting pan. Deglaze the pan by adding water and stirring over heat until all the brown drippings are dissolved or loosened. Add to the stockpot.

6. While the stock is getting started, place the mirepoix in the roasting pan with some of the reserved fat and brown the vegetables well in the oven.

7. Add the tomato product to the mirepoix. Continue to brown until the tomato product turns a rusty brown color. (See alternative procedure below.)

8. When the water in the stockpot comes to a simmer, skim and continue as for white stock.

9. Add the browned vegetables and the tomato product to the stockpot. If desired, they may be held out until 2 to 3 hours before the end of the cooking time.

10. Continue as for white stock.

Figure 7.5 Preparing brown stock.

(a) Roast the bones in a moderately hot oven until well browned.

(b) Place the bones in a stockpot and add the appropriate amount of water.

(c) While the bones are beginning to simmer, brown the mirepoix, using the same roasting pan set on top of the stove or in the oven. Add the browned mirepoix to the stockpot.

(d) Deglaze the roasting pan with water. Add the liquid to the stockpot.

(e) This stock has simmered slowly for 8 hours. Note the sachet is tied to the handle of the pot with twine for easy removal.

(f) Strain the stock through a china cap lined with cheesecloth.

Alternative Procedure

The mirepoix may be browned with the bones. When the bones are half browned, add the mirepoix to the pan and continue roasting until bones and vegetables are browned.

Some chefs use this method because it eliminates some steps. Others prefer to brown the mirepoix separately so it can be added to the stock later in the cooking time.

Tomato paste is the best choice of tomato product if it is browned with the mirepoix, as it contains less water. Tomato purée or canned tomatoes may also be used, but they are more likely to be added directly to the stockpot.

Basic Brown Stock

YIELD: 2 GAL (8 L)

U.S.	METRIC	INGREDIENTS
16 lb	8 kg	Bones: veal or beef
10–12 qt	10–12 L	Water, cold
		Mirepoix:
1 lb	500 g	Onion, chopped
8 oz	250 g	Carrot, chopped
8 oz	250 g	Celery, chopped
4 oz	125 g	Tomato paste (See Note)
		Sachet:
1	1	Bay leaf
¼ tsp	1 mL	Dried thyme
¼ tsp	1 mL	Peppercorns
6–8	6–8	Parsley stems
2	2	Whole cloves

PROCEDURE

1. Review instructions for stock preparation (p. 141).
2. If bones are whole, cut into pieces 3–4 inches (8–10 cm) long with a meat saw. Do not wash.
3. Place bones in a roasting pan in a hot oven (400°F/200°C) and brown them well.
4. Remove bones from pan and place in a stockpot. Cover with water and bring to a simmer. Skim and let stock continue to simmer.
5. Drain and reserve the fat from the roasting pan. Deglaze the pan with water and add to stockpot.
6. Toss the mirepoix with some of the reserved fat and brown well in oven.
7. Add tomato paste to mirepoix. Continue to brown until tomato paste turns a rusty brown color.
8. Add browned mirepoix, tomato product, and sachet to the stockpot.
9. Continue to simmer for required length of time, skimming surface as necessary.

    Veal: 6–8 hours

    Beef: 8–10 hours

    Add water as needed to keep bones covered.
10. Strain through a china cap lined with several layers of cheesecloth.
11. Cool the stock, vented, in a cold-water bath, and refrigerate.

Per 1 fl oz (29.57 mL): Calories, 6; Protein, .5 g; Fat, .1 g (18% cal.); Cholesterol, 0 mg; Carbohydrates, .5 g; Fiber, 0 g; Sodium, 15 mg.

Note: If desired, use 1 lb (500 g) tomato purée or canned tomatoes in place of the tomato paste. Add it to the browned mirepoix and continue to brown, or add it directly to the stockpot without browning.

VARIATIONS

Brown Lamb Stock, Game Stock
Prepare according to basic procedure, substituting appropriate bones.

Preparing Fish Stocks

A standard fish stock is made the same way as a white stock, using the proportions given in the table on page 137. This type of stock is useful for soups and similar seafood preparations. For sauces, chefs usually prefer a more flavorful fish stock called a *fumet*. A fish fumet is made by first sweating the bones and mirepoix in fat. White wine is then added to deglaze, and finally water is added and the fumet finished in the normal manner.

Recipes for a standard fish stock and a fish fumet are given below.

Fish Stock

YIELD: 1 GAL (4 L)

U.S.	METRIC	INGREDIENTS
10–12 lb	5–6 kg	Bones from lean fish
		White mirepoix:
8 oz	250 g	Onion, chopped fine
4 oz	125 g	Celery, chopped fine
4 oz	125 g	Parsnip, chopped fine
		Sachet:
½	½	Bay leaf
¼ tsp	1 mL	Peppercorns
6–8	6–8	Parsley stems
1	1	Whole cloves
1 gal	4 L	Water, cold
24 fl oz	750 mL	White wine (optional)

PROCEDURE
1. Review instructions for stock preparation (pp. 138–139).
2. Place all ingredients in a stockpot. Bring to a simmer.
3. Simmer 45 minutes, skimming as necessary to remove scum.
4. Strain through a china cap lined with several layers of cheesecloth.
5. Cool stock, vented, in a cold-water bath, and refrigerate.

Per 1 fl oz (29.57 mL): Calories, 4; Protein, .8 g; Fat, .3 g (40% cal.); Cholesterol, 0 mg; Carbohydrates, .2 g; Fiber, 0 g; Sodium, 2 mg.

Fish Fumet

YIELD: 1 GAL (4 L)

U.S.	METRIC	INGREDIENTS
1 oz	30 g	Clarified butter
		White mirepoix:
8 oz	250 g	Onion, chopped fine
4 oz	125 g	Celery, chopped fine
4 oz	125 g	Parsnip, chopped fine (optional)
8 oz	250 g	Mushroom trimmings (optional)
11 lb	5.5 kg	Bones from lean fish
24 fl oz	750 mL	White wine (dry)
		Sachet:
½	½	Bay leaf
¼ tsp	1 mL	Peppercorns
6–8	6–8	Parsley stems
1	1	Whole clove
1 gal	4 L	Water, cold

PROCEDURE
1. Butter the bottom of a heavy stockpot or saucepot. Place the mirepoix in bottom of pot and the bones over top of it. Cover bones loosely with a round of brown paper or parchment.
2. Set pot over low heat and cook slowly about 5 minutes, or until bones are opaque and begin to exude juices.
3. Add the wine, bring to a simmer, and then add the sachet and water to cover.
4. Bring to a simmer again, skim, and let simmer 30–45 minutes.
5. Strain through a china cap lined with several layers of cheesecloth.
6. Cool, vented, in a cold-water bath, and refrigerate.

Per 1 fl oz (29.75mL): Calories, 10; Protein, .8 g; Fat, .2 g (17% cal.); Cholesterol, 1 mg; Carbohydrates, .3 g; Fiber, 0 g; Sodium, 3 mg

Figure 7.6 Making fish fumet.

(a) Sweat the mirepoix and fish bones in butter.

(b) Add the white wine and bring to a simmer.

Vegetable Stock

YIELD: 1 GAL (4 L)

U.S.	METRIC	INGREDIENTS
1½ fl oz	45 mL	Oil
		Mirepoix:
1 lb	500 g	Onion, chopped
8 oz	250 g	Carrot, chopped
8 oz	250 g	Celery, chopped
8 oz	250 g	Leeks, chopped
4 oz	125 g	Mushrooms or mushroom trimmings, chopped
4 oz	125 g	Turnip, chopped
2 oz	60 g	Fennel, chopped
½ oz	15 g	Garlic, chopped
4 oz	125 g	Tomatoes, chopped
5 qt	5 L	Water
		Sachet:
1	1	Bay leaf
¼ tsp	1 mL	Dried thyme
¼ tsp	1 mL	Peppercorns
6–8	6–8	Parsley stems
2	2	Whole cloves

PROCEDURE

1. Heat oil in a stockpot over medium heat.
2. Add mirepoix, leeks, mushrooms, turnip, fennel, and garlic. Sweat for 10 minutes. Stir as necessary so vegetables do not brown.
3. Add tomatoes, water, and sachet.
4. Bring to a simmer, and simmer 45 minutes.
5. Strain and cool in a water bath.

Per 1 fl oz (29.57 mL): Calories, 2; Protein, .1 g; Fat, .1 g (27% cal.); Cholesterol, 0 mg; Carbohydrates, .5 g; Fiber, 0 g; Sodium, 3 mg.

VARIATIONS

Other vegetables may be used as desired.
See discussion on page 137.

Remouillage and Other Stock-Related Preparations

Remouillage is a stock made from bones that were already used once to make stock. The literal meaning of the French term is "rewetting." Because not all possible flavor and gelatin is extracted from bones when making a stock, making a remouillage allows the chef to extract a little more value from the bones. The resulting liquid will not be as clear or flavorful as the original stock, but it does have some uses. A remouillage can be used for soups, for braised dishes, and in place of water for making stocks. It can also be reduced to a glaze and used for enriching sauces, soups, and braising liquids.

To make a remouillage, discard the mirepoix and herb sachet after draining a finished stock. Add fresh mirepoix and sachet to the bones, cover with fresh cold water, and simmer about 4 hours. Drain and cool as for regular stock.

Court bouillon is often discussed along with stocks. However, it is rarely used for making soups and sauces, as stocks are.

Basic Japanese stock, called *dashi*, is quickly and easily made from only three ingredients: water; shaved, dried bonito, called *katsuobushi* (kaht soo oh boo shee); and a type of dried seaweed or kelp called *kombu*. Dashi is used in soups and dipping sauces as well as other dishes.

Finally, broths and jus are discussed later in this chapter (page 176).

Dashi 💜

YIELD: 2 QT (2 L)

U.S.	METRIC	INGREDIENTS
4½ pt	2.25 L	Water, cold
2 oz	60 g	Kombu (giant kelp for stock)
1½ oz	50 g	Katsuobushi (dried bonito flakes)

Per 1 fl oz (29.57 mL): Calories, 2; Protein, 0 g; Fat, 0 g (0% cal.); Cholesterol, 0 mg; Carbohydrates, 0 g; Fiber, 0 g; Sodium, 3 mg.

Note: Instant dashi is also available. Its quality is good enough for simmered dishes and miso soup, but not for good clear soup. Follow label instructions.

PROCEDURE

1. Put the water in a pot and add kombu. Bring to a boil over moderately high heat.
2. Just as water comes to a boil, remove the kombu.
3. Remove from heat and immediately add bonito flakes. Let the flakes settle to bottom. This will take 1–2 minutes.
4. Strain through a china cap lined with cheesecloth. Use dashi within 1 day.

VARIATIONS

Vegetarian Dashi
Omit bonito flakes and use only kombu.

Figure 7.7 Dashi ingredients: katsuobushi and kombu.

Reductions and Glazes

Stocks are concentrated by boiling or simmering them to evaporate part of the water. This is called making a *reduction*, or reducing.

Reduction is an important technique in sauce-making and in many other areas of cooking because it produces a more flavorful product by concentrating it. A reduced stock also has more body because the gelatin is concentrated.

What Are Glazes?

A *glaze*—or, in French, *glace* (glahss)—is a stock reduced until it coats the back of a spoon. It is so concentrated—reduced by three-fourths or more—that it is solid and rubbery when refrigerated.

Glazes are used as flavorings in sauce-making and in some meat, poultry, fish, and vegetable preparations. Only small amounts are needed because they are so concentrated.

Glazes diluted to original strength do not taste like the stocks they were made from. The long cooking changes the flavors somewhat.

Procedure for Preparing Glazes

1. Reduce the stock over moderate heat.
2. Skim the surface frequently.
3. When reduced by half to two-thirds, strain into a smaller, heavy saucepan and continue to reduce over lower heat until the liquid is syrupy and coats a spoon.
4. Pour into containers, cool, cover, and refrigerate.
5. Glazes will keep for several weeks or longer if properly stored. They may also be frozen.

Glace de viande

Kinds of Glazes

1. Meat glaze, or *glace de viande* (glahss duh vee awnd)—made from brown stock.

2. Chicken glaze, or *glace de volaille* (voh lye)—made from chicken stock.

3. Fish glaze, or *glace de poisson* (pwah sohn)—made from fish stock.

Convenience Bases

The cost, both in time and materials, of making stocks in modern kitchens has led to the widespread use of concentrated convenience products known as *bases*. These are diluted with water to make flavored liquids similar to stocks.

Glazes can be considered bases and, in fact, they are the original bases, used long before today's manufacturers started producing convenience products.

Judging Quality

Bases vary greatly in quality. The best ones are composed mainly of meat extracts. These are perishable products and must be refrigerated.

Many bases are made primarily from salt, however—an expensive way to buy salt, we might add. *Read the list of ingredients.* Avoid products that list salt first. The best way to judge the quality of a base is to dilute it and compare its flavor to that of a well-made stock.

Using Bases

Bases can be improved with little labor by simmering the diluted or made-up product for a short time with some mirepoix, a sachet, and a few bones or meat trimmings, if possible. This helps give a fresher, more natural taste to a highly processed product.

Bases are also added to stocks to supplement them when only a small quantity of stock is on hand.

Bases are sometimes added to weak stocks to give them more flavor, but this is not as good a practice as making the stock properly in the first place.

Using bases requires taste and judgment, just as other areas of cookery do. If used without care and restraint, bases can detract from the quality of your cooking. But, used carefully, they can be a valuable tool. Always taste and evaluate as you cook.

There is no substitute for a well-made stock. But it is also true that a good base may be better than a poorly made stock. It all depends on the skills you are learning now.

KEY POINTS TO REVIEW

- What are the steps in the procedure for preparing white stock?
- How does making brown stock differ from making white stock?
- What is the best way to cool a stock?
- What is glace de viande? How is it prepared?
- How do you judge the quality of a base?

SAUCES

Like stocks, sauces have lost some of the importance they once had in commercial kitchens—except, of course, in the best restaurants serving what may be considered luxury cuisine. Some of this decline is due to changes in eating habits and to increased labor costs.

However, much of the change is due to misunderstanding. How many times have you heard someone say, "I don't go for all those sauces all over everything. I like good, simple food." No doubt this person puts ketchup—a sweetened tomato sauce—on hamburgers, gravy on mashed potatoes, and tartar sauce on fried fish.

The misunderstandings arise from poorly made sauces. No one likes thick, pasty cream sauces on vegetables or oversalted but otherwise flavorless brown sauces gumming up their meat. But just because some cooks make bad sauces is no reason to reject all sauce cookery.

In fact, many chefs believe good sauces are the pinnacle of all cooking, both in the skill they require and in the interest and excitement they can give to food. Very often, the most memorable part of a really fine meal is the sauce that enhances the meat or fish.

A sauce works like a seasoning. It enhances and accents the flavor of the food; it should not dominate or hide the food.

A good cook knows that sauces are as valuable as salt and pepper. A simple grilled steak is made even better when it has an added touch, something as simple as a slice of seasoned butter melting on it or as refined as a spoonful of béarnaise sauce.

No matter where you work, sauce-making techniques are basic skills you will need in all your cooking. Croquettes, soufflés, and mousses have sauces as their base, nearly all braised foods are served with sauces made of their cooking liquids, and basic pan gravies, favorites everywhere, are made with the same techniques as the classic sauces.

Understanding Sauces

The Functions of Sauces

A *sauce* may be defined as a flavorful liquid, usually thickened, used to season, flavor, and enhance other foods.

A sauce adds the following qualities to foods:

Moistness

Flavor

Richness

Appearance (color and shine)

Interest and appetite appeal

The Structure of Sauces

The major sauces we consider here are made of three kinds of ingredients:

1. A liquid, the body of the sauce

2. A thickening agent

3. Additional seasoning and flavoring ingredients

To understand sauce-making, you must first learn how to prepare these components and then how to combine them into finished sauces.

LIQUID

A liquid ingredient provides the body or base of most sauces. Most classic sauces are built on one of five liquids or bases. The resulting sauces are called *leading sauces* or *mother sauces*.

White stock (chicken, veal, or fish)—for velouté sauces

Brown stock—for brown sauce or espagnole (ess pahn yohl)

Milk—for béchamel

Tomato plus stock—for tomato sauce

Clarified butter—for hollandaise

The most frequently used sauces are based on stock. The quality of these sauces depends on the stock-making skills you learned in the previous section.

THICKENING AGENTS

A sauce must be thick enough to cling lightly to the food. Otherwise, it will just run off and lie in a puddle in the plate. This doesn't mean it should be heavy and pasty. Chefs use the term *nappé* (nap pay; from the French *napper,* meaning "to top") to describe the texture of a sauce that has the right texture to coat foods.

Starches are still the most commonly used thickening agents, although they are used less often than in the past. We discuss starches and other thickening agents in detail below.

OTHER FLAVORING INGREDIENTS

Although the liquid that makes up the bulk of the sauce provides the basic flavor, other ingredients are added to make variations on the basic themes and to give a finished character to the sauces.

Adding specified flavoring ingredients to basic sauces is the key to the catalog of classic sauces. Most of the hundreds of sauces listed in the standard repertoires are made by adding one or more flavoring ingredients to one of the five basic sauces or leading sauces.

As in all of cooking, sauce-making is largely a matter of learning a few building blocks and then building with them.

Roux

Starches as Thickeners

1. Starches are the most common and most useful thickeners for sauce-making. Flour is the principal starch used. Others available to the chef include cornstarch, arrowroot, waxy maize, instant or pregelatinized starch, bread crumbs, and other vegetable and grain products, like potato starch and rice flour. These are discussed later.

2. Starches thicken by *gelatinization,* which, as discussed in Chapter 4, is the process by which starch granules absorb water and swell to many times their original size.

   Another important point made in Chapter 4 is that acids inhibit gelatinization. Whenever possible, do not add acid ingredients to sauces until the starch has fully gelatinized.

3. Starch granules must be separated before heating in liquid to avoid lumping. If granules are not separated, lumping occurs because the starch on the outside of the lump quickly gelatinizes into a coating that prevents the liquid from reaching the starch inside.

   Starch granules are separated in two ways:

   - *Mixing the starch with fat.* This is the principle of the roux, which we discuss now, and of beurre manié, which is discussed in the next section.

   - *Mixing the starch with a cold liquid.* This is the principle used for starches such as cornstarch. It can also be used with flour, but, as we note later, the result is an inferior sauce. A mixture of raw starch and cold liquid is called a *slurry.*

Roux Ingredients

Roux (roo) is a cooked mixture of equal parts by weight of fat and flour.

FAT

The cooking fats employed for making roux are as follows:

Clarified butter is preferred for the finest sauces because of its flavor. The butter is clarified (p. 168) because the moisture content of whole butter tends to gelatinize some of the starch and makes the roux hard to work.

Margarine is widely used in place of butter because of its lower cost. However, its flavor is inferior to butter, so it does not make as fine a sauce. The quality of margarine varies from brand to brand.

Animal fats, such as chicken fat, beef drippings, and lard, are used when their flavor is appropriate to the sauce. Thus, chicken fat can be used for chicken velouté, and beef drippings can be used for beef gravy. When properly used, animal fats can enhance the flavor of a sauce.

Vegetable oil and shortening can be used for roux but, because they add no flavor, they are not preferred. Solid shortening also has the disadvantage of having a high melting point, which gives it an unpleasant fuzzy feeling in the mouth. It is best reserved for the bakeshop and the fry kettle.

Today, roux-thickened sauces are often condemned for health reasons because of the fat content of the roux. It should be remembered, however, that when a roux-bound velouté or brown sauce is properly made, most of the fat is released and skimmed off before the sauce is served.

FLOUR

The thickening power of flour depends, in part, on its starch content. Bread flour has less starch and more protein than cake flour. Eight parts (such as ounces or grams) of cake flour has the same thickening power as 10 parts of bread flour.

Bread flour frequently is used for general cooking purposes in commercial kitchens even though it has less thickening power than cake flour or pastry flour. Most sauce recipes in this book, as well as in other books, are based on bread flour or on all-purpose flour, which has similar thickening power. The proportions of roux to liquid must be adjusted if another flour is used.

Flour is sometimes browned dry in the oven for use in brown roux. A heavily browned flour has only one-third the thickening power of unbrowned flour.

In addition to starch, wheat flour contains proteins and other components. As a roux-thickened sauce is simmered, these components rise to the surface as scum. They then can be skimmed off. Sauces are generally simmered for a time even after the starch is completely gelatinized so these "impurities" can be cooked off. This improves the texture, gloss, and clarity of a sauce. When a high-protein flour such as bread flour is used in a roux, the sauce must be cooked longer and skimmed more often to achieve good clarity.

Sauces made with wheat flour do not freeze well because some of the starch breaks down when frozen, reducing its thickening power.

INGREDIENT PROPORTIONS

Correct amounts of fat and flour—*equal parts by weight*—are important to a good roux. There must be enough fat to coat all the starch granules, but not too much. In fact, Escoffier called for even less fat than our standard proportions (8 parts fat to 9 parts flour).

A good roux is stiff, not runny or pourable. A roux with too much fat is called a *slack roux*. Excess fat increases the cost of the roux unnecessarily; the excess fat rises to the top of the sauce, where it either is skimmed off or makes the sauce look greasy.

Preparing Roux

A roux must be cooked so the finished sauce does not have the raw, starchy taste of flour. The three kinds of roux differ in how much they are cooked.

Figure 7.8 Cooking white roux

White roux is cooked for just a few minutes, just enough to cook out the raw taste. Cooking is stopped as soon as the roux has a frothy, chalky, slightly gritty appearance, before it has begun to color. White roux is used for béchamel and other white sauces based on milk. In spite of its name, white roux is actually a pale yellow because it is made from butter and (usually) unbleached flour. Figure 7.8 illustrates the production of white roux.

Blond roux, or pale roux, is cooked a little longer, just until the roux begins to change to a slightly darker color. Cooking must then be stopped. Blond roux is used for veloutés, or sauces based on white stocks. The sauces have a pale ivory color.

Brown roux is cooked until it takes on a light brown color and a nutty aroma. Cooking must take place over low heat so the roux browns evenly without scorching. For a deeper brown roux, the flour may be browned in an oven before adding it to the fat. A heavily browned roux has only about one-third the thickening power of white roux, but it contributes flavor and color to brown sauces.

Basic Procedure for Making All Roux

1. Melt fat.
2. Add correct amount of flour and stir until fat and flour are thoroughly mixed.
3. Cook to required degree for white, blond, or brown roux.
   Cooking is done in a saucepan on top of the stove, and the roux is stirred for even cooking. Use low heat for brown roux, moderate heat for white or blond roux. Large quantities may be baked in an oven. Some restaurants make up batches large enough to last for several days or a week.

Operations that depend on roux-based sauces and soups generally make quantities of roux in bulk and keep it available throughout the production period for thickening sauces. If you don't make batches of roux as part of the mise en place, you can also make it as part of the production process for an individual sauce. In the recipes in this section, making the roux is part of the recipe. However, they can easily be changed to use a prepared roux. For example, in the Velouté Sauce recipe (p. 160), omit the flour and use just enough butter to sweat the mirepoix. After adding the stock, beat in 8 oz (250 g) prepared blond roux.

Incorporating the Roux

Combining the roux and liquid to obtain a smooth, lump-free sauce is a skill that takes practice to master. It's a good idea to practice the various techniques with water, under the guidance of your instructor, so you understand what you are doing before you start working with valuable stocks.

GENERAL PRINCIPLES

Liquid may be added to roux, or roux may be added to liquid.

The liquid may be hot or cooled, but not ice cold. A very cold liquid will solidify the fat in the roux.

The roux may be warm or cold, but not sizzling hot. Adding a hot liquid to a very hot roux causes spattering and, possibly, lumps.

Most chefs find they get the best results by combining a cold (or cool) liquid with a hot roux, or a hot liquid with a cold roux.

Within these general guidelines, there is room for a number of variations. Two of them are described here. Because successful use of roux is largely a matter of experience, you are advised to profit from your instructors' experience when they demonstrate these techniques or whichever methods they prefer.

Equipment note: Stainless-steel pans are best for white sauces. Whipping in an aluminum pan makes the sauce gray.

Procedures for Incorporating Roux

Method 1: Adding Liquid to Roux

This method is used when a roux is made up specifically for the sauce, gravy, or soup being prepared.

1. Use a heavy saucepot to prevent scorching either the roux or the sauce.

2. When the roux is made, remove the pan from the fire for a few minutes to cool slightly.

3. Slowly pour in the liquid, all the while beating vigorously with a wire whip to prevent lumps from forming.

   If the liquid is hot (such as simmering milk for béchamel sauce), you must beat especially well because the starch will gelatinize quickly.

   If the liquid is cool, you can add a quantity of it, beat to dissolve the roux, and then add the remainder of the liquid, hot or cool.

4. Bring the liquid to a boil, continuing to beat well. The roux does not reach its full thickening power until near the boiling point.

5. Simmer the sauce, stirring from time to time, until all the starchy taste of the flour is cooked out. This takes at least 10 minutes, but the flavor and consistency of the sauce improve if it is cooked longer. Many chefs feel 20 minutes of simmering is a bare minimum. Others cook some sauces for an hour or longer.

6. When the sauce is finished, it may be kept hot in a bain-marie or cooled for later use. Either way, it should be covered or have a thin film of butter melted onto the top to prevent a skin from forming.

Method 2: Adding the Roux to the Liquid

Many restaurants make up large batches of roux to last all day or even all week. This method may be used in these situations.

1. Bring the liquid to a simmer in a heavy pot.

2. Add a small quantity of roux and beat vigorously with a whip to break up all lumps.

3. Continue to beat small quantities into the simmering liquid until the desired consistency is reached. Remember that roux must simmer for a time to thicken completely, so do not add roux too quickly or you risk overthickening the sauce.

4. Continue to simmer until the roux is cooked out and no starchy taste remains.

5. If the sauce is to simmer a long time, underthicken it because it will thicken as it reduces.

Proportions of Roux to Liquid

Table 7.5 indicates the quantities of roux needed to thicken 1 gallon (4 L) liquid to thin, medium, and thick consistencies.

Table 7.5 Roux Proportions in Sauces				
SAUCE	BUTTER	FLOUR	ROUX	LIQUID
Thin or light	6 oz/190 g	6 oz/190 g	12 oz/375 g	1 gal/4 L
Medium	8 oz/250 g	8 oz/250 g	1 lb/500 g	1 gal/4 L
Thick or heavy	12 oz/375 g	12 oz/375 g	1½ lb/750 g	1 gal/4 L

How thick is a thick sauce? Obviously, these are not precise, scientific terms that can be defined easily. Experience can be the only teacher in this case. This is another good reason to practice with roux and water—so you can, with experience, produce the exact consistency you want.

You also have available the techniques of dilution and reduction to adjust the consistency of a sauce (see pp. 153–154), and you will learn how to use beurre manié and other thickening agents.

Other Thickening Agents

Starches

1. *Beurre manié* (burr mahnyay) is a mixture of equal parts soft, raw butter and flour worked together to form a smooth paste. It is used for quick thickening at the end of cooking to finish a sauce. The raw butter adds flavor and gives a sheen to the sauce when it melts.

   To use, drop very small pieces into a simmering sauce and stir with a whip until smooth. Repeat until desired consistency is reached. Simmer just a few minutes more to cook the flour, and then remove from the fire.

2. *Whitewash* is a thin mixture of flour and cold water. Sauces made with whitewash have neither as good a flavor nor as fine a texture as those made with roux. *Whitewash is not recommended for use.*

3. *Cornstarch* produces a sauce that is almost clear, with a glossy texture.

   To use, mix with cold water or other cold liquid until smooth. Stir into the hot liquid. Bring to a boil and simmer until the liquid turns clear and there is no starchy taste. Do not boil for a long period or the starch may break down and the liquid become thin. Sauces thickened with cornstarch may thin out if held on the steam table for long periods. Cornstarch is used extensively in sweet sauces to accompany certain meats as well as in desserts and dessert sauces. It has roughly twice the thickening power of flour.

4. *Arrowroot* is used like cornstarch, but it gives an even clearer sauce. Its use is limited by its high cost. Nevertheless, because of its quality, it is the preferred starch for thickening jus lié. It is less likely than cornstarch to break down when heated for a long time.

5. *Waxy maize* is used for sauces that are to be frozen. Flour and other starches break down and lose their thickening power when frozen. Waxy maize does not. It is handled like cornstarch.

6. *Pregelatinized or instant starches* have been cooked, or gelatinized, and then redried. Thus, they can thicken a cold liquid without heating. These starches are rarely used in sauce-making but are frequently used in the bakeshop.

7. *Bread crumbs* and other crumbs will thicken a liquid quickly because they have already been cooked, like instant starches. Bread crumbs may be used when smoothness of texture is not desired. A common example is the use of gingersnap crumbs to thicken sauerbraten gravy.

8. *Vegetable purées, ground nuts, and other solids* can also be used. A simple tomato sauce is basically a seasoned vegetable purée. The sauce gets its texture from the thickness of the main ingredient. No additional thickener is needed.

   Using this same principle, we can add body or texture to sauces by adding a smooth vegetable purée, or by puréeing mirepoix or other vegetables with the sauce. Other puréed or finely ground ingredients, such as ground nuts, add texture as well as flavor to a sauce.

Egg Yolk and Cream Liaison

In classical cooking, a *liaison* is a mixture of egg yolks and cream, used to enrich and lightly thicken a sauce or other liquid. Egg yolks have the power to thicken a sauce slightly due to the coagulation of egg proteins when heated.

Caution must be used when thickening with egg yolks because of the danger of curdling. This happens when the proteins coagulate too much and separate from the liquid.

Pure egg yolks coagulate at 140° to 158°F (60° to 70°C). For this reason, they are beaten with heavy cream before use. This raises their curdling temperature to 180°–185°F (82°–85°C). (Note this is still well below the boiling point.) The heavy cream also adds thickness and flavor to the sauce.

Egg yolks have only slight thickening power. The liaison is used primarily to give richness of flavor and smoothness of texture to a sauce and only secondarily to give a slight thickening. Also, because of the instability of the egg yolks, it is used only as a finishing technique. Incorporating a liaison is illustrated in Figure 7.9.

(a) Slowly stir a little of the hot sauce (chicken velouté, in this picture) into the mixture of cream and egg yolks to warm it and dilute it.

(b) Stir the tempered liaison back into the remaining sauce.

Procedure for Using a Liaison

1. Beat together the egg yolks and cream in a stainless-steel bowl. Normal proportions are 2–3 parts cream to 1 part egg yolks.
2. Very slowly add a little of the hot liquid to the liaison, beating constantly. This is known as *tempering*.
3. Off the heat, add the warmed, diluted liaison to the rest of the sauce, stirring well as you pour it in.
4. Return the sauce to low heat to warm it gently, but do not heat it higher than 180°F (82°C) or it will curdle. Under no circumstances should it boil.
5. Hold for service above 140°F (69°C) for sanitation reasons, but lower than 180°F (82°C).

Egg Yolk Emulsification

Egg yolks are used as the thickening agent for hollandaise and related sauces, but in this case the principle is entirely different. The entire procedure is discussed in detail when we get to the hollandaise family of sauces, page 171.

Reduction

Simmering a sauce to evaporate some of the water thickens the sauce because only the water evaporates, not the solids. As the solids become more concentrated, the sauce becomes thicker. This technique has always been important for finishing sauces (see the next section). It has become more important as a basic thickening technique as modern chefs use less starch for thickening.

Use caution when reducing stock-based sauces. If such a sauce is reduced too much, the concentration of gelatin may give it a gluey or sticky texture, and it will congeal quickly on plates. Also, the sauce may have a heavily cooked taste that is not as appealing as the fresher, livelier taste of a stock that has not been cooked as much.

Finishing Techniques

Remember that the three basic elements of a finished sauce are a liquid, a thickening agent, and additional seasoning and flavoring ingredients. We have discussed in detail how liquids are combined with thickening agents to make the basic sauces. In the next section, we look at the way families of sauces are built on these bases by the addition of flavoring ingredients.

Sauces may be modified or added to in a great many ways. Among these methods are a number of basic techniques used over and over again for making sauces. Before we study the structure of the sauce families, it will be helpful to look at these basic finishing techniques.

Reduction

1. **Using reduction to concentrate basic flavors.**
   If we simmer a sauce for a long time, some of the water evaporates. The sauce becomes more concentrated, and the resulting product is more flavorful. This is the same technique used when making glazes from stocks. Some reduction takes place in nearly all sauces, depending on how long they are simmered.

2. **Using reduction to adjust textures.**

Concentrating a sauce by reduction also thickens it because only the water evaporates, not the roux or other solids. A skilled sauce chef uses both reduction and dilution to give a sauce the precise texture sought. If a sauce is too thin, it may be simmered until it reaches desired thickness. Or the chef may add a large quantity of stock or other liquid to a thickened sauce to thin it out greatly, then simmer it again until it is reduced to just the right consistency. By doing this, the chef also gives more flavor to the sauce.

3. **Using reduction to add new flavors.**

If we can add a liquid to a sauce, then reduce it to concentrate it, why can't we reduce a liquid first and then add it to a sauce?

In fact, this is one of the most important techniques in sauce-making. We have already mentioned that glazes—reduced stocks—are used to flavor sauces. Reductions of other liquids, especially red and white wines, are used a great deal in this way.

Skip ahead to the recipe for Bordelaise Sauce (p. 165). Note how the red wine is cooked down with shallots, pepper, and herbs to one-fourth its original volume. Not only is the flavor of the wine concentrated but also the flavor from the other spices is extracted. This reduction is a powerful flavoring agent that gives bordelaise sauce its distinctive taste. Reduction allows you to add a great deal of flavor to a sauce without adding much liquid.

TERMINOLOGY

To reduce by one-half means to cook away one-half of the volume so that half is left.

To reduce by three-fourths means to cook away three-fourths of the volume so that only one-fourth is left.

To reduce au sec (oh seck) means to reduce until dry or nearly dry.

Straining

If you have learned how to use a roux properly, you should be able to make a smooth, lump-free sauce. However, to bring a sauce's texture to perfection, to create the velvety smoothness that is important to a good sauce, straining is necessary. Even a slight graininess that you can't see can still be felt on your tongue.

Straining through a china cap lined with several layers of cheesecloth is effective. Very fine sieves are also available for straining sauces. Straining is usually done before final seasoning.

Deglazing

To *deglaze* means to swirl a liquid in a sauté pan or other pan to dissolve cooked particles of food remaining on the bottom.

This term was discussed in relation to the basic technique of sautéing in Chapter 4 and again in connection with the production of brown stock. It is also an important technique for finishing sauces that accompany sautéed items.

A liquid, such as wine or stock, is used to deglaze a sauté pan and then is reduced by one-half or three-fourths. This reduction, with the added flavor of the pan drippings, is then added to the sauce served with the item.

Enriching with Butter and Cream

1. **Liaison.**

In addition to being a thickening agent, a liaison of egg yolks and cream is used to finish a sauce by giving it extra richness and smoothness.

2. **Heavy cream.**

Heavy cream has long been used to give flavor and richness to sauces. The most obvious example is adding cream to basic béchamel sauce to make cream sauce.

3. Butter.

A useful enriching technique, both in classical and in modern cooking, is called *finishing with butter*, or *monter au beurre* (mohn tay oh burr).

To finish a sauce with butter, simply add a few pieces of softened butter to the hot sauce and swirl them in until melted. The sauce should then be served immediately; if it is allowed to stand, the butter may separate.

Finishing a sauce with butter gives it a little extra shine and smoothness as well as adding to it the rich, fresh taste of raw butter.

Seasoning

Whether or not a sauce is to be given a final enrichment of liaison, cream, or butter, it must be checked carefully for seasonings before serving. Remember that the last step in any recipe, whether written or not, is "adjust the seasonings."

1. *Salt* is the most important seasoning for sauces. *Lemon juice* is also important. These two seasonings emphasize the flavors already present by stimulating the taste buds. *Cayenne* and *white pepper* are perhaps third and fourth in importance.

2. *Sherry* and *Madeira* are frequently used as final flavorings. These wines are added at the end of cooking (unlike red and white table wines, which must be cooked in a sauce) because their flavors are easily evaporated by heat.

KEY POINTS TO REVIEW

• What five qualities do sauces add to foods?

• What is roux? How is it made? How is it used?

• What is beurre manié? How is it made? How is it used?

• How do you prepare cornstarch to use in thickening liquids?

• What is a liaison? How is it made? How is it used?

• What is the meaning of the expression *monter au beurre*?

Sauce Families

Leading Sauces

One more time, let's look at the three basic building blocks of sauce cookery, this time from a slightly different angle.

liquid + thickening agent = leading sauce

leading sauce + additional flavorings = small sauce

We have talked about five basic liquids for sauces: milk, white stock, brown stock, tomato purée (plus stock), and clarified butter. From these we get our five *leading sauces*, also known as *grand sauces* or *mother sauces*, as shown in Chart 7.1.

Chart 7.1 **The Leading Sauces**		
LIQUID	THICKENING AGENT	LEADING SAUCE
milk	+ white roux	= béchamel sauce
white stock (veal, chicken, fish)	+ white or blond roux	= velouté (veal velouté, chicken velouté, fish velouté)
brown stock	+ brown roux	= brown sauce or espagnole
tomato plus stock	+ (optional roux, see Note)	= tomato sauce
butter	+ egg yolks	= hollandaise

Note: Roux is not used in all tomato sauces, as tomato purée is naturally thick.

To these five sauces, we add one more: *fond lié* (fone lee ay), meaning "thickened stock." It is sometimes used in place of espagnole.

brown stock + arrowroot or cornstarch = fond lié

You should understand that these charts are a bit oversimplified. Most of these sauces have a few other ingredients for flavoring. Yet knowing this basic structure is the key to making sauces.

Chart 7.2 The Small Sauces

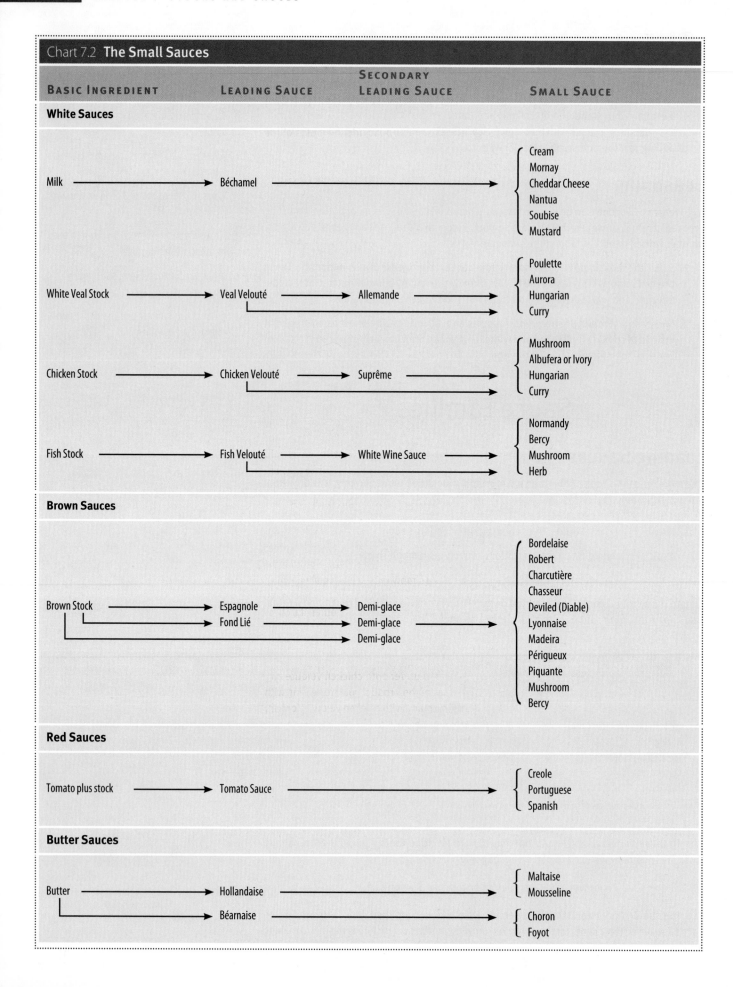

Basic Ingredient	Leading Sauce	Secondary Leading Sauce	Small Sauce
White Sauces			
Milk	Béchamel		Cream, Mornay, Cheddar Cheese, Nantua, Soubise, Mustard
White Veal Stock	Veal Velouté	Allemande	Poulette, Aurora, Hungarian, Curry
Chicken Stock	Chicken Velouté	Suprême	Mushroom, Albufera or Ivory, Hungarian, Curry
Fish Stock	Fish Velouté	White Wine Sauce	Normandy, Bercy, Mushroom, Herb
Brown Sauces			
Brown Stock	Espagnole, Fond Lié	Demi-glace, Demi-glace, Demi-glace	Bordelaise, Robert, Charcutière, Chasseur, Deviled (Diable), Lyonnaise, Madeira, Périgueux, Piquante, Mushroom, Bercy
Red Sauces			
Tomato plus stock	Tomato Sauce		Creole, Portuguese, Spanish
Butter Sauces			
Butter	Hollandaise, Béarnaise		Maltaise, Mousseline; Choron, Foyot

Small Sauces

The major leading sauces—béchamel; veal, chicken, and fish veloutés; and espagnole—are rarely used by themselves as sauces. They are more important as the bases for other sauces, called *small sauces.* Tomato sauce and hollandaise are used as they are, but they, too, are important as bases for small sauces.

Let's expand our sauce family chart one more generation to include examples of the small sauces in order to show the relationships (see Chart 7.2).

Chart 7.2 is probably a little more complicated than you expected because of the extra arrows and the extra category of secondary leading sauces. These are relatively easy to explain.

1. **Secondary leading white sauces.**

   These three sauces—allemande, suprême, and white wine—are really finished sauces, like other small sauces. But they are used so often to build other small sauces that they rate a special category.

   For example, to make suprême sauce, you add cream to chicken velouté.

   To make Albufera sauce, you can add meat glaze (glace de viande) to your suprême sauce. Or, if you don't have suprême sauce, you can make it by adding both cream and meat glaze to chicken velouté. This is why there are two sets of arrows in the chart.

   Allemande, suprême, and white wine sauces are also known as the *main small sauces.* If the concept of secondary leading white sauces seems confusing at first, you may simply think of them as small sauces. The important thing is to understand how the sauces are derived.

2. **Demi-glace.**

   - *Demi-glace* is defined as half brown sauce plus half brown stock, reduced by half. Most chefs prefer demi-glace to espagnole as a base for small sauces because of its more concentrated, more fully developed flavor.

     Note: It is possible to make small sauces directly from espagnole, but they will not be as fine.

   - Some modern chefs feel espagnole is too heavy for modern tastes and that lighter sauces are required. These chefs prepare demi-glace from fond lié by reducing it with mirepoix, white wine, and seasonings, or by simply reducing by half a flavorful brown stock. In other words, demi-glace may be considered a well-flavored brown stock, reduced by half (*demi* means "half"), thickened with roux or other starch, or left unthickened (except by natural gelatin).

3. **Small sauces listed twice.**

   Notice, for example, that mushroom sauce is listed under both chicken velouté and fish velouté. This means you should use the stock of the product you are serving with the sauce. Mushroom sauce for chicken should be made with chicken velouté, for fish, with fish velouté. To be even more confusing, mushroom sauce is also made with brown sauce. Bercy sauce is also made as both a white and a brown sauce. These are considered unrelated sauces that happen to have the same name.

4. **Hollandaise and béarnaise.**

   These are essentially two variations of the same kind of sauce, with different flavorings. Each has its own small family of small sauces.

Standards of Quality for Sauces

1. **Consistency and body.**
   Smooth, with no lumps.
   Not too thick or pasty, but thick enough to coat the food lightly.

2. **Flavor.**
 Distinctive but well-balanced flavor.
 Proper degree of seasoning.
 No starchy taste.
 The flavor should be selected to enhance or complement the food (such as suprême sauce with chicken or white wine sauce with fish) or to provide a pleasing contrast (such as a béarnaise sauce with grilled beef or raisin sauce with ham).

3. **Appearance.**
 Smooth, with a good shine.
 Good color for its type (rich, deep brown for brown sauce, pale ivory for velouté, white—not gray—for cream sauce).

Other Sauces

As usual, not everything fits into one package. Beyond the five major sauce families, a number of other preparations don't follow these basic patterns. We encounter these later in the chapter.

These other preparations include these groups:

Simple and compound butters, including simple browned butter as well as butter combined with flavorings.

Pan gravies, or sauces made with the pan drippings of the meat or poultry they are served with.

Miscellaneous hot sauces, which are not made like any of the five basic sauces. These include such items as raisin sauce (for ham) and sour cream sauce.

Miscellaneous cold sauces include not only sauces for meats, like Cumberland sauce and horseradish sauce, but also vinaigrettes, mayonnaise, and their variations, covered in Chapter 14.

Modern Sauces

Most of the emphasis in this chapter is on techniques for producing classic sauces. It is a mistake to argue that these sauces are not important and that modern sauce-making is entirely different. Modern sauces still depend on the basic classical techniques, even though the emphasis may have changed. For example, a chef in a modern kitchen may prepare a sauce for a sautéed meat item at the last minute by deglazing a sauté pan with a little wine, adding some reduced brown stock, and finishing the sauce by swirling in a little butter. As you can see, these are all techniques used in the production of classical sauces. Learning to make classical sauces is an important foundation for learning modern cooking.

While many of the recipes in this book, especially the traditional ones, incorporate sauces prepared in advance, many of the others, especially the more modern ones, incorporate sauces made at the last minute.

Production

Béchamel

The classic version of the standard white sauce, *béchamel*, was made with lean veal and herbs and spices simmered with the sauce for an hour or with white veal stock added to the sauce and then reduced. This is rarely done today.

Nevertheless, the plain béchamel used today—simply milk and roux—can be improved by simmering the sauce with onion and spices. These may be omitted, of course, but the sauce will have less flavor.

Béchamel Sauce

YIELD: 1 GAL (4 L)

U.S.	METRIC	INGREDIENTS
		Roux:
8 oz	250 g	Clarified butter
8 oz	250 g	Bread flour
1 gal	4 L	Milk
1	1	Bay leaf, small
1	1	Small whole onion, peeled
1	1	Whole clove
to taste	to taste	Salt
to taste	to taste	Nutmeg
to taste	to taste	White pepper

Per 1 fl oz (29.57 mL): Calories, 40; Protein, 1 g; Fat, 3 g (63% cal.); Cholesterol, 10 mg; Carbohydrates, 3 g; Fiber 0 g; Sodium, 30 mg

PROCEDURE

1. Review instructions for making and incorporating roux (pp. 150–151).
2. Heat the butter in a heavy saucepot over low heat. Add the flour and make a white roux. Cool roux slightly.
3. Gradually add the milk to the roux, beating constantly.
4. Bring the sauce to a boil, stirring constantly. Reduce heat to a simmer.
5. Stick the bay leaf to the onion with clove and add to sauce. Simmer at least 15 minutes or, if possible, 30 minutes or more. Stir occasionally while cooking.
6. Adjust consistency with more hot milk, if necessary.
7. Season very lightly with salt, nutmeg, and white pepper. Spice flavors should not dominate.
8. Strain the sauce through a china cap lined with cheesecloth. Cover or spread melted butter on surface to prevent skin formation. Keep hot in a bain-marie, or cool in a cold-water bath for later use.

VARIATIONS

Light Béchamel
Use 12 oz (375 g) roux.

Heavy Béchamel
Use 1½ lb (750 g) roux.

Figure 7.10 Preparing béchamel sauce.

(a) Combine butter and flour to make a roux.

(b) Cook the roux, keeping it white.

(c) Whip in the milk.

(d) Strain the finished sauce through a china cap lined with cheesecloth.

(e) Finished béchamel sauce.

Small Sauces

For each of the following sauces, add the ingredients indicated to *1 qt (1 L) béchamel sauce*. Season to taste.

Cream Sauce
4–8 fl oz (125–250 mL) heavy cream, heated or tempered

Mornay Sauce
4 oz (125 g) grated Gruyère cheese and 2 oz (60 g) parmesan, stirred in until just melted. Finish, off heat, with 2 oz (60 g) raw butter. Thin out with a little hot milk, if necessary, or use a stock or broth appropriate for the dish being prepared.

Mornay Sauce for Glazing or Gratinéeing
Finish Mornay Sauce with liaison of 2 egg yolks and 2 fl oz (60 mL) heavy cream.

Cheddar Cheese Sauce
8 oz (250 g) cheddar cheese, ½ tsp (2 mL) dry mustard, 2 tsp (10 mL) Worcestershire sauce

Mustard Sauce
4 oz (125 g) prepared mustard

Soubise Sauce
1 lb (500 g) onions, finely diced, cooked slowly in 2 oz (60 g) butter without browning. Simmer with sauce 15 minutes and force through a fine sieve.

Tomatoed Soubise Sauce
Add 1 pt (500 mL) thick tomato purée to 1 qt (1 L) soubise sauce

Nantua Sauce
6 oz (175 g) Shrimp Butter (p. 170), 4 fl oz (125 mL) heavy cream

(*Note:* Classic Nantua sauce is made with crayfish, not readily available in many regions.)

Velouté

The three *velouté* sauces are the bases of many variations. Instructions for the small sauces indicate which of the three to use. If more than one is given, the choice depends on what you are serving it with.

Note: In North America, chicken velouté is used much more often than veal velouté. Many of the sauces at one time made with veal stock are now made with chicken stock.

Velouté Sauce (Veal, Chicken, or Fish)

YIELD: 2 QT (2L)

U.S.	METRIC	INGREDIENTS
4 fl oz	125 mL	Clarified butter
4 oz	125 g	White mirepoix, small dice (see Note)
4 oz	125 g	Flour (see Note)
2½ qt	2.5 L	White stock (veal, beef, chicken, or fish)
		Sachet d'épices:
1	1	Bay leaf
½ tsp	2 mL	Dried thyme
½ tsp	2 mL	Peppercorns
3–4	3–4	Parsley stems
as needed	as needed	Salt (see step 7)
as needed	as needed	White pepper (see step 7)

PROCEDURE

1. Review instructions for making and incorporating roux (pp. 150–151).
2. Heat the clarified butter in a heavy saucepot over low heat. Add mirepoix and sweat the vegetables without browning them.
3. Add flour and make a blond roux. Cool roux slightly.
4. Gradually add the stock to the roux, beating constantly. Bring to a boil, stirring constantly. Reduce heat to a simmer.
5. Add the sachet.
6. Simmer the sauce very slowly for 1 hour. Stir occasionally, and skim surface when necessary. Add more stock if needed to adjust consistency.
7. If the velouté is to be used as is, season to taste with salt and white pepper. But if it is to be used as an ingredient in other preparations, do not season velouté.
8. Strain through a china cap lined with cheesecloth. Cover or spread melted butter on surface to prevent skin formation. Keep hot in a bain-marie, or cool in a cold-water bath for later use.

Per 1 fl oz (29.57 mL): Calories, 30; Protein, 1 g; Fat, 2 g (53% cal.); Cholesterol, 5 mg; Carbohydrates, 3 g; Fiber, 0 g; Sodium, 10 mg.

Note: Use a standard white mirepoix, or substitute leeks for the parsnips, as desired.

If you have blond roux on hand, you can use it instead of making roux as part of this procedure. Reduce the clarified butter to 1 fl oz (30 mL). After sweating the mirepoix, add 8 oz (250 g) blond roux.

VARIATION

For a quicker, simpler velouté, omit clarified butter, mirepoix, and sachet.

Figure 7.11 Preparing velouté sauce.

(a) Sweat the mirepoix in butter.

(b) Add the flour and make a blond roux.

(c) Whip in white stock.

(d) As the sauce simmers, skim the surface regularly.

(e) Strain the finished sauce through a china cap lined with cheesecloth.

(f) Finished velouté sauce.

White Wine Sauce

YIELD: 1 GAL (4 L)

U.S.	METRIC	INGREDIENTS
8 fl oz	250 mL	White wine (dry)
2 qt	2 L	Fish velouté
8 fl oz	250 mL	Heavy cream, hot
2 oz	60 g	Butter, in pieces
to taste	to taste	Salt
to taste	to taste	White pepper
to taste	to taste	Lemon juice

Per 1 fl oz (29.57 mL): Calories, 45; Protein, 0 g; Fat, 4 g (85% cal.); Cholesterol, 10 mg; Carbohydrates, 1 g; Fiber, 0 g; Sodium, 30 mg.

PROCEDURE

1. Reduce the wine by half in a saucepan.
2. Add the velouté and simmer until reduced to desired consistency.
3. Slowly stir in the hot (or tempered) cream.
4. Remove from heat and swirl in raw butter pieces.
5. Season to taste with salt, white pepper, and a few drops of lemon juice.
6. Strain through cheesecloth.

VARIATION

Instead of adding hot or tempered heavy cream, make a liaison with 5 egg yolks and 8 fl oz (250 mL) cold heavy cream. Incorporate liaison using the procedure on page 153. Then continue with step 4 in recipe.

Suprême Sauce

YIELD: 2 QT (2 L)

U.S.	METRIC	INGREDIENTS
2 qt	2 L	Chicken velouté
1 pt	500 mL	Heavy cream
2 oz	60 g	Butter, in pieces
to taste	to taste	Salt
to taste	to taste	White pepper
to taste	to taste	Lemon juice

Per 1 fl oz (29.57 mL): Calories, 50; Protein, 1 g; Fat, 5 g (79% cal.); Cholesterol, 20 mg; Carbohydrates, 2 g; Fiber, 0 g; Sodium, 30 mg.

PROCEDURE

1. Place velouté in a saucepan and simmer over moderate heat until reduced by about one-fourth. Stir occasionally.
2. Pour the cream into a stainless-steel bowl and temper it by slowly stirring in a little of the hot sauce. Stir this mixture slowly back into the sauce in the pan and return the sauce just to a simmer.
3. Swirl in raw butter pieces. Season to taste with salt, white pepper, and a few drops of lemon juice.
4. Strain through cheesecloth.

Allemande Sauce

YIELD: 2 QT (2 L)

U.S.	METRIC	INGREDIENTS
2 qt	2 L	Veal velouté (see Note)
		Liaison:
4	4	Egg yolks
8 fl oz	250 mL	Heavy cream
½ fl oz	15 mL	Lemon juice
to taste	to taste	Salt
to taste	to taste	White pepper

PROCEDURE

1. Review instructions for incorporating liaison (p. 153).
2. Place velouté in a saucepan and simmer a few minutes over moderate heat until slightly reduced.
3. Beat the egg yolks and cream together in a stainless-steel bowl.
4. Temper the liaison by slowly beating in about one-third of the hot sauce. Then slowly stir this mixture back into the sauce in the pan.
5. Reheat to just below simmering. Do not boil.
6. Add lemon juice, salt, and white pepper to taste. Strain through cheesecloth.

Per 1 fl oz (29.57 mL): Calories, 40; Protein, 1 g; Fat, 3.5 g (72% cal.); Cholesterol, 25 mg; Carbohydrates, 2 g; Fiber, 0 g; Sodium, 20 mg.

Note: *Allemande sauce, strictly speaking, should be made with veal velouté. However, as chicken velouté is much more common in North America, allemande sauce and the small sauces derived from it are often made with chicken velouté.*

Small Sauces

For each of the following sauces, add the listed ingredients to *1 qt (1 L) veal, chicken, or fish velouté, suprême sauce, allemande sauce, or white wine sauce* as indicated. Season sauce to taste.

Poulette

Simmer 8 oz (250 g) white mushrooms or mushroom trimmings with velouté when making allemande. Make allemande; strain. Finish with 2 tbsp (30 mL) chopped parsley and lemon juice to taste.

Aurora

Add 6 oz (175 g) tomato purée to 1 qt (1 L) veal or chicken velouté, suprême sauce, or allemande sauce.

Hungarian

Sweat 2 oz (60 g) minced onion and 1 tbsp (15 mL) paprika in 1 oz (25 g) butter until soft. Add ½ cup (100 mL) white wine and reduce by half. Add 1 qt (1 L) veal or chicken velouté, simmer 10 minutes, and strain.

Ivory or Albufera

Add 2 oz (60 g) meat glaze (glace de viande) to 1 qt (1 L) suprême sauce.

Curry

Cook 4 oz (125 g) mirepoix, cut brunoise, in 1 oz (25 g) butter until tender but not brown. Add 1 tbsp (15 mL) curry powder, 1 crushed garlic clove, pinch dried thyme, ½ bay leaf, and 2–4 parsley stems and cook another minute. Add 1 qt (1 L) veal, chicken, or fish velouté. Simmer 20 minutes, add ½ cup (125 mL) cream, strain, and season with salt and lemon juice.

Mushroom

Sauté 4 oz (125 g) sliced mushrooms in 1 oz (25 g) butter, adding 1 tbsp (15 mL) lemon juice to keep them white. Add to suprême, allemande, or white wine sauce or to appropriate velouté.

Bercy

Reduce by two-thirds 2 oz (60 g) chopped shallots and ½ cup (125 mL) white wine. Add 1 qt (1 L) fish velouté, reduce slightly, and finish with 2 oz (60 g) raw butter, 2 tbsp (30 mL) chopped parsley, and lemon juice to taste.

Herb

To white wine sauce add chopped parsley, chives, and tarragon to taste.

Normandy

To 1 qt (1 L) fish velouté add 4 oz (125 mL) mushroom cooking liquid (or 4 oz/125 g mushroom trimmings) and 4 oz (125 mL) oyster liquid or fish fumet. Reduce by one-third. Finish with liaison of 4 egg yolks and 1 cup (250 mL) cream. Strain and swirl in 3 oz (75 g) raw butter.

Anchovy

Follow instructions for Normandy sauce but, in place of the raw butter used to finish the sauce, substitute 6 oz (175 g) anchovy butter.

Shrimp

To 1 qt (1 L) white wine sauce add 4 oz (125 g) shrimp butter and a dash of cayenne. If desired, garnish with 4 oz (125 g) diced, cooked shrimp.

Venetian

Combine ½ cup (125 mL) each white wine and tarragon vinegar, ½ oz (15 g) chopped shallots, and 2 tsp (10 mL) chopped fresh chervil. Reduce by two-thirds. Add 1 qt (1 L) white wine sauce and simmer 2–3 minutes. Strain. Add fresh tarragon to taste.

Horseradish

Add 2 oz (60 g) drained horseradish, ½ cup (125 mL) heavy cream, and 2 tsp (10 mL) dry mustard dissolved in 1 fl oz (30 mL) vinegar to 1 qt (1 L) velouté made with beef or veal stock.

Espagnole or Brown Sauce

As one glance at the procedure for making *espagnole* will tell you, this sauce is more complicated than béchamel or velouté. Because it is the starting point for the hearty, flavorful sauces that accompany red meats, it is necessary to give it extra flavor and richness with mirepoix. Some chefs even add more browned bones and cook the sauce as long as a stock.

Note how the roux is made in the espagnole recipe. Though mirepoix is also cooked in the fat, the basic principle is the same as when you make a simple roux in a separate pot.

FOND LIÉ

In its simplest form, fond lié, or jus lié, is a brown stock thickened lightly with arrowroot or cornstarch. Its quality can be improved, however, by applying the technique used for making espagnole—that is, reduce brown stock with browned mirepoix and tomato purée or tomato paste, and then thicken with a starch slurry and strain. You can use the same ratio of stock to mirepoix as for espagnole.

GASTRIQUE

A classic technique to add a balanced sweet-sour accent to a sauce is to add a *gastrique*, which is caramelized sugar dissolved in vinegar. For example, a gastrique gives necessary sweetness and acidity to sauce bigarade, the classic orange sauce served with roast duck.

A quantity of gastrique can be made in advance, stored, and used as needed. Heat 4 oz (120 g) sugar until it melts and then caramelizes to a light golden brown. Let cool briefly. Add 3 fl oz (90 mL) wine vinegar and simmer until the caramel is dissolved.

Brown Sauce or Espagnole

YIELD: 1 GAL (4 L

U.S.	METRIC	INGREDIENTS
		Mirepoix:
1 lb	500 g	Onions, medium dice
8 oz	250 g	Carrots, medium dice
8 oz	250 g	Celery, medium dice
8 oz	250 g	Butter
8 oz	250 g	Bread flour
6 qt	6 L	Brown veal stock
8 oz	250 g	Tomato purée (see Variations)
		Sachet:
½	½	Bay leaf
¼ tsp	1 mL	Thyme
6–8	6–8	Parsley stems

Per 1 fl oz (29.57 mL): Calories, 25; Protein, 1 g; Fat, 1.5 g (53% cal); Cholesterol, 5 mg; Carbohydrates, 2 g; Fiber, 0 g; Sodium, 20 mg.

PROCEDURE

1. Sauté the mirepoix in butter until well browned (**Figure 7.12**).
2. Add the flour and stir to make a roux. Continue to cook until the roux is browned. (See Variations for alternative procedure.)
3. Gradually stir in brown stock and tomato purée, stirring constantly until the mixture comes to a boil.
4. Reduce heat to simmer and skim surface. Add the sachet and let simmer about 2 hours, or until the sauce is reduced to 1 gal (4 L). Skim as often as necessary.
5. Strain through a china cap lined with several layers of cheesecloth. Press on mirepoix gently to extract juices.
6. Cover or spread melted butter on surface to prevent skin formation. Keep hot in a bain-marie, or cool in a cold-water bath for later use.

VARIATIONS

If you have brown roux on hand, you may use it instead of making roux as part of the sauce procedure. Reduce the quantity of butter to 2 oz (60 g), or just enough to brown mirepoix. After adding stock and bringing to a simmer in steps 3 and 4, whip in roux.

2 oz (60 g) tomato paste may be used instead of tomato purée. Add paste to the browned mirepoix and continue to brown until the paste turns a rusty brown color.

Jus de Veau Lié I

Reduce the quantity of butter to 2 oz (60 g). Omit flour. In addition to mirepoix, add veal bones or trimmings if desired. Brown with the mirepoix. After straining (step 5), make a slurry of 1 oz (30 g) arrowroot or cornstarch and enough cold water to make a thin paste. Stir into sauce and simmer until clear and thickened.

Jus de Volaille Lié, Jus d'Agneau Lié, Jus de Canard Lié, or Jus de Gibier Lié

In place of veal stock, use brown chicken stock, lamb stock, duck stock, or game stock. If desired, add appropriate bones or trimmings and brown with mirepoix, as for Jus de Veau Lié.

Figure 7.12 Preparing brown sauce or espagnole.

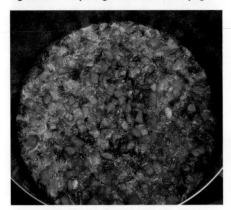

(a) Brown the mirepoix well in fat.

(b) Mix in flour and cook to make a brown roux.

(c) Whip in the stock. Add the sachet and simmer about 2 hours.

(d) Strain the finished sauce through a china cap lined with cheesecloth.

(e) Finished brown sauce or espagnole.

Fond Lié or Jus Lié II

YIELD: 1 QT (1 L)		

U.S.	METRIC	INGREDIENTS
1 qt	1 L	Brown stock
1 oz	30 g	Cornstarch or arrowroot

Per 1 fl oz (29.57 mL): Calories, 5; Protein, 0 g; Fat 0 g (0% cal.); Cholesterol, 0 mg; Carbohydrates, 1 g; Fiber; 0 g; Sodium, 0 mg.

VARIATION
....

For added flavor, the stock can be reduced with browned mirepoix and tomato (as for espagnole) before being thickened. Browned bones may also be added.

PROCEDURE

1. Bring the stock to a boil in a saucepan. Reduce heat to a simmer.
2. Dissolve the starch in a small amount of cold stock or water. Stir it into the simmering stock.
3. Simmer until thickened and clear.

Demi-Glace

U.S.	METRIC	INGREDIENTS
1 gal	4 L	Brown sauce (espagnole)
1 gal	4 L	Brown stock

PROCEDURE

1. Combine the sauce and stock in a saucepan and simmer until reduced by half.
2. Strain through a chinois (fine china cap) or a regular china cap lined with cheesecloth. Cover to prevent a skin from forming. Keep hot in a bain-marie, or cool in a cold-water bath for later use.

Per 1 fl oz (29.57 mL): Calories 25; Protein, 1 g; Fat 1.5 g (53% cal.); Cholesterol, 5 mg; Carbohydrates, 2 g; Fiber, 0 g; Sodium, 20 mg.

Small Sauces

For each of the following sauces, add the listed ingredients to *1 qt (1 L) demi-glace*, as indicated.

Bordelaise
Reduce by three-fourths 1 cup (250 mL) dry red wine, 2 oz (60 g) chopped shallots, ¼ tsp (1 mL) crushed peppercorns, a pinch of dried thyme, and ½ bay leaf. Add 1 qt (1 L) demi-glace, simmer 15 to 20 minutes, and strain. Swirl in 2 oz (60 g) raw butter, cut in pieces. Garnish with diced or sliced beef marrow poached in salted water.

Marchand de Vin (Wine Merchant)
Reduce 6 fl oz (200 mL) red wine and 2 oz (60 g) chopped shallots by three-fourths. Add 1 qt (1 L) demi-glace, simmer, and strain.

Robert
Cook 4 oz (125 g) chopped onion in butter without browning. Add 1 cup (250 mL) white wine and reduce by two-thirds. Add 1 qt (1 L) demi-glace and simmer 10 minutes. Strain and add 2 tsp (10 mL) dry mustard and a pinch of sugar dissolved in a little lemon juice.

Charcutière
Garnish Robert sauce with sour pickles, cut julienne.

Chasseur
Sauté 6 oz (175 g) sliced mushrooms and 2 oz (60 g) minced shallots in 2 oz (60 g) butter. Add 1 cup (250 mL) white wine and reduce by three-fourths. Add 1 qt (1 L) demi-glace and 8 oz (250 g) diced tomato. Simmer 5 minutes and add 2 tsp (10 mL) chopped parsley.

Diable (Deviled)
Reduce by two-thirds 8 fl oz (250 mL) white wine, 4 oz (125 g) chopped shallots, ½ tsp (2 mL) crushed peppercorns. Add 1 qt (1 L) demi-glace and simmer 20 minutes. Season with cayenne to taste and strain.

Madeira
Reduce 1 qt (1 L) demi-glace by about ½ cup (100 mL). Add 3 to 4 fl oz (100 mL) Madeira wine.

Périgueux
Garnish Madeira sauce with finely diced truffle.

Poîvrade
Brown 1 lb (500 g) mirepoix in butter. Add 4 fl oz (125 mL) red wine and 1½ pt (750 mL) Red Wine Marinade for Game and reduce by one-half. Add 1 qt (1 L) demi-glace and reduce by one-third over low heat. Add ½ tsp (2 mL) crushed peppercorns and simmer 10 minutes. Strain.

Port Wine
Follow instructions for Madeira sauce, but use port wine instead of Madeira.

Italian Sauce
Sauté 1 lb (500 g) finely chopped mushrooms and ½ oz (15 g) minced shallots in 2 oz (60 g) butter until all moisture is evaporated. Add 1 cup (250 mL) white wine and reduce by half. Add 1 oz (30 g) tomato paste and 1 qt (1 L) demi-glace and simmer 10 minutes. Add 2 tbsp (30 mL) chopped parsley.

Mushroom
Sauté 8 oz (250 g) sliced mushrooms and 1 oz (30 g) minced shallots in 2 oz (60 g) butter until browned. Add 1 qt (1 L) demi-glace and simmer about 10 minutes. Add 2 oz (60 mL) sherry and a few drops of lemon juice.

Bercy
Reduce by three-fourths 1 cup (250 mL) dry white wine and 4 oz (125 g) chopped shallots. Add 1 qt (1 L) demi-glace and simmer 10 minutes.

Piquante
Reduce by two-thirds 4 oz (125 g) minced shallots, 4 fl oz (125 mL) wine vinegar, and 4 fl oz (125 mL) white wine. Add 1 qt (1 L) demi-glace and simmer until slightly reduced. Add 2 oz (60 g) capers, 2 oz (60 g) sour pickles, cut brunoise, 1 tbsp (15 mL) chopped parsley, and ½ tsp (2 mL) dried tarragon.

Lyonnaise
Sauté 4 oz (125 g) onions in 2 oz (60 g) butter until slightly browned. Add ½ cup (125 mL) white wine vinegar and reduce by half. Add 1 qt (1 L) demi-glace and simmer 10 minutes.

Bigarade
Prepare a gastrique (p. 163) from 6 oz (180 g) sugar and 4 fl oz (125 mL) wine vinegar. Add 8 fl oz (250 mL) orange juice, 3 fl oz (90 mL) lemon juice, 1 qt (1 L) demi-glace, and, if available, juices from a roast duck. Simmer and reduce to desired consistency. Garnish with blanched julienne of orange zest.

Tomato Sauce

Classical tomato sauce, as explained by Escoffier, is made with a roux, but this is rarely done in modern kitchens. The texture of the puréed tomatoes is sufficient to give the sauce the proper texture, even when no starch thickener is used.

This type of sauce may be referred to as a *coulis* (koo-lee). This French term means, in modern kitchens, a purée of vegetables or fruits, used as a sauce. A recipe for another coulis, of sweet peppers, is found on page 179.

Three main techniques are used to purée vegetables and other ingredients for coulis:

1. Puréeing the product in a food processor or blender
2. Passing the product through a food mill
3. Forcing the product through a fine sieve

Of these three methods, the third, forcing through a fine sieve, usually makes the smoothest purée, but it is also the most time-consuming. If you want a smooth purée but the product is difficult to force through a sieve, you can use one of the other methods first, then pass the purée through the sieve to make it smoother.

Tomato Sauce I

YIELD: 1 GAL (4 L)

U.S.	METRIC	INGREDIENTS	PROCEDURE
4 oz	125 g	Salt pork	1. Render the salt pork in a heavy saucepot, but do not brown it.
8 oz	250 g	Onion, medium dice	2. Add the onion and carrots and sauté until slightly softened, but do not brown.
8 oz	250 g	Carrots, medium dice	3. Add the tomatoes and their juice, tomato purée, bones, and sachet. Bring to a boil, reduce heat, and simmer over very low heat (see Note) 1½–2 hours, or until reduced to desired consistency.
4 qt	4 L	Tomatoes, canned or fresh, coarsely chopped	
2 qt	2 L	Tomato purée, canned	4. Remove sachet and bones. Strain sauce or pass it through a food mill.
1 lb	500 g	Ham bones or browned pork bones	5. Adjust seasoning with salt and a little sugar.
		Sachet:	
2 cloves	2 cloves	Garlic, crushed	
1	1	Bay leaf	
¼ tsp	1 mL	Dried thyme	
¼ tsp	1 mL	Dried rosemary	
¼ tsp	1 mL	Peppercorns, crushed	
to taste	to taste	Salt	
to taste	to taste	Sugar	

Per 1 fl oz (29.57 mL): Calories, 20; Protein, 1 g; Fat, 1 g (35% cal.); Cholesterol, 0 mg; Carbohydrates, 3 g; Fiber, 1 g; Sodium, 120 mg.

Note: Tomato sauce scorches easily, so heat must be very low. The sauce may be cooked in a slow oven (300°F/150°C), loosely covered, to reduce the danger of scorching.

VARIATION

Tomato Sauce II (Vegetarian)

Omit the salt pork. Sweat the vegetables in 2 fl oz (60 mL) olive oil. Omit bones.

Tomato Sauce III

See Italian Tomato Sauce for Pasta, page 372.

Small Sauces

For each of the following sauces, add the listed ingredients to *1 qt (1 L) tomato sauce,* as indicated.

Portugaise (Portuguese)

Sauté 4 oz (125 g) onions, cut brunoise, in 1 fl oz (30 mL) oil. Add
1 lb (500 g) tomato concassé (see p. 267) and 1 tsp (5 mL) crushed garlic. Simmer
until reduced by about one-third. Add 1 qt (1 L) tomato sauce, adjust seasonings,
and add 2–4 tbsp (30–60 mL) chopped parsley.

Spanish

Lightly sauté in oil without browning 6 oz (175 g) onion, small dice;
4 oz (125 g) green bell pepper, small dice; and 1 clove garlic, chopped fine. Add 4
oz (125 g) sliced mushrooms and sauté.
Add 1 qt (1 L) tomato sauce, and season to taste with salt, pepper, and hot red
pepper sauce.

Creole

Sauté in oil 4 oz (125 g) onion, small dice; 4 oz (125 g) celery, sliced; 2 oz
(60 g) green bell pepper, small dice; 1 tsp (5 mL) chopped garlic. Add 1 qt
(1 L) tomato sauce, 1 bay leaf, pinch dried thyme, and ½ tsp (2 mL) grated lemon rind.
Simmer 15 minutes. Remove bay leaf and season to taste with salt, pepper, and
cayenne.

Fresh Tomato Coulis with Garlic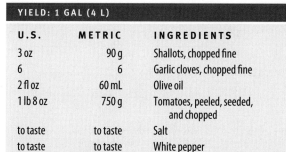

YIELD: 1 GAL (4 L)

U.S.	METRIC	INGREDIENTS	PROCEDURE
3 oz	90 g	Shallots, chopped fine	1. Sweat the shallots and garlic in olive oil until soft.
6	6	Garlic cloves, chopped fine	2. Add the tomatoes and cook until excess liquid has cooked out and the sauce is thick.
2 fl oz	60 mL	Olive oil	3. Season to taste.
1 lb 8 oz	750 g	Tomatoes, peeled, seeded, and chopped	
to taste	to taste	Salt	
to taste	to taste	White pepper	

Per 1 fl oz (29.57 mL): Calories, 45; Protein 1 g; Fat, 3.5 g (66% cal.);
Cholesterol, 0 mg; Carbohydrates, 3 g; Fiber,1 g; Sodium, 5 mg.

Butter Sauces

The fifth leading sauce is hollandaise. Hollandaise and its cousin, béarnaise, are unlike the
sauces we have been studying because their major ingredient is not stock or milk but butter.

Before tackling the complexities of hollandaise, we first look at simpler butter preparations used as sauces.

1. **Melted butter.**

   This is the simplest butter preparation of all, and one of the most widely used, especially as a dressing for vegetables.

   Unsalted or sweet butter has the freshest taste and is ideal for all sauce-making.

2. **Clarified butter.**

   Butter consists of butterfat, water, and milk solids. *Clarified butter* is purified butterfat, with water and milk solids removed (see Figure 7.13). It is necessary for many cooking
   operations. Clarified butter is used in sautéing because the milk solids of unclarified
   butter would burn at such high temperatures. It is used in making hollandaise because
   the water of unclarified butter would change the consistency of the sauce.

3. **Brown butter.**

   Known as *beurre noisette* (burr nwah zett) in French, this is whole melted butter that
   has been heated until it turns light brown and gives off a nutty aroma. It is usually prepared at the last minute and served over fish, white meats, eggs, and vegetables.

Care must be taken not to burn the butter, as the heat of the pan will continue to brown it even after it is removed from the fire.

4. **Black butter.**

Black butter, or *beurre noir* (burr nwahr), is made like brown butter but heated until it is a little darker, and it is flavored with a few drops of vinegar. Capers, chopped parsley, or both are sometimes added.

To avoid dangerous spattering of the vinegar in the hot butter, many chefs pour the butter over the food item, then deglaze the pan with the vinegar and pour that over the item.

5. **Meunière butter.**

This is served with fish cooked à la Meunière. Brown butter is seasoned with lemon juice and poured over the fish, which has been sprinkled with chopped parsley.

As in the case of black butter, dangerous spattering can result when moisture is added to hot butter. To avoid this, cooks often sprinkle the lemon juice directly on the fish before pouring on the brown butter.

Procedure for Clarifying Butter

Method 1

1. Melt the butter in a heavy saucepan over moderate heat.
2. Skim the froth from the surface.
3. Carefully pour off the clear melted butter into another container, leaving the milky liquid at the bottom of the saucepan.

Method 2

1. Melt the butter in a heavy saucepan over moderate heat.
2. Skim the froth from the surface.
3. Leave the pan on the heat and continue to skim the froth from the surface at intervals. The water in the bottom will boil and gradually evaporate.
4. When the butter looks clear and no longer forms a scum on top, strain off the butter through cheesecloth into another container.

You need 1¼ lb (625 g) raw butter to make 1 lb (500 g) clarified butter; 1 lb (500 g) raw butter yields 12 to 13 oz (about 400 g) clarified butter.

Figure 7.13 Clarifying butter.

(a) Skim the foam from the top of the melted butter.

(b) Ladle off the clear, melted fat.

(c) Continue until only the milky liquid remains in the bottom of the pan.

6. **Compound butters.**

Compound butters are made by softening raw butter and mixing it with flavoring ingredients. The mixture is then rolled into a cylinder in waxed paper.

Compound butters have two main uses:

- Slices of the firm butter are placed on hot grilled items at service time. The butter melts over the item and sauces it.

- Small portions are swirled into sauces to finish them and give them a desired flavor.

Easy as they are to make, compound butters can transform a plain broiled steak into a truly special dish.

The favorite compound butter for steaks is maître d'hôtel (may truh doh tel) butter. Variations are given after the recipe (p. 170).

7. Beurre blanc.

Beurre blanc (burr blon) is a sauce made by whipping a large quantity of raw butter into a small quantity of a flavorful reduction of white wine and vinegar so the butter melts and forms an emulsion with the reduction. The technique is basically the same as monter au beurre (p. 155), except the proportion of butter to liquid is much greater.

Beurre blanc can be made quickly and easily by adding cold butter all at once and whipping vigorously over moderately high heat. The temperature of the butter keeps the sauce cool enough to prevent it from separating. Be sure to remove it from the heat before all the butter is melted, and continue whipping. It is better to remove the sauce from the heat too soon rather than too late because it can always be rewarmed slightly if necessary. Figure 7.14 illustrates this procedure.

Some chefs prefer to use low heat and add the butter a little at a time in order to reduce the chance of overheating and breaking the sauce. The process takes a little longer, but the result is the same.

Figure 7.14 Preparing beurre blanc.

(a) Reduce the liquids (usually wine and vinegar) with chopped shallots.

(b) Whip in the raw butter just until the butter is melted and forms a smooth sauce.

(c) Leave in the shallots, or strain them out. Strained beurre blanc has a light, smooth, creamy texture.

Beurre blanc should be held at a warm, not a hot, temperature and stirred or whipped from time to time so the fat and water do not separate. For more stable mixtures of fat and water—called *emulsions*—see the discussion of hollandaise beginning on page 171.

BUTTER-ENRICHED SAUCES

As already noted, the technique for making beurre blanc is the same as monter au beurre, except the proportion of butter is much higher. The same technique can be used to finish a great variety of sauces, usually white sauces, although brown sauces can be finished the same way.

To improvise a butter-enriched version of a classic white sauce, refer to the sauce variations on page 162. In place of the 1 qt (1 L) velouté or other white sauce base, substitute 1 pt (500 mL) concentrated white stock. Combine with the flavoring ingredients indicated in the variation. Reduce to a slightly syrupy consistency. Whip in 8 oz (250 g) raw butter and strain.

Many other sauces for sautéed meat, poultry, or fish items can be improvised using the same technique. Deglaze the sauté pan with wine, stock, or other liquid, add desired flavoring ingredients, reduce, and finish by whipping in a generous quantity of raw butter. Season and strain.

Maître d'Hôtel Butter

YIELD: APPROX. 1 LB (500 G)

U.S.	METRIC	INGREDIENTS
1 lb	500 g	Butter, unsalted (see Note)
2 oz	60 g	Chopped parsley
1½ fl oz	50 mL	Lemon juice
2 tsp	10 mL	Salt (see Note)
pinch	pinch	White pepper

PROCEDURE

1. Using a mixer with the paddle attachment, beat the butter at low speed until smooth and creamy.
2. Add remaining ingredients and beat slowly until completely mixed.
3. Roll the butter into a cylinder about 1 inch (2½ cm) thick in a sheet of parchment or waxed paper. Chill until firm.
4. To serve, cut slices ¼ inch (½ cm) thick and place on broiled or grilled items just before service.

Per 1 ounce (28.35g): Calories, 230; Protein 0 g; Fat, 25 g (98% cal.); Cholesterol, 70 mg; Carbohydrates, 1 g; Fiber, 0 g; Sodium, 300 mg.

Note: If using salted butter, omit the salt.

VARIATIONS

For each kind of seasoned butter, add to *1 lb (500 g) butter* the listed ingredients instead of the parsley, lemon juice, and pepper.

Anchovy Butter
2 oz (60 g) anchovy fillets, mashed to a paste

Garlic Butter
1 oz (30 g) garlic, mashed to a paste (see p. 257)

Escargot (Snail) Butter
Maître d'Hôtel Butter plus 1 oz (30 g) garlic, mashed to a paste

Shrimp Butter
½ lb (250 g) cooked shrimp and shells, ground very fine. Force shrimp butter through a fine sieve to remove pieces of shell.

Mustard Butter
3–4 oz (100 g) Dijon-style mustard

Herb Butter
Chopped fresh herbs to taste

Scallion or Shallot Butter
2 oz (60 g) minced scallions or shallots

Curry Butter
4–6 tsp (20–30 mL) curry powder heated gently with 1 oz (30 g) butter, then cooled

Beurre Blanc

YIELD: 1 PT (500 ML)

U.S.	METRIC	INGREDIENTS
8 fl oz	250 mL	Dry white wine
1½ fl oz	50 mL	White wine vinegar
1 oz	30 g	Shallots, chopped
1 lb	500 g	Cold butter
to taste	to taste	Salt

PROCEDURE

1. Combine wine, vinegar, and shallots in a saucepan. Reduce until about 1 fl oz (30 mL) liquid remains.
2. Cut the butter into small pieces.
3. Add the butter to the hot reduction. Set pan over moderately high heat and whip vigorously. When butter is nearly all melted and incorporated, remove from heat and continue to whip until smooth.
4. Season to taste. Shallots may be left in sauce or strained out.
5. Hold the sauce in a warm, not hot, place until served. Stir or whip it from time to time.

Per 1 fl oz (29.57 mL): Calories, 210; Protein, 0 g; Fat, 23 g (94% cal.); Cholesterol, 60 mg; Carbohydrates, 1 g; Fiber, 0 g; Sodium, 240 mg.

VARIATIONS

Herbed Butter Sauce
Add your choice of chopped fresh herbs to finished beurre blanc, or use an herbed compound butter instead of plain raw butter to make beurre blanc.

Beurre Rouge for Fish
After reducing red wine for Beurre Rouge (following), add 6 fl oz (180 ml) fish stock. Reduce the liquid to 2 fl oz (60 ml).

Beurre Rouge (Red Butter Sauce)
Use dry red wine instead of white wine to make the reduction, and increase the quantity of wine to 1 pt (500 mL). As in basic recipe, reduce the wine to about 1 fl oz. (30 ml). For good color, use a young, bright red wine.

Hollandaise and Béarnaise

Hollandaise is considered an egg-thickened sauce, but the egg doesn't thicken by coagulation as it does in a liaison or in a custard sauce. Instead, it works by emulsification.

An *emulsion* is a uniform mixture of two unmixable liquids. In the case of hollandaise, the two liquids are melted butter and water (including the water in the lemon juice or the vinegar reduction). The two stay mixed and thick because the butter is beaten into tiny droplets and the egg yolks hold the droplets apart. You will encounter emulsion again when you prepare mayonnaise and other salad dressings in Chapter 14.

Two recipes for hollandaise are given. The first is the classic version, flavored with lemon and a vinegar reduction (see Figure 7.15). (You may also see recipes that include shallots in the reduction, in imitation of beurre blanc, but this is not traditional, according to Escoffier.) The second recipe, flavored with just lemon juice, is slightly quicker and easier to make.

Figure 7.15 Making hollandaise sauce.

(a) Combine the egg yolks and reduction in a stainless-steel bowl.

(b) Whip over a hot-water bath.

(c) Continue to whip over a hot water until thick and light.

(d) Very slowly whip in the butter. (Set the bowl in a saucepan lined with a kitchen towel to hold it steady.)

(e) The finished sauce should be thick but pourable.

HOLDING HOLLANDAISE SAUCE

Hollandaise sauce, as well as other sauces in this family, poses a special safety problem. It must be kept warm for service, but it must be held below 140°F (60°C) so the eggs don't curdle. Unfortunately, bacteria grow quickly in this temperature range. Therefore, extra care must be taken to avoid food-borne diseases.

The following sanitation procedures must be observed to avoid the danger of food poisoning:

1. Make sure all equipment is perfectly clean.

2. Hold sauce no longer than 1½ hours. Make only enough to serve in this time, and discard any that is left over.

3. Never mix an old batch of sauce with a new batch.

4. Never hold hollandaise or béarnaise—or any other acid product—in aluminum. Use stainless-steel containers.

Guidelines for Preparing Hollandaise and Béarnaise

Students tend to be afraid of hollandaise because it has a reputation for being difficult to make. True, precautions are necessary to avoid over-cooking the eggs and to get the right consistency. But if you follow the instructions in the recipe carefully and keep in mind these guidelines, you should have no trouble.

Many of these rules have one object in common: Don't overcook the egg yolks, or they will lose their ability to emulsify.

1. **Cool the reduction before adding the yolks, or they will overcook.**

2. **Use the freshest eggs possible for the best emulsification.**
   For safety, pasteurized eggs are recommended.

3. **Beat the yolks over hot water.**
   An experienced cook is able to beat them over direct heat, if care is taken, without making scrambled eggs. Until you have gained some confidence, it is safer to use a hot-water bain-marie.

4. **Use a round-bottomed stainless-steel bowl.**
   The whip must be able to reach all the eggs to beat them evenly. Also, stainless steel will not discolor the sauce or give it a metallic flavor.

5. **Have the butter warm but not hot, or it may overcook the eggs. If it is too cool, it might solidify.**

6. **Add the butter slowly at first.**
   The yolks can absorb only a little at a time. Add a few drops at first and beat in thoroughly before adding more. If you add butter faster than it can be absorbed, the emulsion may break.

7. **Don't add more butter than the egg yolks can hold.**
   Remember this standard proportion:

   6 egg yolks per 1 pound (450 g) clarified butter

8. **Broken or curdled hollandaise can be rescued.**
   First, try adding 1 teaspoon (5 mL) cold water and beating vigorously. If this doesn't work, start over with a couple of egg yolks and repeat the procedure from step 6 in the recipe, adding the broken sauce as you would the butter.

Hollandaise Sauce 1

YIELD: 1 QT (1 L)

U.S.	METRIC	INGREDIENTS	PROCEDURE
2½ lb	1125 g	Butter	1. Review guidelines for preparing hollandaise and béarnaise (above). 2. Clarify the butter (see p. 168). You should have about 2 lb (900 g) clarified butter. Keep the butter warm but not hot.
¼ tsp	1 mL	Peppercorns, crushed	3. Combine peppercorns, salt, and vinegar in a saucepan and reduce until nearly dry (au sec). Remove from heat and add the cold water.
¼ tsp	1 mL	Salt	
6 fl oz	175 mL	White vinegar or wine vinegar	4. Pass the diluted reduction through a fine strainer into a stainless-steel bowl. Use a clean rubber spatula to make sure you transfer all flavoring material to bowl.
4 fl oz	120 mL	Water, cold	
12	12	Egg yolks (see Note after Hollandaise II)	5. Add the egg yolks to bowl and beat well. 6. Hold the bowl over a hot-water bath and continue to beat the yolks until thickened and creamy.
2–4 tbsp	30–60 mL	Lemon juice	7. Remove the bowl from the heat. Using a ladle, slowly and gradually beat in warm clarified butter, drop by drop at first. If the sauce becomes too thick to beat before all the butter is added, beat in a little lemon juice.
to taste	to taste	Salt	
to taste	to taste	Cayenne	8. When all the butter is added, beat in lemon juice to taste and adjust seasoning with salt and cayenne. If necessary, thin the sauce with a few drops of warm water.

Per 1 fl oz (29.57 mL): Calories, 280; Protein, 1 g; Fat, 31 g (99% cal.); Cholesterol, 155 mg; Carbohydrates, 0 g; Fiber, 0 g; Sodium, 310 mg.

9. Strain through cheesecloth if necessary and keep warm (not hot) for service. Hold no longer than 1½ hours (see above).

Hollandaise Sauce II

YIELD: 1 QT (1 L)

U.S.	METRIC	INGREDIENTS
2½ lb	1125 g	Butter
12	12	Egg yolks (see Note)
2 fl oz	60 mL	Water, cold
3 fl oz	100 mL	Lemon juice
to taste	to taste	Salt
to taste	to taste	Cayenne

PROCEDURE

1. Review guidelines for preparing hollandaise and béarnaise (p. 172).
2. Clarify the butter (see p. 168). You should have about *2 lb (900 g) clarified butter*. Keep the butter warm but not hot.
3. Place the egg yolks and cold water in a stainless-steel bowl and beat well. Beat in a few drops of lemon juice.
4. Hold the bowl over a hot-water bath and continue to beat until the yolks are thickened and creamy.
5. Remove the bowl from the heat. Using a ladle, slowly and gradually beat in the warm butter, drop by drop at first. If the sauce becomes too thick to beat before all the butter is added, beat in a little of the lemon juice.
6. When the butter is all added, beat in lemon juice to taste and adjust seasoning with salt and cayenne. If necessary, thin the sauce with a few drops of warm water.
7. Keep warm (not hot) for service. Hold no longer than 1½ hours (see p. 171).

Per 1 fl oz (29.57 mL): Calories, 280; Protein, 1 g; Fat, 31 g (99% cal.); Cholesterol, 155 mg; Carbohydrates, 0 g; Fiber, 0 g; Sodium, 300 mg.

Note: For safety, pasteurized eggs are recommended.

Small Sauces

Maltaise

To 1 qt (1 L) hollandaise add 2–4 fl oz (60–125 mL) orange juice (from blood oranges, if possible) and 2 tsp (10 mL) grated orange rind. Serve with asparagus.

Mousseline

Whip 1 cup (250 mL) heavy cream until stiff and fold into 1 qt (1 L) hollandaise.

Béarnaise Sauce

YIELD: 1 QT (1 L)

U.S.	METRIC	INGREDIENTS
2½ lb	1125 g	Butter
2 oz	60 g	Shallots, chopped
1 cup	250 mL	White wine vinegar
2 tsp	10 mL	Dried tarragon
1 tsp	5 mL	Peppercorns, crushed
12	12	Egg yolks (see Note)
to taste	to taste	Salt
to taste	to taste	Cayenne
to taste	to taste	Lemon juice
2 tbsp	30 mL	Chopped parsley
1 tsp	5 mL	Dried tarragon

PROCEDURE

1. Review guidelines for preparing hollandaise and béarnaise (p. 172).
2. Clarify the butter (see p. 168). You should have about *2 lb (900 g) clarified butter*. Keep the butter warm but not hot.
3. Combine the shallots, vinegar, tarragon, and peppercorns in a saucepan and reduce by three-fourths. Remove from heat and cool slightly.
4. To make it easier to beat with a wire whip, transfer the reduction to a stainless-steel bowl. Use a clean rubber spatula to make sure you get it all. Let the reduction cool a little.
5. Add the egg yolks to the bowl and beat well.
6. Hold the bowl over a hot-water bath and continue to beat the yolks until thickened and creamy.
7. Remove the bowl from the heat. Using a ladle, slowly and gradually beat in the warm clarified butter, drop by drop at first. If the sauce becomes too thick to beat before all the butter is added, beat in a little lemon juice or warm water.
8. Strain the sauce through cheesecloth.
9. Season to taste with salt, cayenne, and a few drops of lemon juice. Mix in the parsley and tarragon.
10. Keep warm (not hot) for service. Hold no longer than 1½ hours (see p. 171).

Per 1 fl oz (29.57 mL): Calories, 280; Protein, 1 g; Fat, 31 g (97% cal.); Cholesterol, 155 mg; Carbohydrates, 1 g; Fiber, 0 g; Sodium, 300 mg.

Note: For safety, pasteurized eggs are recommended.

Small Sauces

Foyot
Add 2 oz (60 g) melted meat glaze (glace de viande) to 1 qt (1 L) béarnaise.

Choron
Add 2 oz (60 g) tomato paste to 1 qt (1 L) béarnaise.

KEY POINTS TO REVIEW

- What are the five leading sauces (also called mother sauces and grand sauces)? Describe the procedure for making each one.

- What is a small sauce?

- What is clarified butter? How is it made? What is it used for?

- What is beurre noisette?

- What is a compound butter?

- What is the procedure for making beurre blanc?

Pan Gravies and Other Integral Sauces

An *integral sauce* is a sauce based on the juices released during the cooking of a meat, poultry, fish, or vegetable item. Most of the sauces we have discussed so far are not integral sauces—that is, they are made separately from and independently of the items they are served with. An integral sauce, on the other hand, can't be made separately because it incorporates cooking juices from the item it is served with.

The most important technique required for integral sauces is deglazing (see pp. 150 and 154). Juices released by sautéed and roasted meats are reduced and caramelized in the bottom of the pan during cooking. Deglazing dissolves these caramelized juices and incorporates them into the desired sauce. For the simplest example, if you sauté a chicken breast and then deglaze the sauté pan with a little stock and season the resulting liquid, you end up with an integral sauce that can be served with the chicken.

The most basic and familiar integral sauces are pan gravy and jus. *Pan gravy* is a sauce made with the juices or drippings of the meat or poultry with which it is being served. Standard pan gravies are similar to brown sauces. Instead of being made with espagnole or demi-glace as a base, however, they are made from pan drippings plus roux plus stock or water and, sometimes, milk or cream.

Jus (zhoo) refers to unthickened juices from a roast. When the roast is served with these clear, natural juices, it is said to be served *au jus* (oh zhoo), meaning "with juice." Stock is usually added to the pan juices to obtain enough quantity to serve.

The preparation of both pan gravy and jus are properly part of meat cookery, and recipes and detailed procedures are included in the meat and poultry chapters. Similarly, recipes for all integral sauces are included as part of the meat, fish, or vegetable in the appropriate chapters.

Now that you have studied sauce-making in detail, read the general procedure for making pan gravies on page 175 so you can see how similar it is to making brown sauce and how the same techniques you have just learned are applied to a different product.

Modern Sauces

As suggested in the introduction to this chapter, sauce-making has changed a great deal since Escoffier's day. Although our basic methods for making many of the sauces in the modern kitchen are derived from classical cuisine, details have changed. Perhaps the most important

Basic Procedure for Making Pan Gravy

Method 2 has fewer steps, but Method 1 is actually quicker for large quantities and gives greater control over final consistency.

Method 1

1. **Remove the roast from the roasting pan.**
   If you did not add mirepoix to the pan during roasting, you can do so now.

2. **Clarify the fat.**
   Set the roasting pan over high heat and cook until all the moisture has evaporated, leaving only the fat, mirepoix, and the brown (caramelized) drippings. Pour off and save the fat.

3. **Deglaze the pan.**
   Pour stock or other liquid into the roasting pan. Stir over heat until the caramelized drippings are dissolved.

4. **Combine with stock and simmer.**
   Pour the deglazing liquid, plus mirepoix, into a large pot with desired amount of stock. Simmer until mirepoix is well cooked. Skim the surface well to remove fat and scum.

5. **Make a roux or, alternatively, a slurry of arrowroot or cornstarch and water.**
   For roux, measure enough of the fat from step 2 to make the correct amount of roux for the volume of gravy. Make a blond or brown roux, as desired. For starch slurry, see page 148.

6. **Thicken the gravy with the roux or starch slurry.**

7. **Strain.**

8. **Adjust seasonings.**

Method 2

1. Remove the roast from the roasting pan.

2. Clarify the fat.

3. Add flour to the roasting pan and make a roux.

4. Add stock. Stir until thickened and the pan is deglazed.

5. Strain. Skim excess fat.

6. Adjust consistency, if necessary, with more stock or more roux.

7. Season.

change is that chefs rely less on roux for thickening a sauce, while reduction has become more important to give sauces body (see pp. 153–154). When starches are used, they are often purer starches, such as arrowroot.

Chefs have also been influenced by other cuisines, such as those of Asia and Latin America, and have borrowed ingredients and procedures from many countries and regions to give variety to their repertoire of sauces.

Because of the ongoing experimentation with and development of new sauces, it is difficult to classify and define them exactly, the way Escoffier did in the last century. We can, however, describe general groups that many of today's popular sauces fall into. The remaining recipes in this chapter include examples of these types of sauces.

A number of other popular sauces, such as barbecue sauce, that don't fit into any of the categories described in the following sections, are included in this chapter. Other sauce recipes are included elsewhere in this book, often as components of other recipes. Among the more important of these are vinaigrette and mayonnaise variations. These are traditionally used as salad dressings but are also used as sauces for meat, seafood, and vegetable items.

BROTHS AND JUS

Beginning with the introduction of nouvelle cuisine in the 1970s, chefs looked for ways to eliminate starch thickeners in sauces in order to make them lighter. The technique of reduction to concentrate a sauce has been the most important tool in this effort. Reduction hasn't been a cure-all, however. First, some of the fresher, lighter flavors of a sauce are lost when a liquid is subjected to the long cooking required for reduction. In addition, reduced sauces sometimes become so gelatinous that they solidify when they cool—not an appetizing result.

Nevertheless, we have become accustomed to sauces that do not cling thickly to the meat, poultry, or seafood. Sauces, often in smaller quantities, are served under or around the item as often as over the top of it, perhaps even more often. Some chefs have gone to the extreme of serving the item in a little broth in place of a sauce. This technique has long been popular with seafood, but it is becoming more common with meat as well. The result is often something like a garnished consommé (pp. 196–197), but with very little consommé and a full portion of meat and garnish.

For a broth to work well as a substitute for a sauce, it should be well flavored and aromatic. Taste the broth, reduce it as necessary to concentrate the flavor, and check the seasonings carefully.

A jus is very much like a broth except it is usually more concentrated, although still unthickened. The term *jus* has two basic meanings:

1. The unthickened, natural juices resulting from a roast. This is the more traditional meaning of *jus* (see p. 174). To make a traditional jus, the drippings of a roast are deglazed with stock or other liquid, reduced slightly, seasoned, strained, and served unthickened.

   To make a meat jus without a roast, follow the procedure below.

2. An unthickened liquid carrying the concentrated flavor of a specific ingredient. This type of jus is often made from vegetables and is sometimes called an *essence*. To make a vegetable essence, the vegetable is simmered with a stock or broth until the liquid is concentrated and flavorful. The recipe for Mushroom Jus (p. 179, also called *mushroom essence*) is an example of this type of preparation.

Procedure for Making a Meat Jus

1. Cut trimmings of the desired meat or poultry product into small pieces. Place them in a heavy pot over moderate heat.
2. Cook until well browned on all sides. Some liquid will be released from the meat. If the trimmings begin to simmer in these juices instead of browning, just let them continue to cook until the liquid has evaporated and browned on the bottom of the pot.
3. Deglaze with a small quantity of white wine or stock. Continue to cook until the liquid is reduced and the juices again caramelize on the bottom.
4. Add enough stock to cover the meat. Stir to dissolve the caramelized juices on the bottom of the pot. Simmer until the liquid is completely reduced and caramelized.
5. Again add enough stock to cover the meat. Stir to dissolve the caramelized juices. Simmer 10 to 15 minutes. Strain and degrease.

PURÉES

Vegetable purées have long been used as sauces. Tomato sauce is the classic example. However, nearly any vegetable can be puréed and used as a sauce, provided it is flavorful, properly seasoned, and of an appropriate consistency or thickness. A vegetable purée is sometimes called a *coulis*.

Purées of starchy vegetables, such as squash or dried beans, may need to be thinned with stock, broth, or water. Even potato purée is sometimes thinned and used as a sauce, usually enriched with a little raw butter stirred in. In addition, potato and other thick purées are used as thickeners for other sauces.

Some vegetables, such as asparagus, make a watery purée. These purées can be reduced to thicken them, but be careful not to lose the fresh vegetable taste and color. This should especially be avoided in the case of green vegetables, which quickly lose their color (see p. 243). Although thin vegetable purées may be thickened with a starch, it is more common to leave them thin or to bind them lightly by finishing them with raw butter (monter au beurre, p. 154) or by reducing them with a little cream until they have the desired consistency.

CREAM REDUCTIONS

In the era of nouvelle cuisine, sauces based on reduced cream became a popular substitute for roux-thickened white sauces. When heavy cream is reduced, it thickens slightly. A common fault with cream reduction sauces is reducing the cream too much, giving it a heavy texture. If it is reduced beyond this point, it is likely to break, and the butterfat will separate. For an appealing, light texture, reduce the cream until it is about two-thirds its original volume.

A reduced cream sauce is a mixture of reduced cream and a concentrated, flavorful stock. White stock is most often used, although brown cream sauces may also be prepared using brown stock. For good results, the stock should be reduced by about three-fourths. Flavored sauces can be made by reducing the stock with flavoring ingredients, as in the recipe for Chipotle Cream Sauce on page 181.

Two methods are possible:

1. Reducing the cream to the desired consistency and then adding it to the stock reduction.

2. Adding fresh cream to the stock reduction and reducing the mixture to the desired consistency.

Many chefs feel the first method is more controllable. See the following procedure:

Procedure for Making a Cream Reduction Sauce

1. Reduce white stock or brown stock by about three-fourths, or until it is concentrated and flavorful.

2. Measure the reduction. For each 1 pint (500 mL) reduction, measure about 1½ pints (750 mL) heavy cream.

3. Place the cream in a heavy saucepan over moderate heat and reduce until lightly thickened, or until reduced by about one-third. Stir from time to time with a whip.

4. Bring the stock reduction to a simmer in a saucepan. Stir in the reduced cream.

5. Check the consistency. Thicken, if necessary, by reducing further, or thin with additional heavy cream.

6. Season and strain.

SALSAS, RELISHES, AND CHUTNEYS

It is said that, in the United States, salsa has become even more popular than ketchup. The salsa referred to is, of course, the Mexican mixture of chopped tomatoes, onions, chiles, herbs, and other ingredients. *Salsa* is actually the Spanish and the Italian word for "sauce," so the word refers to many types of preparations, both raw and cooked, not just this one Mexican relish. Nevertheless, in English-speaking countries, the word *salsa* usually refers to a mixture of raw or cooked chopped vegetables, herbs, and, occasionally, fruits.

Salsas are easily improvised. Select a suitable mixture of vegetables, fruits, or both, and chop coarsely or finely, as desired. Mix with appropriate chopped fresh herbs and season to taste. Salt draws juices out of the ingredients to provide moisture for the mixture. Add citrus juice or vinegar if the mixture is lacking in acidity. Acidity should balance any sweetness from fruits because salsas are usually intended for savory dishes, not desserts.

The words *relish* and *chutney* have no exact definitions. One meaning of *relish* is any raw or pickled vegetable used as an appetizer. For example, a dish of celery sticks, carrot sticks, and olives is sometimes called a *relish dish*, for many years a traditional appetizer in steakhouses and other restaurants. As used in a discussion of sauces, a *relish* is a mixture of chopped vegetables (and sometimes fruits), at least one of which is pickled in vinegar or a salt solution. By this definition, a salsa may be considered a type of relish, especially if it contains an acid such as vinegar or citrus juice.

The word *chutney* originated in India, where it refers to several types of spicy condiments or relishes, including strongly spiced sweet-and-sour cooked fruit or vegetable mixtures, as well as raw or partially cooked mixtures of chopped herbs or vegetables, also spicy and often containing chiles. Almost all chutneys contain an acid ingredient. Western cooks have been especially inspired by the sweet-and-sour types of chutney, so when the word *chutney* appears on a menu, it usually refers to a cooked fruit or vegetable condiment that is sweet, spicy, and tangy.

Several examples of salsas, relishes, and chutneys are included in this chapter.

ASIAN SAUCES

Sauces from many Asian cuisines, including Japanese, Thai, Vietnamese, and Indian, have entered the Western cook's repertoire in recent years. Asia is, of course, a huge continent, and it would take years of study to become familiar with all its varied cooking traditions. This chapter can only begin that familiarization process by providing a selection of popular recipes with sidebars containing background information on ingredients and techniques.

Incidentally, Chinese cuisines have relatively few standalone sauces. Sauces in stir-fried dishes, for example, are made as part of the cooking process by adding liquids and thickeners to the meat and vegetables as they cook. Ready-made condiments such as oyster sauce and hoisin sauce are also used.

When adopting Asian-style sauces into Western cuisine, cooks should have some familiarity with the regional cuisine they are borrowing from and how the sauces are used in that cuisine. Unless the cook is careful, mixing Asian-style sauces with Western dishes can have strange results.

FLAVORED OILS

Flavored oils make a light, interesting alternative to vinaigrettes and other sauces when used to dress a wide variety of dishes. They are especially suitable for simple steamed, sautéed, or grilled items, but they can be used with cold foods as well. When used as a sauce, the oil is usually drizzled around or, sometimes, over the item on the plate. A tablespoon (15 mL) or so per portion is often enough.

The simplest way to flavor an oil is simply to put some of the flavoring ingredient in the oil and let it stand until the oil has taken on enough of the flavor. For most flavorings, however, this is not the best way to extract the most flavor. The flavoring ingredient may need some kind of preparation before adding it to the oil. For example, dry spices develop more flavor if they are first heated gently with a little bit of the oil.

Refrigerating flavored oils is recommended. Botulism is caused by a kind of bacteria that grows in the absence of air. Because oil prevents air from reaching the flavoring ingredients, if any botulism bacteria are present in the flavorings (especially possible with fresh, raw roots), those bacteria could grow while covered with oil if not refrigerated.

The procedure below outlines the basic method for making flavored oils, depending on the type of ingredients. Unless otherwise indicated, use a mild or flavorless oil, such as safflower, canola, corn, or grapeseed. In some cases, as with garlic, the flavoring goes well with olive oil, but usually the goal is to have the pure taste of the flavoring ingredient unmasked by the flavor of the oil.

MOLECULAR GASTRONOMY

As you read in the discussion of molecular gastronomy on page 7, chefs at the forefront of modern cuisine are exploring and inventing new techniques in food preparation and presentation.

Procedure for Making Flavored Oils

1. Prepare the flavoring ingredient in one of the following ways:

    Chop fresh roots (such as horseradish, garlic, shallots, ginger, garlic) or strong herbs (fresh rosemary, sage, thyme, oregano) by hand or in a food processor.

    Grate citrus zests.

    Blanch tender herbs (parsley, basil, tarragon, chervil, cilantro) in boiling water for 10 seconds. Drain immediately and refresh under cold water. Dry well.

    Gently heat dried, ground spices (cinnamon, cumin, curry powder, ginger, mustard, paprika) in a small amount of oil just until they start to give off an aroma.

2. Place the flavoring ingredient in a jar or other closable container. Add oil.

3. Close the jar and shake it well. Let stand 30 minutes at room temperature, then refrigerate.

4. The oil is ready to use as soon as it has taken on the desired flavor, which may be as soon as 1 hour, depending on the ingredient. After 2 days, strain the oil through a chinois lined with a paper coffee filter. Store in the refrigerator.

One category of new techniques is the use of nontraditional thickeners or binding agents for sauces. To give you a taste of a few of these techniques, the end of the chapter features several unusual sauces and other condiments. If you haven't already read the background information on pages 66–68, it would be a good idea to do so before trying these recipes.

KEY POINTS TO REVIEW

- What does the term *integral sauce* mean?
- What is the basic procedure for making a pan gravy?
- What is the basic procedure for making a cream reduction sauce?
- What is the basic procedure for making a flavored oil?

Mushroom Jus

YIELD: 2 QT (2 L)

U.S.	METRIC	INGREDIENTS	PROCEDURE
3 lb	1.5 kg	Mushrooms, cleaned, coarsely chopped	1. Place the mushrooms and the first quantity of water in a stockpot. 2. Bring to a boil. Reduce the heat to a rapid simmer and cook until most of the liquid has evaporated.
2 gal	8 L	Water	
2 gal	8 L	Water	3. Add the second quantity of water and repeat the reduction process.
2 gal	8 L	Water	4. Add the third quantity of water. Reduce by three-quarters. 5. Strain through a china cap lined with cheesecloth, pressing on the mushrooms to extract as much liquid as possible. 6. To use or to finish as a sauce, see Variations.

Per 1 fl oz (29.57 mL): Calories, 5; Protein, 1 g; Fat, 0 g (0% cal.); Cholesterol, 0 mg; Carbohydrates, 1 g; Fiber, 0 g; Sodium, 0 mg.

VARIATIONS

The jus can be used as is, seasoned with salt and pepper. A small amount of arrowroot or other starch may be used to bind the sauce lightly. Alternatively, finish by enriching with cream (see p. 177 for information on cream reductions) or butter (see p. 169). The jus can also be added as a flavoring ingredient to meat or poultry broths and to demi-glace, and it can be used as a deglazing liquid.

Bell Pepper Coulis

YIELD: 2½ PT (1.25 L)

U.S.	METRIC	INGREDIENTS	PROCEDURE
4 lb	2 kg	Red or yellow bell peppers	1. Split peppers in half lengthwise. Remove cores, seeds, and membranes. Chop coarsely.
2 fl oz	60 mL	Olive oil	2. Heat the olive oil in a saucepot over low heat.
2 oz	60 g	Shallots, chopped	3. Add the shallots and peppers. Cover and sweat over low heat until vegetables are soft, about 20 minutes.
4 fl oz	125 mL	Chicken stock, vegetable stock, or water	4. Add the stock or water. Simmer 2–3 minutes. 5. Purée the vegetables and liquid in a blender, then pass through a strainer.
1–4 fl oz	30–125 mL	Additional stock or water	6. Adjust the texture by adding water or stock to thin it.
to taste	to taste	Salt	7. Add salt and white pepper to taste.
to taste	to taste	White pepper	

Per 1 fl oz (29.57 mL): Calories, 25; Protein, 0 g; Fat, 1.5 g (53% cal.); Cholesterol, 0 mg; Carbohydrates, 3 g; Fiber, 1 g; Sodium, 0 mg.

VARIATION

Bell Pepper and Tomato Coulis

Combine bell pepper coulis with an equal volume of tomato purée.

Salsa Verde Cocida

YIELD: 1 QT (1 L)

U.S.	METRIC	INGREDIENTS
4	4	13-oz (368-g) cans whole tomatillos (Mexican green tomatoes)
2 oz	60 g	Onion, chopped
4	4	Garlic cloves, chopped
2–4 oz	60–125 g	Green chiles, such as jalapeño or serrano, canned or fresh
1 oz	30 g	Fresh cilantro leaves (optional)
1 fl oz	30 mL	Oil
to taste	to taste	Salt

PROCEDURE

1. Drain the tomatillos.
2. Combine tomatillos, onion, garlic, chiles, and cilantro in a blender. Blend to a smooth purée.
3. Heat the oil in a large saucepan. Add the purée and cook 4–5 minutes, or until slightly thickened.
4. Season to taste with salt.

Per 1 fl oz (29.57 mL): Calories, 25; Protein, 2 g; Fat, 1 g (27% cal.); Cholesterol, 0 mg; Carbohydrates, 4 g; Fiber, 1 g; Sodium, 55 mg.

VARIATIONS

Salsa Roja

Substitute 2 lb (1 kg) red, ripe tomatoes, peeled, or canned red tomatoes for the tomatillos. Onion may be included or omitted to create slightly different flavors.

Tomato Broth for Chiles Rellenos

Prepare as for Salsa Roja, using onion but omitting chiles and cilantro. After step 3, add 3 pt (1.5 L) pork stock (including the cooking liquid from making Picadillo for the filling for the chiles)
and/or chicken stock. Also, add a sachet containing 6 whole cloves, 10 peppercorns, 2 bay leaves, and 1 small cinnamon stick. Simmer until slightly thickened to the consistency of a thick broth or thin sauce.

Salsa Verde Cocida

Salsa Cruda

YIELD: 1 QT (1 L)

U.S.	METRIC	INGREDIENTS
1 lb 4 oz	600 g	Fresh tomatoes
4 oz, or to taste	125 g, or to taste	Fresh green chiles, such as jalapeño or serrano
6 oz	175 g	Onion
½–1 oz	15–30 g	Fresh cilantro leaves, chopped
1 tbsp	15 mL	Lime juice or vinegar
2–4 fl oz	60–125 mL	Water or tomato juice, cold
1½ tsp	7 mL	Salt

PROCEDURE

1. Chop the tomatoes fine. (You may peel them, but it is not necessary.)
2. Remove the stem ends of the chiles. Chop the chiles fine.
3. Mince the onion.
4. Mix together the tomato, chiles, onion, cilantro, and lime juice or vinegar. Dilute with water or tomato juice to make a thick, chunky sauce.
5. Add salt to taste.

Per 1 fl oz (29.57 mL): Calories, 10; Protein, 0 g; Fat, 0 g (0% cal.); Cholesterol, 0 mg; Carbohydrates, 2 g; Fiber, 0 g; Sodium, 110 mg.

Note: This sauce is used as a table condiment with many dishes, including eggs, broiled meats, tacos, tortillas, and beans. It is best if used within a few hours.

Cucumber Raita

YIELD: 1½ PT (750 ML)

U.S.	METRIC	INGREDIENTS	PROCEDURE
½ tsp	2 mL	Cumin seed	1. In a small, dry skillet over moderate heat, toast the cumin seeds until aromatic and a slightly darker shade of brown. Remove from the heat and grind in a spice grinder.
8 oz	250 g	Cucumber	2. Peel and grate the cucumbers coarsely.
1 pt	500 mL	Plain yogurt	3. Place the yogurt in a bowl and whip until smooth.
1 tsp	5 mL	Salt	4. Add the ground cumin, grated cucumber, salt, pepper, and cayenne. Mix well.
⅛ tsp	1 mL	Black pepper	
⅛–¼ tsp	1–2 mL	Cayenne	

Per 1 fl oz (29.57 mL): Calories, 15; Protein, 1 g; Fat, 1 g (53% cal.); Cholesterol, 0 mg; Carbohydrates, 1 g; Fiber, 0 g; Sodium, 105 mg.

Cucumber Raita

Indonesian Peanut Sauce

YIELD: 1 PT (500 ML)

U.S.	METRIC	INGREDIENTS	PROCEDURE
8 oz	250 g	Peanut butter	1. Combine all ingredients in a food processor. Process until the mixture forms a smooth sauce.
8 fl oz	250 mL	Hot water	2. Refrigerate.
4–6	4–6	Garlic cloves, crushed to a paste	
2–3	2–3	Serrano chiles, seeded, chopped fine	
1 tbsp	15 mL	Fresh ginger root, peeled and chopped fine	
1 tbsp	15 mL	Brown sugar	
1 tbsp	15 mL	Lime juice	
1 fl oz	30 mL	Soy sauce	

Per 1 fl oz (29.57 mL): Calories, 90; Protein, 4 g; Fat, 7 g (66% cal.); Cholesterol, 0 mg; Carbohydrates, 4 g; Fiber, 1 g; Sodium, 190 mg.

Barbecue Sauce

YIELD: ½ GAL (2 L)

U.S.	METRIC	INGREDIENTS
1 qt	1 L	Tomato purée
1 pt	500 mL	Water
⅔ cup	150 mL	Worcestershire sauce
½ cup	125 mL	Cider vinegar
½ cup	125 mL	Vegetable oil
8 oz	250 g	Onion, chopped fine
4 tsp	20 mL	Finely chopped garlic
2 oz	60 g	Sugar
1 tbsp	15 mL	Dry mustard
2 tsp	10 mL	Chili powder
1 tsp	5 mL	Black pepper
to taste	to taste	Salt

PROCEDURE

1. Place all ingredients in a heavy saucepan and bring to a boil. Reduce heat and simmer about 20 minutes, or until slightly reduced and flavors are well blended. Stir occasionally during cooking so the sauce does not scorch on the bottom.

2. Adjust seasoning.

Per 1 fl oz (29.57 mL): Calories, 25; Protein, 0 g; Fat, 2 g (60% cal.); Cholesterol, 0 mg; Carbohydrates, 3 g; Fiber, 0 g; Sodium, 30 mg.

Note: This sauce is not intended to be eaten as is but to be cooked with other foods. .

Chile Barbecue Sauce

YIELD: 2½ PT (1.25 L)

U.S.	METRIC	INGREDIENTS
1½ pt	750 mL	Bottled chili sauce
8 fl oz	250 mL	Soy sauce
2 oz	60 g	Dark brown sugar
1½ fl oz	45 mL	Worcestershire sauce
1 pt	500 mL	Water
6 fl oz	175 mL	Lemon juice
1 tbsp	15 mL	Hot red pepper sauce
2	2	Whole chipotle chiles
3 tbsp	45 mL	Chili powder

PROCEDURE

1. Combine all ingredients in a heavy saucepot. Bring to a boil.
2. Simmer 15 minutes.
3. Strain.
4. Adjust seasoning with salt if necessary. (It is not likely more salt will be needed; soy sauce is salty.)

Per 1 fl oz (29.57 mL): Calories, 35; Protein, 1 g; Fat, 0 g (0% cal); Cholesterol, 0 mg; Carbohydrates, 8 g; Fiber, 1 g; Sodium, 620 mg.

Shallot Oil

YIELD: 1 PT (500 ML)

U.S.	METRIC	INGREDIENTS
2–3 tbsp	30 g	Shallots, chopped
1 pt	500 mL	Flavorless oil, such as canola, corn, safflower, or grapeseed

PROCEDURE

1. Combine the chopped shallots and the oil in a jar. Shake well.
2. Let stand 30 minutes. Refrigerate.
3. The oil is ready to use as soon as it has taken on the desired flavor, which may be in 1–2 hours. After 2 days, strain the oil through a paper coffee filter. Store in refrigerator.

Per 1 fl oz (29.57 mL): Calories, 240; Protein, 0 g; Fat, 27 g (100% cal.); Cholesterol, 0 g; Carbohydrates, 0 g; Fiber, 0 g; Sodium, 0 mg.

VARIATIONS

Ginger Oil, Horseradish Oil, or Garlic Oil

Substitute ginger root, horseradish, or garlic for shallots in the basic recipe. For best results, chop ginger or horseradish very fine in a food processor, or grate with a fine-holed grater. For garlic oil, substitute olive oil for the flavorless oil if desired.

Lemon or Orange Oil

Substitute 3–4 tbsp (30 g) grated lemon or orange zest for shallots in the basic recipe.

Rosemary Oil, Sage Oil, Thyme Oil, or Oregano Oil

Substitute 3½ oz (100 g) chopped fresh rosemary, sage, thyme, or oregano for shallots in the basic recipe.

Cinnamon Oil, Cumin Oil, Curry Oil, Ginger Oil, or Paprika Oil

Substitute 3 tbsp (45 mL) of one of the above ground, dried spices for shallots in the basic recipe. In a small pan, combine the spice with just enough oil to make a thin paste. Heat gently just until the spice starts to give off an aroma. Be careful not to burn the spice. Paprika, especially, darkens quickly. Add the spice mixture to remaining oil. Let stand, refrigerate, and filter as in basic recipe.

Basil Oil, Parsley Oil, Chervil Oil, or Cilantro Oil

Select the desired quantity of one of the above fresh herbs. Drop into boiling water. Blanch 10 seconds. Drain and refresh under cold water. Drain again and pat dry with towels. Put the herbs in a blender and add a small amount of olive oil. Blend to make a paste. Measure the volume of the paste and add 4 times that volume of olive oil. Shake and let stand. Refrigerate and strain as in basic recipe.

Fruit Salsa

YIELD: 2 LB (1 KG)

U.S.	METRIC	INGREDIENTS
8 oz	250 g	Honeydew melon, seeded, rind removed
8 oz	250 g	Papaya, peeled and seeded
8 oz	250 g	Mango, peeled and pitted
4 oz	125 g	Red bell pepper, cored and seeded
1 oz	30 g	Jalapeño, stemmed and seeded
3 oz	90 g	Red onion, cut brunoise
4 fl oz	125 mL	Lime juice
2 tbsp	30 mL	Chopped cilantro
to taste	to taste	Salt

PROCEDURE

1. Chop the melon, papaya, mango, bell pepper, and jalapeño into fine dice. Be careful to save the juices that are released.
2. Combine the chopped fruit with their juices, peppers, onion, lime juice, and cilantro in a bowl.
3. Season to taste with salt.
4. Refrigerate until served.

Per 1 ounce (28.35 g): Calories, 15; Protein, 0 g; Fat, 0 g (0% cal.); Cholesterol, 0 mg; Carbohydrates, 3 g; Fiber, 0 g; Sodium, 0 mg.

Fruit Salsa

Tartar Sauce

YIELD: APPROX. 1 QT (1 L)

U.S.	METRIC	INGREDIENTS
4 oz	125 g	Dill pickles or sour gherkins
2 oz	60 g	Onions
2 oz	60 g	Capers
1 qt	1 L	Mayonnaise
2 tbsp	30 mL	Chopped parsley

PROCEDURE

1. Chop pickles and onions very fine. Chop the capers if large, or leave whole if small.

2. Press the pickles and capers in a fine sieve, or squeeze out in a piece of cheesecloth so they don't make the sauce too liquid.

3. Combine all ingredients in a stainless-steel bowl and mix well.

Per 1 fl oz (29.57 mL): Calories, 200; Protein, 0 g; Fat, 22 g (98% cal.); Cholesterol, 15 mg; Carbohydrates, 1 g; Fiber, 0 g; Sodium, 240 mg.

VARIATION

Rémoulade Sauce

Add 1 tbsp (15 mL) anchovy paste or mashed anchovies to tartar sauce.

Aïoli I

YIELD: APPROX. 1 PT 4 OZ (600 ML)

U.S.	METRIC	INGREDIENTS
10	10	Garlic cloves
⅛ tsp	0.5 mL	Salt
3	3	Egg yolks
1 pt	500 mL	Olive oil
1–2 tbsp	15–30 mL	Lemon juice

PROCEDURE

1. Crush the garlic to a fine paste with the salt.

2. Add the egg yolks and beat until thoroughly combined.

3. A few drops at a time, begin adding the olive oil, beating constantly. Do not add oil any faster than it can be absorbed.

4. After about half the oil is added, the mixture will be very stiff. Add a few drops of the lemon juice at this point.

5. Continue adding the remaining oil gradually. From time to time, add a few more drops of the lemon juice. The finished aïoli should be like a stiff mayonnaise. Adjust seasoning with salt if necessary.

Per 1 fl oz (29.57 mL): Calories, 200; Protein, 1 g; Fat, 22 g (99% cal.); Cholesterol, 30 mg; Carbohydrates, 1 g; Fiber, 0 g; Sodium, 15 mg.

Cocktail Sauce

YIELD: 2 QT (2 L)

U.S.	METRIC	INGREDIENTS
1 qt	1 L	Ketchup
2½ cups	600 mL	Chili sauce
1 cup	250 mL	Prepared horseradish
4 fl oz	125 mL	Lemon juice
2 tbsp	30 mL	Worcestershire sauce
dash	dash	Hot red pepper sauce

PROCEDURE

1. Combine all ingredients and mix.
2. Chill.

Per 1 fl oz (29.57 mL): Calories, 30; Protein, 1 g; Fat, 0 g (0% cal.); Cholesterol, 0 mg; Carbohydrates, 7 g; Fiber, 0 g; Sodium, 330 mg.

Note: Serve as a dip with shrimp, crab, lobster, raw clams, or raw oysters.

Mignonette Sauce

YIELD: 1 QT (1 L)

U.S.	METRIC	INGREDIENTS
1 qt	1 L	Wine vinegar, red or white
8 oz	250 g	Shallots, cut brunoise
1 tsp	5 mL	Salt
1 tsp	5 mL	White pepper
2 tsp	5 mL	Dried tarragon

PROCEDURE

1. Combine all ingredients.
2. Chill.
3. Serve 1 fl oz (30 mL) per portion as a cocktail sauce for oysters or clams on the half-shell.

Per 1 fl oz (29.57 mL): Calories, 5; Protein, 0 g; Fat, 0 g (0% cal.) Cholesterol, 0 mg; Carbohydrates, 1 g; Fiber, 0 g; Sodium, 75 mg.

Mignonette Sauce

Parmesan Foam

YIELD: VARIABLE

U.S.	METRIC	INGREDIENTS
5 fl oz	150 mL	Milk
4 oz	125 g	Grated parmesan cheese
4 fl oz	125 mL	Heavy cream
to taste	to taste	Salt

Per 1 ounce (28.35 g): Calories, 70; Protein, 4 g; Fat, 6 g (73% cal.); Cholesterol, 20 mg; Carbohydrates, 1 g; Fiber, 0 g; Sodium, 140 mg.

PROCEDURE

1. In a small saucepan, bring the milk to a boil.
2. Remove from the heat, add the cheese, and stir.
3. Let stand 30 minutes at room temperature.
4. Strain through a chinois. Press on the solids to extract all the liquid, but do not force the solids through strainer.
5. Mix in cream. Add salt to taste and refrigerate.
6. Pour the cream mixture into a foaming canister. Close canister and charge with a nitrous oxide (N_2O) cartridge. Make foam by inverting canister and pulling on lever.

Raspberry Beads

YIELD: VARIABLE

U.S.	METRIC	INGREDIENTS
3.3 oz	100 g	Apple juice
1.3 oz	40 g	Raspberry juice
½ oz	15 g	Sugar
0.03 oz	1 g	Sodium alginate
0.08 oz	2.5 g	Calcium chloride
8 fl oz	250 g	Water

Per 1 ounce (28.35 g): Calories, 10; Protein, 0 g; Fat, 0 g (0% cal.); Cholesterol, 0 mg; Carbohydrates, 2 g; Fiber, 0 g; Sodium, 0 mg.

PROCEDURE

1. Combine the apple juice, raspberry juice, sugar, and sodium alginate in a blender. Blend until well combined.
2. Let the mixture stand several hours in the refrigerator.
3. Dissolve the calcium chloride in water.
4. Using a syringe, drop droplets of raspberry mixture into the calcium solution. Leave in calcium bath about 1 minute (the longer they are left in, the firmer they become).
5. Remove the beads from calcium bath and rinse in a strainer.

TERMS FOR REVIEW

stock	sauce	au sec	clarified butter
broth	leading sauce	deglaze	beurre noisette
mirepoix	mother sauce	monter au beurre	compound butter
sachet d'épices	nappé	leading sauce	emulsion
bouquet garni	slurry	fond lié	integral sauce
venting	roux	small sauce	pan gravy
remouillage	white roux	demi-glace	jus
reduction	blond roux	béchamel	au jus
glaze	brown roux	velouté	salsa
glace de viande	beurre manié	espagnole	relish
glace de volaille	whitewash	gastrique	chutney
glace de poisson	liaison	coulis	

QUESTIONS FOR DISCUSSION

1. Which bones make a more gelatinous stock, beef or veal?
2. The stockpot is often considered a good way to use trimmings from meats and vegetables. Do you agree? Explain.
3. How should vegetables for mirepoix be cut?
4. Explain the importance of blanching bones before making stocks.
5. Why should stock not be boiled? Should a stockpot be covered? Why or why not?
6. Explain the procedure for cooling stock. Why is it important?
7. Why is an understanding of stocks important even if you work in an establishment that uses only bases?
8. You have just prepared a suprême sauce, but your supervisor says it's too thin. It must be served in five minutes. What can you do to correct the sauce?
9. What are the two methods for preparing starches so they can be incorporated into hot liquids? Why are they necessary, and how do they work?
10. Why is it necessary to be able to thicken a sauce with a roux without making lumps if the sauce is going to be strained anyway?
11. You are preparing a gravy for a batch of Swiss steaks that are to be frozen for later use. What thickening agent will you use?
12. Name the five leading sauces and their major ingredients. List at least two small sauces made from each.
13. What precautions must be taken when finishing and holding allemande sauce?
14. What are the similarities between espagnole and pan gravy? the differences?
15. What precautions are necessary when making hollandaise to avoid overcooking the eggs or curdling the sauce?

Chapter 8

Wisconsin Cheddar and Broccoli Soup, page 205.

Soups

The popularity of soups today may be due to increased nutrition consciousness, to a desire for simpler or lighter meals, or to an increased appreciation of how appetizing and satisfying soups can be. Whatever the reasons, they emphasize the importance of soup-making skills.

If you have already studied the preparation of stocks and sauces in Chapter 7, you now have at your disposal the major techniques for the preparation of soups. You know how to make stocks and how to use thickening agents such as roux and liaison.

A few more techniques are necessary for you to master before you are able to prepare all the types of soups that are popular today. As in sauce-making, basic techniques are the building blocks you can use to create a wide variety of appetizing soups.

After reading this chapter, you should be able to

1. Describe three basic categories of soups.
2. Identify standard appetizer and main-course portion sizes for soups.
3. State the procedures for holding soups for service and for serving soups at the proper temperature.
4. Prepare clarified consommé.
5. Prepare vegetable soups and other clear soups.
6. Prepare cream soups.
7. Prepare purée soups.
8. Prepare bisques, chowders, specialty soups, and national soups.

UNDERSTANDING SOUPS

Soup, according to the dictionary, is a liquid food derived from meat, poultry, fish, or vegetables. This definition is all right as far as it goes, but there's a lot it doesn't tell us. Is a stock, straight from the stockpot, a soup? Is beef stew liquid enough to be called a soup?

We're interested more in production techniques than in definitions. However, a few more definitions are necessary before we can go into the kitchen, so we can talk to each other in the same language. Definitions aren't rules, so don't be alarmed if you hear other books or chefs use these terms differently. What matters is that you learn the techniques and are able to adapt them to many uses.

Classifications of Soups

Soups can be divided into three basic categories: clear or unthickened soups, thick soups, and special soups that don't fit the first two categories.

Most of these soups, no matter what their final ingredients may be, are based on stock. Thus, the quality of the soup depends on the stock-making skills discussed in Chapter 7.

Clear Soups

Clear soups are all based on a clear, unthickened broth or stock. They may be served plain or garnished with a variety of vegetables and meats.

1. *Broth* and *bouillon* are two terms used in many ways. In general, they both refer to simple, clear soups without solid ingredients. We have already defined broth (Chapter 7) as a flavorful liquid obtained from the simmering of meats and/or vegetables. Broths are discussed in more detail on page 193.

2. *Vegetable soup* is a clear, seasoned stock or broth with the addition of one or more vegetables and, sometimes, meat or poultry products and starches.

3. *Consommé* is a rich, flavorful stock or broth that has been clarified to make it perfectly clear and transparent. The process of clarification is a technique we study in detail.

   Far from being just a plain old cup of broth, a well-made consommé is one of the greatest of all soups. Its sparkling clarity is a delight to the eye, and its rich, full flavor, strength, and body make it a perfect starter for an elegant dinner.

Thick Soups

Unlike clear soups, thick soups are opaque rather than transparent. They are thickened either by adding a thickening agent, such as a roux, or by puréeing one or more of their ingredients to provide a heavier consistency.

1. *Cream soups* are soups thickened with roux, beurre manié, liaison, or other added thickening agents, plus milk and/or cream. They are similar to velouté and béchamel sauces—in fact, they may be made by diluting and flavoring either of these two leading sauces.

   Cream soups are usually named after their major ingredient, as in cream of chicken or cream of asparagus.

2. *Purées* are soups naturally thickened by puréeing one or more of their ingredients. They are not as smooth and creamy as cream soups.

   Purées are normally based on starchy ingredients. They may be made from dried legumes (such as split pea soup) or from fresh vegetables with a starchy ingredient, such as potatoes or rice, added. Purées may or may not contain milk or cream.

3. *Bisques* are thickened soups made from shellfish. They are usually prepared like cream soups and are almost always finished with cream.

   The term *bisque* is sometimes used on menus for a variety of vegetable soups. In these cases, it is really a marketing term rather than a technical term, so it is impossible to give a definition that covers all uses.

4. *Chowders* are hearty soups made from fish, shellfish, and/or vegetables. Although they are made in many ways, they usually contain milk and potatoes.

5. *Potage* is a term sometimes associated with thick, hearty soups, but it is actually a general term for soup. A clear soup is called a *potage clair* in French.

Specialty and National Soups

This is a catch-all category for soups that don't fit well into the main categories and soups that are native to particular countries or regions.

Specialty soups are distinguished by unusual ingredients or methods, such as turtle soup, gumbo, peanut soup, and cold fruit soup.

Cold soups are sometimes considered specialty soups, and, in fact, some of them are. But many other popular cold soups, such as jellied consommé, cold cream of cucumber soup, and vichyssoise (vee shee swahz) are simply cold versions of basic clear and thick soups.

Vegetarian Soups and Low-Fat Soups

A great variety of vegetable-based soups are suitable for vegetarian menus. Vegetable soups for vegans must contain no meat or any other animal product and must be made with water or vegetable stock. To bind thick soups, use a starch slurry or a roux made with oil rather than butter. Lacto-vegetarians, on the other hand, accept soups containing butter, milk, or cream.

Because the appeal of vegetarian vegetable soups depends entirely on the freshness and the quality of the vegetables and not on the richness of meat stocks, be especially careful to use high-quality ingredients and to avoid overcooking.

Clear soups are especially suitable for people seeking low-fat foods. Consommés and clear vegetable soups are virtually fat-free, especially if the vegetables were not sweated in fat before being simmered.

Thick soups can be kept low in fat by thickening them with a slurry of starch (such as arrowroot, potato starch, or cornstarch) and cold water rather than with a roux. For cream soups, reduce or omit the cream and instead use evaporated skim milk. Purée soups are usually more adaptable than cream soups to low-fat diets because the vegetable purée adds body and richness to the soup without requiring added fat. A little yogurt or evaporated skim milk can be used to give creaminess to a purée soup. Even garnishing a serving of soup with a teaspoonful of whipped cream gives a feeling of richness while adding only a gram or two of fat.

Service of Soups

Standard Portion Sizes

Appetizer portion: 6 to 8 oz (200 to 250 mL)

Main course portion: 10 to 12 oz (300 to 350 mL)

Temperature

Serve hot soups hot, in hot cups or bowls.

Serve cold soups cold, in chilled bowls or even nested in a larger bowl of crushed ice.

Holding for Service

Strangely enough, some chefs who take the greatest care not to overcook meats or vegetables nevertheless keep a large kettle of soup on the steam table all day. You can imagine what a vegetable soup is like after four or five hours at that temperature.

1. Small-batch cooking applies to soups as well as to other foods. Heat small batches frequently to replenish the steam table with fresh soup.

2. Consommés and some other clear soups can be kept hot for longer periods if the vegetable garnish is heated separately and added at service time.

Garnish

Soup garnishes may be divided into three groups.

1. **Garnishes in the soup.**
   Major ingredients, such as the vegetables in clear vegetable soup, are often considered garnishes. This group of garnishes also includes meats, poultry, seafood, pasta products, and grains such as barley or rice. They are treated as part of the preparation or recipe itself, not as something added on.

   Consommés are generally named after their garnish, such as consommé brunoise, which contains vegetables cut into brunoise shape [⅛-inch (3-mm) dice].

   Vegetable cream soups are usually garnished with carefully cut pieces of the vegetable from which they are made.

   An elegant way to serve soup with a solid garnish is to arrange the garnish attractively in the bottom of a heated soup plate. This plate is set before the diner, and then the soup is ladled from a tureen by the dining room staff.

2. **Toppings.**
   Clear soups are generally served without toppings to let the attractiveness of the clear broth and the carefully cut vegetables speak for themselves. Occasional exceptions are toppings of chopped parsley or chives.

   Thick soups, especially those that are all one color, are often decorated with a topping. Toppings should be placed on the soup just before service so they won't sink or lose their fresh appearance. Their flavors must be appropriate to the soup.

   Do not overdo soup toppings. The food should be attractive in itself. Topping suggestions for thick soups include the following:

Fresh herbs (parsley, chives), chopped	Croutons
Fine julienne of vegetables	Grated parmesan cheese
Sliced almonds, toasted	Crumbled bacon
Grated cheese	Paprika
Sieved egg yolks	Flavored butters
Chopped or riced egg whites	Flavored oils

   Fried herbs, such as parsley, sage, chervil, celery leaves, leek julienne

   Sour cream, crème fraîche, or whipped cream, either plain or flavored with herbs or spices

3. **Accompaniments.**
   American soups are traditionally served with crackers. In addition to the usual saltines, other suggestions for crisp accompaniments are:

Melba toast	Cheese straws
Corn chips	Whole-grain wafers
Breadsticks	

   Profiteroles (tiny unsweetened cream-puff shells)

CLEAR SOUPS

Broths

The difference between a broth and a stock is that a broth, according to the most common definition, is made by simmering meat and vegetables, while a stock is made by simmering bones and vegetables. Because of this difference, a well-made stock is generally richer in gelatin content than a broth, because gelatin is derived from cartilage and connective tissue. A broth, on the other hand, usually has a more pronounced flavor of meat or poultry than a stock. A more neutral flavor is desired in a stock, which is used as the base for many sauces as well as soups. A broth, on the other hand, is an excellent choice as the base of a soup when a distinct meat flavor is desired.

Nevertheless, broths are not often specially made in food-service operations. The cost of the meat makes them expensive, unless the meat can be used for another purpose, or unless the restaurant has a good supply of meat trimmings that might otherwise be wasted. Instead, broth is usually a byproduct of simmering meat or poultry.

Note that the broths resulting from both these recipes are white. Flavorful cuts such as beef shank, chuck, and neck are good for making broths.

Broths can be served as is, with only seasoning and perhaps a light garnish added. For example, plain chicken broth is commonly served as a restorative for invalids. More often, however, broths are used in place of stocks in vegetable soups and other clear soups, as discussed in the section beginning on page 197.

Like stock, broth can be made with water. For especially rich, flavorful broths, use stock in place of water in the broth recipe.

Consommé

When we define *consommé* as a clarified stock or broth, we are forgetting the most important part of the definition. The word *consommé* means, literally, "completed" or "concentrated." In other words, a consommé is a strong, concentrated stock or broth. In classical cuisine, this was all that was necessary for a stock to be called a consommé. In fact, two kinds were recognized: ordinary (or unclarified) consommé and clarified consommé.

Rule number one for preparing consommé is that the stock or broth must be strong, rich, and full-flavored. Clarification is second in importance to strength. A good consommé, with a mellow but full aroma and plenty of body (from the natural gelatin) you can feel in your mouth, is one of the great pleasures of fine cuisine. But clarification is an expensive and time-consuming procedure, and, quite frankly, it's not worth the trouble if the soup is thin and watery.

How Clarification Works

Coagulation of proteins was an important subject in our discussion of stock-making because one of our major concerns was how to keep coagulated proteins from making the stock cloudy. Strangely enough, this same process of *coagulation* enables us to clarify stocks to perfect transparency.

Remember that some proteins, especially those called *albumins*, dissolve in cold water. When the water is heated, they gradually solidify or coagulate and rise to the surface. If we control this process carefully, these proteins collect all the tiny particles that cloud a stock and carry them to the surface. The stock is then left perfectly clear.

If, on the other hand, we are not careful, these proteins break up as they coagulate and cloud the liquid even more, just as they can do when we make stock.

Basic Ingredients

The mixture of ingredients we use to clarify a stock is called the *clearmeat* or the *clarification*.

1. *Lean ground meat* is one of the major sources of protein that enables the clearmeat to do its job. It also contributes flavor to the consommé. The meat must be lean because fat is undesirable in a consommé. Beef shank, also called *shin beef*, is the most desirable meat because it is high in albumin proteins as well as in flavor and gelatin, and it is very lean.

   Beef and/or chicken meat are used to clarify chicken consommé. Meat is not used, obviously, to make fish consommé. Ground lean fish may be used, but it is normal to omit flesh altogether and use only egg whites.

2. *Egg whites* are included in the clearmeat because, being mostly albumin, they greatly strengthen its clarifying power.

3. *Mirepoix* and other seasoning and flavoring ingredients are usually included because they add flavor to the finished consommé. They do not actually help in the clarification, except possibly to give solidity to the raft. The *raft* is the coagulated clearmeat, floating in a solid mass on top of the consommé.

   The mirepoix must be cut into fine pieces so it will float with the raft.

   A large amount of a particular vegetable may be added if a special flavor is desired, as in, for example, essence of celery consommé.

4. *Acid ingredients* (tomato products for beef or chicken consommé, lemon juice or white wine for fish consommé) are often added because the acidity helps coagulate the protein. They are not absolutely necessary—the heat will coagulate the protein anyway—but many chefs like to use them.

Procedure for Preparing Consommé

1. Start with a well-flavored, cold, strong stock or broth. If your stock is weak, reduce it until it is concentrated enough, then cool it before proceeding, or plan on simmering the consommé longer to reduce while clarifying.

2. Select a heavy stockpot or soup pot, preferably one with a spigot at the bottom. The spigot enables you to drain off the finished consommé without disturbing the raft.

3. Combine the clearmeat ingredients in the soup pot and mix them vigorously.

4. Optional step: Mix in a small amount of cold water or stock—4 to 8 oz per pound (250 to 500 mL per kg) of meat—and let stand 30 to 60 minutes. This allows more opportunity for the proteins that do the clarifying to dissolve out of the meat.

   Note: Chefs disagree on the importance of this step. Some let the mixture stand overnight in the refrigerator. Others skip the step altogether. Check with your instructor.

5. Gradually add the cold, degreased stock and mix well with the clearmeat.

   The stock must be cold so it doesn't cook the proteins on contact.

   Mixing distributes the dissolved proteins throughout the stock so they can collect all the impurities more easily.

6. Set the pot over a moderately low fire and let it come to a simmer very slowly.

7. Stir the contents occasionally so the clearmeat circulates throughout the stock and doesn't burn to the bottom.

8. When the simmering point is approaching, stop stirring. The clearmeat will rise to the surface and form a raft.

9. Move the pot to lower heat so the liquid maintains a slow simmer. Do not cover. Boiling would break up the raft and cloud the consommé. The same principle operates in stock-making.

10. Let simmer 1½ hours without disturbing the raft.

11. Strain the consommé through a china cap lined with several layers of cheesecloth.

    If you are not using a stockpot with a spigot, ladle the consommé out carefully without breaking up the raft.

    Let the liquid drain through the cheesecloth by gravity. Do not force it, or fine particles will pass through and cloud the consommé.

12. Degrease.
    Remove all traces of fat from the surface. Strips of clean brown paper passed across the surface are effective in absorbing every last speck of fat without absorbing much consommé.

13. Adjust the seasonings.
    Kosher salt is preferred to regular table salt because it has no impurities or additives that could cloud the stock.

Figure 8.1 Preparing consommé.

(a) The stock is well mixed with the clarification ingredients and set on a burner to begin heating.

(b) The raft begins to rise to the top.

(c) The raft has almost completely formed. The consommé will continue to simmer for a total of 1½ hours.

Emergency Procedures

1. **Clarifying hot stock.**

   If you do not have time to cool the stock properly before clarifying, at least cool it as much as you can. Even 10 minutes in a cold-water bath helps. Then, mix ice cubes or crushed ice with the clearmeat. This will help keep it from coagulating when the hot stock hits it. Proceed as in the basic method.

   Finally, review your production planning so you can avoid this emergency in the future.

2. **Clarifying without meat.**

   In a pinch, you can clarify a stock with egg whites alone. Use at least 3 or 4 egg whites per gallon (4 L) stock, plus mirepoix if possible. Great care is necessary because the raft will be fragile and easily broken up.

   Egg whites and mirepoix alone are often used for clarifying fish stocks.

3. **Failed clarification.**

   If the clarification fails because you let it boil, or for some other reason, it can still be rescued, even if there is no time for another complete clarification.

   Strain the consommé, cool it as much as you can, then slowly add it to a mixture of ice cubes and egg whites. Carefully return to a simmer as in the basic method and proceed with the clarification.

   This should be done in emergencies only. The ice cubes dilute the consommé, and the egg white clarification is risky.

4. **Poor color.**

   Beef or veal consommé made from brown stock should have an amber color. It is not dark brown like canned consommé. Chicken consommé is a very pale amber.

   It is possible to correct a pale consommé by adding a few drops of caramel color to the finished soup, but for best results, check the color of the stock before clarification. If it is too pale, cut an onion in half and place it cut side down on a flattop range until it is black, or char it under a broiler. Add this to the clearmeat. The caramelized sugar of the onion will color the stock.

Consommé

| YIELD: 1 GAL (4 L) | PORTIONS: 16 | PORTION SIZE: 8 FL OZ (250 ML) |
| | 20 | 6 FL OZ (250 ML) |

U.S.	METRIC	INGREDIENTS	PROCEDURE
1 lb	500 g	Lean beef, preferably shin, ground	1. Review the information on preparing consommé, page 195.
		Mirepoix, chopped into small pieces:	2. Combine the beef, mirepoix, egg whites, tomatoes, herbs, and spices in a tall, heavy stockpot. Mix vigorously with a wooden paddle or a heavy whip.
8 oz	250 g	Onion	
4 oz	125 g	Celery	
4 oz	125 g	Carrot	
8 oz	250 g	Egg whites	
8 oz	250 g	Canned tomatoes, crushed	
6–8	6–8	Parsley stems, chopped	
pinch	pinch	Dried thyme	
1	1	Bay leaf	
2	2	Whole cloves	
½ tsp	2 mL	Peppercorns, crushed	
5 qt	5 L	Beef or veal stock, cold (brown or white)	3. Add about 1 pint (500 mL) cold stock and stir well. Let stand about 30 minutes. (Optional step: see p. 195 for explanation.)

Per serving: Calories, 30; Protein, 3 g; Fat; 1 g (31% cal.); Cholesterol, 15 mg; Carbohydrates, 2 g; Fiber, 0 g; Sodium, 75 mg.

VARIATIONS

Double Consommé

Use twice the quantity of beef in basic recipe. Add 8 oz (250 g) leeks to mirepoix.

(Variations continue on next page)

4. Gradually stir in the remaining cold stock. Be sure the stock is well mixed with the other ingredients.
5. Set the pot on moderately low heat and let it come to a simmer very slowly. Stir occasionally.
6. When the simmering point is approaching, stop stirring.
7. Move the pot to lower heat and simmer very slowly about 1½ hours. Do not stir or disturb the raft that forms on top.
8. Very carefully strain the consommé through a china cap lined with several layers of cheesecloth.
9. Degrease thoroughly.
10. Season to taste.

VARIATIONS *(continued)*

Chicken Consommé

Use chicken stock instead of beef or veal stock. Add to the clearmeat 8 oz (250 g) chicken trimmings (such as wing tips and necks) that have been chopped and browned in a hot oven. Omit tomato and add 1 fl oz (30 mL) lemon juice.

Cold Jellied Consommé

Unflavored gelatin must often be added to consommé to make jellied consommé. Amount needed depends on the strength of the stock and amount of jelling desired. Classically, a chilled consommé is only half jelled, more like a thick syrup. Some people, however, prefer a gelatin content high enough to solidify the consommé. In the following guidelines, use the lower quantity of gelatin for a partially jelled soup, the higher quantity for a fully jelled soup. Also, for tomatoed consommé (madrilène), increase the gelatin slightly because the acidity of the tomatoes weakens the gelatin.

1. If stock is thin when cold, add 1–2 oz (30–60 g) gelatin per gallon (4 L).
2. If stock is slightly jelled and syrupy when cold, add ½–1 oz (15–30 g) gelatin per gallon (4 L).
3. If stock is jelled when cold, no gelatin is needed. Add up to ½ oz (15 g) per gallon (4 L) if firmer texture is desired.

Gelatin may be added to clearmeat (in step 2 of recipe). This is the best method because there is no danger of clouding the consommé. It may also be added to finished consommé after softening it in cold water. See page 432 for instructions on use of gelatin.

Consommé Madrilène

Increase the tomatoes in the basic recipe to 24 oz (750 g). Use beef, veal, or chicken stock. Serve hot or jellied.

Essence of Celery Consommé

Increase the celery in the basic recipe to 1 lb (500 g).

Consommé au Porto

Flavor finished consommé with 6–8 fl oz (200–250 mL) port wine per gallon (4 L).

Consommé au Sherry

Flavor finished consommé with 6–8 fl oz (200–250 mL) sherry wine per gallon (4 L).

GARNISHED CONSOMMÉS

For the following consommés, prepare and cook the garnish separately. At service time, add 1–2 tbsp (15–30 mL) garnish to each portion. See page 119 for description of cuts. All cuts should be small enough to fit the bowl of a spoon. For example, julienne may need to be cut shorter than for other applications.

Consommé Brunoise

Onion or leek, carrot, celery, and turnip (optional), cut brunoise. Sweat lightly in butter and simmer in a little consommé until tender.

Consommé Julienne

Onion or leek, carrot, and celery, cut julienne. Prepare like brunoise garnish.

Consommé Printanière

Small dice of spring vegetables: carrot, turnip, celery, green beans. Prepare like brunoise garnish.

Consommé Paysanne

Thin slices of leeks, carrots, celery, turnip, and cabbage. Prepare like brunoise garnish.

Consommé with Pearl Tapioca

Cooked pearl tapioca.

Consommé Vermicelli

Cooked broken vermicelli (very thin spaghetti).

Consommé Fettuccine

YIELD: 10 OZ (300 G)

U.S.	METRIC	INGREDIENTS
10 fl oz	300 mL	Consommé
0.2 oz (2 tsp)	6 g	Agar-agar

Per serving: Calories, 5; Protein, 0 g; Fat; 0 g (0% cal.); Cholesterol, 0 mg; Carbohydrates, 1 g; Fiber, 1 g; Sodium, 10 mg.

PROCEDURE

1. Place the consommé in a saucepan and mix in the agar-agar.
2. Bring to a boil, then remove from heat. Whip with a wire whip to be sure the agar-agar is thoroughly mixed in.
3. Select a half-sheet pan that is perfectly level. Have ready a refrigerator shelf that is perfectly level.
4. Pour the consommé into the sheet pan. Refrigerate until set. This will take only a few minutes.
5. Cut the jelled consommé lengthwise into uniform strips ¼ inch (6 mm) wide. Remove from pan.
6. To serve, mound a small portion on a plate. Garnish as desired (see Variation for suggestion).

MOLECULAR SOUP

One of the ways chefs working in molecular gastronomy (see page 67) surprise diners' expectations and thus get them to focus on the food is to transform foods into unexpected shapes and forms. The recipe for Consommé Fettuccine, transforming soup into noodles, based on an idea developed by the Spanish chef Ferran Adrià, is an example of this approach.

Vegetable Soups

Clear vegetable soups are made from a clear stock or broth, not necessarily clarified, with the addition of one or more vegetables and, sometimes, meat or poultry and/or pasta or grains. Most vegetable soups are made from meat or poultry stock or broth. Meatless or vegetarian soups are made from vegetable broth or water.

Guidelines for Preparing Vegetable Soups

Procedures for making these soups are not complicated. Most of them are made simply by simmering vegetables in stock until done. But care and attention to details are still necessary for producing a high-quality soup.

1. **Start with a clear, flavorful stock or broth.**
   This is one reason it's important to be able to make stocks that are clear, not cloudy.

2. **Select vegetables and other ingredients whose flavors go well together.**
   Don't just throw in everything you've got. Judgment, combined with experience, must be used to create a pleasing combination. Five or six vegetables are usually enough. More than that often makes a jumble.

3. **Cut vegetables uniformly.**
   Neat, careful cutting means uniform cooking and attractive appearance. Sizes of cuts are important, too. Pieces should be large enough to be identifiable but small enough to eat conveniently with a spoon.

4. **Cooking vegetables slowly in a little butter before combining with liquid improves their flavor and gives the soup a mellower, richer taste.**

5. **Cook starches such as grains and pasta separately and add to the soup later.**
   Cooking them in the soup makes it cloudy. Potatoes are sometimes cooked directly in the soup, but they should be rinsed of excess starch after cutting if you want to keep the soup as clear as possible.

6. **Observe differences in cooking times.**
   Add long-cooking vegetables first, short-cooking vegetables near the end. Some vegetables, like tomatoes, should be added to the hot soup only after it is removed from the fire.

7. **Don't overcook.**
   Some cooks feel soups must be simmered a long time to extract flavors into the liquid. But you should already have done this when you made the stock! Vegetables in soup should be no more overcooked than vegetable side dishes, especially as the soup will probably spend a longer time in the steam table.

Clear Vegetable Soup

YIELD: 6 QT (6 L)   PORTIONS: 24   PORTION SIZE: 8 FL OZ (250 ML)

U.S.	METRIC	INGREDIENTS
4 oz	125 g	Butter or chicken fat
1½ lb	750 g	Onions, small dice
1 lb	500 g	Carrots, small dice
1 lb	500 g	Celery, small dice
12 oz	375 g	Turnip, small dice
6 qt	6 L	Chicken stock
1 lb	500 g	Drained canned tomatoes, coarsely chopped
to taste	to taste	Salt
to taste	to taste	White pepper
12 oz	375 g	Frozen peas, thawed

PROCEDURE

1. Heat the butter in a heavy saucepot over medium-low heat.
2. Add the onions, carrots, celery, and turnip. Sweat vegetables in the butter over low heat until about half cooked. Do not let them brown.
3. Add the stock. Bring to a boil and skim carefully. Simmer until vegetables are just barely tender.
4. Add the tomatoes and simmer another 5 minutes.
5. Degrease the soup and season with salt and white pepper.
6. Just before serving, add the peas.

Per serving: Calories, 80; Protein, 3 g; Fat, 4.5 g (46% cal.); Cholesterol, 15 mg; Carbohydrates, 9 g; Fiber, 2 g; Sodium, 125 mg.

VARIATIONS

Other vegetables may be used in addition to or in place of one or more of the vegetables in basic recipe. Add with the vegetables sweated in butter:

Leeks
Rutabagas
Green cabbage
Parsnips

Add to simmering soup, timing the addition so all vegetables are done at the same time:

Potatoes
Green beans
Lima beans
Corn

Other cuts may be used for the vegetables instead of small dice, such as bâtonnet, julienne, or paysanne (see p. 119).

Vegetable Rice Soup
Add 1½–2 cups (350–500 mL) cooked rice to finished soup.

Chicken Vegetable Rice Soup
Add 12 oz (375 g) cooked, diced chicken to vegetable rice soup.

Vegetable Beef Soup
Use beef stock instead of chicken stock. Add 12 oz (375 g) cooked, diced beef when the tomatoes are added. Also, add the juice from the tomatoes.

Vegetable Beef Barley Soup
Add 1½–2 cups (350–500 mL) cooked barley to vegetable beef soup.

Clear Vegetable Soup with Cranberry Beans

Other Clear Soups

In addition to vegetable soups, many other clear or unthickened soups are known to various cuisines. They range from simple broths to elaborate concoctions of meats, vegetables, starches, and other ingredients. Although many contain vegetables, we don't classify them as vegetable soups because other ingredients are generally more prominent.

KEY POINTS TO REVIEW

- What are the three basic categories of soup? What are some examples of each?
- What are normal portion sizes for soups?
- After soups are cooked, how are they best held for service?
- What is the procedure for making consommé?
- How are clear vegetable soups made?

THICK SOUPS

Cream Soups

Learning to cook professionally, as you have already heard, is not learning recipes but learning basic techniques you can apply to specific needs.

The basic techniques of sauce-making were discussed in Chapter 7. If we tell you that cream soups are simply diluted velouté or béchamel sauces, flavored with the ingredient for which they are named, you should almost be able to make a cream of celery soup without further instructions.

It's not *quite* that simple. There are some complications, but they are mostly a matter of detail. You already know the basic techniques.

The Classic Cream Soups

In the great kitchens of several decades ago, cream soups were exactly as we have just described: diluted, flavored sauces. In fact, what we now call *cream soups* were divided into two groups, veloutés and creams.

These methods were natural to large kitchens that always had quantities of velouté and béchamel sauces on hand. Making a soup was simply a matter of finishing off a sauce.

Modern cooks view these methods as complicated and have devised other methods that seem simpler. But most of the sauce steps are involved—you still have to thicken a liquid with roux (or other starch), cook and purée the ingredients, and add the milk or cream.

The classical method is still important to learn. It will give you versatility, it makes excellent soup, and besides, it really isn't any harder or longer, in the final analysis. In addition, we explain two other methods much in use today.

But first, we consider a problem frequently encountered with cream soups.

Curdling

Because cream soups contain milk or cream or both, curdling is a common problem. The heat of cooking and the acidity of many of the other soup ingredients are the causes of this curdling.

Fortunately, we can rely on one fact to avoid curdling: *Roux and other starch thickeners stabilize milk and cream*. Caution is still necessary because soups are relatively thin and do not contain enough starch to be completely curdle-proof.

Observe the following guidelines to help prevent curdling:

1. Do not combine milk and simmering soup stock without the presence of roux or other starch. Do one of the following:

   - Thicken the stock before adding milk.

   - Thicken the milk before adding it to the soup.

2. Do not add cold milk or cream to simmering soup. Do one of the following:

   - Heat the milk in a separate saucepan.

   - Temper the milk by gradually adding some of the hot soup to it. Then add it to the rest of the soup.

3. Do not boil soups after milk or cream is added.

Standards of Quality for Cream Soups

1. **Thickness.**
   About the consistency of heavy cream. Not too thick.

2. **Texture.**

Smooth; no graininess or lumps (except garnish, of course).

3. **Taste.**

Distinct flavor of the main ingredient (asparagus in cream of asparagus, etc.). No starchy taste from uncooked roux.

Basic Procedures for Making Cream Soups

The following methods apply to most cream soups. Individual ingredients may require variations.

Method 1

1. Prepare Velouté Sauce (p. 160) or Béchamel Sauce (p. 159), using roux.

2. Prepare the main flavoring ingredients. Cut vegetables into thin slices. Sweat them in butter about 5 minutes to develop flavor. Do not brown. Green leafy vegetables must be blanched before stewing in butter. Cut poultry and seafood into small pieces for simmering.

3. Add flavoring ingredients from step 2 to the velouté or béchamel and simmer until tender. Exception: Finished tomato purée is added for cream of tomato; further cooking is not necessary.

4. Skim any fat or scum carefully from the surface of the soup.

5. Purée the soup using a food mill (Figure 8.2) or an immersion blender (Figure 8.3), and then strain it through a fine china cap. Alternatively, just strain it through a fine china cap, pressing down hard on the solid ingredients to force out the liquid and some of the pulp. The soup should be very smooth.

   Poultry and seafood ingredients may be puréed or reserved for garnish.

6. Add hot white stock or milk to thin the soup to proper consistency.

7. Adjust seasonings.

8. At service time, finish with liaison (p. 153) or heavy cream.

Method 2

1. Sweat vegetable ingredients (except tomatoes) in butter; do not let them color.

2. Add flour. Stir well to make a roux. Cook the roux a few minutes, but do not let it start to brown.

3. Add white stock, beating with a whip as you slowly pour it in.

4. Add any vegetables, other solid ingredients, or flavorings that were not sautéed in step 1.

5. Simmer until all ingredients are tender.

6. Skim any fat that rises to the surface.

7. Purée and/or strain (as in Method 1).

8. Add hot white stock or milk to thin soup to proper consistency.

9. Adjust seasonings.

10. At service time, finish with heavy cream or liaison.

Method 3

1. Bring white stock to a boil.

2. Add vegetables and other flavoring ingredients. If desired, first slowly cook some or all of the vegetables in butter a few minutes to develop flavors.

3. Simmer until all ingredients are tender.

4. Thicken with roux, beurre manié, or other starch.

5. Simmer until no starch taste remains.

6. Skim fat from surface.

7. Purée and/or strain (as in Method 1).

8. Add hot or tempered milk and/or cream. A light cream sauce may be used, if desired, to avoid thinning the soup or curdling the milk.

9. Adjust seasonings.

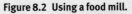

Figure 8.2 Using a food mill.

(a) Purée soft foods by turning the crank of the mill to force them through small holes.

(b) Scrape the solids from the bottom of the mill after all the food is forced through the plate.

Figure 8.3 Using an immersion blender to purée a soup.

Cream of Celery Soup (Cream Soup Method 1)

YIELD: 6 QT (6 L)   PORTIONS: 24   PORTION SIZE: 8 FL OZ (250 ML)

U.S.	METRIC	INGREDIENTS	PROCEDURE
3 lb	1.5 kg	Celery, small dice	1. Review cream soup guidelines and Method 1 (p. 201).
12 oz	375 g	Onion, small dice	2. Sweat the celery and onions in the butter in a heavy saucepot until almost tender. Do
3 oz	90 g	Butter	not let them brown.
4½ qt	4.5 L	Velouté sauce, made with chicken or veal stock (see Note)	3. Add the velouté to the pot. Simmer until vegetables are very tender. 4. Skim any fat or scum from the soup. 5. Pass the soup through a food mill to purée it. 6. Pass the puréed soup through a fine china cap or cheesecloth.
3 pt	1.5 L	Milk or white stock, hot	7. Add enough hot milk or stock to bring the soup to the proper consistency.
to taste	to taste	Salt	8. Heat the soup again, but do not let it boil.
to taste	to taste	White pepper	9. Season to taste.
3 cups	750 Ml	Heavy cream, hot (see Note) Optional garnish:	10. At service time, add the cream. Add garnish if desired.
6 oz	175 g	Celery, cut julienne, cooked	

Per serving: Calories, 320; Protein, 5 g; Fat, 27 g (75% cal.); Cholesterol, 90 mg; Carbohydrates, 15 g; Fiber, 1 g; Sodium, 240 mg.

Note: Béchamel may be used in place of velouté if desired. This is often done for vegetarian menus.
   The quantity of cream may be decreased as desired to reduce dietary fat.

VARIATIONS, METHOD 1

For the following cream soups, make substitutions in the basic recipe as indicated. Frozen and canned vegetables may be used, where appropriate, in place of fresh. Also, trimmings may be used if clean and of good quality, such as bottom ends of asparagus and broccoli stalks.

Cream of Asparagus
Use 3 lb (1.5 kg) asparagus stalks in place of celery. Optional garnish: cooked asparagus tips.

Cream of Broccoli
Use 3 lb (1.5 kg) broccoli in place of celery. Optional garnish: small cooked broccoli florets.

Cream of Carrot
Use 3 lb (1.5 kg) carrots in place of celery. Garnish: chopped parsley.

Cream of Cauliflower
Use 3 lb (1.5 kg) cauliflower in place of celery. Optional garnish: tiny cooked cauliflower florets.

Cream of Corn
Use 3 lb (1.5 kg) whole-kernel corn (fresh, frozen, or canned) in place of celery. Do not sweat the corn with the onions. Instead, sweat the onions alone, add velouté, then add corn. Garnish: corn kernels.

Cream of Cucumber
Use 3 lb (1.5 kg) peeled, seeded cucumber in place of celery. Optional garnish: small, diced, cooked cucumber.

Cream of Mushroom
Use 1½ lb (750 g) mushrooms in place of celery. Optional garnish: julienne, brunoise, or sliced cooked mushrooms.

Cream of Pea
Use 3 lb (1.5 kg) frozen green peas in place of celery. Do not sweat the peas with the onions. Add them after velouté is added.

Cream of Spinach
Use 3 lb (1.5 kg) fresh spinach or 2 lb (900 g) frozen spinach in place of celery. Do not sweat the spinach with the onion. Blanch it, drain well, and add to velouté in step 3.

Cream of Watercress
Use 1½ lb (750 g) watercress in place of celery.

Cream of Chicken
Reduce celery to 6 oz (175 g) and add 6 oz (175 g) carrot (note that, together with the onion, this makes 1½ lb [750 g] mirepoix). Use a velouté sauce made with a strong, flavorful chicken stock. After soup is strained, add 6 oz (175 g) cooked chicken meat, cut into julienne or fine dice.

Cold Cream Soups
Most cream soups are delicious cold as well as hot. For example, cold cream of cucumber soup is a special favorite in summer. Procedure:

1. Chill soup after step 9 in recipe.
2. Add cold cream after soup is well chilled.
3. Dilute with extra milk, cream, or stock if soup becomes too thick.
4. Season carefully. Cold foods require more seasonings.

Cream of Mushroom Soup (Cream Soup Method 2)

YIELD: 6 QT (6 L)   PORTIONS: 24   PORTION SIZE: 8 FL OZ (250 ML)

U.S.	METRIC	INGREDIENTS	PROCEDURE
12 oz	375 g	Butter	1. Review cream soup guidelines and Method 2 (p. 201).
12 oz	375 g	Onion, chopped fine	2. Heat the butter in a heavy saucepot over moderate heat.
1½ lb	750 g	Mushrooms, chopped	3. Add the onions and mushrooms. Sweat the vegetables without letting them brown.
9 oz	275 g	Flour	4. Add the flour and stir to make a roux. Cook the roux a few minutes, but do not let it start to brown.
4½ qt	4.5 L	White stock, chicken or veal, hot	5. Gradually beat in the stock. Bring to a boil, stirring with a whip as it thickens.
			6. Simmer until vegetables are very tender.
			7. Skim the soup carefully.
			8. Pass the soup through a food mill to purée it.
			9. Pass the puréed soup through a fine china cap or cheesecloth.
3 pt	1.5 L	Milk, hot	10. Add enough hot milk to bring the soup to the proper consistency.
to taste	to taste	Salt	11. Heat the soup again, but do not let it boil.
to taste	to taste	White pepper	12. Season to taste.
3 cups	750 mL	Heavy cream, hot (see Note)	13. At service time, add the cream. Add garnish, if desired.
		Optional garnish:	
6 oz	175 g	Mushrooms, cut brunoise, sautéed in butter	

Per serving: Calories, 300; Protein, 5 g; Fat 25 g (75% cal.); Cholesterol, 85 mg; Carbohydrates, 14 g; Fiber, 1 g; Sodium, 170 mg.

Note: The quantity of cream may be decreased as desired to reduce dietary fat.

VARIATIONS, METHOD 2

For each variation, replace the mushrooms with the vegetable in quantity indicated. See Note to the variations for Cream of Celery Soup, page 202.

Cream of Asparagus
3 lb (1.5 kg) asparagus

Cream of Broccoli
3 lb (1.5 kg) broccoli

Cream of Carrot
3 lb (1.5 kg) carrots

Cream of Cauliflower
3 lb (1.5 kg) cauliflower

Cream of Celery
3 lb (1.5 kg) celery

Cream of Corn
3 lb (1.5 kg) whole-kernel corn

Cream of Cucumber
3 lb (1.5 kg) peeled, seeded cucumber

Cream of Green Pea
3 lb (1.5 kg) frozen peas. Add after step 5.

Cream of Spinach
3 lb (1.5 kg) fresh or 2 lb (900 g) frozen spinach. Blanch, drain, and add after step 5.

Cream of Watercress
1½ lb (750 g) watercress

Cream of Chicken
6 oz (175 g) celery and 6 oz (175 g) carrot. Use strong chicken stock. Add 6 oz (175 g) cooked chicken meat, cut into julienne or fine dice, to finished soup after straining.

Cream of Broccoli Soup (Cream Soup Method 3)

YIELD: 6 QT (6 L)   PORTIONS: 24   PORTION SIZE: 8 FL OZ (250 ML)

U.S.	METRIC	INGREDIENTS	PROCEDURE
4½ qt	4.5 L	White stock, chicken or veal	1. Bring the stock to a boil in a heavy saucepot.
3 lb	1.5 kg	Broccoli (fresh or frozen), chopped	2. Add broccoli and onion. (Optional: Vegetables may be sweated in butter first to develop flavors.)
12 oz	375 g	Onion, chopped fine	3. Simmer until the vegetables are tender. Do not overcook, or the broccoli will lose its fresh green color.
9 oz	275 g	Butter, clarified	4. Combine the butter and flour in a saucepan to make a roux. Cook the roux a few minutes, but do not let it color. Cool the roux slightly. (Note: Beurre manié may be used instead of roux.)
9 oz	275 g	Flour	5. Beat the roux into the soup. Simmer until no starch taste remains.
			6. Pass the soup through a food mill, then through a fine china cap or cheesecloth.
3 pt	1.5 L	Milk, hot	7. Add enough hot milk to bring the soup to proper consistency.
to taste	to taste	Salt	8. Heat the soup again, but do not let it boil.
to taste	to taste	White pepper	9. Season to taste.
3 cups	750 mL	Heavy cream, hot (see Note) Optional garnish:	10. At service time, add the heavy cream. If desired, add garnish.
6 oz	175 g	Small broccoli florets, cooked	

Per serving: Calories, 280; Protein, 6 g; Fat, 22 g (69% cal.); Cholesterol, 75 mg; Carbohydrates, 16 g; Fiber, 2 g; Sodium, 150 mg.

Note: The quantity of cream may be decreased as desired to reduce dietary fat.

VARIATIONS, METHOD 3

For other cream soups, replace the broccoli with 3 lb (1.5 kg) of any of the following:

Asparagus	Carrots	Cauliflower	Celery
Corn	Green peas	Spinach	

Wisconsin Cheddar and Broccoli Soup

YIELD: 3 QT (3 L)   PORTIONS: 12   PORTION SIZE: 8 FL OZ (250 ML)

U.S.	METRIC	INGREDIENTS	PROCEDURE
8 oz	250 g	Butter	1. Heat the butter in a heavy saucepot over moderate heat.
6 oz	180 g	Onion, chopped fine	2. Add the onion, celery, broccoli stems, and mushrooms. Sweat the vegetables without letting them brown.
4 oz	125 g	Celery, chopped fine	
8 oz	250 g	Broccoli stems, coarsely chopped	3. Add the flour and stir to make a roux. Cook the roux a few minutes, but do not let it start to brown.
4 oz	125 g	Mushrooms, chopped	
4½ oz	140 g	Flour	
4½ pt	2250 mL	White stock	4. Gradually beat in the stock. Bring to a boil, stirring with a whip, as it thickens.
			5. Simmer until the vegetables are very tender.
			6. Skim the soup carefully.
			7. Pass the soup through a food mill to purée it.
			8. Pass the puréed soup through a chinois or fine strainer.
1 pt	500 mL	Milk, hot	9. Add the hot milk to the soup.
12 oz	375 g	Broccoli florets, cooked	10. Heat the soup again, but do not let it boil.
			11. Separate the broccoli florets into pieces small enough to be eaten with a soup spoon. Add them to the soup.
			12. If the soup is to be served at once, proceed to the next step. Otherwise, cool in a cold-water bath and refrigerate until service time. Reheat soup to a simmer when ready to finish.
1 lb	500 g	Sharp cheddar cheese, grated	13. Add the cheese to the soup and stir until entirely melted.
8 fl oz	250 mL	Heavy cream, hot (see Note)	14. Carefully reheat the soup, but do not let it boil, or else the cheese may curdle or separate.
to taste	to taste	Salt	15. Stir in the heavy cream.
to taste	to taste	White pepper	16. Season to taste with salt and white pepper.

Per serving: Calories, 460; Protein, 13 g; Fat, 38 g (75% cal.); Cholesterol, 115 mg; Carbohydrates, 15 g; Fiber, 2 g; Sodium, 410 mg.

Note: The quantity of cream may be decreased as desired to reduce dietary fat.

Wisconsin Cheddar and Broccoli Soup

Purée Soups

Techniques

Purée soups are made by simmering dried or fresh vegetables, especially high-starch vegetables, in stock or water, then puréeing the soup. Thus, they are relatively easy to prepare. Purée soups are not as smooth and refined as cream soups but are heartier and coarser in texture and character.

Techniques vary greatly depending on the ingredients and the desired result.

Basic Procedure for Making Purée Soups

1. Sweat mirepoix or other fresh vegetables in fat.

2. Add liquid.

3. Add dried or starchy vegetables.

4. Simmer until vegetables are tender. Fresh vegetables should be completely cooked but not overcooked or falling apart.

5. Purée soup in a food mill or with an immersion blender.

   Variation: Some soups made from dried legumes, such as bean soup and lentil soup, are not puréed but are served as is or slightly mashed.

6. Purée soups are generally not bound with an added starch but rely on the starches present in the vegetables. Some fresh vegetable purées, however, settle out. These may be thickened with a little starch if desired.

7. Add cream if required.

8. Adjust seasonings.

Figure 9.4 Preparing a purée soup.

(a) Sweat onions, mirepoix, or other fresh vegetables in fat.

(b) Add stock or other liquid.

(c) Add starchy vegetables or other remaining vegetables.

(d) Purée the soup with an immersion blender, a food processor, or food mill.

Purée of Carrot Soup (Potage Crècy)

YIELD: 6 QT (6 L)   PORTIONS: 24   PORTION SIZE: 8 FL OZ (250 ML)

U.S.	METRIC	INGREDIENTS
4 oz	125 g	Butter
4 lb	2 kg	Carrots, small dice
1 lb	500 g	Onions, small dice
5 qt	5 L	Chicken stock or white veal stock
1 lb	500 g	Potatoes, small dice
to taste	to taste	Salt
to taste	to taste	White pepper

PROCEDURE

1. Heat the butter in a heavy saucepot over moderately low heat.
2. Add the carrots and onions, and sweat the vegetables until they are about half cooked. Do not let them brown.
3. Add the stock and potatoes. Bring to a boil.
4. Simmer until the vegetables are tender.
5. Purée the soup by passing it through a food mill or by using an immersion blender.
6. Bring the soup back to a simmer. If necessary, add more stock to thin the soup to the proper consistency.
7. Season to taste.

		Optional:
1½–2 cups	350–500 mL	Cream, hot

8. If desired, finish the soup with hot cream at service time.

Per serving: Calories, 90; Protein, 2 g; Fat, 4.5 g (40% cal.); Cholesterol, 15 mg; Carbohydrates, 13 g; Fiber, 3 g; Sodium, 95 mg.

VARIATIONS

Rice may be used in place of potatoes as the binding agent in the above recipe or in any variation below except purée of potato, purée of potato and leek, and purée of watercress. Use 8 oz (250 g) raw rice in place of 1 lb (500 g) potatoes. The soup must be simmered until the rice is very soft.

Purée of Cauliflower Soup (Purée Dubarry)
Use 4 lb (2 kg) cauliflower in place of carrots.

Purée of Celery or Celery Root Soup
Use 4 lb (2 kg) celery or celery root in place of carrots.

Purée of Jerusalem Artichoke Soup
Use 4 lb (2 kg) Jerusalem artichoke in place of carrots.

Purée of Potato Soup (Potage Parmentier)
Omit carrots from basic recipe, add 10 oz (300 g) leeks to the onions, and increase the potatoes to 5 lb (2.5 kg).

Purée of Potato and Leek Soup
Use 2 lb (1 kg) leeks in place of the carrots. Increase the potatoes to 2½ lb (1.25 kg).

Purée of Turnip Soup
Use 4 lb (2 kg) white turnips in place of carrots.

Purée of Watercress Soup
Prepare like purée of potato soup, but add 5 bunches watercress, chopped, when the potatoes are almost tender.

Purée of Mixed Vegetable Soup
Decrease carrots to 1¼ lb (600 g). Add 10 oz (300 g) each celery, turnips, leeks, and cabbage.

Potage Solferino
Combine equal parts purée of potato and leek soup and cream of tomato soup.

Purée of Split Pea Soup

YIELD: 6 QT (6 L)   PORTIONS: 24   PORTION SIZE: 8 FL OZ (250 ML)

U.S.	METRIC	INGREDIENTS
6 oz	175 g	Salt pork
		Mirepoix:
10 oz	300 g	Onion, small dice
5 oz	150 g	Celery, small dice
5 oz	150 g	Carrot, small dice
6 qt	6 L	Ham stock (see Note)
1	1	Ham bone or ham hock (optional)
3 lb	1.5 kg	Green split peas
		Sachet:
1	1	Bay leaf
2	2	Whole cloves
6	6	Peppercorns
to taste	to taste	Salt
to taste	to taste	Pepper

PROCEDURE

1. Cut the salt pork into fine dice or pass through a grinder.
2. Cook the salt pork slowly in a heavy saucepot to render the fat. Do not brown the pork.
3. Add the mirepoix and sweat in the fat until the vegetables are slightly softened.
4. Add the ham stock and ham bone. Bring to a boil.
5. Rinse the split peas under cold water. Drain in a strainer and add to the stock. Add the sachet.
6. Cover and simmer until the peas are tender, about 1 hour.
7. Remove the ham bone and sachet.
8. Pass the soup through a food mill.
9. Bring the soup back to a simmer. If it is too thick, bring it to proper consistency with a little stock or water.
10. Season to taste.
11. If a ham hock was used, trim off the meat. Dice it, and add to the soup.

Per serving: Calories, 230; Protein, 13 g; Fat, 7 g (26% cal.); Cholesterol, 5 mg; Carbohydrates, 32 g; Fiber, 12 g; Sodium, 590 mg.

Note: Water may be used if ham stock is not available. In this case, the optional ham bone or ham hock should be used to provide flavor. Simmer the water and bone together for 1 hour or more before making the soup to extract more flavor.

VARIATIONS

For a coarser, more rustic texture, do not pass the soup through a food mill but serve as is. In this case, name soup simply Split Pea Soup rather than Purée of Split Pea Soup. Other bean, pea, and lentil soups may also be served without puréeing.

Other dried vegetables are made into soups using the same procedure. Most dried beans should be soaked in cold water overnight to reduce cooking time. (Split peas may be soaked, but they cook quickly enough without soaking.)

Purée of White Bean Soup

Use 3 lb (1.5 kg) navy beans. Soak the beans overnight. Use chicken or veal stock in place of ham stock.

Purée of Yellow Split Pea Soup

Use yellow split peas instead of green.

Purée of Lentil Soup

Use 3 lb (1.5 kg) brown lentils. Soak overnight. Use either ham stock or white stock. Garnish with diced cooked bacon or ham or sliced frankfurters.

Purée of Kidney Bean Soup

Use 3 lb (1.5 kg) red kidney beans. Soak beans overnight. Use white stock and add 2½ cups (600 mL) red wine to the soup when the beans are almost tender. Garnish with croutons sautéed in butter.

Purée of Black Bean Soup

Use 3 lb (1.5 kg) black turtle beans. Soak beans overnight. Use white stock and ham bone. Add 8 oz (250 mL) Madeira or sherry to the finished soup. Garnish with lemon slices and chopped hard-cooked egg.

Purée Mongole

Combine 3 qt (3 L) purée of green split pea soup and 2 qt (2 L) tomato purée. Dilute to proper consistency with about 1–2 qt (1–2 L) white stock. Garnish with cooked peas and cooked julienne of carrots and leeks.

Nonpuréed Bean Soups

Prepare any of the above soups as directed, but purée only about one-fourth of the beans. Add this purée to the soup as a thickening agent.

Bisques

A bisque (bisk) is a cream soup made with shellfish. At one time, bisques were thickened with rice, but today they are more frequently thickened with roux. Bisques are made basically like other cream soups, but they seem more complex because of the handling of the shellfish and the variety of flavoring ingredients often used. Expensive to prepare and rich in taste, they are considered luxury soups.

The term *bisque* has come to be used for a great variety of soups, primarily because the word sounds nice. In this book, we reserve the term for shellfish cream soups. Nevertheless, you will also see the word *bisque* applied to many of the vegetable purée soups and cream soups discussed in earlier sections.

BISQUE

Linguists say the most likely origin of the word *bisque* is Biscay, the name of the bay off the coast of southwestern France and northwestern Spain.

It is sometimes said the word comes from *biscuit*, because the soup was once thickened by dried bread, but language experts say there is no evidence for this origin.

Shrimp Bisque

YIELD: 2 QT (2 L)   PORTIONS: 10   PORTION SIZE: 6 FL OZ (200 ML)

U.S.	METRIC	INGREDIENTS
1 oz	30 g	Butter
2 oz	60 g	Onions, cut brunoise
2 oz	60 g	Carrots, cut brunoise
1 lb	500 g	Small shrimp, shells on
small piece	small piece	Bay leaf
pinch	pinch	Dried thyme
4	4	Parsley stems
1 oz	30 g	Tomato paste
2 oz	60 mL	Burnt brandy (see Note)
6 oz	200 mL	White wine
1 qt	1 L	Fish velouté
1 pt	500 mL	Fish stock
1 cup	250 mL	Heavy cream, hot
to taste	to taste	Salt
to taste	to taste	White pepper

Per serving: Calories, 220; Protein, 8 g; Fat 17 g (70% cal.); Cholesterol, 110 mg; Carbohydrates, 6 g; Fiber, 0 g; Sodium, 180 mg.

Note: Burnt brandy is brandy that has been heated in a saucepan and flamed (carefully) to burn off the alcohol.

PROCEDURE

1. Heat the butter in a saucepan over medium heat.
2. Add onions and carrots. Sauté until lightly browned.
3. Add the shrimp, bay leaf, thyme, and parsley stems. Sauté until the shrimp turn red.
4. Add the tomato paste and stir well.
5. Add the brandy and wine. Simmer until reduced by half.
6. Remove the shrimp. Peel and devein them. Return shells to the saucepan.
7. Cut the shrimp into small dice and reserve for garnish.

8. Add the fish velouté and stock to the saucepan. Simmer 10–15 minutes.
9. Strain. Return the soup to the saucepan and bring back to a simmer.
10. At service time, add the hot cream and the diced shrimp. Season to taste.

VARIATIONS

This recipe is based on Method 1 for making cream soups (p. 201) in that it uses velouté as a base. You can also use fish stock instead of velouté and thicken the soup in other ways:

1. Beat in beurre manié (p. 152), a little at a time, after step 8, until properly thickened.
2. Stir in a cornstarch slurry (cornstarch in cold water), a little at a time.
3. Simmer 2 oz (60 g) rice in 1 pt (500 mL) of the stock until the rice is completely cooked. Liquefy in a blender or force through a fine sieve to purée the rice, and add to the soup. (This is the classical method.)

To reduce food cost, you may reduce the quantity of shrimp and add extra shrimp shells for flavor. Or, instead of using all the cooked shrimp for garnish, save most of them for another use.

Paprika is often used instead of tomato paste to color and flavor bisques. Substitute 1 tbsp (15 mL) Spanish paprika for the 1 oz (30 g) tomato paste.

Lobster Bisque

In place of shrimp, use live lobster. (Alternatively, to reduce food costs, use crushed lobster shells or rock lobster tails.)

Chowders

Chowders are chunky, hearty soups so full of good things they sometimes are more like stews than soups. Many types of chowder are simply cream soups or purée soups that are not puréed but left chunky. Like other specialty regional soups, chowders resist categorization. However, most of them are based on fish or shellfish or vegetables, and most contain potatoes and milk or cream.

KEY POINTS TO REVIEW

- What are the three basic procedures for making cream soups?

- What is a purée soup? Describe the basic procedure for making a purée soup.

- What is a bisque? Describe the basic procedure for making a shrimp bisque.

- What is a chowder?

Potato Chowder

YIELD: 6 QT (6 L)   PORTIONS: 24   PORTION SIZE: 8 FL OZ (250 ML)

U.S.	METRIC	INGREDIENTS	PROCEDURE
8 oz	250 g	Salt pork	1. Grind the salt pork or cut into very fine dice.
12 oz	375 g	Onions, medium dice	2. Render the pork fat in a heavy saucepot.
3 oz	90 g	Celery, medium dice	3. Add the onions and celery. Cook in the fat over moderate heat until nearly tender. Do not brown.
4 oz	125 g	Flour	4. Add the flour. Stir into the fat to make a roux. Cook the roux slowly 4–5 minutes, but do not let it brown.
3½ qt	3.5 L	Chicken stock	5. Using a wire whip, slowly stir in the stock. Bring to a boil, stirring to make sure the liquid is smooth.
3 lb	1.5 kg	Potatoes, medium dice	6. Add the potatoes. Simmer until all the vegetables are tender.
3 pt	1.5 L	Milk, hot	7. Stir in the hot milk and cream.
1 cup	250 mL	Heavy cream, hot	8. Season to taste with salt and white pepper.
to taste	to taste	Salt	
to taste	to taste	White pepper	
as needed	as needed	Chopped parsley	9. Sprinkle each portion with a little chopped parsley for garnish.

Per serving: Calories, 210; Protein, 5g; Fat 14g (59% cal.); Cholesterol, 35 mg; Carbohydrates, 18g; Fiber, 1 g; Sodium, 180 mg.

VARIATIONS

Corn Chowder

Version 1. Prepare as in basic recipe, but reduce potatoes to 2¼ lb (1.1 kg). When vegetables are tender, add 3 lb (1.5 kg) frozen or drained canned whole-kernel corn. (If using canned corn, replace part of the chicken stock with corn liquid.)

Version 2. Prepare as in basic recipe, but reduce potatoes to 1½ lb (750 g). Add 3 lb (1.5 kg) canned cream-style corn when vegetables are tender.

New England Clam Chowder

YIELD: 6 QT (6 L) PORTIONS: 24 PORTION SIZE: 8 FL OZ (250 ML)

U.S.	METRIC	INGREDIENTS
2 qt	2 L	Canned, minced clams, with their juice, or fresh shucked clams, with their juice (see Note)
1½ qt	1.5 L	Water
10 oz	300 g	Salt pork, ground or cut into fine dice
1 lb	500 g	Onions, small dice
4 oz	125 g	Flour
2 lb	1 kg	Potatoes, small dice
2½ qt	2.5 L	Milk, hot
1 cup	250 mL	Heavy cream, hot
to taste	to taste	Salt
to taste	to taste	White pepper

PROCEDURE

1. Drain the clams, reserving the juice. If you are using fresh clams, chop them, being sure to save all the juice.
2. Combine the juice and water in a saucepan. Bring to a boil.
3. Remove from the heat and keep the liquid hot for step 7.
4. In a heavy saucepot or stockpot, render the salt pork over medium heat.
5. Add the onions and cook slowly until soft, but do not brown.
6. Add the flour and stir to make a roux. Cook the roux slowly 3–4 minutes, but do not let it brown.
7. Using a wire whip, slowly stir the clam liquid and water into the roux. Bring to a boil, stirring constantly to make sure the liquid is smooth.
8. Add the potatoes. Simmer until tender. (If you are using large, tough chowder clams, pass them once through a grinder and add with the potatoes.)
9. Stir in the clams and hot milk and cream. Heat gently, but do not boil.
10. Season to taste with salt and white pepper.

Per serving: Calories, 300; Protein, 16 g; Fat, 17 g (52% cal.); Cholesterol, 65 mg; Carbohydrates, 19 g; Fiber, 1 g; Sodium, 350 mg.

Note: If whole clams in the shell are used, you will need about 8–10 qt (8–10 L). Scrub them well. Combine with the 1½ qt (1½ L) water in a stockpot and simmer until the shells open. Remove the clams from the shells and chop. Strain the liquid.

VARIATIONS

Manhattan Clam Chowder

Substitute 4 fl oz (125 mL) oil or 4 oz (125 g) butter for the salt pork. Add 10 oz (300 g) celery, small dice; 10 oz (300 g) carrots, small dice; and 1 tsp (5 mL) chopped garlic to the onions in step 5. Omit flour. Instead of milk, use 2½ qt (2½ L) chopped canned tomatoes and their juices. Omit cream.

New England Fish Chowder

Follow the procedure for New England Clam Chowder, but omit clams and water. Use 3 qt (3 L) fish stock instead of the clam juice and water mixture in step 7. Remove all skin and bones from 1¼ lb (625 g) haddock fillets. Cut into ¾-in. (2-cm) chunks. Add to the finished soup and keep hot (do not boil) until the fish is cooked, about 5 minutes.

SPECIALTY SOUPS AND NATIONAL SOUPS

French Onion Soup Gratinée

YIELD: 7½ QT (7.5 L)　PORTIONS: 24　PORTION SIZE: 10 FL OZ (300 ML)

U.S.	METRIC	INGREDIENTS
4 oz	125 g	Butter
5 lb	2.5 kg	Onions, sliced thin
6½ qt	6.5 L	Beef stock, or half beef and half chicken stock
to taste	to taste	Salt
to taste	to taste	Pepper
4–6 fl oz	125–175 mL	Sherry (optional)
as needed	as needed	French bread (see procedure)
1½ lb	750 g	Gruyère or Swiss cheese, or a mixture, coarsely grated

Per serving: Calories, 320; Protein, 15 g; Fat, 15 g (42% cal.); Cholesterol, 50 mg; Carbohydrates, 31 g; Fiber, 3 g; Sodium, 410 mg.

PROCEDURE

1. Heat the butter in a stockpot over moderate heat. Add the onions and cook until golden. Stir occasionally. *Note:* The onions must cook slowly and become evenly browned. This is a slow process and will take about 30 minutes. Do not brown too fast or use high heat.

2. Add the stock and bring to a boil. Simmer until the onions are very tender and the flavors are well blended, about 20 minutes.

3. Season to taste with salt and pepper. Add the sherry, if desired.

4. Keep the soup hot for service.

5. Cut the bread into slices about ⅜ in. (1 cm) thick. You need 1 or 2 slices per portion, or just enough to cover the top of the soup in its serving crock.

6. Toast bread slices in the oven or under the broiler.

7. For each portion, fill an individual-service soup crock with hot soup. Place 1 or 2 slices of the toast on top and cover with cheese. Pass under the broiler until the cheese is bubbling and lightly browned. Serve immediately.

VARIATIONS

Onion soup may be served without gratinéeing and with cheese croutons prepared separately. Toast the bread as in basic recipe. Place on a sheet pan. Brush lightly with butter and sprinkle each piece with grated cheese. (Parmesan may be mixed with the other cheese.) Brown under the broiler. Garnish each portion with

1 cheese crouton. (This method is less expensive because it uses much less cheese.)

French Onion Soup Gratinée

Minestrone

YIELD: 6 QT (6 L) PORTIONS: 24   PORTION SIZE: 8 FL OZ (250 ML)

U.S.	METRIC	INGREDIENTS	PROCEDURE
4 fl oz	125 mL	Olive oil	1. Heat the oil in a heavy pot over medium heat.
1 lb	500 g	Onions, sliced thin	2. Add the onions, celery, carrots, and garlic. Sweat them in the oil until almost tender. Do not brown.
8 oz	250 g	Celery, small dice	
8 oz	250 g	Carrots, small dice	3. Add the cabbage and zucchini. Stir to mix the vegetables. Continue to sweat another 5 minutes.
2 tsp	10 mL	Garlic, chopped	
8 oz	250 g	Green cabbage, shredded (see p. 253 for technique)	
8 oz	250 g	Zucchini, medium dice	
1 lb	500 g	Canned tomatoes, crushed	4. Add the tomatoes, stock, and basil. Bring to a boil, reduce heat, and simmer until the vegetables are almost cooked. (Do not overcook. The soup will continue to cook when the pasta is added.)
5 qt	5 L	White stock	
1 tsp	5 mL	Dried basil	
6 oz	175 g	Small macaroni, such as ditalini	5. Add the pasta and continue to simmer the soup until the pasta is cooked. (Alternatively, cook pasta separately and add to the soup just before serving.)
1½ lb	750 g	Drained, canned cannellini or other white beans (2 No.2 cans)	6. Add the beans and return soup to a boil.
¼ cup	60 mL	Chopped parsley	7. Add the parsley. Season to taste with salt and pepper.
to taste	to taste	Salt	
to taste	to taste	Pepper	
as needed	as needed	Parmesan cheese, grated	8. Just before service, top with the parmesan cheese, or serve cheese separately.

Per serving: Calories, 150; Protein, 7 g, Fat, 7 g (40% cal.); Cholesterol, 10 mg; Carbohydrates, 17 g; Fiber, 3 g; Sodium, 200 mg.

Minestrone

Gazpacho

YIELD: 2½ QT (2.5 L)   PORTIONS: 12   PORTION SIZE: 6 FL OZ (200 ML)

U.S.	METRIC	INGREDIENTS
2½ lb	1.2 kg	Tomatoes, peeled and chopped fine
1 lb	500 g	Cucumbers, peeled and chopped fine
8 oz	250 g	Onions, peeled and chopped fine
4 oz	125 g	Green bell peppers, seeded and chopped fine
½ tsp	2 mL	Crushed garlic
2 oz	60 g	Fresh white bread crumbs
1 pt	500 mL	Water or tomato juice, cold
3 fl oz	90 mL	Red wine vinegar
4 fl oz	125 L	Olive oil
to taste	to taste	Salt
to taste	to taste	Pepper
to taste	to taste	Cayenne or hot red pepper sauce
to taste	to taste	Lemon juice or vinegar
		Garnish:
2 oz	60 g	Onion, small dice
2 oz	60 g	Cucumber, small dice
2 oz	60 g	Green pepper, small dice

PROCEDURE

1. If a blender is available, combine all ingredients in the blender and process until liquefied.

2. If a blender is not available, combine all ingredients except olive oil. Pass through a food mill. If a smoother soup is desired, then pass through a fine sieve. Rub the solids through the sieve to purée them. Place the mixture in a stainless-steel bowl. Using a wire whip, slowly beat in the olive oil.

3. Add salt, pepper, and cayenne or pepper sauce to taste.

4. If necessary, adjust tartness by adding a little lemon juice or vinegar.

5. Chill the soup thoroughly.

6. Combine garnish ingredients in a small bowl or bain-marie.

7. At service time, ladle 6 oz (200 mL) gazpacho into chilled soup cups. Top with 1–2 tbsp (15–30 g) diced vegetable garnish. If desired, gazpacho may be served with ice cubes.

Per serving: Calories, 130; Protein, 2 g; Fat, 10 g (63% cal.); Cholesterol, 0 mg; Carbohydrates, 11 g; Fiber, 2 g; Sodium, 36 mg.

Gazpacho

TERMS FOR REVIEW

clear soup	cream soup	chowder	clearmeat
vegetable soup	purée soup	potage	clarification
consommé	bisque	coagulation	raft

QUESTIONS FOR DISCUSSION

1. You have 3 gallons (12 L) vegetable soup in the walk-in, prepared by a cook on the morning shift. You are going to serve the soup this evening, and your dinner service lasts from 6 until 10 p.m. How should you prepare the soup for service?
2. What are the most important characteristics of a good consommé?
3. Why is it important not to boil consommé during clarification?
4. What is the function of egg whites in clearmeat? mirepoix? tomato product?

5. In what order would you add the following items to a vegetable soup during cooking?

   Carrots   Shredded cabbage   Tomatoes

   Barley   Diced cooked beef

6. Using Method 1 or 2, describe how you would prepare cream of watercress soup.

Chapter 9

Cinnamon Raisin French Toast, page 234.

Breakfast Preparation

When we speak of breakfast cookery, we are not just talking about a particular meal. We are referring to a particular small group of foods that appears on perhaps every breakfast menu. These items not only appear on breakfast menus but also are popular for brunches, snacks, and late suppers. Many establishments offer a breakfast menu all day long.

Eggs, of course, are the most popular breakfast food, and they are the primary subject of this chapter. In addition, the chapter examines the preparation of other breakfast staples: pancakes, waffles, French toast, and breakfast meats.

After reading this chapter, you should be able to

1. Describe the composition of eggs and the major differences among grades.

2. Store eggs properly.

3. Prepare the following egg items: hard-, medium-, and soft-cooked eggs; poached eggs; fried eggs; baked eggs; scrambled eggs; omelets; entrée soufflés; and savory custards.

4. List the key differences between waffle batter and pancake batter, and prepare each.

5. Prepare French toast, and identify the common variations possible by changing the basic ingredients.

6. Prepare each of the two general types of breakfast cereal.

7. Identify the three most common breakfast meats and prepare them.

EGGS

Contrary to popular opinion, there is no law that says one must have eggs or cereal or pancakes or pastries for breakfast and must not have shrimp curry or chili or spaghetti and meatballs. Although most of us would think these last suggestions rather strange for the morning meal, there is probably no food that someone, somewhere, does not enjoy for breakfast. No doubt many Japanese, who have soybean soup, sour pickles, and rice for their first meal of the day, think Western breakfast habits are strange.

However, the egg remains a favorite breakfast food, even as we become more adventurous and explore ethnic cuisines. For such apparently simple items, eggs are used in many ways in the kitchen and require special study. We examine not only the usual breakfast preparation but other egg dishes as well, such as soufflés and custards.

Understanding Eggs

Composition

A whole egg consists primarily of a yolk, a white, and a shell. In addition, it contains a membrane that lines the shell and forms an air cell at the large end, and two white strands called chalazae that hold the yolk centered. Figure 9.1 is a cross-sectional diagram that shows the location of these features.

1. The *yolk* is high in both fat and protein, and it contains iron and several vitamins. Its color ranges from light to dark yellow, depending on the diet of the chicken.

2. The *white* is primarily albumin protein, which is clear and soluble when raw but white and firm when coagulated. The white also contains sulfur.

   The white has two parts: a thick portion that surrounds the yolk, and a thinner, more liquid portion outside of this.

3. The *shell* is not the perfect package, in spite of what you may have heard. Not only is it fragile but it is also porous, allowing odors and flavors to be absorbed by the egg and allowing the egg to lose moisture even if unbroken.

BROWN EGGS

Many consumers like to buy brown-shelled eggs, even pay more for them, because they think they are more nutritious, more flavorful, or somehow more natural. In fact, shell color is determined by the breed of the hen and has no relation to the flavor, purity, or nutritional value of the egg.

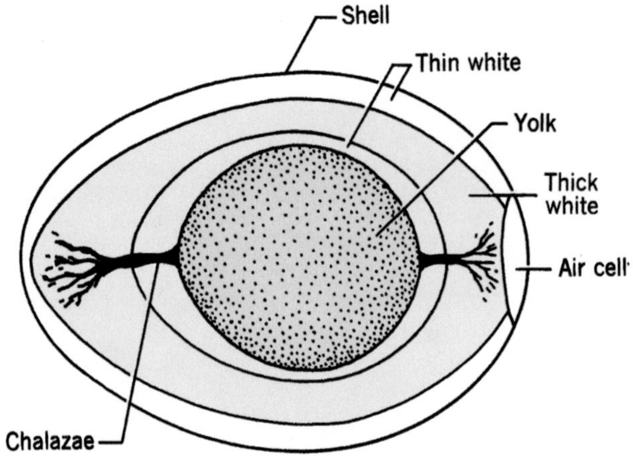

Figure 9.1 The parts of an egg. The diagram shows, in simplified form, the location of the parts of an unbroken egg, as described in the text.

Grades and Quality

GRADES

In the United States, eggs are graded for quality by the USDA. The three grades are AA, A, and B.

The best grade (AA) has a firm yolk and white that stand up high when broken onto a flat surface and do not spread over a large area. In the shell, the yolk is well centered, and the air sac is small.

As eggs age, they lose density. The thin part of the white becomes larger, and the egg spreads over a larger area when broken. Also, the air sac becomes larger as the egg loses moisture through the shell. Figure 9.2 shows the differences among grades AA, A, and B.

Figure 9.2 Egg grades.
Courtesy of the USDA.

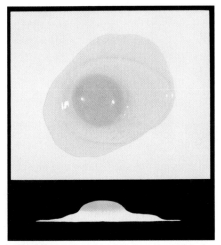

(a) Grade AA.

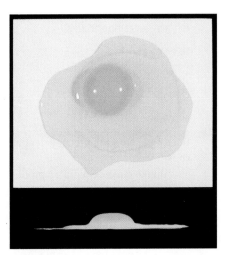

(b) Grade A.

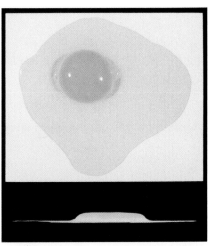

(c) Grade B eggs, as seen from the top and side. Note how the white and yolk lose thickness and spread more in the lower grades.

MAINTAINING QUALITY

Proper storage is essential for maintaining quality. Eggs keep for weeks if held at 36°F (2°C) but lose quality quickly if held at room temperature. In fact, they can lose a full grade in one day at warm kitchen temperatures. There's no point in paying for Grade AA eggs if they are Grade B by the time you use them.

Store eggs away from foods that might pass on undesirable flavors or odors.

GRADES AND USE

One glance at Figure 9.2 will show you why Grade AA is the best to use for fried or poached eggs. Lower grades spread too much to produce a high-quality product.

For hard-cooked eggs, use either Grade A eggs or Grade AA eggs that have been held a few days in the refrigerator. Very fresh eggs are difficult to peel when cooked in the shell.

Grade B eggs are suitable for use in baking. If you are certain they have developed no strong flavors, they may be used for scrambled eggs, where the firmness of the whole egg is less important.

Size

Eggs are also graded by size. Table 9.1 gives the minimum weight per dozen (including shell) according to size category. Note that each size differs from the next by 3 ounces or 85 grams.

Most food-service operations use large eggs, and recipes in most books are based on this size.

Table 9.1
Egg Size Classifications

	MINIMUM WEIGHT PER DOZEN	
SIZE	U.S.	METRIC
Jumbo	30 oz	850 g
Extra-large	27 oz	765 g
Large	24 oz	680 g
Medium	21 oz	595 g
Small	18 oz	510 g
Peewee	15 oz	425 g

Market Forms

1. **Fresh eggs or shell eggs.**

   These are most often used for breakfast cookery and are the main subject of this section.

2. **Frozen eggs.**

   - Whole eggs

   - Whites

   - Yolks

   - Whole eggs with extra yolks

   Frozen eggs are usually made from high-quality fresh eggs and are excellent for use in scrambled eggs, omelets, French toast, and in baking. They are pasteurized and are usually purchased in 30-pound (13.6-kg) cans. These take at least two days to thaw at refrigerator temperatures.

3. **Dried eggs.**

   - Whole eggs

   - Yolks

   - Whites

   Dried eggs are used primarily for baking. They are not suggested for use in breakfast cookery.

   Unlike most dehydrated products, dried eggs are not shelf-stable and must be kept refrigerated or frozen, tightly sealed.

SANITATION

In recent years, cases of salmonella food poisoning have been caused by raw or undercooked eggs. As a result, cooks have been made more aware of egg-related sanitation concerns. Pasteurized egg products are used in more operations.

Egg Substitutes

Egg yolks, in addition to being high in fat, are also high in cholesterol. Efforts to reduce cholesterol in the diet have led to the development of commercial egg substitutes. These are of two types:

1. Egg substitutes that can be used to make such dishes as scrambled eggs, omelets, and custards are made of pasteurized egg whites with the addition of a blend of ingredients to substitute for the yolks, such as vegetable oil, milk solids, vegetable gums, salt, emulsifiers, and vitamin additives. They are sold in bulk liquid form, usually frozen, and can be substituted, ounce for ounce, for whole liquid eggs in most egg preparations.

2. Eggless egg substitutes contain no egg product. They are made of flours or other starches, plus vegetable gums and stabilizers, and, sometimes, soy protein. They are intended for use in baked goods only and are not suitable for use in breakfast egg preparations or custards. If they contain no milk products (read ingredient lists on individual products), they may be used in vegan diets.

General Cooking Principles

The most important rule of egg cookery is simple: *Avoid high temperatures and long cooking times*. In other words, do not overcook. This should be a familiar rule by now.

Overcooking produces tough eggs, causes discoloration, and affects flavor.

COAGULATION

Eggs are largely protein, so the principle of coagulation (p. 53) is important to consider.

Eggs coagulate at the following temperatures:

Whole eggs, beaten	about 156°F (69°C)
Whites	140°–149°F (60°–65°C)
Yolks	144°–158°F (62°–70°C)
Custard (whole eggs plus liquid)	175°–185°F (79°–85°C)

Note that whites coagulate or cook before yolks do. This is why it is possible to cook eggs with firm whites but soft yolks.

Note also that when eggs are mixed with a liquid, they become firm at a higher temperature. However, 185°F (85°C) is still much lower than the temperature of a sauté pan or skillet over high heat. As the temperature of coagulation is reached, the eggs change from semiliquid to solid, and they become opaque. If their temperature continues to rise, they become even firmer. *An overcooked egg is tough and rubbery.* Low temperatures produce the best-cooked eggs.

If egg-liquid mixtures such as custards and scrambled eggs are overcooked, the egg solids separate from the liquids, or *curdle*. This is often seen as tough, watery scrambled eggs.

SULFUR

The familiar green ring you often see in hard-cooked eggs is caused by cooking at high temperatures or cooking too long. The same green color appears in scrambled eggs that are overcooked or held too long in the steam table.

This ring results when the sulfur in the egg whites reacts with the iron in the yolk to form iron sulfide, a compound that has a green color and a strong odor and flavor. The best way to avoid green eggs is to use *low temperatures and short cooking and holding times.*

FOAMS

Whipped egg whites are used to give lightness and rising power to soufflés, puffy omelets, cakes, some pancakes and waffles, and other products. The following guidelines will help you handle beaten egg whites properly (see Figure 9.3).

1. **Fat inhibits foaming.**
   When separating eggs, be careful not to get any yolk in the whites. Yolks contain fats. Use very clean equipment when beating whites.

2. **Mild acids help foaming.**
   A small amount of lemon juice or cream of tartar gives more volume and stability to beaten egg whites. Use about 2 teaspoons cream of tartar per pound of egg whites (20 mL per kg).

3. **Egg whites foam better at room temperature.**
   Remove them from the cooler 1 hour before beating.

4. **Do not overbeat.**
   Beaten egg whites should look moist and shiny. Overbeaten eggs look dry and curdled and have lost much of their ability to raise soufflés and cakes.

5. **Sugar makes foams more stable.**
   When making sweet puffed omelets and dessert soufflés, add some of the sugar to the partially beaten whites and continue to beat to proper stiffness. (This will take longer than when no sugar is added.) The soufflé will be more stable before and after baking.

Figure 9.3 **Whipping egg whites.**

(a) **The whites are just beginning to whip into a foam.**

(b) **The whites have reached the soft-peak stage.**

(c) **The whites have reached the firm-peak stage. Note the smooth texture. Whipping beyond this stage will cause the foam to break.**

> ### KEY POINTS TO REVIEW
>
> - What are the three components of a whole shell egg? Describe each of these components.
> - How are eggs graded for size and quality? What are the grades?
> - How should egg products be stored?
> - What are five guidelines to keep in mind when whipping egg white foams?

Cooking Eggs

Simmering in the Shell

The term *hard-boiled egg* is not a good one to use because eggs should be simmered instead of boiled.

Eggs may be simmered in water to the soft-, medium-, or hard-cooked stage according to the following methods.

Procedures for Simmering Eggs in the Shell

Method 1

1. Collect equipment and food items.

2. Bring eggs to room temperature by (a) removing them from the cooler 1 hour before cooking, or (b) placing them in warm water for 5 minutes and draining. Cold eggs are more likely to crack when placed in boiling water.

3. Place eggs in boiling water and return the water to a simmer.

4. Simmer, do not boil, for the required time:

    Soft-cooked   3 to 4 minutes

    Medium-cooked   5 to 7 minutes

    Hard-cooked   12 to 13 minutes

    Exact cooking time depends on temperature of eggs, size of eggs, and amount of water used.

5. Drain immediately and cool under cold running water to stop the cooking. Cool just a few seconds if eggs are to be served hot. Cool further if they are to be held for later use.

6. To peel, crack the shell and pull it away, starting at the large end (where the air sac is located). For easier peeling, peel while still warm, and hold under running water to help loosen shell. Very fresh eggs are hard to peel. Eggs for cooking in the shell should be several days old.

Method 2

1. Collect equipment and food items.

2. Place eggs in saucepan and cover with cold water.

3. Bring water to a boil.

4. Reduce heat and simmer for the required time:

    Soft-cooked   1 minute

    Medium-cooked   3 to 5 minutes

    Hard-cooked   8 to 9 minutes

Method 3; for Hard-Cooked Eggs Only

Proceed as in Method 2, but remove pan from heat and cover as soon as it comes to a boil. Let stand off heat 20 minutes.

Poaching

The principles of cooking eggs in the shell are applicable to poached eggs. The only difference between the two items is the shell.

This difference, of course, complicates the cooking process, as emphasized in the following procedure. The object is to keep the eggs egg-shaped—that is, in a round, compact mass rather than spread all over the pan.

STANDARDS OF QUALITY FOR POACHED EGGS

1. Bright, shiny appearance.

2. Compact, round shape, not spread or flattened.

3. Firm but tender whites; warm, liquid yolks.

Procedure for Poaching Eggs

1. Collect equipment and food items.

2. Use the freshest Grade AA eggs whenever possible for best results. These maintain their shape best because the yolks and whites are firm.

3. If eggs are not very fresh, add 1 teaspoon salt and 1 tablespoon distilled vinegar per quart of water (5 mL salt and 15 mL vinegar per L). The vinegar helps coagulate the egg white faster so it keeps a better shape.

   Vinegar is not necessary if very fresh eggs are used. Omit in this case because whites will be tougher and not as shiny if cooked with vinegar.

4. Bring water to a simmer.
   If water is boiling, eggs will toughen and may be broken up by the agitation.
   If water is not hot enough, eggs will not cook quickly enough and will spread.

5. Break eggs, one at a time, into a dish or a small plate and slide into the simmering water. Eggs will hold their shape better if they slide in against the edge of the pan.

6. Simmer 3 to 5 minutes, until whites are coagulated but yolks are still soft.

7. Remove eggs from pan with slotted spoon or skimmer.

8. To serve immediately, drain very well. For better appearance, trim ragged edges.

9. To hold for later service, plunge immediately into ice water to stop the cooking. At service time, reheat briefly in hot water.

Eggs Benedict

YIELD: 1 PORTION (SEE NOTE)

U.S.	METRIC	INGREDIENTS
½	½	English muffin
as needed	as needed	Butter
1	1	Egg, fresh Grade AA
1 slice	1 slice	Canadian bacon or ham, cooked (about 2 oz/60 g)
1½ fl oz	50 mL	Hollandaise Sauce (p. 171)

PROCEDURE

1. Toast the muffin half. Spread it with butter and place on a serving plate.

2. Poach the egg according to the basic procedure given in this section.

3. While the egg is poaching, heat the Canadian bacon or ham for 1 minute on a hot griddle or in a sauté pan. Place the meat on the toasted muffin.

4. Drain the poached egg well and place it on the Canadian bacon.

5. Ladle hollandaise over the top. Serve immediately.

Per serving: Calories, 660; Protein, 19 g; Fat, 58 g (79% cal.); Cholesterol, 480 mg; Carbohydrates, 15 g; Fiber, 1 g; Sodium, 1260 mg.

Note: To prepare Eggs Benedict in quantity, the eggs may be poached ahead of time, cooled in ice water, and refrigerated. At service time, reheat the eggs in simmering water 30–60 seconds. Drain, plate, and serve.

VARIATIONS

Eggs Florentine
Instead of the muffin and bacon, place the egg on a bed of hot, buttered cooked spinach (about 2 oz/60 g). Cover with Mornay sauce instead of hollandaise. Optional: Sprinkle with parmesan cheese and brown under the salamander or broiler.

Eggs Bombay
Instead of the muffin and bacon, place the egg on a bed of hot rice pilaf (about 2 oz/60 g). Cover with curry sauce instead of hollandaise.

Frying

Fried eggs are an especially popular breakfast preparation. They should always be cooked to order and served immediately. For best quality, observe each step in the following procedure. The choice of cooking fat is a matter of taste and budget. Butter has the best flavor, but margarine or oil may be used. Use bacon fat only if that flavor is desired by the customer.

Procedure for Frying Eggs to Order

1. Collect all equipment and food items.
   Eggs may be fried in small, individual sauté pans (omelet pans) or on the griddle. Griddled eggs are not as attractive because they tend to spread more. See page 227 for the procedure for conditioning sauté pans to avoid sticking.

2. Select very fresh Grade AA eggs for best results.

3. Add about ⅛ inch (2 mm) fat to the sauté pan and set it over moderate heat, or preheat the griddle to 325°F (165°C) and ladle on a small quantity of fat. Too much fat will make the eggs greasy. Not enough will cause them to stick, unless a pan with a nonstick coating is used.

4. Break the eggs into a dish. This lessens the chance of breaking the yolks.

5. When the fat is hot enough so a drop of water sizzles when dropped into it, slide the eggs into the pan (or onto the griddle).
   If the fat is not hot enough, the eggs will spread too much and may stick. If it is too hot, the eggs will become tough or even crisp.

6. Reduce heat to low (if using sauté pan) and cook the eggs to order as indicated below. See Figures 9.4 and 9.5 for flipping and turning techniques.

Figure 9.4 Flipping eggs in a pan.

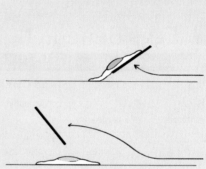

(a) Lift the handle of the pan and slide the eggs to the far edge with a quick jerk.

(b) With a quick flip of the wrist, as shown by the arrow, turn the eggs over. Do not flip the eggs too hard, or the yolks may break when they land.

Figure 9.5 When frying eggs on a griddle, turn them with one smooth motion of the spatula, as shown. The left corner of the egg never actually leaves the surface of the griddle.

- *Sunny side up.* Cook slowly without flipping until white is completely set but yolk is still soft and yellow. Heat must be low, or bottom will toughen or burn before top is completely set.

- *Basted.* Do not flip. Add a few drops of water to pan and cover so steam cooks the top. A thin film of coagulated white will cover the yolk, which should remain liquid. *Note:* This preparation is sometimes called *country style.* The term *basted* is used because the same effect may be achieved by spooning hot fat over the egg as it fries. This method may make the eggs excessively greasy, however.

- *Over easy.* Fry and flip over. Cook just until the white is just set but the yolk is still liquid.

- *Over medium.* Fry and flip over. Cook until the yolk is partially set.

- *Over hard.* Fry and flip over. Cook until the yolk is completely set.

KEY POINTS TO REVIEW

- What are the procedures for simmering eggs in the shell?

- What are the steps in the procedure for poaching eggs?

- What are the steps in the procedure for frying eggs to order?

STANDARDS OF QUALITY FOR FRIED EGGS

1. White should be shiny, uniformly set, and tender, not browned, blistered, or crisp at edges.

2. Yolk should be set properly according to desired doneness. Sunny-side-up yolks should be yellow and well rounded. In other styles, the yolk is covered with a thin layer of coagulated white.

3. Relatively compact, standing high. Not spread out and thin.

Huevos Rancheros

YIELD: 1 PORTION

U.S.	METRIC	INGREDIENTS
as needed	as needed	Vegetable oil
1	1	Corn tortilla
2	2	Eggs
4 fl oz	125 mL	Salsa Roja (p. 180)
1 oz	30 g	Monterey jack or fresh Mexican white cheese, grated or crumbled

Per serving: Calories, 400; Protein, 22 g; Fat, 27 g (60% cal.); Cholesterol, 450 mg; Carbohydrates, 19 g; Fiber, 3 g; Sodium, 340 mg.

PROCEDURE

1. Heat a thin layer of oil in a sauté pan.
2. Fry the tortilla briefly in the oil, turning it once, until softened.
3. Remove from the pan and drain on paper towels.
4. Fry the eggs sunny side up or basted, following the procedure on page 224.
5. Place the tortilla on a warm dinner plate.
6. Top with the eggs.
7. Ladle the sauce over the whites of the eggs, leaving the yolks uncovered.
8. Top with the grated cheese.
9. If desired, add a portion of Frijoles Refritos (p. 342) to the plate.

Huevos Rancheros

Baked Eggs

Baked eggs are baked in individual serving dishes. They are also called *shirred eggs* and *eggs en cocotte.*

They may also be baked with or garnished with a variety of meats and sauces, as indicated in the variations that follow.

Baked Egg Variations

Any of the following may be placed in the buttered egg dish before adding the egg:

    Ham or Canadian bacon, thin slice, lightly browned on griddle or in sauté pan

    Bacon, cooked crisp, 3 or 4 half-strips

    Corned beef hash, beef hash, or ham hash

    Cheese, such as cheddar, Swiss, or Gruyère, grated

    Diced chicken in cream sauce

    Tomato concassé, sautéed in butter

Procedure for Making Baked Eggs

1. Collect equipment and food items.
2. Butter individual-portion ramekins or baking dishes.
3. Break eggs into dish.
4. Place in oven at 350°F (175°C) and cook to desired doneness.
5. Serve in the same dish or ramekin.

Baked eggs with sausages

Any of the following may placed on top of the eggs, either before or after baking. Place solid garnish to one side. Spoon sauces around the outside. Do not cover the yolk.

Heavy cream, hot	Sautéed chicken livers and brown sauce
Brown sauces such as bordelaise, Madeira, or demi-glace	Small grilled sausages
Tomato sauce	Mushrooms sautéed in butter or cream sauce
Soubise sauce	Asparagus tips

Scrambled Eggs

Like other egg preparations, scrambled eggs are best if cooked to order. However, they may be made in larger quantities. They should be undercooked if they are to be held for volume service, as they will cook more in the steam table.

If scrambled eggs must be held over 30 minutes, they will be more stable if the eggs are mixed with a medium white sauce (béchamel) before cooking. Use about 8 ounces sauce per quart of eggs (250 mL per L).

Do not overcook scrambled eggs or hold them too long. Overcooked eggs are tough and watery, and they eventually turn green in the steam table.

Scrambled eggs should be soft and moist, unless the customer requests "scrambled hard."

Procedure for Scrambling Eggs

1. Collect equipment and food items.
2. Break eggs into a stainless-steel bowl and beat until well blended. Season with salt and white pepper. Do not use aluminum, which may discolor the eggs.
3. If desired, add a small amount of milk or cream, about 1 to 1½ tablespoons (15 to 20 mL) for 2 eggs, or 8 to 12 ounces per quart of eggs (250 to 375 mL per L).
   Too much liquid may make cooked eggs watery, and it dilutes the flavor. Heavy cream adds richness but also adds cost.
4. Heat butter in a small sauté pan (for cooking to order) or in a large skillet, as for fried eggs.
   Note: Steam kettles or tilting skillets may be used for scrambling large quantities of eggs.
5. When fat is just hot enough to make a drop of water sizzle, pour in eggs.
6. Cook over low heat, stirring gently from time to time as the eggs coagulate. Lift portions of coagulated egg so uncooked egg can run underneath.
   Too much stirring breaks up eggs into very small particles.
   Do not let the eggs brown. Keep heat low.
7. When eggs are set but still soft and moist, remove from heat. Turn out onto plate or into steam table pan.

ADDITIONS TO SCRAMBLED EGGS

Flavor variations may be created by adding any of the following ingredients to scrambled eggs before serving:

Chopped parsley and/or other herbs	Sautéed diced onion and green bell pepper
Grated cheese (cheddar, Swiss, parmesan)	Diced smoked salmon
Diced ham	Sliced cooked breakfast sausage
Crumbled bacon	

Omelets

Making omelets is like riding a bicycle. When you are learning, it seems difficult, and you can't imagine how anyone can do it. But once you have mastered the technique, it seems easy, and you don't understand how anyone could have trouble doing it.

We are talking about the plain or French omelet. There are several kinds, as described below, but the French omelet remains the most popular. Making it is a technique worth mastering.

FRENCH OMELET

Omelets may be described as sophisticated scrambled eggs. The first part of the technique is similar to that for making scrambled eggs. But the similarities end there, and the omelet emerges from the pan not as a shapeless pile of curds but an attractive oval with a light, delicate texture.

Two elements are necessary for making omelets:

1. High heat. This seems like a contradiction to our basic principle of low-temperature egg cookery. But the omelet cooks so fast that its internal temperature never has time to get too high.

2. A conditioned omelet pan. First, the pan must have sloping sides and be the right size so the omelet can be shaped properly. Second, it must be well seasoned or conditioned to avoid sticking.

Procedure for Conditioning an Omelet Pan

The following method is only one of many. Your instructor may show you another. The object is to seal the surface of the metal with a layer of baked-on oil.

1. Rub the clean pan with a thin film of vegetable oil.
2. Set the pan over moderately high heat until it is very hot.
3. Remove from heat and let cool.
4. Do not scour the pan or wash with a detergent after use. Rub with salt, which will scour the pan without harming the primed surface. Rinse only after pan has cooled, or wipe with a clean towel.
5. Reseason as often as necessary, or after each day's use.

Procedure for Making a French Omelet

Figure 9.6 Making a French omelet. Read the accompanying text for a full description of the steps shown here.

(a) As soon as the eggs are added to the hot pan, shake the pan back and forth with one hand and stir the eggs in a circular motion with a fork.

(b) When the eggs are almost set, tilt the pan and shake the eggs down to the opposite side of the pan. Rapping the handle sharply helps move the eggs.

(c) Spoon the filling, if used, across the center.

See Figure 9.6 for illustration of technique.

1. Collect all equipment and ingredients.
2. Beat 2 or 3 eggs in a small bowl just until well mixed. Do not whip until frothy. Season with salt and pepper.
   If desired, 1 tablespoon (15 mL) water may be added to make the omelet lighter.
   For extended service, beat a large quantity of eggs. Measure each portion with a ladle.
3. Place an omelet pan over high heat.
4. When the pan is hot, add about 1 tablespoon (15 mL) clarified butter and swirl it around to coat the inside of the pan. Give it a second to get hot.
   Raw butter may be used, but great care is necessary to keep it from burning.
5. Add the eggs to the pan. They should begin to coagulate around the edges and on the bottom in a few seconds.
6. With one hand (the left, if you are right-handed), vigorously shake the pan back and forth. At the same time, stir the eggs with a circular motion with the bottom side of a fork, but do not let the fork scrape the pan.
   This is the difficult part. The most common errors are not shaking and stirring vigorously enough and using heat that is too low. The purpose of this action is to keep the eggs in motion so they coagulate uniformly.
7. Stop shaking and stirring when the eggs are almost set but still very moist. If you continue stirring, you will have scrambled eggs instead of an omelet.
8. Tilt the handle up and shake the pan so the omelet slides to the opposite side of the pan and begins to climb up the opposite slope.
9. For a filled omelet, spoon the filling across the center of the egg, perpendicular to the handle.
10. With the fork, fold the sides of the omelet over the center. The omelet should now be resting in the corner of the pan and have an approximately oval shape.
11. Grasp the handle of the pan with your palm underneath and tilt the omelet out onto a plate so it inverts and keeps an oval shape.
    The whole procedure should take less than 1 minute.
    The finished omelet should be moist on the inside, tender on the outside, and yellow or only slightly browned.

(d) Fold over the side of the omelet to make an oval shape.

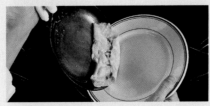

(e) Grasp the handle of the pan with your palm underneath and tilt the omelet onto a plate.

(f) The finished omelet should have a neat, oval shape. Some chefs prefer omelets that are lightly browned. Others feel they should not be browned at all.

SUGGESTED OMELET FILLINGS

Cheese

Sautéed or creamed mushrooms

Creamed or curried chicken

Creamed or buttered spinach

Sautéed onions, with or without bacon

Sautéed onions and diced potatoes

Seafood Newburg or seafood in a cream sauce

Red caviar

Thick Spanish Sauce (p. 167)

Ratatouille (p. 299)

AMERICAN-STYLE OR FOLDED OMELET

This style of omelet is often called a *French omelet*, but it is not a French omelet. It was probably devised by cooks who hesitated to tackle the French method.

It is made somewhat like a French omelet, except low heat is used and the eggs are not stirred or agitated. Instead, the edges of the cooked portion are lifted with a fork or spatula, allowing the uncooked portion to flow underneath. The finished omelet may be folded in half or like a French omelet.

The advantage of this method is that it is easier to learn.

The disadvantages are that the omelet is not as light or delicate in texture and the method is much slower.

FLUFFY OMELET OR SOUFFLÉ OMELET

These omelets are made by beating the egg whites separately and folding them into the beaten yolks, which may have some milk added. The mixture is poured into a hot, buttered omelet pan, and the omelet is finished in the oven. It is folded in half for service.

Fluffy omelets are not often made in food service because of the time they take to make.

FRITTATAS AND OTHER FLAT OMELETS

A *frittata* is a flat omelet that originated in Italy. The same basic techniques are used for many popular American preparations. Flat omelets are made by mixing beaten eggs with a variety of ingredients, such as vegetables, meats, or cheese, and cooking the mixture over low heat without stirring. To finish, it is either flipped over or run under the broiler or into the oven until the top is set.

A popular American frittata (actually derived from the Chinese egg foo yung) is the Western omelet, containing diced sautéed onion, green bell pepper, and ham.

Soufflés

Soufflés are not normally featured on breakfast menus. However, they are important basic egg preparations with which you should be familiar.

Amateur cooks often consider soufflés difficult to make. Actually, they are relatively easy preparations. Many restaurants have no difficulty turning out large numbers of soufflés to order. The only hard part is making sure the waiter picks up the order when it is ready.

A standard entrée soufflé consists of three elements:

1. Base—usually a heavy béchamel sauce.

2. Flavor ingredient—cheese, vegetables, seafood, etc.

3. Egg whites, beaten.

General Procedure for Preparing Entrée Soufflés

1. Prepare a heavy béchamel sauce.
2. Combine the sauce with egg yolks.
3. Prepare the flavor ingredients—grate cheese, cook and chop vegetables, and so on.
4. Combine the base and the flavor ingredients.
5. Beat egg whites and fold in.
6. Bake in a soufflé dish that has been buttered and dusted with parmesan cheese.
7. Serve immediately.

À la Carte Service

Prepare through step 4 and hold in refrigerator.

If several flavors are offered, prepare a single large batch of base and keep the flavor ingredients separate.

For each order, beat egg whites and combine with measured amount of base.

KEY POINTS TO REVIEW

- What are the steps in the procedure for making baked eggs?
- What are the steps in the procedure for making scrambled eggs?
- What are the steps in the procedure for making a French omelet?
- What are the steps in the procedure for making entrée soufflés?

Summer Squash, Spinach, and Leek Frittata

YIELD: 4 PORTIONS

U.S.	METRIC	INGREDIENTS	PROCEDURE
4 oz	125 g	Leeks, white part and a little of the green, trimmed and cleaned	1. Split the leeks in half lengthwise, and then slice them crosswise into thin slices. 2. Trim and slice the squash. 3. Heat the butter in a sauté pan over moderate heat. 4. Add the leeks and sauté until wilted. 5. Add the squash and sauté until just tender. 6. Remove from the pan and cool. 7. Blanch the spinach in boiling water until wilted. 8. Drain and cool the spinach in cold water. Drain again and squeeze dry. 9. Chop the spinach coarsely and mix it with the squash.
10 oz	300 g	Yellow summer squash or zucchini	
1 oz	30 g	Butter	
8 oz	250 g	Spinach leaves (no stems)	
6	6	Eggs	10. Beat the eggs and add them to the vegetables. 11. Add salt and pepper to taste 12. Heat the butter over moderate heat in a well-seasoned or, preferably, a nonstick 10-in. (25-cm) sauté pan (see Note). 13. Add the egg mixture. Immediately lower the heat as low as possible. Cover loosely. 14. Cook slowly until the eggs are mostly set but creamy in the middle. 15. Place the pan under the broiler until the eggs are set. 16. Slide the frittata onto a plate. 17. Cut into 4 wedges. Serve immediately.
to taste	to taste	Salt	
to taste	to taste	Pepper	
½ oz	15 g	Butter	

Per serving: Calories, 230; Protein, 12 g; Fat, 17 g (65% cal.); Cholesterol, 340 mg; Carbohydrates, 9 g; Fiber, 3 g; Sodium, 220 mg.

Note: To make individual portions to order, cook one-fourth of the egg mixture in a 6-in. (15-cm) sauté pan.

Summer Squash, Spinach, and Leek Frittata

Cheese Soufflé

PORTIONS: 12   PORTION SIZE: 4 OZ (125 G)

U.S.	METRIC	INGREDIENTS	PROCEDURE
as needed	as needed	Butter	1. Select three 1½-qt (1½-L) soufflé dishes (4 portions each) or two 2-qt (2-L) dishes (6 portions each). Butter the insides of the dishes well. Sprinkle with cheese or crumbs so the bottom and sides are completely coated.
as needed	as needed	Parmesan cheese or dry bread crumbs	
		Roux:	2. Make a white roux with the butter and flour. Cook the roux a few minutes.
2½ oz	75 g	Butter	3. Beat in the hot milk. Bring to a boil while stirring. Cool and stir until very thick and smooth.
2½ oz	75 g	Flour	
1½ pt	750 mL	Milk, hot	4. Remove from the heat. Stir in the salt, pepper, cayenne, and nutmeg.
1½ tsp	7 mL	Salt	
1 tsp	5 mL	White pepper	
pinch	pinch	Cayenne	
pinch	pinch	Nutmeg	
12	12	Egg yolks	5. Add the egg yolks to the hot sauce and quickly mix in with a wire whip.
10 oz	300 g	Gruyère cheese, coarsely grated (see Note)	6. Stir in the cheese.
12–15	12–15	Egg whites	7. Beat the egg whites with the salt until they form stiff peaks. (The larger number of egg whites will make a lighter soufflé.)
¼ tsp	1 mL	Salt	

8. Fold the egg whites into the cheese mixture.

9. Pour the mixture into the prepared soufflé dishes.

Per serving: Calories, 290; Protein, 17 g; Fat, 21 g (65% cal.); Cholesterol, 265 mg; Carbohydrates, 8 g; Fiber, 0 g; Sodium, 600 mg.

10. Place the dishes in a preheated 375°F (190°C) oven. Bake 40 minutes without opening the oven door. After this time, check for doneness by *very gently* shaking the dishes. If the centers are firm and do not jiggle, the soufflés are done. If necessary, bake another 5–10 minutes.

Note: Other cheeses may be used: sharp cheddar, Swiss, a mixture of Swiss and Gruyère, or a mixture of Swiss or Gruyère and parmesan.

11. Remove from oven and serve *immediately*.

VARIATIONS

À la Carte Service: Prepare the basic recipe through step 6. Chill mixture quickly and hold in refrigerator. For each order, scale 3½ oz (100 g) of the mixture. Beat 1 egg white and fold in. Bake in an individual soufflé dish 20–30 minutes.

Mushroom Soufflé
Reduce cheese to 5 oz (150 g). Add 4 oz (125 g) cooked chopped mushrooms.

Spinach Soufflé
Reduce cheese to 5 oz (150 g). Add 5 oz (150 g) well-drained, chopped cooked spinach.

Other Vegetable Soufflés
Follow the procedure for Spinach Soufflé, using chopped cooked vegetables such as broccoli, asparagus, or carrots.

Spinach and Ham Soufflé
Add 2 oz (60 g) ground or finely chopped ham to Spinach Soufflé.

Salmon Soufflé
Make the sauce base with milk plus liquid from canned salmon. Add 1½ oz (45 g) tomato paste to the base. Reduce cheese to 4 oz (125 g) and add 8 oz (250 g) flaked canned salmon.

Custards

A *custard* is a liquid that is thickened or set by the coagulation of egg protein.

There are two basic kinds of custard:

1. *Stirred custard,* which is stirred as it cooks and remains pourable when done.

2. *Baked custard,* which is not stirred and which sets firm.

One basic rule governs the preparation of both custards: *Do not heat custards higher than an internal temperature of 185°F (85°C).*

This temperature, as you know, is the point at which egg-liquid mixtures coagulate. If they are heated more than this, they are likely to curdle. An overbaked custard becomes watery because the moisture separates from the toughened protein.

Most custards are sweet. These preparations are covered in the baking and dessert section of this book.

The *quiche* (keesh), which is a custard baked in a pastry shell, is probably the most popular form of savory custard. The following recipe illustrates the technique for preparing savory custards.

Quiche au Fromage (Cheese Tart)

YIELD: FOUR 8-INCH (20-CM) TARTS   PORTIONS: 24   PORTION SIZE: ⅙ OF TART
16   ¼ OF TART

U.S.	METRIC	INGREDIENTS	PROCEDURE
2 lb	900 g	Mealy Pie Dough	1. Scale the dough into 4 pieces, 8 oz (225 g) each. 2. Roll the dough into 4 circles, ⅛ in. (3 mm) thick. 3. Fit the dough into four 8-in. (20-cm) pie pans or tart pans. 4. Hold the pie shells in the refrigerator until needed (see Note).
1 lb	450 g	Swiss or Gruyère cheese, grated	5. Sprinkle 4 oz (110 g) cheese into the bottom of each tart shell. 6. Beat together the eggs, cream, milk, and seasonings. Pour into the tart shells. 7. Place the tarts in a 375°F (190°C) oven on the bottom shelf or, if using a deck oven, directly on the deck. 8. Bake until the filling is set, about 20–30 minutes. 9. Serve hot or cold. Cut into wedges of desired size.
12	12	Eggs, beaten	
1 pt	500 mL	Heavy cream	
2 pt	950 mL	Milk	
2 tsp	10 mL	Salt	
¼ tsp	1 mL	White pepper	
⅛ tsp	0.5 mL	Nutmeg	

Per ⅙ tart: Calories, 370; Protein, 12 g; Fat, 30 g (69% cal.); Cholesterol, 155 mg; Carbohydrates, 18 g; Fiber, 3 g; Sodium, 450 mg.

Note: Pastry shells may be partially baked before filling if uncooked bottoms tend to be a problem. This is sometimes the case if you are using shiny aluminum pie pans or if the bottom heat of the oven isn't strong enough.

VARIATIONS

Quiche Lorraine
Dice 1 lb (450 g) bacon strips and cook until crisp. Drain and add to pie shell in step 5. Omit cheese or leave it in, as desired. (Quiche Lorraine was originally made without cheese.)

Onion Quiche
Sauté 2 lb (900 g) sliced onions very slowly in 2 oz (60 g) butter until golden and tender. Cool and add to empty pie shells. Reduce cheese to 8 oz (225 g).

Spinach Quiche
Sauté 3 oz (90 g) chopped onion in 3 oz (90 g) butter until soft. Add 1½ lb (700 g) cooked, drained chopped spinach. Sauté until most of the liquid evaporates. Cool and add to empty pie shell. Omit cheese.

Mushroom Quiche
Sauté 2 lb (900 g) sliced mushrooms and 3 oz (90 g) chopped onion in 3 oz (90 g) butter. Add 1 tbsp (15 mL) lemon juice to keep the mushrooms white. Cook until juices evaporate. Cool and add to the empty pie shell. Omit cheese.

Seafood Quiche
Substitute 8 oz (225 g) cooked diced shrimp and 8 oz (225 g) cooked diced crabmeat for the cheese. Add 3 fl oz (90 mL) sherry and 2 oz (60 g) tomato paste to the egg mixture.

BREAKFAST BREADS, CEREALS, AND MEATS

Bread items probably play a more important role at breakfast than even eggs. Hardly an order of eggs is sold without an order of toast on the side. And for the diner who prefers a continental breakfast, coffee and a bread item such as a roll or pastry constitute the entire breakfast.

Except for toast, few breakfast breads are prepared to order. Most operations purchase such items ready-made. These products include muffins, doughnuts, Danish pastries, sweet rolls, and regional favorites such as bagels and cornbread.

In this section, we consider three items that are made to order: pancakes, waffles, and French toast. You may not think of pancakes and waffles as breads, but they are actually a form of quick bread, a category of foods we consider in more detail in the baking section of this book.

Pancakes and Waffles

Waffles and pancakes, also called *griddle cakes* and *hot cakes*, are made from pourable batters. Pancakes are made on a griddle, while waffles are made on a special tool called a *waffle iron*.

Both items should be cooked to order and served hot. Waffles lose their crispness very quickly, and pancakes toughen as they are held. However, batters may be prepared ahead and are often mixed the night before.

Serve with butter and with maple syrup or syrup blends (pure maple syrup is expensive). Other condiments that may accompany these items are fruit syrups, jams and preserves, applesauce, and fruits such as strawberries or blueberries.

Ingredients and Procedures

Compare the basic pancake and waffle recipes and note how much alike the batters are, with important exceptions:

1. Waffle batter contains more fat.

2. Waffle batter contains less liquid, so it is slightly thicker.

3. Waffles are given extra lightness when the egg whites are beaten separately and folded into the batter. (Some recipes omit this step.)

A standard-size pancake requires ¼ cup (60 mL) batter. The amount of batter needed for waffles depends on the size of the waffle iron.

Pre-preparation for Volume Service

Pancake and waffle batters leavened by *baking powder only* may be mixed the night before and stored in the cooler. Some rising power may be lost, so baking powder may have to be increased.

Batters leavened by baking soda should not be made too far ahead because the soda will lose its power. Mix dry ingredients and liquid ingredients ahead and combine just before service.

Batters using beaten egg whites and baking powder may be partially made ahead, but *incorporate the egg whites just before service*.

Buttermilk Pancakes

YIELD: 3½ PT (1.75 L) BATTER, ENOUGH FOR 25–30 LARGE OR 50 MEDIUM PANCAKES

U.S.	METRIC	INGREDIENTS	PROCEDURE
1 lb	500 g	Pastry flour or all-purpose flour	1. Sift together the flour, sugar, salt, baking powder, and baking soda.
2 oz	60 g	Sugar	
1 tsp	5 mL	Salt	
1 tbsp	15 mL	Baking powder	
1½ tsp	7 mL	Baking soda	
4	4	Eggs, beaten	2. Mix the beaten eggs, buttermilk, and butter or oil.
1 qt	1 L	Buttermilk	3. Add the liquid ingredients to the dry ingredients. Mix just until the dry ingredients are thoroughly moistened. Do not overmix. (*Note:* Buttermilk makes a thick batter. Thin with a little skim milk or water if the batter seems too thick.)
4 fl oz	125 mL	Melted butter or oil	

Per 2-ounce (56.7-g) pancake: Calories, 120; Protein, 4 g; Fat, 5 g (36% cal.); Cholesterol, 40 mg; Carbohydrates, 16 g; Fiber, 0 g; Sodium, 250 mg.

4. Depending on the size pancake desired, measure 1–2 fl oz (30–60 mL) portions of the batter onto a greased, preheated griddle (375°F/190°C), allowing space for spreading.

5. Griddle the pancakes until the tops are full of bubbles and begin to look dry and the bottoms are golden brown. Turn and brown the other side.

6. Remove from the griddle and serve.

Waffles

YIELD: 3½ PT (1.75 L) BATTER

U.S.	METRIC	INGREDIENTS	PROCEDURE
1 lb 4 oz	625g	Pastry flour or all-purpose flour	1. Sift together the flour, salt, and baking powder.
1 tsp	5 mL	Salt	
2 tbsp	30 mL	Baking powder	
6	6	Egg yolks, beaten	2. Mix the egg yolks, milk, and butter or oil.
1½ pt	750 mL	Milk	3. Add the liquid ingredients to the dry ingredients. Mix just until the dry ingredients are thoroughly moistened. Do not overmix.
8 fl oz	250 mL	Melted butter or oil	
6	6	Egg whites	4. Whip the egg whites until they form soft peaks. Add the sugar and whip until stiff peaks form.
2 oz	60 g	Sugar	5. Fold the egg whites into the batter.

Per 1 fl oz (29.57 mL) batter: Calories, 80; Protein, 2 g; Fat, 4 g (45% cal.); Cholesterol, 30 mg; Carbohydrates, 9 g; Fiber, 0 g; Sodium, 100 mg.

6. Pour enough batter onto a lightly greased, preheated waffle iron to almost cover the surface with a thin layer. Close the iron.

7. Cook waffles until signal light indicates they are done or until steam is no longer emitted.

8. Remove from the iron and serve.

French Toast

French toast in different versions is popular in many regions, and it has the advantage of being an excellent way to utilize day-old bread.

Basic French toast consists of slices of bread dipped in a batter of eggs, milk, a little sugar, and flavorings. French toast is cooked on a griddle like pancakes.

Variations may be created by changing the basic ingredients:

Bread. White pullman bread is standard. Specialty versions can be made with French bread, rich egg bread, or whole-grain breads.

Batter. Milk is the usual liquid, mixed with egg in various proportions. Deluxe versions may include cream or sour cream.

Flavorings. Vanilla, cinnamon, and nutmeg are popular choices. Other possibilities are grated lemon and orange rind, ground anise, rum, and brandy.

The most common fault in making French toast is not soaking the bread long enough to allow the batter to penetrate. If the bread is just dipped in the batter, the final product is just dry bread with a little egg on the outside.

French toast is dusted with powdered sugar and served, like pancakes, with accompanying butter, syrups, preserves, or fruits.

Cinnamon Raisin French Toast

PORTIONS: 6   PORTION SIZE: 2 SLICES

U.S.	METRIC	INGREDIENTS	PROCEDURE
6	6	Eggs	1. Beat together the eggs, milk, cream, sugar, vanilla, cinnamon, nutmeg, and salt until the sugar is dissolved.
12 fl oz	375 mL	Milk	
4 fl oz	125 mL	Heavy cream	2. Soak the bread in the egg mixture until the bread is soaked through, but do not leave so long that it falls apart.
4 oz	125 g	Sugar	
1 tbsp	15 mL	Vanilla extract	
1 tsp	5 mL	Cinnamon	
⅛ tsp	0.5 mL	Nutmeg	
⅛ tsp	0.5 mL	Salt	
12 slices	12 slices	Cinnamon raisin bread, ¾ in. (2 cm) thick	
1½ oz	45 g	Butter	3. For each portion, heat 1½ tsp (7 mL) butter in a sauté pan large enough to hold 2 slices of bread.
as needed	as needed	Confectioners' sugar	4. Put 2 slices of bread in the pan and brown the bottoms.

Per serving: Calories, 470; Protein, 15 g; Fat, 23 g (43% cal.); Cholesterol, 260 mg; Carbohydrates, 51 g; Fiber, 2 g; Sodium, 400 mg.

5. Turn the bread over and cook 30 seconds.

6. Transfer the sauté pan to an oven preheated to 375°F (190°C). Bake 10 minutes. The bread should be cooked through and slightly puffed up.

7. Plate, dust with confectioners' sugar, and serve immediately.

VARIATION

The amount of batter in the recipe is enough to soak about 24 thin slices of sliced bread. Regular slices of bread are thin enough to be cooked from start to finish on a griddle or in a sauté pan.

Cinnamon Raisin French Toast

Cereals

Hot Cooked Cereals

Cooked cereals are of two types:

1. Whole, cracked, or flaked cereals, such as oatmeal (rolled oats), Scotch oatmeal (cracked oats), and cracked wheat. The particles are large and can be added to boiling water without lumping.

2. Granular cereals, such as farina and cornmeal. The particles are small and tend to lump when added to boiling water.

For more information on cooking grains, see Chapter 13.

Procedure for Cooking Whole, Cracked, or Flaked Cereals

1. Collect equipment and ingredients.
2. Measure the correct amount of water and salt into a pot and bring to a boil. Read package directions for quantities.
   Using milk or part milk makes a richer cereal, but a more expensive one. Be careful not to scorch the milk if you use it.
3. Measure the correct amount of cereal.
4. Add the cereal slowly, stirring constantly.
5. Stir until some thickening takes place, then stop stirring. Too much stirring makes cereal gummy.
6. Reduce heat to a slow simmer, cover, and cook until desired doneness and consistency are reached. Cooking times vary greatly.
7. Keep covered until service to prevent drying.

Procedure for Cooking Granular Cereals

The procedure is the same as above, except the cereal is mixed with a little cold water before being added to boiling water. This separates the grains and prevents lumping. The cold water must be calculated as part of the total amount of liquid. Alternatively, mix the cereal with all the cold liquid, then bring to a boil and simmer until done.

Cold Cereals

Cold, dry cereals are purchased ready prepared and need no preparation by the kitchen. Like hot cereals, they are served with accompanying milk or cream, sugar, and, sometimes, fruit such as berries or sliced bananas.

Breakfast Meats

Meats and meat cooking methods are covered in previous chapters, but we mention them again because three meats in particular—bacon, sausage, and ham—appear on most breakfast menus.

Bacon

Bacon is a cured, smoked pork product. It is available in whole slabs but is almost always purchased sliced. Thickness of slices is specified by number of slices per pound, usually 18 to 22 (40 to 48 per kg).

Low-temperature cooking applies to bacon as well as to other meats. Bacon is about 70 percent fat and shrinks a great deal. However, cooking at low temperatures minimizes shrinkage. The oven is most often used for cooking bacon in quantity, though a griddle or sauté pan may also be used.

To cook in the oven, lay out the bacon strips on sheet pans in a single layer, or, even better, on racks over sheet pans. (Bacon may be purchased already laid out on parchment.) Bake at 300° to 350°F (150° to 175°C) until about three-fourths done. Remove from the oven, being careful not to spill the hot fat. Finish individual portions to order on the griddle or in the oven, cooking them until crisp.

Ham

Ham for breakfast service is almost always precooked. Slices in 3- to 4-ounce (90- to 115-g) portions need only be heated and browned slightly on a griddle or under the broiler.

Canadian bacon is boneless pork loin that is cured and smoked like ham. It is handled like ham in the kitchen.

Sausage

Breakfast sausage is simply fresh pork that has been ground and seasoned. It is available in three forms: patties, links, and bulk.

Because it is fresh pork, sausage must be cooked well done. This does not mean, however, that it should be cooked until it is just hard, dry, shrunken little nuggets, as it often is.

Most kitchens cook sausages by the same methods as bacon. For volume service, sausage is partially cooked in the oven and then finished to order. Link sausages hold better than patties because the links are protected from drying by their casings.

KEY POINTS TO REVIEW

- How does pancake batter differ from waffle batter?

- How can a basic French toast recipe be modified to create variety?

- What are the steps in the procedure for cooking whole, cracked, or flaked cereals? What are the steps in the procedure for cooking granular cereals?

- How are bacon, ham, and sausages prepared for breakfast service?

TERMS FOR REVIEW

yolk	sunny side up	over hard	custard
white	basted	baked egg	quiche
shell	over easy	frittata	breakfast sausage
curdle	over medium	soufflé	

QUESTIONS FOR DISCUSSION

1. Which grade of egg would you choose to prepare poached eggs? hard-cooked eggs? fried eggs? scrambled eggs? Why?

2. Is it possible to prepare hard-cooked eggs in a pressure steamer? Give reasons for your answer.

3. When separating eggs, many chefs advise breaking them one by one over a small bowl, then transferring each white to the larger bowl as it is separated. Can you give a reason for this advice?

4. Give two reasons for being careful not to add too much vinegar to the poaching water for eggs.

5. In the recipe for waffles, what is the purpose of beating the sugar into the egg whites rather than combining it with the other dry ingredients?

6. What precautions might you take if you were making French toast from thick slices of French bread?

Chapter 10

Ragout of Summer Vegetables, page 290.

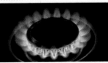

Understanding Vegetables

Vegetables were, at one time, abused and neglected, relegated to the minor role of unimportant side dishes, to be taken or left, or not even noticed on the table.

Today, however, lowly vegetables are much more appreciated, not only for their nutritional importance but for the variety, flavor, eye appeal, and even elegance and sophistication they bring to the menu. Modern cooks owe it to themselves and their customers to treat vegetables with understanding, respect, and imagination.

Because they are so perishable, vegetables require extra care from receiving to service. Freshness is their most appealing and attractive quality, and one must be especially careful to preserve it. The goals of proper vegetable cookery are to preserve and enhance fresh flavor, texture, and color, and to prepare and serve vegetables that are not just accepted but sought after.

After reading this chapter, you should be able to

1. Describe the factors that influence texture, flavor, color, and nutritional changes when cooking vegetables.

2. Cook vegetables to their proper doneness.

3. Judge quality in cooked vegetables based on color, appearance, texture, flavor, seasonings, and appropriateness of combination with sauces or other vegetables.

4. Perform pre-preparation tasks for fresh vegetables.

5. Determine the quality of frozen, canned, and dried vegetables.

6. Prepare vegetables using the batch cooking method and the blanch-and-chill method.

7. Store fresh and processed vegetables.

CONTROLLING QUALITY CHANGES DURING COOKING

As a cook, you have a choice of many kinds of vegetables and many cooking methods. Not surprisingly, then, you are also faced with the necessity of learning many rules for cooking vegetables.

Many guides to vegetable cookery simply present a long list of rules to memorize. You will be able to understand the principles more easily, however, if you first learn how vegetables change as they are cooked and how to control those changes. In other words, it is suggested you not just memorize what to do but understand why you do it.

Cooking affects vegetables in four ways. It changes the following:

1. Texture.

2. Flavor.

3. Color.

4. Nutrients.

How much these four characteristics change determines whether your final product is attractive and delicious to the customer or whether it ends up in the garbage. You can control these changes if you understand how they occur.

Unfortunately, there is still legitimate controversy among chefs about proper vegetable cooking techniques. Modern technology has not yet solved all the problems experienced chefs tackle successfully every day in the kitchen.

Controlling Texture Changes

Changing texture is one of the main purposes of cooking vegetables.

Fiber

The fiber structures of vegetables (including cellulose and pectins) give them shape and firmness. Cooking softens some of these components.

The *amount of fiber* varies

1. In different vegetables. Spinach and tomatoes have less fiber than carrots and turnips, for example.

2. In different examples of the same vegetables. Old, tough carrots have more fiber than young, fresh carrots.

3. In the same vegetable. The tender tips of asparagus and broccoli have less fiber than their tougher stalks.

Fiber is made *firmer* by

1. **Acids.**
   Lemon juice, vinegar, and tomato products, when added to cooking vegetables, extend the cooking time.

2. **Sugars.**
   Sugar strengthens cell structure. You will use this principle primarily in fruit cookery. For firm poached apples or pears, for example, cook in a heavy syrup. For applesauce, cook apples until soft before sweetening.

Fiber is *softened* by

1. **Heat.**
   In general, longer cooking means softer vegetables.

2. **Alkalis.**
   Do not add baking soda to green vegetables. Not only does it destroy vitamins but it also makes the vegetables unpleasantly mushy.

Starch

Starch is another vegetable component that affects texture.

1. *Dry starchy foods* like dried legumes (beans, peas, lentils), rice, and macaroni products must be cooked in enough water for the starch granules to absorb moisture and soften. Dried beans are usually soaked before cooking to replace lost moisture.

2. *Moist starchy vegetables* like potatoes and sweet potatoes have enough moisture of their own, but they must still be cooked until the starch granules soften.

Doneness

A vegetable is said to be done when it reaches the desired degree of tenderness. This stage varies from vegetable to vegetable. Some, such as winter squash, eggplant, and braised celery, are considered properly cooked when they are quite soft. Most vegetables, however, are best cooked very briefly, until they are crisp-tender or *al dente* (firm to the bite). At this stage of tenderness they not only have the most pleasing texture but also retain maximum flavor, color, and nutrients.

Guidelines for Achieving Proper Doneness in Vegetables

1. Don't overcook.
2. Cook as close to service as possible. Holding vegetables in a steam table continues to cook them.
3. If vegetables must be cooked in advance, slightly undercook them, cool rapidly in cold water, drain, and refrigerate, then reheat to order.
4. For uniform doneness, cut vegetables into pieces of uniform size before cooking.
5. Vegetables with both tough and tender parts need special treatment so the tender parts are not overcooked by the time the tougher parts are done. For example,

   Peel the woody stalks of asparagus.

   Peel or split broccoli stalks.

   Pierce the base of Brussels sprouts with a sharp knife.

   Remove the heavy center stalks of lettuce leaves before braising.

6. Don't mix batches of cooked vegetables. They are likely to be cooked to slightly different levels of doneness.

Controlling Flavor Changes

Cooking Produces Flavor Loss

Many flavors are lost during cooking by dissolving into the cooking liquid and by evaporation. The longer a vegetable is cooked, the more flavor it loses.

Flavor loss can be controlled in several ways:

1. Cook for as short a time as possible.

2. Use boiling salted water. Starting vegetables in boiling water shortens cooking time. The addition of salt helps reduce flavor loss.

3. Use just enough water to cover to minimize leaching. Note that this rule contradicts rule 1 in that adding vegetables to a small quantity of water lowers the temperature more, so cooking time is extended. Save your questions on this until you have finished reading the sections on color and nutritional changes.

4. Steam vegetables whenever appropriate. Steam cooking reduces leaching out of flavor and shortens cooking time.

STRONG-FLAVORED VEGETABLES

With certain strong-flavored vegetables, it is desirable to lose some of the flavor to make them more appealing to the taste. These include the onion family (onions, garlic, leeks, shallots), the cabbage family (cabbage, Brussels sprouts, cauliflower, broccoli), and some root vegetables (turnips, rutabagas).

When cooking strong-flavored vegetables, leave uncovered to allow these flavors to escape, and use larger amounts of water.

Cooking Produces Flavor Changes

Cooked vegetables do not taste like raw vegetables because cooking produces certain chemical changes. As long as the vegetables are not overcooked, this change is desirable. It produces the flavors one looks for in vegetable dishes.

Overcooking produces undesirable changes in members of the cabbage family. They develop a strong, unpleasant flavor. Cabbage and its relatives should be cooked quickly, uncovered.

Cooking and Sweetness

Young, freshly harvested vegetables have a relatively high sugar content that makes them taste sweet. As they mature, or as they sit in storage, the sugar gradually changes to starch. This is especially noticeable in corn, peas, carrots, turnips, and beets.

To serve sweet-tasting vegetables:

1. Try to serve young, fresh vegetables that have been stored as short a time as possible.

2. For older vegetables, especially those just listed, add a small amount of sugar to the cooking water to replace lost sweetness.

Controlling Color Changes

It is important to preserve as much natural color as possible when cooking vegetables. Because customers may reject or accept a vegetable on the basis of its appearance, it can be said that its visual quality is as important as its flavor or nutritional value.

Pigments are compounds that give vegetables their color. Different pigments react in different ways to heat and to acids and other elements that may be present during cooking, so it is necessary to discuss them one at a time. Table 10.1 summarizes this information.

White Vegetables

Pigments called *anthoxanthins* (an tho zan thins) and *flavonoids* range from pale yellow to white. These are the primary coloring compounds in potatoes, onions, cauliflower, and white cabbage and in the white parts of such vegetables as celery, cucumbers, and zucchini.

White pigments stay white in acid and turn yellow in alkaline water. To keep vegetables such as cauliflower white, add a little lemon juice or cream of tartar to the cooking water. (Don't add too much, though, as this may toughen the vegetable.) Covering the pot also helps keep acids in.

Cooking for a short time, especially in a steamer, helps maintain color (and flavor and nutrients as well). Overcooking or holding too long in a steam table turns white vegetables dull yellow or gray.

Table 10.1	Vegetable Color Changes During Cooking			
COLOR	EXAMPLES OF VEGETABLES	COOKED WITH ACID	COOKED WITH ALKALI	OVERCOOKED
White	Potatoes, turnips, cauliflower, onions, white cabbage	White	Yellowish	Yellowish, gray
Red	Beets, red cabbage (not tomatoes, whose pigment is like that in yellow vegetables)	Red	Blue or blue-green	Greenish blue, faded
Green	Asparagus, green beans, lima beans, broccoli, Brussels sprouts, peas, spinach, green peppers, artichokes, okra	Olive green	Bright green	Olive green
Yellow (and orange)	Carrots, tomatoes, rutabagas, sweet potatoes, squash, corn	Little change	Little change	Slightly faded

Red Vegetables

Red pigments, called *anthocyanins*, are found in only a few vegetables, mainly red cabbage and beets. Blueberries also are colored by these red pigments. (The red color of tomatoes and red peppers is due to the same pigments that color carrots yellow or orange.)

Red pigments react very strongly to acids and alkalis.

Acids turn them a brighter red.

Alkalis turn them blue or blue-green (not a very appetizing color for red cabbage).

Red beets and red cabbage, therefore, have their best color when cooked with a small amount of acid. Red cabbage is often cooked with tart apples for this reason.

When a strongly acid vegetable is desired, as for Harvard beets or braised red cabbage, add just a small amount of acid at first. Acids toughen vegetables and prolong cooking time. Add the rest when the vegetables are tender.

Red pigments dissolve easily in water. This means

1. Use a short cooking time. Overcooked red vegetables lose a lot of color.

2. Use only as much water as is necessary.

3. Cook beets whole and unpeeled, with root and an inch of stem attached, to protect color. Skins easily slip off cooked beets.

4. When steaming, use solid pans instead of perforated pans to retain the red juices.

5. Whenever possible, serve the cooking liquid as a sauce with the vegetable.

Green Vegetables

Green coloring, or *chlorophyll*, is present in all green plants. Green vegetables are common in the kitchen, so it is important to understand the special handling required by this pigment.

Acids are enemies of green vegetables. Both *acid* and *long cooking* turn green vegetables a drab olive green.

Protect the color of green vegetables by

1. Cooking uncovered to allow plant acids to escape.

2. Cooking for the shortest possible time. Properly cooked green vegetables are tender-crisp, not mushy.

3. Cooking in small batches rather than holding for long periods in a steam table.

Steaming is rapidly becoming the preferred method for cooking green vegetables. Steam cooks food rapidly, lessens the dissolving out of nutrients and flavor, and does not break up delicate vegetables. Overcooking, however, can occur rapidly in steamers.

Do not use baking soda to maintain green color. Soda destroys vitamins and makes texture unpleasantly mushy and slippery.

How much water should be used when boiling? A large quantity of water helps dissolve plant acids, helps preserve colors, and speeds cooking. But some cooks feel an excessive amount of nutrients are lost. See the next section for further discussion.

Yellow and Orange Vegetables

Yellow and orange pigments, called *carotenoids*, are found in carrots, corn, winter squash, rutabaga, sweet potatoes, tomatoes, and red peppers. These pigments are very stable. They are little affected by acids or alkalis. Long cooking can dull the color, however. Short cooking not only prevents dulling of the color but also preserves vitamins and flavors.

Controlling Nutrient Losses

Vegetables are an important part of our diet because they supply a wide variety of essential nutrients. They are our major sources of vitamins A and C and are rich in many other vitamins and minerals. Unfortunately, many of these nutrients are easily lost.

Six factors are responsible for most nutrient loss:

1. High temperature.

2. Long cooking.

3. Leaching (dissolving out).

4. Alkalis (baking soda, hard water).

5. Plant enzymes (which are active at warm temperatures but destroyed by high heat).

6. Oxygen.

Some nutrient loss is inevitable because it is rarely possible to avoid all of these conditions at the same time. For example,

- Pressure steaming shortens cooking time, but the high temperature destroys some vitamins.

- Braising uses low heat, but the cooking time is longer.

- Baking eliminates the leaching out of vitamins and minerals, but the long cooking and high temperature cause nutrient loss.

- Boiling is faster than simmering, but the higher temperature can be harmful and the rapid activity can break up delicate vegetables and increase loss through leaching.

- Cutting vegetables into small pieces decreases cooking time, but it increases leaching by creating more exposed surfaces.

- Even steaming allows some leaching out of nutrients into the moisture that condenses on the vegetables and then drips off.

Cooking in a Little Liquid Versus a Lot of Liquid

This is an area of controversy with good arguments on both sides.

1. Using a lot of liquid increases vitamin loss by leaching. Use just enough liquid to cover. Save the cooking liquid for reheating the vegetables or for stocks or soups.

2. Using a little liquid increases cooking time. When the vegetables are combined with the small quantity of boiling water, the temperature is lowered greatly and the vegetables must sit in warm water while it again heats up. Also, plant enzymes may destroy some vitamins before the water again becomes hot enough to destroy them.

Tests have shown that, for these reasons, no more nutrients are lost when vegetables are cooked in a lot of water than when vegetables are cooked in just enough water to cover.

When cooking green vegetables, there is an added advantage to using a lot of water. Plant acids are more quickly diluted and driven off, better preserving the color.

The best cooking methods, nutritionally, are usually those that produce the most attractive, flavorful products.

- They are more likely to be eaten. Discarded vegetables benefit no one, no matter how nutritious they are.

- Factors that destroy nutrients are often those that also destroy color, flavor, and texture.

General Rules of Vegetable Cookery

Now that you understand how vegetables change as they cook, let's summarize that information in some general rules. You should now be able to explain the reasons for each of these rules.

- Don't overcook.

- Cook as close to service time as possible, and in small quantities. Avoid holding for long periods on a steam table.

- If the vegetable must be cooked ahead, undercook slightly and chill rapidly. Reheat at service time.

- Never use baking soda with green vegetables.

- Cut vegetables uniformly for even cooking.

- Start with boiling, salted water when boiling green vegetables and other vegetables that grow above the ground. Roots and tubers are started in cold, salted water for more even cooking.

- Cook green vegetables and strong-flavored vegetables uncovered.

- To preserve color, cook red and white vegetables in a slightly acid (not strongly acid) liquid. Cook green vegetables in a neutral liquid.

- Do not mix a batch of freshly cooked vegetables with a batch of the same vegetable that was cooked earlier and kept hot in a steam table.

Standards of Quality in Cooked Vegetables

1. **Color.**
   Bright, natural colors.
      Green vegetables, in particular, should be a fresh, bright green, not olive green.

2. **Appearance on plate.**
   Cut neatly and uniformly. Not broken up.
      Attractively arranged or mounded on plate or dish.
      Not swimming in cooking water.
      Imaginative and appropriate combinations and garnishes are always well received.

3. **Texture.**
   Cooked to the right degree of doneness.
      Most vegetables should be crisp-tender, not overcooked and mushy, but not tough or woody either.

KEY POINTS TO REVIEW

- What factors affect changes in texture when vegetables are cooked?

- What are the guidelines for achieving proper doneness in vegetables?

- What factors affect changes in flavor when vegetables are cooked?

- What factors affect changes in color when vegetables are cooked? Describe factors specific to white vegetables, green vegetables, red vegetables, and orange and yellow vegetables.

- What steps can you take to maintain the highest nutritional values when cooking vegetables?

- What standards are used to judge the quality of cooked vegetables?

Vegetables intended to be soft (potatoes, squash, sweet potatoes, tomatoes, vegetable purées) should be cooked through, with a pleasant, smooth texture.

4. **Flavor.**
Full, natural flavor and sweetness, sometimes called *garden-fresh flavor*. Strong-flavored vegetables should be pleasantly mild, with no off flavors or bitterness.

5. **Seasonings.**
Lightly and appropriately seasoned. Seasonings should not be too strong and should not mask the natural garden flavors.

6. **Sauces.**
Butter and seasoned butters should be fresh and not used heavily; vegetables should not be greasy.
Cream sauces and other sauces should not be too thick or too heavily seasoned. As with seasonings, sauces should enhance, not cover up.

7. **Vegetable combinations.**
Interesting combinations attract customers.
Flavors, colors, and shapes should be pleasing in combination.
Vegetables should be cooked separately and then combined to allow for different cooking times.
Acid vegetables (like tomatoes) added to green vegetables will discolor them. Combine just before service.

HANDLING VEGETABLES

Fresh Vegetables

Washing

1. Wash all vegetables thoroughly.

2. Root vegetables that are not peeled, such as potatoes for baking, should be scrubbed very well with a stiff vegetable brush.

3. Wash green, leafy vegetables in several changes of cold water. Lift the greens from the water so the sand can sink to the bottom. Pouring off into a colander dumps the sand back onto the leaves.

4. After washing, drain well and refrigerate lightly covered. The purpose of covering is to prevent drying, but covering too tightly cuts off air circulation. This can be a problem if the product is stored more than a day because mold is more likely to grow in a damp, closed space. Use a drain insert in the storage container to allow drainage.

Soaking

1. With a few exceptions, do not soak vegetables for long periods. Flavor and nutrients leach out.

2. Cabbage, broccoli, Brussels sprouts, and cauliflower may be soaked 30 minutes in cold salted water to eliminate insects, if necessary.

3. Limp vegetables can be soaked briefly in cold water to restore crispness.

4. Dried legumes are soaked for several hours before cooking to replace moisture lost in drying. Dried beans absorb their weight in water.

Peeling and Cutting

1. Peel most vegetables as thinly as possible. Many nutrients lie just under the skin.

2. Cut vegetables into uniform pieces for even cooking.

3. Peel and cut vegetables as close to cooking time as possible to prevent drying and loss of vitamins through oxidation.

4. For machine paring, sort vegetables for evenness of size to minimize waste.

5. Treat vegetables that brown easily (potatoes, eggplant, artichokes, sweet potatoes) with an acid, such as lemon juice, or an antioxidant solution, or hold under water until ready to use (some vitamins and minerals will be lost).

6. Save edible trim for soups, stocks, and vegetable purées.

Classifying Vegetables

Many people are bothered by the fact that tomatoes are referred to as vegetables when they are, in fact, fruits. Yes, tomatoes are fruits, and carrots are roots, and spinach is a leaf, and they are all vegetables.

To a botanist, the term *fruit* refers to a specific part of a plant, just as do the terms *stem*, *root*, and *leaf*. A fruit is defined as the ripened ovary or ovaries of a seed-bearing plant, and it contains the seeds. In other words, if it has seeds, it's a fruit. We shouldn't be misled by the fact that a few fruits are sweet. Many, if not most, fruits in nature are not sweet at all. Some examples of fruits used in the vegetable kitchen are tomatoes, eggplant, peppers, green beans, okra, cucumbers, squash, pea pods, walnuts, and avocados.

There are many ways of classifying vegetables. Some are more helpful to the cook than others. Putting vegetables into groups based on their botanical origin is not always helpful. For example, okra and eggplant are both fruits, but they are handled and cooked so differently that this information doesn't really help us.

The following vegetable categories are based, in part, on how the vegetables are used in the kitchen. For example, the vegetables listed as roots and tubers come from several unrelated families, but they all have fairly solid, uniform textures and are handled in similar ways. This is not a scientific classification, and it is not the only way to group vegetables.

Note that the first three categories are all fruits or, in a few cases, seeds from fruits.

- The gourd family: cucumber, winter and summer squashes, pumpkin, chayote (Some sources put eggplant in the gourd family, but this is incorrect; see below.)

- Seeds and pods: beans, peas, corn, okra

- Other tender-fruited vegetables: avocado, eggplant, sweet and hot peppers, tomato (Eggplant, tomato, and peppers are all members of the nightshade family; the avocado is unrelated.)

- Roots and tubers: beet, carrot, celery root, parsnip, radish, turnip, rutabaga, Jerusalem artichoke, potato, sweet potato, jícama

- The cabbage family: cabbage, broccoli, cauliflower, Brussels sprouts, kohlrabi, bok choy

- The onion family: onion, scallion, leek, garlic, shallot

- Leafy greens: spinach, beet greens, lettuces, endive and chicory, Swiss chard, sorrel, watercress, collards, kale, turnip greens (The last three are also members of the cabbage family.)

- Stalks, stems, and shoots: globe artichoke, asparagus, celery, fennel, fiddlehead ferns, bamboo shoots

- Mushrooms

ORGANIC FOODS

As noted in Chapter 5, the law in many countries, including the United States, regulates the use of the term *organic*. Although many foods, including meats and poultry, can qualify for the organic label, organic vegetables, fruits, and other plant products have long been most prominent in the market.

First of all, for a food item or an ingredient in a processed food to be labeled organic in the United States, it must not contain hormones, antibiotics, synthetic pesticides, irradiated components, genetically modified organisms, or reprocessed sewage. Second, food products may be labeled in one of four ways, depending on how organic they are:

1. The label "100 percent organic" can be used only on products that contain only organic ingredients.

2. The label "organic" may be used on products that contain at least 95 percent organic ingredients by weight.

3. If a product contains 70 percent or more organic ingredients by weight, it can be labeled "made with organic ingredients." Up to three of those ingredients may be listed on the packaging.

4. If a product contains less than 70 percent organic ingredients by weight, those ingredients may be listed on the ingredient information panel, but the product may not use the word "organic" on the front of the package.

The green and white "USDA ORGANIC" seal may be used on the packaging of only those products in the first two of these categories.

Fresh Vegetables: Evaluating and Preparing

This section lists the fresh vegetables commonly used in North American kitchens, including many products that have become familiar from Asian and Latin cuisines. Tips for evaluation and trimming the products, as well as the average trimming yield, are indicated. Vegetables are listed alphabetically, rather than by family classification, to make them easier to find.

ARTICHOKES, GLOBE

Identification: Artichokes are the unopened or immature flowers of a type of thistle. They vary in size and coloration but are usually round to somewhat elongated, colored light to medium green, sometimes with purple tints.

Related Varieties: Baby artichokes are not actually babies but come from a different place on the plant and are at their full size. Especially young baby artichokes may be tender enough to eat whole, with little trimming except for removing the top points of the leaves.

Evaluation: Look for compact, tight leaves; heavy for size; few or no brown blemishes.

Preparation: Wash. Cut 1 inch (2–3 cm) off tops. Cut off stem and lower leaves. Scrape out choke (fuzzy center) with melon ball cutter. (Remove choke before or after cooking.) Dip in lemon juice immediately. To prepare bottoms, see Figures 10.1 and 10.2.

Percentage Yield: 80% (whole, trimmed), 30% (bottoms only)

Figure 10.1 Trimming artichoke bottoms.

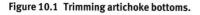

(a) Cut or break off the stem flush with the bottom of the artichoke, as shown.

(b) Break off the outer leaves.

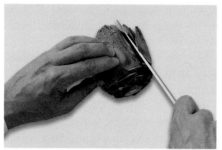

(c) Alternatively, trim the outer leaves with a knife as shown, being careful not to cut into the base of the artichoke.

(d) Cut off the remaining leaves above the base.

(e) With a paring knife, trim off the green outer peel to give the base a smooth, neat appearance.

(f) With a ball cutter or tablespoon, scrape out the fuzzy choke.

(g) A trimmed artichoke bottom on the left; a trimmed whole artichoke on the right. Note that the points of the leaves have been cut off and the center choke removed.

Figure 10.2 To keep the cut stem end of an artichoke from darkening during steaming or boiling, tie a slice of lemon over the cut surface.

ARTICHOKES, JERUSALEM

See Sunchoke.

ASPARAGUS

Identification: Spear-shaped new shoot or stem that emerges from the plant's roots in the spring. The pointed spear tip sprouts branches when the shoot is allowed to grow.

Related Varieties: *White asparagus* is the same plant as green, but soil is mounded over the shoots, protecting them from the sun so they do not turn green. In Europe, white asparagus is more common than green. The flavor is milder than that of green, although North American white asparagus is usually more bitter than European. *Purple asparagus* turns dark green when cooked. It is tender and sweet.

Evaluation: Look for tightly closed tips; firm, not withered, stalks. For white asparagus, buy only product that has been kept chilled for its entire storage time; unchilled white asparagus becomes fibrous.

Preparation: Break off woody lower ends. Remove lower scales, which may harbor sand, or peel lower part of stalk. Figure 10.3 shows an alternative method. Cut tips to uniform lengths and/or tie them in bundles for cooking. White asparagus should be peeled the entire length of the stalk. Purple asparagus needs no peeling; just trim the bottoms.

Percentage Yield: 55% (green, peeled)

Figure 10.3 Trimming asparagus.

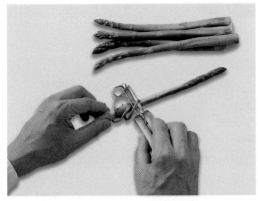

(a) With a vegetable peeler, pare the stalk from about 2 in. (5 cm) below the tip down to the base.

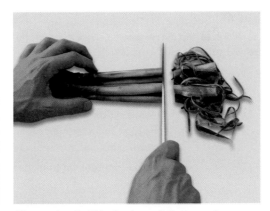

(b) Cut or break off the hard, woody bottoms of the stems.

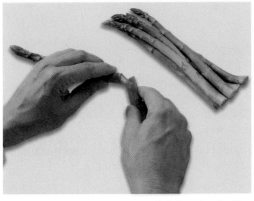

(c) Another method used by many chefs is to break off the stems first . . .

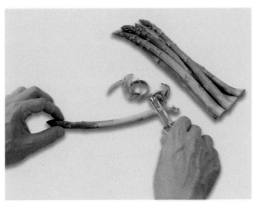

(d) . . . and then peel the stem.

AVOCADOS

Identification: The egg-shaped fruit of a small tree, with a leathery skin, tender, pale-green flesh, and a single large seed or pit in the center.

Related Varieties: There are several varieties that fall into two main categories: (1) The Mexican or Californian avocados, mostly the Hass variety, which have rough, dark green skins that turn black when ripe. These have a rich, buttery flesh with a high oil content. (2) The West Indian or Florida type, which has smoother skin that remains green. These are juicier and have a lower oil content.

Evaluation: Look for fresh appearance; fruit heavy for size; no blemishes or bruises.

Preparation: Ripen at room temperature, 2 to 5 days. Cut in half lengthwise and remove pit (see Figure 10.4). Peel (skin pulls away easily from ripe fruit). Dip into or rub with lemon juice immediately to prevent browning.

Percentage Yield: 75%

Figure 10.4 Preparing avocados.

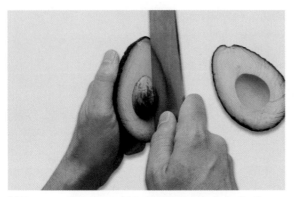

(a) To remove the pit or seed from the cut avocado, strike it sharply (but carefully) with the heel of a chef's knife.

(b) Twist the knife slightly and pull out the pit.

BAMBOO SHOOTS

Identification: The young shoots of various species of bamboo plants, harvested as they just begin to emerge from the ground. They are roughly cone-shaped, with tough brown skins and a creamy, crisp, tender interior.

Evaluation: Look for solid, heavy shoots with no soft spots or cracks; no trace of sour smell.

Preparation: Peel down to the creamy white or pale yellowish cone-shaped core. Slice and boil in salted water until tender, then cut as desired for use in recipes.

Percentage Yield: Varies greatly, depending on size of shoots, which range from a few ounces to a pound (less than 100 grams to 500 grams) or more.

BEANS, DRIED

See Chapter 13.

BEANS, FAVA

Identification: Also called *broad bean*. Unlike most of our common beans, which originated in the Western Hemisphere, favas are Old World beans. The large pods hold four to six beans in a soft, white lining. The flat beans slightly resemble limas, but they are not as starchy. Flavor is subtle and nutlike.

Evaluation: Select small to medium pods that are fresh green in color, not overly large. Yellowing pods may be too mature. Some spots on pods is normal.

Preparation: Preparation is labor-intensive. Shell the beans, parboil, then peel off skins or husks (Figure 10.5).

Percentage Yield: 15–20%

Figure 10.5 Preparing fava beans.

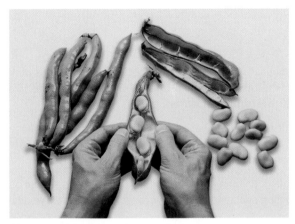

(a) Split open the pods and remove the beans.

(b) Blanch the beans for a few minutes. This cooks the beans and loosens the skins. Peel off the outer skins. Unpeeled beans are on the left, peeled beans on the right.

BEANS, FRESH SHELL

Identification: These are the fresh, moist versions of the many types of dried beans.

Related Varieties: Although many types of beans are grown to be shelled, most of these are dried, and, with the exception of *cranberry* or *borlotti beans*, *southernpeas* or *cowpeas*, and *black-eyed peas*, few are available fresh. Soybeans and lima beans have their own entries below.

Evaluation: Look for firm, fresh, moderately filled-out pods containing firm but not hard seeds. Avoid yellow or brownish pods, which are likely to be too mature.

Preparation: Shell and rinse. Cook before serving; raw beans can be harmful.

Percentage Yield: 40%

BEANS, LIMA

Identification: Flat, pale-green beans in flat, slightly fuzzy pods, with three or four beans per pod. Larger limas tend to be starchier than small or baby limas.

Related Varieties: Many varieties are grown, but they are not usually distinguished from one another in the market.

Evaluation: Beans should be plump, with tender skins.

Preparation: Shell, wash, and drain.

Percentage Yield: 40%

BEANS, SNAP

Identification: Fresh green beans and other varieties are in the same family as shell beans, except they are grown to be picked immature for their tender, edible pods.

Related Varieties: Green beans are the most common. Some green varieties, picked when very small and tender, are known as *haricots verts* (ah ree coh vehr, French for "green beans"). Other varieties include yellow or wax beans, purple beans, and flat, Italian-style green beans.

Evaluation: Look for firm and straight beans, with few shriveled ends; even color, without blemishes. Should be tender and crisp enough to break when bent to a 45-degree angle. Enclosed seeds should be small, not large and bulging.

Preparation: Wash. Cut or snap off ends. Remove any spots. Leave whole or cut into desired lengths.

Percentage Yield: 88%

Green beans

BEANS, SOY
See Soybeans.

BEETS

Red beets

Identification: A tender, bulbous, somewhat sweet root, usually but not always dark red. The tops can also be cooked like other greens; handle and treat beet tops like Swiss chard (see below), which is in the beet family.

Related Varieties: Beets come in several shapes and colors in addition to the common red, including yellow, pink, orange or brick red, and white. Chioggia (kee oh ja) are striped red and white. Shapes include round, elongated oval, and cylindrical.

Evaluation: Look for firm, round, uniform size; smooth skin. Tops, if any, should be fresh or just wilted, but not yellow or deteriorated. Large, rough beets are often woody.

Preparation: Cut off tops, leaving 1 inch (2–3 cm) of stem attached to beets. Leave roots on to avoid loss of color and juice during cooking. Scrub well. Steam, boil, or bake before peeling.

Percentage Yield: 40–45% (75% if purchased without tops)

BOK CHOY

Bok Choy

Identification: An Asian member of the cabbage family, related to Chinese cabbage, except the stalk is thicker and fleshier and the green portion is smoother and darker in color. Leaves and stalks are tender, crisp, and juicy.

Related Varieties: Several varieties all form compact, elongated bunches. The most common variety forms large heads or bunches with white stems. *Shanghai bok choi* is smaller, with pale green stems. *Choy sum* is allowed to become more mature, so the central stem or core is longer, and there may be small yellow flowers among the leaves.

Evaluation: Fresh, green appearance for all varieties, with no wilting or discoloration.

Preparation: Cut in half lengthwise and wash under running water to remove soil from the crooks of the stalks. Trim bottom by cutting off a thin slice, or cut out core. Cut as desired. Small varieties may be cooked whole.

Percentage Yield: 80%

BROCCOLI

Figure 10.6 Prepare tough bottoms of broccoli stalks by pulling off the fibrous peel, as shown.

Identification: A green vegetable in the cabbage family, consisting of tight clusters of tiny green flower buds on fleshy stalks.

Related Varieties: Pale green *broccoflower* is closer in character to cauliflower than to broccoli and should be handled like cauliflower. *Broccolini* is a relatively new broccoli hybrid with slender stems and small, loose florets (flower bud heads). *Broccoli rabe* (also called *broccoli raab, broccoletti di rape, rapini,* and *cima de rapa*), like broccolini, has slender stems and loose florets, but it also has tender leaves attached to the stems, and the stems are slightly ribbed rather than smooth. Broccoli has a stronger, more mustardy flavor. Several varieties of *Chinese broccoli* are similar to broccoli rabe in both shape and flavor, but the stems are smoother and fleshier.

Evaluation: Look for dark green, tightly closed buds in regular broccoli and broccoflower. Broccoli rabe and Asian types should be dark green with crisp, not wilted, leaves.

Preparation: Wash well. Soak in salted water 30 minutes if necessary to remove insects. Split large stalks into smaller sizes for portioning. Split thick stalks partway for faster cooking, or cut tops from stalks. Tougher stalks may be peeled (Figure 10.6).

Percentage Yield: 65–75%

BRUSSELS SPROUTS

Identification: This cabbage relative resembles a tiny cabbage head. The clusters of leaves grow in rows along a thick stalk. Flavor is somewhat stronger than that of green cabbage.

Related Varieties: Red or purple (the color of red cabbage) Brussels sprouts exist but are not often seen, probably because their flavor and texture is less appealing to most people.

Evaluation: Look for bright green, tight heads; uniform size.

Preparation: Trim bottom ends and remove yellowed outer leaves (but don't cut off too much of the bottom or you will lose too many leaves). For more even cooking, pierce base with sharp knife point. Rinse well. Rinse in cold salted water 30 minutes if necessary to remove insects.

Percentage Yield: 80%

Brussels sprouts

CABBAGE: GREEN, RED, AND SAVOY

Identification: Cabbages are large leaf clusters in dense, round heads (heads may also be flat or elongated, depending on the variety). Cabbage and mustard are in the same family, a relationship that can be detected in the faintly peppery taste.

Evaluation: For both green and red cabbage, look for a firm head, heavy for size. Good color. Crisp leaves, finely ribbed. Savoy cabbage is not as heavy, with darker green, ruffled leaves.

Preparation: Remove coarse or discolored outer leaves. Remove core and rinse whole, or cut into quarters and then remove core. For wedges, core is left in, but with bottom trimmed, to hold sections together. (See Figure 10.7)

Percentage Yield: 80%

Green cabbage

Figure 10.7 Cutting and shredding cabbage.

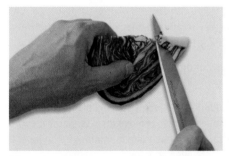

(a) Cut the cabbage head into quarters. Then cut out the core as shown.

(b) With a French knife, cut into thin shreds.

Red cabbage

CABBAGE, CHINESE

Identification: Heads of tender, crinkly, pale green leaves with broad, flat center stalks. The flavor is mild and slightly spicy.

Related Varieties: The two main varieties have different head shapes, although their flavor and texture are virtually the same. The head of *napa cabbage* is stout and barrel-shaped. A more elongated, slender head cabbage is often called *celery cabbage* for its shape. See also Bok Choy, a closely related cabbage.

Evaluation: Look for firm, tightly packed heads with no dry or browned tips, crisp and not limp or wilted.

Preparation: Wash. Cut as desired, discarding the center core.

Percentage Yield: 85%

Savoy cabbage

CACTUS PADS OR NOPALES

Cactus pad

Identification: Nopales are tender pads of the prickly pear cactus. When cooked, their texture is slippery, like that of okra, and their flavor slightly resembles cooked green pepper or possibly green beans with a slight sourness.

Evaluation: Try to purchase pads with the spines removed. Look for full, firm, crisp pads, not wilted or soft ones.

Preparation: If spines are present, wear rubber gloves and brush them vigorously under running water, then with a vegetable peeler remove the eyes that held the spines. Trim the base if necessary. Cut as desired. Can be sautéed, boiled, steamed, or grilled.

Percentage Yield: 90%

CARROTS

Identification: Long, pointed, orange roots. Among the most widely used vegetables. Specialty carrots are also available in other colors, including yellow, red, and purple.

Evaluation: Look for bright orange color; crisp, straight, and well shaped shaft; smooth surface. Large carrots are sometimes woody.

Preparation: Trim top and bottom ends. Pare with hand peeler.

Percentage Yield: 75–80%

Carrot
Courtesy of Grimmway Farms

CAULIFLOWER

Cauliflower

Identification: White or off-white, tight cluster of tiny flowers (florets) branching off a central stalk. Member of the cabbage family.

Related Varieties: *Broccoflower* is a light green relative that looks like a cross between broccoli and cauliflower. Handle like regular cauliflower.

Evaluation: Look for white color, not yellow or brownish; fine-grained, tightly closed buds; fresh green, well-trimmed leaves.

Preparation: Remove leaves and trim tough part of stalk. Cut away discolored parts. Wash. Soak in salted water 30 minutes if necessary to remove insects. Separate into florets, leaving portion of center stalk attached to each one to minimize trim loss. If cooking whole, cut out center of stalk for more even cooking.

Percentage Yield: 55%

Figure 10.8 Cauliflower disassembly.

(a) With a paring knife or small utility knife, cut out the central core.

(b) Separate the cauliflower into florets.

CELERY

Identification: Pale green stems that form bunches or clusters attached at root end. One of the most common vegetables.

Evaluation: Look for bunches that are straight, compact, well trimmed; fresh green color.

Preparation: Cut off root end. Separate stems and scrub well. Reserve leaves and tough outer stems for stocks, soups, mirepoix. Ribbed outer side of stems may be peeled to remove strings.

Percentage Yield: 75%

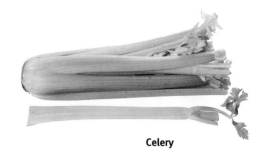

Celery

CELERY ROOT OR CELERIAC

Identification: A variety of celery grown for its round, fleshy white root.

Evaluation: Select firm and heavy roots. Large ones are often soft and spongy in the center.

Preparation: Wash well, peel, and cut as desired.

Percentage Yield: 75%

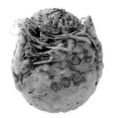

Celery root

CHAYOTE

Identification: A member of the gourd or squash family, this vegetable has a crisp texture and a mild flavor somewhere between zucchini and cucumber. It is roughly pear-shaped, although more rounded, with a thin yellow-green skin and creamy white flesh. It is also known as *mirliton* and *vegetable pear*.

Evaluation: Look for firm, solid chayotes without blemishes.

Preparation: Skin can be left on if served raw, but peel chayotes to be cooked, because the skin toughens. The soft seed in the middle can also be eaten.

Percentage Yield: 100% if unpeeled; 85–90% if peeled

Chayote

CHESTNUT

Identification: Chestnuts are the seed or nut of a variety of trees grown primarily in Europe. They have a thin, hard, dark brown outer shell and a bitter inner skin surrounding a soft, starchy meat.

Evaluation: Look for plump, firm nuts with no blemishes on the shells.

Preparation: The shell and skin must be removed before use. With the point of a paring knife, cut an *X* in the shell on the flat side of each nut. Roast at 350°F (180°C) for 15 minutes, or blanch in boiling water. Peel while still hot.

Percentage Yield: 75%

CORN

Identification: Corn is a grain used as a vegetable if immature. It grows in rows on the outside of a central woody cob and is covered with a leafy husk. Varieties grown for vegetable use are sweeter than grain varieties.

Evaluation: Look for fresh, moist husks, not dry; no worm damage; kernels well filled, tender, and milky when punctured.

Preparation: Strip off husks, remove silk, and cut off bottom stump. Cut into two or three sections as desired, if serving on cob, or cut from cob. Keep refrigerated and use as soon as possible.

Percentage Yield: 28% after husking and cutting from cob

Corn

Figure 10.9 Cucumber garnishes can be made more decorative by scoring the cucumber before slicing or cutting.

(a) Scoring with a fork.

(b) Scoring with a channel knife.

CUCUMBER

Identification: A member of the gourd family, like squash, the cucumber has a thin green skin and a crisp, mild, juicy off-white flesh.

Related Varieties: Cucumbers are of two types, slicing and pickling. The common green slicing cucumber, with dark green skin, is most often used in food service. The long, slender hothouse cucumber, also called *seedless* and *burpless*, is another common slicing cucumber. Pickling cucumbers, also called *Kirbys*, range in size from tiny gherkins to the large ones used to make dill pickles. They are somewhat drier and a little more flavorful than the slicing types. Their green skin is a little lighter in color than that of slicing cucumbers, and the surface is bumpy.

Evaluation: Look for vegetables that are firm, crisp, dark green, well shaped. Yellow color means the cucumber is overmature.

Preparation: Wash. Trim ends. Peel if skin is tough or has been waxed. Skin may be scored to make decorative slices (see Figure 10.9).

Percentage Yield: 75–95%, depending on peeling

EGGPLANT

Identification: Eggplants are members of the same family as tomatoes, peppers, and potatoes. They have purple, white, or pale green skin and a firm but spongy off-white flesh containing tiny edible seeds.

Related Varieties: Worldwide, there are dozens of varieties. In the West, the most common is the large, oblong, purple-skinned variety. Smaller, elongated varieties are sometimes called *Italian eggplant*. White-skinned varieties are round, egg-shaped (the origin of the name *eggplant*), or long and slender. *Japanese eggplants* are small, long, and slender, with a purple instead of green stem. Asian types include small round, green-skinned fruits, including a Thai eggplant no larger than a pea. The flesh of these varieties is similar in flavor, varying in texture or density from soft to almost hard.

Evaluation: Eggplants should be firm, not soft. Common purple types should be shiny, dark purple color; heavy and plump; without blemishes or soft spots.

Preparation: Wash. Trim off stem end. Peel if skin is tough. Cut just before use. Dip in lemon juice or antioxidant solution to prevent discoloration if not to be cooked within a few minutes after peeling and cutting.

Percentage Yield: 90% (75% if peeled)

Italian eggplant

White eggplant

Fennel

FENNEL

Identification: The clustered or bunched stems form a bulbous base. The fleshy bulb is white with a pale hint of green, while the stems are darker green. The aroma and flavor have a faint suggestion of licorice.

Related Varieties: The vegetable fennel is more properly known as *Florence fennel*, to distinguish it from the varieties grown as a spice (seed) and herb. The vegetable is sometimes incorrectly called *anise*, which is a different plant.

Evaluation: Look for bright, pale green color with few or no brown spots. Fresh green tops, not wilted or spoiled. Compact, heavy for size.

Preparation: Trim stems and feathery leaves. Split in half through the base. If the fennel is large, cut out the core as for cabbage if it is fibrous or tough.

Percentage Yield: 80%

FIDDLEHEAD FERN

Identification: This spring vegetable is the early shoot of a fern, usually ostrich fern, harvested just as it emerges from the ground. It consists of a tightly curled stem lined with the tiniest beginnings of leaves. It is usually handled and cooked like tender asparagus.

Evaluation: Look for jade green, firm and resilient, not wilted, fiddleheads with fresh-looking, not spoiled, cut ends and leaf tips.

Preparation: Trim the cut ends. Rinse well.

Percentage Yield: 85%

Fiddlehead ferns

GARLIC

Identification: A pungent member of the onion family, garlic forms bunches of cloves attached at the root end and covered with a papery skin.

Related Varieties: There are many varieties, with white or purplish skins. Some are more pungent than others. Elephant garlic is the size of an apple, with relatively few large cloves; it is milder than other varieties.

Evaluation: Skin may be white or pink. No brown spots, soft spots, or spoilage; dry skin; no green shoots.

Preparation: Separate cloves as needed, or strike whole bulb with heel of hand to separate. To peel cloves, crush slightly with side of heavy knife. Peel and trim root end (see Figure 10.10).

Percentage Yield: 88%

Figure 10.10 Peeling and crushing garlic.

(a) **Place the garlic on the worktable. Hold a broad knife blade over it as shown and strike it firmly with the palm of the hand.**

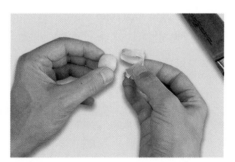

(b) **You can now peel the garlic easily.**

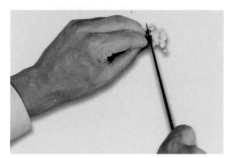

(c) **Chop or mince the garlic.**

(d) **To make a paste of the garlic, sprinkle it with salt and mash it firmly with the back of the knife blade.**

Collard greens

Turnip greens

Kale

GREENS, CABBAGE FAMILY (COLLARDS, TURNIP GREENS, KALE)

Identification: These sturdy, flavorful greens are nearly always cooked because they are too tough to eat raw, unless very young. The kale varieties have curly or ruffled dark green leaves (except the ornamental varieties, which may have touches of red or other colors). Turnip greens resemble large, lobed mustard or arugula leaves. Collards are similar, generally with heavier stems and more rounded leaves.

Evaluation: Avoid browned, yellowed, or dried leaves. Look for smaller leaves that are dark green and have a moist feel.

Preparation: Strip the leaves off the stems if they are tough. Cut off any discolored parts. Wash well in several changes of water.

Percentage Yield: 80%

JÍCAMA

Identification: Jícama (HEE kama) is a large, round tuber with a thin brown skin and crisp, mild, juicy, creamy white flesh similar to water chestnuts.

Evaluation: Look for smooth, almost shiny skin with no blemishes.

Preparation: Peel. Cut as desired.

Percentage Yield: 85%

Jícama

KOHLRABI

Identification: Kohlrabi, when trimmed, resembles a root vegetable, but it is actually a swollen stem. A member of the cabbage family, its pale white, crisp flesh resembles, in texture and flavor, the interior of a broccoli stem. The skin is tough and must be removed.

Related Varieties: Purple-skinned kohlrabi are similar to the more common green variety, except for skin color.

Evaluation: Look for uniform light green color; 2–3 inches (5–8 cm) in diameter. Crisp and firm. No woodiness.

Preparation: Peel like turnips, being sure to remove the full thickness of skin.

Percentage Yield: 55%

Kohlrabi

LEEKS

Identification: A long, slender member of the onion family with distinctive flavor, milder than onions.

Related Varieties: *Ramps* are wild leeks with broad, flat leaves and bulbs that resemble those of scallions. They have a pungent, garlicky flavor.

Evaluation: Look for fresh green leaves; 2–3 inches (5–8 cm) of white. White part should be crisp and tender, not fibrous.

Preparation: Cut off roots and green tops. Cut deeply through white part, separate the layers slightly, and wash carefully to remove all embedded soil (see Figure 10.11).

Percentage Yield: 50%

LETTUCE

Identification: See Chapter 14 for full description of salad greens.

Percentage Yield: 75%

Figure 10.11 Cleaning leeks.

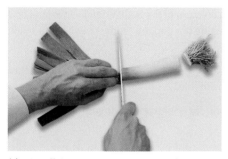

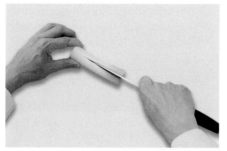

(a) Trim off the root end and as much of the green as desired.

(b) Make one or two deep cuts to within 1 in. (2.5 cm) of the root end.

(c) Spread apart the layers, as shown. Carefully wash out all embedded dirt under running water.

MUSHROOMS, WHITE

Identification: Mushrooms are the fruiting body of a fungus—that is, the part of the fungus that produces spores for reproduction.

Evaluation: Select firm, white caps, closed at the stem. Stems should be relatively short. No dark spots, bruises, or mold.

Preparation: Trim bottoms of stems. Just before cooking, wash quickly in cold water; drain well. If you desire to keep the mushrooms white, add a small amount of acid (lemon juice, vinegar, ascorbic acid) to the rinse water. To flute mushrooms, see Figure 10.12.

Percentage Yield: 90%

White mushrooms

MUSHROOMS, EXOTIC AND WILD VARIETIES

See pages 267–268.

Figure 10.12 Basic method for fluting mushrooms.

(a) Grasping the blade of a paring knife, hold the edge against the center of the mushroom cap at a sharp angle.

(b) The first cut is completed.

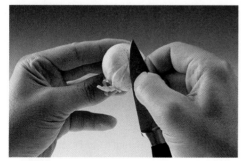

(c) Continue making cuts all around the mushroom.

(d) The fluted mushroom cap.

OKRA

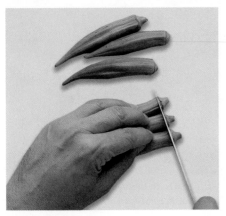

Figure 10.13 To prepare okra, cut off the stem ends.

Identification: Okra is the pod or fruit of a member of the mallow family. It is long and tapered, with ridges running its length. Inside the pod are tender seeds and a thick, sticky juice. The flavor is very mild.

Related Varieties: Common okra varieties are green. Red-skinned varieties, which turn green when cooked, are uncommon but available.

Evaluation: Look for tender, full pods, not dry or shriveled. Ridges should be soft. Seeds should be soft and white. Uniform color.

Preparation: Wash. Trim ends (see Figure 10.13). Slice or leave whole.

Percentage Yield: 82%

ONIONS, DRY

Yellow onions

Identification: A pungent, many-layered bulbous root that is the kitchen's most common vegetable.

Related Varieties: Onions come in almost limitless varieties, from tiny white, yellow, and red pearl onions and cipolline (chip oh lee neh, Italian pearl onions) to medium and large yellow onions, the workhorse of the kitchen, to large red and white onions. Mild varieties include Vidalia, Walla Walla, and Maui. These are often said to be sweeter, but they do not contain more sugar than regular varieties. Rather, they have less of the chemical compounds that make onions strong.

Evaluation: Select onions that are clean, hard, well shaped; no mold or black fungus; no green shoots. Skins should be very dry.

Preparation: Cut off root and stem ends. Peel. Wash. Cut or slice as needed (see Figure 7.10).

Percentage Yield: 90%

Red onions

White onion

Pearl onions

ONIONS, GREEN (SCALLIONS)

Scallions

Identification: These are very young, immature bulb onions, sold with their stems. Scallions are almost always white varieties of onion, although red varieties can sometimes be found.

Evaluation: Scallions should have fresh, crisp green tops; little or no bulb formation at white part.

Preparation: Cut off roots and wilted ends of green tops. Amount of green left on varies with recipe or use.

Percentage Yield: 60–70%

PARSLEY

Identification: Parsley is the most common fresh herb used in kitchens. It is used in such quantities that it is included here with vegetables.

Related Varieties: The two main varieties are curly parsley and flat or Italian parsley.

Evaluation: Select bright green, unwilted leaves with no rot.

Preparation: Wash well and drain. Remove yellow leaves and large stems (save stems for stocks). Separate into sprigs for garnish, or chop leaves.

Percentage Yield: 85%

PARSNIPS

Identification: The parsnip is a long, conical root vegetable that looks like a carrot, only more tapered and with a wider top. Its skin is tan and its interior is yellow-beige, with a distinctive, sweet flavor.

Evaluation: Look for firm, smooth, well-shaped parsnips, with light, uniform color. Large ones are often woody.

Preparation: Refrigerating for two weeks develops sweetness. Trim ends and peel. Rinse.

Percentage Yield: 70–75%

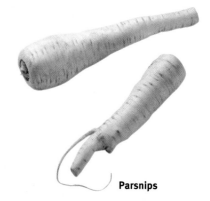

Parsnips

PEA GREENS OR PEA SHOOTS

Identification: These are the tender tips, with leaves, of pea vines, usually snow peas.

Evaluation: Look for fresh, medium-green leaves and tender, not woody, stems.

Preparation: Wash well; trim ends of stems, especially if tough. Cook like spinach.

Percentage Yield: 90–95%

PEAS, GREEN

Identification: The tender, immature seed of a legume (see Chapter 13).

Evaluation: Look for firm, fresh, moderately filled-out pods. Peas lose sweetness quickly after harvest, so locally grown, just-harvested peas are best. Frozen peas are likely to be sweeter than fresh peas that have been stored for some time.

Preparation: Shell and rinse. (Peas are not often purchased by food-service operations because of the labor required for shelling.)

Percentage Yield: 40%

Pea shoots

PEAS, EDIBLE POD

Identification: Unlike shell peas, above, whose pods are too fibrous to be eaten, these peas have tender, edible pods and so are always served in the pod.

Related Varieties: The two main varieties are the flat-podded snow pea, with tiny undeveloped seeds, and the rounder *sugar pea* or *sugar snap pea*, with larger seeds.

Evaluation: Look for fresh green color, crisp pods, no blemishes.

Preparation: Remove stem end. Pull off strings at side veins. Wash.

Percentage Yield: 90%

Snow peas

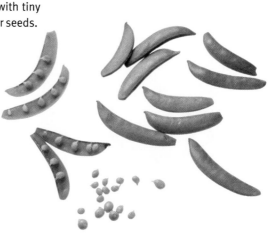

Sugar snap peas

Figure 10.14 Roasting peppers.

(a) Roast the peppers over an open flame until the skins blacken. For large quantities, you may do this under a broiler or in a hot oven. In this case, the skins will not darken as much but can still be peeled off.

(b) Wrap the peppers in plastic film while they are still hot. This helps loosen the skins.

(c) Peel off the loosened skin. You may do this under running water to help rinse off charred skin, but nutrients and flavor may be lost.

PEPPERS, SWEET

Identification: Peppers are the fruit of a plant related to tomatoes, eggplant, and potatoes. Both sweet and hot peppers are members of the *Capsicum* family. They have fleshy walls and a hollow interior, with a seedy core just below the stem. Also called *bell peppers.*

Related Varieties: Green, red, yellow, orange, and purple peppers are widely available.

Evaluation: Shiny color; well shaped; no soft spots or shriveling.

Preparation: Wash. Cut in half lengthwise and remove core, seeds, and white membranes. Peppers to be julienned or diced may have the interior ribs trimmed. Or leave whole (as for stuffed peppers) and cut out core from the end. Peppers are often roasted and peeled as preparation for use in recipes (see Figure 10.14).

Percentage Yield: 82%

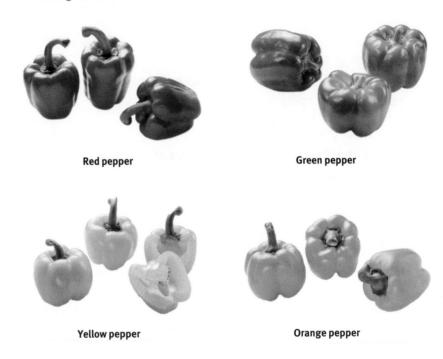

Red pepper   Green pepper

Yellow pepper   Orange pepper

PEPPERS, HOT, OR CHILES

Identification: Relatives of sweet peppers, but containing a compound called *capsaicin*, which makes them spicy hot. (*Chile* is the original Spanish spelling; also spelled *chili* and *chilli*.)

Related Varieties: Many varieties are available worldwide. The heat of any particular pepper is determined by how much capsaicin it contains and is measured in Scoville units. A mildly hot jalapeño averages 2,500–3,000 units, while the intensely hot habanero averages around 200,000 units. Commonly used fresh chiles include the jalapeño, serrano, poblano, California, New Mexico, Thai green, and cayenne.

Evaluation: See Peppers, Sweet.

Green cayenne chiles

Italian hot peppers

Jalapeños and cherry peppers

Preparation: Larger fresh chile peppers, such as ancho, mulato, New Mexico, and Anaheim, are usually roasted and prepared like sweet peppers (see p. 262). Small peppers, such as cayenne, jalapeño, and serrano, are usually chopped or sliced and used as seasoning. Remove core, veins, and seeds carefully; wear rubber gloves if you are sensitive to the hot oils, and avoid touching the eyes or any sensitive part of the skin after working with chiles.

Percentage Yield: 80–90%

Hot pepper varieties: red habanero, caribe, orange habanero, and green chiles

POTATOES, WHITE

Identification: See Chapter 12.

Percentage Yield: 80%

POTATOES, SWEET

Identification: Sweet potatoes are any of several types of tubers, usually bulbous, with tapered or pointed ends. They are unrelated to potatoes and to yams. (True yams are an entirely different vegetable, with starchy white flesh. They are not often seen in North America, except in Hispanic and some other specialty markets.)

Related Varieties: There are two basic groups of sweet potatoes, those with a creamy white or pale yellow flesh and those with orange flesh. The variety that has a moister, deeper orange flesh is sometimes referred to, incorrectly, as the *yam*. These varieties are interchangeable for most purposes. Skin colors range from beige to orange to red, depending on the variety.

Evaluation: Look for clean, dry surface. Firm, not shriveled or blemished. Fat, regular shapes are preferable because of less waste in trimming and portioning.

Preparation: Scrub, boil, or steam, then peel. May be peeled before cooking but must be dipped in antioxidant to prevent discoloring. Machine paring is wasteful with irregular shapes.

Percentage Yield: 80%

Sweet potato

RADISHES

Identification: Crisp, juicy root vegetables in the mustard family, with a peppery taste.

Related Varieties: In North America and Western Europe, the word *radish* usually indicates the small, round or tapered, red-skinned and white-fleshed variety, or sometimes the white icicle radish. Other important radishes are the turnip-size *black radish*, eaten raw or cooked, and the very large, long Asian *daikon* (the name is Japanese for "big root"), with white skin and flesh, also served raw or cooked. Cooked radishes are somewhat like turnips both in flavor and texture.

Evaluation: Select firm, tender, crisp radishes, with good shape and color.

Preparation: Cut off root and stem ends. Wash. Decorative cuts are shown in Figure 10.15.

Percentage Yield: 90%

Radishes

Black radish

Daikon

Figure 10.15 Radishes can be cut into many decorative forms, including those shown here.

RUTABAGAS

See Turnip.

SALSIFY

Salsify

Identification: The name *salsify* (sal si fee) refers to either of two distantly related long, slender root vegetables with off-white flesh and a flavor, when cooked, sometimes said to resemble artichoke.

Related Varieties: True salsify, or white salsify, has brownish-white roots, often forked and branched, with many root hairs attached. Scorzonera (score tso nerra), or black salsify, is straight, long, and slender, with dark brown skin. Both have off-white flesh.

Evaluation: Select medium-size roots, as larger ones may be fibrous. They should be as smooth as possible.

Preparation: Scrub with a brush. Peel with a swivel peeler and immediately drop into water containing an acid, such as lemon juice or vinegar, to prevent discoloration. Wear gloves to prevent staining the hands.

Percentage Yield: 65–70%

SHALLOTS

Identification: Shallots are small, dry-skinned onions that grow in clusters attached at the root end. They have a brown, papery skin and white and purple flesh. Their flavor is milder than that of onions.

Evaluation: Same as for dry onions.

Preparation: Same as for dry onions.

Percentage Yield: Same as for dry onions.

Shallots

SORREL

Sorrel

Identification: A tender leafy green with a tart, astringent taste, used in small quantities, usually to flavor sauces. The leaf resembles spinach but is longer and not as dark green.

Evaluation: Same as for spinach.

Preparation: Pull off coarse stems. Wash in several changes of water if sandy. For most purposes, sorrel is cut into chiffonade (p. 124).

Percentage Yield: 90%

SOYBEAN

Identification: Most soybeans are allowed to mature and dry and are harvested and processed as a grain. The use of tender, unripe soybeans, known as *edamame* (edd ah mah meh), is a popular adoption from Japanese cuisine. The small, fuzzy pods usually hold three light green, roundish beans.

Evaluation: Same as shell beans.

Preparation: Rinse, boil in the pod until the beans are tender, and shell.

Percentage Yield: 50%

Green soybeans

Soybeans in the pod

SPINACH

Identification: A tender, dark green leaf, probably the most popular of leafy vegetables after lettuce.

Related Varieties: Two main types are curly-leafed and flat-leafed.

Evaluation: Look for fresh, crisp, dark green leaves. No rot or slime or badly bruised leaves.

Preparation: Remove stems and damaged leaves (Figure 10.16). Wash in several changes of water. Use a large quantity of water and lift spinach up and down to float off sand and dirt. Lift from water and drain well.

Percentage Yield: 50–70%

Figure 10.16 When trimming spinach leaves, remove the heavy center rib along with the stem.

SQUASH, SUMMER

Identification: Several types of tender-skinned members of the gourd family are called *summer squash*. All have tender seeds in a firmly filled seed cavity, unlike the hard seeds encased in a fibrous mesh in the hollow interior of winter squash.

Related varieties: Green-skinned *zucchini* is well known and the most popular. *Yellow straight* and *crookneck* squashes are similar in flavor and use. *Pattypan* squash has a squat, round shape, slightly resembling the popular idea of a flying saucer. They can be yellow, dark green, or pale green. Many other, less common types are available.

Evaluation: Look for firm, heavy, and crisp squash, with tender skin, no blemishes.

Preparation: Wash or scrub well. Trim ends.

Percentage Yield: 90%

Yellow summer squash

Zucchini

SQUASH, WINTER, INCLUDING PUMPKIN

Identification: Winter squash are mature members of the gourd family, with thick skins and hard seeds in a hollow cavity. They are starchier and less moist than summer squash and, unlike summer squash, are not generally eaten raw.

Related Varieties: Many types, of all sizes and shapes, are available, including Hubbard, acorn, butternut, buttercup, kabocha, turban, delicata, sweet dumpling, and pumpkin. Spaghetti squash has a fibrous flesh that, when cooked and scraped out of the shell, resembles a tangled pile of spaghetti.

Evaluation: Heavy and firm. Hard rind. No blemishes.

Preparation: Wash. Cut in half. Scrape out seeds and fibers. Cut into portion sizes. For puréed or mashed squash either steam or bake, then remove peel; or peel, dice, then steam.

Percentage Yield: 65–85%

Spaghetti squash

Acorn squash

Butternut squash

Buttercup squash

SQUASH BLOSSOMS

Squash blossoms

Identification: Young, yellow blossoms of any summer squash.

Related Varieties: Female flowers are attached to the ends of new squashes. They fall off after the squash is a day or two old so must be harvested, attached to the tiny fruit, in a timely manner. Male blossoms contain the pollen and grow on a separate part of the same plant. Both types are used, often for stuffing, or simply sliced and sautéed.

Evaluation: Squash blossoms should be fresh and bright yellow, not wilted. They are best if used within a day or two of harvest.

Preparation: Open the flower petals gently and carefully rinse in water.

Percentage Yield: 100%

SUNCHOKES OR JERUSALEM ARTICHOKES

Identification: Sunchoke is a relatively new marketing term for a Jerusalem artichoke, created because the vegetable is not an artichoke and has nothing to do with Jerusalem. Sunchokes are knobby brown tubers with crisp, creamy white flesh.

Sunchokes

Evaluation: Look for firm sunchokes with clean brown skin, no soft or green spots, and no sprouts.

Preparation: Wash and peel off brown skin.

Percentage Yield: 80%

SWISS CHARD

Red-stemmed Swiss chard

Identification: A leafy green related to the beet. Chard leaves resemble beet greens in both flavor and appearance, but the center stalks of chard are broader.

Related Varieties: Red-stemmed, white-stemmed, and yellow-stemmed chard are available.

Evaluation: Fresh, dark green color, not wilted. Crisp, not wilted or rubbery stalks.

Preparation: Wash thoroughly. Trim ends of stalks. Remove leafy greens from stalks by cutting along the margins of the stalk down the center of the leaf. Center stalks may be cooked separately like asparagus.

White-stemmed Swiss chard

Percentage Yield: 85%

TOMATOES

Identification: One of the most widely used vegetables, the fruit of a plant in the nightshade family, related to eggplant, potatoes, and peppers.

Related Varieties: In addition to the common red slicing tomato and the small cherry tomato, dozens of varieties of heirloom tomatoes are grown and marketed. These come in all shades of red, pink, yellow, and green, all with somewhat different flavors.

Evaluation: Firm but not hard, with little or no green core. Smooth, without bruises, blemishes, cracks, or discoloration. If underripe, let stand two to three days at room temperature. Do not refrigerate.

Figure 10.17 Preparing tomato concassé.

(a) Blanch and peel the tomato and cut it in half crosswise. Gently squeeze out the seeds, as shown.

Tomato varieties

Preparation: For use with skin on: Wash, remove core. To peel: Plunge into boiling water 10–20 seconds (riper tomatoes take less time). Cool immediately in ice water. Slip skins off and remove core. (Note: Many chefs core the tomatoes and cut a shallow x in the skin at the bottom before blanching in boiling water. Other chefs, wishing to avoid even the slightest loss of flavor and nutrients from the exposed flesh into the water, first blanch the tomatoes and then core them and pull off the skins, which slip off just as easily.) See Figure 10.17 for further techniques.

Percentage Yield: 90% (peeled)

(b) Dice the seeded tomato, or chop it coarsely.

TOMATILLOS

Identification: A small green fruit vegetable resembling a green cherry tomato encased in a papery husk. It is not a tomato, although it is in the same family as tomatoes, eggplant, peppers, and potatoes. Widely used in Mexican cuisine.

Evaluation: Look for hard, dry tomatillos with tight husks.

Preparation: Remove the husks and rinse.

Percentage Yield: 95%

Tomatillos

TURNIPS AND RUTABAGAS

Identification: Root vegetables in the mustard family, related to cabbages.

Related Varieties: Turnips are white with purple skin around the stem end. The flesh is white. Rutabagas, also called *swedes*, are much larger and have yellow-orange flesh.

Evaluation: Look for roots that are firm and heavy, with good color and no blemishes. White turnips over 2½ inches (6–7 cm) in diameter may be woody or spongy.

Preparation: Peel heavily by hand or in machine to remove thick skin (see Figure 10.18). Rinse.

Percentage Yield: 75–80%

Figure 10.18 Peel rutabagas and turnips deeply enough to remove the full thickness of skin, as pointed out in this photograph.

WATER CHESTNUTS

Identification: Water chestnuts are corms, or swollen underground stem bases, of plants that grow in moist, warm environments. They are small and roundish, with dark brown skin and crisp white flesh.

Evaluation: Look for solid water chestnuts with no sign of softness, bruising, rot, or shriveling. They spoil easily.

Preparation: Scrub well with a brush, as they are often muddy. Peel with a paring knife.

Percentage Yield: 75%

WATERCRESS

Watercress

Identification: See discussion of salad greens in Chapter 14.

Evaluation: Bright green, crisp, unbruised leaves.

Preparation: Wash well. Remove heavy stems and discolored leaves.

Percentage Yield: 90%

Mushrooms: A Special Topic

Because of the great interest today in exotic mushrooms, and because eating some poisonous species of wild mushroom can be fatal, it is important for the cook to be familiar with at least the most popular varieties of exotic mushrooms, both cultivated and wild.

Although hundreds of mushroom varieties are edible, until recently only the common cultivated button mushroom was used with any frequency in most commercial kitchens. Now, however, many varieties are available. Some of these mushrooms, especially the wild ones, are expensive, but the demand always seems to exceed the supply.

Strictly speaking, the term *wild* should be used only for those mushrooms that are not cultivated but rather hunted and gathered in the wild. In the kitchen and on menus, however, exotic cultivated varieties, such as shiitakes, are often referred to as "wild mushrooms" because they are seen as rare and unusual, like true wild mushrooms, and they are generally more flavorful than the button mushroom.

One important advantage of cultivated exotic mushrooms is that they are available all year, while certain wild mushrooms may be in season only a few weeks annually.

CULTIVATED EXOTIC MUSHROOMS

Shiitake mushrooms

1. **Shiitake.**
   Sometimes known as *Black Forest mushroom* or *golden oak mushroom*, the shiitake is also available in dried form as *Chinese black mushroom*. The fresh mushroom is golden brown to dark brown. It has a firm, fleshy texture and a broad, dome-shaped cap with creamy white gills. The stem is rather tough, so it is trimmed off and chopped fine or used in stocks.

2. **Oyster mushroom.**
   Also called *pleurotte*, it is a light tan or cream-colored fan-shaped mushroom with a short stem at the side. Tender, with delicate flavor, it is best prepared simply so its mild flavor is not overwhelmed by stronger-tasting ingredients. (*Note:* The name *oyster* refers to the shape of the mushroom, not its taste.)

Oyster mushrooms

3. **Enoki mushroom.**
   Also called *enokitake* or *enokidake*, this mushroom has a tiny white cap on a long, slender stem, and it grows in clusters or bunches attached at the base. The base is trimmed off before use. The enoki mushroom has a crisp texture and a fruity, slightly acidic but sweet flavor. It is often used raw (for example, in salads or as garnish) or in clear soups. When used in cooked dishes, it should be added in the last few minutes so as not to be overcooked.

4. **Cremini mushroom.**

   The cremini is a variety of the common cultivated button mushroom, but it has a brown or tan skin. It may have a slightly more robust flavor than white cultivated mushrooms.

5. **Portobello mushroom.**

   This is a mature cremini whose cap has opened and spread into a broad, flat disk. It may be 6 inches (15 cm) or more across. Portobello (note the correct spelling) mushrooms are often grilled, brushed with olive oil, and served plain as a first course.

Cremini mushrooms

WILD MUSHROOMS

Of the many varieties of edible wild mushrooms, those described here are among the most prized as well as the most likely to be found on menus. As a rule, they are expensive and of limited availability.

Wild mushrooms should be carefully examined for spoilage and insect infestation. Cut away any damaged parts.

The four varieties described here are also available dried (see p. 272). Dried mushrooms have a high price per pound but are more economical to use than fresh wild mushrooms because they are equivalent to 7 or 8 times their weight of fresh mushrooms. In addition, they have a more intense, concentrated flavor, so a little goes a long way.

Caution: Never eat any wild mushroom that has not been identified by an expert. Many mushrooms are poisonous, and some are deadly. Many species are difficult to identify, and some poisonous varieties resemble edible ones.

Chanterelle mushrooms

1. **Morel.**

   Several varieties exist, including black, golden, and nearly white. The morel is shaped somewhat like a conical sponge, with a pitted surface, on a smooth stem. It is completely hollow. The most prized of spring mushrooms, it is usually sautéed in butter or cooked in a sauce and is especially good with cream.

2. **Bolete.**

   Other names for this mushroom include *cep*, *cèpe* (sepp; the French term), *porcino* (por chee no; the Italian term; the plural is *porcini* [por chee nee]), and *steinpilz* (shtine pilts; the German term). It is a brown-capped mushroom with a light-colored, bulbous stem. The interior flesh is creamy white. The underside of the cap has no gills but many tiny pores. With a meaty but smooth texture and rich, earthy flavor, it is often sautéed or braised with garlic and olive oil or butter. It is available late summer to fall.

3. **Chanterelle.**

   Also called *girolle*, the chanterelle is yellow to orange in color and shaped like an umbrella that has turned inside out. The underside of the cone-shaped cap has ridges instead of gills. It has a rich, woodsy aroma and flavor and is best cooked simply, such as sautéed in butter, perhaps with garlic. It is available summer and fall.

4. **Black trumpet.**

   This mushroom is closely related to the chanterelle but is black in color and has much thinner flesh. It is also called *black chanterelle*, *horn of plenty*, and *trompette de la mort* (French name, meaning "trumpet of death," so called because of its black color). In spite of this French name, it is edible and delicious.

> ### KEY POINTS TO REVIEW
>
> - What basic preparation techniques are common to all vegetables?
>
> - For each vegetable commonly used in food service, what standards are used to evaluate freshness?
>
> - For each vegetable commonly used in food service, what basic preparation techniques are used?
>
> - Outside of standard white button mushrooms, what are the five most commonly used varieties of cultivated mushroom? Name four varieties of wild mushroom that are often purchased dried.

Processed Vegetables

It is generally agreed that the quality of frozen and canned vegetables can never equal that of the best-quality fresh product at its peak of maturity, prepared properly, and cooked while still fresh. However, because of the high perishability of fresh produce, seasonal variations in availability and price, and the amount of labor required to handle fresh produce in commercial kitchens, food service relies, to a great extent, on processed vegetables. Therefore, it is important to know how to handle processed foods properly. Your goal should be to make them as close as possible in quality to the best fresh produce.

The quality of processed vegetables varies greatly. For example, frozen cauliflower always lacks the slightly crunchy texture of properly cooked fresh cauliflower. In fact, most frozen vegetables are a bit mushier than fresh because cell walls rupture during freezing. On the other hand, frozen peas are almost universally accepted, not just for their convenience but for their dependably high quality in comparison with the highly perishable fresh product.

In the section of Chapter 6 called "Handling Convenience Foods," we learned that convenience foods are products that are partially or completely prepared or processed by the manufacturer. This means you should treat frozen and canned vegetables as though they are partially or fully cooked fresh vegetables, which deserve the same care in handling, heating, seasoning, and presentation.

Handling Frozen Vegetables

CHECKING QUALITY

Examine all frozen products when received to make sure they have experienced no loss of quality. Check in particular for the following:

1. **Temperature.**
   Check the temperature inside the case with a thermometer. Is it still 0°F (−18°C) or below, or have the vegetables begun to thaw during shipment?

2. **Large ice crystals.**
   A little frost is normal, but lots of ice means poor handling.

3. **Signs of leaking on the carton.**
   This is another obvious sign of thawing.

4. **Freezer burn.**
   Open a package and check the vegetables themselves. Is the color bright and natural, or is there yellowing or drying on the surface?

COOKING

Frozen vegetables are partially cooked, so final cooking time is shorter than for fresh products.

Cook from the frozen state. Most vegetables need no thawing. They can go directly into steamer pans or boiling salted water.

Exceptions: Corn on the cob and vegetables that freeze into a solid block, such as spinach and squash, should be thawed in the cooler first for more even cooking.

Seasoning: Most frozen vegetables are slightly salted during processing, so add less salt than you would to fresh products.

Handling Canned Vegetables

CHECKING QUALITY

1. **Reject damaged cans on receipt.**
   Puffed or swollen cans indicate spoilage. Small dents may be harmless, but large dents may mean the can's protective lining has been damaged. Avoid rusted or leaking cans.

2. **Know the drained weight.**
   This varies with different grades of different vegetables and should be specified when ordering. Typical drained weights are 60 to 65 percent of total contents. You must know this drained weight in order to calculate the number of servings the can contains.

   Some canned products, such as tomato sauce and cream-style corn, have no drained weight because the entire contents are served.

3. **Check the grade.**
   Grades are determined by the packers or by federal inspectors. They are based on factors like color, absence of defect, and *sieve size* (size of individual pieces). Check to make sure you receive the grade you ordered (and paid for).

In the United States, the federal grades are

U.S. Grade A or Fancy

U.S. Grade B or Extra Standard (for vegetables) or Choice (for fruits)

U.S. Grade C or Standard

COOKING

1. Wipe the top of the can clean before opening. Use a clean can opener.

2. Drain the vegetable and place half the liquid in a cooking pot. Bring it to a boil. This shortens the heating time of the vegetable.

3. Add the vegetable and heat to serving temperature. Do not boil for a long time. Canned vegetables are fully cooked—in fact, usually overcooked. They need reheating only.
   Note: Health officials recommend holding vegetables at 190°F (88°C) 10 minutes or more—20 to 30 minutes for nonacid vegetables like beets, green beans, or spinach—to eliminate the danger of botulism.

4. Heat as close to serving time as possible. Do not hold in steam table for long periods.

5. Season and flavor with imagination. Canned vegetables require more creativity in preparation than fresh because they can be dreary when served plain.

6. Season the liquid while it is coming to a boil, before you add the vegetable. This will give the flavors of the herbs and spices time to blend.

7. Butter enhances the flavor of most vegetables, and it carries the flavors of the other seasonings you choose to add.

8. Dress up the vegetables with flavors and garnishes, such as beets or sauerkraut with caraway, limas or green beans with crisp crumbled bacon, corn with sautéed minced onion and green or red pepper, carrots with butter and tarragon or orange juice and brown sugar.

The combinations suggested in the table in Chapter 11 apply to canned vegetables as well as to fresh and frozen.

Handling Dried Vegetables

There are two basic kinds of dried vegetable.

DRIED LEGUMES

Dried beans and peas have been used as food for thousands of years, and they continue to be important foods today. In fact, with today's increased interest in healthful eating and in vegetables of all sorts, many more interesting varieties of beans are widely available now than only a few years ago.

Although legumes are dried forms of seed vegetables, they are hard and starchy and handled much like grains (which are also dried seeds). Grains and legumes are discussed in more detail in Chapter 13.

FREEZE-DRIED AND OTHER DEHYDRATED VEGETABLES

Drying has always been an important method for preserving vegetables, especially before modern canning and freezing techniques were developed. Modern technology has developed new methods for drying foods, so a great variety of dried products is on the market, including dried potatoes, onions, carrots, celery, beans, peppers, tomatoes, and mushrooms.

Follow manufacturers' directions for reconstituting these products. Many must be soaked in cold or warm water for specific lengths of time. They continue to absorb water as they are simmered.

Instant dried products, especially potatoes, require only the addition of a boiling liquid and seasonings to be ready to serve. Again, manufacturers' directions vary with their brands.

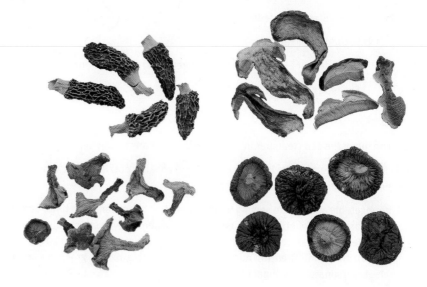

Dried mushrooms, clockwise from top left: morels, porcini, shiitake, chanterelles.

An important category of dried vegetable is dried mushrooms. Many flavorful wild mushrooms are in season for only a short time and are in limited supply at high prices. They are available year round in dried form, however. The most popular types—morels, chanterelles, and porcini—are illustrated, along with dried shiitake, a cultivated mushroom that originated in Japan and China.

Dried mushrooms should be soaked in hot water until soft, then drained and lightly squeezed before being cooked. The flavorful soaking liquid is strained and used as a flavoring for cooking liquids and sauces.

Production and Holding Problems in Quantity Cooking

We have emphasized throughout this chapter that vegetables should be cooked as close as possible to serving time. They lose quality rapidly when held in a steam table.

In quantity cooking, however, it is rarely possible to cook individual vegetable portions to order. After 20 to 30 minutes at steam table temperatures, even carefully prepared vegetables are usually overcooked.

Two systems have been devised to help solve this problem. *Batch cooking* is especially well suited to set meal service, and the *blanch-and-chill* method is most helpful in extended meal service. Needs vary from institution to institution, and you will probably find both techniques useful in one kitchen.

Batch Cooking

Rather than cooking all your vegetables in one batch large enough for the entire meal service, this method (described in Chapter 6, p. 115) involves dividing the food into smaller batches and cooking them one at a time, as needed.

Blanch-and-Chill Method

It is usually impractical to cook vegetables completely to order. Too much time is required. But if the vegetables have been partially cooked, the time needed to finish them to order is short.

Partially cooking, chilling, and finish-cooking is not as good, nutritionally, as cooking completely to order, but it is almost as good. It's certainly better than holding vegetables for hours at serving temperature, and it gives the cook complete control over the degree of doneness when served.

Procedure for Batch Cooking

1. Steamers and small tilting trunnion kettles behind the service line are the most useful kinds of equipment for vegetable batch cooking.

2. Divide each vegetable into batches small enough to be served within 20 to 30 minutes. Arrange in steamer pans ready to be placed in steamers or in containers ready for pouring into the kettles.

3. Keep the prepped vegetables in the cooler until needed.

4. Cook batches as needed. In planning, allow time for loading and unloading the equipment, for cooking, for finishing the product with the desired seasoning, sauce, or garnish, and for carrying to the serving line.

5. Undercook slightly if the vegetable must be held before serving.

6. Have all your seasonings, sauces, and garnishes ready for finishing the dish.

7. Do not mix batches. They will be cooked to different degrees, and colors and textures usually will not match.

Procedure for Blanching and Chilling

1. Steam or simmer the vegetable until partially cooked to the desired degree. (In the case of French fries, blanch by deep-frying.)

   The amount of cooking required depends on the vegetable and on the method by which it will be reheated or finished. Frozen vegetables need less cooking than fresh. Often, they need only be thawed.

2. Chill immediately in ice water. (Needless to say, French fries are an exception.)

3. Drain and keep chilled until needed.

4. Finish to order by desired cooking method.

   For example, one or more portions can be placed in a strainer and lowered briefly into a ready pot of boiling water.

   Sautéing in butter is a popular method for finishing such items as peas, green beans, and carrots.

   Potato croquettes are an example of a more complicated application of this same method. The potatoes are boiled or steamed, puréed, seasoned, formed, and breaded in advance. They are then deep-fried to order.

Storage

Fresh Vegetables

1. Potatoes, onions, and winter squash are stored at cool temperatures (50–65°F/ 10–18°C) in a dry, dark place.

2. Other vegetables must be refrigerated. To prevent drying, they should be kept covered or wrapped, or the humidity in the cooler must be high. Allow for some air circulation to help prevent mold.

3. Peeled and cut vegetables need extra protection from drying and oxidation. Cover or wrap, and use quickly to prevent spoilage. Potatoes, eggplants, and other vegetables that brown when cut should be treated with an acid or antioxidant. As an alternative, they can be blanched to destroy the enzymes that cause browning. Raw cut potatoes are sometimes held in cold water for a short time.

4. Store all fresh vegetables as short a time as possible. They lose quality rapidly. Peas and corn lose sweetness even after a few hours in storage.

5. Keep refrigerators and storage areas clean.

Frozen Vegetables

1. Store at 0°F (−18°C) or colder, in original containers, until ready for use.

2. Do not refreeze thawed vegetables. Quality will be greatly reduced.

Dried Vegetables

1. Store in a cool (less than 75°F/24°C), dry, well-ventilated place.

2. Keep well sealed and off the floor.

Canned Vegetables

1. Keep in a cool, dry place, away from sunlight and off the floor.

2. Discard cans that show signs of damage or spoilage (swollen, badly dented, or rusted cans). When in doubt, throw it out.

Leftovers

1. The best way to store leftovers is not to create them in the first place. Careful planning and small-batch cooking reduce leftovers.

2. Don't mix batches.

3. Store leftover creamed vegetables for one day only. Then either use or discard. Before storing, cool rapidly by placing the container on ice.

KEY POINTS TO REVIEW

- How do you check frozen vegetables and canned vegetables for quality?

- What guidelines are used for handling and cooking frozen vegetables and canned vegetables?

- What are the steps in the procedure for batch-cooking vegetables? For what kind of meal service is this method usually used?

- What are the steps in the blanch-and-chill method for cooking vegetables? For what kind of meal service is this method usually used?

- What guidelines are used for storing fresh vegetables? Frozen vegetables? Canned vegetables? Dried vegetables? Vegetable leftovers?

TERMS FOR REVIEW

al dente	flavonoids	carotenoids	batch cooking
pigment	anthocyanins	sieve size	blanch-and-chill
anthoxanthins	chlorophyll		

QUESTIONS FOR DISCUSSION

1. Give two reasons for not adding baking soda to the cooking water for green vegetables.
2. Besides appearance, why is proper uniform cutting of vegetables important?
3. What are some advantages of steam-cooking vegetables over boiling or simmering?
4. You are trying a recipe for blueberry muffins. When you break open a finished muffin, you see the baked dough around each berry is green. What caused this? How can you correct it? (*Hint:* The batter is made with buttermilk and leavened with baking soda. Even though berries aren't discussed in this chapter, the information about color changes will enable you to answer this question.)
5. Discuss the reasons for cooking green vegetables in a large quantity of water and in just enough water to cover.

Chapter 11

Spinaci alla Romana, page 289

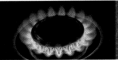
Cooking Vegetables

Now that you have studied the whys and wherefores of vegetable cooking, you should be able to proceed to actual preparation with a clear understanding of what you are doing.

This chapter outlines the basic methods of vegetable preparation. Successful performance of these methods relies on your knowledge of the principles we have discussed.

The recipes given here reinforce your understanding through actual practice. The emphasis is on the method rather than on the particular vegetable used because each method applies to many vegetables. For this reason, variations are listed after basic recipes rather than presented as separate complete recipes. As in other chapters, recipes for sauces that appear in Chapter 7 and are used as components of subsequent preparations are not repeated here.

Most of the recipes are applicable to fresh, frozen, or canned vegetables, even though variations are not listed for each. You have learned how to handle these products in order to make proper substitutions. Review pages 269–271 if necessary.

Potatoes and other starchy foods, such as rice and pasta, are covered in the next chapter. However, the basic cooking methods here apply to potatoes as well as to other vegetables.

After reading this chapter, you should be able to

1. Identify vegetables that are well suited to the different vegetable cooking methods.
2. Cook vegetables by boiling and steaming.
3. Cook vegetables by sautéing and pan-frying.
4. Cook vegetables by braising.
5. Cook vegetables by baking.
6. Cook vegetables by broiling and grilling.
7. Cook vegetables by deep-frying.

Boiling and Steaming

Nearly all vegetables may be cooked by boiling or by steaming. These are the two most frequently used methods because they are easy, economical, and adaptable to a great variety of preparations.

Boiling and steaming are basic cooking methods. In most cases, additional steps are required after the basic cooking is completed in order to make the product ready for serving. These steps include adding butter, seasonings, flavorings, and sauces.

Unless they are to be served immediately, boiled or simmered vegetables are drained as soon as they are cooked and then cooled quickly under cold water. This is called *shocking* or *refreshing*, and it prevents the vegetables from being overcooked in their retained heat. Normally, they are then reheated quickly by sautéing in butter or other fat. Seasonings and sauces can be added at this stage. We classify this cooking method as boiling even though the vegetables are finished by sautéing to reheat them. This section includes recipes for boiled vegetables finished with a variety of sauces, flavorings, and seasonings.

In other cases, the product is only partially cooked by boiling or steaming and is finished by another cooking method, such as sautéing or baking. Recipes of this sort are usually included under the final cooking method.

We speak of the cooking method as *boiling* even though, in many cases, *simmering* is a more appropriate term. Green vegetables are generally boiled so they cook quickly, preserving color and nutrients. In many cases, however, the agitation and high temperature of boiling break up delicate vegetables, and simmering is more appropriate.

Steaming as a method for cooking vegetables is becoming more and more widely used, especially as more varieties of advanced equipment become available. It may be the ideal method for cooking certain vegetables, such as broccoli, that easily break or turn watery or mushy when simmered.

A useful technique that combines boiling and steaming is called **pan-steaming**. In this method, vegetables are cooked in a covered pan in a small amount of water—not enough water to cover them—so they are partly cooked by the steam trapped in the pan. After the vegetables are cooked, they are removed from the pan, and the flavorful cooking liquid may be reduced to a glaze or made into a sauce. This is a quick method for cooking many vegetables and so is useful for cooking small quantities to order.

Finally, this section also contains a recipe for artichokes cooked sous vide. It is essential that you read the discussion of sous vide cooking, and especially the safety precautions, on page 66 before you try this recipe.

Procedure for Boiling Vegetables

1. Collect all equipment and food products.
2. Trim, peel, and cut vegetables as required. See pages 248–268 for prep requirements.
3. Add the required amount of water to the pot (saucepot, steam-jacketed kettle, tilting skillet, or whatever equipment you are using).
   Most vegetables are cooked in just enough water to cover, but many green vegetables and strong-flavored vegetables may be cooked in a large quantity of water (2 or 3 times their volume). See page 244 for discussion.
4. Add salt (1½–2 tbsp per gal water/6–8 g per L) and bring to a boil.
5. Place the vegetables in the pot and return the water to a boil.
6. Reduce heat to a simmer and cook the vegetables, covered or uncovered, as indicated, to required doneness.
   Green vegetables and strong-flavored vegetables are cooked uncovered. Other vegetables are cooked covered.
7. Drain the vegetables quickly to avoid overcooking.
8. If the vegetables are to be served at once, complete the recipe and serve.
9. If the vegetables are not to be served at once, cool them (except potatoes and starchy vegetables) in cold water, drain as soon as cool, and refrigerate until needed.

Procedure for Steaming Vegetables

This method is used both for pressurized and nonpressurized compartment steam cookers and for simple rangetop steamers that consist of a perforated basket over a pot of boiling water.

1. Know your equipment. Read all operating instructions supplied with your equipment. Each model is a little different.

2. Collect all equipment and food products.

3. Trim and cut vegetables as required.

4. Preheat the steamer.

5. Arrange vegetables in pans or baskets for cooking. Make shallow, even layers for uniform cooking.
   - Use perforated pans for best steam circulation.
   - Use solid pans if cooking liquid must be retained.

6. Insert pans or baskets in steamer and close door or lid (Figure 11.1).

7. Steam for required period. Consult timing charts supplied with your model of steamer.

8. Remove vegetables from steamer. If it is a pressure steamer, pressure must return to zero before door is opened.

9. Finish vegetables according to recipe and serve at once, or cool quickly for later use.

Figure 11.1 Compartment steaming

Vegetables that form compact layers do not steam well. They do not allow the steam to circulate, so they cook unevenly. Examples: spinach and other greens, peas, whole-kernel corn, frozen puréed squash.

Procedure for Pan-Steaming Vegetables

1. Collect all equipment and food products.

2. Trim, peel, and cut vegetables as required. See pages 248–268 for prep requirements.

3. Add the vegetables and a small amount of water to an appropriate pan, such as a sautoir, large enough to hold the vegetables in a shallow layer. The amount of water needed depends on the cooking time of the vegetable. Use less liquid for quick-cooking vegetables, more liquid for long-cooking vegetables. In most cases, the water should cover the vegetables by no more than about three-quarters.

4. Add salt, and bring the water to a boil (Figure 11.2). Other seasonings may be added to the water if desired.

5. Add the vegetable and any other seasonings or ingredients as directed by the recipe.

6. Cover the pan and, if necessary, lower the heat to maintain a simmer. Cook until the vegetable is done. During cooking, remove the cover from time to time to check doneness and to make sure the water hasn't all evaporated. Add more water if the pan is going dry.

7. Remove the vegetable with a slotted spoon.

8. If desired, reduce the liquid to a glaze to toss with the vegetable. As an alternative, reduce the liquid as desired and finish it to make a sauce. For example: Thicken with a starch slurry or monter au beurre.

Figure 11.2 Pan-steaming vegetables.

(a) Place the vegetables in a sauté pan and add a small amount of water. Bring to a boil, and then cover.

(b) When the vegetables are cooked, remove them from the pan with a slotted spoon.

(c) Reduce the cooking liquid and finish the sauce as desired, such as with butter.

(d) Return the vegetables to the pan and toss with the sauce. Add herbs or other flavorings and seasonings as desired.

Puréeing Vegetables

Vegetable purées are served as side dishes or garnishes, and they are also used as ingredients in other preparations.

Purées were introduced in the discussion of soups in Chapter 8. The vegetable purées we are discussing here are similar, although they are of course much thicker than soups. Procedures for puréeing vary depending on the vegetable and how the purée is to be used, but some general guidelines can be stated:

Guidelines for Puréeing Vegetables

1. Vegetables to be puréed should be cooked until tender. Undercooked vegetables make a grainy purée. Be careful not to overcook green vegetables, which discolor when cooked too long.

   Exception: A few vegetables, such as avocados and tomatoes, are tender enough to be puréed raw. Whether or not they are cooked depends on the vegetable and the desired use for the purée.

2. Vegetables for puréeing can be cooked by any method, but the most commonly used methods are boiling, steaming, and baking. Baking is used most often for starchy vegetables such as sweet potatoes and white potatoes.

3. Vegetables cooked by boiling or simmering should be drained well when done. If a stiff purée is desired, it may be necessary to dry the cooked vegetable before puréeing. Place the colander of drained vegetables on a sheet pan and set in a moderate oven for a few minutes to dry.

4. Always purée cooked vegetables while they are still hot. Cold vegetables are harder to purée to a smooth texture.

5. Select appropriate equipment. Ricers, food processors, vertical cutter/mixers (VCMs), food mills, and sieves can be used for puréeing. Food mills, ricers, and sieves make lump-free purées, but they may leave a grainy texture, depending on the vegetable, although a fine drum sieve (tamis) makes a very smooth purée (Figure 11.3). Food processors and VCMs can create a smooth texture, especially with starchy vegetables, but they do not eliminate vegetable fibers and may leave a few lumps. First using a processor and then passing the purée through a food mill or tamis yields the smoothest result.

6. Season and finish the purée as desired. Butter or cream is often used to finish vegetable purées. Alternatively, use the purée as an ingredient in another recipe as directed.

Figure 11.3 Puréeing vegetables using a tamis.

(a) Rub the cooked vegetable through the tamis using a pestle (as shown) or a plastic scraper.

(b) Scrape the purée from the bottom of the sieve.

KEY POINTS TO REVIEW

- What are the steps in the procedure for boiling vegetables?

- What are the steps in the procedure for steaming vegetables? for pan-steaming vegetables?

- Vegetables to be puréed should be cooked to what doneness? What equipment is used to purée vegetables? List other guidelines for making puréed vegetables.

Peas, Carrots, and Pearl Onions with Tarragon Butter

PORTIONS: 15   PORTION SIZE: 3 OZ (100 G)

U.S.	METRIC	INGREDIENTS
12 oz	375 g	Pearl onions
1 lb	500 g	Carrots
1 lb 8 oz	750 g	Peas, frozen
2 oz	60 g	Butter
1½ tsp	7 mL	Dried tarragon
1 tbsp	15 mL	Chopped parsley
to taste	to taste	Salt
to taste	to taste	White pepper

Per serving: Calories, 90; Protein, 3 g; Fat, 3.5 g (34% cal.); Cholesterol, 10 mg; Carbohydrates, 12 g; Fiber, 3 g; Sodium, 90 mg.

PROCEDURE

1. Blanch the onions 20 seconds in boiling water. (Blanching makes them easier to peel.) Drain, refresh under cold water, and drain again. Peel the onions.
2. Bring salted water to a boil in a saucepan. Add the onions, return to a boil, reduce heat to a simmer, and simmer until tender. Drain, refresh under cold water, and drain again.
3. Peel the carrots and cut into bâtonnet.
4. Bring salted water to a boil in a saucepan. Add the carrots, return to a boil, reduce heat to a simmer, and simmer until tender. Drain, refresh briefly, and drain again.
5. Bring a third pan of salted water to a boil. Add the frozen peas. Return to a boil, reduce heat, and simmer until tender. This takes only a few seconds. Frozen peas have already been blanched and need very little cooking. Drain, refresh, and drain again.
6. Mix together the three vegetables.
7. Heat the butter in as many sauté pans as necessary to hold the vegetables without overcrowding.
8. Add the vegetables and the tarragon. Toss over heat until the vegetables are hot and coated with the butter. Add the parsley and toss to mix.
9. Season to taste with salt and white pepper.

VARIATIONS

Herbs may be omitted for a simpler preparation, if desired.

Quantity Preparation: Cook and drain the vegetables and combine in a steam table pan. Heat the butter with the herbs and ladle over the vegetables. Season and serve.

Buttered Vegetables

The following vegetables may be cooked by simply boiling or steaming and dressed with butter for service, as in the basic recipe:

Asparagus	Cabbage	Parsnips
Beans, green or yellow	Carrots	Peas
Beans, lima	Cauliflower (see Note)	Rutabagas
Beets	Celery	Spinach
Broccoli (see Note)	Corn (on cob or whole kernel)	Turnips
Brussels sprouts	Kohlrabi	

Note: Dress each portion of broccoli spears with butter just when served. Butter runs off broccoli quickly. Do not sauté for à la carte service. Reheat in boiling water, then add butter. Other large vegetables, such as cauliflower, may also be prepared like broccoli.

Herbed Vegetables

Season buttered vegetables with fresh chopped parsley or other appropriate fresh or dried herbs (see table on p. 311). Dried herbs should be heated with the vegetable a few minutes to release flavor.

Amandine

Especially for green beans, broccoli, celery, cauliflower. For each 2 lb (900 g) EP of vegetable, sauté 2 oz (60 g) slivered or sliced almonds in 2–3 oz (60–90 g) butter until lightly browned. (Caution: Almonds darken quickly.) Combine with cooked vegetable.

Hollandaise

Especially for broccoli, asparagus, cauliflower, Brussels sprouts, leeks, and artichoke hearts or bottoms. At service time, nap each portion of vegetable with 2 fl oz (60 mL) hollandaise sauce.

Polonaise

Especially for cauliflower, broccoli, Brussels sprouts, and, sometimes, asparagus and green beans. For each 5 lb (2.3 kg) EP of vegetable, sauté 1½ pt (750 mL) fresh bread crumbs in about 6 oz (175 g) butter until golden. Chop the whites and yolks of 2–4 hard-cooked eggs separately. Combine the crumbs, chopped egg, and 4 tbsp (60 mL) chopped parsley. Sprinkle this mixture over the cooked vegetable immediately before serving.

Peas, Carrots, and Pearl Onions with Tarragon Butter

Creamed Spinach

PORTIONS: 25   PORTION SIZE: 3½ OZ (100 G)

U.S.	METRIC	INGREDIENTS
10 lb AP	4.5 kg AP	Spinach, fresh
2½ pt	1.2 L	Cream sauce, hot
to taste	to taste	Nutmeg
to taste	to taste	Salt
to taste	to taste	White pepper

Per serving: Calories, 120; Protein, 6 g; Fat, 7 g (50% cal.); Cholesterol, 20 mg; Carbohydrates, 10 g; Fiber, 3 g; Sodium, 150 mg.

Note: For frozen chopped spinach, partially thaw 2½ packages (2½ lb/1.1 kg each). Cover with boiling salted water and break spinach apart. Cook only until hot and drain. Squeeze out excess liquid and combine with cream sauce.

PROCEDURE

1. Trim spinach and wash carefully in several changes of water. Drain. (See Note.)
2. Place 2 in. (5 cm) water in a heavy pot, cover, and bring to a boil. Add the spinach. Stir several times so it cooks evenly.
3. As soon as the spinach is thoroughly wilted, drain in a colander, pressing with the back of a kitchen spoon to squeeze out excess liquid.
4. Chop the spinach coarsely.
5. Combine with the cream sauce in a hotel pan. Season to taste with nutmeg, salt, and pepper. (The spinach must not taste strongly of nutmeg.)

VARIATIONS

Creamed Vegetables

The following vegetables, cut into small pieces if necessary, may be cooked by boiling or steaming and combined with cream sauce, as in the basic recipe. For 25 portions, use 5–6 lb (about 2½ kg) EP vegetables and 2½–3½ pt (1.2–1.7 L) cream sauce.

Asparagus	Cabbage	Okra
Beans, green or yellow	Carrots	Onions, small white
Beans, lima	Cauliflower	Peas
Broccoli	Celery	
Brussels sprouts	Kohlrabi	

Broccoli Mornay

PORTIONS: 24   PORTION SIZE: 3½ OZ (100 G) BROCCOLI, 2 FL OZ (60 ML) SAUCE

U.S.	METRIC	INGREDIENTS
7½ lb	3.4 kg	Broccoli
1½ qt	1.5 L	Mornay sauce, hot

Per serving: Calories, 160; Protein, 9 g; Fat, 10 g (53% cal.); Cholesterol, 30 mg; Carbohydrates, 11 g; Fiber, 4 g; Sodium, 180 mg.

Note: This method of cooking in a shallow pan is used to prevent damaging the blossom ends, which are easily broken. Other delicate vegetables, such as asparagus, are also sometimes cooked in shallow water in hotel pans or sauté pans.

Broccoli may be cooked in a steamer, following the basic steaming method.

PROCEDURE

1. Trim and wash broccoli. Separate large pieces into smaller serving pieces. Split or peel stems for even cooking.
2. Arrange broccoli in hotel pan with flowers to the outside, stems in center.
3. Pour in boiling salted water to partially cover. Cover with clean, wet towels and set on rangetop.
4. Simmer until blossom parts are nearly tender. Fold back towels from edges to uncover blossoms. This releases steam and helps avoid overcooking. Leave stems covered and continue to simmer until stems feel tender but al dente when pierced with a knife, Drain well.
5. Nap each portion with 2 fl oz (60 mL) Mornay sauce at service time. Ladle the sauce across the stems without covering the blossoms.

VARIATIONS

Other vegetables may be served with cheese sauce, such as cauliflower and Brussels sprouts.

Broccoli with Cheddar Cheese Sauce

Prepare as in the basic recipe, but substitute cheddar cheese sauce for the Mornay sauce.

Puréed Butternut Squash

PORTIONS: 25　PORTION SIZE: 3 OZ (90G)

U.S.	METRIC	INGREDIENTS
7½ lb	3.5 kg	Butternut squash
6 oz	175 g	Butter
3 oz	90 g	Brown sugar
2 tsp	10 mL	Salt
to taste	to taste	White pepper
to taste	to taste	Nutmeg or ground ginger

Per serving: Calories, 90; Protein, 1 g; Fat, 6 g (51% cal.); Cholesterol, 15 mg; Carbohydrates, 12 g; Fiber, 2 g; Sodium, 250 mg.

Note: If squash is too wet, cook out some of the moisture in a shallow pan over medium heat after step 2.

PROCEDURE

1. Peel the squash, cut in half, and scrape out seeds. Cut into large dice.
2. Place in perforated steamer pan. Steam until tender. (Alternative *pan-steaming method*: Place in heavy pot. Add 1 in. [3 cm] water, cover, and cook slowly until tender. Drain well.)
3. Purée the squash with a food mill. Add the butter, sugar, and seasonings. Whip until light, but do not overwhip or squash will become watery.

VARIATIONS

Add 3–4 fl oz (90–125 mL) heavy cream, heated. Sugar may be reduced or omitted if the squash has a good flavor.

Mashed Rutabagas or Yellow Turnips

Prepare as in the basic recipe. If desired, add a small amount of whipped potato.

Cauliflower au Gratin

PORTIONS: 25　PORTION SIZE: 3 OZ (90 G) CAULIFLOWER, 1½ OZ (45 G) SAUCE AND TOPPING

U.S.	METRIC	INGREDIENTS
5 lb EP	2.3 kg EP	Cauliflower
1 tbsp	15 mL	Lemon juice (see Note)
1 qt 6 fl oz	1.2 L	Béchamel or Mornay sauce, hot
1½ oz	45 g	Dry bread crumbs
1½ oz	45 g	Parmesan cheese, grated
2½ oz	75 g	Butter, melted

Per serving: Calories, 60; Protein, 3g; Fat, 3.5 g (50& cal.); Cholesterol, 10mg; Carbohydrates, 5 g; Fiber, 2 g; Sodium, 80 mg.

Note: Adding lemon juice to cooking water helps keep white vegetables white. It may be omitted if desired.

VARIATIONS

Substitute cheddar cheese sauce for the béchamel or Mornay, and use grated cheddar cheese instead of parmesan for topping.

Other vegetables may be prepared au gratin, such as asparagus, Belgian endive, broccoli, Brussels sprouts, celery, celery root, leeks, and turnips.

PROCEDURE

1. Separate the cauliflower into florets.
2. Place the cauliflower and lemon juice in boiling salted water. Return to boil, lower heat, and cover. Simmer until just tender. Do not overcook, as the cauliflower will cook further in the sauce. Drain.
3. Butter the bottom of a baking pan or hotel pan and place the cauliflower in it about 2 in. (5 cm) deep. (Individual ovenproof serving dishes may be used instead.)
4. Cover with the hot sauce.
5. Mix together the bread crumbs and cheese and sprinkle evenly over the top. Drizzle melted butter over the top.
6. Bake at 350°F (175°C) about 20 minutes to heat through. Brown the top under the broiler or salamander.

Cauliflower au Gratin

Green Beans with Sesame Dressing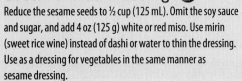

PORTIONS: 16   PORTION SIZE: 2 OZ (60 G)

U.S.	METRIC	INGREDIENTS
1 cup	250 mL	White sesame seeds
1½ fl oz	50 mL	Soy sauce
2 tbsp	30 g	Sugar
2 fl oz	60 mL	Dashi (p. 145) or water
2 lb	1 kg	Green beans

Per serving: Calories, 80; Protein, 3 g; Fat, 4.5 g (48% cal.); Cholesterol, 0 mg; Carbohydrates, 8 g; Fiber, 3 g; Sodium, 150 mg.

PROCEDURE

1. Toast the sesame seeds in a dry skillet, stirring and tossing regularly, until light golden.
2. Using a spice grinder or mortar and pestle, grind the sesame seeds to a paste.
3. Mix in the soy sauce and sugar. Thin with dashi or water. Set aside.
4. Wash the green beans and trim the ends. Cut into 1-in. (2.5-cm) lengths.
5. Cook the beans in boiling salted water until crisp-tender. Drain, cool under cold running water, and drain again.
6. Mix the beans with the dressing.

VARIATIONS

Other mild green vegetables, such as spinach and asparagus, can be served the same way.

Sesame Miso Dressing

Reduce the sesame seeds to ½ cup (125 mL). Omit the soy sauce and sugar, and add 4 oz (125 g) white or red miso. Use mirin (sweet rice wine) instead of dashi or water to thin the dressing. Use as a dressing for vegetables in the same manner as sesame dressing.

Green Beans with Sesame Dressing

Pan-Steamed Kohlrabi with Parsley

PORTIONS: 12   PORTION SIZE: 3 OZ (90 G)

U.S.	METRIC	INGREDIENTS
2 lb 4 oz	1.1 kg	Kohlrabi, medium dice
½ tsp	2 mL	Salt
2 oz	60 g	Butter
1½ tsp	7 mL	Chopped parsley

Per serving: Calories, 60; Protein, 2 g; Fat, 4 g (53% cal.); Cholesterol, 10 mg; Carbohydrates, 6 g; Fiber, 3 g; Sodium, 125 mg.

PROCEDURE

1. Select a sautoir or saucepan large enough to hold the kohlrabi in a layer no more than 2 in. (5 cm) deep.
2. Put about ½ in. (1 cm) of water in the pan and add the salt. Bring to a boil.
3. Add the kohlrabi. Cover the pan, lower the heat to a simmer, and cook until the kohlrabi is tender but not too soft, about 5 minutes.
4. Uncover and remove the kohlrabi with a slotted spoon.
5. Reduce the cooking liquid over moderately high heat to about 2 fl oz (60 mL).
6. Add the butter and swirl in the pan to melt.
7. Return the kohlrabi to the pan and add the parsley. Toss over heat so the liquid reduces to a glaze and coats the vegetable.
8. Taste and add more salt if necessary. Serve immediately.

Green Beans with Roasted Peppers and Bacon

PORTIONS: 16   PORTION SIZE: 3½ OZ (100 G)

U.S.	METRIC	INGREDIENTS	PROCEDURE
3 lb	1.35 kg	Green beans	1. Trim the stem ends from the green beans.
			2. Wash and drain the beans.
			3. Boil the beans in a large pot of salted water until just tender. Drain.
			4. Rinse under cold water to cool the beans and stop the cooking, or drop them into ice water. Drain again. Refrigerate until needed.
1 lb	450 g	Red bell peppers	5. Roast and peel the peppers (see p. 262). Trim and discard the stem, seed core, and inner membranes.
			6. Cut the peppers into bâtonnet.
8 oz	225 g	Slab bacon	7. Cut the bacon into bâtonnet about 1 in. (2.5 cm) long.
to taste	to taste	Salt	8. In a heavy sauté pan, cook the bacon over moderate heat until crisp.
			9. Remove the bacon from the pan with a slotted spoon and reserve. Reserve about 2 oz (60 g) of the fat in the pan, discarding the rest.
			10. Add the beans and the red peppers to the pan with the bacon fat and toss over heat until hot.
			11. Taste and add salt if necessary. The salt from the bacon may be enough.
			12. Add the crisp bacon and toss to mix.
			13. Serve immediately.

Per serving: Calories, 90; Protein, 4 g; Fat, 6 g (53% cal.); Cholesterol, 10 mg; Carbohydrates, 8 g; Fiber, 3 g; Sodium, 115 mg.

VARIATIONS

Green Beans with Pecans and Browned Shallots

Omit the bacon and peppers. Brown 12 oz (360 g) thinly sliced shallots in butter. Add 12 oz (360 g) broken pecans and continue to cook until the pecans are hot. Reheat the beans in butter instead of bacon fat, and toss with the shallots and pecans.

Collards with Ham

PORTIONS: 16   PORTION SIZE: 4 OZ (125 G)

U.S.	METRIC	INGREDIENTS	PROCEDURE
2 lb	1 kg	Smoked ham hocks	1. Simmer the ham hocks in water to cover until the meat is tender, 1½ to 2 hours.
			2. Remove the hocks from the liquid, and reserve the liquid in the pot.
			3. Remove the meat from the bone and cut into small dice.
6 lb	3 kg	Collard greens	4. Trim the stems from the greens. Wash the greens in several changes of cold water.
to taste	to taste	Black pepper	5. Add the greens to the ham stock. Simmer until very tender, 45 to 60 minutes.
2 tsp, or	20 mL, or	Hot pepper sauce	6. Drain the greens, reserving the liquid.
to taste	to taste		7. Chop the greens coarsely.
			8. Combine the greens with the ham.
			9. Add enough of the reserved cooking liquid to moisten the greens well. Reheat as necessary.
			10. Add pepper and hot pepper sauce to taste.
			11. Serve with vinegar on the side, for diners to add to taste.
as needed	as needed	Cider vinegar	

Per serving: Calories, 240; Protein, 20 g; Fat, 14 g (51% cal.); Cholesterol, 60 mg; Carbohydrates, 10 g; Fiber, 6 g; Sodium, 95 mg.

Note: This is a traditional Southern preparation that disregards all the rules of cooking green vegetables and preserving vegetable color.

VARIATIONS

Turnip greens, mustard greens, or kale may be substituted for the collards.

Onion Compote

YIELD: 1 LB 8 OZ (800 G)

U.S.	METRIC	INGREDIENTS	PROCEDURE
4 lb	2 kg	Onions, sliced	1. In a nonreactive saucepan (such as stainless steel), combine the onions and the first quantity of water. Cover and simmer 5 minutes.
8 fl oz	250 mL	Water	
3 pt	1.5 L	Red wine	2. Add the red wine and the second quantity of water. Simmer, uncovered, very slowly until the onions are tender and most of the liquid has evaporated.
2 pt	1 L	Water	
8 fl oz	250 mL	Red wine vinegar	3. Add the vinegar. Mix well and continue to simmer.
			4. By the time the vinegar has reduced, the onions should be very tender. If not, add a little more water, cover, and steam gently until they are soft. Remove the cover and reduce again.
4 oz	125 g	Butter	5. Stir in the butter and sugar. Stir and heat gently until the sugar is dissolved.
2 oz	60 g	Sugar	6. Season with salt and pepper.
to taste	to taste	Salt	7. Serve as a condiment with meat, poultry, and fish dishes.
to taste	to taste	Pepper	

Per serving: Calories, 135; Protein, 1 g; Fat, 4 g (27% cal.); Cholesterol, 10 mg; Carbohydrates, 12 g; Fiber, 1 g; Sodium, 40 mg.

Onion Compote

Artichokes Clamart

PORTIONS: 10   PORTION SIZE: 1 ARTICHOKE HEART, 1 OZ (30 G) PEAS

U.S.	METRIC	INGREDIENTS	PROCEDURE
10	10	Artichokes, large	1. Prepare artichoke bottoms by trimming. Rub the cut surfaces with the lemon as you work to keep them from darkening.
1	1	Lemon, cut in half	
1 oz	30 g	Flour	2. Mix the flour with a little water, then add it to the remaining water in a saucepan. Add the lemon juice and salt. Bring to a boil. This mixture is called a *blanc*. It helps keep the artichokes white as they cook.
3 pt	1.5 L	Water, cold	
1½ fl oz	50 mL	Lemon juice	
1 tbsp	15 mL	Salt	3. Add the artichokes to the blanc and simmer until just tender, about 30 minutes. Drain.
10 oz	300 g	Peas, frozen	4. Place the peas in a saucepan with boiling salted water and simmer until just heated through. Drain.
3 oz	90 g	Butter	5. Heat 1 oz (30 g) of the butter in a sauté pan and sauté the peas briefly. Season with salt, pepper, and basil, tossing over heat briefly so the basil can release its flavor.
to taste	to taste	Salt	
to taste	to taste	White pepper	
pinch	pinch	Dried basil	6. At the same time, heat the remaining 2 oz (60 g) butter in another sauté pan. Place the cooked artichoke bottoms in the pan and sauté over medium heat until the artichokes are well coated with butter and are hot. Season with salt and pepper.
			7. Arrange artichokes in a hotel pan and fill with the peas. (Do not do this in advance because the lemon juice in the artichokes will discolor the peas.)

Per serving: Calories, 150; Protein, 6 g; Fat, 7 g (38% cal.); Cholesterol, 20 mg; Carbohydrates, 20 g; Fiber, 9 g; Sodium, 580 mg.

VARIATIONS

Artichoke bottoms can be filled with other vegetables, such as asparagus tips, tiny tournéed carrots, tournéed turnips, or mushrooms. They may also be used as containers for a sauce served with grilled meat items. Either way, they are used mostly as garnish for meats.

Cipolline in Agrodolce (Sweet-Sour Onions)

PORTIONS: 16   PORTION SIZE: 3½ OZ (100 G)

U.S.	METRIC	INGREDIENTS	PROCEDURE
4½ lb	2 kg	Pearl onions	1. Blanch the onions 1 minute. Drain and peel.
1 pt	500 mL	Water	2. Put the onions in a sauté pan in a single layer. Add the water and butter and cook slowly, uncovered, about 20 minutes, or until fairly tender. Add a little water if necessary during cooking so that the pan does not become dry. Stir gently from time to time.
2 oz	60 g	Butter	
3 fl oz	90 mL	Wine vinegar	3. Add the vinegar, sugar, and salt. Cover lightly. Cook over low heat until the onions are very tender and the liquid is syrupy, about 30 minutes. If necessary, remove the cover toward the end of the cooking time to let the liquid reduce. The onions should be lightly browned by the time they are done.
1½ oz	45 g	Sugar	
1½ tsp	7 mL	Salt	

Per serving: Calories, 120; Protein, 2 g; Fat, 3 g (23% cal.); Cholesterol, 10 mg; Carbohydrates, 21 g; Fiber, 1 g; Sodium, 270 mg.

Glazed Root Vegetables

| PORTIONS: 12 | PORTION SIZE: 3½–4 OZ (110–120 G) |
| PORTIONS: 25 | PORTION SIZE: 3 OZ (90 G) |

U.S.	METRIC	INGREDIENTS
3 lb	1.4 kg	Carrots
1½ lb	600 g	Parsnips
2½ lb	1 kg	Turnips
3 oz	90 g	Butter
2 oz	60 g	Sugar
to taste	to taste	Salt

Per serving: Calories, 90; Protein, 1 g; Fat, 3 g (30% cal.); Cholesterol, 5 mg; Carbohydrates, 15 g; Fiber, 4 g; Sodium, 85 mg.

VARIATIONS

Single vegetables as well as other combinations of vegetables may be glazed by this method, including celery root, pearl onions, rutabagas, and chestnuts, in addition to carrots, parsnips, and turnips.

PROCEDURE

1. Trim and peel the carrots, parsnips, and turnips. Tournéed root vegetables are often prepared by this method.
2. Place the vegetables in a saucepan with boiling salted water to cover. Simmer until tender. Drain.
3. Heat the butter in a sauté pan. Add the vegetables and sprinkle with the sugar. Season to taste with salt. Sauté until the vegetables are well glazed.

Glazed Carrots

Glazed Carrots (Carrots Vichy)

| PORTIONS: 25 | PORTION SIZE: 3 OZ (90 G) |

U.S.	METRIC	INGREDIENTS
6½ lb	3 kg	Carrots
as needed	as needed	Water (see Note)
5 oz	150 g	Butter
2 tbsp	30 g	Sugar
2 tsp	10 mL	Salt
to taste	to taste	White pepper
as needed	as needed	Chopped parsley

Per serving: Calories, 100; Protein, 2 g; Fat, 5 g (43% cal.); Cholesterol, 10 mg; Carbohydrates, 13 g; Fiber, 2 g; Sodium, 240 mg.

Note: Sometimes Vichy water or other bottled mineral water is used, but it is not necessary.

PROCEDURE

1. Trim, peel, and slice the carrots.
2. Place them in a saucepan or straight-sided sauté pan. Add water to barely cover. Add the butter, sugar, and salt.
3. Bring to a boil. Lower heat and simmer until the carrots are tender and the water is nearly evaporated. If done properly, these should happen at the same time. Toss the carrots so they are well coated with the glaze left in the pan.
4. Season with pepper. Garnish with chopped parsley.

Spinaci alla Romana (Roman-Style Spinach)

PORTIONS: 16   PORTION SIZE: 3 OZ (90 G)

U.S.	METRIC	INGREDIENTS
6 lb	2.7 kg	Spinach
1½ fl oz	45 mL	Olive oil
1½ oz	45 g	Fat from prosciutto or pork, small dice
1½ oz	45 g	Pine nuts
1½ oz	45 g	Raisins
to taste	to taste	Salt
to taste	to taste	Pepper

Per serving: Calories, 100; Protein, 5 g; Fat, 7 g (57% cal.); Cholesterol, 5 mg; Carbohydrates, 7 g; Fiber, 3 g; Sodium, 90 mg.

PROCEDURE

1. Trim and wash the spinach. Cook in a small quantity of boiling water until wilted. Drain, cool under running water, and drain again. Press excess water out of the spinach, but do not squeeze too dry.

2. Heat the oil in a pan. Add the fat and render it. Remove and discard the cracklings (solid pieces remaining from the fat).

3. Add the spinach, pine nuts, and raisins. Sauté until hot.

4. Season with salt and pepper.

VARIATIONS

Chopped garlic may be sautéed in the fat before the spinach is added.

Lean prosciutto, sliced thin, then diced, may be added.

Spinaci alla Piemontese

Omit the oil, fat, nuts, and raisins. Heat 8 chopped anchovy fillets and 2 chopped garlic cloves in 4 oz (125 g) butter, then add the boiled, drained spinach and sauté.

Spinaci alla Romana

Ragoût of Summer Vegetables

PORTIONS: 12   PORTION SIZE: 4 OZ (120 G)

U.S.	METRIC	INGREDIENTS
9 oz	270 g	Carrots, trimmed and peeled
9 oz	270 g	Yellow summer squash, trimmed
9 oz	270 g	Green beans, trimmed
9 oz	270 g	Baby turnips, peeled
6 oz	180 g	Lima beans, shelled
6 oz	180 g	Pearl onions, blanched and peeled
5 fl oz	150 mL	Vegetable stock, vegetable cooking liquid, or chicken stock
3 oz	90 g	Butter, cut into small pieces
2 tsp	10 mL	Fresh chervil, chopped
2 tsp	10 mL	Fresh chives, chopped
2 tsp	10 mL	Parsley, chopped
to taste	to taste	Salt
to taste	to taste	White pepper

PROCEDURE

1. Cut the carrots into bâtonnet.
2. Cut the squash into medium dice.
3. Cut the green beans into 2-in. (5-cm) lengths
4. Quarter the turnips.
5. Cook the six vegetables separately in a steamer or in boiling salted water until crisp-tender. Shock each vegetable in ice water as soon as it is cooked. Drain and refrigerate.
6. Bring the desired stock or cooking liquid to a simmer in a sauté pan large enough to hold the vegetables in a shallow layer. (Of course, do not choose chicken stock as the cooking liquid if the dish is for a vegetarian menu.)
7. Add the vegetables to the pan and toss over heat until the vegetables are hot (see Note).
8. Add the butter and the herbs. Toss just until the butter is melted and coats the vegetables.
9. Season to taste with salt and white pepper.

Per serving: Calories, 110; Protein, 2 g; Fat, 6 g (49% cal.); Cholesterol, 15 mg; Carbohydrates, 12 g; Fiber, 3 g; Sodium, 75 mg.

Note: As an alternative finishing method, heat the stock in a saucepan, reduce slightly, monter au beurre, and season. Reheat the vegetables separately and mix with the butter sauce.

Ragout of Summer Vegetables

Artichokes Cooked Sous Vide, in a Warm Vinaigrette with Aromatic Vegetables

PORTIONS: 10   PORTION SIZE: 1 ARTICHOKE

U.S.	METRIC	INGREDIENTS
2 qt	2 L	Water, cold
3 fl oz	90 mL	Lemon juice
10	10	Artichokes, large
as needed	as needed	Lemon halves
3 fl oz	90 mL	Olive oil
1 tsp	5 mL	Salt

PROCEDURE

1. Review the guidelines for safe sous vide cooking on page 66.
2. Prepare acidulated water: Mix the water and lemon juice in a bowl large enough to hold the artichokes.
3. Trim the artichoke bottoms as shown in **Figure 10.1**, but leave 1 in. (2.5 cm) of stem attached. Rub cut surfaces with cut lemon as you work to keep the artichokes from darkening. Drop into acidulated water as soon as each one is finished.
4. Vacuum-pack as follows: Remove each artichoke bottom from the water, dry quickly on clean towels, and dip in olive oil to coat. Sprinkle lightly with salt. Place in plastic bags and vacuum-pack.
5. Cook in a hot-water bath at 194°F (90°C) for 45 minutes, or until the artichokes are tender.
6. If the artichokes are not to be served immediately, cool in an ice-water bath. Refrigerate, unopened, until needed.

3 oz	90 g	Carrots, brunoise
3 oz	90 g	Shallots, brunoise
1	1	Garlic clove, minced
3 fl oz	90 mL	Olive oil
to taste	to taste	Salt
1 fl oz	30 mL	Lemon juice
1 tbsp	15 mL	Chopped parsley

7. Over low heat, sweat the carrots, shallots, and garlic in half the olive oil just until tender. Do not let them brown.
8. Remove from the heat and add salt to taste.
9. Add the remaining olive oil and the lemon juice.
10. Reheat the artichokes, in their plastic bags, in a hot-water bath.
11. Remove the artichokes from their bags and cut each into 8 wedges.
12. Toss the artichokes with the warm mixture of olive oil, lemon juice, and aromatic vegetables. Plate at once and sprinkle with a little chopped parsley.

Per serving: Calories, 190; Protein, 2 g; Fat, 17 g (76% cal.); Cholesterol, 0 mg; Carbohydrates, 10 g; Fiber, 5 g; Sodium, 280 mg.

VARIATION

If sous vide equipment is not available, cook the artichokes in a *blanc*, following steps 2 and 3 in the recipe for Artichokes Clamart, p. 287.

Sautéing and Pan-Frying

Remember that the main differences between sautéing and pan-frying are the amount of fat used and the cooking time. *Sautéing* means cooking quickly in a small amount of fat. The product is often tossed or flipped in the pan over high heat. *Pan-frying* means cooking in a larger amount of fat, usually for a longer time at lower heat, and the product is not tossed or flipped. In practice, the two methods are similar, and the distinction between them is hard to draw.

Both methods may be used for finish-cooking precooked or blanched vegetables as well as for completely cooking vegetables from the raw state. Sautéing in butter is especially popular for finishing precooked and chilled vegetables for service.

Stir-frying is a quick-cooking technique used in Asian cookery. In effect, it is similar to sautéing, except the pan is left stationary and the items being cooked are stirred and flipped in hot fat with spatulas or other tools.

Procedure for Sautéing Vegetables

This method is used for precooked or blanched vegetables and for tender, small-cut vegetables that cook quickly.

1. Collect all equipment and food products.

2. Prepare vegetables as required.

3. Place sauté pan on high heat.

4. When the pan is hot, add a small amount of clarified butter, oil, or other fat, enough to coat the bottom of the pan. (Clarified butter is used because the milk solids in whole butter burn quickly at the high heat necessary for sautéing.)

Flipping action of wrist

Figure 11.4 To flip foods in a sauté pan, give the handle a sharp twist upward with the wrist. Be sure to move the pan back far enough to catch the foods as they come down.

5. As soon as the fat is hot, add the vegetable. Do not overload the pan, or the temperature will be lowered too much and the vegetables will simmer instead of sauté.

6. After the heat has recovered, flip the pan a few times to turn and toss the vegetables (see Figure 11.4). Let the pan set again over the heat.

7. Continue to flip the vegetables as often as necessary for them to cook or heat evenly and become coated with the cooking fat. (Don't flip more than necessary, however. It may be fun and a good way to show off, but it's a waste of time and accomplishes nothing except breaking fragile vegetables. Also, the heat must have time to recover between flips.)

8. As soon as the vegetables are cooked, or heated through if precooked, remove from the pan and serve. Browning may or may not be desirable, depending on the vegetable and the particular preparation.

Procedure for Pan-Frying Vegetables

Note: A griddle is often used for this procedure if only a small amount of fat is required.

1. Collect all equipment and food products.

2. Prepare vegetables as required.

3. Place a sauté pan or cast-iron skillet on moderately high heat. Add required amount of fat to the pan and let it heat.

4. Place prepared vegetables in the pan. Adjust the heat so the product cooks through with the desired amount of browning but without burning the outside.

5. Turn vegetables with a spatula and continue to cook until done.

6. Remove from pan. If necessary, drain on absorbent paper to eliminate excess fat.

Zucchini Sauté Provençale

PORTIONS: 25   PORTION SIZE: 3½ OZ (100 G)

U.S.	METRIC	INGREDIENTS
6 lb	2.7 kg	Zucchini
6 fl oz	175 mL	Olive oil
6 oz	175 g	Shallots or onions, minced
4–6	4–6	Garlic cloves, chopped
to taste	to taste	Chopped parsley
to taste	to taste	Salt
to taste	to taste	White pepper

Per serving: Calories, 80; Protein, 1 g; Fat, 7g (72% cal.); Cholesterol, 0 mg; Carbohydrates, 5 g; Fiber 1 g; Sodium, 5 mg.

PROCEDURE

1. Wash and trim the zucchini. Cut crosswise into thin slices.
2. Heat the oil in two or three sauté pans (or sauté in several batches—do not overload the pans). Add the shallot or onion and the garlic. Sauté until soft but not browned.
3. Add the zucchini and sauté until slightly browned but still somewhat crisp.
4. Add the parsley and toss to mix. Season to taste.

VARIATIONS

Cut the zucchini into other shapes, but keep them small enough to cook quickly. Examples: bâtonnet, julienne, dice, and shredded on a coarse grater.

Shredded Zucchini with Shallots
Shred the zucchini on a coarse grater. Sauté with shallots as in basic recipe, but without browning. Omit the garlic and parsley.

Zucchini with Tomatoes
Sauté as in the basic recipe. When half cooked, add 2½ pt (1.2 L) drained, chopped, canned tomatoes or fresh tomatoes concassé (p. 267). Finish cooking. Season with oregano and basil.

Zucchini with Cream
Shred zucchini on grater. Salt lightly and let stand in a colander 30 minutes. Press out excess liquid. Sauté as in basic recipe, but without browning. Add 2½ cups (600 mL) heavy cream and simmer 2 minutes.

Sautéed Mushrooms

PORTIONS: 25   PORTION SIZE: 3½ OZ (100 G)

U.S.	METRIC	INGREDIENTS
6½ lb	3 kg	Mushrooms, fresh
10 oz	300 g	Clarified butter or half oil, half butter
to taste	to taste	Salt
to taste	to taste	Pepper

Per serving: Calories, 120; Protein, 2 g; Fat, 11 g (80% cal.); Cholesterol, 30 mg; Carbohydrates, 4 g; Fiber, 2 g; Sodium, 115 mg.

Note: If mushrooms must be kept light in color, add lemon juice to the pan with the mushrooms. Use about 1 fl oz (29.57 mL) lemon juice per 1 lb (500 g) mushrooms.

PROCEDURE

1. Rinse the mushrooms quickly and dry them with towels. Trim the bottoms of the stems and slice the mushrooms.
2. Heat two or three sauté pans over high heat (or sauté in several batches— do not overload pans). Add the fat to the pans. Place the mushrooms in the pans and sauté over high heat until browned. Do not overcook, or the mushrooms will shrivel and lose a great deal of moisture.
3. Season with salt and pepper.

VARIATIONS

Garnish with chopped parsley.

Instead of slicing, leave small mushroom caps whole, or cut in halves or quarters.

Creamed Mushrooms
Prepare as in the basic recipe, using lemon juice to keep light color. Combine with 2½ pt (1.2 L) hot cream sauce. Season with a little nutmeg.

Duxelles
Chop mushrooms very fine. Squeeze out moisture in a towel. Sauté in butter with 3 oz (90 g) minced shallot or onion until dry. Season with salt, pepper, nutmeg. Use in vegetable and meat stuffings. May be moistened with heavy cream or stretched with bread crumbs.

Pan-Fried Eggplant with Tomato Sauce

PORTIONS: 24 PORTION SIZE: 3½ OZ (100 G) EGGPLANT, 2 FL OZ (60 ML) SAUCE

U.S.	METRIC	INGREDIENTS	PROCEDURE
6½ lb	3 kg	Eggplant	1. Wash and trim eggplants. Pare if skins are tough. Cut crosswise into ¼-in. (0.5-cm) slices.
		Breading:	2. Hold in strongly salted cold water up to 30 minutes. (This step may be omitted, but it helps prevent darkening and eliminates some bitter flavors.)
6 oz	175 g	Flour	
1½ tsp	7 mL	Salt	3. Set up breading station, seasoning the flour with the salt and pepper.
½ tsp	2 mL	White pepper	4. Drain the eggplants and dry them well. Pass through Standard Breading Procedure (see p. 128).
1 pt	500 mL	Egg wash	
1¼ lb	600 g	Bread crumbs	5. Heat ¼ in. (0.5 cm) oil in a heavy iron skillet or sauté pan. Pan-fry the breaded eggplant on both sides until browned. Remove from pan with slotted spatula and drain on absorbent paper.
as needed	as needed	Oil for frying	
1½ qt	1.5 L	Tomato sauce	6. Serve 2–3 slices per portion, depending on size. Nap each portion with 2 fl oz (60 mL) tomato sauce. Ladle the sauce in a band across the eggplant; do not cover completely.

Per serving: Calories, 260; Protein, 7 g; Fat, 13 g (44% cal.); Cholesterol, 70 mg; Carbohydrates, 30 g; Fiber, 4 g; Sodium, 490 mg.

VARIATIONS

Instead of Standard Breading Procedure, simply dredge slices in seasoned flour and pan-fry.

Pan-Fried Eggplant Creole
Use Creole sauce instead of tomato sauce.

Eggplant Parmigiana
Pan-fry as in the basic recipe. Top each fried slice with a thin slice of mozzarella cheese. Arrange in layers in a baking pan, covering each layer with tomato sauce and sprinkling with parmesan cheese. Bake 30 minutes at 350°F (175°C).

Corn with Poblanos

PORTIONS: 12 PORTION SIZE: 3 OZ (90 G)

U.S.	METRIC	INGREDIENTS	PROCEDURE
12 oz	360 g	Poblano chiles	1. Roast and peel the chiles as illustrated on page 262. Remove and discard the stem, seeds, and inner membranes.
2 lb	900 g	Corn, fresh or frozen	2. Cut the chiles into bâtonnet.
1½ fl oz	45 mL	Olive oil	3. If the corn is frozen, drop into boiling water until thawed, then drain.
8 oz	240 g	Onion, chopped fine	4. Heat the olive oil in a sauté pan over moderately high heat.
1 tsp	5 mL	Dried oregano	5. Add the onion and sauté until it is soft and beginning to brown.
to taste	to taste	Salt	6. Add the poblanos, corn, and oregano. Sauté until hot and well blended.
to taste	to taste	Pepper	7. Add salt and pepper to taste.

Per serving: Calories, 180; Protein, 6 g; Fat, 7 g (30% cal.); Cholesterol, 0 mg; Carbohydrates, 30 g; Fiber, 9 g; Sodium, 25 mg.

VARIATIONS

Gratin of Corn and Poblanos
Prepare as in the basic recipe. Transfer to a gratin dish and cover with a generous layer of Monterey jack or similar mild cheese. Place under a salamander or broiler until the cheese is melted and lightly browned.

Corn and Poblanos in Cream
Prepare as in the basic recipe, but in step 6 add 12 fl oz (360 mL) heavy cream. Simmer until the cream is thickened and reduced by about one-third.

Stir-Fried Mixed Vegetables

PORTIONS: 16   PORTION SIZE: 4 OZ (125 G)

U.S.	METRIC	INGREDIENTS
1½ lb	750 g	Chinese cabbage
16	16	Dried black mushrooms
6 oz	175 g	Bamboo shoots, drained
4 oz	125 g	Celery
4 oz	125 g	Carrots
15-oz can	425-g can	Baby corn
4	4	Scallions
2–3 fl oz	60–90 mL	Oil
1	1	Garlic cloves, crushed (optional)
5 slices	5 slices	Fresh ginger root
1 tsp	5 mL	Salt
12 fl oz	350 mL	Water or chicken stock
1 fl oz	30 mL	Soy sauce (optional)
¼ cup	25 g (60 mL)	Cornstarch
3 fl oz	100 mL	Water, cold
1 tsp	5 mL	Sesame oil (optional)

Per serving: Calories, 90; Protein, 2 g; Fat, 4 g, (36% cal.); Cholesterol, 0 mg; Carbohydrates, 14 g; Fiber, 3 g; Sodium, 165 mg.

VARIATIONS

This is a basic procedure for stir-fried vegetables. One or two vegetables, or any harmonious assortment, can be cooked using the same recipe, merely substituting different vegetable ingredients.

PROCEDURE

1. Cut off the root end of the cabbage and separate the leaves. Cut out the thick center ribs, then cut them crosswise into 2-in. (5-cm) chunks. Cut the thin, leafy parts into shreds.

2. Soak the mushrooms in boiling water to cover. When soft, drain and squeeze dry, reserving the liquid. Discard the stems and cut the caps into julienne.

3. Cut the bamboo shoots into thin slices.

4. Cut the celery on the diagonal into thin slices.

5. Cut the carrots into julienne.

6. Drain the baby corn.

7. Slice the scallions into shreds at a sharp angle.

8. Heat the oil in a wok or large sauté pan.

9. Add the garlic and cook about 15 seconds to flavor the oil, then remove and discard the garlic.

10. Add the ginger and salt and let cook about 15 seconds.

11. Add the cabbage ribs and stir-fry 1–2 minutes.

12. Add the remaining vegetables, except the shredded cabbage leaves. Continue to stir-fry another 1–2 minutes. Add the shredded cabbage.

13. Add the stock and soy sauce and continue to stir and cook until the vegetables are cooked but still crisp.

14. Mix the cornstarch with the cold water, then stir it, a little at a time, into the vegetables to thicken the sauce. Do not add it all at once because you may not need it all. The sauce should not be too thick but rather the consistency of a light velouté sauce.

15. Stir in the sesame oil and serve at once.

Brussels Sprouts with Walnuts

PORTIONS: 12   PORTION SIZE: 3½ OZ (100 G)

U.S.	METRIC	INGREDIENTS
3 lb	1.5 kg	Brussels sprouts
2 oz	60 g	Butter
6 oz	180 g	Walnut pieces
to taste	to taste	Salt

PROCEDURE

1. Trim the bases of the sprouts and remove any damaged leaves.
2. Blanch the sprouts in a large quantity of boiling salted water until half to three-fourths cooked.
3. Drain and refresh the sprouts in ice water. Drain again. (If the sprouts are to be finished immediately, refreshing can be omitted.)
4. Cut the sprouts in half lengthwise.
5. Heat the butter in a sauté pan large enough to hold the sprouts in a thin layer.
6. Add the sprouts and the walnuts to the pan. Sauté until the sprouts are tender and lightly browned.
7. Add salt to taste.

Per serving: Calories, 183; Protein, 6 g; Fat, 15 g (65% cal.); Cholesterol, 10 mg; Carbohydrates, 12 g; Fiber, 5 g; Sodium, 60 mg.

VARIATION

For a vegan version of this recipe, substitute walnut oil for the butter.

Brussels Sprouts with Walnuts

Braising

Braising, as you know, is a slow, moist-heat cooking method using a small amount of liquid. When meats are braised, they are seared or browned in fat before liquid is added. Braised vegetables are not always cooked in fat before liquid is added, although some kind of fat is used in the preparation.

Braised vegetable preparations tend to be more complex than boiled or steamed vegetables, and the cooking times are longer. Unfortunately, there are so many variations of braised vegetable that it is not possible to prescribe a single basic procedure. Instead, we discuss the procedures in general terms and use the recipes to illustrate them.

Characteristics of Vegetable Braising Procedures

1. Fat is added to a braising or baking pan or a saucepan and heated. Finely diced mirepoix or other flavoring ingredients may be cooked briefly in the fat. The fat contributes to flavor and eating quality.
2. The vegetable (blanched or raw) is placed in the pan. It may or may not be cooked in the fat before the liquid is added, depending on the recipe.
3. Liquid is added—stock, water, wine, or a combination of liquids. The liquid generally covers the vegetable only partway.
4. The pot or saucepan is covered and the vegetable is cooked slowly in the oven or on the rangetop.
5. The flavorful cooking liquid is served with the vegetable. It is sometimes drained off and reduced over high heat before serving in order to concentrate flavor.

Braised Red Cabbage

PORTIONS: 25   PORTION SIZE: 5 OZ (150 G)

U.S.	METRIC	INGREDIENTS
6 lb	3 kg	Red cabbage
12 oz	375 g	Bacon, diced
1 lb	500 g	Onions, sliced
1 oz	30 g	Sugar
1½ pt	750 mL	White stock (chicken, pork, veal) or water
1 lb	500 g	Apples (unpeeled), cored and diced
4	4	Cloves
6	6	Whole allspice
1	1	Cinnamon stick
4 fl oz or more	125 mL or more	Cider vinegar or red wine vinegar
1 cup	250 mL	Red wine (or more vinegar)
to taste	to taste	Salt
to taste	to taste	Pepper

Per serving: Calories, 130; Protein, 3 g; Fat, 8 g (54% cal.); Cholesterol, 10 mg; Carbohydrates, 11 g; Fiber, 3 g; Sodium, 110 mg.

PROCEDURE

1. Remove the outer leaves of the cabbage and cut it into quarters. Remove the core and shred the cabbage with a knife or a power shredder attachment. Do not chop; cabbage should be in long, fine shreds.

2. Render the bacon in a large, heavy pot. Add the onions and sugar and cook until the onion is soft.

3. Add the cabbage and stir over heat until it is coated with fat.

4. Add the stock, apples, and spices, tied in a cheesecloth bag. Cover and simmer until cabbage is nearly tender, about 30 minutes.

5. Add the vinegar and red wine and simmer another 10 minutes. Remove spice bag.

6. Taste and correct seasoning. If not tart enough or color is not red enough, add more vinegar.

VARIATIONS

Substitute lard, salt pork, or chicken fat for the bacon. Vegetable oil may be used, but it does not contribute to flavor.

Eliminate cinnamon, cloves, and allspice. Add 1 tbsp (15 mL) caraway seeds to onions when sautéing them.

Braised Green or White Cabbage

Prepare as in the basic recipe, but season with 1 bay leaf, 6–8 parsley stems, 6 peppercorns, and a pinch of thyme instead of the cinnamon, cloves, and allspice. Omit sugar, apples, wine, and vinegar. Butter may be used as the cooking fat, if desired.

Braised Red Cabbage

Peas à la Française

PORTIONS: 16   PORTION SIZE: 3 OZ (90 G)

U.S.	METRIC	INGREDIENTS
3 oz	90 g	Butter
2 oz	60 g	Onion, chopped, or whole tiny pearl onions, peeled
2½ lb	1.1 kg	Peas, frozen
8 oz	225 g	Lettuce, shredded
2 tbsp	30 mL	Chopped parsley
1 tsp	5 mL	Salt
2 tsp	10 mL	Sugar
4 fl oz	125 mL	Chicken stock or water, hot
1 tbsp	15 mL	Beurre manié

PROCEDURE

1. Heat the butter in a saucepan. Add the onions and sauté lightly.

2. Add the peas, lettuce, parsley, salt, and sugar. Cook over moderate heat, stirring a few times, until the vegetables begin to steam.

3. Add the stock or water. Bring to a boil, cover, and simmer over low heat or in the oven until peas are tender.

4. Stir in a little beurre manié to thicken the cooking liquid, and simmer another 2–3 minutes. Adjust seasoning. (For larger quantities, drain off liquid and thicken separately.)

Per serving: Calories, 100; Protein, 4 g; Fat, 5 g (43% cal.); Cholesterol, 15 mg; Carbohydrates, 11 g; Fiber, 4 g; Sodium, 250 mg.

Braised Celery

PORTIONS: 25   PORTION SIZE: 3 OZ (90 G)

U.S.	METRIC	INGREDIENTS
6 lb	3 kg	Celery
4 oz	125 g	Butter
3 pt (approximately)	1.5 L (approximately)	Brown stock or chicken stock
to taste	to taste	Salt
to taste	to taste	Pepper
as needed	as needed	Beurre manié (optional)

PROCEDURE

1. Trim and wash the celery. If it is very stringy, peel the outside of the ribs, or use the tender inner stems and save the outside ones for mirepoix. Cut into 1½-in. (4-cm) lengths. Split broad pieces lengthwise so all pieces are about the same size.

2. Heat the butter in a braising pot and add the celery. Cook over moderate heat until the celery is just beginning to soften.

3. Add enough stock to cover the celery by about two-thirds. Season with salt and pepper to taste. Cover and cook slowly in the oven or on the rangetop until tender, 20–30 minutes.

4. Drain the celery and keep it warm in a steam table pan. Reduce the stock over high heat to about 2½ pt (1.25 L). If desired, thicken slightly with beurre manié. Adjust the seasonings and pour the sauce over the celery.

Per serving: Calories, 50; Protein, 1 g; Fat, 4 g (64% cal.); Cholesterol, 10 mg; Carbohydrates, 4 g; Fiber, 2 g; Sodium, 130 mg.

VARIATIONS

Bacon fat may be used instead of butter. For extra flavor, add finely diced mirepoix to the fat in the pan before adding celery.

Braised Celery Hearts
Prepare as in the basic recipe, but use celery hearts (the tender inner stalks, connected at the root), cut into wedges.

Braised Celery with Brown Sauce
Add 2½ pt (1.25 L) brown sauce or demi-glace to the reduced cooking liquid and reduce again to reach desired consistency. Add to celery.

Braised Celery Root
Prepare as in the basic recipe, using sliced, blanched knob celery (celeriac) instead of stalk celery.

Braised Lettuce
Blanch romaine lettuce to wilt leaves. Fold leaves into neat, portion-size bundles. Arrange on finely cut sautéed mirepoix and braise as in the basic recipe, without sautéing the lettuce.

Ratatouille

The method for this preparation is unlike that for the other braised vegetables in this section because no liquid is added. It is classified as a braised item because the vegetables are first sautéed in fat, then simmered in their own juices.

PORTIONS: 20   PORTION SIZE: 4 OZ (125 G)

U.S.	METRIC	INGREDIENTS
1 lb	500 g	Zucchini
1 lb	500 g	Eggplant
1 lb	500 g	Onions
4	4	Green bell peppers
4	4	Garlic cloves
2 lb	1 kg	Tomatoes (canned may be used if necessary)
6 oz, or more as needed	200 mL, or more as needed	Olive oil
½ cup	125 mL	Chopped parsley
1	1	Bay leaf
¼ tsp	1 mL	Dried thyme
to taste	to taste	Salt
to taste	to taste	Pepper

PROCEDURE

1. Prepare the vegetables: Cut the zucchini into ½-in. (1-cm) slices. Peel the eggplant and cut into large dice. Slice the onions. Remove the cores and seeds of the peppers and cut into 1-in. (2.5-cm) dice. Chop the garlic. Peel and seed the tomatoes and cut into large dice (leave canned tomatoes whole; they will break up during cooking).

2. Sauté the zucchini in a little of the olive oil until it is about half cooked. Remove from pan.

3. Sauté the eggplant in olive oil until half cooked. Remove from pan.

4. Sauté the onions and peppers until half cooked. Add the garlic and sauté another minute.

5. Combine all vegetables and seasonings in brazier or heavy saucepan. Cover and cook in a slow oven (325°F/160°C) about 30 minutes, or until vegetables are tender and flavors are well blended. If the vegetables are too juicy, cook uncovered on a rangetop for a few minutes to reduce. Be careful not to scorch the vegetables on the bottom.

6. Adjust seasonings. Serve hot or cold.

Per serving: Calories, 110; Protein, 1 g; Fat, 9 g (67% cal.); Cholesterol, 0 mg; Carbohydrates, 9 g; Fiber, 2 g; Sodium, 5 mg.

Ratatouille

Lecsó

PORTIONS: 16   PORTION SIZE: 4 OZ (125 G)

U.S.	METRIC	INGREDIENTS
1 lb 8 oz	750 g	Onions
3 lb	1.5 kg	Green peppers or Hungarian or Italian frying peppers
3 oz	100 g	Tomatoes, as ripe as possible
3 tbsp	20 g	Lard
to taste	to taste	Hungarian paprika
pinch	pinch	Salt

PROCEDURE

1. Peel the onion and cut into fine dice.

2. Core and seed the peppers. Cut into thin slices.

3. Peel, seed, and chop the tomatoes.

4. Heat the lard over low heat. Add the onion and cook slowly 5–10 minutes, until it is quite soft.

5. Add the peppers and cook another 5–10 minutes.

6. Add the tomatoes and paprika. Cover and simmer 15–20 minutes, or until vegetables are tender.

7. Season to taste with salt. Add 1–2 pinches of sugar if desired.

Per serving: Calories, 110; Protein, 2 g; Fat, 6 g (46% cal.); Cholesterol, 5 mg; Carbohydrates, 14 g; Fiber, 3 g; Sodium, 10 mg.

VARIATIONS

This dish may be used as a vegetable or an appetizer, or served with rice or boiled noodles. Smoked sausages are often added to it as a luncheon dish, or it may be served with eggs prepared in a variety of ways. The portion size indicated is rather large because this dish is often served as part of a main course. For a side-dish portion, you may want to reduce the portion size to 2½–3 oz (75–100 g)..

Gratin of Fennel

PORTIONS: 12   PORTION SIZE: 3½ OZ (100 G)

U.S.	METRIC	INGREDIENTS	PROCEDURE
4½ lb	2 kg	Fennel bulbs	1. Trim the stems and root ends of the fennel bulbs.
12 oz	360 g	Onion (optional)	2. Cut lengthwise—that is, from stem end to root end—into quarters. If the bulbs are large, cut each quarter into 2 wedges.
3 oz	90 g	Butter	
1 tsp, or to taste	5 mL, or to taste	Salt	3. Cut the onion into thin slices.
			4. Heat the butter in a sauté pan over moderate heat.
¼ tsp, or to taste	1 mL, or to taste	White pepper	5. Add the fennel and onion. Sauté 2–3 minutes, turning the fennel to coat it with the butter.
8 fl oz	250 mL	Water, chicken stock, or vegetable stock	6. Sprinkle with the salt and white pepper. Add the water or stock.
			7. Cover tightly. Cook over very low heat or in an oven heated to 325°F (165°C) until the fennel is tender, about 20 minutes. Check once or twice during cooking to make sure the liquid hasn't all evaporated. Add a little more liquid if necessary to keep the vegetables moist.
			8. When the fennel is tender, the liquid should be nearly all evaporated. If it is not, set the pan over moderate heat, uncovered, to cook off the liquid.
4 oz	125 g	Parmesan cheese, grated	9. Transfer the fennel to individual-portion gratin dishes or to one or more larger gratin dishes.
			10. Distribute the grated cheese over the top of the fennel.
			11. Place under a broiler or salamander or in a hot oven until the top is browned.

Per serving: Calories, 140; Protein, 6 g; Fat, 9 g (53% cal.); Cholesterol, 20 mg; Carbohydrates, 12 g; Fiber, 5 g; Sodium, 490 mg.

Baking

You could, if you wished, cook carrots by placing them in a pot of boiling water, placing the pot in a hot oven, and cooking until tender. This is not baking, however. It's plain old simmering. You'd just be using the heat of the oven rather than the rangetop to simmer the water.

When we talk about baking vegetables, we usually mean one of two things:

1. Cooking starchy vegetables, such as potatoes, winter squash, and sweet potatoes, and other moist, dense-textured vegetables such as tomatoes, beets, eggplant, onions, and turnips, from the raw to the finished state. Starch vegetables are baked because the dry heat produces a desirable texture. Baked potatoes, for example, do not have the same texture as boiled or steamed potatoes.

   In some areas, it is fashionable to refer to baked vegetables as *roasted*.

   In theory, any vegetable with enough moisture can be baked like potatoes, but the drying effects of the oven and the long cooking time make it undesirable for most small vegetables, such as peas and green beans.

2. Finishing certain vegetable combinations, sometimes known as *casseroles*. The vegetables in these items are usually parcooked by simmering or steaming before they are baked.

   Vegetable casseroles are baked for either of two reasons:

   • The slow, all-around heat allows the product to cook undisturbed. The agitation and stirring of rangetop cooking is not always desirable. Baked beans could be finished on top of the range, but they would be mushier and more broken. Custard-based timbales would be pourable, not firmly set.

   • The dry heat produces desirable effects, such as browning and caramelizing of sugars. For example, you could put a pan of candied sweet potatoes in a steamer, but the moist heat would not allow a glaze to form.

Procedure for Baking Vegetables

1. Collect all equipment and food products.
2. Prepare vegetables as required.
3. Place in appropriate pan and set in preheated oven.
4. Bake to desired doneness.

Baked Acorn Squash

PORTIONS: 24   PORTION SIZE: ½ SQUASH

U.S.	METRIC	INGREDIENTS
12	12	Acorn squash, small
as needed	as needed	Butter, melted
5 oz	150 g	Brown sugar
2½ tsp	12 mL	Salt
2 fl oz	60 mL	Sherry (optional)

Per serving: Calories, 130; Protein, 2 g; Fat, 2 g (13% cal.); Cholesterol, 5 mg; Carbohydrates, 28 g; Fiber, 3 g; Sodium, 270 mg.

VARIATIONS

Hubbard, buttercup, and other winter squash varieties may be cut into portion sizes and baked as in basic recipe.

Gingered Squash

Mix 1½ tsp (7 mL) ground ginger with the sugar in the basic recipe.

Puréed Squash

Bake cut Hubbard squash until tender. Remove from shell and purée in food mill. Add butter, salt, and pepper to taste.

PROCEDURE

1. Wash and cut squash in half lengthwise. Scrape out seeds. (If using large squash, cut into portion sizes.)

2. Brush cut surfaces and cavity with melted butter. Place close together, cut side down, on baking sheet. (This helps squash cook faster without drying by retaining steam.)

3. Bake at 350°F (175°C) until almost tender, about 30–40 minutes.

4. Turn the squash cut side up and brush again with butter. Sprinkle the cavities with sugar and salt. Add a few drops of sherry to each if desired.

5. Bake 10–15 minutes more, or until surface is glazed.

Baked Acorn Squash

Roasted Winter Vegetables

PORTIONS: 16   PORTIONS SIZE: 4 OZ (125 G)

U.S.	METRIC	INGREDIENTS
12 oz	375 g	Carrots, peeled
12 oz	375 g	Celery root, peeled
8 oz	250 g	Turnips, peeled
8 oz	250 g	Parsnips, peeled
12 oz	375 g	Waxy potatoes, peeled
8 oz	250 g	Butternut squash, peeled and seeded
12	12	Shallots, peeled
12	12	Garlic cloves, peeled
4 fl oz	125 mL	Olive oil
1½ tsp	7 mL	Dried thyme
1½ tsp	7 mL	Coarse salt
1 tsp	5 mL	Coarsely ground black pepper

Per serving: Calories, 120; Protein, 1 g; Fat, 7 g (51% cal.); Cholesterol, 0 mg; Carbohydrates, 14 g; Fiber, 3 g; Sodium, 230 mg.

PROCEDURE

1. Cut the carrots, celery root, turnips, parsnips, potatoes, and squash into 1-in. (2.5-cm) dice.

2. Place these cut vegetables, plus the shallots and garlic cloves, in a baking pan.

3. Pour the olive oil over the vegetables and sprinkle with the thyme, salt, and pepper. Toss or mix until the vegetables are well coated with oil. Add more oil if necessary.

4. Bake at 375°F (190°C) about 45 minutes, or until the vegetables are tender and lightly browned. Turn or stir the vegetables several times during baking so they cook evenly. Do not allow them to become too browned, or they may be bitter.

VARIATIONS

Vegetable proportions may be varied as desired. Other vegetables, such as sweet potatoes, stalk celery, onions, and rutabagas may be added.

Roasted Onions

Substitute 4 lb (2kg) onions, sliced ¼ in. (5 mm) thick, for all the vegetables in the basic recipe. Bake as in the basic recipe, cooking until the onions are browned and caramelized. Onions lose a lot of moisture during baking, so total yield is only about 2¼ lb (1.1 kg).

Roasted Summer Vegetables

Omit the parsnips, turnips, celeriac, and butternut squash. Substitute an assortment of summer vegetables in desired proportions, such as eggplant, summer squash, fennel, bell peppers, cherry tomatoes, and baby turnips. Season with fresh chopped basil and parsley.

Roasted Winter Vegetables

Roasted Beets with Beet Greens

PORTIONS: 12   PORTION SIZE: 3 OZ (90 G)

U.S.	METRIC	INGREDIENTS	PROCEDURE
3 lb	1.5 kg	Beets, large (without tops)	1. Trim the beets as necessary, but leave the root and 1–2 in. (3-5 cm) of the stems attached. Wash well. 2. Place in a baking pan and roast at 375°F (190°C) until tender, about 1 hour for large beets (**Figure 11.5**). Test by piercing with a thin-bladed knife. 3. Cool and refrigerate until needed.
1 lb	480 g	Beet greens	4. Trim the beet greens, discarding the stems. Wash well in several changes of water, and drain. 5. Blanch the greens in boiling salted water. Drain and refresh in ice water. Drain again. Squeeze out excess water. 6. Chop the greens coarsely.
2 oz to taste to taste	60 g to taste to taste	Butter Salt Pepper	7. Peel the roasted beets (**Figure 11.6**). Cut them into small dice. 8. Heat the butter in a sauté pan. Add the diced beets and chopped greens and sauté until hot. 9. Season to taste with salt and pepper.

Per serving: Calories, 100; Protein, 3 g; Fat, 4 g (33% cal.); Cholesterol, 10 mg; Carbohydrates, 15 g; Fiber, 4 g; Sodium, 230 mg.

Roasted Beets with Beet Greens

Figure 11.5 Roast beets, uncovered, until tender.

Figure 11.6 With a paring knife, pull the peels from the beets.

Roasted Garlic

YIELD: APPROXIMATELY 6 OZ (175 G) GARLIC PULP

U.S.	METRIC	INGREDIENTS
6	6	Garlic heads, whole
1 fl oz	30 mL	Olive oil

Per 1 ounce: Calories, 90; Protein, 2 g; Fat, 5 g (48% cal.); Cholesterol, 0 mg; Carbohydrates, 10 g; Fiber, 1 g; Sodium, 5 mg.

VARIATION

For whole roasted heads of garlic to use as garnish, cut off the tops (the pointed end) of the heads before rubbing with oil.

PROCEDURE

1. Preheat an oven to 400°F (200°C).

2. Rub the heads of garlic with olive oil.

3. Place on a sheet pan in the oven. Roast about 30 minutes, or until soft.

4. Remove from the oven and cool slightly.

5. For roasted garlic pulp, cut the heads in half crosswise and squeeze out the pulp.

6. For roasted garlic cloves to use as garnish, separate the cloves. Serve peeled or unpeeled.

Roasted Garlic

Glazed Sweet Potatoes

PORTIONS: 25   PORTION SIZE: 5 OZ (150 G)

U.S.	METRIC	INGREDIENTS
8 lb	3.6 kg	Sweet potatoes

PROCEDURE

1. Scrub the sweet potatoes and boil or steam until nearly tender. Do not overcook.

2. Spread the potatoes on a sheet pan to cool.

3. Peel the potatoes when they are cool enough to handle. Remove dark spots. Cut into neat, uniform pieces for easy portioning. Arrange in a buttered baking pan.

U.S.	METRIC	INGREDIENTS
6 fl oz	175 mL	Water
1½ cups	350 mL	Light corn syrup or maple syrup
6 oz	175 g	Brown sugar
8 fl oz	250 mL	Orange juice
2 fl oz	60 mL	Lemon juice
2 oz	60 g	Butter
1 tsp	5 mL	Cinnamon
¼ tsp	1 mL	Ground cloves
½ tsp	2 mL	Salt

4. Place the water, syrup, and sugar in a saucepan. Stir over heat until sugar is dissolved. Add the remaining ingredients and boil until the mixture is reduced to about 1½ pt (700–800 mL) and forms a heavy syrup.

5. Pour the syrup over the potatoes.

6. Bake at 350°F (175°C) until potatoes are thoroughly cooked and glazed, about 45–60 minutes. Baste with the syrup several times during baking.

Per serving: Calories, 190; Protein, 2 g; Fat, 2 g (9% cal.); Cholesterol, 5 mg; Carbohydrates, 44 g; Fiber, 2 g; Sodium, 100 mg.

Spaghetti Squash with Tomato Confit

PORTIONS: 12   PORTION SIZE: 2¾ OZ (80 G) SQUASH, 1½ OZ (45 G) TOMATO CONFIT

U.S.	METRIC	INGREDIENTS
¼ oz	7 g	Garlic, sliced
2½ fl oz	75 mL	Olive oil
1 lb 12 oz EP	850 g EP	Tomatoes, peeled, seeded, and chopped
2½ tbsp	37 mL	Capers, rinsed and drained
1½ oz	45 g	Black olives, European type such as Kalamata, pitted and sliced
to taste	to taste	Salt
4½ lb	2.2 kg	Spaghetti squash
1½ fl oz	45 mL	Olive oil (optional)

Per serving: Calories, 120; Protein, 2 g; Fat, 7 g (50% cal.); Cholesterol, 0 mg; Carbohydrates, 14 g; Fiber, 3 g; Sodium, 150 mg.

VARIATION

Alternative Baking Method: Cut the raw squash in half lengthwise and scrape out the seeds. Place cut side down in a hotel pan and add about 1 in. (2.5 cm) water to the pan. Cover with foil and bake as above. Do not allow the squash to become too tender, as it will become too soft and lose its spaghettilike quality.

PROCEDURE

1. Over moderate heat, sweat the garlic in the olive oil until lightly cooked. Do not brown.

2. Add the tomatoes. Stir and cook until the liquid evaporates and the tomatoes are very thick.

3. Add the capers and olives. Cook another minute.

4. Season to taste with salt.

5. If making in advance, cool and refrigerate until needed.

6. Pierce the squash in several places with the tip of a sharp knife, to allow steam to escape.

7. Place in a hotel pan or baking pan. Add about 1 in. (2.5 cm) water to the pan. Cover with foil. Bake at 375°F (190°C) for 1 hour. Test for doneness by inserting a sharp knife to determine if the squash is tender.

8. Carefully cut the squash in half. Scrape out the seeds and discard.

9. With a fork, scrape out the spaghetti-like strands of squash flesh from the shells.

10. For service, the squash may be finished in one of two ways. Reheat the tomato mixture, if necessary, and toss with the squash. Alternatively, toss the squash with the olive oil, if desired, and plate. Top with a spoonful of the tomato mixture.

Spaghetti Squash with Tomato Confit

Broiling and Grilling

Grilled quick-cooking vegetables such as peppers, zucchini, large mushroom caps, and eggplant are pleasant accompaniments to grilled and roasted meats and poultry. Cut the vegetables into broad slices, brush with oil, and grill until lightly cooked and lightly browned. Heavy browning may produce an unpleasant burned taste. Grilled vegetables are often dressed with vinaigrette.

Broiling is also used to finish cooked or partially cooked vegetables by browning or glazing them on top. Bread crumbs are sometimes used to give a pleasing brown color and to prevent drying. Casseroles or gratin dishes that do not brown sufficiently in the oven may be browned for a few seconds under the broiler or salamander.

Procedure for Broiling or Grilling Vegetables

1. Collect equipment and food supplies.
2. Prepare the vegetables as necessary, including cutting them into required shapes and seasoning or marinating them.
3. Preheat the broiler or grill.
4. If necessary, brush the grill with a wire brush to clean it of any charred food particles.

Figure 11.7 Grilling vegetables

5. Place the vegetables directly on the grill or broiler grate. Alternatively, place tender vegetables on broiler platters or sheet pans and set under the broiler. Cook the vegetables to the desired doneness and color, turning them as necessary (Figure 11.7).
6. Remove from broiler or grill and serve immediately.

Grilled Vegetable Medley

YIELD: ABOUT 3 LB (1.5 KG)   PORTIONS: 9   PORTION SIZE: 5 OZ (150 G)

U.S.	METRIC	INGREDIENTS
3–3½ lb	1.5–1.75 kg	Assorted vegetables:
		Small eggplants
		Zucchini
		Yellow summer squash
		Bell peppers
		Radicchio
		Large onions
as needed	as needed	Olive oil
to taste	to taste	Salt
as needed	as needed	Balsamic vinegar

Per serving: Calories, 180; Protein, 1 g; Fat, 16 g (78% cal.); Cholesterol, 0 mg; Carbohydrates, 9 g; Fiber, 2 g; Sodium, 10 mg.

PROCEDURE

1. Prepare the vegetables: Trim the stem ends of the eggplants and cut them lengthwise into thick slices. If they are very small, just cut them in half lengthwise. Trim the stem ends of the zucchini and yellow squash. Cut lengthwise into thick slices. Core and seed the peppers and cut into quarters lengthwise. Remove any bruised outer leaves of the radicchio and cut in halves or quarters through the base, leaving the core in to hold the leaves together. Cut the onion into thick slices, holding the rings of each slice together with a bamboo skewer.

2. Brush the vegetables with olive oil and sprinkle them with salt.

3. Grill the vegetables over medium heat, turning as necessary, until they are tender and lightly grill-marked. Cooking time will vary by vegetable. Regulate the heat or distance from the flame so the vegetables cook without browning too much.

4. Remove from the grill and brush with a little balsamic vinegar, and, if desired, a little more olive oil. Serve warm.

VARIATIONS

Other vegetables and vegetable assortments may be grilled in the same manner. Suggestions include large mushroom caps, Belgian endive, blanched potatoes, fennel, asparagus, leeks, and scallions. Grilled vegetables may be served with various sauces, such as aïoli, sauce Vierge, salsa cruda, and vinaigrette variations.

Grilled Vegetable Medley

Deep-Frying

The principles of deep-frying you have already learned are applied to vegetables as well as to other foods.

- Review "Deep-Frying," Chapter 4, page 63.

- Review "Breadings" and "Batters," Chapter 6, pages 128–130.

Potatoes (covered in the next chapter) and onion rings are the most popular fried vegetables, but many others may be fried, too.

Deep-fried vegetables may be divided into five categories:

1. Vegetables dipped in batter and fried.

2. Vegetables breaded and fried.

3. Vegetables fried without a coating.

    Potatoes are the obvious example. Other starchy vegetables, such as sweet potatoes, may be fried without breading or batter if they are cut thin to reduce cooking time. The sugar in them burns easily if they are cooked too long.

    Thin slices and shavings of vegetables, deep-fried until light and crisp, make an attractive and interesting garnish for many dishes. Root vegetables, such as beets, celery root, and parsnips, can be sliced thin and fried like potato chips (slice long roots like parsnips lengthwise). Other vegetables, such as leeks and celery, can be cut into thin shreds or julienne and fried. These may be dusted in flour before frying.

4. Small vegetables or cuts mixed with a batter and dropped with a scoop into hot fat. The term *fritter* is used for this preparation, as well as for that in category 1.

5. Croquettes: thick vegetable purées or mixtures of small pieces of vegetable and a heavy béchamel or other binder, formed into shapes, breaded, and fried.

Procedure for Deep-Frying Vegetables

1. Collect all equipment and food products.

2. Preheat fryer to proper temperature.
   Most vegetables are fried at 325°–350°F (160°–175°C).

3. Prepare food items as required. Apply breading or batter if necessary.

4. Place proper amount of food in fryer. Do not overload.

5. Fry to desired doneness.

6. Remove food from fryer and let fat drain from it.

7. Serve at once, or, if necessary, hold uncovered in a warm place for the shortest possible time.

Vegetables for Deep-frying

Most vegetables large enough to coat with breading or batter may be fried. Tender, quick-cooking vegetables can be fried raw. Others may be precooked by simmering or steaming briefly to reduce the cooking time they need in the frying fat.

Raw vegetables for frying in breading or batter:

Eggplant	Onion rings	Tomatoes
Mushrooms	Peppers	Zucchini

Blanched or precooked vegetables for frying in breading or batter:

Artichoke hearts	Carrots	Fennel
Asparagus	Cauliflower	Okra
Beans, green and yellow	Celery	Parsnips
Broccoli	Celery root	Turnips
Brussels sprouts	Cucumbers	

KEY POINTS TO REVIEW

- What are the two basic kinds of baked vegetable preparation?

- What are the steps in the procedure for broiling or grilling vegetables?

- What are the basic kinds of deep-fried vegetable preparations?

- What are the steps in the procedure for deep-frying vegetables?

Onion Rings

PORTIONS: 20   PORTION SIZE: 3 OZ (90 G), 8–10 PIECES

U.S.	METRIC	INGREDIENTS	PROCEDURE
2	2	Egg yolks, beaten	1. Combine the egg yolks and club soda in a bowl.
1 pt	500 mL	Club soda	2. Sift together the flour, baking powder, and salt.
10 oz	300 g	Flour	3. Add the dry ingredients to the liquid and mix to make a smooth batter.
2 tsp	10 mL	Baking powder	
½ tsp	2 mL	Salt	
2	2	Egg whites	4. Whip the egg whites to soft peaks.
			5. Fold into the batter.
3 lb	1.4 kg	Onions, large	6. Peel the onions and cut crosswise into ¼-in. (0.5-cm) slices. Separate into rings (save unusable pieces for another purpose).
as needed	as needed	Flour	7. Place the onions in cold water, if they are not used immediately, to maintain crispness.
			8. Drain and dry the onions thoroughly.
			9. Dredge with flour and shake off excess. (This step isn't always necessary, but it helps the batter adhere.)
			10. Dip a few pieces at a time in the batter and fry in deep fat (350°F/175°C) until golden brown.
			11. Drain and serve immediately.

Per serving: Calories, 150; Protein, 3 g; Fat, 7 g (40% cal.); Cholesterol, 20 mg; Carbohydrates, 21 g; Fiber, 2 g; Sodium, 85 mg.

VARIATIONS

Beer Batter
Substitute light beer for the club soda.

Other Fried Vegetables
Any of the vegetables on the list at the beginning of this section may be fried in this batter.

Onion Rings

Vegetable Fritters

PORTIONS: 20   PORTION SIZE: 3 OZ (90 G), 2 PIECES

U.S.	METRIC	INGREDIENTS
		Batter:
6	6	Eggs, beaten
1 pt	500 mL	Milk
1 lb	500 g	Flour
2 tbsp	30 mL	Baking powder
1 tsp	5 mL	Salt
1 oz	30 g	Sugar
1½ lb EP	700 g EP	Vegetables: Choice of corn, cooked diced carrots, baby lima beans, diced asparagus, diced celery or celery root, turnip, eggplant, cauliflower, zucchini, parsnips

Per serving: Calories, 140; Protein, 4 g; Fat, 6 g (37% cal.); Cholesterol, 45 mg; Carbohydrates, 19 g; Fiber, 1 g; Sodium, 230 mg.

PROCEDURE

1. Combine the eggs and milk.
2. Mix together the flour, baking powder, salt, and sugar. Add to the milk and eggs and mix until smooth.
3. Let the batter stand for several hours in a refrigerator.
4. Stir the cold, cooked vegetables into the batter.
5. Drop with a No. 24 scoop into deep fat at 350°F (175°C). Hold the scoop just above the hot fat when dropping. Fry until golden brown.
6. Drain well and serve.

VARIATIONS

For lighter fritters, beat egg whites separately and fold into batter.

Fruit Fritters

Increase sugar to 2 oz (60 g). Use fresh, frozen, or canned fruits such as blueberries, diced pineapple, or apple. Fruit must be well drained.

Dust each portion with powdered sugar at service time. (Batter may be seasoned with cinnamon, vanilla, brandy, or other appropriate flavoring.)

Chiles Rellenos

PORTIONS: 16   PORTION SIZE: 1 PEPPER

U.S.	METRIC	INGREDIENTS
16	16	Chiles poblanos (see Note)
3 lb (approximately)	1.4 kg (approximately)	Picadillo (see Note)
12	12	Egg yolks
1 fl oz	30 mL	Water
1 oz	30 g	Flour, sifted
½ tsp	2 mL	Salt
12	12	Egg whites
as needed	as needed	Flour for dredging
3–4 pt	1.5–2 L	Tomato Broth for Chiles Rellenos (p. 180)

Per serving: Calories, 430; Protein, 24 g; Fat, 30 g (62% cal.); Cholesterol, 210 mg; Carbohydrates, 17 g; Fiber, 2 g; Sodium, 460 mg.

Note: Anaheim peppers or frying peppers may be used if poblanos are not available, but the results will not be as flavorful. The exact amount of filling needed depends on the size of the peppers.

VARIATIONS

For cheese-filled chiles, use chunks of American Muenster or Monterey jack cheese instead of the picadillo.

For baked chiles rellenos, omit the egg batter and simply bake the stuffed chiles in a casserole until they are heated through. Serve with the tomato broth as in the basic recipe.

PROCEDURE

1. Char the chiles over a gas flame until the skin is blackened. Rub off the blackened skin under running water.
2. Slit one side of each pepper and remove the seeds, but be careful to keep the peppers intact.
3. Stuff the peppers with the picadillo.
4. Beat the egg yolks and water slightly, then mix in the flour and salt.
5. Whip the whites until they form soft peaks. Fold them into the yolk mixture.
6. Carefully dust the filled peppers with flour, then dip in the egg batter. Deep-fry at 350°F (175°C) until lightly browned. (*Hint:* Carefully lower each pepper into the fat with the slit side up. If the slit tends to open, spoon a little of the batter over the slit. This helps keep the opening sealed and the filling inside the pepper.)
7. For each portion, ladle 3–4 fl oz (90–125 mL) broth into a broad serving bowl or soup plate. Place 1 chile in the center of the bowl and serve at once.

Chile Relleno

Suggested Vegetable Seasonings, Flavorings, and Combinations

Asparagus	Lemon juice, brown butter, mustard sauce, parmesan cheese; hard-cooked egg, peas, artichokes, mushrooms
Beans, green	Dill, basil, tarragon, oregano, garlic, brown butter, soy sauce; almonds, sesame seed, onion, tomato, celery, mushrooms, bacon
Beans, lima	Oregano, sage, thyme, sour cream, cheddar cheese; corn, peas, onions, mushrooms, pimiento, bacon
Beets	Lemon, allspice, caraway, cloves, dill, ginger, horseradish, bay leaf, orange, sour cream, onion
Broccoli	Lemon, mustard sauce, almonds, buttered and toasted bread crumbs, hard-cooked egg
Brussels sprouts	Caraway, dill, parmesan cheese, cheddar cheese, chestnuts
Cabbage	Caraway, celery seed, dill, mustard, nutmeg, garlic; bacon, ham, carrots, onion
Carrots	Parsley, dill, fennel, tarragon, ginger, nutmeg, bay leaves, caraway, mint, orange; celery, peas, zucchini
Cauliflower	Dill, nutmeg, mustard, curry, cheese, tomato sauce; hard-cooked egg, peas, almonds
Celery	Parsley, tarragon, onion, green or red pepper, potatoes
Corn	Chili powder, mild cheddar or jack cheese, tomato, bacon, lima beans
Cucumber	Dill, garlic, mint, tarragon; peas
Eggplant	Garlic, marjoram, oregano, parsley, parmesan cheese; tomato, chopped walnuts
Mushrooms	Nutmeg, parsley, lemon, paprika, dill, sherry, parmesan cheese, cayenne, heavy cream; peas, spinach, artichokes, green beans
Okra	Garlic, coriander, sage; tomatoes, corn
Onions	Nutmeg, sage, thyme, cheese sauce, sour cream; peas
Peas	Mint, basil, dill, sage; mushrooms, pearl onions, turnips, potatoes, carrots, water chestnuts, Jerusalem artichokes
Spinach	Nutmeg, garlic, heavy cream; mushrooms, hard-cooked egg, cheese
Squash, summer (including zucchini)	Cumin, basil, oregano, mustard seed, rosemary, garlic, parmesan cheese, parsley; tomato, carrots (with zucchini), onion, almonds, walnuts
Squash, winter	Cinnamon, nutmeg, allspice, cloves, ginger; apples, bacon, pecans
Sweet potatoes	Allspice, cinnamon, cloves, nutmeg, ginger, brandy, orange; almonds, apples, bananas
Tomatoes	Basil, bay leaf, garlic, celery seed, oregano, thyme, rosemary, chili powder; peppers, black olives
Turnips	Parsley, chives, nutmeg; mushrooms, potatoes, peas

QUESTIONS FOR DISCUSSION

1. Which vegetables would you simmer uncovered?

Asparagus	Cauliflower
Green beans	Peas
Beets	Sweet potatoes
Brussels sprouts	Rutabagas
Carrots	Turnips

2. Why are greens such as spinach not well suited to cooking in a compartment steamer?

3. In the recipe for Peas, Carrots, and Pearl Onions (p. 281), why could you not save a step and cook the three vegetables together in one pot?

4. Why is it important to drain vegetables well before combining with a cream sauce?

5. Which of the two methods for making glazed root vegetables (see Glazed Root Vegetables, p. 288, and Glazed Carrots, p. 288) might be more appropriate for à la carte service, or cooking to order? Why?

6. We have learned that green vegetables should be cooked in a neutral liquid because acids destroy green pigments. But the recipe for artichokes says to cook them with lemon juice. What's going on here?

7. Describe briefly how you would make breaded, fried onion rings rather than onion rings with batter.

Chapter 12

Potato and Eggplant Stew with Cilantro, page 319.

Potatoes

T**he eating habits** of most nations place a great deal of importance on a category of foods we call *starches*. In fact, for a large portion of the world's peoples, starch is the mainstay of the diet and supplies most of the day's calories. In North America and Europe, the most important starches are potatoes, rice, pasta, and bread. It is true we do not depend on these high-carbohydrate foods as much as many of the world's people, who eat far less meat than we do. Nevertheless, even as diet fashions and fads come and go, starches appear at nearly all our meals.

Because we eat them often and have devised a great many ways of preparing them, starchy foods require extra study beyond that which we give other vegetables. In this chapter, we turn our attention primarily to the preparation of our most important vegetable, the potato. Grains and other starches are discussed in Chapter 13.

After reading this chapter, you should be able to

1. Classify potatoes into two types, describe the general properties of each type, and identify the most suitable cooking method for each type.
2. Identify characteristics of high-quality potatoes, and describe how to store them.
3. Cook potatoes by boiling and steaming.
4. Prepare potato purée.
5. Cook potatoes by baking, sautéing, pan-frying, and deep-frying.

Understanding Potatoes

In classical cuisine, the potato is one of the most important of all foods. To many of us today, potatoes are considered an ordinary and humble food. Escoffier, however, treated the potato with great respect. His *Guide Culinaire* lists more than 50 potato preparations, far more than for any other vegetable or starch.

Considering how important the potato is in the cuisines of Europe and North America, it is surprising to think this vegetable wasn't widely used until the last half of the eighteenth century. Although the potato had been brought to Europe from the New World a few hundred years earlier, it wasn't until then that an army pharmacist named Antoine-Auguste Parmentier began promoting its use. To this day, many classical recipes featuring the potato are called *Parmentier* (par mawn tyay).

Botanically, the potato is a tuber, which is an enlarged underground stem with buds (or eyes) that become new shoots. Traditional main courses in western cooking feature a protein item, one or more vegetables, and a starch. The potato is, of course, a vegetable, but because of its high starch content it usually serves the same function on the menu as grains and other starchy foods.

Potatoes are traditionally classified as either starchy, low-moisture varieties or as waxy, high-moisture varieties. The following section summarizes the main characteristics of these two categories as well as traditional uses for each. Today, many potato varieties are available that were largely unknown not long ago. As always, chefs love to experiment with new foods and to find new uses for them. For example, they don't feel limited to russets for baking. So, after reading about the two main categories of potatoes below, continue to the next section for an introduction to some of the many varieties available today.

Types

Potatoes are classified according to their starch content. The amount of starch determines the use for which they are usually considered most suitable. Keep in mind that these categories are only general. Within each group is a range of starch and moisture content. For example, different varieties of *waxy potatoes* have different moisture content, depending not only on the variety of potato but also on the growing and storage conditions.

1. **Waxy potatoes.**

   High moisture content, high sugar content, low starch content.

   Usually small and round in shape, but some varieties can be large, and some may be elongated. Flesh is white, yellow, or even blue or purple. Skin is white, red, yellow, or blue.

   Hold shape well when cooked. Firm, moist texture. Use for boiling whole, for salads, soups, hash browns, and any preparation where the potato must hold its shape.

   Do not use for deep-frying. High sugar content will cause dark streaks and poor texture.

Waxy potatoes, clockwise from top left: small and large red-skinned potatoes, white potatoes, large and small yellow potatoes.

2. **Mature or starchy potatoes.**
   High starch content, low moisture and sugar. Light, dry, and mealy when cooked.

   - *Russets* or Idahos.
       Long, regularly shaped potatoes with slightly rough skin.
       Ideal choice for the traditional baked potato. Best potato for French fries because the high starch content produces an even, golden color and good texture. Also, the regular shape means little trimming loss.
       May be mashed, but is generally too expensive for that purpose.
       Sizes are indicated by count per 50-pound carton. For example, 100s average 8 ounces each.

   - *All-purpose potatoes* (sometimes called *chef potatoes*).
       Not as dry and starchy as russets.
       Irregularly shaped. Less expensive than russets.
       Suitable for most purposes, but not usually used for baking because of irregular shape. Especially useful for puréeing or mashing, or any preparation in which the shape of the whole potato is not important.
       Note: Very knobby potatoes are wasteful when pared in a mechanical peeler.

Starchy potatoes, left to right: russet potatoes, all-purpose or chef potatoes.

Varieties

For most of us, selecting the right potato for a particular preparation means selecting from among russets, all-purpose potatoes, and red- or white-skinned boiling potatoes, as these are often the only types found in the kitchen. For basic potato cookery, then, the information in the preceding section tells us what we need to know. Today's chefs, however, can use more information in order to take advantage of the many varieties of potato available today, as growers discover new varieties and rediscover heirloom potato varieties. The following are some of the many potatoes available.

First, the term *new potato* needs explanation. Not all small potatoes are new potatoes, and not all new potatoes are small. Normally, potatoes are not harvested until the green, bushy tops turn brown and die back. At this point, the potatoes are mature. Their skin has thickened, and their starch content has developed. Any potato harvested before it is mature, while leaves and stems are still green, is a new potato. Because new potatoes have not matured, they have a lower starch content and tender, thin skin. Although most new potatoes are small, usually less than 1½ inches (4 cm) in diameter, this is not always the case.

New potatoes are shipped and sold as soon as they are harvested. By contrast, potatoes that are harvested mature are held at a controlled temperature and humidity for about two weeks in order to toughen their skins further and heal cuts and other damage. This curing process gives the potatoes greater keeping quality.

Russets, often called *Idaho potatoes* because so many russets are grown in that state, are high-starch potatoes with a regular, elongated shape, brown or reddish-brown, rough skin, and white flesh. These are the standard choice for baking and deep-frying.

All-purpose potatoes are also white-fleshed potatoes. They have a moderate starch content and moderate moisture, making them suitable for many kinds of preparations, indicated in the previous section. White-fleshed potatoes may also be harvested young, when they have more moisture, less starch, and a thin skin. Young white potatoes are used mostly for boiling.

Yellow-fleshed potatoes include many varieties. *Yukon Gold* is a round, medium-size potato that ranges from waxy to somewhat starchy, depending on age and growing conditions. They are used for many purposes, including baking. *Yellow Finn* is also used for baking; it has a smooth, creamy texture when baked, unlike the grainy, starchy texture of baked russets. Other yellow potatoes include *Bintje* (waxy), *Butte* (fairly starchy), *Concord* (waxy), *Charlotte* (waxy), and *Island Sunshine* (medium starch).

Blue potatoes (All-Blue)

Fingerling potatoes

Red-skinned varieties may have white, pink, or yellow flesh. Most of them are of the waxy type. *Red Bliss* has long been one of the most popular waxy potatoes. Other red-skinned potatoes include *All-Red* (pink flesh), *Early Ohio* (white flesh), *Early Rose* (white flesh), and *Rose Gold* (yellow flesh).

Blue-skinned, white-fleshed varieties are similar to red-skinned varieties, except their skins range in color from dark reddish blue to purple. When cooked, the skins may keep their color or turn brown, grayish, or another color, depending on the variety. Several varieties are grown, including *Blue Pride*, *Caribe*, and *Kerry Blue*.

Blue- or purple-fleshed varieties are the novelty item among potatoes. They may be waxy or somewhat starchy, depending on the variety. The two most common purple-fleshed potatoes are *Peruvian Blue*, also called *Purple Peruvian*, with dark violet flesh that lightens somewhat when cooked, and *All-Blue*, with purple or reddish purple flesh that becomes lavender when cooked.

Fingerling potatoes are small potatoes, usually firm and waxy, with a long, narrow shape. Most popular fingerlings are yellow-skinned and yellow-fleshed, but red-skinned, yellow-fleshed fingerlings, red-skinned, pink-fleshed fingerlings, and purple fingerlings are also grown. Among the available varieties are *Austrian Crescent* (yellow), *French Fingerling* (red skin, yellow flesh), *Russian Banana* (yellow), *La Ratte* (yellow), *Ruby Crescent* (pinkish yellow skin, yellow flesh), and *Red Thumb* (red skin, pink flesh).

Each of these varieties has a slightly different flavor, texture, and cooking characteristics. Experiment with any variety you find available and adapt it to the most appropriate preparations.

Checking for Quality

Look for these signs of high-quality potatoes:

1. Firm and smooth, not soft or shriveled.

2. Dry skin.

3. Shallow eyes.

4. No sprouts. Sprouting potatoes are high in sugar.

5. No green color. Green areas develop on potatoes stored in light. These areas contain a substance called *solanine*, which has a bitter taste and is poisonous in large quantities. All green parts should be cut off before cooking.

6. Absence of cracks, blemishes, and rotten spots.

Storing and Handling

Keep potatoes in a cool, dry, dark place, ideally at 55°–60°F (13°–16°C). If they will be used quickly, you may keep them at room temperature.

Do not refrigerate. Temperatures below 45°F (7°C) convert potato starch to sugar. Refrigerated potatoes must be stored at 50°F (10°C) for two weeks to change the sugar back to starch.

New potatoes do not keep well. Purchase only one week's supply at a time.

Potatoes begin to turn brown as soon as they are peeled. To prevent browning, place peeled potatoes in cold water immediately. Potatoes may be peeled in advance and stored a short time under water, although some nutrients will be lost.

Remove all green parts when peeling potatoes (see "Checking for Quality" above).

Market Forms

The demands of time and labor have made processed potato products widely used, and many forms are available. Many of these products are very good, and there is no doubt they save time. However, for best quality, there is no substitute for fresh potatoes, *if they are well prepared.*

1. **Fresh, unprocessed.**

2. **Peeled. Treated to prevent browning.**
   Keep refrigerated (below 40°F/4°C) for five to seven days.

3. **Canned whole, cooked.**

4. **French fries. Blanched in deep fat and frozen.**
   Available in a wide variety of sizes and cuts. Cook from the frozen state.
   Refrigerated French fries are also available.

5. **Other frozen, prepared products.**
   Available as hash browns, puffs, stuffed baked, and croquettes; in casseroles with a
   variety of sauces.

6. **Dehydrated.**
   Granules or flakes for mashed potatoes to be reconstituted with hot water or milk and
   butter or other desired flavorings.
   Other products: many varieties and preparations. May need soaking in water
   before cooking.

KEY POINTS TO REVIEW

- What are the differences between waxy and starchy potatoes? Give examples of each, and indicate what kinds of preparation each is appropriate for.

- How do you check potatoes for quality?

- How should potatoes be stored?

Cooking Potatoes

Some potato recipes are simple, but many are complex and use a combination of cooking methods. For example, to make potato croquettes, you must first boil or steam the potatoes, purée them and combine the purée with other ingredients, shape them, bread them, and, finally, deep-fry them.

Cooking methods are essentially the same as the methods for vegetables discussed in the previous chapter. If necessary, review these methods before proceeding with the following recipes.

Boiling and Steaming Potatoes

These methods for cooking potatoes are given in the first recipe in this section. Boiled or steamed potatoes are served as is and are also the basis for many other preparations.

Potatoes are peeled or left unpeeled for boiling and steaming. For most purposes, they are peeled. Peel thoroughly with a swivel peeler and remove all eyes. Place peeled potatoes immediately in a container of cold water to prevent browning.

If potatoes are cooked with the skins on and peeled after cooking, it is best to peel while they are still hot because the skins pull off more easily. New potatoes are usually cooked and served with the skins on. Fingerling potatoes are peeled after cooking if the skins are tough, or they may be served with the skins on if tender.

Two additional points should be noted:

1. Boiled potatoes are generally started in cold water rather than hot. This allows for more even cooking and heat penetration from outside to inside during the relatively long cooking time required.

2. Potatoes are never cooled in cold water, unlike most vegetables. This would make them soggy.

Boiled Potatoes (Pommes Natures)

PORTIONS: 25   PORTION SIZE: 5 OZ (150 G)

U.S.	METRIC	INGREDIENTS
10 lb	4.5 kg	Potatoes

Per serving: Calories, 140; Protein, 3 g; Fat, 0 g (0% cal.); Cholesterol, 0 mg; Carbohydrates, 32 g; Fiber, 3 g; Sodium, 10 mg.

Note: Potatoes may be cut, shaped, or trimmed as desired. They may be left in neat but irregular shapes, trimmed or tournéed into large, medium, or small sizes, or cut with a ball scoop for parisienne boiled potatoes. Allow for greater trimming loss if preparing tournéed or parisienne potatoes.

VARIATIONS

Steamed Potatoes (Pommes Vapeurs)
Prepare as in basic recipe, but steam in perforated pan instead of boiling.

Parsley Potatoes
Prepare as in basic recipe. Brush or pour 4 oz (125 mL) melted butter onto the potatoes and sprinkle with chopped parsley.

New Potatoes
Prepare as in basic recipe, using small new potatoes. Scrub well, but do not peel. Serve 1–3 per portion, depending on size.
Optional: Peel a narrow band around each potato before cooking to prevent skin from splitting.

Creamed Potatoes
Prepare new potatoes or all-purpose potatoes as in basic recipe. Cut or slice to desired size, or leave small new potatoes whole. Combine with 2 qt (2 L) hot cream sauce. Heat over low heat, but do not boil, and hold for service.

PROCEDURE

1. Peel and eye potatoes. Be sure all traces of dark peel are removed.

2. Cut potatoes into 25 uniform portions, 1 or 2 pieces per portion. Trim pieces to shape (see Note). Save the trimmings for other use.

3. Place in a pot and cover with salted water. Bring to boil, lower heat, and simmer until tender.

4. Drain and let the potatoes steam dry in the colander for a minute. Alternatively, spread on a sheet pan and dry in a warm oven just until they stop steaming.

5. Serve immediately or place in a hotel pan, cover with a clean, damp towel, and hold for service.

Potato and Eggplant Stew with Cilantro

PORTIONS: 12   PORTION SIZE: 6 OZ (180 G)

U.S.	METRIC	INGREDIENTS	PROCEDURE
2 fl oz	60 mL	Vegetable oil	1. Heat the oil in a large saucepot over moderate heat.
2 tsp	10 mL	Cumin seeds	2. Add the cumin. Cook until the seeds are aromatic and start to darken, 15 to 20 seconds.
12 oz	337 mL	Onion, chopped fine	
2 tbsp	30 mL	Finely chopped garlic	3. Add the onion, garlic, ginger, and turmeric. Sauté until the onions are soft and lightly browned.
2 tbsp	30 mL	Grated fresh ginger root	
½ tsp	2 mL	Turmeric	4. Add the eggplant and stir together with the onion. Sauté 2 minutes.
1½ lb	750 g	Eggplant, peeled, medium dice	5. Add the potatoes, tomatoes, and water. Cover and simmer until the potatoes are tender. Stir occasionally, and add a little more water if the potatoes become dry.
2 lb	1 kg	Potatoes, medium dice	
1 lb	500 g	Tomatoes, canned, chopped, with their juice	
6 fl oz	180 mL	Water	6. Stir in the cilantro.
4 tbsp	60 mL	Chopped fresh cilantro	7. Season with salt.
to taste	to taste	Salt	

Per serving: Calories, 140; Protein, 3 g; Fat, 5 g (31% cal.); Cholesterol, 0 mg; Carbohydrates, 22 g; Fiber, 4 g; Sodium, 55 mg.

Potato and Eggplant Stew with Cilantro

Potato Purée

Potato purée is an important product in most kitchens, even though it is not served as is. It is the basis of many popular preparations, including mashed or whipped potatoes, *duchesse potatoes*, and potato croquettes. (Please note that this usage of the term is different from classic European usage, where *purée de pommes de terre* indicates mashed or whipped potatoes.)

Starchy potatoes are usually used for purées. The flesh of starchy potatoes breaks apart easily and can absorb large quantities of butter, milk, and other enriching ingredients. Moderately waxy potatoes can also be puréed. The flesh doesn't break apart as easily, however, so they are harder to purée. Also, they don't absorb as much fat or liquid.

Avoid excessive mixing of potato purée. Too much whipping or mixing damages cell walls, releasing excess starch that makes the purée gluey in texture.

Following is the basic procedure for making potato purées.

Procedure for Making Potato Purée

1. Select starchy or moderately waxy potatoes.

2. Wash, peel, and eye carefully.

3. Cut into uniform sizes for even cooking.

4. Simmer or steam until tender. Potatoes for purée must be thoroughly cooked, or the purée will be grainy, but they must not be overcooked, or it will be watery.

5. Drain in a colander (if simmered). Set the colander on a sheet pan and place in an oven for several minutes to dry out the potatoes. If potatoes are too moist, they will be too loose or slack when liquid is added later.

6. While the potatoes are still hot, pass them through a food mill or ricer to purée. A mixer with the paddle attachment may be used to break up the potatoes for whipped potatoes, but there is no guarantee it will remove all lumps.

   Equipment used for puréeing should not be cold, or it will cool the potatoes too much. Heat equipment under hot water before use.

7. Add ingredients to the purée as indicated in the individual recipe. Avoid excessive mixing in order to prevent glueyness.

KEY POINTS TO REVIEW

- What guidelines should be observed when boiling potatoes?

- What are the steps in the basic procedure for making potato purée?

- What are the ingredients in duchesse potatoes?

 # Mashed or Whipped Potatoes

PORTIONS: 25   PORTION SIZE: 5 OZ (150 G)

U.S.	METRIC	INGREDIENTS
9 lb	4 kg	Potatoes
6 oz	175 g	Butter
1 cup	250 mL	Light cream, hot
as needed	as needed	Milk, hot
to taste	to taste	Salt
to taste	to taste	White pepper

Per serving: Calories, 190; Protein, 3 g; Fat, 8 g (36% cal.); Cholesterol, 20 mg; Carbohydrates, 29 g; Fiber, 3g; Sodium, 65 mg.

PROCEDURE

1. Peel and eye the potatoes and cut them into uniform sizes. Simmer in salted water to cover until tender.

2. Drain well and let the potatoes steam dry for a few minutes.

3. Pass the potatoes through a food mill or ricer into the bowl of a mixer. Alternative method: Place potatoes in mixer with paddle attachment. Mix until well broken up. Replace paddle with whip and beat until well puréed. Do not overwhip, or potatoes will become pasty.

4. Beat in butter, then cream.

5. Add enough hot milk to bring potatoes to proper consistency. They should be soft and moist, but firm enough to hold their shape, not runny.

6. Add salt and white pepper to taste.

7. If desired, whip *briefly* at high speed until potatoes are light and fluffy. Do not overwhip.

VARIATIONS

Garlic Mashed Potatoes

Method 1: Simmer 6–8 whole, peeled cloves of garlic with the potatoes. Purée the garlic and the potatoes together.

Method 2: Purée 1 or 2 heads roasted garlic (p. 304) and mix into the potatoes before adding cream.

Duchesse Potatoes

PORTIONS: 25   PORTION SIZE: 4 OZ (100 G)

U.S.	METRIC	INGREDIENTS
7 lb	3 kg	Potatoes, peeled and quartered
4 oz	100 g	Butter, melted
to taste	to taste	Salt
to taste	to taste	White pepper
to taste	to taste	Nutmeg
10	10	Egg yolks
as needed	as needed	Egg wash (optional)

PROCEDURE

1. Steam the potatoes or simmer them in salted water until tender. Drain in a colander and let dry in an oven several minutes.

2. Pass the potatoes through a food mill or ricer.

3. Add butter and mix to a smooth paste. Season to taste with salt, pepper, and just a little nutmeg (the potatoes should not taste strongly of nutmeg).

4. If the potatoes are very moist, stir over a low flame to stiffen. They must be much stiffer than mashed potatoes.

5. Add the egg yolks (off the fire) and beat until smooth.

6. Put the mixture in a pastry bag with a star tube and bag out into desired shapes on sheet pans or as platter borders (see **Figure 11.1**). Cone-shaped spiral mounds are most popular for individual portion service.

7. If desired, brush lightly with egg wash for greater browning.

8. At service time, place potatoes in hot oven (400°–425°F/200°–230°C) until lightly browned. Platter borders may be browned under the salamander.

Per serving: Calories, 150; Protein, 3 g; Fat, 6 g (34% cal.); Cholesterol, 95 mg; Carbohydrates, 23 g; Fiber, 2 g; Sodium, 45 mg.

VARIATION

Duchesse potato mixture is also used as the base for Potato Croquettes (p. 334). It is considered one of the basic hot kitchen preparations.

Figure 11.1 Using the pastry bag: duchesse potatoes.

(a) Turn down the top of the pastry bag as shown. Slip your hand under this collar and hold the top open with your thumb and forefinger while you fill it with duchesse potato mixture.

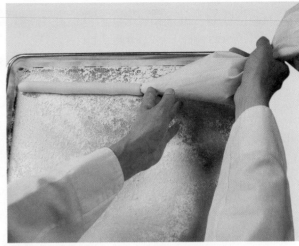

(b) Turn the top of the bag up again and gather the loose top together as shown. Hold the bag shut with your thumb and forefinger. To force out the potatoes, squeeze the top of the bag in the palm of your hand. Use your free hand to guide the tip or hold the item being filled or decorated. You can make potato croquettes quickly by forcing out the potato mixture in long strips, using a large plain tube. Cut the strips into 2-in. (5-cm) lengths with a knife.

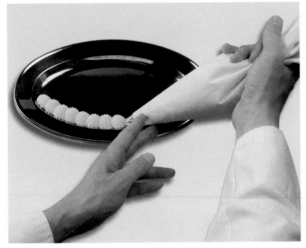

(c) Duchesse potatoes are often used to decorate platters, as in this illustration. This technique is also used in decorating cakes and desserts with icing, whipped cream, or meringue.

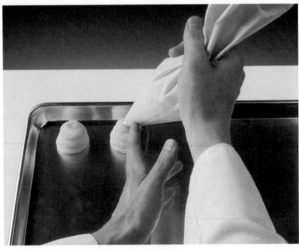

(d) Single portions of duchesse potatoes are usually piped out into a tall spiral shape. They are then browned in the oven.

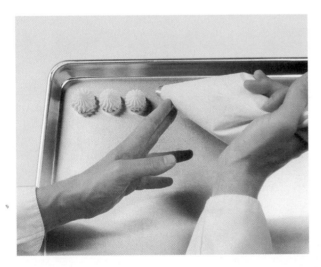

(e) Dauphine and Lorette potatoes may be bagged out into many shapes, such as these small stars. Some cookies are also shaped this way.

Baking

Preparing baked potatoes is a simple procedure that is widely misunderstood and therefore needlessly complicated. Properly baked potatoes are white, fluffy, mealy, and steamy, and they have a dry skin that crackles slightly when pressed. Poorly baked potatoes, unfortunately common, are gray and soggy and have a damp, soft skin.

Russet potatoes are most often used for baked potatoes. However, many varieties are now available, some of which are excellent for baking and yield different flavors and textures. Don't be afraid to experiment with some of the varieties listed on pages 315–316.

Procedure for Baking Potatoes

1. For standard baked potatoes, select russets or other regularly shaped starchy potatoes.

2. Scrub well and pierce the ends with a fork or skewer so steam can escape.

3. For crisp skins, rub lightly with oil. For more tender skins, leave dry.

4. Place on sheet pans or on sheet pan racks in a preheated 400°F (200°C) oven and bake until done, about 1 hour. To test doneness, squeeze gently. Done potatoes yield to gentle pressure.

    Note: Using sheet pan racks eliminates the hard spot that forms where the potato is in contact with the sheet pan.

5. Remove from oven.

6. To hold for service, keep warm and uncovered so the potatoes will not be made soggy by trapped steam. Hold no more than 1 hour, if possible, though they will keep longer with some loss of quality.

    Note that nothing was said about wrapping potatoes in foil. Foil-wrapped potatoes do not bake but rather steam in their own moisture. The texture of a steamed potato is entirely different from that of a baked potato. Save yourself the trouble and expense of wrapping in foil and serve a better product.

 # Baked Potatoes

PORTION SIZE: 1 POTATO

U.S.	METRIC	INGREDIENTS
as needed	as needed	Idaho or baking potatoes
as needed	as needed	Vegetable oil (optional)

Per serving: Calories, 130; Protein, 3 g; Fat, 0 g (0% cal.); Cholesterol, 0 mg; Carbohydrates, 31 g; Fiber, 3 g; Sodium, 10 mg.

PROCEDURE

1. Scrub the potatoes well and pierce the ends with a skewer or fork to allow steam to escape.

2. Lightly oil the potatoes if a crisp skin is desired. Leave them dry for a somewhat softer skin.

3. Place on sheet pan in 400°F (200°C) oven. Bake until done, about 1 hour. Test for doneness by squeezing a potato gently.

Stuffed Baked Potatoes

PORTIONS: 10   PORTION SIZE: 1 POTATO

U.S.	METRIC	INGREDIENTS
10	10	Baking potatoes, 7–8 oz (200–225 g) each
2 oz	60 g	Butter, melted
4 oz	100 mL	Light cream or milk, hot
to taste	to taste	Salt
to taste	to taste	White pepper
3 tbsp	45 mL	Dry bread crumbs
1 oz	30 g	Butter, melted
3 tbsp	45 mL	Parmesan cheese, grated

Per serving: Calories, 270; Protein, 5 g; Fat, 10 g (32% cal.); Cholesterol, 30 mg; Carbohydrates, 42 g; Fiber, 4 g; Sodium, 140 mg.

PROCEDURE

1. Bake the potatoes according to the basic method.

2. Remove from the oven. Cut a slice off the top of each potato and scoop out the pulp, leaving a shell about ¼ in. (½ cm) thick.

3. Pass the pulp through a food mill or ricer. Beat in the butter and enough cream or milk to make a smooth purée. Season to taste. (Note that this preparation is basically the same as whipped potatoes.)

4. Fill the potato shells with the purée, using a pastry bag or kitchen spoon. (A pastry bag is faster and neater.) Place them on a baking sheet.

5. Mix the bread crumbs and melted butter until all the crumbs are moistened. Then mix in the parmesan cheese and top the potatoes with this mixture.

6. Place in hot oven (400°F/200°C) until potatoes are heated through and tops are browned, about 15 minutes.

VARIATIONS

For each variation listed, add the indicated ingredients to the potato purée mixture. Proportions are for 2½–3 lb (1.1–1.4 kg) purée.

1. 2 oz (60 g) grated parmesan cheese
2. 8 oz (225 g) minced onion, sautéed in butter
3. 4 oz (100 g) cooked ham, small dice
   4 oz (100 g) mushrooms, chopped and sautéed in butter
4. 8 oz (225 g) bacon, diced and cooked crisp
   1 green pepper, chopped and sautéed in butter or bacon fat

Macaire Potatoes

Scoop out the pulp completely and discard the skins. Mash the pulp with a kitchen fork or break it up with the paddle of a mixer. Omit the melted butter and cream or milk. Instead, mix in 7 oz (200 g) soft butter. Season. Form into small cakes and pan-fry in clarified butter until golden brown on both sides.

Oven Roast Potatoes

PORTIONS: 25   PORTION SIZE: 4 OZ (125 G)

U.S.	METRIC	INGREDIENTS
10 lb AP	4.5 kg AP	Potatoes
as needed	as needed	Vegetable oil or olive oil
to taste	to taste	Salt
to taste	to taste	White pepper

Per serving: Calories, 160; Protein, 3 g; Fat, 2.5 g (14% cal.); Cholesterol, 0 mg; Carbohydrates, 32 g; Fiber, 3 g; Sodium, 10 mg.

PROCEDURE

1. Peel and eye potatoes. Cut into 25 uniform portions and trim pieces to shape. Save the trimmings for other use.

2. Dry the potatoes well and rub with oil. Place in oiled baking pan and season with salt and pepper.

3. Place in 400°F (200°C) oven and bake until browned and cooked through, about 1 hour. Halfway through baking time, turn potatoes and brush with additional oil.

Roasted New Potatoes with Herbs and Garlic

PORTIONS: 10   PORTION SIZE: 4 OZ (125 G)

U.S.	METRIC	INGREDIENTS
3 lb	1.5 kg	New potatoes, fingerling potatoes, or other small potatoes
3 fl oz	90 mL	Olive oil
2 tbsp	30 mL	Fresh rosemary, coarsely chopped
1 tbsp	15 mL	Fresh thyme
2 tbsp	30 mL	Finely chopped garlic
2 tsp	10 mL	Salt

Per serving: Calories, 270; Protein, 5 g; Fat, 8 g (26% cal.); Cholesterol, 0 mg; Carbohydrates, 45 g; Fiber, 4 g; Sodium, 480 mg.

PROCEDURE

1. Wash the potatoes, drain, and let dry.
2. Cut round potatoes in half, or, if using small fingerlings, leave them whole.
3. Place the potatoes in a roasting pan.
4. Pour the oil over the potatoes and sprinkle with the herbs, garlic, and salt. Toss or mix so all the potatoes are coated.
5. Bake at 400°F (200°C) until the potatoes are tender, about 45 minutes.

Roasted New Potatoes with Herbs and Garlic

Baked "En Casserole"

A number of preparations call for potatoes baked in a baking pan or casserole, with or without liquid added. The best-known is scalloped potatoes. A characteristic of most of these preparations is that they are baked uncovered at least part of the time so a brown crust forms on top. (Note that two versions of Gratin Dauphinoise are included here. The first is a modern version, while the second is a more traditional version.)

Scalloped Potatoes

PORTIONS: 25   PORTION SIZE: 5 OZ (150 G)

U.S.	METRIC	INGREDIENTS
2½ qt	2.5 L	Milk
3 oz	90 g	Butter
3 oz	90 g	Flour
2 tsp	10 mL	Salt
to taste	to taste	White pepper
7½ lb	3.5 kg	Potatoes

Per serving: Calories, 200; Protein, 6 g; Fat, 6 g (27% cal.); Cholesterol, 20 mg; Carbohydrates, 31 g; Fiber, 2 g; Sodium, 80 mg.

Note: Unthickened milk may be used instead of a thin white sauce, but the milk is more likely to curdle. The roux helps prevent curdling.

PROCEDURE

1. Make a thin white sauce (béchamel) using the ingredients listed (see p. 159). Keep hot while preparing the potatoes.
2. Peel and eye the potatoes. Cut into slices ⅛ in. (3 mm) thick.
3. Place the potatoes in a buttered baking pan, making several layers.
4. Pour in the white sauce. Lift the potatoes slightly so the sauce can run between the layers.
5. Cover with foil or greased paper and place in oven at 350°F (175°C) for 30 minutes.
6. Uncover and continue to bake until top is lightly browned and potatoes are tender.

VARIATIONS

Scalloped Potatoes with Onions
Add 1¼ lb (600 g) sliced onions to baking pan with the potatoes.

Scalloped Potatoes with Cheese
Add 1 lb (500 g) shredded cheddar cheese to baking pan with potatoes. Top with additional cheese before browning.

Scalloped Potatoes with Ham
Add 2½ lb (1.4 kg) diced ham.

Gratin Dauphinoise I

PORTIONS: 24   PORTION SIZE: 4 OZ (125 G)

U.S.	METRIC	INGREDIENTS
5 lb	2.5 kg	Firm-fleshed potatoes
2 tsp	10 mL	Salt
¼ oz	7 g	Garlic, chopped
1 qt	1 L	Cream
1 pt	500 mL	Milk
to taste	to taste	White pepper

Per serving: Calories, 300; Protein, 4 g; Fat, 23 g (67 % cal.); Cholesterol, 85 mg; Carbohydrates, 21 g; Fiber, 2 g; Sodium, 490 mg.

PROCEDURE

1. Peel the potatoes and cut into thin slices (as for potato chips). Do not place the sliced potatoes in water.
2. Toss the potatoes in the salt and garlic and arrange in an even layer in a buttered full-size hotel pan or a roasting pan of equivalent size.
3. Mix the cream and milk and lightly season with pepper. Bring to a boil.
4. Pour over the potatoes, then place the pan in the oven at 400°F (200°C) for about 30 minutes, or until the potatoes are tender and the sauce is thick.

Gratin Dauphinoise

Gratin Dauphinoise II

PORTIONS: 15   PORTION SIZE: 5 OZ (150 G)

U.S.	METRIC	INGREDIENTS
3 lb	1.4 kg	Potatoes
to taste	to taste	Salt
to taste	to taste	White pepper
to taste	to taste	Nutmeg
½ lb	225 g	Gruyère cheese, grated
1 pt	500 mL	Milk
1 cup	250 mL	Heavy cream
3	3	Egg yolks

Per serving: Calories, 220; Protein, 8 g; Fat, 13 g (53% cal.); Cholesterol, 85 mg; Carbohydrates, 18 g; Fiber, 1g; Sodium, 80 mg.

PROCEDURE

1. Peel and eye the potatoes. Cut into very thin slices.
2. Place some of the potatoes in a layer in a buttered baking pan. Season with salt, pepper, and a very small amount of nutmeg. Sprinkle with a little of the cheese. Repeat until all the potatoes and about three-fourths of the cheese are used up.
3. Combine the milk and half the cream and heat to a simmer. Beat the egg yolks with the remaining cream. Slowly stir in the hot milk mixture.
4. Pour the milk mixture over the potatoes. Top with remaining cheese.
5. Bake uncovered at 350°F (175°C) until done, 45–60 minutes.

VARIATION

Savoyarde Potatoes
Prepare as above, but use chicken stock instead of milk.

Boulangère Potatoes

PORTIONS: 25   PORTION SIZE: 5 OZ (150 G)

U.S.	METRIC	INGREDIENTS
2½ lb	1.1 kg	Onions, sliced
5 oz	150 g	Butter or fat drippings from roast (see Note)
7½ lb	3.5 kg	Potatoes, peeled and cut into thick slices
1 qt	1 L	Stock, chicken or lamb (if available), hot
to taste	to taste	Salt
to taste	to taste	Pepper

PROCEDURE

1. Sauté the onions in butter or fat until they are translucent and just beginning to brown.
2. Add the potatoes and toss until coated with fat.
3. Place in a baking pan or in a roasting pan under a partially cooked roast. Pour in the hot stock. Season.
4. Bake 1–1½ hours at 350°F (175°C) or at the roasting temperature of lamb, until potatoes are done. Add more stock during cooking if necessary to keep potatoes from drying out.

Per serving: Calories, 160; Protein, 3 g; Fat, 5 g (27% cal.); Cholesterol, 15 mg; Carbohydrates, 28 g; Fiber, 3 g; Sodium, 55 mg.

Note: Boulangère potatoes may be cooked separately, but they are usually cooked with a roast, especially leg of lamb.

If the potatoes are cooked with a roast, they must be added to the pan at the right time so they will be done at the same time as the meat.

Potatoes au Gratin

PORTIONS: 25   PORTION SIZE: 6 OZ (175 G)

U.S.	METRIC	INGREDIENTS
7½ lb	3.5 kg	Potatoes
2 qt	2 L	Cheddar Cheese Sauce (p. 160), hot
⅔ cup	150 mL	Dry bread crumbs
2 tsp	10 mL	Paprika
2 oz	60 g	Butter, melted (optional)

PROCEDURE

1. Scrub the potatoes and simmer or steam them until tender but still firm.
2. Drain and spread on sheet pan to cool.
3. When the potatoes are cool enough to handle, peel and cut them into uniform ⅜-in. (1-cm) dice.
4. Combine with the hot cheese sauce in a baking pan.
5. Mix the bread crumbs and paprika and sprinkle over the potatoes. Drizzle the butter evenly over the top.
6. Bake at 350°F (175°C) about 30 minutes, or until hot and browned.

Per serving: Calories, 190; Protein, 7 g; Fat, 6 g (29% cal.); Cholesterol, 20 mg; Carbohydrates, 26 g; Fiber, 2 g; Sodium, 150 mg.

Note: Cream sauce may be used instead of cheese sauce. Grated cheese (cheddar or parmesan) may be sprinkled over the potatoes before topping them with bread crumbs.

Anna Potatoes

PORTIONS: 10   PORTION SIZE: 5 OZ (150 G)

U.S.	METRIC	INGREDIENTS
4 lb AP	1.8 kg AP	Boiling potatoes
12 oz	350 g	Butter
to taste	to taste	Salt
to taste	to taste	White pepper

Per serving: Calories, 260; Protein, 3 g; Fat, 14 g (47 % cal.); Cholesterol, 35 mg; Carbohydrates, 32 g; Fiber, 3 g; Sodium, 150 mg.

Note: Small molds may be used instead of the large pan for individual service.

PROCEDURE

1. Select round, uniformly sized potatoes. The appearance of this dish is important, so the slices should be neat and even.

2. Peel and eye the potatoes and cut into thin slices. Hold in cold water until ready to use.

3. Clarify the butter (see p. 168).

4. Heat about ¼ in. (0.5 cm) butter in a heavy 9-in. (23-cm) cast-iron skillet. The skillet must be well seasoned so the potatoes will not stick. Remove from heat.

5. Drain the potatoes and dry them well. Select the most uniform slices for the bottom layer. Arrange the slices in circles in the bottom of the pan. Shingle the slices and reverse the direction of each circle. See **Figure 11.2** for illustration of this technique. Season this layer with salt and pepper and ladle some clarified butter over it.

6. Continue making layers, seasoning and buttering each layer, until the ingredients are used up. The potatoes will be mounded over the top of the pan, but they will compress as they cook. There will be a great deal of butter in the pan, but it will be drained after cooking and can be reused.

7. Place the pan over a moderate fire and heat until the pan is sizzling. Shake the pan lightly to make sure the potatoes are not sticking.

8. Cover with foil and bake in a hot oven (450°F/230°C) about 40 minutes, or until potatoes are tender. Test for doneness by piercing center with paring knife. Remove the foil and bake 10 minutes more.

9. Drain off excess butter (remember that it's hot!) and carefully invert the potato cake onto a baking sheet. The potatoes should have stayed intact in a round cake, but if any slices fall off, put them back in place. Set the potatoes back in the oven if necessary for even browning.

10. Cut into wedges for service.

VARIATION

Voisin Potatoes

Prepare as in basic recipe, but sprinkle each layer of potatoes with grated Swiss cheese.

Figure 11.2 Anna Potatoes.

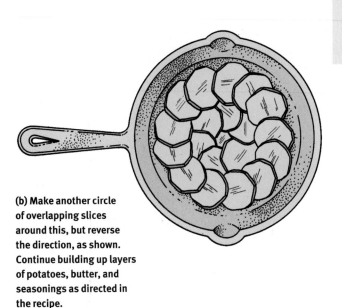

(a) Place one potato slice in the center of the prepared pan. Make a circle of overlapping slices around it.

(b) Make another circle of overlapping slices around this, but reverse the direction, as shown. Continue building up layers of potatoes, butter, and seasonings as directed in the recipe.

Sautéing and Pan-Frying

The procedures for sautéing and pan-frying potatoes are basically the same as for other vegetables (p. 292).

There are many sautéed and pan-fried potato preparations. Some are made with raw potatoes, others with precooked or blanched potatoes. Many of these recipes are especially useful because they are excellent ways to utilize leftover boiled potatoes.

This group of recipes may be divided into two categories based on production technique.

1. **Potatoes mixed or tossed while cooking.**

   The procedure for sautéing vegetables, page 292, is used for these preparations. The potatoes are cut into pieces or into small shapes and cooked in a small amount of fat. They are turned or tossed in the pan so they brown on all sides. This category includes rissola, parisienne, noisette, château, and American fried or home-fried potatoes.

2. **Potatoes cooked and served in compact cakes.**

   The procedure for pan-frying vegetables (see p. 292) is the basic method used for these preparations. The potatoes are not mixed while cooking but are made into cakes, which are browned on both sides. This category includes hash browns and variations as well as potato pancakes and macaire potatoes (see p. 324).

 # Rissolé or Cocotte Potatoes

PORTIONS: 25   PORTIONS SIZE: 4 OZ (125 G)

U.S.	METRIC	INGREDIENTS
14 lb	7 kg	Potatoes (see Note)
10 oz	300 g	Clarified butter
to taste	to taste	Salt
to taste	to taste	White pepper

Per serving: Calories, 290; Protein, 4 g; Fat, 11g (34% cal.); Cholesterol, 30 mg; Carbohydrates, 45 g; Fiber, 4 g; Sodium, 125 mg.

Note: The quantity of potatoes needed varies depending on how heavily they are trimmed. Save trimmings for purées or other uses.

PROCEDURE

1. Peel and eye the potatoes and trim or tourné them into small oval shapes about 1½ in. (4 cm) long.
2. Place the potatoes in a saucepan, cover with salted water, and bring to a boil. Reduce heat and simmer 7–8 minutes, or until about three-fourths cooked.
3. Drain and turn out onto a sheet pan to steam dry.
4. Heat the clarified butter in a large sauté pan. Add the potatoes and sauté over moderate heat until golden brown and fully cooked. (Potatoes may also be browned in deep fat if speed of service is critical.)
5. Season with salt and pepper.

VARIATIONS

Alternative Method: Potatoes may be sautéed without prior blanching. Sauté over low heat and keep covered during the first half or three-fourths of the cooking period so the potatoes cook fully without overbrowning. Potatoes cooked this way absorb more butter than those that are blanched first. Thus they are tastier, but they also are higher in calories.

Parisienne and Noisette Potatoes

Prepare as in basic recipe, but cut potatoes with a melon ball cutter. Parisienne potatoes are cut with a scoop slightly larger than 1 in. (about 3 cm). Noisette potatoes are smaller than 1 in. (about 2.5 cm). Blanch 3–5 minutes or cook from raw state.

Château Potatoes

Prepare as in basic recipe, but tourné the potatoes into larger ovals, about 2 in. (5 cm) long.

Hash Brown Potatoes

PORTIONS: 25   PORTION SIZE: 4½ OZ (125 G)

U.S.	METRIC	INGREDIENTS
7½ lb	3.4 kg	Boiled potatoes, cooled and peeled
10 oz	275 g	Oil, clarified butter, or a mixture of oil and clarified butter
to taste	to taste	Salt
to taste	to taste	Pepper

Per serving: Calories, 180; Protein, 2 g; Fat, 7 g (35% cal.); Cholesterol, 0 mg; Carbohydrates, 27 g; Fiber, 2 g; Sodium, 5 mg.

VARIATIONS

Any of the following can be added to the potatoes to vary the flavor: chopped parsley, chives, bacon, hard-cooked egg, grated cheese, and garlic.

Rösti Potatoes

Shred boiled potatoes on the large holes of a hand grater, or use a machine. Prepare as in basic recipe. Potatoes should be very crisp. (These are sometimes called *hash brown potatoes* but, strictly speaking, hash browns are made with chopped potatoes, as *hash* means "to chop.")

Lyonnaise Hash Browns

Combine 1¼ lb (600 g) onion, chopped and sautéed in butter, with the chopped or shredded potatoes before pan-frying.

PROCEDURE

1. Chop the potatoes into small pieces.
2. Ladle a thin layer of oil or butter into a well-seasoned 6-in. (15-cm) sauté pan and set it over high heat. A griddle may also be used for this preparation.
3. When the fat is hot, add 1 portion of potatoes and flatten them into a round cake. Shake the pan back and forth to keep the potatoes from sticking.
4. When the potatoes are well browned on the bottom, flip them over or turn them with an offset spatula. Try to keep the potato cake unbroken. Season with salt and pepper.
5. When the second side is done, tilt the pan to drain off any excess fat for reuse, holding the potatoes in the pan with the spatula. Slide the potatoes out of the sauté pan onto a plate.
6. Repeat with remaining portions.

Lyonnaise Potatoes

PORTIONS: 25   PORTION SIZE: 4½ OZ (125 G)

U.S.	METRIC	INGREDIENTS
6½ lb	3 kg	Boiled potatoes, cooled and peeled
1½ lb	700 g	Onions
8 oz	225 g	Clarified butter, vegetable oil, or mixture of oil and butter
to taste	to taste	Salt
to taste	to taste	White pepper

Per serving: Calories, 190; Protein, 2 g; Fat, 9 g (42% cal.); Cholesterol, 25 mg; Carbohydrates, 26 g; Fiber, 2 g; Sodium, 95 mg.

Note: This preparation may be made on a griddle instead of in a sauté pan.

VARIATIONS

Home Fries or American Fries
Prepare as in basic recipe, but omit onions.

Potatoes O'Brien
Cook 10 oz (300 g) diced bacon until crisp. Remove bacon from pan. Sauté 10 oz onion (300 g), cut in fine dice, and 10 oz (300 g) green bell pepper, cut in fine dice, in bacon fat. Sauté 6½ lb (3 kg) diced potatoes as in basic recipe and add vegetables.

Add the crisp bacon and 4 oz (125 g) diced pimiento to finish, and season to taste.

PROCEDURE

1. Cut the potatoes into slices about ¼ in. (0.5 cm) thick.
2. Peel the onions, cut in half lengthwise, and slice into julienne.
3. Heat half the fat in a sauté pan and sauté the onions until they are golden. Remove from the pan with a slotted spoon and set aside.
4. Put the rest of the fat into the pan. Set the pan on high heat and add the potatoes.
5. Sauté the potatoes, tossing them in the pan until well browned on all sides.
6. Add the onions and continue to sauté for another minute, or until onions and potatoes well mixed and the flavors are blended.
7. Season to taste.

Lyonnaise Potatoes

Potato Pancakes

PORTIONS: 20   PORTION SIZE: 2 PANCAKES, ABOUT 2 OZ (60 G) EACH

U.S.	METRIC	INGREDIENTS
6 lb	2.7 kg	Potatoes
1 lb	450 g	Onions
2	2	Lemons
6	6	Eggs
¼ cup	60 mL	Chopped parsley (optional)
2 tsp	10 mL	Salt
½ tsp	2 mL	White pepper
2 oz or more	60 g or more	Flour (see Note)
as needed	as needed	Oil for pan-frying

Per serving: Calories, 220; Protein, 5 g; Fat, 10 g (40% cal.); Cholesterol, 65 mg; Carbohydrates, 29 g; Fiber, 3 g; Sodium, 260 mg.

Note: Matzoh meal or dried potato starch may be used instead of flour for binding the batter.

PROCEDURE

1. Peel the potatoes and onions. Grate them together into a stainless-steel bowl. Juice the lemons, add the juice to the potatoes to prevent discoloration, and toss to mix.
2. Place the potatoes in a china cap and squeeze out the excess liquid. Hold the liquid and let the starch settle out. Drain the liquid from the starch.
3. Return the potatoes to a stainless-steel bowl and add the potato starch.
4. Beat in the eggs, parsley, salt, and pepper.
5. Stir in enough flour to bind the potato mixture. (If the batter is too thin, the pancakes will fall apart in the pan. Test-fry a little first, and add more flour if necessary.)
6. Pour about ¼ in. (½ cm) oil into a heavy iron skillet. Heat the oil over moderately high heat. The oil should reach about 325°F/160°C.
7. Measuring with a solid kitchen spoon, place portions of the batter in the pan to make individual pancakes.
8. Pan-fry, turning once, until golden brown on both sides.
9. Remove from the pan with a slotted spoon or spatula and drain briefly on absorbent paper.
10. *Alternative method:* Lightly brown in oil and place in one layer on a sheet pan. Finish in the oven (375°F/190°C) until brown and crisp.

Deep-Frying

All the rules of deep-frying that you learned in Chapter 4 apply to potatoes. Review page 63 to refresh your memory.

There are two kinds of deep-fried potato preparations:

1. **Potatoes fried raw.**
   These are potatoes that are simply cut into shapes and deep-fried until golden and crisp. They include all the varieties of French fries as well as potato chips.

   Russet or Idaho potatoes are most suitable for frying because of their high starch content and their regular shape, which permits less trimming loss.

2. **Preparations made from cooked, puréed potatoes.**
   Most of these products are made from duchesse potato mixture. They include potato croquette variations, Dauphine potatoes, and Lorette potatoes.

   Starchy potatoes are used for these recipes, as they are for duchesse potatoes, because they make a good dry, mealy purée.

French Fries

Because French fries, or deep-fried potatoes, are one of the most popular items in North American food service, you must know how to prepare them well. Most French fries served are made from blanched, frozen product, but it is important to know how to make them from fresh potatoes.

The recipe on page 333 gives the complete procedure for preparing French fries. Note that they are fried in two stages. It is possible to cook them in one step, but this is impractical in a volume operation because of the long cooking time. The more common practice is to blanch them in frying fat. This is done at a lower temperature so they cook through without browning. They are then drained and refrigerated until service time. Portions can then be finished to order in a few minutes.

Frozen products have been prepared through step 5 in the recipe and then frozen. To use them, simply begin with step 6.

KEY POINTS TO REVIEW

- What are the steps in the procedure for baking potatoes?
- What are the two basic categories of sautéed or pan-fried potato preparations?
- What are the steps in the procedure for making French fries?
- What are potato croquettes? How are they made?

 # French Fries

PORTIONS: AS NEEDED (2¼ LB AP/1 KG AP POTATOES YIELDS ABOUT 1 LB/450 G COOKED POTATOES)

U.S.	METRIC	INGREDIENTS
as needed	as needed	Idaho potatoes

Per 3.2 oz (90.7 g): Calories, 290; Protein, 4 g; Fat, 15 g (46% cal.); Cholesterol, 0 mg; Carbohydrates, 36 g; Fiber, 3 g; Sodium, 200 mg.

PROCEDURE

1. Peel and eye the potatoes.

2. Cut the potatoes into strips ⅜ in. (1 cm) square and about 3 in. (7.5 cm) long. Hold the cut potatoes in cold water until needed, to prevent discoloration.

3. Line sheet pans with several layers of brown paper and have them ready by the deep fryer.

4. Drain and dry the potatoes well. Deep-fry in fat heated to 325°F (160°C) until they are just beginning to turn a pale golden color. At this point, they should be cooked through and soft.

5. Remove the potatoes from the fryer and turn them out onto the sheet pans in a single layer to drain. Refrigerate.

6. At service time, fry the potatoes in small quantities in fat heated to 350°–375°F (175°–190°C) until brown and crisp.

7. Drain well. Salt them lightly away from the fryer, or let customers salt their own. Serve immediately.

VARIATIONS

Pont-Neuf Potatoes

Prepare as in basic recipe, but cut the potatoes in thicker strips, about ½ in. (1.25 cm) square or slightly larger. Blanching time will be slightly longer.

Allumette Potatoes (Shoestring or Matchstick Potatoes)

Cut the potatoes into thin strips, slightly less than ¼ in. thick (about 0.5 cm). Because they are so thin, they are usually fried in one step (without blanching) until very crisp.

Straw Potatoes

Cut into very thin strips, about ⅛ in. (3 mm) thick. Fry in one step in hot fat (375°F/190°C).

Steakhouse Fries

Scrub but do not peel potatoes. Cut in half lengthwise, then cut each half lengthwise into 4–6 wedges, depending on size. Prepare as in basic recipe.

Potato Chips

Cut potatoes into very thin slices, less than ⅛ in. (3 mm) thick. Fry in one step in hot fat (375°F/190°C).

Waffle or Gaufrette Potatoes

Set the fluted blade of a mandoline to cut very thin slices. Cut potatoes into round slices, turning the potato about 90 degrees between slices so you cut waffle shapes (see **Figure 11.3**). Fry like potato chips.

Figure 11.3 Gaufrette Potatoes.

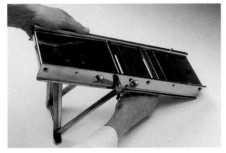  

(a) Set the fluted blade of the mandoline so it cuts very thin slices.

(b) Slice the potatoes, turning the potato about 90 degrees between slices so the ridges on the two sides of each slice cross each other.

(c) You may need to adjust the thickness of the cut after the first slice or two. The slices should be thin enough to have holes.

Potato Croquettes

These are made from duchesse potato mixture. The procedure for duchesse potatoes is repeated here for the sake of convenience.

PORTIONS: 20   PORTION SIZE: 3 PIECES, 1½ OZ (40 G) EACH

U.S.	METRIC	INGREDIENTS	PROCEDURE
7 lb	3 kg	Potatoes, peeled and quartered	1. Steam the potatoes or simmer in salted water until tender. (Steaming is preferable because it results in a drier product.) Drain in a colander (if simmered) and let dry in an oven a few minutes.
4 oz	100 g	Butter	2. Pass the potatoes through a food mill or ricer.
to taste	to taste	Salt	3. Add the butter and mix to a smooth paste. Season to taste with salt, pepper, and nutmeg.
to taste	to taste	White pepper	
to taste	to taste	Nutmeg	4. Set over moderate heat and stir the mixture to dry it out well. If it is not dry enough, the croquettes will not hold their shape. *Alternative method:* Add enough cornstarch or dry potato starch to absorb excess moisture and stiffen the mixture.
10	10	Egg yolks	

Procedure (continued):

5. Remove from the fire, add the egg yolks, and beat in thoroughly.

6. To shape croquettes, two methods are available: (a) Spread the mixture to cool in a pan, cover with plastic or buttered paper to keep a crust from forming, and refrigerate. Dust hands with flour and shape potatoes by hand into cylinders the shape of corks, about 2 in. (5 cm) long and about 1½ oz (40 g) each. (b) Dust sheet pans with flour. Place the warm potato mixture in a pastry bag fitted with a large, plain tip. Bag out the potatoes into long strips on the pans (see **Figure 11.1**).
With a knife, cut the strips into 2-in. (5-cm) lengths.

U.S.	METRIC	INGREDIENTS	PROCEDURE
		Standard Breading Procedure:	7. Set up a breading station and pass the potatoes through Standard Breading Procedure (p. 128).
as needed	as needed	Flour	
as needed	as needed	Egg wash	8. At service time, fry croquettes in deep fat at 350°F (175°C) until golden brown. Drain well.
as needed	as needed	Bread crumbs	

9. Serve immediately, 3 pieces per portion.

Per serving: Calories, 443; Protein, 9 g; Fat, 20 g (42% cal.); Cholesterol, 155 mg; Carbohydrates, 54 g; Fiber, 3 g; Sodium, 315 mg.

VARIATIONS

Other shapes may be used as desired.

Add 8 oz (225 g) of any one of the following to the potato mixture:

Grated cheese
Minced, sautéed onion
Chopped, sautéed mushrooms
Chopped ham
Finely chopped nuts

Berny Potatoes

Shape into small balls. Bread with finely slivered almonds instead of bread crumbs. (In classical cuisine, minced truffles are added to the potato mixture.)

Lorette Potatoes

Prepare like Dauphine potatoes and add 1 oz grated parmesan cheese per pound of mixture (60 g per kg). Shape as desired (the classic shape is a small crescent) and fry without breading.

Dauphine Potatoes

Method 1: For each pound of duchesse or croquette potato mixture, add ⅓ lb (150 g) Pâte à Choux or cream puff paste, made without sugar and with half the amount of butter. To fry, bag out into desired shapes onto greased brown paper. Slide into hot fat. Remove paper when potatoes float loose.

Method 2: Hold pastry bag over deep fryer. Force out potato mixture and cut off short lengths with the back of a knife, letting them drop into the hot fat.

TERMS FOR REVIEW

waxy potato	new potato	solanine
russet	all-purpose	duchesse potatoes

QUESTIONS FOR DISCUSSION

1. True or false: French fries made from fresh potatoes are always better than French fries made from frozen, blanched potato strips. Explain.

2. If mature, starchy potatoes are best for puréeing (mashed, duchesse, etc.), then why doesn't everyone use russets or Idahos, which are the starchiest?

3. Why is it not a good idea to put parisienne potatoes on your menu unless you are also serving a puréed potato product?

4. Many of the potato recipes in this chapter do not indicate what type of potato to use. For those recipes, indicate whether you would select all-purpose, russet, or waxy potatoes.

Chapter 13

Quinoa Salad with Bell Peppers, page 419.

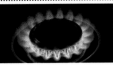

Legumes, Grains, Pasta, and Other Starches

This chapter continues the discussion of starchy foods. The previous chapter focuses on a fresh vegetable, the potato, one of the most important starches on European and North American menus. This chapter, by contrast, discusses preparations based on dried foods: legumes and grains.

For most of human history—and prehistory—grains have been the most important source of nutrients and calories to sustain life, and this remains true today in many parts of the world. For example, in parts of Asia, rice is eaten at nearly every meal. In Japan, the standard words for *breakfast*, *lunch*, and *dinner* can be translated as "morning rice," "noon rice," and "evening rice."

In many regions, dried beans, eaten together with rice, are a more common source of protein than meat or fish. Dried legumes are actually matured, dried versions of some of the fresh vegetables discussed in earlier chapters and are not immediately thought of as starches. However, they do have a high starch content and, because of their dried nature, are handled much like grains.

Pastas and noodles are important starchy foods made from grains, usually wheat, but also rice and other grains. In this chapter we look primarily at the noodle products inherited from Italian cuisine, but we also learn about noodles from other cuisines.

After reading this chapter, you should be able to

1. Distinguish the major types of dried legumes.
2. Cook dried legumes.
3. Distinguish the major types of rice.
4. Distinguish the major types of other grains used in food service.
5. Prepare grains by simmering and by the pilaf and risotto methods.
6. Distinguish major kinds and shapes of commercial pasta, and determine their quality.
7. Prepare fresh and commercial pasta products, and list the steps involved in the alternate steam-table method of its preparation.

Dried Legumes

A *legume* is a plant that bears seed pods that split along two opposite sides when ripe. Legumes include beans, peas, lentils, and a number of other plants. In culinary usage, we use the word to refer to the seeds from these pods, especially when they are mature and dried. (Do not confuse the English meaning of *legume* with that of the French word *legume*, which means "vegetable.")

Dried beans and peas have been used as food for thousands of years, and they continue to be important foods today. In fact, with today's increased interest in healthful eating and in vegetables of all sorts, as well as a greater knowledge of cuisines from around the world, many more interesting varieties of beans are widely available now than only a few years ago.

Legumes are high in protein and, thus, are important in vegetarian diets. They are rich in B vitamins and minerals. Some legumes, like the soybean, are also rich in fat.

Types and Varieties

The three most important types of dried legumes in Western kitchens are kidney beans, peas, and lentils. Several unrelated legumes, including chickpeas, fava beans, soybeans, and lima beans, play smaller roles on the menu. The following descriptions include most of the commonly available beans.

KIDNEY BEANS

Most of the many-colored beans in the illustrations are types of kidney bean. These are all varieties of one species of plant—the same plant that gives us the common green bean. Their flavors and textures vary slightly, but their cooking and handling characteristics are similar, although some may require longer cooking times than others.

A subgroup of this family is sometimes called *haricot beans* (*haricot* is the French word for "bean"). These are all varieties of green bean (*haricots verts*) that are allowed to ripen until the seeds are mature and dry. The members of this group are white beans of various sizes. The term *kidney bean* is then used for the remaining beans in this family, which have colors other than white.

The most common kinds of kidney bean and haricot bean are summarized in Table 13.1.

PEAS

Dried *green* and *yellow* peas are the same peas we eat as a fresh vegetable, but they are left on the vine until mature and dry. They are usually split, with the hull removed, in order to speed cooking time, although whole peas are also available.

Split peas cook quickly without preliminary soaking.

Black-eyed peas and *pigeon peas* are popular in the southern United States as well as in parts of Africa and the Caribbean. They are not related to green or yellow peas nor to kidney beans but, like regular peas, are often sold fresh in the pod as well as dried. Black-eyed peas are small, white, kidney-shaped beans with a black spot where the bean attaches to the pod. Pigeon peas are small and round or oval, with beige skin flecked with brown.

LENTILS

Lentils are small, lens-shaped legumes. They have a shorter cooking time than kidney beans, even when whole, and do not need soaking. If desired, however, they may be soaked, resulting in an even shorter cooking time.

The most prized lentils are the tiny *green lentils*, commonly known as *Le Puy* lentils because the best ones are grown in Le Puy, France. (*Note:* Only lentils actually grown in Le Puy should be given this name. If grown elsewhere, they are simply called *green lentils*.) They have a dark green or gray-green hull and, unlike other lentils, keep their shape fairly well when cooked.

The larger *brown lentils* are the most common lentils in Western kitchens. They range in color from medium brown to greenish-brown.

Table 13.1 The Kidney Bean/Haricot Bean Family

NAME	DESCRIPTION
Haricot beans	
Navy bean	small, oval white bean
Pea bean	similar to but smaller than navy bean
Rice bean	tiny white bean slightly larger than a grain of cooked rice
Great Northern bean	medium-small white bean
White kidney bean, cannellini	large, white kidney-shaped bean
Soissons (swah sohn)	medium white bean
Flageolet	small, pale green bean, harvested while immature and then dried
Kidney beans	
Red kidney bean	dark red-brown medium bean with tough skin
Pink kidney bean	pink-red bean similar to red kidney
Pinto bean	medium kidney bean with tan skin splotched with pink-brown
Black bean or turtle bean	small, black, oval kidney bean
Cranberry bean or borlotti bean	medium kidney bean, pale pink skin spotted with red
Brown or Swedish bean	small, oval, brown-skinned bean
Calypso bean	medium oval bean, white with black patches
Appaloosa bean	medium kidney-shaped bean with black and white skin

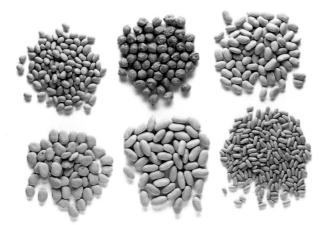

Top row: navy beans, garbanzo beans or chickpeas, Great Northern beans. Bottom row: baby lima beans, cannellini beans or white kidney beans, rice beans.

Top row: black turtle beans, dried fava beans. Bottom row: Swedish brown beans, calypso beans, flageolet beans.

Top row: red kidney beans, pink beans, appaloosa beans. Bottom row: cranberry beans or borlotti, Christmas lima beans, pinto beans.

Top row: yellow split peas, green lentils, green split peas. Bottom row: brown lentils, red lentils, black-eyed peas.

Red lentils have long been a mainstay in India and have become popular in the West only recently. They are tiny, salmon-pink lentils that have been split, with the dark hull removed. Red lentils turn yellow when cooked and break apart to form a purée.

Yellow lentils are small split lentils similar to red lentils, but less often seen.

OTHER LEGUMES

A number of other legumes are also important.

Lima beans, also called *butter beans*, are flat, broad beans ranging from creamy white to pale pastel green in color, in a range of sizes from large to small. They have a starchy texture and a distinctive flavor unlike that of any of the kidney beans. Like peas, they are often harvested when they are immature and moist and eaten as a fresh vegetable.

Chickpeas, also called *garbanzos* or, in Italian, *ceci* (chay chee), are round, hard, yellow-brown beans about twice the size of peas and best known as the main ingredient in hummus. They stay firm and whole when cooked and have a nutty flavor. Dried chickpeas are also ground into flour.

Fava beans are broad, flat beans, the matured dried form of the vegetable discussed on pages 250–251. The brilliant green of the immature vegetable turns a creamy brown color when the bean is dried. The skin of the dried fava is tough and the texture is starchy.

Soybeans are one of the world's most important bean crops because of their high protein content as well as their rich oil content. Fresh soybeans are used as a vegetable (p. 264). Dried soybeans are very hard and require a long cooking time, but they are not often cooked and eaten directly. Rather, they are used to make a variety of other foods, such as soy sauce, soybean paste or *miso*, and tofu or bean curd.

Mung beans are small, round beans with a dark green skin and white interior. They are often sprouted to make the bean sprouts widely used in Chinese cooking. As dried legumes, they are available whole or hulled and split. The split form has a much shorter cooking time. Split mung beans break apart when cooked to make a purée. Mung beans belong to the same family as pigeon peas and black-eyed peas.

Adzuki beans are small, oval beans with a thick red skin. They are used primarily in Asian cooking in sweet as well as savory dishes.

Dal, or *dhal*, is the generic term in India for dried legume. Legumes used in Indian cuisine include *moong dal* (mung bean), *masoor dal* (red lentil), *urad dal* (a tiny, white split lentil), and *chana* (chickpea).

Cooking Legumes

Because dried beans, peas, and lentils are dry and hard, they must be rehydrated—that is, they must absorb water—in order to be made edible. Thus, the primary cooking method used to prepare dried legumes is simmering. Once the beans are cooked and tender, they can be finished in a variety of ways. The recipes in this section give a sample of ways to prepare legumes. Additional recipes are included in Chapter 8 ("Soups") and Chapter 14 ("Salads and Salad Dressings").

KEY POINTS TO REVIEW

- What are the three major types of dried legumes? Give examples of each.

- In addition to the three main types of legumes, what are six other important legumes used in the kitchen? Describe them.

- What are the steps in the basic procedure for preparing dried legumes?

Procedure for Preparing Dried Legumes

1. Pick over to remove any foreign particles. Rinse well.

2. Soak overnight in 3 times the volume of water. (Split peas and some lentils do not require soaking. Check package directions.)

3. Drain the beans. Place them in a pot and add fresh cold water to cover by 1–2 inches (2.5–5 cm).

4. Bring to a boil. Reduce heat and simmer, covered, until tender. Do not boil, or the legumes may toughen. Some beans require up to 3 hours of simmering.

5. Check texture for doneness. A properly cooked bean is soft and creamy in texture, not hard or grainy. Unless a purée or soup is desired, kidney beans should remain intact, not cooked so long they are falling apart. Other peas and beans will form a purée or remain whole, depending on the type.

6. If you forget to soak beans overnight, an alternative method can be used. Put the beans in a cooking pot with 3 times their volume of cold water. Bring to a boil. When water just starts to boil, cover tightly and remove from the heat. Let stand 1 hour. Then proceed with step 3 above.

White Beans, Bretonne Style

YIELD: ABOUT 6 LB (3 KG)   PORTIONS: 20   PORTION SIZE: 5 OZ (150 G)

U.S.	METRIC	INGREDIENTS	PROCEDURE
2 lb	1 kg	Dried white beans	1. Soak the beans overnight in cold water.
1	1	Carrot, small	2. Drain the beans and place in a pot with enough water to cover by 1 in. (2.5 cm). Add the carrot, celery, onion, and sachet. Simmer until the beans are tender but not soft or broken (1–3 hours, depending on the beans). Drain, but save the liquid. Discard the vegetables and sachet.
1 stem	1 stem	Celery	
1	1	Onion, small, peeled	
		Sachet d'épices:	
1	1	Bay leaf	
6–8	6–8	Parsley stems	
3–4	3–4	Peppercorns	
1	1	Clove	
pinch	pinch	Thyme	
4 oz	125 g	Butter	3. Heat the butter in a large saucepot or brazier. Sauté the onion and garlic until soft. Add the tomatoes and cook a few minutes to reduce liquid.
8 oz	250 g	Onion, diced	
2	2	Garlic cloves, chopped	4. Add the beans to this mixture and stir carefully. Simmer until heated through and flavors are blended. If too dry, add some of the bean cooking liquid. Add pan drippings, if you are using them. Season to taste.
1 lb	500 g	Canned tomatoes, with juice, coarsely chopped	
as needed	as needed	Pan juices from roast lamb (optional; see Note)	
to taste	to taste	Salt	
to taste	to taste	Pepper	

Per serving: Calories, 200; Protein, 11 g; Fat, 5 g (22% cal.); Cholesterol, 10 mg; Carbohydrates, 29 g; Fiber, 7 g; Sodium, 90 mg.

Note: This preparation is often served with roast leg of lamb or other lamb roast. If so, the pan drippings may be used to flavor the beans.

White Beans, Bretonne Style

Baked Beans, New England Style

PORTION: 20   PORTION SIZE: 4½ OZ (125 G)

U.S.	METRIC	INGREDIENTS	PROCEDURE
2 lb	900 g	Dried beans, navy or Great Northern	1. Soak the beans overnight in enough water to cover by 2 in. (5 cm.).
		Bouquet garni:	2. Place the beans and liquid in a pot and add the bouquet garni. Bring to a boil and skim foam. Reduce heat to a simmer. Cover and simmer 45 minutes–1 hour, or until beans are just tender but not soft. Add more water if necessary during cooking.
1	1	Bay leaf	
6–8	6–8	Parsley stems	
¼ tsp	1 mL	Dried thyme	
a few	a few	Celery tops	3. Drain the beans, reserving the cooking liquid. Discard the bouquet garni.
1 cup	250 mL	Molasses	4. Mix the molasses, brown sugar, dry mustard, salt, and 1 qt (1 L) of the bean cooking liquid. If there is not enough bean liquid, add water to make up the difference.
2 oz	60 g	Brown sugar	
1 tbsp	15 mL	Dry mustard	5. Mix the beans, molasses mixture, and salt pork in a 4-qt (4-L) pot or deep baking pan.
1 tbsp	15 mL	Salt	6. Bake, covered, at 300°F (150°C) for 2–2½ hours. Add more liquid if necessary during baking.
8 oz	225 g	Salt pork, medium dice	

Per serving: Calories, 290; Protein, 10 g; Fat, 10 g (31% cal.); Cholesterol, 10 mg; Carbohydrates, 41 g; Fiber, 7 g; Sodium, 520 mg.

VARIATIONS

Michigan Baked Beans

Reduce molasses to ¼ cup (60 mL) and add 2 cups (500 mL) tomato sauce or tomato purée.

Frijoles de la Olla (Mexican Pinto Beans)

PORTIONS: 16–20   PORTION SIZE: 4 OZ (125 G)

U.S.	METRIC	INGREDIENTS
1½ lb	750 g	Dried pinto beans or pink beans
3 qt	3 L	Water, cold (see Note)
6 oz	175 g	Onion, sliced thin
1–2	1–2	Garlic cloves, chopped
1	1	Jalapeño or other green chile, chopped (optional)
2 oz	60 g	Lard or rendered pork fat
2 tsp	10 mL	Salt

Per serving: Calories, 170; Protein, 8 g; Fat, 4 g (20% cal.); Cholesterol, 5 mg; Carbohydrates, 27 g; Fiber, 9 g; Sodium, 290 mg.

Note: The beans may be soaked overnight, if desired (although many Mexican cooking authorities feel the results are not as good). If they are soaked, reduce the water for cooking to 1½ pt (750 mL).

PROCEDURE

1. Combine the beans, water, onion, garlic, and jalapeño in a pot. Bring to a boil, reduce heat, and simmer, covered, 1½ hours. Check the pot from time to time and add more water, if needed, to keep the beans covered.

2. Add the lard and salt. Continue to simmer until the beans are tender. Do not let the beans go dry. There should always be some broth. Add hot water if necessary.

3. The beans will hold refrigerated for several days.

VARIATIONS

Frijoles Refritos

For the quantity of beans in the basic recipe, make in at least 3 batches. Mash the beans coarsely. Heat 2 oz (60 g) lard in a large sauté pan. Add 2 oz (60 g) chopped onion and fry until soft, but do not brown. Add one-third of the cooked, mashed beans (about 1½ lb/750 g, including broth) to the pan. Stir and mash the beans over heat until the beans start to dry out and pull away from the sides of the pan. Roll the mass out of the pan like an omelet. Sprinkle with grated cheese (mild cheddar or Monterey jack) and serve with tortilla chips.

Vegetarian Pinto Beans

Omit the lard or pork fat from the basic recipe.

Green Lentils with Celery Root and Mustard

YIELD: 3 LB 12 OZ (1.8 KG)   PORTIONS: 12   PORTION SIZE: 5 OZ (150 G)

U.S.	METRIC	INGREDIENTS
1 lb 4 oz	600 g	Green (Le Puy) lentils
1	1	Onion, small, whole
		Sachet d'épices (p. 136):
¼ tsp	1 mL	Dried thyme
6	6	Peppercorns
1	1	Bay leaf
8–10	8–10	Parsley stems
1	1	Whole cloves
1	1	Garlic clove
4 oz	120 g	Celery root, small dice
1½ oz	45 g	Onion, brunoise
1½ oz	45 g	Carrot, brunoise
1 fl oz	30 mL	Olive oil
1 fl oz	30 mL	Dijon-style mustard
to taste	to taste	Salt
to taste	to taste	Pepper

PROCEDURE

1. Rinse and drain the lentils.
2. Place the lentils, onion, and sachet in a saucepan and add enough water to cover the lentils by 2 in. (5 cm).
3. Bring to a simmer and cook until tender but still firm. This may take from 10 minutes to more than 30, depending on the lentils. Add more water if necessary if the cooking time is long.
4. Drain the lentils, reserving the cooking liquid. Discard the onion and sachet.
5. Sweat the celery root, onion brunoise, and carrot in the olive oil 1 minute.
6. Add a little of the lentil cooking liquid to moisten the vegetables and continue to cook until the celery root is tender. Add more liquid from time to time as needed.
7. When the vegetables are tender, stir in the mustard.
8. Add the lentils and stir. Cook just until the lentils are hot.
9. Add salt and pepper to taste.

Per serving: Calories, 200; Protein, 13 g; Fat, 2.5 g (11% cal.); Cholesterol, 0 mg; Carbohydrates, 32 g; Fiber, 8 g; Sodium, 90 mg.

Green Lentils with Celery Root and Mustard

Pasta e Fagioli

PORTIONS: 12   PORTION SIZE: 8 FL OZ (240 ML)

U.S	METRIC	INGREDIENTS
12 oz	360 g	Dried cranberry beans
4 fl oz	120 mL	Olive oil
6 oz	180 g	Pancetta (unsmoked Italian-style bacon), ground or chopped fine
6 oz	180 g	Onion, chopped fine
3 oz	90 g	Carrot, chopped fine
3 oz	90 g	Celery, chopped fine
4	4	Fresh sage leaves, chopped
1 tbsp	15 mL	Fresh rosemary, chopped
3 tbsp	45 mL	Chopped fresh parsley
2½ qt	2.5 L	Water
1 oz	30 g	Tomato paste
to taste	to taste	Salt
1 lb	450 g	Dried fettuccine, broken
12 tsp	60 mL	Grated parmesan cheese
3 fl oz	90 mL	Olive oil

PROCEDURE

1. Clean and rinse the beans. Soak in cold water overnight.
2. Heat the olive oil in a heavy saucepot over moderate heat. Add the pancetta and cook, stirring from time to time, until crisp. Remove with a slotted spoon, leaving the fat in the pot.
3. Add the onion, carrot, celery, sage, rosemary, and parsley to the pot. Sweat in the reserved fat just until the vegetables start to become tender.
4. Drain the beans and add them to the pot. At the same time, add the water. Bring to a boil, reduce heat, and simmer until the beans are almost tender, about 45 minutes.
5. Add the tomato paste. Continue to simmer until the beans are very tender.
6. Remove about half of the soup and pass it through a food mill to purée it. Return it to the pot with the rest of the soup.
7. Season to taste with salt.
8. At this point the soup should be thick but still liquid enough to cook the pasta when it is added. If necessary, add a little more water.
9. Add the pasta and simmer until it is tender.
10. Stir in the reserved pancetta.
11. Serve each portion topped with 1 teaspoon (5 mL) cheese and a drizzle of olive oil.

Per serving: Calories, 440; Protein, 15 g; Fat, 22 g (44% cal.); Cholesterol, 10 mg; Carbohydrates, 48 g; Fiber, 9 g; Sodium, 350 mg.

Note: If cranberry beans are not available, use white kidney beans.

Pasta e Fagioli

Purée of Flageolet Beans with Garlic

YIELD: 4 LB (2 KG)   PORTIONS: 16   PORTION SIZE: 4 OZ (125 G)

U.S.	METRIC	INGREDIENTS
1½ lb	750 g	Dried flageolet beans
1	1	Sachet d'épices (p. 136)
3 pt	1.5 L	Water or light vegetable stock
6–8	6–8	Garlic cloves, peeled and chopped
2 tsp	10 mL	Salt
12 fl oz	375 mL	Olive oil
3 fl oz	90 mL	Lemon juice
to taste	to taste	Additional salt
to taste	to taste	Pepper

PROCEDURE

1. Rinse and drain the beans. Soak overnight in enough cold water to cover by several inches (5 cm or more).
2. Drain. Add the sachet and the water or stock. Simmer until the beans are tender, about 45 minutes. Discard the sachet.
3. Mash the chopped garlic with the salt.
4. Drain the beans. Place the beans in a food processor with the garlic and olive oil. Blend to a purée.
5. With the motor running, pour in the lemon juice. The purée should have the consistency of soft mashed potatoes.
6. Adjust seasoning to taste with salt and pepper if necessary.
7. Serve warm as a vegetable accompaniment (reheat as necessary) or cold as a dip.

Per serving: Calories, 320; Protein, 9 g; Fat, 22 g (60% cal.); Cholesterol, 0 mg; Carbohydrates, 24 g; Fiber, 8 g; Sodium, 290 mg.

VARIATIONS

Other beans, such as white kidney beans and pinto beans, may be substituted.

Flageolet Beans with Wilted Arugula

Cook the beans as in the basic recipe, but do not purée. Use 3 cloves garlic and 4 fl oz (125 mL) olive oil. Chop the garlic and sauté in the olive oil. Add 1 lb (500 g) coarsely chopped arugula and sauté just until wilted. Add this mixture to the drained, hot beans. Season to taste.

Masoor Dal (Red Lentils with Spices)

PORTIONS: 12   PORTION SIZE: 8 FL OZ (240 ML)

U.S.	METRIC	INGREDIENTS
1 lb 4 oz	575 g	Red lentils
2½ qt	2.5 L	Water
4	4	Garlic cloves, chopped
4 thin slices	4 thin slices	Fresh ginger root
2 tbsp	30 mL	Chopped fresh cilantro
2 tsp	10 mL	Turmeric
½ tsp	2 mL	Cayenne
1½ fl oz	45 mL	Lemon juice
to taste	to taste	Salt
2 fl oz	6 mL	Vegetable oil
2 tsp	10 mL	Cumin seed

PROCEDURE

1. Sort, rinse, and drain the lentils.
2. Put the lentils and water in a saucepot. Bring to a boil. Skim off any froth that rises to the top.
3. Add the garlic, ginger, cilantro, turmeric, and cayenne. Simmer until the lentils are very tender and falling apart, about 1½ hours.
4. Add the lemon juice and salt to taste.
5. To finish the dal, heat the oil in a small sauté pan. When it is very hot, add the cumin seed and cook a few seconds, until the cumin is aromatic.
6. Pour the oil and seeds into the dal and stir in.

Per serving: Calories, 200; Protein, 12 g; Fat, 5 g (21% cal.); Cholesterol, 0 mg; Carbohydrates, 30 g; Fiber, 8 g; Sodium, 20 mg.

Grains

Wheat and rice are without doubt the world's two most important grains. Unlike rice, wheat is rarely cooked and eaten as a whole grain. Rather, its primary use is to be ground into flour for making breads and other baked goods. The use of grain flours in baked goods is the subject matter of the last seven chapters of this book. In this section, we look at other uses of grains in food-service kitchens.

Types of Grains

Grains are the edible seeds of various members of the grass family. Each seed consists of four parts:

- The husk—an inedible fibrous outer layer that is removed during processing

- The endosperm—the starchy mass that forms most of the kernel

- The bran—a tough but edible layer covering the endosperm

- The germ—the tiny embryo that forms the new plant when the seed sprouts

A product labeled *whole grain* consists of the *endosperm*, *bran*, and *germ*. The grain may be polished or milled to remove the bran and germ. White rice and other polished grains are only the endosperm.

Although rice appears on menus more often than other grain starches, several other grains can also be served as side dishes to add variety to your menu. The most popular of these grains are described following the section on rice.

RICE

Regular milled white rice has been milled to remove the outer bran coating. This process removes some vitamins and minerals, but it produces a white, lighter-textured product most people prefer. White rice appears in several forms:

Enriched rice has received a coating of vitamins to compensate for some of the nutrients lost in milling.

Short-grain and **medium-grain** rice have small, round kernels that become sticky when cooked. They are used for such preparations as rice pudding and rice molds. In addition, the regular boiled rice used in Japanese cuisine for everyday eating and for making sushi is short-grain rice.

Long-grain rice has long, slender grains that stay separate and fluffy when properly cooked. It is used for side dishes, entrées, casseroles, and so on.

Top row: basmati rice, glutinous rice, plain long-grain rice.
Bottom row: Japanese short-grain rice, jasmine rice, Arborio rice.

Top row: true wild rice, Wehani rice, cultivated wild rice.
Bottom row: parboiled or converted rice, brown long-grain rice.

Parboiled or *converted* rice is a specially processed long-grain rice. It has been partially cooked under steam pressure, re-dried, and then milled or polished. This process results in a higher vitamin and mineral content, compared with regular milled white rice.

Parboiled rice is the most widely used in food service. The grains stay firm, separate, and light, and the product holds well in the steam table without becoming mushy or sticky. However, the flavor and texture are not like those of regular long-grain rice, so it is not preferred by all customers.

Converted rice takes slightly more liquid and time to cook.

Instant rice has been precooked and dried so it can be prepared quickly. It does not hold well after cooking, and the grains quickly lose their shape and become mushy.

Brown rice has the bran layer left on, giving it a light brown color, a slightly coarse, crunchy texture, and nutty flavor. Brown rice is available as short, medium, or long grain. Brown rice takes about twice as long to cook as white rice.

Arborio rice is one of several Italian varieties of a type of short-grain rice essential for making the highest-quality risotto (see p. 356). It is the variety most often found in North America and the one specified in recipes. Two other varieties, less widely available, used for risotto are *carnaroli* and *vialone nano*.

Basmati rice is an extra-long-grain rice widely used in India and surrounding countries. It has a distinctive nutty flavor. Brown basmati rice is also available.

Jasmine rice is a long-grain white rice from Thailand and other parts of Southeast Asia. It is fragrant, a little like basmati rice but more delicate or floral.

Wehani rice is another aromatic rice, red in color, with a rich, earthy flavor.

Wild pecan rice is a cultivated, not wild, long-grain rice from Louisiana. It is aromatic, with a nutty flavor, from which it gets the name *pecan*.

Glutinous rice, also called **sticky rice** and **sweet rice**, is a sweet-tasting short-grain rice that becomes quite sticky and chewy when cooked. It is used for a number of special dishes, including desserts, in Chinese and Japanese cuisines. It is often cooked by soaking and steaming rather than boiling. Contrary to what you may read elsewhere, it is *not* the rice used for sushi, which is made with regular Japanese short-grain rice.

Wild rice is not a type of rice but an unrelated grain, so it is discussed with specialty grains below.

CORN

Unlike other grains, which have a husk covering each seed, **corn** has a set of husks covering the entire seed head, or ear. Also unlike other grains, corn is eaten as a fresh vegetable, although different varieties are grown as grain and as a vegetable.

Corn as a grain is not often cooked whole. More often, it is ground into **cornmeal** and cooked into a porridge or used in baked goods. *Meal* can be defined as a coarsely ground grain, as distinguished from *flour*, which is finely ground grain. Common cornmeal is yellow or white, depending on the variety of corn it is made from.

Polenta is Italian-style cornmeal. Polenta has become popular in North America in recent years. Its preparation and uses are explained and illustrated on pages 362–363.

Hominy is corn that has been treated with lye. When it is cracked into a coarse meal, it becomes **grits**, popular in the southern United States and wherever the foods of the South are appreciated. Hominy in whole-grain form is known in Mexican cuisine as **pozole** (poh soh leh). It requires several hours of simmering.

Blue corn, usually available as blue cornmeal, is derived from early varieties of corn grown by Native Americans.

WHEAT

The most common use of wheat is to be made into flour. The milling process for white flour separates the bran and germ. **Wheat germ** and **wheat bran** can be purchased separately. They are usually used as additions to baked goods and some other dishes to enrich their nutritional content and to add flavor interest.

Whole wheat grains that have been cut into smaller pieces are called **cracked wheat**. This product is often added to breads and also can be cooked like pilaf (see p. 353).

Wheatberries are the whole grain minus the hulls. They are generally cooked by boiling or simmering, but cooking time can be several hours. Soaking overnight reduces the cooking time to about 1 hour.

Top row: Egyptian green wheat, hulled wheatberries. Bottom row: couscous, kasha, farro.

Bulgur is a type of cracked wheat that has been partially cooked or parched. It is usually available in coarse, medium, and fine granulations. Its cooking time is shorter than regular cracked wheat and, in fact, the fine granulations can be prepared simply by pouring boiling water over them and letting them stand for ½ hour. This type of bulgur is often served cold, mixed with lemon juice, olive oil, chopped scallions, and fresh herbs.

Green wheat is wheat that is harvested while immature and then dried. It can be cooked like cracked wheat.

Couscous (koose koose) is not actually a grain, although it resembles one. It is made from semolina wheat, a variety of high-protein wheat, and is sort of a granular pasta. See the discussion of couscous in the pasta section of this chapter (p. 367).

OTHER GRAINS

Wild rice is not actually rice but rather the seed of an unrelated grass native to the northern United States and Canada. The grains are long, slender, hard, and dark brown or nearly black in color. Because of its unique nutty flavor, scarcity, and high price, wild rice is considered a luxury food.

Wild rice is now widely cultivated, but the cultivated type is slightly different from that harvested in the wild. Grains of cultivated wild rice are generally larger and firmer, but the texture of the cooked rice is coarser and the flavor less complex. Cultivation has helped reduce the price of wild rice, however.

Farro (far oh) is a wheatlike grain that may be an ancestor of modern wheat. It has been used in the Mediterranean region for thousands of years and is still widely known in Tuscany and other parts of Italy. Farro has a flavor similar to that of wheat. It is higher in protein than wheat and can often be eaten by people who have wheat allergies. In North America, farro is known as **spelt**, although the Italian name is catching on. (Some sources argue that spelt and farro are different grains, but according to the International Plant Genetic Resources Institute, "the only registered varieties of farro belong to *T. spelta* or spelt."

Kamut (kah moot), like farro, is an ancient relative of wheat. It is similar to spelt in composition and flavor.

Buckwheat is technically not a grain because it is the seed not of a grass but of a plant with branched stems and broad, arrow-shaped leaves. Whole buckwheat is often ground into flour. When the grains are crushed into coarse pieces, they are called **buckwheat groats** and can be cooked like rice. Toasted buckwheat is called **kasha**. The toasting gives it a nutty flavor. Kasha is popular in Eastern European and Jewish cooking. Kasha is also cooked like pilaf (p. 353).

Barley is usually purchased as **pearled barley**, which has been milled to remove the outer bran layers. It is commonly used in soups, but it can also be cooked by the pilaf method and served like rice, although it has a longer cooking time.

Oats are most familiar in North America as a breakfast food. **Steel-cut oats** are whole grains that have been cut into small pieces, somewhat resembling cracked wheat. They are usually cooked as a porridge. **Rolled oats** are whole grains that have been steamed until soft and then flattened between rollers. This processing reduces their cooking time considerably. If they are cooked and not just softened during the steaming process, they become **instant oats**. These need no additional cooking, only reconstituting with boiling water.

Millet is a small, round yellow grain that is an important food source in much of Africa and Asia. It has a high protein content and a mild flavor. Millet is often used as bird seed in North America. It can be cooked like rice.

Quinoa (keen wah) is a grain native to the South American Andes that has only recently become an occasional feature of North American menus. Quinoa is high in good-quality protein and lower in carbohydrates than other grains. It is a tiny, round grain with an ivory color and a mild, delicate flavor. When cooked, the germ of the grain unwinds, making it look as though each grain has a tail. Before cooking, quinoa must be washed and rinsed well to remove a bitter coating that occurs naturally on the grain.

Triticale is a high-protein hybrid of wheat and rye. It is often ground into flour, but it can also be cooked whole like rice. Triticale has a nutty, sweet flavor.

Amaranth is a tiny, yellow-brown seed with a somewhat spicy, nutty flavor when cooked. It contains high-quality protein and thus is useful in vegetarian diets.

Flaxseeds are technically not a grain because they are not seeds of a grass. Flax has recently gained popularity because it is thought to have some health benefits due to its beneficial fiber as well as a high quantity of omega-3 fatty acids. The seeds are used mostly in small quantities in breads and in commercial breakfast cereal preparations. Consuming them in large quantities can cause digestive problems.

Top row: quinoa, triticale, pearl barley. Bottom row: blue cornmeal, pozole, bulgur wheat.

Storing and Handling Grains

Store raw grains at room temperature in a dark, dry place and in a tightly sealed container to keep out moisture and insects. Milled grains such as white rice that have had the germ removed will keep for many months. Whole grains are somewhat more perishable because the fat content of the germ can become rancid.

Depending on the source, whole grains may need to be picked over like dried beans (see p. 339) to remove foreign matter such as tiny stones or bits of soil. In addition, whole grains usually should be washed and drained before cooking.

Rice, our most commonly cooked grain, should be rinsed in cold water before boiling or steaming. This removes the excess starch that makes it sticky. The rice industry recommends *not* washing rice because it removes some of the vitamin coating of enriched rice. But that's probably a small price to pay for a more attractive product. This is a decision you will have to make in your own operation.

Do not buy low-grade rice, which tends to be dirty, or rice that has been coated with talc.

Rice cooked by the pilaf method (p. 353) does not need to be washed (unless it is dirty) because the fat coating each kernel helps keep the grains separate and reduces stickiness.

Converted rice and instant rice do not need to be washed.

KEY POINTS TO REVIEW

- What are the four parts of a grain kernel? Which of these parts are included in products labeled *whole grain*?

- What are the most important kinds of rice used in the kitchen? Describe them.

- What are the most important corn products used in the kitchen?

- In addition to rice and corn products, what other important whole-grain items are used as ingredients in the kitchen? Describe each.

- How should grains and grain products be stored?

Cooking Grains

Most grains are cooked by one of three cooking methods: the simmering method, the pilaf method, and the risotto method.

SIMMERING METHODS

The most common method for cooking rice and other whole grains is to place the washed grain in a heavy pot with the right amount of water or other liquid to hydrate it, bring it to a simmer, cover, and cook slowly until all the water is absorbed. The exact amount of liquid needed varies considerably, depending on these factors:

1. The type of grain, its age, and its moisture content.

2. Tightness or looseness of the cover (degree of moisture loss during cooking).

3. Desired moistness of the finished product.

Because of all these factors, it is difficult to be precise when determining how much liquid to use. It is better to add too much liquid than too little. With too little moisture, the grain will not cook to tenderness. If a little too much is added, remove the pan from the heat, keeping it tightly covered, and let it stand for a few minutes. Liquid remaining in the bottom of the pan is likely to be absorbed. If there is much excess liquid, drain it off.

A second method, called the *pasta method*, can be used. It is so called because, like pasta, the item is cooked in a large quantity of water and drained. This method is good for producing separate, unsticky grains. However, some nutrients are lost in the cooking water, so chefs disagree about the value of the method.

Procedure for Simmering Rice and Other Grains

1. For whole grains, wash the grain in cold water as necessary. Drain.
2. Combine the grain with the proper amount of water or other liquid in a heavy saucepot. Bring to a boil. Stir.
3. Cover and cook over very low heat for the proper cooking time, depending on the grain.
4. Test for doneness. Cook a few additional minutes if necessary.
5. Remove from the heat. Drain excess liquid if necessary. Let stand, covered, to allow moisture to be absorbed uniformly by the grain.
6. For rice and any grains that stick together, fluff with a fork and turn out into a hotel pan to let steam escape and stop the cooking.

Variation: Pasta Method

1. Drop the washed, drained grain into a large pot of boiling salted water.
2. When just tender, pour into a strainer and drain well.
3. Place in a hotel pan. Cover and steam dry in oven 5 to 10 minutes, or leave uncovered and place in a steamer to steam dry.

Boiled and Steamed Rice

YIELD: ABOUT 3 LB (1.4 KG)	PORTIONS: 10	PORTION SIZE: 4½–5 OZ (140 G)
	12	4 OZ (115 G)
	16	3 OZ (90 G)

PROPORTIONS	U.S.	METRIC
Regular long-grain white rice		
Rice	1 lb	475 g
Water	1 qt	1 L
Salt	1 tsp	5 mL
Butter	1 oz	30 g
Parboiled long-grain rice		
Rice	1 lb	475 g
Water	4½ cups	1.1 L
Salt	1 tsp	5 mL
Butter	1 oz	30 g
Medium-grain white rice		
Rice	18 oz	525 g
Water	1 qt	1 L
Salt	1 tsp	5 mL
Butter	1 oz	30 g
Brown rice		
Rice	12 oz	350 g
Water	1 qt	1 L
Salt	1 tsp	5 mL
Butter	1 oz	30 g

Per 4½–5 oz (140 g) serving: Calories 200; Protein, 4 g; Fat, 2.5 g (12% cal.); Cholesterol, 5 mg; Carbohydrates, 39 g; Fiber 1 g; Sodium, 260 mg.

PROCEDURES

Rangetop

1. Wash rice in cold water until water runs clear (optional step; see p. 349 for note on washing rice).
2. Combine all ingredients in a heavy pot. Bring to boil. Stir. Cover and cook over very low heat.

   Cooking times:
   Long- and medium-grain:
      15–20 minutes
   Parboiled: 20–25 minutes
   Brown: 40–45 minutes
3. Test rice for doneness. Cook 2–4 minutes more if necessary.
4. Turn rice out into a hotel pan. Fluff with fork or slotted spoon to let steam escape.

Oven

1. Wash rice in cold water until water runs clear (optional step; see p.349 for note on washing rice).
2. Bring salted water to boil. Combine all ingredients in a shallow steamer pan. Cover with foil or tight lid. Place in 375°F (175°C) oven.

   Cooking times:
   Long- and medium-grain:
      25 minutes
   Parboiled: 30–40 minutes
   Brown: 1 hour
3. Test rice for doneness. Bake 2–4 minutes more if necessary.
4. Fluff rice with fork or slotted spoon to let steam escape.

Steamer

1. Wash rice in cold water until water runs clear (optional step; see p. 349 for note on washing rice).
2. Bring salted water to boil. Combine all ingredients in a shallow steamer pan.
   Place uncovered pan in steamer for cooking time recommended by equipment manufacturer.

   Cooking times depend on
   type of steamer.
3. Test rice for doneness. Steam 2–4 minutes more if necessary.
4. Fluff rice with fork or slotted spoon to let steam escape.

SIMMERING MEALS AND CEREALS

Procedures for cooking meals and cereals such as polenta and oatmeal differ somewhat from procedures for cooking whole grains. Cracked or flaked cereals such as rolled oats consist of large particles. They are usually stirred into boiling water. Because of the size of the particles, there is little danger of lumping.

Granular meals such as cornmeal can be stirred into boiling water if care is taken to add the grain slowly and to stir constantly and vigorously while doing so, in order to avoid lumps. See the recipe for polenta (p. 362). Alternatively, combine the meal with cold liquid, stir, and bring to a simmer while continuing to stir. Mixing the meal with cold liquid separates the granules to prevent lumping.

Procedure for Simmering Whole, Cracked, or Flaked Cereals

1. Measure the correct amount of liquid into a pot and bring to a boil.
2. Measure the correct amount of meal or cereal.
3. Add the cereal slowly to the boiling liquid, stirring constantly.
4. Stir until some thickening takes place. Depending on the grain, continue to stir constantly, or stir only occasionally. Some cereals, such as oatmeal, become gummy with excessive stirring.
5. Reduce heat to a slow simmer and cook to desired doneness and consistency.
6. To prevent drying, keep the cooked grain covered until serving.

Variation: Simmering Meals and Granular Cereals

The procedure is the same as above, except the cereal is mixed with cold liquid. This separates the grains to prevent lumping. Place the mixture in a pot, bring to a simmer, and cook as in the basic procedure.

THE PILAF METHOD

The pilaf method is equivalent to braising. The grain is first sautéed in fat and then cooked in liquid—preferably in the oven for uniform heating—until the liquid is absorbed (see Figure 13.1). The fat helps keep the grains separate and adds flavor.

Figure 13.1 Making rice pilaf.

(a) Sweat the onion or shallot.

(b) Add the rice and sauté briefly.

(c) Pour in the hot stock or other liquid.

(d) Bring to a boil and cover. Cook at low heat on top of the stove or in the oven for the required time.

(e) The finished pilaf.

It is normal to measure rice by volume when making pilaf, as the proportions are based on volume measure. One pint of raw rice weighs about 14 ounces, or 1 pound measures about 2¼ cups (1 L weighs about 875 g; or 1 kg measures 1.15 L). Regarding exact measurements, see the note following the pilaf recipe.

Procedure for Cooking Grain by the Pilaf Method

1. Heat the desired fat (such as butter or olive oil) in a heavy pan. Add chopped onion or other aromatic vegetable, if desired, and sauté until soft but not browned.
2. Add the grain. Stir to coat the grains with fat.
3. Cook the grain in the fat, stirring, to toast the grain lightly.
4. Add the proper amount of hot liquid.
5. Bring to a simmer, stirring occasionally.
6. Cover tightly. Cook on the stovetop or, preferably, in an oven, for the correct length of time, depending on the grain.
7. Remove from the heat and let stand, covered, to allow the moisture to be absorbed uniformly by the grain.

THE RISOTTO METHOD

Risotto is a classic Italian preparation made by a special procedure that is like neither the boiling method nor the pilaf method. After sautéing the rice, add a small amount of hot stock or other liquid and stir until the liquid is absorbed. Repeat this procedure until the rice is cooked but still firm. Risotto should be served quickly, as it does not hold well. The finished product has a creamy consistency due to the starch that is cooked out of the rice. The grains are not fluffy and separate.

The word *risotto* comes from the Italian word *riso*, meaning "rice." Other grains can be cooked using the same method, although strictly speaking they should not be called *risotto*. In Italy, farro cooked by the risotto method is called *farrotto*, and orzo pasta cooked this way is called *orzotto*. In the English-speaking world, however, the word *risotto* is more likely to be understood and is often used on menus, but with the grain specified if any type other than rice is used. For example, farrotto might be called *farro risotto*.

Procedure for Cooking Grain by the Risotto Method

1. Heat the desired fat (such as butter or olive oil) in a heavy pan. Add chopped onion or other aromatic vegetable, if desired, and sauté until soft but not browned.
2. Add the grain. Stir to coat the grains with fat.
3. Cook the grain in the fat, stirring, to toast the grain lightly.
4. Add a small amount of boiling liquid. Cook slowly, stirring, until the liquid is absorbed by the grain.
5. Add a second small quantity of liquid and repeat the procedure.
6. Continue adding a small quantity of liquid at a time, stirring constantly, and waiting until the liquid is absorbed before adding more.
7. Stop adding liquid when the grain is tender but still firm. It should be moist and creamy but not runny.

KEY POINTS TO REVIEW

- What are the steps in the basic procedure for simmering rice and other grains?
- How is the procedure for cooking cracked and flaked cereals different from cooking meals or granular cereals?
- What are the steps in the procedure for cooking grain by the pilaf method?
- What are the steps in the procedure for cooking grain by the risotto method?

Rice Pilaf

YIELD: ABOUT 3 LB (1.4 KG)	PORTIONS: 10	PORTION SIZE: 5 OZ (150 G)
	12	4 OZ (125 G)
	16	3 OZ (90 G)

U.S.	METRIC	INGREDIENTS
2 oz	60 g	Butter
3 oz	90 g	Onions, fine dice
1 pt (see Note)	500 mL (see Note)	Long-grain rice
1½–2 pt (see Note)	750 mL–1 L (see Note)	Chicken stock or water, boiling
to taste	to taste	Salt

Per 5-oz (150-g) serving: Calories, 190; Protein, 4 g; Fat, 5 g (23% cal.); Cholesterol, 15 mg; Carbohydrates, 33 g; Fiber, 1 g; Sodium, 50 mg.

Note: Rice for pilaf is measured by volume rather than by weight. Use 1½–2 times its volume in stock or water (1¾ times is the normal proportion for long-grain rice). For example, use 2 pints liquid per pint of rice (1 L liquid per 0.5 L rice) if you desire a moister product or if you are using parboiled rice. Use 1½ pints (0.75 L) liquid if you desire a drier product and if your cover is tight enough to retain most of the steam.

PROCEDURE

1. Heat the butter in a heavy saucepan. Add the onion and sauté until it begins to soften. Do not brown.

2. Add the rice, without washing. Stir over heat until the rice is completely coated with butter.

3. Pour in the boiling liquid. Return the liquid to a boil with the rice. Taste and adjust seasonings; cover tightly.

4. Place in a 350°F (175°C) oven and bake 18–20 minutes, or until liquid is absorbed and rice is dry and fluffy. Taste the rice and, if it is not done, replace in oven 3–5 minutes.

5. Turn out into a hotel pan and fluff the rice with a fork. This releases steam and prevents further cooking. Keep hot for service.

6. If desired, additional raw butter may be stirred into finished rice.

VARIATIONS

Tomato Pilaf

Prepare as in the basic recipe, using 12–16 oz (375–500 mL) chicken stock and 1½ lb (700 g) chopped tomatoes with juice.

Spanish Rice

Prepare like Tomato Pilaf, but use bacon fat and sauté 6 oz (175 g) diced green bell pepper, 1 crushed garlic clove, and 1 tbsp (15 mL) paprika with the onion.

Turkish Pilaf

Sauté ¼ tsp (1 mL) turmeric with the rice. To finished rice, add 4 oz (125 g) tomato concassé or drained, chopped canned tomatoes, 4 oz (125 g) cooked peas, and 4 oz (125 g) raisins (soaked and drained). Let stand 10–15 minutes before serving.

Cracked Wheat Pilaf

Prepare as in the basic recipe, using cracked wheat instead of rice.

Orzo Pilaf

Prepare as in the basic recipe, using orzo (rice-shaped pasta) instead of rice.

Barley Pilaf

Prepare as in the basic recipe, using pearled barley instead of rice. Use 2½ pints (1.25 L) stock and bake 45 minutes. Mushrooms are often added to barley pilaf.

Additions to Rice Pilaf

Pimiento	Spinach, chopped
Chopped nuts	Mushrooms
Celery, diced	Olives, chopped or sliced
Carrot, diced or grated	Ham, diced or cut julienne
Scallions	Raisins or currants
Peas	Water chestnuts
Green bell pepper, diced	Bacon

Basic Fried Rice

PORTIONS: 16　PORTION SIZE: 6 OZ (175 G)

U.S.	METRIC	INGREDIENTS
4 lb	1.8 kg	Cooked rice, cold
4–6 fl oz	125–175 mL	Oil
1 lb	450 g	Cooked meat (cut into shreds) or seafood (flaked or sliced)
3 oz	90 g	Scallions, sliced thin
1 lb	450 g	Vegetables (see Variations), shredded or small dice
4–6 fl oz	125–175 mL	Soy sauce (optional)
to taste	to taste	Salt
4–8	4–8	Eggs, beaten

PROCEDURE

1. Break up the rice to remove all lumps.
2. Divide the rice and other ingredients into two or more batches, depending on the size of the pan or wok. Do no more than 1–2 lb (0.5–1 kg) rice at one time. If you fry too much at once, it will not fry properly.
3. Heat a small amount of oil in the wok. Add the meat and stir-fry 1–2 minutes.
4. Add the scallions and stir-fry 1 minute.
5. Add any raw vegetables and stir-fry until almost done.
6. Add the rice and stir-fry until it is hot and lightly coated with oil.
7. Add any cooked vegetables and mix in.
8. Add soy sauce, if used, and salt.
9. Add beaten egg and mix in. Stir-fry lightly to cook the egg, then serve.

Per serving: Calories, 280; Protein, 11 g; Fat, 10 g (33% cal); Cholesterol, 70 mg; Carbohydrates, 35 g; Fiber, 2 g; Sodium, 35 mg.

VARIATIONS

The quantities given in the basic recipe are only guidelines, but rice should be the predominant ingredient. You can omit the meat or fish items.

For plain rice, you can omit the vegetables too.

Eggs can be omitted, or they can be added to fried rice in several other ways:

1. Remove the meat and vegetables from the pan when they are cooked. Add the egg to the pan and scramble. Add the rice, return the meat and vegetables to the pan, and continue with the recipe.
2. In step 9, push the rice to the sides of the pan. Add the egg to the well in the middle. When it starts to set, gradually mix in the rice.
3. Scramble the eggs separately and add to the rice at the end.
4. Mix the raw beaten egg with the cold cooked rice before cooking.

Suggested Ingredients

Meats: cooked pork, beef, chicken, duck, ham, bacon, Chinese sausage

Seafood: shrimp (diced or whole), crab, lobster

Vegetables: bamboo shoots, bean sprouts, celery, peas, mushrooms, onions, peppers, water chestnuts

Bulgur Pilaf with Lemon

PORTIONS: 12　PORTION SIZE: 2½ OZ (75 G)

U.S.	METRIC	INGREDIENTS
1 oz	30 g	Butter or vegetable oil
4 oz	125 g	Onion, chopped fine
8 oz	250 g	Bulgur, coarse
4 tsp	20 mL	Grated lemon zest
1½ pt	750 mL	Chicken stock or vegetable stock, hot
to taste	to taste	Salt
to taste	to taste	Pepper
4 tbsp	60 mL	Chopped chives

PROCEDURE

1. Heat the butter in a saucepan. Add the chopped onion and sauté gently without browning until the onion is soft.
2. Add the bulgur. Stir to coat with butter. Stir over heat 1 minute to lightly toast the grain.
3. Add the grated lemon zest and stir to mix.
4. Stir in the hot stock. Add salt and pepper to taste. Bring to a simmer.
5. Cover the pot and cook over low heat or in an oven heated to 350°F (175°C) until the bulgur is tender, about 20 minutes.
6. Uncover and fluff the grain with a kitchen fork. Add the chives and toss to mix in.

Per serving: Calories, 90; Protein, 3 g; Fat, 2 g (20% cal.); Cholesterol, 25 mg; Carbohydrates, 15 g; Fiber, 4 g; Sodium, 25 g.

Risotto alla Parmigiana

PORTIONS: 10   PORTION SIZE: 5 OZ (150 G)

U.S.	METRIC	INGREDIENTS
1 oz	30 g	Butter
1 fl oz	30 mL	Vegetable oil
1 oz	30 g	Onion, chopped fine
1 lb	450 g	Italian Arborio rice
1½ qt (approximately)	1.4 L (approximately)	Chicken stock, hot

PROCEDURE

1. Heat the butter and oil in a large, straight-sided sauté pan. Add the onion and sauté until soft. Do not brown.

2. Add the rice and sauté until well coated with the fat.

3. Using a 6-oz (150-mL) ladle, add one ladle of stock to the rice. Stir the rice over medium heat until the stock is absorbed and the rice is almost dry.

4. Add another ladle of stock and repeat procedure. Do not add more than one ladleful of stock at a time.

5. Stop adding stock when the rice is tender but still firm. It should be very moist and creamy, but not runny. The cooking should take about 30 minutes.

U.S.	METRIC	INGREDIENTS
1 oz	30 g	Butter
3 oz	90 g	Parmesan cheese, grated
to taste	to taste	Salt

6. Remove from the heat and stir in the raw butter and parmesan cheese. Salt to taste.

Per serving: Calories, 260; Protein, 7 g; Fat, 11 g (38% cal.); Cholesterol, 25 mg; Carbohydrates, 34 g; Fiber, 3g; Sodium, 210 mg.

VARIATIONS

Restaurant Method: Prepare basic pilaf (p. 354) using 1 lb Italian Arborio rice to 1 qt chicken stock (500 g rice to 1 L stock). To finish for service, place desired number of portions in a sauté pan and moisten with additional stock. Simmer until slightly moist and creamy, as in basic recipe. Finish with raw butter and parmesan cheese.

Risotto Milanese

Prepare as in basic recipe, but add ¼–½ tsp (1–2 mL) saffron soaked in 1 cup (200 mL) stock near the end of cooking.

Risotto with Mushrooms

Add 4–8 oz (100–200 g) mushrooms, chopped and sautéed in butter, near the end of cooking time.

Risi Bisi

Add 1 lb (450 g) cooked peas and ¼ cup (60 mL) chopped parsley to basic risotto. (This is not authentic Risi Bisi, which is considered a thick soup in Italy. However, it is similar.)

Risotto Milanese

Figure 13.2 Making risotto.

(a) Sauté the onion or shallot until soft.

(b) Add the rice. Sauté until coated with the fat.

(c) Add a ladleful of stock to the rice. Stir until the liquid is absorbed.

(d) Continue adding stock and stirring until the rice is cooked.

(e) For Risotto Milanese, add saffron steeped in hot stock near the end of the cooking period.

(f) Finish by stirring in parmesan cheese and butter.

Arroz à la Mexicana

PORTIONS: 16   PORTION SIZE: 4½ OZ (125 G)

U.S.	METRIC	INGREDIENTS
1½ lb	700 g	Long-grain rice
3 fl oz	90 mL	Oil
12 oz	350 g	Tomato purée
3 oz	90 g	Onion, chopped fine
2	2	Garlic cloves, mashed to a paste
3½ pt	1.75 L	Chicken stock
1 tbsp	15 mL	Salt

Per serving: Calories, 230; Protein, 4 g; Fat, 6 g (24% cal.); Cholesterol, 5 mg;
Carbohydrates, 39 g; Fiber, 1 g; Sodium, 440 mg.

PROCEDURE

1. Rinse the rice well to remove excess starch. Soak in cold water at least 30 minutes. Drain well.

2. Heat the oil in a pot and add the rice. Stir over moderate heat until it begins to brown lightly.

3. Add the tomato purée, onion, and garlic. Cook until the mixture is dry. Be careful not to let it burn.

4. Add the chicken stock and salt. Stir. Simmer, uncovered, over medium heat until most of the liquid is absorbed.

5. Cover, turn the heat to very low, and cook 5–10 minutes, or until the rice is tender.

6. Remove from the heat and let it stand, without removing the cover, 15–30 minutes before serving.

VARIATION

Arroz Verde

Omit the tomato purée. Purée the onion and garlic in a blender along with the following: 6 fl oz (175 mL) water, 3 tbsp (45 mL) chopped fresh cilantro leaves, ¾ cup (45 g or 200 mL) chopped parsley, and 3 oz (90 g) green chiles (or part green chiles and part green bell peppers). Use this purée in place of the tomato purée. Reduce the quantity of stock to 3 pt (1.5 mL). You may use water instead of stock.

Arroz à la Mexicana

Wheatberries with Pecans and Poblanos

PORTIONS: 12   PORTION SIZE: 4 OZ (125 G)

U.S.	METRIC	INGREDIENTS
1 lb 8 oz	750 g	Whole wheatberries, rinsed and soaked overnight in cold water (see Note)
2 qt	2 L	Water, cold
2 fl oz	60 mL	Olive oil
3 oz	90 g	Chopped pecans
3 oz	90 g	Roasted poblano chile, diced
to taste	to taste	Salt

PROCEDURE

1. Drain the soaking water from the wheatberries. Add the wheatberries to the cold water in a pot. Bring to a boil. Reduce heat to a simmer, cover, and simmer until the wheatberries are tender but still slightly crunchy, about 1 hour. Remove from heat and allow to stand, covered, 10 minutes. Drain.

2. Heat the olive oil in a sauté pan. Add the pecans and diced poblanos. Sauté about 1 minute.

3. Add the cooked wheatberries. Toss over heat until the mixture is hot. Season to taste.

Per serving: Calories, 280; Protein, 8 g; Fat, 10 g (31% cal.); Cholesterol, 0 mg; Carbohydrates, 42 g; Fiber, 7 g; Sodium, 0 mg.

Note: This recipe was developed using soft wheatberries with the bran left on. Other types of wheatberry may be used, but the yields and cooking times will vary. For example, the white wheatberries shown in the illustration on page 348 cook in less than 30 minutes and yield 3 times their dry weight (about 4½ lb/2.25 kg for this recipe). When using a new type of product, test cooking time and yield with a small quantity before adapting it to production.

VARIATIONS

Substitute any green chile or any sweet bell pepper for the poblanos.

Brown Rice, Barley, Farro, or Cracked Wheat with Pecans and Poblanos

Substitute cooked brown rice, cooked barley, cooked farro, or cracked wheat pilaf for the cooked wheatberries.

Wheatberries with Pecans and Poblanos

Paella

PORTIONS: 16   PORTION SIZE: SEE PROCEDURE

U.S.	METRIC	INGREDIENTS
2	2	Chickens, 2½–3 lb (1.1–1.4 kg) each
as needed	as needed	Olive oil
8 oz	225 g	Chorizo sausage (see Note)
2 lb	900 g	Lean pork, cut into large dice
16	16	Large shrimp, peeled and deveined
2 lb	900 g	Squid, cleaned, cut into rings
2	2	Red bell peppers, large dice
2	2	Green bell peppers, large dice
16	16	Small clams
16	16	Mussels
8 fl oz	250 mL	Water
as needed	as needed	Chicken stock
1 tsp	5 mL	Saffron
12 oz	350 g	Onion, small dice
6	6	Garlic cloves, minced
2 lb	900 g	Tomatoes, chopped
2 tsp	10 mL	Dried rosemary
2 lb	900 g	Short-grain rice, such as Italian Arborio
2 tsp	10 mL	Salt
to taste	to taste	Pepper
4 oz	125 g	Cooked green peas
16	16	Lemon wedges

PROCEDURE

1. Cut each chicken into 8 pieces.

2. In a large sauté pan, brown the chicken in olive oil. Remove and set aside.

3. Using additional oil as needed, briefly sauté the sausage, pork, shrimp, squid, and peppers. Do each ingredient separately, then remove to separate containers.

4. Combine the clams and mussels with the water in a covered pot. Steam just until they open.

5. Remove the shellfish and set them aside. Strain the liquid, then add enough chicken stock to measure 2 qt (2 L).

6. Add the saffron to the stock mixture.

7. In the skillet used for browning the meats, sauté the onion and garlic until soft. Use additional olive oil if necessary.

8. Add the tomatoes and rosemary. Cook until most of the liquid has evaporated and the tomatoes form a rather dry paste.

9. Add the rice and stir. Add the chicken, sausage, pork, squid, and peppers.

10. Bring the stock mixture to a boil in a separate pot, then add to the rice and stir. Add salt and pepper to taste.

11. Bring to a simmer, cover, and put in a 350°F (175C) oven for 20 minutes. (This dish is traditionally made uncovered on top of the stove, but making it in the oven is more practical for restaurants because it requires less attention.)

12. Remove the pan from the oven. Check the moisture level and add more stock, if necessary. It should be quite moist but not soupy.

13. Sprinkle the peas over the rice. Arrange the shrimp, clams, and mussels on top. Cover loosely and let stand 10 minutes to heat the shellfish.

14. For each portion, allow 8 oz (225 g) rice and vegetables, 1 shrimp, 1 clam, 1 mussel, 1 piece of chicken, and at least 1 piece each of pork, sausage, and squid. Garnish each portion with 1 lemon wedge.

Per serving: Calories, 630; Protein, 52 g; Fat, 22 g (32% cal.); Cholesterol, 260 mg; Carbohydrates, 52 g; Fiber, 5 g; Sodium, 630 mg.

Note: If chorizo is not available, use pepperoni or other hard, spicy sausage. You may cut the sausage into ½-ounce (15-g) chunks before sautéing or cut them up just before serving.

Paella

Farrotto with Pecorino Cheese

PORTIONS: 10   PORTION SIZE: 4 OZ (1150 G)

U.S.	METRIC	INGREDIENTS	PROCEDURE
1 lb	450 g	Farro	1. Soak the farro in cold water 45 minutes. Drain.
			2. Boil the farro in boiling salted water 20 minutes. Drain. At this point, the farro should be about half-cooked.
2 fl oz	60 mL	Olive oil	3. Heat the olive oil in a sauté pan over moderate heat.
1 oz	30 g	Onion, chopped fine	4. Sweat the onion in the oil until soft.
1½ qt (approximately)	1.5 L (approximately)	Vegetable stock, hot	5. Add the farro. Stir and cook over moderate heat 2 minutes.
			6. Ladle in 4 fl oz (125 mL) stock. Stir over moderate heat until the stock is absorbed and the farro is almost dry.
			7. Add another ladleful of stock and repeat the procedure.
			8. Stop adding stock when the farro is tender.
1 oz	30 g	Butter	9. Stir in the butter and cheese. Serve immediately.
4 oz	120 g	Pecorino cheese, grated	

Per serving: Calories, 260; Protein, 8 g; Fat, 12 g (39% cal.); Cholesterol, 15 mg; Carbohydrates, 34 g; Fiber, 0 g; Sodium, 102.7 mg.

Farrotto with Pecorino Cheese

Polenta

YIELD: ABOUT 5 LB (2.5 KG)

U.S.	METRIC	INGREDIENTS
5 pt	2.5 L	Water
1 tbsp	15 mL	Salt
1 lb	500 g	Polenta (Italian coarse-grained yellow cornmeal)

Per 1 ounce (28.35 g): Calories, 20; Protein, 0 g; Fat, 0 g (0% cal.); Cholesterol, 0 mg; Carbohydrates, 4 g; Fiber, 0 g; Sodium, 90 mg.

PROCEDURE

1. Bring the water and salt to a boil in a saucepot.
2. Very slowly sprinkle the cornmeal into the boiling water, stirring constantly. This must be done slowly and carefully to avoid lumps (see **Figure 13.3**).
3. Cook over low heat, stirring almost constantly. The polenta will become thicker as it cooks and eventually start to pull away from the sides of the pot. This will take 20–30 minutes.
4. Lightly moisten a large, flat surface, such as a wooden board or a platter.
5. Pour the polenta onto this board or platter. Serve immediately, hot, or let cool and use in any of a number of ways, including the variations below.

VARIATIONS

Freshly made hot polenta is good with many kinds of stews and other braised dishes that provide plenty of flavorful juices for the polenta to soak up. It is also served with grilled dishes.

Polenta con Sugo di Pomodoro

Serve hot polenta with tomato sauce or Meat Sauce (p. 372).

Polenta con Salsicce

Serve hot polenta with pork sausages cooked with tomatoes or tomato sauce.

Polento al Burro e Formaggio

Stir 6 oz (175 g) fresh butter and 2–3 oz (60–90 g) grated parmesan cheese into hot polenta as soon as it is cooked.

Polenta Fritta or Grigliata

Let polenta cool and cut it into slices ½ in. (1 cm) thick. Pan-fry in oil until a thin crust forms. Alternatively, heat slices on a grill or broiler until hot and lightly grill-marked.

Polenta Grassa

This can be prepared in two ways.

1. Pour a layer of hot polenta into a buttered baking dish. Cover with sliced fontina cheese and dot with butter. Cover with another layer of polenta, then another layer of cheese and butter. Bake until very hot.
2. Prepare as in the first method, but instead of the hot, freshly made polenta, use cold polenta cut into thin slices.

Polenta Pasticciata

Prepare Meat Sauce (p. 372), using pork sausage in addition to the beef. Also, add sautéed sliced mushrooms to the sauce. Cut cold polenta into thin slices. Fill a baking pan with alternating layers of polenta slices, meat sauce, and parmesan cheese. Bake until hot.

Polenta Pasticciata

Figure 13.3 Making polenta.

(a) Slowly sprinkle the polenta into the simmering water, stirring constantly to avoid lumps.

(b) Simmer while stirring until the polenta reaches the desired texture. Serve at once, or proceed to the next step.

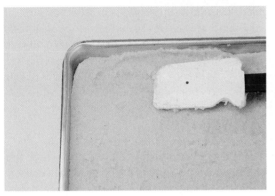

(c) Pour the polenta into a sheet pan and cool.

(d) Cut into desired shapes.

Grits with Cheddar Cheese

PORTIONS: 12   PORTION SIZE: 6 OZ

U.S.	METRIC	INGREDIENTS
2 cups	500 mL	Hominy grits
2 qt	2 L	Water
1 tsp	5 mL	Salt
8 oz	250 g	Cheddar cheese, grated

Per serving: Calories, 170; Protein, 7 g; Fat, 7 g (35% cal.); Cholesterol, 20 mg; Carbohydrates, 22 g; Fiber, 1 g; Sodium, 310 mg.

VARIATIONS

For regular grits, omit the cheese. Serve topped with a pat of butter.
If desired, substitute milk for one-third of the water.

PROCEDURE

1. Stir the grits into the water in a saucepan.

2. If you are using stone-ground grits, let them settle, then skim off any hulls that float to the surface.

3. Bring the mixture to a boil while stirring.

4. Simmer the grits, stirring every 5–10 minutes. If you are using quick-cooking grits, they will be done in 7–10 minutes but can be cooked longer if a thicker product is desired. If you are using regular grits, cooking time is about 45 minutes, and you may have to add water as they thicken. In any case, continue to cook until creamy, adding water as necessary.

5. Stir in salt to taste.

6. Add the cheese and stir until it is melted.

Grits

Pasta, Noodles, and Dumplings

Macaroni products, or pastas, are popular alternatives to other starch foods. The word *pasta* is Italian for "paste," so called because pasta is made from a mixture of wheat flour and water and, sometimes, eggs.

Not so many years ago, many of us knew only spaghetti with tomato sauce and elbow macaroni with cheese, among all pasta products. Today, thanks to the influence of Italian cooks, we have a choice of a great variety of pasta dishes.

In addition, noodle products play an important role in other cuisines, notably those of Asia. These include not only wheat noodles but also noodles made of rice and other starches. Although most of our attention here is devoted to Italian-style pastas, we take a look at these other products as well.

Italian-Style Pastas

Italian pastas have spread beyond their original borders to become one of the most popular foods in North America and Europe. Please note that when we use the term *Italian-style pasta* we are referring only to the noodle products themselves, not to the dishes prepared from them. Appearing on menus are many dishes that are made with Italian-style pastas but that are not recognizably Italian in any way, as they use ingredients from other cuisines, including those of Asia and Latin America. Adopted by chefs from many cultures, Italian pastas have become citizens of the world.

KINDS, CHARACTERISTICS, AND QUALITY FACTORS

Commercial dried pasta is made from dough that has been shaped and dried. To refer to this category of food, we sometimes use the term *macaroni*, meaning any dried pasta made from flour and water. These include spaghetti, lasagna, elbow macaroni, and many other shapes.

The best dried macaroni pastas are made from *semolina*, a high-protein flour from the inner part of durum wheat kernels. Lower-quality products are made from farina, a softer flour.

Specialty pastas include ingredients in addition to semolina and water. Whole wheat pasta may be made with all whole wheat flour or a mixture of semolina and whole wheat. Other grain flours, including buckwheat and farro (spelt), are used in other specialty items.

Spinach pasta is perhaps the most popular of the pastas that contain vegetable purées. Others include red peppers, hot chile, seaweed, beet, tomato, and pumpkin.

Pasta containing *squid ink* is black in color and goes well with seafood sauces.

When purchasing macaroni products (unflavored), look for a good yellow color, not gray-white. The product should be very hard, brittle, and springy, and it should snap with a clean, sharp-edged break. When cooked, it should be firm and hold its shape well. Poor-quality pastas are soft and pasty when cooked.

In addition to pastas made of flour and water, dried *egg pastas* are also available. They contain at least 5.5 percent egg solids in addition to the flour and water. They are usually sold as flat noodles of various widths.

Fresh egg pasta is made from flour and eggs and, sometimes, a small quantity of water and/or oil. Use a regular all-purpose or bread flour. Hard semolina flour, used for factory-made spaghetti and macaroni, is not appropriate for fresh egg pasta. Softer flour makes a more tender pasta. Soft egg noodle products are also available fresh and frozen from manufacturers. They take less time to cook than dried macaroni products.

Other flours, such as whole wheat flour, can be used to make fresh noodles. When you are making them yourself, you can experiment with ingredients. Keep in mind that flours other than wheat flour don't form much gluten, so they should be mixed with some wheat flour. Buckwheat flour added to white flour makes especially tasty noodles that are featured in a northern Italian classic called *Pizzoccheri*.

Vegetable purées and other flavoring ingredients are often added to fresh egg pasta. Spinach, tomato, beet, mushrooms, fresh herbs, dried chile, grated lemon zest, saffron, and squid ink are among the many possibilities.

SHAPES AND THEIR USES

Pasta is made in hundreds of shapes and sizes. Each shape is appropriate for different preparations because of the way different kinds of sauce cling to them or the way their textures
complement the texture of the topping. The illustration shows some of the most popular
kinds. Table 13.2 describes the most common shapes and gives suggestions for use.

Remember that fresh egg pasta and factory-made spaghetti and macaroni are different
products. It makes no sense to say that one type is better than the other. Italian cooks use
fresh and dried pasta in different ways, with different recipes for each type. Factory pasta has
a chewy, robust texture, good with robust sauces, while fresh egg pasta is tender and more
delicate. Fresh egg pasta absorbs sauces more deeply than factory macaroni products. In
general, factory-made pasta is ideal for olive oil–based sauces, and fresh homemade pasta
is better with butter or cream-based sauces.

Table 13.2 Commercial Pasta Shapes and Uses

NAME	DESCRIPTION	SUGGESTED USES
Spaghetti	Long, round	With great variety of sauces, especially tomato sauces
Spaghettini	Thin, long, round	Like spaghetti, especially with olive oil and seafood sauces
Vermicelli	Very thin	With light, delicate sauces and, broken, in soups
Linguine	Looks like slightly flattened spaghetti	Like spaghetti; popular with clam sauces
Perciatelli	Looks like thick, hollow spaghetti	Like spaghetti, but can handle heavy, chunky sauces
Fusilli	Long, shaped like a corkscrew	Thick, creamy sauces
Macaroni	Long, hollow tubes	Especially good with hearty meat sauces
Elbow macaroni	Short, bent macaroni	Cold, in salads; baked, in casseroles
Penne or mostaccioli	Hollow tubes, cut diagonally; may be smooth or ridged	Baked, with meat sauce or with tomato sauce and cheese; freshly cooked, with tomato sauce
Ziti	Short, hollow tubes, cut straight	
Rigatoni	Larger tubes, with ridges	
Manicotti (sometimes called cannelloni, which are actually rolled from fresh egg noodle dough)	Large hollow tubes, sometimes with ridges	Stuff with cheese or meat filling
Orecchiette	Little ears	Chunky vegetable sauces
Rotelle, ruote	Wheels	Chunky tomato, meat, or vegetable sauces; in soups
Radiatore	Radiators; curled, ruffled shapes	Cold, in salads; hot, with chunky sauces
Fettuccine	Flat egg noodles	Rich cream sauces or meat sauces
Tagliagelle	Wide, flat egg noodles	
Lasagna	Broad, flat noodles, often with rippled edges	Baked with meat, cheese, or vegetable fillings
Conchiglie	Shells	With seafood or meat sauces; small sizes can be used in salads
Bow ties or farfalle	Look like bow ties	With sauces containing chunks of meat, sausage, or vegetable
Pastina (little pasta)		In soups; cold, in salads; buttered, as a side dish
Ditalini	Very short, hollow tubes	
Orzo	Rice-shaped	
Stelline	Tiny stars	
Acini di pepe	Peppercorns	
Pepe bucato	Peppercorns with holes	
Rotelline	Little wheels	
Semi di melone	Melon seeds	

Top row: elbow macaroni, pepe bucato, radiatore, ziti, conchiglie. Middle row: fettuccine; spaghettini; fusilli; (three small piles, from top to bottom) orzo, stelline, and ditalini; lasagna; spaghetti; (two small piles, from top to bottom) gemelli and rigatoni. Bottom row: bow ties (farfalle), penne, manicotti.

Other Noodle Products

Asian countries have a wide variety of noodle products. We can divide these into two categories: wheat noodles and noodles made of other starches.

NOODLES MADE OF WHEAT

Most of the Asian wheat noodles we know in the West are from China and Japan.

Chinese noodles are made from either flour and water or flour, water, and egg. If they contain egg, they are usually labeled as *egg noodles*. Flat noodles come in a variety of widths, from very thin to nearly an inch (2.5 cm) wide. Round noodles come in a variety of thicknesses, from thin vermicelli to thicker, spaghetti-like noodles.

Cantonese noodles are a special type of Chinese wheat noodle made by stretching a single large piece of dough in one length until it is as thin as spaghetti. Some restaurants feature a skilled noodle maker performing this amazing feat in the dining room. Cantonese noodles are available fresh or dried.

Japanese wheat noodles come in several varieties. **Udon** are thick, white noodles made from wheat flour. They are available fresh in vacuum packs or dried. **Somen** are thin, white wheat noodles usually packaged in small bundles. Tamago somen are made with egg in addition to wheat flour and water (*tamago* means "egg").

Soba are thin noodles made with buckwheat in addition to wheat flour. A special variety of buckwheat noodle is **chasoba**, made with powdered green tea in addition to the buckwheat.

In spite of the *soba* in the name, **chukasoba** contain no buckwheat. They are wheat noodles made with flour and water, with an alkali such as sodium carbonate added to the water. The noodles are yellow in color, leading some people to think they are egg noodles, but they contain no egg. These noodles are used in the popular ramen dishes familiar in the West from the single-portion packages of noodles and soup stock, found in nearly every supermarket.

NOODLES MADE OF OTHER STARCHES

With the increased popularity of Southeast Asian and Chinese cuisines in the West, *rice noodles* have become familiar. Rice noodles are available as very fine, almost hairlike noodles called **rice vermicelli,** and as flat noodles of various widths. Rice noodles are sometimes known as **rice sticks.**

Rice vermicelli are often cooked by deep-frying the dry noodles, without using any water. The noodles puff up and become crisp and tender. Rice vermicelli can also be broken apart and stir-fried, as long as enough liquid is added to the stir-fry to rehydrate them.

Rice noodles of all types are not usually boiled in water because they become too soft and sticky. Rather, they are covered with hot water and soaked until tender. This takes from a few minutes to about an hour, depending on the thickness of the noodle and the temperature of the water. The noodles are drained and added to stir-fried dishes and soups at the last minute of cooking.

Bean thread noodles, also called **cellophane noodles,** are made with mung bean starch. They are very thin noodles that resemble rice vermicelli. Like rice noodles, they are either deep-fried or soaked in hot water until tender and then added to soups and braised dishes.

COUSCOUS

Couscous is a kind of granular pasta made from semolina flour (see sidebar). It is cooked by soaking and then steaming, using a fairly time-consuming process. **Instant couscous** is prepared by simply adding the dry product to hot or boiling water and letting it stand 5 minutes. The accompanying procedures outline the methods for making both classic and instant couscous.

Procedure for Steaming Traditional Couscous

1. Place the couscous in a bowl and add enough cold water to cover it by several inches (cm). Stir the couscous and then drain off the excess water through a fine sieve. Smooth the couscous in the bowl and let stand 15 minutes, allowing the couscous to absorb the moisture that coats it.

2. With wet hands, stir and rub the grains to break up all lumps.

3. Line the top of a couscousière with a double layer of cheesecloth. Place the couscous inside. If you don't have a couscousière, select a colander that will fit over a large saucepan or similar pot. Line with cheesecloth and put the couscous in it.

4. Set the couscousière top or colander over a simmering stew (or simmering water). Steam, uncovered, 20 minutes.

5. Empty the couscous into a hotel pan and spread it into a flat layer. Sprinkle with a little salt and just enough water to moisten it slightly. Coat your hands with oil and stir and rub the couscous to break up all lumps. Let stand 10 minutes. At this point, if the couscous feels dry, sprinkle with a little more water and stir.

6. Give the couscous a second steaming by repeating step 4.

7. Turn out the finished couscous into a hotel pan or other container for service. Stir lightly to break up any lumps.

Procedure for Preparing Instant Couscous

1. Measure equal parts by volume dry instant couscous and water.

2. Place the water in a saucepan and bring to a boil. Add ½ tsp (2 mL) salt and 2 tsp (10 mL) butter per pint (0.5 L) water.

3. When the water boils, add the couscous and stir. Remove from the heat, cover, and let stand 5 minutes.

4. Before serving, stir with a fork to break up lumps.

COUSCOUS

Couscous is a classic dish of North Africa, especially Morocco and Algeria. The word refers to both the grainlike product and the dish made from it. After soaking, couscous is steamed in the perforated top section of a double kettle called a *couscousière* (koos koos yair), while a spicy stew cooks in the lower section.

Rather than being made from a smooth dough like noodles are, couscous is made by sprinkling water into a bowl of semolina flour and stirring with the hand, forming tiny granules of dough. The granules are then sifted out and dried, and the process is repeated.

A related product called *Israeli couscous* is made in the lands at the eastern end of the Mediterranean. Israeli couscous is made from regular wheat rather than semolina, and it is formed into larger, spherical grains. It is typically served in place of rice.

Cooking Pasta

DONENESS

Pasta should be cooked *al dente*, or "to the tooth." This means cooking should be stopped when the pasta still feels firm to the bite, not soft and mushy. Much of the pleasure of eating pasta is its texture (that's why there are so many shapes), and this is lost if it is overcooked.

TESTING DONENESS AND SERVING

Many suggestions have been made for testing doneness, but none is more reliable than breaking off a very small piece and tasting it. As soon as the pasta is al dente, the cooking must be stopped at once. Half a minute extra is enough to overcook it.

Cooking times differ for every shape and size of pasta. Timing also depends on the kind of flour used and the moisture content. Times indicated on packages are often too long.

Fresh egg pasta, if it has not been allowed to dry, takes only 1 to 1½ minutes to cook after the water returns to a boil.

Italian practice is to toss the pasta with the sauce the minute it is drained. The sauce immediately coats all surfaces of the pasta, and cheese, if there is any, melts in the heat of the boiling hot noodles. If you are attempting to serve an authentic Italian pasta dish, follow this practice rather than simply topping the pasta with the sauce.

Pasta is best if cooked and served immediately. Whenever possible, you should try to cook pasta to order. Fresh pasta, in particular, cooks so quickly there is little reason to cook it in advance. In volume operations, however, commercial pasta may have to be cooked ahead of time. The following procedures can be used for quantity cookery.

YIELDS

One pound (450 g) uncooked dried pasta yields about 3 pounds (1.4 kg) cooked pasta. This is enough for four to six main-course portions or eight to ten side-dish or first-course portions.

One pound (450 g) uncooked fresh pasta yields 2 to 2½ pounds (900 to 1100 g) cooked pasta.

Procedure for Cooking Pasta in Large Quantities

1. Use at least 4 quarts boiling salted water per pound of pasta (4 L per 500 g). Use about 1½ tablespoons (25 g) salt per 4 quarts (4 L) water.

2. Have the water boiling rapidly and drop in the pasta. As it softens, stir gently to keep it from sticking together and to the bottom.

3. Continue to boil, stirring a few times.

4. As soon as the pasta is al dente, drain it immediately in a colander and rinse with cold running water until completely cooled. Otherwise, it would continue to cook and become too soft. (If you are cooking just a few portions to serve immediately, just drain well and do not rinse. Sauce and serve without a moment's delay.)

   If the pasta is to be used cold in a salad, it is ready to be incorporated into the recipe as soon as it has cooled.

5. If the pasta is to be held, toss gently with a small amount of oil to keep it from sticking.

6. Measure portions into mounds on trays. Cover with plastic film and refrigerate until service time. (Do not store pasta in cold water. The pasta will absorb water and become soft, as though it had been overcooked.)

7. To serve, place the desired number of portions in a china cap and immerse in simmering water to reheat. Drain, plate, and add sauce.

Alternative Method: Steam Table Service

Pasta gradually becomes soft and mushy when kept hot for service, but it will hold reasonably well for 30 minutes. It will not be as good as if freshly cooked, however. This method should not be used unless cooking pasta to order is not possible in a particular food-service operation.

1. Follow steps 1 to 3 above.

2. Drain the pasta while still slightly undercooked. Rinse briefly in cool water, enough to stop the cooking and rinse off starch but not enough to cool the pasta. Pasta should still be quite warm.

3. Transfer the pasta to a steam table pan and toss with oil to prevent sticking.

4. Hold for up to 30 minutes.

Fresh Egg Pasta

YIELD: 1½ LB (700 G)

U.S.	METRIC	INGREDIENTS
1 lb	450 g	Bread flour
5	5	Eggs
½ fl oz	15 mL	Olive oil
pinch	pinch	Salt

Per 1 ounce (28.35 g): Calories, 90; Protein, 4 g; Fat, 2 g (20% cal.); Cholesterol, 45 mg; Carbohydrates, 14 g; Fiber, 0 g; Sodium, 20 mg.

PROCEDURE

1. Mound the flour on a work surface. Make a well in the center and add the eggs, oil, and salt.

2. Working from the center outward, gradually mix the flour into the eggs to make a dough.

3. When it is firm enough to knead, begin kneading the dough, incorporating more flour. If the dough is still sticky when all the flour is incorporated, add more flour, a little at a time. Knead well for at least 15 minutes.

4. Cover the dough and let it rest at least 30 minutes.

5. Cut the dough into 3 to 5 pieces. Set the rollers of a pasta machine at the widest opening. Pass the pieces of dough through the machine, folding them in thirds after each pass and dusting them lightly with flour to keep them from getting sticky. Continue passing each piece through the machine until it is smooth. See **Figure 13.4**.

6. Working with one piece of dough at a time, decrease the width between the rollers one notch and pass the dough through them again. After each pass, turn the rollers one notch narrower, dust the dough with flour, and pass it through again. Continue until the dough is as thin as desired. The pasta is now ready to cut into desired shapes and to cook. See below for cutting instructions.

VARIATIONS

Cutting Instructions

Fettuccine or *Tagliatelle*: Roll dough thin and cut with wide cutting rollers.

Taglierini: Roll dough thin and cut with narrow cutting rollers.

Papardelle: Cut by hand, using a fluted cutting wheel, into long noodles about ¾ in. (18 mm) wide.

Tonnarelli: Roll dough to the same thickness as the width of the narrow cutting roller. Cut with the narrow cutting rollers. The result is like square spaghetti.

Bow ties: Cut into rectangles about 1½ × 3 in. (4 × 8 cm). Pinch in the middle to make a bow.

Lasagne: Cut by hand into broad strips about 8–12 in. (20–30 cm) long.

Spinach Pasta

Clean 1 lb (450 g) AP spinach, discarding stems. Simmer 5 minutes in salted water. Drain, rinse in cold water, and squeeze dry. Chop as fine as possible. Incorporate in basic pasta recipe, adding it to the flour at the same time as the eggs. Reduce the quantity of eggs to 4.

Other Colored Pastas

Other colored vegetables, in small quantities, cooked until tender and puréed or chopped fine, can be substituted for spinach to color pasta. For example, experiment with beets, red bell peppers, and carrots.

Whole Wheat Pasta

Substitute whole wheat flour for half of the white flour.

Buckwheat Pasta

In place of the 1 lb (450 g) white flour, use 10 oz (280 g) buckwheat flour and 6 oz (180 g) white flour. Omit the olive oil.

Figure 13.4 Working with fresh egg pasta.

(a) Set the rollers of the machine at their widest setting. Pass the piece of dough through the rollers, fold in thirds, and repeat until the dough is smooth.

(b) Decrease the opening between the rollers one notch at a time and pass the dough through them to roll to desired thickness.

(c) Pass the rolled-out dough through the appropriate cutters to make pasta of desired size and shape.

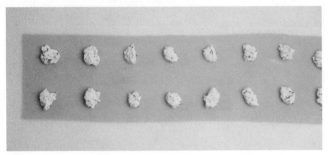

(d) To make ravioli, lay a thin sheet of pasta on the workbench. Deposit portions of filling on the dough using a spoon, small scoop, or pastry bag.

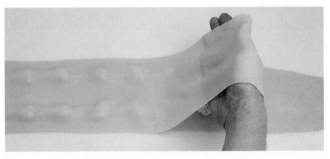

(e) Cover with another sheet of pasta.

(f) Press down between the mounds of filling to seal the layers of pasta together. Try to remove air bubbles from between the layers.

(g) Cut out the ravioli with cutters, or cut them apart with a pastry wheel.

Ravioli with Cheese Filling

PORTIONS: 25   PORTION SIZE: 5 OZ (150 G) UNCOOKED OR APPROXIMATELY 7 OZ (200 G) COOKED

U.S.	METRIC	INGREDIENTS	PROCEDURE
3 lb	1.4 kg	Ricotta cheese	1. Mix together the ricotta, parmesan, egg yolks, parsley, and seasonings.
8 oz	250 g	Parmesan cheese, grated	
5	5	Egg yolks	
¾ cup	50 g	Chopped parsley	
½ tsp	2 mL	Nutmeg	
to taste	to taste	Salt	
to taste	to taste	White pepper	
4½ lb	2 kg	Fresh pasta	2. Roll the pasta into thin sheets.

Per serving: Calories, 410; Protein, 21 g; Fat, 17g (38% cal.); Cholesterol, 205 mg; Carbohydrates, 42 Fiber, 1 g; Sodium, 270 mg.

3. Over half the pasta, make small mounds of cheese filling, about 1 tsp (5 mL) each, arranging them in a checkerboard pattern 1½–2 in. (4–5 cm) apart.

4. Lay the remaining pasta over the top and press down between the mounds of cheese to seal well (see **Figure 13.4**). While doing this, try to avoid sealing large air bubbles inside the ravioli. *Note:* If the pasta is fresh and moist, the layers will seal together if pressed firmly. If it is dry, moisten the bottom layer lightly between the mounds of cheese, using a brush dipped in water. Do not get the pasta too wet.

5. Cut the ravioli apart with a pastry wheel. Check each piece to be sure it is completely sealed.

6. The cheese filling does not keep well, so the ravioli should be cooked the same day they are made. They can be held briefly on sheet pans covered with dry, clean towels; turn them over from time to time so they do not stick. Alternatively, cook them immediately in boiling salted water, keeping them slightly underdone. Drain and rinse under cold water, drain, and toss with oil or melted butter. Spread in a single layer on a sheet pan and refrigerate. They can then be reheated to order by sautéing them briefly in butter or oil or by dipping them in boiling water.

7. Serve with your choice of sauce, such as tomato sauce, meat sauce, Bolognese sauce, tomato cream sauce, or just melted butter and parmesan cheese.

Italian Tomato Sauce for Pasta

YIELD: 3 QT (3 L)   PORTIONS: 32   PORTION SIZE: 3 FL OZ (ML)

U.S.	METRIC	INGREDIENTS
1 pt	500 mL	Olive oil (see Note)
½ lb	225 g	Onion, chopped fine
½ lb	225 g	Carrot, chopped fine
½ lb	225 g	Celery, chopped fine
1 No. 10 can	1 No. 10 can	Whole tomatoes
2	2	Garlic cloves, minced
1 oz	30 g	Salt
1 tbsp	15 mL	Sugar

Per serving: Calories, 190; Protein, 1 g; Fat, 18 g (82% cal.); Cholesterol, 0 mg; Carbohydrates, 8 g; Fiber, 2 g; Sodium, 660 mg.

Note: The quantity of olive oil may seem high, but it is only 1 tbsp for a 3-oz portion (15 mL per 90 g). These are typical proportions for basic tomato sauce in Italy, where sauces are not used in such large quantities as in North America. The olive oil is intended to be a major ingredient, not just a sautéing medium for the mirepoix, so use a good, flavorful oil. If a lower-fat sauce is desired, oil may be cut in half. Except for meat sauce, most Italian sauces are cooked less than American-style tomato sauce and have fewer ingredients. As a result, they have a more pronounced fresh tomato taste.

PROCEDURE

1. Heat the olive oil in a large saucepot. Add the onions, carrots, and celery and sauté lightly for a few minutes. Do not let the vegetables brown.

2. Add remaining ingredients. (See Appendix 2 for can sizes and substitutions.) Simmer, uncovered, about 45 minutes, until reduced and thickened.

3. Pass through a food mill. Taste and adjust seasonings.

4. For service, this sauce should be tossed with the freshly cooked spaghetti or other pasta in a bowl before being plated, rather than simply ladled over the pasta.

VARIATIONS

Omit onion, carrot, and celery. Reduce oil to 8 fl oz (250 mL). Add fresh chopped parsley and basil to taste.

Meat Sauce

Brown 2 lb (1 kg) ground beef, ground pork, or a mixture of beef and pork, in oil or rendered pork fat. Add 8 fl oz (250 mL) red wine, 2 qt (2 L) tomato sauce, 1 qt (1 L) beef or pork stock, and parsley, basil, and oregano to taste. Simmer 1 hour, uncovered.

Tomato Cream Sauce

Use 8 oz (250 g) butter instead of the olive oil in the basic recipe. At service time, add 1 cup heavy cream per quart of tomato sauce (250 mL per L). Bring to simmer and serve.

Tomato Sauce with Sausage

Slice 3 lb (1.4 kg) fresh Italian sausage and brown in oil. Drain and add to basic tomato sauce. Simmer 20 minutes.

Tomato Sauce with Sausage and Eggplant

Prepare like Tomato Sauce with Sausage, but use 1½ lb (700 g) each sausage and peeled, diced eggplant.

Tomato Sauce with Ham and Rosemary

Cook 1 lb (450 g) ham, cut into fine dice, and 2 tbsp (30 mL) dried rosemary leaves in a little olive oil for a few minutes. Add to basic tomato sauce (after it has been passed through the food mill) and simmer 5 minutes.

Pesto (Fresh Basil Sauce)

YIELD: ABOUT 3 CUPS (750 ML)   PORTIONS: 12   PORTION SIZE: 2 OZ (60 ML)

U.S.	METRIC	INGREDIENTS
2 qt	2 L	Fresh basil leaves
1½ cups	375 mL	Olive oil
2 oz	60 g	Walnuts or pine nuts (pignoli)
6	6	Garlic cloves
1½ tsp	7 mL	Salt
5 oz	150 g	Parmesan cheese, grated
1½ oz	50 g	Romano cheese, grated

Per 1 fl oz (29.57 mL): Calories, 350; Protein, 8 g; Fat, 35 g (88% cal.); Cholesterol, 15 mg; Carbohydrates, 3 g; Fiber, 1 g; Sodium, 550 mg.

PROCEDURE

1. Wash the basil leaves and drain well.

2. Put the basil, oil, nuts, garlic, and salt in a blender or food processor. Blend to a paste, but not so long that the mixture is smooth. It should have a slightly coarse texture.

3. Transfer the mixture to a bowl and stir in the cheese.

4. To serve, cook pasta to order according to the basic procedure. Just before the pasta is done, stir a little of the hot cooking water into the pesto to thin it, if desired. Toss the drained pasta with the pesto and serve immediately. Pass additional grated cheese.

Fettuccine Alfredo

PORTIONS: 10   PORTION SIZE: 6–7 OZ (175–200 G)

U.S.	METRIC	INGREDIENTS
1 cup	250 mL	Heavy cream
2 oz	60 g	Butter
1½ lb	700 g	Fresh fettuccine
1 cup	250 mL	Heavy cream
6 oz	175 g	Freshly grated parmesan cheese
to taste	to taste	Salt
to taste	to taste	Pepper

PROCEDURE

1. Combine 1 cup (250 mL) cream and the butter in a sauté pan. Bring to a simmer, reduce by one-fourth, and remove from heat.

2. Drop the noodles into boiling salted water, return to a full boil, and drain. The noodles must be slightly undercooked because they will cook further in the cream mixture.

3. Put the drained noodles in the pan with the hot cream and butter mixture. Over low heat, toss the noodles with two forks until they are well coated.

4. Add the remaining 1 cup (250 mL) cream and the cheese, and toss to mix well. (If the noodles seem dry at this point, add a little more cream.)

5. Add salt and pepper to taste.

6. Plate and serve immediately. Offer additional grated cheese at the table.

Per serving: Calories, 500; Protein, 17 g; Fat, 32 g (56% cal.); Cholesterol, 195 mg; Carbohydrates, 35 g; Fiber, 1 g; Sodium, 430 mg.

VARIATIONS

Fettuccine with Vegetables I (Fettuccine Primavera)

Fresh, lightly cooked vegetables can be added to fettuccine to make a great variety of dishes. In the basic recipe, use about half the quantity of cream. Select 4–6 fresh vegetables, cut them into appropriately small sizes and shapes, cook them al dente, and add

them to the pasta when it is being tossed in the cream. The following are examples of appropriate vegetables:

Mushrooms	Tiny green beans
Peas	Asparagus
Broccoli	Artichoke hearts
Red or green bell pepper	Zucchini

Small quantities of finely diced ham, prosciutto, or bacon can also be added as a flavor accent.

Fettuccine with Vegetables II

Prepare like Fettuccine with Vegetables I, but omit all butter and cream. Instead, toss the freshly cooked fettuccine and cooked vegetables with olive oil. Add parmesan cheese as desired.

Fettuccine Bolognese

Serve the freshly cooked fettuccine with Bolognese Sauce (p. 374) instead of the cream sauce.

Fettuccine with Seafood

Use half the quantity of cream and cheese in the basic recipe. Prepare like Fettuccine with Vegetables I, adding only 1 to 3 types of vegetables. At the same time, add the desired quantity of cooked seafood, such as shrimp, scallops, crab, or lobster. For a fuller flavor, reduce a small amount of fish stock and white wine with the cream in the first step.

Fettuccine with Gorgonzola

Prepare as in the basic recipe, except use light cream instead of heavy cream in the first step. Omit the second quantity of heavy cream, and instead add 6 oz (175 g) gorgonzola cheese (Italian blue cheese). Reduce the quantity of parmesan cheese to 2 oz (60 g).

Fettuccini with Vegetables II

Bolognese Sauce (Ragù Bolognese)

YIELD: 1 QT (1 L)   PORTIONS: 32

U.S.	METRIC	INGREDIENTS	PROCEDURE
1 fl oz	30 mL	Vegetable oil	1. Heat the oil and butter in a heavy saucepot over moderate heat. Add the onion, celery, and carrot. Sweat the vegetables until they just begin to soften.
2½ oz	75 g	Butter	
3 oz	90 g	Onion, chopped fine	2. Add the ground beef, along with a little salt and pepper. Stir to break up lumps, and cook until the meat has all lost its red color, but do not brown.
3 oz	90 g	Celery, chopped fine	
3 oz	90 g	Carrot, chopped fine	
1½ lb	720 g	Ground beef, preferably chuck	
to taste	to taste	Salt	
to taste	to taste	Pepper	
12 fl oz	360 mL	Milk	3. Add the milk and nutmeg. Simmer slowly until the milk has almost completely reduced.
¼ tsp	1 mL	Nutmeg	
1 pt	500 mL	Dry white wine	4. Add the wine. Continue to simmer until the wine has almost completely reduced.
1 lb 8 oz	720 g	Canned Italian-style tomatoes, chopped, with their juice	5. Stir in the tomatoes. Simmer over low heat, barely bubbling, about 3 hours, or until the sauce is quite thick. Stir from time to time as it cooks.
to taste	to taste	Salt	6. Taste and adjust the seasonings with salt and pepper.
to taste	to taste	Pepper	

Per serving: Calories, 90; Protein, 5 g; Fat, 5 g (53% cal.); Cholesterol, 20 mg; Carbohydrates, 2 g; Fiber, 0 g; Sodium, 70 mg.

Spaghettini Puttanesca

PORTIONS: 10   PORTION SIZE: APPROXIMATELY 12 OZ (350 G)

U.S.	METRIC	INGREDIENTS	PROCEDURE
3½ lb	1.6 kg	Tomatoes, preferably fresh	1. Peel, seed, and dice the tomatoes, and let them stand in a colander. If using canned tomatoes, drain them and chop them coarsely.
2 fl oz	60 mL	Olive oil	2. Heat the first quantity of olive oil in a sauté pan over moderate heat. Add the garlic and sauté for 1 minute.
5	5	Garlic cloves, chopped	
15	15	Anchovy fillets, chopped	3. Add the anchovy fillets and sauté for a few seconds.
3 tbsp	30 g	Capers, drained	4. Add the tomatoes, capers, and olives. Bring to a boil. Cook 2–3 minutes.
5 oz	150 g	Black olives, pitted and sliced	5. Remove from heat. Add the oregano, the parsley, and the second quantity of olive oil. Season to taste with salt and pepper.
½ tsp	2 mL	Dried oregano	
3 tbsp	45 mL	Chopped parsley	
1 fl oz	30 mL	Olive oil	
to taste	to taste	Salt	
to taste	to taste	Pepper	
2 lb	900 g	Spaghettini	6. Boil the spaghettini, drain, toss with the sauce, and serve immediately. Grated cheese is usually not served with this dish.

Per serving: Calories, 500; Protein, 16 g; Fat 13 g (23% cal.); Cholesterol, 5 mg; Carbohydrates, 80 g; Fiber, 9 g; Sodium, 460 mg.

Spaghetti Carbonara

PORTIONS: 10   PORTION SIZE: 11 OZ (330 G)

U.S.	METRIC	INGREDIENTS
2 fl oz	60 mL	Olive oil
12 oz	360 g	Pancetta, cut into short bâtonnet
2	2	Garlic cloves, chopped fine
3 fl oz	90 mL	Dry white wine
2 lb	1 kg	Spaghetti
4	4	Whole eggs, preferably pasteurized, lightly beaten
5 oz	150 g	Parmesan cheese, grated
¼ tsp or to taste	1 mL or to taste	Black pepper
1 oz	30 g	Chopped parsley
as needed	as needed	Salt

PROCEDURE

1. Heat the oil in a sauté pan over moderate heat. Add the pancetta and sauté until most of the fat has rendered and it begins to crisp.

2. Add the garlic and cook another few seconds.

3. Add the wine. Reduce by three-fourths.

4. While the pancetta is cooking, boil the spaghetti. Drain.

5. Reduce the heat under the sauté pan to low and add the spaghetti. Toss to coat with the fat from the pancetta.

6. Add the eggs, cheese, pepper, and parsley. Mix well over low heat until the spaghetti is well coated and the eggs are coagulated. Heat only until the pasta has a creamy appearance. Do not cook so long that the eggs set hard.

7. Taste for seasonings. Because of the salt in the pancetta, you may not need salt, but add a little if needed.

8. Serve immediately.

Per serving: Calories, 620; Protein, 25 g; Fat, 25 g (37% cal.); Cholesterol, 125 mg; Carbohydrates, 71 g; Fiber, 4 g; Sodium, 940 mg.

Spaghetti Carbonara

SPAGHETTI CARBONARA

According to legend, spaghetti carbonara originated outside Rome as a hearty meal for coal miners (Italian for "coal" is *carbone*) or charcoal makers. Whatever its origins, the dish has become popular both inside and outside Italy. Although most versions served in North American restaurants contain cream, in Italy, the authentic spaghetti carbonara is made without cream, like the version here. In addition, the authentic version is made with *guanciale* (gwan chah leh), or cured pork jowl, but pancetta is a good substitute if guanciale is not available.

Linguine with White Clam Sauce

PORTIONS: 10   PORTION SIZE: APPROXIMATELY 12 OZ (350 G)

U.S.	METRIC	INGREDIENTS	PROCEDURE
4 dozen	4 dozen	Cherrystone clams	1. Open the clams. Strain and reserve 1 pt (500 mL) of their juice. Chop the clams coarsely.
1 cup	250 mL	Olive oil	2. Heat the olive oil in a large sauté pan. Add the garlic and brown it very lightly. Do not let it get too brown, or it will be bitter.
4–6	4–6	Garlic cloves, sliced thin	3. Add the red pepper and then, very carefully, add the wine. (If the pan is very hot, you may want to cool it a little first to prevent dangerous spattering when the liquid is added.) Reduce the wine by half.
½ tsp	2 mL	Red pepper flakes	4. Add the reserved clam juice and reduce by half.
½ cup	125 mL	Dry white wine (optional)	5. Add the oregano.
2 tsp	10 mL	Dried oregano	
2 lb	900 g	Linguine	6. Drop the linguine into boiling, salted water and boil al dente. Drain and plate.
4 tbsp	60 mL	Chopped parsley	7. While the linguine is boiling, add the chopped clams and the parsley to the olive oil mixture. Heat gently, just until the clams are hot. Do not overcook them, or they will be tough.
to taste	to taste	Black pepper	8. Add pepper to taste. (Because clams are salty, the sauce will probably not need any salt, but taste to make sure.)

Per serving: Calories, 600; Protein, 21 g; Fat, 24 g (36% cal.); Cholesterol, 25 mg; Carbohydrates, 74 g; Fiber, 7 g; Sodium, 40 mg.

9. Spoon the sauce over the hot linguine and serve at once.

10. Many people prefer this dish without parmesan cheese, but provide it on the side for those who want it.

Baked Lasagne (Lasagne al Forno)

PORTIONS: 24   PORTION SIZE: 8 OZ (225 G)

U.S.	METRIC	INGREDIENTS	PROCEDURE
1½ lb	700 g	Ricotta cheese	1. Mix together the ricotta, parmesan, and eggs. Season to taste with salt and pepper.
2 oz	60 g	Parmesan cheese, grated	
2	2	Eggs	
to taste	to taste	Salt	
to taste	to taste	Pepper	
2 lb	900 g	Fresh pasta or spinach pasta	2. Cut the fresh pasta into lasagna noodles. Cook them in boiling salted water, drain, and rinse in cold water. Lay them out in a single layer on oiled sheet pans.
3 qt	3 L	Meat Sauce (p. 372) or Bolognese Sauce (p. 374)	3. Ladle a little meat sauce into a standard hotel pan, 12 × 20 in. (20 × 50 cm). Spread it across the bottom.
1½ lb	700 g	Mozzarella cheese, shredded	4. Arrange a layer of noodles in the pan. Then add a layer of the ricotta mixture, a layer of noodles, a layer of sauce, and a layer of mozzarella.
4 oz	125 g	Parmesan cheese, grated	5. Continue making layers of noodles, ricotta, sauce, and mozzarella until all ingredients are used. Top with parmesan cheese.

Per serving: Calories, 450; Protein, 26 g; Fat, 25 g (50% cal.); Cholesterol, 150 mg; Carbohydrates, 29 g; Fiber, 2 g; Sodium, 590 mg.

6. Bake at 375°F (190°C) about 45 minutes. Cover lightly with foil at first to keep it from drying out, but remove the foil for the last 15 minutes of baking time.

VARIATIONS

Other ingredients can be added to lasagne, such as sliced cooked meatballs, sausages, zucchini, eggplant, and so forth. It is best to add only one or two ingredients so the lasagne doesn't seem like a catchall for leftovers.

If meat items are added to the lasagne, you may use plain tomato sauce instead of meat sauce. The ricotta mixture may also be omitted, especially if other protein items are added or if the quantity of mozzarella is increased.

Rigatoni or Penne with Sausage and Clams

PORTIONS: 8   PORTION SIZE: APPROXIMATELY 10 OZ (300 G) PASTA AND SAUCE, PLUS 3 CLAMS

U.S.	METRIC	INGREDIENTS
1 fl oz	30 mL	Olive oil
8 fl oz	250 g	Italian sausage, cut into ½-in. (1-cm) slices
4 oz	125 g	Onion, chopped
4 oz	125 g	Green bell pepper, diced
4 oz	125 g	Red bell pepper, diced
6 oz	180 g	Tomatoes, peeled, seeded, chopped
pinch	pinch	Saffron
to taste	to taste	Hot red pepper flakes
1 lb	500 g	Rigatoni or penne
24	24	Littleneck clams, well scrubbed
to taste	to taste	Salt
to taste	to taste	Pepper
8 tsp	40 mL	Chopped parsley

PROCEDURE

1. Heat the oil in a sauté pan. Add the sausage and sauté until just cooked. Remove with a slotted spoon.
2. Add the onion and diced peppers to the fat in the pan. Sauté briefly until just starting to get tender.
3. Add the tomatoes, saffron, and hot pepper. Simmer about 5 minutes.
4. Meanwhile, add the penne or rigatoni to boiling salted water and boil al dente.
5. Shortly before the pasta is cooked, return the sausage to the pan with the vegetable mixture. Set over moderately high heat. Add the clams and cover. Cook just until the clams open. Do not overcook, or they will be tough. Season with salt and pepper.
6. Drain the pasta and immediately transfer to pasta bowls for serving.
7. Top with the contents of the pan, dividing the clams, sausage, and vegetables evenly among the servings.
8. Sprinkle with chopped parsley. Serve immediately.

Per serving: Calories, 340; Protein, 18 g; Fat, 9 g (24% cal); Cholesterol, 30 mg; Carbohydrates, 47 g; Fiber, 6 g; Sodium, 170 mg.

VARIATIONS

Mussels may be substituted for clams. Adjust the quantity as desired. If neither clams nor mussels are available, the dish can be made with shrimp, although its flavor and character will be quite different.

Rigatoni or Penne with Sausage, Peppers, and Tomatoes

Omit the seafood from the recipe and double the quantity of sausage.

Macaroni and Cheese

PORTIONS: 15   PORTION SIZE: 6 OZ (175 G)

U.S.	METRIC	INGREDIENTS
1 lb	450 g	Elbow macaroni
1 qt	1 L	Medium Béchamel, hot (p. 159)
1 tsp	5 mL	Dry mustard
dash	dash	Tabasco
1 lb	450 g	Cheddar cheese, grated
		Garnish:
as needed	as needed	Bread crumbs
as needed	as needed	Paprika

PROCEDURE

1. Cook macaroni according to basic method for boiling pasta. Drain and rinse in cold water.
2. Flavor the béchamel with the dry mustard and Tabasco.
3. Mix the macaroni with the cheese. Combine with the béchamel.
4. Pour into a buttered half-hotel pan. Sprinkle with bread crumbs and paprika.
5. Bake at 350°F (175°C) until hot and bubbling, about 30 minutes.

Per serving: Calories, 330; Protein, 14 g; Fat, 17 g (46% cal.); Cholesterol, 50 mg; Carbohydrates, 31 g; Fiber, 1 g; Sodium, 290 mg.

Note: Cheese sauce may be used instead of béchamel. If you do so, reduce grated cheese to 4 oz (100 g) or omit.

Dumplings

Dumplings are starch products made from soft doughs or batters and cooked by simmering or steaming. They are served as side dishes and in soups and stews. Many national cuisines have their own kinds of dumpling.

<table>
<tr><td colspan="2" align="center">KEY POINTS TO REVIEW</td></tr>
</table>

- What are the major kinds and shapes of commercial pasta?
- What are the quality factors to look for in commercial pasta?
- How should pasta be cooked for à la carte service?
- What procedure should be used if pasta is to be cooked ahead in quantity?
- How are rice noodles prepared for cooking?

Potato Dumplings

PORTIONS: 10   PORTION SIZE: 5 OZ (150 G)

U.S.	METRIC	INGREDIENTS
2½ lb	1.1 kg	Boiled potatoes, peeled, cold
12 oz	350 g	Flour
2 tsp	10 mL	Salt
2	2	Eggs
4 oz	125 g	Butter
4 oz	125 g	Dry bread crumbs

PROCEDURE

1. Grate the potatoes into a mixing bowl.
2. Add the flour and salt and mix lightly until just combined.
3. Add the eggs and mix well to form a stiff dough. Work in more flour if necessary.
4. Divide the dough into 20 equal portions. Roll each piece into a ball. Refrigerate 1 hour. Dumplings may be made ahead up to this point.

5. Heat the butter in a sauté pan and add the bread crumbs. Sauté for a few minutes, until the crumbs are toasted and brown. Set aside.
6. Place the dumplings in a pot of boiling salted water. Stir so they rise to the top and don't stick to the bottom of the pan. Simmer 10 minutes.
7. Remove with a slotted spoon and place in a single layer in a hotel pan (or onto serving plates).
8. Top with the toasted buttered bread crumbs. Serve 2 pieces per order. (Dumplings may also be served with melted butter or pan gravy.)

Per serving: Calories, 360; Protein, 8 g; Fat, 11 g (28% cal); Cholesterol, 65 mg; Carbohydrates, 57 g; Fiber, 3 g; Sodium, 680 mg.

VARIATIONS

One or more of the following may be added to the dough: ¼ cup (60 mL) chopped parsley; 4 oz (125 g) diced bacon, cooked crisp; 2 oz (60 g) onion, chopped fine and sautéed in butter or bacon fat.

Spaetzle

PORTIONS: 15   PORTION SIZE: 4 OZ (125 G)

U.S.	METRIC	INGREDIENTS
6	6	Eggs
1½ cups	375 mL	Milk or water
1 tsp	5 mL	Salt
⅛ tsp	0.5 mL	Nutmeg
⅛ tsp	0.5 mL	White pepper
1 lb or more	450 g or more	Flour
as needed	as needed	Butter, for service

Per serving: Calories, 260; Protein, 7 g; Fat, 15 g (52% cal.); Cholesterol, 120 mg; Carbohydrates, 24 g; Fiber, 1 g; Sodium, 310 mg.

PROCEDURE

1. Beat the eggs in a bowl and add the milk or water, salt, nutmeg, and pepper.

2. Add the flour and beat until smooth. You should have a thick batter. If it is too thin, beat in a little more flour.

3. Let the batter stand 1 hour before cooking to relax the gluten.

4. Set a colander or perforated hotel pan (or a spaetzle machine, if available) over a large pot of boiling salted water (see **Figure 13.5**). The colander should be high enough so the steam doesn't cook the batter in the colander.

5. Place the batter in the colander and force it through the holes with a spoon or plastic scraper.

6. After the spaetzle float to the top of the water, let them simmer 1–2 minutes, then remove them with a skimmer. Cool quickly in cold water and drain well.

7. Cover and refrigerate until service.

8. Sauté portions to order in butter until hot. Serve immediately.

Figure 13.5 Making spaetzle.

(a) Force the batter through the holes of the perforated pan into simmering water.

(b) Remove the spatzle from the simmering water with a skimmer and drop into ice water.

Potato Gnocchi with Tomato Sauce

PORTIONS: 16   PORTION SIZE: 4½ OZ (140G)

U.S.	METRIC	INGREDIENTS
4 lb	2 kg	All-purpose potatoes (see Note)
1 lb	500 g	Flour

PROCEDURE

1. Wash the potatoes, but do not peel. Boil until tender.
2. Peel the potatoes while they are still hot, and force them though a food mill.
3. Add about three-fourths of the flour to the potatoes and knead to make a soft, sticky mixture. Continue to work in more flour to form a soft, smooth dough. It should still be somewhat sticky. You may not need all the flour.
4. Divide the dough into smaller pieces. Roll each piece into a sausage shape about ½ in. (1.25 cm) thick. Cut into pieces about ¾ in. (2 cm) long.
5. To shape the gnocchi, pick up one piece of the dough and press it with your fingertip against the times of a fork. Then flip the piece with the finger and allow it to drop on the worktable. This will give the piece grooves on one side and an indentation on the other side.

U.S.	METRIC	INGREDIENTS
3 pt	1.5 L	Italian Tomato Sauce for Pasta (p. 372)
1½ cup	350 mL	Grated parmesan cheese

6. Drop the gnocchi into a large quantity of boiling salted water. When they float to the surface, let them boil 10–15 seconds, then remove with a skimmer or slotted spoon.
7. Plate the gnocchi. Top each portion with 2 fl oz (60 mL) tomato sauce and 1 tbsp (15 mL) grated parmesan cheese.

Per serving: Calories, 380; Protein, 10 g; Fat, 17 g (40% cal.); Cholesterol, 5 mg; Carbohydrates, 47 g; Fiber, 4 g; Sodium, 680 mg.

Note: All-purpose potatoes give the best results in this recipe. If you are using either very starchy potatoes, such as russets, or very waxy potatoes, add 2 beaten eggs to the mixture in step 3 to help the gnocchi hold together when cooking.

VARIATIONS

Gnocchi may be served with other pasta sauces, such as pesto, or simply with melted butter and grated cheese.

TERMS FOR REVIEW

legume	germ	bulgur	egg pasta
haricot bean	parboiled or converted rice	pasta	rice noodle
lentil	Arborio rice	commercial dried pasta	couscous
dal	polenta	macaroni	al dente
endosperm	hominy	semolina	dumpling
bran			

QUESTIONS FOR DISCUSSION

1. Describe how to prepare dried beans, lentils, and peas for cooking.
2. What is the main difference between cooking dried kidney beans and dried lentils?
3. Describe the three basic methods for cooking grains.
4. Should rice be washed before cooking? Always, sometimes, or never? Discuss.
5. Can wild rice and long-grain rice be cooked together to decrease the portion cost of wild rice? Explain.
6. What factors determine how much water is needed to cook rice?
7. Describe two ways in which rice noodles are cooked or prepared.
8. Describe the procedure for making cheese ravioli, starting with a freshly made piece of pasta dough.

Chapter 14

Salade Niçoise, page 429.

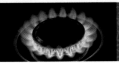
Salad Dressings and Salads

In the days before modern refrigeration, the pantry was the storeroom where food products were kept before being brought into the kitchen. Because this room was cooler than the kitchen, it was especially suited as a work area for the production of cold food, especially aspics, chaud-froids, and other elaborate buffet preparations. In kitchens around the world, this department is often referred to by its French name, *garde manger* (gard mawn zhay).

Today, the pantry is the department responsible for cold foods and related items. This does not mean that no cooking is done in the pantry. On the contrary, garde manger chefs must be masters of a wide range of cooking techniques. In addition, they must have artistic judgment as well as the patience and dexterity to perform a great many hand operations quickly and efficiently.

This chapter deals with two groups of items prepared in the pantry: salads and salad dressings.

After reading this chapter, you should be able to

1. Identify the major salad dressing ingredients.
2. Prepare the following: oil and vinegar dressings, mayonnaise and mayonnaise-based dressings, cooked dressings, and specialty dressings.
3. Identify and describe five salad types, and select appropriate recipes for use as appetizer, accompaniment, main course, separate course, or dessert salad.
4. Identify a dozen popular salad greens, list six categories of other salad ingredients, and recognize several examples from each category.
5. Judge the quality of fruits, and complete the pre-preparation procedures for fruit.
6. Identify the four basic parts of a salad.
7. Prepare and arrange salads that achieve maximum eye appeal.
8. Set up an efficient system for producing salads in quantity.
9. Prepare the following types of salads: green, vegetable, bound, fruit, combination, and gelatin.
10. Set up a successful salad bar and buffet service.

SALAD DRESSINGS

Salad dressings are liquids or semiliquids used to flavor salads. They are sometimes considered cold sauces, and they serve the same functions as sauces—that is, they flavor, moisten, and enrich.

Most of the basic salad dressings used today can be divided into three categories:

1. Oil and vinegar dressings (most unthickened dressings).

2. Mayonnaise-based dressings (most thickened dressings).

3. Cooked dressings (similar in appearance to mayonnaise dressings, but more tart, and with little or no oil content).

A number of dressings have as their main ingredient such products as sour cream, yogurt, and fruit juices. Many of these are designed specifically for fruit salads or for low-calorie diets.

Ingredients

Because the flavors of most salad dressings are not modified by cooking, their quality depends directly on the quality of the ingredients.

Most salad dressings are made primarily of an oil and an acid, with other ingredients added to modify the flavor or texture.

Oils

KINDS

Corn oil is widely used in dressings. It has a light golden color and is nearly tasteless, except for a mild cornmeal-type flavor.

Cottonseed oil, soybean oil, canola oil, and *safflower oil* are bland, nearly tasteless oils. *Vegetable oil* or *salad oil* is a blend of oils and is popular because of its neutral flavor and relatively low cost.

Peanut oil has a mild but distinctive flavor and may be used in appropriate dressings. It is somewhat more expensive.

Olive oil has a distinctive, fruity flavor and aroma and a greenish color. The best olive oils are called *virgin* or *extra-virgin,* which means they are made from the first pressing of the olives. Because of its flavor, olive oil is not an all-purpose oil but may be used in specialty salads such as Caesar salad.

Walnut oil has a distinctive flavor and a high price. It is occasionally used in fine restaurants featuring specialty salads. Other nut and seed oils, such as *hazelnut oil* and *grapeseed oil*, are sometimes used.

QUALITY FACTORS

All-purpose oils for dressings should have a mild, sweet flavor. Strongly flavored oils can make excellent salad dressings but are not appropriate with every food.

Winterized oil should be used with dressings that are to be refrigerated. These oils have been treated so they remain a clear liquid when chilled.

Rancidity is a serious problem with oils because even a hint of a rancid flavor can ruin an entire batch of dressing. A thin film of oil, such as might be left on containers through careless washing, becomes rancid very quickly. Clean all dressing containers thoroughly, and never pour a fresh batch into a jar containing older dressing.

Vinegar

KINDS

Cider vinegar is made from apples. It is brown in color and has a slightly sweet apple taste.

White or *distilled vinegar* is distilled and purified so that it has a neutral flavor.

Wine vinegar may be white or red, and it has, naturally, a winy flavor.

Flavored vinegars have had another product added to them, such as tarragon, garlic, or raspberries.

Sherry vinegar is made from sherry wine and, consequently, has the distinctive flavor of that wine.

Balsamic vinegar is a special wine vinegar aged in wooden barrels (see sidebar). It is dark brown in color and has a noticeably sweet taste.

Other specialty vinegars include malt vinegar, rice vinegar, and vinegars flavored with fruits.

QUALITY FACTORS

Vinegars should have a good, clean, sharp flavor for their type.

Strength of acidity determines the tartness of the vinegar—and of the dressing made from it. Most salad vinegars are about 5 percent acidity, but some range as high as 7 or 8 percent. Read the label for this information. Vinegar that is too strong should be diluted with a little water before it is measured for a recipe.

White vinegar is used when a completely neutral flavor is desired for a dressing. Other vinegars are used for their characteristic flavors. Wine vinegars are usually preferred for the best-quality oil-and-vinegar dressings.

Lemon Juice

Fresh lemon juice may be used in place of or in addition to vinegar in some preparations, when its flavor is desired.

Egg Yolk

Egg yolk is an essential ingredient in mayonnaise and other emulsified dressings. For safety, pasteurized eggs should be used and the finished product should be refrigerated to guard against spoilage.

Seasonings and Flavorings

Nearly any herb or spice can be used in salad dressings. Fresh herbs are preferable to dried herbs as flavorings, especially when the dressings are used for simple, light mixed green salads. Remember that dried herbs and spices need extra time to release their flavors if they are not heated in the product. This is why most dressings are best made at least two or three hours before serving. Review Chapter 4 to refresh your memory on the use of herbs and spices.

Other ingredients added for flavoring include mustard, ketchup, Worcestershire sauce, and cheeses.

A note on blue cheese and *Roquefort cheese*: Many restaurants sell "Roquefort dressing" that is actually blue cheese dressing. Roquefort is a brand name for a special kind of blue cheese made in Roquefort, France. It is made of sheep's milk, has a distinctive taste, and is expensive. Do not use the term *Roquefort* for blue cheese dressings unless you are actually using this brand of cheese.

Emulsions in Salad Dressings

As you know, oil and water do not normally stay mixed but separate into layers. Salad dressings, however, must be evenly mixed for proper service, even though they are made primarily of oil and vinegar. A uniform mixture of two unmixable liquids is called an *emulsion*. One liquid is said to be in *suspension* in the other.

BALSAMICO TRADIZIONALE (TRADITIONAL BALSAMIC VINEGAR)

True balsamic vinegar is made by small artisan producers, as distinguished from the industrial product found in most kitchens and supermarkets. It is made not from wine or wine vinegar but from grape juice, usually from white Trebbiano grapes, although four other grapes are permitted by Italian law. Balsamico tradizionale is aged in a series of small wooden barrels for at least 10 but as long as 50 years. The result is an intensely flavorful, thick, almost syrupy, dark brown liquid.

Because of the small production and the long aging, true balsamic vinegar is very expensive, the oldest bottlings being among the most expensive foods anywhere.

The familiar inexpensive balsamico vinegars most of us are familiar with are made in large quantities from wine vinegar and caramelized sugar, sometimes with the addition of a quantity of aged balsamico. The quality of inexpensive balsamic vinegars ranges from terrible to good. The better ones can be excellent salad ingredients. True balsamic tradizionale is too costly to be mixed with salad dressings. It is generally used by itself as a condiment, measured out in mere drops.

Temporary Emulsions

A simple oil-and-vinegar dressing is called a *temporary emulsion* because the two liquids always separate after being shaken or beaten together. In a standard vinaigrette, the vinegar is broken into tiny droplets. These droplets are mixed evenly, or *suspended*, throughout the oil.

The harder the mixture is beaten or shaken, the longer it takes for it to separate. This is because the vinegar is broken into smaller droplets, so the droplets take longer to recombine with each other and separate from the oil. When a mixture of oil and vinegar is mixed in a blender, the resulting mixture stays in emulsion considerably longer.

Some ingredients act as stabilizers (see sidebar). For example, when mustard is added to the mixture, the vinaigrette stays emulsified longer. Other ingredients that work this way include vegetable purées and stocks with a good gelatin content. Even these mixtures, however, will separate when they stand long enough. They should be mixed again before use.

Permanent Emulsions

Mayonnaise is also a mixture of oil and vinegar, but the two liquids do not separate. This is because the formula also contains egg yolk, which is a strong emulsifier. The egg yolk forms a layer around each of the tiny droplets and holds them in suspension (see sidebar).

The harder the mayonnaise is beaten to break up the droplets, the more stable the emulsion becomes. All emulsions, whether permanent or temporary, form more easily at room temperature, because chilled liquid is harder to break up into small droplets.

Other stabilizers are used in some preparations. Cooked dressing uses starch in addition to eggs. Commercially made dressings may use such emulsifiers as gums, starches, and gelatin.

Oil-and-Vinegar Dressings

Basic *vinaigrette*, the first recipe in this section, is a simple mixture of oil, vinegar, and seasonings. It can be used as is, but it is usually the base for other dressings, such as the variations that follow.

The ratio of oil to vinegar in a basic vinaigrette is 3 parts oil to 1 part vinegar. This is not a divine law, however, and the proportions may be changed to taste. Some chefs prefer a 2:1 ratio, while others prefer a 4:1 or even 5:1 ratio. Less oil makes the dressing more tart, while more oil makes it taste milder and oilier.

A very strong vinegar, more than 5 percent acid, may have to be diluted with water before being measured and added to the recipe.

For guidelines in the preparation of vinaigrettes, review the discussion of temporary emulsions above. The emulsion in the basic vinaigrette recipe holds only a short time because the formula contains no stabilizers, with the minor exception of a little pepper. To make a good emulsion, mix some mustard with the vinegar, as in the first variation of the basic recipe.

Basic Vinaigrette

YIELD: 1 QT (1 L)

U.S.	METRIC	INGREDIENTS
1 cup	250 mL	Wine vinegar
1 tbsp	15 mL	Salt
1 tsp	5 mL	White pepper
3 cups	750 mL	Salad oil, olive oil, or part salad oil and part olive oil

PROCEDURE

1. Mix the vinegar, salt, and white pepper until the salt is dissolved.
2. Using a wire whip, a mixing machine, or a blender, begin adding the oil a few drops at a time. Gradually increase the oil to a thin stream. (See discussion of temporary emulsions, p. 386.)
3. Mix again before using. (The best way to re-emulsify a separated vinaigrette is to put it in a blender and spin at high speed until it is recombined.)

Per 1 fl oz (29.57 mL): Calories, 180; Protein, 0 g; Fat, 21 g (100% cal.); Cholesterol, 0 mg; Carbohydrates, 0 g; Fiber, 0 g; Sodium, 220 mg.

VARIATIONS

Mustard Vinaigrette

Add 1–2 oz (30–60 g) prepared mustard (French or Dijon type) to the basic recipe. Mix with the vinegar in step 1.

Herbed Vinaigrette

Add to the basic recipe or to the Mustard Vinaigrette variation ½ cup or 1 oz (30 g) chopped parsley, 1 tsp (5 mL) chopped fresh basil, 1 tsp (5 mL) chopped fresh marjoram or oregano, and 2 tsp (10 mL) chopped chives. If fresh herbs are not available, use half their volume of dried herbs.

Lemon Vinaigrette

In place of the wine vinegar in the basic recipe or the Mustard Vinaigrette variation, use 2½ fl oz (75 mL) wine vinegar and 5½ fl oz (175 mL) fresh lemon juice.

Balsamic Vinaigrette

Use balsamic vinegar in place of half to three-quarters of the wine vinegar in the basic recipe.

Italian Dressing

Use all or part olive oil. Add to the basic recipe 1½ tsp (7 mL) minced garlic, 1 tbsp (15 mL) dried oregano, and ¼ cup (60 mL) chopped parsley.

Piquante Dressing

Add to the basic recipe 2 tsp (10 mL) dry mustard, 2 tbsp (30 mL) finely chopped onion, and 2 tsp (10 mL) paprika.

Chiffonade Dressing

Add to the basic recipe the following ingredients, all chopped fine: 2 hard-cooked eggs, 4 oz (125 g) cooked or canned red beets (drained), 2 tbsp (30 mL) chopped parsley, and 1 oz (30 g) onion or scallions.

Avocado Dressing

Add 1 lb (500 g) puréed avocado to the basic recipe or to Herbed Vinaigrette. Beat until smooth. Increase salt to taste.

Blue Cheese or Roquefort Vinaigrette

Mix 4 oz (125 g) crumbled blue cheese or Roquefort cheese and 4 fl oz (125 mL) heavy cream in a mixer with a paddle attachment or by hand in a stainless-steel bowl. Gradually beat in 1½ pt (750 mL) Basic Vinaigrette.

American French or Tomato French Dressing

YIELD: 2 QT (2 L)

U.S.	METRIC	INGREDIENTS
4 oz	125 g	Onion
12 oz	375 mL	Cider vinegar
2½ cups	625 mL	Ketchup
4 oz	125 g	Sugar
1 tsp	5 mL	Mashed garlic
1 tbsp	15 mL	Worcestershire sauce
1 tsp	5 mL	Paprika
¼ tsp	1 mL	Hot pepper sauce (such as Tabasco)
½ tsp	2 mL	White pepper
1 qt	1 L	Salad oil

PROCEDURE

1. Grate the onion on a hand grater or grind in food chopper.
2. Combine all ingredients except the oil in a stainless-steel bowl.
3. Mix with a wire whip until well combined and sugar is dissolved.
4. Using a wire whip or a mixing machine, gradually beat in the oil.
5. Beat or stir again before serving.

Per 1 fl oz (29.57 mL): Calories, 140; Protein, 0 g; Fat, 14 g (86% cal.); Cholesterol, 0 mg; Carbohydrates, 5 g; Fiber, 0 g; Sodium, 115 mg.

Sauce Gribiche

U.S.	METRIC	INGREDIENTS	PROCEDURE
6	6	Hard-cooked egg yolks	1. Mash the yolks or force them through a sieve into a bowl.
1½ tbsp	45 mL	Prepared mustard, French or Dijon-style	2. Add the mustard, salt, and pepper, and mix well.
to taste	to taste	Salt	3. As when making mayonnaise (see p. 390), very gradually beat in the olive oil a few drops at a time at first, then in a thin stream.
to taste	to taste	Pepper	4. Because the cooked yolks do not enable a stable emulsion like raw yolks do, the mixture curdles easily. When it does, beat in a little hot water. Continue adding oil alternately with hot water. The mixture should have the consistency of a thin mayonnaise.
1 pt	475 mL	Olive oil	
as needed	as needed	Wine vinegar or water	5. Add just enough vinegar to give the dressing a slightly tart taste.
2 tbsp	30 mL	Chopped parsley	6. Stir in the herbs, capers, cornichons, and egg whites.
2 tbsp	30 mL	Chopped fresh chervil	7. Taste and add more salt if necessary.
2 tbsp	30 mL	Chopped fresh tarragon	
2 tbsp	30 mL	Capers	
2 tbsp	30 mL	Cornichons or sour gherkin pickles, chopped	
6	6	Hard-cooked egg whites, cut julienne	

Per 1 fl oz (29.57 mL): Calories, 180; Protein, 2 g; Fat, 19 g (96% cal.); Cholesterol, 50 mg; Carbohydrates, 0 g; Fiber, 0 g; Sodium, 70 mg.

Oriental Vinaigrette

U.S.	METRIC	INGREDIENTS	PROCEDURE
¾ cup	200 mL	Rice vinegar or white vinegar	1. Combine all ingredients except the oils and salt in a bowl and mix well.
¼ cup	60 mL	Soy sauce	2. Taste the dressing and add salt if necessary (the soy sauce may contain enough salt).
1 tbsp	15 mL	Grated fresh ginger root	
2 tsp	10 mL	Pepper	3. Using a wire whip or a mixing machine, gradually beat in the salad oil and then the sesame oil.
¼ tsp	1 mL	Crushed garlic	
½ tsp	2 mL	Hot pepper sauce (such as Tabasco)	4. Mix or stir again before using.
1¾ cups	425 mL	Salad oil	
¼ cup	60 mL	Sesame oil	
as needed	as needed	Salt	

Per 1 fl oz (29.57 mL): Calories, 160; Protein, 0 g; Fat, 18 g (100% cal.); Cholesterol, 0 mg; Carbohydrates, 0 g; Fiber, 0 g; Sodium, 150 mg.

Reduced-Fat Vinaigrette

U.S.	METRIC	INGREDIENTS	PROCEDURE
1 cup	250 mL	Wine vinegar	1. Mix the vinegar, jus lié, salt, and white pepper until the salt is dissolved.
1 pt	500 mL	Jus Lié (p. 163) made with white stock, vegetable stock, or vegetable juice	2. Using a wire whip or a mixing machine, mix in the oil.
1 tbsp	15 mL	Salt	3. Mix or stir again before using.
1 tsp	5 mL	White pepper	
1 cup	250 mL	Salad oil, olive oil, or part salad oil and part olive oil	

Per 1 fl oz (29.57 mL): Calories, 60; Protein, 0 g; Fat, 7 g (100% cal.); Cholesterol, 0 mg; Carbohydrates, 0 g; Fiber, 0 g; Sodium, 220 mg.

Fat-Free Vinaigrette

YIELD: 10 FL OZ (300 ML)

U.S.	METRIC	INGREDIENTS
8 oz	250 g	Onions, whole, with peel
2 tbsp	30 mL	Prepared mustard, French or Dijon style
2 fl oz	60 mL	Wine vinegar
4 fl oz	125 mL	Vegetable stock or juice
2 tbsp	30 mL	Chopped parsley
to taste	to taste	Salt
to taste	to taste	Black pepper

PROCEDURE

1. Roast the onions at 350°F (175°C) until they are completely soft, 45 to 60 minutes.
2. Cool until they are cool enough to handle. Peel.
3. Purée the onions in a blender or food processor.
4. Add the mustard, vinegar, and stock. Blend to mix well.
5. Stir in the chopped parsley.
6. Season to taste with salt and pepper.

Per 1 fl oz (29.57 mL): Calories, 15; Protein, 0 g; Fat, 0 g (0% cal.); Cholesterol, 0 mg; Carbohydrates, 3 g; Fiber, 0 g; Sodium, 80 mg.

VARIATIONS

Substitute chicken stock for the vegetable stock.

Fat-Free Roasted Garlic Vinaigrette

Substitute roasted garlic for the roasted onions in the basic recipe.

See the variations following Basic Vinaigrette for other flavoring ideas.

Emulsified Dressings

Mayonnaise is the most important emulsified dressing. It is sometimes used by itself as a salad dressing, but more often it serves as the base for a wide variety of other dressings. Mayonnaise-based dressings are generally thick and creamy. In fact, many of them are made with the addition of sour cream.

Emulsified French dressing is similar to basic French dressing, except egg yolk is added to keep the oil and vinegar from separating. Its preparation is similar to that of mayonnaise. Emulsified French dressing is given a red-orange color and a subtle flavoring through the addition of Spanish paprika.

Preparation of Mayonnaise

Good-quality prepared mayonnaise is readily available on the market, and few establishments make their own. But it is such a basic preparation and, like the mother sauces you studied in Chapter 7, the foundation of many others. Therefore, it is important to know how to make it.

Homemade mayonnaise is not as stable as the commercial product, which is prepared with special equipment that creates a finer emulsion and which may have added stabilizers to increase its shelf life. Also, the commercial product is usually less expensive. Nevertheless, making mayonnaise in your operation takes only minutes with a power mixer, and by carefully selecting your ingredients you can make a superior-tasting product.

To make mayonnaise, you must observe several conditions in order to get an emulsion. Study the guidelines on the next page before proceeding with the recipe.

Guidelines for Making Mayonnaise

1. **Use fairly bland ingredients if the mayonnaise is to be used as a base for other dressings.**
   The mayonnaise will be more versatile as a base if it has no strong flavors. Olive oil and other ingredients with distinctive flavors may be used for special preparations.

2. **Use the freshest eggs possible for the best emulsification. For safety, use pasteurized eggs.**

3. **Have all ingredients at room temperature.**
   Cold oil is not easily broken into small droplets, so it is harder to make an emulsion.

4. **Beat the egg yolks well in a bowl.**
   Thorough beating of the yolks is important for a good emulsion.

5. **Beat in the seasonings.**
   It is helpful to add a little of the vinegar at this time as well. The emulsion will form more easily because the acidity of the vinegar helps prevent curdling of the egg yolk proteins. Also, the vinegar helps disperse the spices and dissolve the salt.

6. **Begin to add the oil very slowly, beating constantly.**
   It is critical to add the oil slowly at first, or the emulsion will break. When the emulsion has begun to form, the oil may be added more quickly. But never add more oil at once than the amount of mayonnaise that has already formed in the bowl, or the emulsion may break.

7. **Gradually beat in the remaining oil alternately with the vinegar.**
   The more oil you add, the thicker the mayonnaise gets. Vinegar thins it. Add a little vinegar whenever the mayonnaise gets too thick to beat.
      Beating with a power mixer using the wire whip attachment makes a more stable emulsion than beating by hand.

8. **Add no more than 8 ounces (240 mL) oil per large egg yolk, or no more than 1 quart (950 mL) per 4 yolks.**
   The emulsion may break if more oil is added than the egg yolks can handle.

9. **Taste and correct the seasonings.**
   Finished mayonnaise should have a smooth, rich, but neutral flavor, with a pleasant tartness. Its texture should be smooth and glossy, and it should be thick enough to hold its shape.

10. **If the mayonnaise breaks, it can be rescued.**
    Beat an egg yolk or two or some good prepared mayonnaise in a bowl, and very slowly begin to beat in the broken mayonnaise, as in step 6. Continue until all the mayonnaise has been added and re-formed.
       Alternative repair method: Place the broken mayonnaise in a blender and spin until the emulsion is re-formed.

Figure 14.1 Making mayonnaise by hand.

(a) Whip the egg yolks until light. Whip in this first quantity of vinegar and seasonings.

(b) Slowly pour in the oil in a thin stream, whipping constantly.

(c) The finished mayonnaise should be thick enough to hold its shape.

Mayonnaise

YIELD: 2 QT (2 L)

U.S.	METRIC	INGREDIENTS	PROCEDURE
8	8	Egg yolks, preferably pasteurized	1. Review the guidelines for making mayonnaise on page 390.
2 tbsp	30 mL	Vinegar	2. Place the egg yolks in the bowl of a mixer and beat with the whip attachment until well beaten.
2 tsp	10 mL	Salt	
2 tsp	10 mL	Dry mustard	3. Add 2 tbsp (30 mL) vinegar and beat well.
pinch	pinch	Cayenne	4. Mix the dry ingredients and add to the bowl. Beat until well mixed.
3¼ pt	1.7 L	Salad oil	5. Turn the mixer to high speed. Very slowly, almost drop by drop, begin adding the oil. When the emulsion forms, you can add the oil slightly faster.
4 tbsp	60 mL	Vinegar	6. When the mayonnaise becomes thick, thin with a little of the second quantity of vinegar.
3–4 tbsp	50–60 mL	Lemon juice	7. Gradually beat in the remaining oil alternately with the vinegar. (If the emulsion breaks, see step 10 in the basic procedure to repair it.)

Per 1 fl oz (29.57 mL): Calories, 220; Protein, 0 g; Fat, 25 g (100% cal.); Cholesterol, 25 mg; Carbohydrates, 0 g; Fiber, 0 g; Sodium, 75 mg.

8. Adjust the tartness and the consistency by beating in a little lemon juice.

Mayonnaise-Based Dressings

For each of the following dressings, add the listed ingredients to *2 qt (2 L) mayonnaise*, as indicated.

Thousand Island Dressing

1 pt (500 mL) chili sauce, 2 oz (60 g) minced onion, 4 oz (125 g) finely chopped green bell pepper, 4 oz (125 g) chopped drained pimiento, and (optional ingredient) 3 chopped hard-cooked eggs.

Louis Dressing

Prepare Thousand Island Dressing without the chopped eggs. Add 1 pt (500 mL) heavy cream.

Russian Dressing

1 pt (500 mL) chili sauce or ketchup, ½ cup (125 mL) drained horseradish, 2 oz (60 g) minced onion, and (optional ingredient) 1 cup (500 mL) lumpfish or whitefish caviar.

Chantilly Dressing

1 pt (500 mL) heavy cream, whipped. Fold the whipped cream into the mayonnaise carefully to retain volume. Do this as close as possible to service time.

Blue Cheese Dressing

½ cup (125 mL) white vinegar, 2 tsp (10 mL) Worcestershire sauce, a few drops of hot red pepper sauce, and 1 lb (500 g) crumbled blue cheese. Thin to desired consistency with 1–2 cups (250–500 mL) heavy cream or half-and-half. *Variation:* Substitute sour cream for up to half of the mayonnaise.

Ranch Dressing

1½ qt (1.5 L) sour cream, 2½ pt (1.25 L) buttermilk, 8 oz (250 mL) wine vinegar, 6 oz (175 mL) lemon juice, 6 oz (175 mL) Worcestershire sauce, 6 tbsp (90 mL) chopped parsley, 4 tbsp (60 mL) chopped chives, 6 crushed garlic cloves, 4 chopped scallions, 2 oz (60 mL) prepared mustard, 1 tbsp (15 mL) celery seed.

Aïoli II

Mash 2–4 oz (60–125 g) garlic with the salt in the basic recipe. Add this to the egg yolks. Use olive oil or half olive oil and half salad oil. For another version of Aïoli, see page 184.

Emulsified French Dressing

YIELD: 2 QT (2 L)

U.S.	METRIC	INGREDIENTS	PROCEDURE
2	2	Eggs, preferably pasteurized	1. Place the eggs in the bowl of a mixer and beat with the whip attachment until well beaten.
1 tbsp	15 mL	Salt	
1 tbsp	15 mL	Paprika	2. Mix the dry ingredients and add to the bowl. Beat until well mixed.
1 tbsp	15 mL	Dry mustard	3. Turn the mixer to high speed. Very slowly begin adding the oil, as when making mayonnaise.
½ tsp	2 mL	White pepper	
3 pt	1.4 L	Salad oil	4. When the dressing becomes thick, thin with a little of the vinegar.
8 fl oz	250 mL	Cider vinegar	5. Gradually beat in the remaining oil alternately with the vinegar.
4 fl oz	125 mL	Lemon juice	6. Beat in the lemon juice.
as needed	as needed	Vinegar, lemon juice, or water	7. The dressing should be pourable, not thick like mayonnaise. If it is too thick, taste for seasonings first. If the dressing is not tart enough, thin with a little vinegar or lemon juice. If it is tart enough, thin with water.

Per 1 fl oz (29.57 mL): Calories, 190; Protein, 0 g; Fat, 21 g (100% cal.); Cholesterol, 5 mg; Carbohydrates, 0 g; Fiber, 0 g; Sodium, 110 mg.

Caesar Dressing

YIELD: 1 QT (1 L)

U.S.	METRIC	INGREDIENTS	PROCEDURE
25	25	Anchovy fillets (see Note)	1. Mash the anchovies and garlic together to make a paste.
2 tsp	10 mL	Crushed garlic	
4	4	Eggs, pasteurized	2. Place the eggs in the bowl of a mixer and whip with the whip attachment until well beaten.
3 fl oz	90 mL	Lemon juice	3. Add the anchovy and garlic paste and the first quantity of lemon juice. Whip until well mixed.
2½ cups	600 mL	Olive oil	4. With the mixer on high speed, slowly begin adding the oil, as when making mayonnaise.
3 fl oz	90 mL	Lemon juice	5. When the dressing becomes thick, add a little of the remaining lemon juice.
2 oz	60 g	Parmesan cheese, grated	6. Gradually beat in the rest of the oil alternating with the rest of the lemon juice.
to taste	to taste	Salt	7. Mix in the parmesan cheese and salt.

Per 1 fl oz (29.57 mL): Calories, 170; Protein, 2 g; Fat, 18 g (93% cal.);
Cholesterol, 30 mg; Carbohydrates, 1 g; Fiber, 0 g; Sodium, 160 mg.

Note: Anchovies are a main ingredient in traditional Caesar salads but may be omitted according to taste.

KEY POINTS TO REVIEW

- What kinds of oils and vinegars are used in salad dressings? What are their quality factors?

- In addition to oil and vinegar, what are the other major ingredients in most salad dressings?

- What is an emulsion? Describe how the emulsions work in a basic vinaigrette and in mayonnaise. What is the function of stabilizers and emulsifiers in these dressings?

- How do you make a basic vinaigrette?

- How do you make mayonnaise?

Other Dressings

Cooked salad dressing is similar in appearance to mayonnaise, but it has a more tart flavor, while mayonnaise is richer and milder. Cooked dressing is made with little or no oil and with a starch thickener. It may be made in the kitchen or purchased already prepared. Formerly, it was little used in commercial kitchens because of its strong flavor and tartness, but now it is preferred to mayonnaise in some regions.

You will find in many cookbooks a great variety of dressings based on neither mayonnaise nor oil and vinegar. They include dressings based on sour cream and on fruit juice and yogurt (for fruit salads), and low-calorie dressings that appeal to the dieter. The important thing to remember is that these dressings should have well-balanced flavors with a pleasant tartness, and they should harmonize with and complement the salad with which they are served.

Sour Cream Fruit Salad Dressing

YIELD: ABOUT 2½ PT (1.25 L)

U.S.	METRIC	INGREDIENTS	PROCEDURE
4 oz	125 g	Currant jelly	1. Place the jelly and lemon juice in a stainless-steel bowl. Set over hot water or low heat and stir until melted.
4 fl oz	125 mL	Lemon juice	2. Remove from heat and beat in the sour cream a little at a time. Chill the dressing.
2 pt	1 L	Sour cream	

Per 1 fl oz (29.57 mL): Calories, 60; Protein, 1 g; Fat, 5 g (74% cal.);
Cholesterol, 10 mg; Carbohydrates, 3 g; Fiber, 0 g; Sodium, 15 mg.

VARIATION

Yogurt Fruit Salad Dressing

Prepare as in the basic recipe, using 1 cup (250 mL) sour cream and
3 cups (750 mL) plain yogurt instead of all sour cream.

Cooked Salad Dressing

YIELD: 2 QT (2 L)

U.S.	METRIC	INGREDIENTS	PROCEDURE
4 oz	125 g	Sugar	1. Mix the sugar, flour, salt, mustard, and cayenne in a stainless-steel bowl.
4 oz	125 g	Flour	2. Add the eggs and yolks and beat until smooth.
2 tbsp	30 mL	Salt	3. Place the milk in a saucepan and bring to a simmer. Be careful not to scorch it.
2 tbsp	30 mL	Dry mustard	4. Gradually beat about half the milk into the egg mixture. Then return the mixture to the saucepan.
¼ tsp	1 mL	Cayenne	
4	4	Eggs	5. Cook over low heat, stirring constantly, until very thick and no raw flour taste remains.
4	4	Egg yolks	
3 pt	1.5 L	Milk	
4 oz	125 g	Butter	6. Remove from heat and stir in the butter.
12 fl oz	375 mL	Cider vinegar	7. When the butter is melted and mixed in, stir in the vinegar.
			8. Immediately transfer the dressing to a stainless-steel container. Cover and cool.

Per 1 fl oz (29.57 mL): Calories, 50; Protein, 2 g; Fat, 3 g (49% cal.); Cholesterol, 35 mg; Carbohydrates, 5 g; Fiber, 0 g; Sodium, 250 mg.

Honey Lemon Dressing

YIELD: 1 PT (500 ML)

U.S.	METRIC	INGREDIENTS	PROCEDURE
1 cup	250 mL	Honey	1. Mix honey and lemon juice until thoroughly mixed.
1 cup	250 mL	Lemon juice	2. Serve with fruit salads.

Per 1 fl oz (29.57 mL): Calories, 70; Protein, 0 g; Fat, 0 g (0% cal.); Cholesterol, 0 mg; Carbohydrates, 19 g; Fiber, 0 g; Sodium, 0 mg.

VARIATIONS

Honey Cream Dressing
Mix 1 cup (250 mL) heavy cream with the honey before adding the lemon juice.

Honey Lime Dressing
Use lime juice instead of lemon juice.

Fruit Salad Dressing

YIELD: 1 QT (1 L)

U.S.	METRIC	INGREDIENTS	PROCEDURE
6 oz	175 g	Sugar	1. Mix the sugar and cornstarch in a stainless-steel bowl.
1 oz	30 g	Cornstarch	2. Add the eggs and beat until the mixture is smooth.
4	4	Eggs	
1 cup	250 mL	Pineapple juice	3. Heat the fruit juices in a saucepan and bring to a boil.
1 cup	250 mL	Orange juice	4. Gradually beat the hot juices into the egg mixture.
½ cup	125 mL	Lemon juice	5. Return the mixture to the saucepan and bring to a boil, stirring constantly.
			6. When the mixture has thickened, immediately pour it into a stainless-steel bowl or bain-marie and chill.
1 cup	250 mL	Sour cream	7. Beat the sour cream into the chilled fruit mixture.

Per 1 fl oz (29.57 mL): Calories, 60; Protein, 1 g; Fat, 2 g (31% cal.); Cholesterol, 30 mg; Carbohydrates, 9 g; Fiber, 0 g; Sodium, 10 mg.

Low-Fat Buttermilk Yogurt Dressing

YIELD: 1 PT 12 FL OZ (850 ML)

U.S.	METRIC	INGREDIENTS
1 pt	500 mL	Fat-free or low-fat yogurt, unflavored
8 fl oz	250 mL	Buttermilk
1 tbsp	15 mL	Prepared mustard, French or Dijon style
1 fl oz	30 mL	Wine vinegar
1 fl oz	30 mL	Lemon juice
1 fl oz	30 mL	Worcestershire sauce
1½ tbsp	22 mL	Chopped parsley
1 tsp	5 mL	Finely chopped garlic
½ oz	15 g	Shallots, chopped fine
½ tsp	2 mL	Celery seed
4 tsp	20 mL	Sugar
to taste	to taste	Salt
to taste	to taste	Pepper

PROCEDURE

1. Mix all ingredients until uniformly blended.

Per 1 fl oz (29.57 mL): Calories, 15; Protein, 1 g; Fat, 0 g (0% cal.); Cholesterol, 0 mg; Carbohydrates, 3 g; Fiber, 0 g; Sodium, 45 mg.

SALADS

Because the number and variety of salad combinations is nearly endless, it is helpful to divide salads into categories in order to understand how they are produced. For the pantry chef, the most useful way to classify salads is by ingredients: green salads, vegetable salads, fruit salads, and so on. This is because production techniques are slightly different for each kind. We use this classification when we discuss specific recipes later in this chapter.

Before the pantry chef can produce the salads, first he or she must decide exactly what salads should be made. Therefore, you should know what kinds of salad are best for which purposes. For this reason, salads are also classified according to their function in the meal. Keep in mind that there are no exact dividing lines between the types of salad discussed below. For example, a salad suitable as the first course of a dinner may also be an excellent main course on a luncheon menu.

Types of Salads

Today, the variety of salads on offer seems to be greater than ever in memory. Restaurants that once listed no more than two or three salads on their menu now devote an entire page to the category. New kinds of salad fill bin after bin in the prepared-food sections of supermarkets and delicatessens.

At the same time, more traditional salads have not lost their importance. In schools, hospitals, nursing homes, neighborhood diners, and mom-and-pop restaurants, cooks who never heard of mesclun still must know how to clean a head of iceberg lettuce and how to prepare flavored gelatins.

The following classification of salad types describes the roles salads fill in modern menus. These categories apply to both traditional and modern recipes. Examples of both are included later in this chapter.

Appetizer Salads

Many establishments serve salads as a first course, often as a substitute for a more elaborate first course. Not only does this ease the pressure on the kitchen during service but it also gives the customers a satisfying food to eat while their dinners are being prepared.

In addition, more elaborate composed salads are popular as appetizers (and also as main courses at lunch) in many elegant restaurants. These often consist of a poultry, meat, or fish item, plus a variety of vegetables and garnishes, attractively arranged on a bed of greens.

Appetizer salads should stimulate the appetite. This means they must have fresh, crisp ingredients; a tangy, flavorful dressing; and an attractive, appetizing appearance.

Preportioned salads should not be so large as to be filling, but they should be substantial enough to serve as a complete course in themselves. (Self-service salad bars, of course, avoid this problem.) Tossed green salads are especially popular for this reason, as they are bulky without being filling.

The combination of ingredients should be interesting, not dull or trite. Flavorful foods like cheese, ham, salami, shrimp, and crabmeat, even in small quantities, add appeal. So do crisp raw or lightly cooked vegetables. A bowl of poorly drained iceberg lettuce with a bland dressing is hardly an exciting way to start a meal.

Attractive arrangement and garnish are important because visual appeal stimulates the appetite. A satisfying, interesting starter puts the customer in a good frame of mind for the rest of the meal.

Accompaniment Salads

Salads can also be served with the main course. They serve the same function as other side dishes (vegetables and starches).

Accompaniment salads must balance and harmonize with the rest of the meal, like any other side dish. For example, don't serve potato salad at the same meal at which you are serving French fries or another starch. Sweet fruit salads are rarely appropriate as accompaniments, except with such items as ham or pork.

Side-dish salads should be light and flavorful, not too rich. Vegetable salads are often good choices. Heavier salads, such as macaroni or high-protein salads containing meat, seafood, cheese, and so on, are less appropriate, unless the main course is light. Combination salads with a variety of elements are appropriate accompaniments to sandwiches.

Main-Course Salads

Cold salad plates have become popular on luncheon menus, especially among nutrition- and diet-conscious diners. The appeal of these salads is in variety and freshness of ingredients.

Main-course salads should be large enough to serve as a full meal and should contain a substantial portion of protein. Meat, poultry, and seafood salads, as well as egg salad and cheese, are popular choices.

Main-course salads should offer enough variety on the plate to form a balanced meal, both nutritionally and in flavors and textures. In addition to the protein, a salad platter should offer a variety of vegetables, greens, and/or fruits. Examples are chef's salad (mixed greens, raw vegetables, and strips of meat and cheese), shrimp or crabmeat salad with tomato wedges and slices of avocado on a bed of greens, and cottage cheese with an assortment of fresh fruits.

The portion size and variety of ingredients give the chef an excellent opportunity to use imagination and creativity to produce attractive, appetizing salad plates. Attractive arrangements and good color balance are important.

Separate-Course Salads

Many fine restaurants serve a refreshing, light salad after the main course. The purpose is to cleanse the palate after a rich dinner and to refresh the appetite and provide a pleasant break before dessert.

Salads served after the main course were the rule rather than the exception many years ago, and the practice deserves to be more widespread. A diner who may be satiated after a heavy meal is often refreshed and ready for dessert after a light, piquant salad.

Separate-course salads must be very light and in no way filling. Rich, heavy dressings, such as those made with sour cream and mayonnaise, should be avoided. Perhaps the ideal choice is a few delicate greens, such as Bibb lettuce or Belgian endive, lightly dressed with vinaigrette. Fruit salads are also popular choices.

Dessert Salads

Dessert salads are usually sweet and may contain items such as fruits, sweetened gelatin, nuts, and cream. They are often too sweet to be served as appetizers or accompaniments and are best served as dessert or as part of a buffet or party menu.

Ingredients

Freshness and variety of ingredients are essential for high-quality salads. Lettuce, of course, is the first choice for most people, but many other foods can make up a salad.

The following tables list, by category, most of the ingredients used in popular salads. You will be able to think of others. Add them to the lists as they occur to you or as they are suggested by your instructor. The lists will be useful when you are creating your own salad ideas.

Following these lists are detailed descriptions of two groups of food that have not been covered in previous chapters and belong especially in the pantry: salad greens and fresh fruits.

Salad Greens

Iceberg lettuce	Dandelion greens
Romaine lettuce	Watercress
Boston lettuce	Arugula
Bibb or limestone lettuce	Radicchio
Loose-leaf lettuce	Mesclun
Escarole	Tatsoi
Chicory or curly endive	Mâche
Frisée	Microgreens
Belgian endive	Sprouts
Chinese cabbage or celery cabbage	Edible flowers
Spinach	

Vegetables, Raw

Avocado	Cucumbers
Bean sprouts	Sunchokes (Jerusalem artichokes)
Broccoli	Kohlrabi
Cabbage, white, green, and red	Mushrooms
Carrots	Onions and scallions
Cauliflower	Peppers, red, green, and yellow
Celery	Radishes
Celeriac (celery root)	Tomatoes

Vegetables, Cooked, Pickled, and Canned

Artichoke hearts	Hearts of palm
Asparagus	Leeks
Beans (all kinds)	Olives

Beets	Peas
Carrots	Peppers, roasted and pickled
Cauliflower	Pimientos
Corn	Potatoes
Cucumber pickles (dill, sweet, etc.)	Water chestnuts

Starches

Dried beans (cooked or canned)	Macaroni products	Bread (croutons)
Potatoes	Grains	

Fruits, Fresh, Cooked, Canned, or Frozen

Apples	Grapes	Peaches
Apricots	Kiwi fruit	Pears
Bananas	Kumquats	Persimmons
Berries	Mandarin oranges and tangerines	Pineapple
Cherries	Mangoes	Plums
Coconut	Melons	Prunes
Dates	Nectarines	Pomegranates
Figs	Oranges	Prickly pear
Grapefruit	Papayas	Raisins

Protein Foods

Meats (beef, ham)	Bacon
Poultry (chicken, turkey)	Eggs, hard-cooked
Fish and shellfish (tuna, crab, shrimp, lobster, salmon, sardines, anchovies, herring, any fresh cooked fish)	Cheese, cottage
	Cheese, aged or cured types
Salami, prosciutto, luncheon meats, etc.	

Miscellaneous

Gelatin (plain or flavored)	Nuts

Lettuce and Other Salad Greens

ICEBERG LETTUCE

The most popular salad ingredient. Firm, compact head with crisp, mild-tasting pale green leaves. Valuable for its texture because it stays crisp longer than other lettuces. Can be used alone but is best mixed with more flavorful greens, such as romaine, because it lacks flavor itself. Keeps well.

ROMAINE OR COS LETTUCE

Elongated, loosely packed head with dark green, coarse leaves. Crisp texture, with full, sweet flavor. Keeps well and is easy to handle. Essential for Caesar salad. For elegant service, the center rib is often removed.

BOSTON LETTUCE

Small, round head with soft, fragile leaves. Deep green outside shading to nearly white inside. The leaves have a rich, mild flavor and delicate, buttery texture. Bruises easily and does not keep well. Cup-shaped leaves excellent for salad bases.

Iceberg lettuce

Romaine or cos lettuce

Boston lettuce

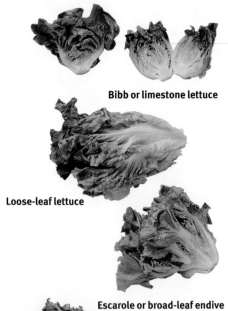

Bibb or limestone lettuce

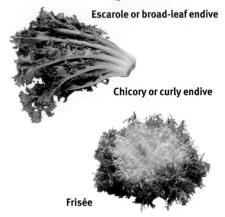

Loose-leaf lettuce

Escarole or broad-leaf endive

Chicory or curly endive

Frisée

Belgian endive or witloof chicory

Chinese cabbage

Spinach

Watercress

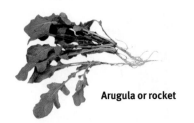

Arugula or rocket

BIBB OR LIMESTONE LETTUCE

Similar to Boston lettuce, but smaller and more delicate. A whole head may be only a few inches (less than 10 cm) across. Color ranges from dark green outside to creamy yellow at the core. Its tenderness, delicate flavor, and high price make it a luxury in some markets. The small, whole leaves are often served by themselves, with a light vinaigrette dressing, as an after-dinner salad.

LOOSE-LEAF LETTUCE

Forms bunches rather than heads. Soft, fragile leaves with curly edges. May be all green or with shades of red. Wilts easily and does not keep well, but is inexpensive and gives flavor, variety, and interest to mixed green salads.

ESCAROLE OR BROAD-LEAF ENDIVE

Broad, thick leaves in bunches rather than heads. Texture is coarse and slightly tough, and flavor is somewhat bitter. Mix with sweeter greens to vary flavor and texture, but do not use alone because of the bitterness. Escarole is frequently braised with olive oil and garlic and served as a vegetable in Italian cuisine.

CHICORY OR CURLY ENDIVE

Narrow, curly, twisted leaves with firm texture and bitter flavor. Outside leaves are dark green; core is yellow or white. Attractive when mixed with other greens or used as a base or garnish, but may be too bitter to be used alone.

FRISÉE

Frisée is the same plant as curly endive or chicory, but it is grown in a way that makes it more tender and less bitter. Except for the outer layer, the leaves are pale yellow, slender, and feathery, with a distinct but mild taste.

BELGIAN ENDIVE OR WITLOOF CHICORY

Narrow, lightly packed, pointed heads resembling spearheads, 4 to 6 inches (10 to 15 cm) long. Pale yellow-green to white in color. Leaves are crisp, with a waxy texture and pleasantly bitter flavor. Usually expensive. Often served alone, split in half or into wedges, or separated into leaves, accompanied by a mustard vinaigrette dressing.

CHINESE CABBAGE

Elongated, light green heads with broad, white center ribs. Available in two forms: narrow, elongated head, often called *celery cabbage*, and thicker, blunt head, called *napa cabbage*. Tender but crisp, with a mild cabbage flavor. Adds excellent flavor to mixed green salads. Also used extensively in Chinese cooking.

SPINACH

Small, tender spinach leaves are excellent salad greens, either alone or mixed with other greens. A popular salad is spinach leaves garnished with sliced raw mushrooms and crisp, crumbled bacon. Spinach must be washed thoroughly, and the coarse stems must be removed.

WATERCRESS

Most commonly used as a garnish, watercress is also excellent in salads. Small, dark green, oval leaves with a pungent, peppery flavor. Remove thick stems before adding to salads.

ARUGULA

Also known as *rugula* or *rocket*, these pungent, distinctively flavored greens are related to mustard and watercress. They are tender and perishable, and they often are sandy, so they must be washed carefully. Arugula was once found almost exclusively in Italian restaurants, but it has since become more widely available and is increasingly popular.

MESCLUN

Mesclun is a mixture of tender baby lettuces. It is available as a mixture, but some chefs prefer to buy individual baby lettuces and make their own mixture.

Mesclun

BABY LETTUCES

The small, tender leaves that make up a mesclun mix are also available separately. These include baby Bibb (both red and green), baby romaine, baby red oak leaf, and lola rossa (a red lettuce with ruffled leaves).

Lola rossa   Red oak leaf

Alfalfa sprouts

SPROUTS

Sprouts are young plants that have just emerged from their seeds, before the true leaves develop. Sprouts from mung beans are commonly used in Chinese cooking. Alfalfa, daikon radish, and mustard sprouts are often used in delicate salads. Alfalfa sprouts have a mild flavor, while radish and mustard sprouts have a peppery flavor.

MICROGREENS

These are the first true leaves that develop after a seed sprouts. Tiny herb leaves and tiny leaves from lettuce and other salad greens, younger and smaller than baby lettuces, are used mostly as garnish for other dishes, both hot and cold.

Microgreens

TATSOI

Tatsoi is a small, round, dark green leaf. Its flavor has a pleasant bite similar to that of arugula, watercress, and other members of the mustard family. It is sometimes included in mesclun mixtures, although it is not actually a lettuce.

Tatsoi

MIZUNA

Mizuna, also known as *Japanese mustard greens*, is a dark green leaf with jagged edges resembling dandelion leaves. It has a mild, mustardy taste.

Mizuna

MÂCHE

Also called *corn salad*, *lamb's lettuce*, *lamb's tongue*, and *field salad*, mâche is a small, very tender green with spoon-shaped leaves. It has a delicate, nutty flavor.

Mâche

RADICCHIO

Radicchio (ra dik ee oh), a red-leafed Italian variety of chicory, has creamy white ribs or veins and generally comes in small, round heads. It has a crunchy texture and a slightly bitter flavor. Radicchio is expensive, but only a leaf or two are needed to add color and flavor to a salad.

Radicchio

TREVISO

Treviso is a red-leafed plant like radicchio, but with elongated leaves somewhat like Belgian endive. Like radicchio and endive, it belongs to the chicory family and has a slightly bitter flavor.

Treviso

DANDELION GREENS

The familiar lawn ornament is also cultivated for use in the kitchen. Only young, tender leaves may be used. Older leaves are coarse and bitter, though cultivated varieties are milder than wild dandelion. Best in spring.

Dandelion greens

PRECLEANED, PRECUT SALAD GREENS

Precut greens are sold in large, sealed plastic bags. They save labor costs in large operations but are more perishable than unprocessed greens. Keep refrigerated, and do not open until ready to use. Unopened bags will keep for two or three days. Taste before serving to make sure the greens do not have too much antioxidant on them, making them bitter.

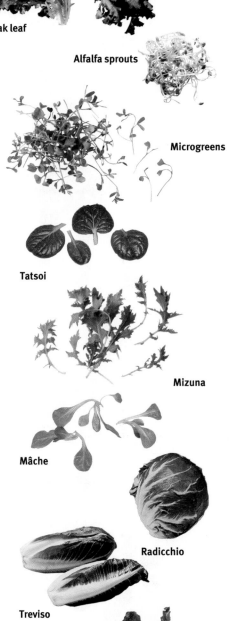

Granny Smith apple

Golden Delicious apple

Rome apple

Round Gala apple

Macintosh apples

Red Delicious apples

Apricots

Bananas

Fresh Fruits: Evaluating and Preparing

The following is a summary of the most commonly available fresh fruits. Emphasis is on the qualities to look for when purchasing them and on how to trim and prepare the fruit for use. In addition, identification information is included for certain exotic items. Nearly everyone knows what apples, bananas, and strawberries are, but not everyone can identify a persimmon or a passion fruit. Trimming yields are also given. How to use these percentages is explained on pages 103–104.

APPLES

Mature apples have a fruity aroma, brown seeds, and a slightly softer texture than unripe fruit. Overripe or old apples are soft and sometimes shriveled. Avoid apples with bruises, blemishes, decay, or mealy texture. Summer varieties (sold until fall) do not keep well. Fall and winter varieties keep well and are available for a longer period. Apples with a good acid content are usually better for cooking than bland eating varieties like Red Delicious. Granny Smith and Golden Delicious are widely used for cooking. To prepare, wash; pare if desired. Quarter and remove core, or leave whole and core with a special coring tool. Use a stainless-steel knife for cutting. After paring, dip in solution of lemon juice (or other tart fruit juice) or ascorbic acid to prevent browning.

Percentage yield: 75%

APRICOTS

Only tree-ripened apricots have sufficient flavor, and they keep for a week or less under refrigeration. They should be golden yellow, firm, and plump, not mushy. Avoid fruit that is soft, blemished, or decayed.

Wash, split in half, and remove pit. Peeling is not necessary for most purposes.

Percentage yield: 94%

BANANAS

Look for plump, smooth bananas without bruises or spoilage. All bananas are picked green, so you don't need to avoid unripe fruit. Avoid overripe fruit, however.

Ripen at room temperature for three to five days; fully ripe fruit is all yellow with small brown flecks and no green. Do not refrigerate, or fruit will discolor. Peel and dip in fruit juice to prevent browning.

Percentage yield: 70%

BERRIES

This category includes blackberries, blueberries, cranberries, black currants (cassis), red currants, white currants, lingonberries, raspberries, and strawberries. Berries should be full, plump, and clean, with bright, fully ripe color. Watch for moldy or spoiled fruits. Wet spots on carton indicate damaged fruit.

Refrigerate in original container until ready to use in order to reduce handling. Except for cranberries, berries do not keep well. Sort out spoiled berries and foreign materials. Wash with gentle spray and drain well. Remove stems from strawberries. Red currants for garnishing are often left on the stem. Handle berries carefully to avoid bruising.

Percentage yield: 92–95%

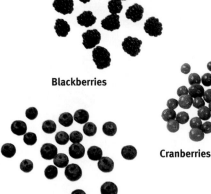

Blackberries

Blueberries

Cranberries

White currants

Raspberries

Strawberries

CHERRIES

Look for plump, firm, sweet, juicy cherries. Bing or black cherries should be uniformly dark to almost black.

Refrigerate in original container until ready to use. Just before use, remove stems and sort out damaged fruit. Rinse and drain well. Pit with a special pitting tool.

Percentage yield: 82% (pitted)

COCONUTS

Shake to hear liquid inside; fruits with no liquid are dried out. Avoid cracked fruits and fruits with wet eyes.

Pierce eye with ice pick or nail and drain liquid. Crack with hammer and remove meat from shell (easier if placed in 350°F/175°C oven 10 to 15 minutes first). Peel brown skin with paring knife or vegetable peeler.

Percentage yield: 50%

FIGS

Calimyrna figs, also called *Smyrna figs*, are light green; Black Mission figs and Black Spanish figs (also called *Brown Turkey*) are purple. All figs are sweet when ripe, and soft and delicate in texture. They should be plump and soft, without spoilage or sour odor.

Keep refrigerated (although firm, unripe figs can be left at room temperature, spread in one layer, for a few days to ripen slightly). Rinse and drain, handling carefully. Trim off hard stem ends.

Percentage yield: 95% (80–85% if peeled)

GRAPEFRUIT

Select fruit that is heavy for its size and has a firm, smooth skin. Avoid puffy, soft fruits and those with pointed ends, which have low yield and a lot of rind. Cut and taste for sweetness.

For sections and slices, peel with a chef's knife, removing all white pith (see p. 124). Free sections from membrane with a small knife.

Percentage yield: 45–50% (flesh without membrane); 40–45% (juiced)

GRAPES

Look for firm, ripe, good-colored fruits in full bunches. Grapes should be firmly attached to stems and should not fall off when shaken. Watch for rotting or shriveling at stem ends.

Refrigerate in original container. Wash and drain. Except for seedless varieties, cut in half and remove seeds with the point of a paring knife.

Percentage yield: 90%

GUAVA

There are many varieties of these small, tropical fruits. They may be round, oval, or pear-shaped, with aromatic flesh that may be green, pink, yellow, red, or white, sometimes full of seeds and sometimes nearly seedless. The flavor is complex and ranges from sweet to sour. Select tender fruits with a full aroma

Cut in half and scoop out the flesh. For many uses, the flesh is puréed in a food processor or blender, seeds and all. Alternatively, cut into dice or other shapes as desired.

Percentage yield: 80%

KIWI FRUIT

Kiwis are firm when unripe; they become slightly softer when ripe but do not change color significantly. Common kiwis have green flesh; golden kiwis are also available. Allow them to ripen at room temperature. Avoid fruits with bruises or soft spots.

Pare thin outer skin. Cut crosswise into slices.

Percentage yield: 80%

KUMQUATS

These look like tiny, elongated oranges, about the size of a medium olive. The skin and even the seeds can be eaten. In fact, the skin is sweet, while the flesh and juice are tart. Avoid soft or shriveled fruit. Kumquats keep well and are usually in good condition in the market.

Wash, drain well, and cut as desired.

Percentage yield: 95–100%

Cherries

Coconut

Figs

Calimyrna figs

Black mission figs

Grapefruit

Red grapefruit

Grapes

Guava

Kiwi fruit

Kumquats

Lemons

Limes

LEMONS AND LIMES

Look for firm, smooth skins. Colors may vary: Limes may be yellow, and lemons may have green on skin.

Cut in wedges, slices, or other shapes for garnish, or cut in half crosswise for juicing. Wash first if using the zest.

Percentage yield: 40–45% (juiced)

LITCHIS (OR LYCHEES)

This Chinese fruit is about the size of a walnut or Ping-Pong ball. Its rough, leathery outer skin, which ranges from reddish to brown, is easily peeled away to reveal aromatic, juicy white flesh that surrounds an inedible pit. Look for heavy, plump fruit with good color.

Peel, cut in half, and remove the seed.

Percentage yield: 50%

Litchis

MANGOES

This tropical fruit comes in two main types: oval, with a skin that ranges from green to orange to red, and kidney-shaped, with skin that is more uniformly yellow when ripe. Mangoes have a thin but tough skin and yellow to yellow-orange flesh that is juicy and aromatic. Fruit should be plump and firm, with clear color and no blemishes. Avoid rock-hard fruit, which may not ripen properly.

Mangoes

Let ripen at room temperature until slightly soft. Peel and cut flesh away from center stone, or cut in half before peeling, working a thin-bladed knife around both sides of the flat stone.

Percentage yield: 75%

MELONS

Look for the following characteristics when selecting melons:

Cantaloupes: Smooth scar on stem end, with no trace of stem (called *full slip*, meaning the melon was picked ripe). Yellow rind, with little or no green. Heavy, with good aroma.

Honeydew: Good aroma, slightly soft, heavy, creamy white to yellowish rind, not too green. Large sizes have best quality.

Crenshaw, Casaba, Persian, Canary, Santa Claus: Heavy, with a rich aroma and slightly soft blossom end.

Watermelon: Yellow underside, not white. Firm and symmetrical. Large sizes have best yield. Velvety surface, not too shiny. When cut, look for hard, dark brown seeds and no white heart (hard white streak running through center).

Cantaloupe

Honeydew

Canary melon

To prepare hollow melons, wash, cut in half, and remove seeds and fibers. Cut into wedges and cut flesh from rind, or cut balls with ball cutter. For watermelon, wash, cut in half or into pieces, and cut balls with ball cutter, or cut flesh from rind and remove seeds.

Percentage yield: Watermelons: 45%; others: 50–55%

Watermelon

Crenshaw melon

Piel de sapo melon

Nectarines

NECTARINES

See Peaches and Nectarines.

ORANGES, MANDARINS, AND TANGERINES

To buy high-quality oranges, use the same guidelines as for grapefruit. Mandarins may feel puffy, but they should be heavy for their size. Unusual varieties include blood oranges, with dark red flesh and juice and intense flavor, and Seville oranges, with tart rather than sweet flesh. Seville oranges are prized for making marmalade.

Peel mandarins by hand and separate the sections. For juicing, cut oranges in half crosswise. For sections, see Grapefruit.

Percentage yield: 60–65% (sections with no membranes); 50% (juiced)

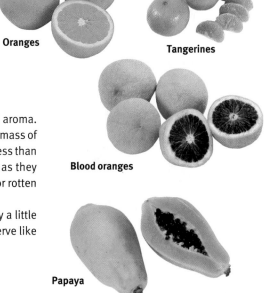

Oranges

Tangerines

Blood oranges

PAPAYAS

Papayas are pear-shaped tropical fruits with a mild, sweet flavor and slightly floral aroma. The flesh is yellow or pinkish, depending on the variety, and the center cavity holds a mass of round, black seeds. Papayas may weigh from less than 1 pound to several pounds (less than 500 g to more than 1 kg) each. Their skin is green when unripe, becoming yellow as they ripen. For best quality, select fruits that are firm and symmetrical, without bruises or rotten spots. Avoid dark green papayas, which may not ripen properly.

Let ripen at room temperature until slightly soft and nearly all yellow, with only a little green. Wash. Cut in half lengthwise and scrape out the seeds. Peel, if desired, or serve like cantaloupe.

Percentage yield: 65%

Papaya

PASSION FRUIT

These are tropical fruits about the size of eggs, with a brownish purple skin that wrinkles when ripe. (There is also a yellow-skinned variety.) They are mostly hollow when ripe, with juice, seeds, and a little flesh inside. The tart juice has an intense, exotic flavor and aroma greatly prized by pastry chefs. Select fruits that are large and heavy for their size. If they are smooth, let ripen at room temperature until the skin is wrinkled.

To use, cut in half, taking care not to lose any juice. Scrape out the seeds, juice, and pulp. Seeds can be eaten, so do not discard. If you need only the juice, it is much more economical to buy the frozen juice, as fresh fruits are expensive.

Percentage yield: 40–45%

Passion fruits

PEACHES AND NECTARINES

Peaches should be plump and firm, without bruises or blemishes. Avoid dark green fruits, which are immature and will not ripen well. Avoid fruits refrigerated before ripening, as they may be mealy. Select freestone varieties of peaches. Clingstone varieties require too much labor (they are used primarily for canning).

Let ripen at room temperature, then refrigerate. Peel peaches by blanching in boiling water 10 to 20 seconds, until skin slips off easily, and cool in ice water. (Nectarines do not need to be peeled.) Cut in half, remove pits, and drop into fruit juice, sugar syrup, or ascorbic acid solution to prevent darkening.

Percentage yield: 75%

Peaches

PEARS

Pears should be clean, firm, and bright, with no blemishes or bruises.

Pears for eating raw should be fully ripe and aromatic. For cooking, they are better if slightly underripe, as fully ripe pears are very soft when cooked. Wash, pare, cut in halves or quarters, and remove core. To prevent browning, dip in fruit juice.

Percentage yield: 75% (peeled and cored)

Bartlett pears

Bosc pears

Butter French pear
Courtesy of the California
Pear Advisory Board

Comice pear
Courtesy of the California
Pear Advisory Board

Forelle pear
Courtesy of the California
Pear Advisory Board

Seckel pear
Courtesy of the California
Pear Advisory Board

Starcrimson pear
Courtesy of the California
Pear Advisory Board

Taylor gold pear
Courtesy of the California
Pear Advisory Board

PERSIMMONS

Persimmons are orange-red fruits available in two varieties. The most common is Hachiya, which is shaped somewhat like a large acorn (about 8 oz/250 g each). It is extremely tannic when unripe, making it nearly inedible until it ripens to a soft, jellylike mass. Ripe persimmons are sweet, juicy, and mild but rich in flavor. The other variety, Fuyu, is smaller and more squat in shape. It lacks the tannin content of Hachiya persimmons and can be eaten even when not fully ripe. Select plump persimmons with good red color and stem cap attached.

Ripen at room temperature until very soft, then refrigerate. Remove stem cap, cut as desired, and remove seeds, if there are any.

Percentage yield: 80%

Hachiya persimmons

PINEAPPLES

Pineapples should be plump and fresh-looking, with an orange-yellow color and abundant fragrance. Avoid soft spots, bruises, and dark, watery spots.

Store at room temperature for a day or two to allow some tartness to disappear, then refrigerate. Pineapples may be cut in many ways. For slices, chunks, and dice, cut off top and bottom and pare the rough skin from the sides, using a stainless-steel knife. Remove all eyes. Cut into quarters lengthwise and cut out the hard center core. Slice or cut as desired.

Percentage yield: 50%

Pineapple

PLUMS

Plums should be plump and firm but not hard, with good color and no blemishes.

Wash, cut in half, and remove pits, or serve whole.

Percentage yield: 95% (pitted only)

Prune plums

Red plums

Black freestone plums

Santa Rosa plums

POMEGRANATES

The pomegranate is a subtropical fruit about the size of a large apple. It has a dry red skin or shell enclosing a mass of seeds. Each seed is surrounded by a small sphere of juicy, bright red pulp. Pomegranates are used mostly for their red, tart-sweet juice. The seeds, with their surrounding pulp, can also be used as an attractive garnish for desserts and even meat dishes. Look for heavy fruits without bruises. When squeezed, they should yield to gentle pressure; if they are too hard, they may be dried out.

To prepare, lightly score the skin without cutting into the seeds and carefully break the fruit into sections. Separate the seeds from the membranes. Juicing is difficult. Some methods crush the seeds and make the juice bitter. This method makes a better juice: Roll the whole pomegranate on the countertop under the palm of the hand to break the juice sacs. Then pierce a hole in the side and squeeze out the juice.

Percentage yield: 55%

Pomegranates

PRICKLY PEARS OR CACTUS PEARS

This is a barrel-shaped fruit about the size of a large egg. Its skin color ranges from magenta to greenish red, and it has a bright pinkish red, spongy interior with black seeds. The pulp is sweet and aromatic, but with a mild flavor. Good-quality fruits are tender but not mushy, with a good skin color, not faded. Avoid fruits with rotten spots.

If the fruit is firm, allow to ripen at room temperature, then refrigerate. As it is the fruit of a cactus, thorns grow on the skin. These are removed before shipping, but small, hard-to-see thorns may remain. To avoid getting stung, hold the fruit with a fork while you slice off the top and bottom. Still holding it with a fork, pare the sides with a knife and discard the peels without touching them. Cut or slice the pulp as desired, or force it through a sieve to purée it and remove the seeds.

Percentage yield: 70%

Prickly pears

QUINCES

Quinces grow in temperate climates and were once very popular in Europe and North America. Many old, neglected quince trees remain in New England and elsewhere. The fruit resembles a large, yellow, lumpy pear with a smooth or slightly downy skin. The raw fruit is never eaten, as it is dry and hard. When cooked (usually stewed or poached in a sugar syrup), it becomes aromatic, flavorful, and sweet, and the color of the flesh turns slightly pink. The fruit keeps well. Select fruit with good color and free of bruises or blemishes.

Cut, pare, and core like apples or pears, then cook.

Percentage yield: 75%

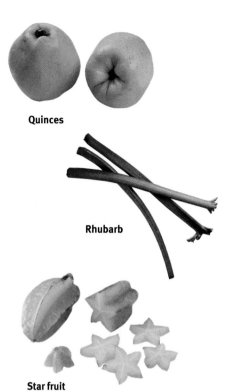

Quinces

Rhubarb

Star fruit

RHUBARB

Rhubarb is a stem, not a fruit, but it is used like a fruit. Buy firm, crisp, tender rhubarb with thick stalks, not thin and shriveled.

Cut off all traces of leaf, which is poisonous. Trim root end, if necessary. Peel with a vegetable peeler if desired, or omit this step if the skin is tender. Cut into desired lengths.

Percentage yield: 85–90% (if purchased without leaves)

STAR FRUIT OR CARAMBOLA

The star fruit is a shiny, yellow, oblong fruit with five ridges running the length of the fruit, so it forms stars when sliced crosswise. It is fragrant, ranging from tart to sweet, with a crisp texture. Look for full, firm fruits. Avoid fruits with ribs that have browned and shrunk.

Wash and slice crosswise.

Percentage yield: 99%

KEY POINTS TO REVIEW

- What are the five main types of salad, as categorized by their place in menus? What kinds of salad are appropriate for each category?

- What are the main categories of salad ingredients? Give examples of each.

- What are the most important varieties of salad greens? Describe them.

- What fruits are used in the kitchen? How is each kind judged for quality? What pre-preparation techniques are used for each?

Arrangement and Presentation

The Structure of a Salad

A plated salad may have as many as four parts: base, body, dressing, and garnish. All salads have body, and most have dressing, but base and garnish are parts of only some salads, as you will see in the following discussion.

Of course this discussion refers only to individual plated salads. When we use the term *salad* to refer to a bulk mixture, as in "two pounds of potato salad," references to the *four parts of a salad* do not apply.

BASE OR UNDERLINER

A scoop of potato salad looks bare when served by itself on a salad plate as a side dish. Placing it on a bed of lettuce leaves makes it more appealing and also emphasizes its identity as a salad. Although most tossed green salads and many composed salads are presented without an underliner, bound salads and some other vegetable salads may be more attractive and appetizing when served on a bed of leafy greens.

Cup-shaped leaves of iceberg or Boston lettuce make attractive bases. They give height to salads and help confine loose pieces of food.

A layer of loose, flat leaves (such as romaine, loose-leaf, or chicory) or of shredded lettuce may be used as a base. This kind of base involves less labor and food cost, as it is not necessary to separate whole cup-shaped leaves from a head.

BODY

This is the main part of the salad and, as such, receives most of our attention in this chapter.

GARNISH

A garnish is an edible decorative item added to a salad for eye appeal, though it often adds to the flavor as well. It should not be elaborate or dominate the salad. Remember this basic rule of garnishing: Keep it simple.

Garnish should harmonize with the rest of the salad ingredients and, of course, be edible. It may be mixed with the other salad ingredients (for example, shreds of red cabbage mixed into a tossed green salad), or it may be added at the end.

Often, the main ingredients of a salad form an attractive pattern in themselves, and no garnish is necessary. In the case of certain combination salads and other salads with many ingredients or components, there may be no clear distinction between a garnish and an attractive ingredient that is part of the body. In general, if a salad is attractive and balanced without an added garnish, don't add one.

Nearly any of the vegetables, fruits, and protein foods listed on pages 396–397, cut into simple, appropriate shapes, may be used as garnish.

DRESSING

Dressing is a seasoned liquid or semiliquid added to the body of the salad for flavor, tartness, spiciness, and moistness.

The dressing should harmonize with the salad ingredients. In general, use tart dressings for green salads and vegetable salads and use slightly sweetened dressings for fruit salads. Soft, delicate greens like Boston or Bibb lettuce require a light dressing. A thick, heavy dressing will turn them to mush.

Dressings may be added at service time (as for green salads), served separately for the customer to add, or mixed with the ingredients ahead of time (as in potato salad, tuna salad, egg salad, and so on). A salad mixed with a heavy dressing, like mayonnaise, to hold it together is called a *bound salad*.

Remember: Dressing is a *seasoning* for the main ingredients. It should accent their flavor, not overpower or drown them. Review the rules of seasoning in Chapter 4.

Arranging the Salad

Perhaps even more than with most other foods, the appearance and arrangement of a salad are essential to its quality. The colorful variety of salad ingredients gives the chef an opportunity to create miniature works of art on the salad plate.

Unfortunately, it is nearly as difficult to give rules for arranging salads as it is for painting pictures because the principles of composition, balance, and symmetry are the same for both arts. It is a skill you must develop an eye for, by experience and by studying good examples.

Guidelines for Arranging Salads

1. **Keep the salad off the rim of the plate.**
   Think of the rim as a picture frame and arrange the salad within this frame. Select the right plate for the portion size, not too large or too small.

2. **Strive for a good balance of colors.**
   Plain iceberg lettuce looks pale and sickly all by itself, but it can be enlivened by mixing in darker greens and perhaps a few shreds of carrot, red cabbage, or other colored vegetable. On the other hand, don't go overboard. Sometimes just a few shades of green creates a beautiful effect. Too many colors may look messy.

3. **Height helps make a salad attractive.**
   Ingredients mounded on the plate are more interesting than if they are spread flat. Lettuce cups as bases add height. Often just a little height is enough. Arrange ingredients like fruit wedges or tomato slices so they overlap or lean against each other rather than lie flat on the plate.

4. **Cut ingredients neatly.**
   Ragged or sloppy cutting makes the whole salad look sloppy and haphazard.

5. **Make every ingredient identifiable.**
   Cut every ingredient into large enough pieces that the customer can recognize each immediately. Don't pulverize everything in the buffalo chopper or VCM. Bite-size pieces are the general rule, unless the ingredient can be cut easily with a fork, such as tomato slices. Seasoning ingredients, like onion, may be chopped fine.

6. **Keep it simple.**
   A simple, natural arrangement is pleasing. An elaborate design, a gimmicky or contrived arrangement, or a cluttered plate is not pleasing. Besides, elaborate designs take too long to make.

Recipes and Techniques

Thorough mise en place is extremely important in salad-making. Little cooking is involved, but a great deal of time-consuming handwork is. Salads can be made quickly and efficiently only if the station is set up properly.

Green Salads

PRINCIPLES

Salad greens must be fresh, clean, crisp, cold, and well drained, or the salad will be of poor quality. Good greens depend on proper preparation.

Moisture and air are necessary to keep greens crisp.

1. Leaves wilt because they lose moisture. Crispness can be restored by washing and refrigeration. The moisture that clings to the leaves after thorough draining is usually enough. Too much water drowns them and dissolves out flavor and nutrients.

2. Air circulation is essential for the greens to breathe. Do not seal washed greens too tightly or pack them too firmly. Refrigerate in colanders covered with clean, damp towels, or in specially designed perforated plastic bins. These protect from drying while allowing air circulation.

Browning or rusting occurs when cut greens are held too long. This can be partially avoided by rinsing them in a mild antioxidant and by using stainless-steel knives. Better yet, plan purchasing and production so you don't need to hold them too long.

Procedure for Quantity Salad Production

When salads are made in quantity, an assembly-line production system is most efficient. Figure 14.2 illustrates this technique.

Remember the rules of safe food handling. Most salad ingredients are eaten without further cooking, so it is essential to avoid cross-contamination. Use sanitary tools and work surfaces. Wash hands properly before beginning work. In some places, local health laws require the use of gloves whenever you are handling ready-to-eat foods.

1. Prepare all ingredients. Wash and cut greens. Prepare cooked vegetables. Cut all fruits, vegetables, and garnish. Mix bound and marinated salads (egg salad, potato salad, three-bean salad, etc.). Have all ingredients chilled.

2. Arrange salad plates on worktables. Line them up on trays for easy transfer to refrigerator.

3. Place bases or underliners on all plates.

4. Arrange body of salad on all plates.

5. Garnish all salads.

6. Refrigerate until service. Do not hold more than a few hours, or the salads will wilt. Holding boxes should have high humidity.

7. Do not add dressing to green salads until service, or they will wilt.

Figure 14.2 Efficient production of salads in quantity.

(a) Prepare all ingredients ahead. Arrange cold salad plates on trays for easy refrigeration.

(b) Place lettuce bases on all plates.

(c) Place body of salad (in this case, potato salad) on all plates.

(d) Garnish all salads. Refrigerate until service.

Basic Procedure for Making Green Salads

1. **Wash greens thoroughly.**
Remove core from head lettuce by striking the core gently against a flat surface, such as a cutting board or the side of a vegetable sink, and twisting it out. Do not smash it, or you'll bruise the entire head. Cut through the core of other greens or separate the leaves so all traces of grit can be removed. Wash in several changes of cold water, until completely clean. For iceberg lettuce, run cold water into the core end (after removing core), then turn over to drain.

2. **Drain greens well.**
Lift greens from the water and drain in a colander. Tools and machines are available that quickly spin-dry greens. Poor draining results in a watered-down dressing and a soupy, soggy salad.

3. **Crisp the greens.**
Refrigerate greens in a colander covered with damp towels or in a perforated storage bin to allow air circulation and complete drainage.

4. **Cut or tear into bite-size pieces.**
Many people insist on tearing leaves instead of cutting, but this is a slow method if you have a large quantity to do. Also, you are more likely to crush or bruise the leaves.
Use sharp stainless-steel knives for cutting. Bite-size pieces are important as a convenience to the customer. It is difficult to eat or cut large leaves with a salad fork.

5. **Mix the greens.**
Toss gently until uniformly mixed. Nonjuicy raw vegetable garnish such as green pepper strips or carrot shreds may be mixed in at this time. Just make sure the vegetables are not cut into compact little chunks that will settle to the bottom of the bowl. Broad, thin slices or shreds stay better mixed.
For tossed salads to be served immediately, add the dressing to the greens in the bowl. Toss to coat the greens with the dressing. Plate (step 6) and serve immediately. For pre-plated salads, proceed with steps 6 through 9.

6. **Plate the salads (including underliners, if used).**
Cold plates, please. Don't use plates right out of the dishwasher.
Avoid plating salads more than an hour or two before service, or they are likely to wilt or dry.

7. **Garnish.**
Exceptions: (a) Garnish that is tossed with the greens in step 5. (b) Garnish that will not hold well (croutons will get soggy, avocado will discolor, etc.). Add these at service time.

8. **Refrigerate.**

9. **Add dressing immediately before service, or serve it on the side.**
Dressed greens wilt rapidly.

KEY POINTS TO REVIEW

- What are the four parts of a salad? Do all salads have all four parts?
- What are the basic guidelines for arranging salads?
- What are the steps in the basic procedure for making green salads?

Mixed Green Salad

PORTIONS: 25   PORTION SIZE: 2½–3 OZ (70–90 G)

U.S.	METRIC	INGREDIENTS
4½ lb	2 kg	Assorted salad greens
1–1½ pt	500–750 mL	Basic Vinaigrette or variation (p. 387)

Per serving: Calories, 130; Protein, 1 g; Fat, 13 g (91% cal.); Cholesterol, 0 mg; Carbohydrates, 2 g; Fiber, 2 g; Sodium, 160 mg.

VARIATIONS

Any combination of salad greens may be used. When using head lettuces, make allowances for variations in trimming yields. Plan on an EP weight of 2½–3 oz (70–90 g) per portion.

Vegetable ingredients, if they are not juicy, may be tossed with the greens. See page 396 for a listing. Shredded carrot and red cabbage are useful because a small amount gives an attractive color accent.

Garnishes may be added after the salads are plated, such as

Tomato wedges	Pepper rings
Cherry tomatoes	Red onion rings
Cucumber slices	Croutons
Radishes	Hard-cooked egg wedges or slices

Service variation: Instead of tossing the salads with the dressing, plate the greens and hold for service. Ladle dressing over salads just before service, or serve dressing in a separate container.

PROCEDURE

1. Review guidelines and procedure for preparing green salads (p. 409).
2. Wash and drain the greens thoroughly. Chill in refrigerator.
3. Cut or tear the greens into bite-size pieces.
4. Place the salad greens in a large mixing bowl and toss gently until uniformly mixed.
5. Immediately before service, add the dressing and toss to coat all the leaves with the dressing.
6. Place on cold salad plates and serve immediately.

Spinach Salad

PORTIONS: 25   PORTION SIZE: 3 OZ (90 G)

U.S.	METRIC	INGREDIENTS
3 lb	1.4 kg	Spinach leaves, trimmed (no stems)
12 oz	350 g	Bacon
1 lb	450 g	Fresh white mushrooms
6	6	Hard-cooked eggs

Per serving: Calories, 60; Protein, 5 g; Fat, 3.5 g (50% cal.); Cholesterol, 55 mg; Carbohydrates, 3 g; Fiber, 2 g; Sodium, 130 mg.

Note: Bacon may be added to salads when they are assembled (step 9). However, it will be less appetizing because the fat congeals in the refrigerator. For best quality, cook the bacon as close to serving time as possible.

PROCEDURE

1. Wash the spinach leaves in several changes of cold water until there is no trace of sand on them. Drain well. Chill in the refrigerator.
2. Cook the bacon until crisp on a griddle or in the oven on a sheet pan. Drain and let cool.
3. Crumble the bacon.
4. Wash the mushrooms and dry them well. Trim the bottoms of stems. Cut the mushrooms into thin slices.
5. Chop the eggs coarsely.
6. Place the spinach in a large bowl. Tear large leaves into smaller pieces. Smaller leaves may be left whole.
7. Add the mushrooms. Toss to mix thoroughly.
8. Portion the salad onto cold salad plates.
9. Sprinkle the salad with the chopped eggs.
10. Hold for service in refrigerator.
11. At serving time, sprinkle with the crumbled bacon.
12. Serve with a vinaigrette variation or with emulsified French dressing.

Caesar Salad (Method 1: Tableside Preparation)

PORTIONS: 8   PORTION SIZE: 4 OZ (125 G) PLUS DRESSING

U.S.	METRIC	INGREDIENTS	PROCEDURE
2 lb	1 kg	Romaine leaves	1. Wash and drain the greens thoroughly. Chill in the refrigerator
4 oz	125 g	White bread	2. Trim the crusts from the bread. Cut the bread into small cubes measuring about ⅜ in. (1 cm).
1–1½ fl oz	30–45 mL	Olive oil	3. Heat a thin layer of olive oil in a sauté pan over moderately high heat. Add the bread cubes and sauté in the oil until golden and crisp. Add more oil as needed.
			4. Remove the croutons from the pan and hold for service. Do not refrigerate.
1–2	1–2	Garlic cloves	5. Have all ingredients prepared ahead of time and arranged on a cart in the dining room.
4–8	4–8	Anchovy fillets	6. Ask the customers how much garlic they would like. Depending on their answer, either rub the bowl with a cut clove of garlic and remove it, or leave it in the bowl and crush it with the anchovies.
8 fl oz	250 mL	Olive oil	
2	2	Eggs, pasteurized	7. Ask the customers how many anchovies, if any, they would like.
2½ fl oz	75 mL	Lemon juice	8. Mash the garlic and anchovies to a paste in the salad bowl.
1 oz	30 g	Parmesan cheese, grated	9. Beat in about half the olive oil.
to taste	to taste	Salt	10. Add the greens and toss to coat with the oil mixture.
			11. Break the egg over the bowl and drop it in. Toss the lettuce well.
			12. Add the lemon juice, the rest of the oil, the parmesan cheese, and a little salt. Toss again until well mixed.
			13. Add the croutons and toss a final time.
			14. Plate and serve.

Per serving: Calories, 370; Protein, 6 g; Fat, 33 g (80% cal.); Cholesterol, 55 mg; Carbohydrates, 12 g; Fiber, 2 g; Sodium, 270 mg.

VARIATIONS

Caesar Salad (Method 2: Pantry Preparation)

Prepare the croutons and salad greens as in the basic recipe. Toss the greens with Caesar Dressing (p. 392). Plate and garnish with croutons.

Grilled Chicken Caesar

Top Caesar salads with sliced, grilled chicken breast.

Caesar Salad

Garden Salad

PORTIONS: 25   PORTION SIZE: 3 OZ (90 G) PLUS GARNISH

U.S.	METRIC	INGREDIENTS
3½ lb	1.6 kg	Mixed salad greens (see Note)
8 oz	250 g	Cucumbers
4 oz	125 g	Celery
4 oz	125 g	Radishes
4 oz	125 g	Scallions
4 oz	125 g	Carrots
1½ lb	700 g	Tomatoes

Per serving: Calories, 25; Protein, 2 g; Fat, 0.5 g (14% cal.); Cholesterol, 0 mg; Carbohydrates; 5 g; Fiber, 2 g; Sodium, 25 mg.

Note: Include some firm-textured, crisp lettuce in the mixed greens, such as romaine or iceberg.

PROCEDURE

1. Wash and drain the greens thoroughly. Chill in the refrigerator.
2. Score the cucumbers lengthwise with a fork (see p. 256), or peel them if they are waxed. Cut into thin slices.
3. Cut the celery into thin slices on the bias.
4. Trim the radishes and cut into thin slices.
5. Trim the roots and wilted tops of the scallions. Cut in half crosswise. Then slice lengthwise into thin shreds.
6. Trim and peel the carrots. Shred on a medium grater.
7. Remove the core end of the tomatoes. Cut into wedges, 8–10 per tomato, depending on size.
8. Cut or tear the lettuce and other greens into bite-size pieces.
9. Place all ingredients except tomatoes in a large mixing bowl. Toss until evenly mixed.
10. Plate the salads on cold plates or bowls.
11. Garnish with tomato wedges.
12. Hold for service in refrigerator.
13. Serve with an appropriate dressing.

Vegetable, Grain, Legume, and Pasta Salads

PRINCIPLES

Vegetable salads are salads whose main ingredients are vegetables other than lettuce or other leafy greens. Some vegetables are used raw, such as celery, cucumbers, radishes, tomatoes, and green peppers. Some are cooked and chilled before including in the salad, such as artichokes, green beans, beets, and asparagus. See pages 396–397 for lists of vegetables that can be used.

Starchy items such as grains, pastas, and dried legumes can also form the body of a salad. These ingredients usually have a bland, flat taste, so they are enhanced by a well-seasoned, tart dressing. Raw or cooked vegetables are usually added to the starch item to enhance the color, flavor, and nutritional balance of the salad. Depending on the proportion of vegetables and starch item, it is not always possible to classify the salad as a vegetable or starch salad. However, the guidelines below apply to the preparation of all these salads.

In addition, protein items such as poultry, meat, seafood, and cheese may be added to vegetable and starch salads.

Some bound salads, discussed on page 421, could be considered as a subcategory of vegetable and starch salads. However, many bound salads have a protein item as a main ingredient, so we discuss them as a separate category. There is no exact dividing line between these types. Coleslaw with mayonnaise dressing, for example, may be considered to be in either category.

Guidelines for Making Vegetable, Legume, Grain, and Pasta Salads

1. Neat, accurate cutting of ingredients is important because the shapes of the vegetables add to eye appeal. The design or arrangement of a vegetable salad is often based on different shapes, such as long, slender asparagus and green beans, wedges of tomato, slices of cucumber, strips or rings of green pepper, and radish flowers.

2. Cut vegetables as close as possible to serving time, or they may dry or shrivel at the edges.

3. Cooked vegetables should have a firm, crisp texture and good color. Mushy, overcooked vegetables are unattractive in a salad. See Chapter 11 for vegetable cooking principles.

4. After cooking, vegetables must be thoroughly drained and chilled before being included in the salad.

5. Starches, pastas, and legumes should be cooked until completely tender, but not overcooked. Starches absorb liquid from the dressing, so they may become mushy if they were overcooked. Undercooked grains and dried beans may be unpleasantly firm when cooled.

6. Vegetables are sometimes marinated, or soaked in a seasoned liquid, before being made into salads, as for Mixed Bean Salad (p. 418) and Mushrooms à la Grecque (p. 414). The marinade is usually some form of oil and vinegar dressing that also serves as the dressing for the salad. Do not plate marinated salads too far ahead of time, or the lettuce base will wilt. Use crisp, sturdy greens (such as iceberg, romaine, or chicory) as bases, as they do not wilt as quickly.

7. Grains and pastas may also be marinated for a short time, but avoid marinating for more than a few hours, as they are likely to absorb too much liquid and become very soft. This is especially true of cooked pasta. Legumes should not be marinated long either, but for the opposite reason. The acid in the marinade may toughen the proteins in the beans or lentils.

Coleslaw

PORTIONS: 25   PORTION SIZE: 3 OZ (100 G)

U.S	METRIC	INGREDIENTS
1½ pt	750 mL	Mayonnaise
2 fl oz	60 mL	Vinegar
1 oz	30 g	Sugar (optional)
2 tsp	10 mL	Salt
½ tsp	2 mL	White pepper
4 lb EP	2 kg EP	Cabbage, shredded
25	25	Lettuce cups

PROCEDURE

1. Combine the mayonnaise, vinegar, sugar, salt, and pepper in a stainless-steel bowl. Mix until smooth.
2. Add the cabbage and mix well.
3. Taste and, if necessary, add more salt and/or vinegar.
4. Arrange the lettuce leaves as underliners on cold salad plates.
5. Using a No. 12 scoop, place a mound of coleslaw in the center of each plate.
6. Hold for service in refrigerator.

Per serving: Calories, 230; Protein, 2 g; Fat, 24 g (89% cal.); Cholesterol, 25 mg; Carbohydrates, 5 g; Fiber, 2 g; Sodium, 270 mg.

VARIATIONS

1. Use Cooked Salad Dressing (p. 393) instead of mayonnaise. Reduce or omit vinegar.
2. Substitute sour cream for half of the mayonnaise.
3. Substitute heavy cream for 1 cup (250 mL) mayonnaise.
4. Substitute lemon juice for the vinegar.
5. Use 1 pt (500 mL) basic vinaigrette and omit mayonnaise and vinegar. Flavor with 2 tsp (10 mL) celery seed and 1 tsp (5 mL) dry mustard.
6. Add 2 tsp (10 mL) celery seed to the basic mayonnaise dressing.

Mixed Cabbage Slaw

Use half red cabbage and half green cabbage.

Carrot Coleslaw

Add 1 lb (500 g) shredded carrots to the basic recipe. Reduce cabbage to 3½ lb (1.7 kg).

Garden Slaw

Add the following ingredients to the basic recipe: 8 oz (250 g) carrots, shredded; 4 oz (125 g) celery, chopped or cut julienne; 4 oz (125 g) green bell pepper, chopped or cut julienne; 2 oz (60 g) scallions, chopped. Reduce cabbage to 3½ lb (1.7 kg).

Coleslaw with Fruit

Add the following ingredients to the basic recipe: 4 oz (125 g) raisins, soaked in hot water and drained; 8 oz (250 g) unpeeled apple, cut in small dice; 8 oz (250 g) pineapple, cut in small dice. Use sour cream dressing (dressing variation 2 above) and use lemon juice instead of vinegar.

Roasted Pepper Salad

PORTIONS: 12   PORTION SIZE: 3½ OZ

U.S.	METRIC	INGREDIENTS
1 lb 12 oz	840 g	Red bell peppers
1 lb 12 oz	840 g	Yellow bell peppers
10 fl oz	300 mL	Vinaigrette (p. 387), made with olive oil and red wine vinegar
½ oz	15 g	Fresh basil, chopped

PROCEDURE

1. Roast and peel the peppers, following the procedure illustrated on page 262.

2. Cut the peppers into strips ½-in. (1 cm) wide.

3. Mix the peppers, vinaigrette, and basil. Check for seasonings and add salt and pepper if desired, although none may be needed if the dressing is well seasoned.

Per serving: Calories, 190; Protein, 1 g; Fat, 17 g (83% cal.); Cholesterol, 0 mg; Carbohydrates, 9 g; Fiber, 2 g; Sodium, 180 mg.

Mushrooms à la Grecque

PORTIONS: 25   PORTION SIZE: 2½ OZ (75 G)

U.S.	METRIC	INGREDIENTS
4½ lb	2 kg	Small whole mushrooms
1 qt	1 L	Water
1 pt	500 mL	Olive oil
6 fl oz	175 mL	Lemon juice
1	1	Celery rib
2 tsp	10 mL	Salt
		Sachet:
2	2	Garlic cloves, crushed
1½ tsp	7 mL	Peppercorns, lightly crushed
2 tsp	10 mL	Coriander seeds
1	1	Bay leaf
1 tsp	5 mL	Dried thyme
25	25	Lettuce cups
¼ cup	60 mL	Chopped parsley

PROCEDURE

1. Wash and dry mushrooms. Trim the bottoms of the stems. Leave the mushrooms whole. (If only large ones are available, cut them into quarters.)

2. Place the water, olive oil, lemon juice, celery, and salt in a stainless-steel saucepan. Tie the sachet ingredients in cheesecloth and add to the pan.

3. Bring to a boil. Simmer 15 minutes to extract flavors from the spices.

4. Add the mushrooms. Simmer 5 minutes.

5. Remove from heat. Cool the mushrooms in the liquid.

6. Remove the celery and the sachet. Marinate the mushrooms overnight in the refrigerator. (The mushrooms will keep several days in the marinade.)

7. Arrange the lettuce leaves as underliners on cold salad plates.

8. Just before service, place a 2½-oz (75-g) portion of mushrooms in each lettuce cup, using a slotted spoon.

9. Sprinkle with chopped parsley.

Per serving: Calories, 180; Protein, 3 g; Fat, 19 g (88% cal.); Cholesterol, 0 mg; Carbohydrates, 3 g; Fiber, 1 g; Sodium, 190 mg.

VARIATIONS

Other vegetables may be prepared à la Grecque using this recipe. Increase cooking time as necessary, but keep the vegetables crisp.

Artichoke hearts	Leeks
Carrots, sliced or diced	Pearl onions
Cauliflower florets	

Carrot Salad

PORTIONS: 25   PORTION SIZE: 3 OZ (100 G)

U.S.	METRIC	INGREDIENTS
5 lb	2.5 kg	Carrots
1½ cups	375 mL	Mayonnaise
1 cup	250 mL	Vinaigrette
to taste	to taste	Salt
25	25	Lettuce cups
13	13	Pitted black olives

Per serving: Calories, 200; Protein, 1 g; Fat, 18 g (79% cal.); Cholesterol, 10 mg; Carbohydrates, 10 g; Fiber, 3 g; Sodium, 20 mg.

PROCEDURE

1. Peel the carrots. Shred them on a coarse grater.
2. Combine the mayonnaise and vinaigrette. Mix until smooth.
3. Add the carrots and mix. Season to taste with salt.
4. Arrange the lettuce cups as underliners on cold salad plates.
5. Using a No. 12 scoop, place a mound of carrot salad in each lettuce cup.
6. Cut the olives in half lengthwise. Garnish the top of each salad with an olive half.

VARIATIONS

Carrot Raisin Salad
Simmer 8 oz (250 g) raisins in water 2 minutes. Cool, then drain. Mix raisins with the carrots.

Carrot Pineapple Salad
Mix 12 oz (375 g) drained pineapple tidbits with the carrots.

Carrot Celery Salad
Reduce the carrots to 3½ lb (1.7 kg). Mix 1½ lb (750 g) celery (cut julienne) or celery root (shredded) with the carrots.

Celery Salad
Use celery or celery root instead of carrots in basic recipe. Cut stalk celery into thin slices instead of shredding it. Add 2 tbsp (30 mL) French or Dijon-type mustard to the dressing.

Carrot Raisin Salad

Mixed Vegetable Salad with Pasta

PORTIONS: 25   PORTION SIZE: 4 OZ (125 G)

U.S.	METRIC	INGREDIENTS
1½ lb	700 g	Cooked ditalini pasta, cold
1 lb	450 g	Cooked chickpeas or other dried beans, cold
12 oz	350 g	Zucchini, medium dice, raw or blanched
12 oz	350 g	Green beans, cooked, cut into ½-in. (1-cm) lengths
8 oz	250 g	Red onions, diced
6 oz	175 g	Small pitted black olives
6 oz	175 g	Celery, diced
4 oz	125 g	Green bell pepper, diced
4 oz	125 g	Red bell pepper, diced
¼ cup	60 mL	Capers, drained
4 oz	125 g	Parmesan cheese, grated
1½ pt	700 mL	Italian Dressing (p. 387)
25	25	Lettuce leaves for underliners
25	25	Tomato wedges or cherry tomatoes

PROCEDURE

1. Combine the pasta, beans, vegetables, and cheese in a large bowl. Toss to mix

2. No more than 1–2 hours before service, add the dressing and toss.

3. Arrange the lettuce leaves on cold salad plates.

4. Just before service, place a 4-oz (125-g) portion of the salad on each lettuce leaf.

5. Garnish each salad with a tomato wedge.

Per serving: Calories, 290; Protein, 6 g; Fat, 22 g (67% cal.); Cholesterol, 5 mg; Carbohydrates, 18 g; Fiber, 4 g; Sodium, 420 mg.

VARIATIONS

Add 1 lb (450 g) diced or sliced salami, pepperoni, or mozzarella cheese to the salad mixture.

Heirloom Tomato Salad

PORTIONS: 12   PORTION SIZE: ABOUT 4 OZ (125 G)

U.S.	METRIC	INGREDIENTS
3 lb	1.5 kg	Assorted ripe heirloom tomatoes, 3 or 4 varieties (see Procedure)
12 small bunches	12 small bunches	Mixed baby greens
6 fl oz	180 mL	Extra-virgin olive oil
3 fl oz	90 mL	Balsamic vinegar
to taste	to taste	Coarse salt
to taste	to taste	Black pepper

PROCEDURE

1. Select the tomatoes: Use 3 or 4 types of ripe, flavorful tomatoes of varied colors (yellow, green, orange, different shades of red), depending on availability. Include at least one type of small tomato, such as cherry tomato.

2. Prepare the tomatoes: Peel large tomatoes by blanching them 10 seconds in boiling water, cutting out the core end, and pulling off the skins. Small tomatoes with tender skins can be left unpeeled. Cut large tomatoes into slices. Cut small tomatoes into quarters or halves or leave whole, depending on size.

3. Arrange the tomatoes attractively on large salad plates.

4. Place a small bunch of greens on each plate.

5. Drizzle the tomatoes with a little olive oil and then a little vinegar.

6. Sprinkle lightly with coarse salt and black pepper.

Per serving: Calories, 150; Protein, 1 g; Fat, 14 g (82% cal.); Cholesterol, 0 mg; Carbohydrates, 6 g; Fiber, 1 g; Sodium, 100 mg.

VARIATIONS

Instead of the oil and vinegar, drizzle the salad with Balsamic Vinaigrette (p. 387) or Mustard Vinaigrette (p. 387).

Insalata Caprese

Use only one variety of large, red tomato. Peel and slice. Alternate overlapping slices of tomato and fresh mozzarella on a plate or platter. Sprinkle with fresh basil, cut chiffonade, coarse salt, and pepper. Drizzle with olive oil.

Greek Salad

PORTIONS: 12

U.S.	METRIC	INGREDIENTS
		Vinaigrette:
1½ fl oz	45 mL	Lemon juice
½ tsp	2 mL	Salt
⅛ tsp	0.5 mL	Pepper
1 tbsp	15 mL	Dried oregano
4½ fl oz	135 mL	Olive oil
12 oz	360 g	Cucumber, cut in half lengthwise and sliced
1 lb 8 oz	720 g	Tomatoes, large dice
9 oz	270 g	Feta cheese, crumbled
6 oz	180 g	Red onion, in thin slices
4 oz	120 g	Pitted Kalamata olives
1 lb 2 oz	540 g	Romaine lettuce, cut into bite-size pieces

PROCEDURE

1. Prepare vinaigrette, using the ingredients listed and following the procedure on p. 387.

2. Combine the cucumber, tomatoes, cheese, onion, and olives in a bowl.

3. Add the vinaigrette and toss to mix.

4. Divide the lettuce among individual serving bowls (1½ oz or 45 g per portion).

5. Spoon the vegetable and cheese mixture onto the lettuce.

Per serving: Calories, 210; Protein, 5 g; Fat, 18 g (74% cal.); Cholesterol, 20 mg; Carbohydrates, 9 g; Fiber, 2 g; Sodium, 500 mg.

VARIATION

Instead of dicing the tomatoes, cut them into wedges. Garnish each plated salad with 2 or 3 wedges.

Panzanella

PORTIONS: 10   PORTION SIZE: 4 OZ (125 G)

U.S.	METRIC	INGREDIENTS
12 oz	375 g	Firm, white Italian bread
1½ lb	750 g	Ripe tomatoes, peeled
1½ oz	45 g	Red onion, chopped fine
½ oz	15 g	Fresh basil, torn into small pieces
4 fl oz	125 mL	Olive oil
2 fl oz	60 mL	Red wine vinegar
⅛ tsp	0.5 mL	Red pepper flakes
to taste	to taste	Salt
to taste	to taste	Pepper

PROCEDURE

1. Use a hearty, firm bread for this recipe. If necessary, let it sit out to dry for a few hours, or dry it slightly in an oven.

2. Tear the bread into bite-size pieces. Place in a large bowl.

3. Chop the tomatoes coarsely into ½-in. (1-cm) pieces. Add to the bowl.

4. Add the remaining ingredients. Toss to mix.

5. Let stand about 1 hour, or until the bread has absorbed the juices and softened.

VARIATIONS

Add either or both of the following ingredients to the mixture: 8 oz (250 g) peeled, seeded cucumber, chopped; 4 oz (125 g) hearts of celery, sliced.

Per serving: Calories, 200; Protein, 4 g; Fat, 12 g (53% cal.); Cholesterol, 0 mg; Carbohydrates, 20 g; Fiber, 2 g; Sodium, 200 mg.

Mixed Bean Salad with Olives and Tomatoes

PORTIONS: 12   PORTION SIZE: 4 OZ (125 G)

U.S.	METRIC	INGREDIENTS
8 oz	250 g	Chickpeas, cooked or canned, drained
8 oz	250 g	Red kidney beans, cooked or canned, drained
8 oz	250 g	Navy or white kidney beans, cooked or canned, drained
10 oz	300 g	Tomatoes, peeled, seeded, small dice
2 oz	60 g	Green olives, pitted, sliced
2 oz	60 g	Black olives, pitted, sliced
2 oz	60 g	Red onion, chopped fine
8 fl oz	250 mL	Mustard Vinaigrette (p. 387)
2 tbsp	30 mL	Chopped parsley
12	12	Lettuce leaves

PROCEDURE

1. Combine the chickpeas and beans in a bowl. Add the tomatoes, olives, and onion. Toss gently.

2. Add the vinaigrette. Mix.

3. Cover and refrigerate 2–4 hours.

4. Before serving, mix in the chopped parsley.

5. Arrange the lettuce leaves on cold salad plates.

6. Mound the salad mixture on the lettuce leaves.

Per serving: Calories, 220; Protein, 5 g; Fat, 16 g (62% cal.); Cholesterol, 0 mg; Carbohydrates, 17 g; Fiber, 6 g; Sodium, 320 mg.

VARIATION

White Bean Salad
Instead of the mixture of beans, use only white kidney beans.

Mixed Bean Salad with Olives and Tomatoes

Quinoa Salad with Bell Peppers

PORTIONS: 12 PORTION SIZE: 4½ OZ (135 G)

U.S.	METRIC	INGREDIENTS
9 oz	275 g	Quinoa
1½ pt	750 mL	Water
¼ tsp	1 mL	Salt
4 oz	125 g	Red bell pepper, small dice
4 oz	125 g	Green bell pepper, small dice
2 oz	60 g	Scallion, chopped fine
6 oz	180 g	Cucumber, peeled and seeded, small dice
3 oz	90 g	Dried apricots, chopped fine
8 fl oz	250 mL	Italian Dressing (p. 387)
to taste	to taste	Salt
12	12	Lettuce or radicchio leaves

PROCEDURE

1. Rinse the quinoa thoroughly in cold water. Drain.
2. Combine with the water and salt. Bring to a boil. Lower heat, cover, and simmer slowly until the grain is cooked, about 15 minutes.
3. Spread the cooked grain in a shallow pan to cool.
4. Combine the cooled quinoa, bell peppers, scallions, cucumber, and apricots in a bowl.
5. Add the dressing and toss to mix.
6. Add salt to taste.
7. Arrange the lettuce leaves on cold salad plates.
8. Mound the salad mixture on the lettuce leaves.

Per serving: Calories, 220; Protein, 4 g; Fat, 14 g (56% cal.); Cholesterol, 0 mg; Carbohydrates, 21 g; Fiber, 2 g; Sodium, 200 mg.

VARIATIONS

This salad can also be made with brown rice, farro, or couscous.

Quinoa Salad with Bell Peppers

Lentil Salad

PORTIONS: 10 PORTION SIZE: 4 OZ (125 G)

U.S.	METRIC	INGREDIENTS
12 oz	375 g	Green lentils
1 qt	1 L	Water
4 oz	125 g	Celery, cut brunoise
4 oz	125 g	Carrot, cut brunoise
1½ oz	45 g	Red onion, cut brunoise
1 oz	30 g	Parsley, chopped
4 fl oz	145 mL	Olive oil
2 fl oz	60 mL	Lemon juice
to taste	to taste	Salt
to taste	to taste	Pepper
12	12	Lettuce leaves

PROCEDURE

1. Pick over, rinse, and drain the lentils.
2. Place them in a saucepan with the water. Bring to a boil, reduce heat, and simmer until the lentils are just tender and not falling apart, about 25 minutes.
3. Drain the lentils and place them in a bowl.
4. While the lentils are still warm, add the celery, carrot, onion, parsley, olive oil, and lemon juice. Toss to mix.
5. Season to taste with salt and pepper.
6. Arrange the lettuce leaves on salad plates.
7. Serve the lentil salads warm or cold. Mound the salad on the lettuce leaves.

Per serving: Calories, 200; Protein, 9 g; Fat, 11 g (44% cal.); Cholesterol, 0 mg; Carbohydrates, 23 g; Fiber, 6 g; Sodium, 35 mg.

Tabbouleh

PORTIONS: 12   PORTION SIZE: 4 OZ (125 G)

U.S.	METRIC	INGREDIENTS	PROCEDURE
12 oz	375 g	Bulgur wheat, fine or medium texture	1. Place the bulgur wheat in a bowl. Pour over it about twice its volume of boiling water. 2. Cover and let stand until completely cool. The bulgur should have absorbed most or all of the water and should be tender enough to eat. If any liquid remains, drain it and squeeze out the grain gently. Fluff with a fork.
1 lb	500 g	Cucumber	3. Peel the cucumbers and quarter them lengthwise. Scoop out and discard the seeds. Slice the cucumbers ¼ in. (6 mm) thick.
1½ tsp	7 mL	Coarse salt	4. Toss with the coarse salt in a bowl and let stand 30 minutes. 5. Rinse, drain, and pat dry.
1½ oz	45 g	Parsley, chopped	6. Mix the bulgur, cucumbers, parsley, scallions, tomato, lemon juice, and olive oil.
1½ oz	45 g	Scallions, sliced thin	7. Add salt and pepper to taste.
6 oz	180 g	Tomato, peeled, seeded, and chopped	
3 fl oz	90 mL	Lemon juice	
3 fl oz	90 mL	Olive oil	
to taste	to taste	Salt	
to taste	to taste	Pepper	
12	12	Lettuce leaves	8. Arrange the lettuce leaves on cold salad plates. 9. Mound the tabbouleh on the lettuce leaves.

Per serving: Calories, 170; Protein, 4 g; Fat, 7 g (36% cal.); Cholesterol, 0 mg; Carbohydrates, 24 g; Fiber, 6 g; Sodium, 240 mg.

Wheatberry Salad with Mint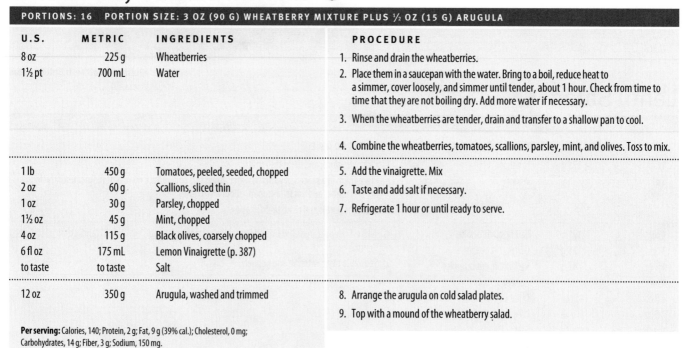

PORTIONS: 16   PORTION SIZE: 3 OZ (90 G) WHEATBERRY MIXTURE PLUS ½ OZ (15 G) ARUGULA

U.S.	METRIC	INGREDIENTS	PROCEDURE
8 oz	225 g	Wheatberries	1. Rinse and drain the wheatberries.
1½ pt	700 mL	Water	2. Place them in a saucepan with the water. Bring to a boil, reduce heat to a simmer, cover loosely, and simmer until tender, about 1 hour. Check from time to time that they are not boiling dry. Add more water if necessary. 3. When the wheatberries are tender, drain and transfer to a shallow pan to cool. 4. Combine the wheatberries, tomatoes, scallions, parsley, mint, and olives. Toss to mix.
1 lb	450 g	Tomatoes, peeled, seeded, chopped	5. Add the vinaigrette. Mix
2 oz	60 g	Scallions, sliced thin	6. Taste and add salt if necessary.
1 oz	30 g	Parsley, chopped	7. Refrigerate 1 hour or until ready to serve.
1½ oz	45 g	Mint, chopped	
4 oz	115 g	Black olives, coarsely chopped	
6 fl oz	175 mL	Lemon Vinaigrette (p. 387)	
to taste	to taste	Salt	
12 oz	350 g	Arugula, washed and trimmed	8. Arrange the arugula on cold salad plates. 9. Top with a mound of the wheatberry salad.

Per serving: Calories, 140; Protein, 2 g; Fat, 9 g (39% cal.); Cholesterol, 0 mg; Carbohydrates, 14 g; Fiber, 3 g; Sodium, 150 mg.

Bound Salads

PRINCIPLES

Bound salads are mixtures of foods held together, or bound, with a dressing, usually a thick dressing such as mayonnaise. The term bound is used most often for traditional mixtures of cooked protein, starch, and vegetable items with mayonnaise, such as chicken salad, tuna salad, egg salad, and potato salad.

As noted in the discussion of vegetable and starch salads on page 412, there is no exact dividing line between that category and bound salads, so you should keep in mind the guidelines for preparing both kinds of salads when preparing bound salads.

Some of these salads, mainly those made with protein items, are also used as sandwich fillings. Sandwich filling ingredients must usually be chopped fine or cut into small dice to be practical for this use. Plated salads, by contrast, may contain larger cuts if desired.

Popular choices for cooked salads are the following:

Chicken	Lobster
Turkey	Eggs
Ham	Potatoes
Tuna	Pastas
Salmon	Rice
Crab	Mixed vegetables
Shrimp	

Guidelines for Making Bound Salads

1. Cooked ingredients must be thoroughly cooled before being mixed with mayonnaise, and the completed salad mixture must be kept chilled at all times. Mayonnaise-type salads are ideal breeding grounds for bacteria that cause food poisoning.

2. Bound salads are good ways to use leftovers such as chicken, meat, or fish, but the ingredients must have been handled according to the rules of good sanitation and food handling. The product will not be cooked again to destroy any bacteria that might grow in the salad and cause illness.

3. Potatoes for salads should be cooked whole, then peeled and cut, in order to preserve nutrients.

4. Except in the case of sandwich fillings, don't cut ingredients too small, or the final product will be like mush or paste, with no textural interest.

5. Crisp vegetables are usually added for texture. Celery is the most popular, but other choices are green peppers, carrots, chopped pickles, onions, water chestnuts, and apples. Be sure the flavors go together, however.

6. Bland main ingredients, such as potatoes and some seafoods, may be marinated in a seasoned liquid such as vinaigrette before being mixed with the mayonnaise and other ingredients. Any marinade not absorbed should be drained first to avoid thinning the mayonnaise.

7. Fold in thick dressings gently to avoid crushing or breaking the main ingredients.

8. Bound salads are usually portioned with a scoop. This has two advantages: (a) It provides portion control. (b) It gives height and shape to the salad.

9. For plated salads, serve on a base of greens, and choose attractive, colorful garnishes when appropriate. A scoop of potato or chicken salad looks pale and uninteresting when plated without a base or garnish.

Chicken or Turkey Salad

PORTIONS: 25   PORTION SIZE: 3½ OZ (100 G)

U.S.	METRIC	INGREDIENTS
3 lb	1.4 kg	Cooked chicken or turkey, ½-in. (1-cm) dice
1½ lb	700 g	Celery, ¼-in. (0.5-cm) dice
1 pt	500 mL	Mayonnaise
2 fl oz	60 mL	Lemon juice
to taste	to taste	Salt
to taste	to taste	White pepper
25	25	Lettuce cups
as needed	as needed	Parsley or watercress sprigs

PROCEDURE

1. Combine all ingredients in a mixing bowl. Toss gently until thoroughly mixed.

2. Arrange lettuce as underliners on cold salad plates.

3. Using a No. 10 scoop, place a mound of chicken salad on each plate. Garnish with parsley or watercress.

4. Hold for service in refrigerator.

Per serving: Calories, 200; Protein, 15 g; Fat, 22 g (74% cal.); Cholesterol, 60 mg; Carbohydrates, 2 g; Fiber, 1 g; Sodium, 170 mg.

VARIATIONS

Add any of the following ingredients to the basic recipe:

6 oz (175 g) broken walnuts or pecans

6 hard-cooked eggs, chopped

8 oz (225 g) seedless grapes, cut in half, and 3 oz (90 g) chopped or sliced almonds

8 oz (225 g) drained, diced pineapple

8 oz (225 g) diced avocado

1 lb (450 g) peeled, seeded, diced cucumber, *substituted for* 1 lb (450 g) of the celery

8 oz (225 g) sliced water chestnuts

Egg Salad

Substitute 28 diced hard-cooked eggs for the chicken in the basic recipe.

Tuna or Salmon Salad

Substitute 3 lb (1.4 kg) drained, flaked canned tuna or salmon for the chicken in the basic recipe. Add 2 oz (60 g) chopped onion. Optional ingredient: 4 oz (100 g) chopped pickles or drained capers.

Macedoine of Vegetables Mayonnaise

PORTIONS: 25   PORTION SIZE: 4 OZ (125 G)

U.S.	METRIC	INGREDIENTS
2 lb	1 kg	Cooked carrots, ¼-in. (0.5-cm) dice
2 lb	1 kg	Cooked white turnips, ¼-in. (0.5-cm) dice
1 lb	500 g	Cooked green beans, sliced in ¼-in. (0.5-cm) pieces
1 lb	500 g	Cooked green peas
1 pt or as needed	500 mL or as needed	Mayonnaise
to taste	to taste	Salt
to taste	to taste	White pepper
25	25	Lettuce cups
25	25	Tomato wedges

PROCEDURE

1. Chill all ingredients before combining.

2. Place vegetables and mayonnaise in a bowl and mix until evenly combined. Use just enough mayonnaise to bind. Season to taste with salt and white pepper.

3. Place lettuce bases as underliners on cold salad plates.

4. Using a No. 10 scoop, place a mound of salad on each plate. Garnish with 1 tomato wedge.

Per serving: Calories, 180; Protein, 3 g; Fat, 14 g (68% cal.); Cholesterol, 10 mg; Carbohydrates, 12 g; Fiber, 4 g; Sodium, 150 mg.

Ham Salad

PORTIONS: 25   PORTION SIZE: 3½ OZ (105 G)

U.S.	METRIC	INGREDIENTS
3 lb	1.44 kg	Cooked smoked ham, small dice
1 lb	480 g	Celery, small dice
8 oz	240 g	Chopped pickles (sweet or dill) or drained pickle relish
2 oz	60 g	Onion, chopped fine
1 pt	500 mL	Mayonnaise
2 fl oz	60 mL	Vinegar
25	25	Lettuce leaves for underliners
50	50	Tomato wedges (optional)

Per serving: Calories, 150; Protein, 1 g; Fat, 15 g (87% cal.); Cholesterol, 5 mg; Carbohydrates, 4 g; Fiber, 1 g; Sodium, 170 mg.

PROCEDURE

1. Combine ham, celery, pickles, onion, mayonnaise, and vinegar in a mixing bowl. Toss gently until evenly mixed. Adjust seasonings.
2. Refrigerate until ready for use.
3. Serve a 3½-oz (105-g) portion on a bed of lettuce.
4. If desired, garnish with tomato wedges.

VARIATIONS

Ham Salad Spread
Grind the ham, or chop very fine. Chop the celery very fine. Use for sandwiches.

Deviled Ham
Grind the ham. Add 3 tbsp (45 mL) prepared mustard and 1 tsp (5 mL) hot red pepper sauce to the basic recipe. Increase the onion to 4 oz (120 g). Use as a canapé spread.

Corned Beef Salad
Substitute corned beef for the ham in the basic recipe.

Macaroni and Ham Salad
Reduce the ham to 12 oz (360 g) and add 3 lb (1.44 kg) cooked, drained, chilled elbow macaroni. Omit the pickles and add 6 oz (180 g) green pepper, cut in small dice.

Potato Salad

PORTIONS: 25   PORTION SIZE: 4 OZ (125 G)

U.S.	METRIC	INGREDIENTS	PROCEDURE
5 lb AP	2.5 kg AP	Waxy potatoes (see Note)	1. Scrub the potatoes. Steam or boil until tender, but do not overcook. 2. Drain the potatoes. Leave in the colander or spread out on a sheet pan until cool enough to handle.
1½ cups 1½ tsp ¼ tsp	375 mL 7 mL 1 mL	Basic Vinaigrette (p. 387) Salt White pepper	3. Peel the warm potatoes. Cut into ½-in. (1-cm) dice. 4. Combine the dressing, salt, and pepper. Add the potatoes and mix carefully to avoid breaking or crushing them. 5. Marinate until cold. For the purpose of food safety, chill the potatoes in the refrigerator before proceeding with the next step.
12 oz 4 oz	375 g 125 g	Celery, small dice Onion, chopped fine (Optional ingredients—see Variations below)	6. If any vinaigrette has not been absorbed by the potatoes, drain it off. 7. Add the celery, onion, and, if desired, any of the optional ingredients listed below. Mix gently.
1 pt	500 mL	Mayonnaise	8. Add the mayonnaise. Mix carefully until evenly blended. 9. Keep refrigerated until ready to use.
25 50	25 50	Lettuce cups Pimiento strips	10. Arrange the lettuce as underliners on cold salad plates. 11. Using a No. 10 scoop, place a 4-oz (125-g) mound of potato salad on each plate. 12. Garnish each salad with 2 strips pimiento placed crosswise on top. 13. Hold for service in refrigerator.

Per serving: Calories, 290; Protein, 2 g; Fat, 24 g (74% cal.); Cholesterol, 10 mg; Carbohydrates, 17 g; Fiber, 2 g; Sodium, 360 mg.

Note: See pages 314–315 for explanation of potato types. Do not use starchy, mealy potatoes for salad because they will not hold their shape.

VARIATIONS

Optional ingredients, to be added in step 7:

   4–6 hard-cooked eggs, diced

   2 oz (60 g) green bell peppers, small dice

   2 oz (60 g) pimientos, small dice

   4 oz (125 g) chopped pickles or capers or sliced olives

   ¼ cup (60 mL) chopped parsley

Vinaigrette marination (steps 4–5) may be omitted if necessary. In this case, chill the potatoes before mixing with the dressing. Add 2 fl oz (60 mL) vinegar to the mayonnaise and check carefully for seasonings. Refrigerate 2 hours or more before serving.

French Potato Salad

PORTION: 25   PORTION SIZE: 4 OZ (125 G)

U.S.	METRIC	INGREDIENTS
7 lb	3.5 kg	Waxy potatoes
8 fl oz	250 mL	Salad oil
6 fl oz	200 mL	Wine vinegar (white or red)
4 oz	125 g	Onions or shallots, chopped fine
¼ tsp	1 mL	Garlic, chopped fine
¼ cup	60 mL	Chopped parsley
1 tbsp	15 mL	Dried tarragon
to taste	to taste	Salt
to taste	to taste	Pepper

Per serving: Calories, 180; Protein, 2 g; Fat, 9 g (46% cal.); Cholesterol, 0 mg; Carbohydrates, 22 g; Fiber, 2 g; Sodium, 5 mg.

PROCEDURE

1. Scrub the potatoes. Steam or boil until tender, but do not overcook.
2. Drain the potatoes. Leave in the colander or spread out on a sheet pan until cool enough to handle.
3. Peel the potatoes while still hot. Cut into slices ¼-in. (0.5-cm) thick or into ½-in. (1-cm) dice.
4. Mix the potatoes with the remaining ingredients. Allow to stand at least 15 minutes while the potatoes absorb the dressing.
5. Serve warm or cold. This salad is a popular accompaniment to hot cooked sausages.

VARIATION

Hot German Potato Salad

Omit oil and tarragon from the basic recipe. Cook 8 oz (250 g) diced bacon until crisp. Add the bacon, the bacon fat, and 1 cup (250 mL) hot chicken stock to the dressing ingredients. (More stock may be needed if the potatoes absorb a great deal.) Place the mixed salad in a hotel pan, cover, and heat in a 300°F (150°C) oven about 30 minutes. Serve hot.

Dilled Shrimp Salad

PORTION: 25   PORTION SIZE: 3½ OZ (100 G)

U.S.	METRIC	INGREDIENTS
3 lb	1.4 kg	Cooked, peeled, deveined shrimp
1½ lb	700 g	Celery, small dice
1 pt	500 mL	Mayonnaise
2 tbsp	30 mL	Lemon juice
2 tsp	10 mL	Dried dill weed (or 2 tbsp/30 mL chopped fresh dill)
½ tsp	2 mL	Salt
25	25	Lettuce cups
50	50	Tomato wedges

Per serving: Calories, 200; Protein, 12 g; Fat, 15 g (67% cal.); Cholesterol, 115 mg; Carbohydrates, 5 g; Fiber, 1 g; Sodium, 300 mg.

PROCEDURE

1. Cut the shrimp into ¼-in. (0.5-cm) pieces. (If the shrimp are very small, leave them whole.)
2. Combine the celery and shrimp in a bowl.
3. Mix the mayonnaise, lemon juice, dill, and salt.
4. Add the dressing to the shrimp mixture. Mix in thoroughly.
5. Arrange the lettuce leaves as underliners on cold salad plates.
6. Using a No. 10 scoop, place a mound of shrimp salad on each plate.
7. Garnish with tomato wedges, using 2 per salad.

VARIATIONS

Crab or Lobster Salad

Prepare as in the basic recipe, using crab or lobster meat instead of shrimp.

Crab, Shrimp, or Lobster Louis

Use Louis Dressing (p. 391) instead of the mixture of mayonnaise, lemon juice, and dill. Serve on shredded lettuce. If food cost permits, omit celery and increase shellfish to 4½ lb/2 kg.

Rice and Shrimp Salad

Reduce shrimp in the basic recipe to 1 lb (450 g), and add 2 lb (900 g) cooked rice.

Curried Rice Salad with Shrimp

Prepare Rice and Shrimp Salad, but omit the dill. Instead, flavor the dressing with 1 tsp (5 mL) curry powder heated lightly in 1 teaspoon (5 mL) oil and cooled. Optional: Substitute diced green bell pepper for half the celery.

Fruit Salads

PRINCIPLES

As their name indicates, *fruit salads* have fruits as their main ingredients. They are popular as appetizer salads, as dessert salads, and as part of combination luncheon plates, often with a scoop of cottage cheese or other mild-tasting protein food.

Guidelines for Making Fruit Salads

1. Fruit salads are often arranged rather than mixed or tossed because most fruits are delicate and easily broken. An exception is the Waldorf salad, made of firm apples mixed with nuts, celery, and a mayonnaise-based dressing.

2. Broken or less attractive pieces of fruit should be placed at the bottom of the salad, with the more attractive pieces arranged on top.

3. Some fruits discolor when cut and should be dipped into an acid such as tart fruit juice. See pages 400–405 for pre-preparation guidelines for individual fruits.

4. Fruits do not hold as well as vegetables after being cut. If both vegetable and fruit salads are being prepared for a particular meal service, the vegetable salads should usually be prepared first.

5. Drain canned fruits well before including them in the salad, or the salad will be watery and sloppy. The liquid from the canned fruit may be reserved for use in fruit salad dressing or other preparations.

6. Dressings for fruit salads are often slightly sweet, but a little tartness is usually desirable as well. Fruit juices are often used in dressings for fruit salad.

KEY POINTS TO REVIEW

- What are the guidelines for making vegetable, legume, grain, and pasta salads?
- What is a bound salad? What are the guidelines for making bound salads?
- What are the guidelines for making fruit salads?

Waldorf Salad

PORTIONS: 25   PORTION SIZE: 3 OZ (90 G)

U.S.	METRIC	INGREDIENTS	PROCEDURE
1½ cups	350 mL	Chantilly Dressing (p. 391)	1. Prepare the dressing. Place it in a large stainless-steel bowl and have it ready in the refrigerator. (See Note.)
4 lb AP	1.8 kg AP	Crisp, red eating apples	2. Core the apples and dice them to ½ in. (1 cm) without peeling them.
1 lb	450 g	Celery, small dice	3. As soon as the apples are cut, add them to the dressing and mix in to prevent darkening.
4 oz	100 g	Walnuts, coarsely chopped	4. Add the celery and walnuts. Fold in until evenly mixed.
25	25	Lettuce cups	5. Arrange the lettuce bases as underliners on cold salad plates.
2 oz	60 g	Chopped walnuts (optional)	6. Using a No. 12 scoop, place a mound of salad on each plate.
			7. If desired, garnish each salad with about 1 tsp (5 mL) chopped nuts.
			8. Hold for service in refrigerator.

Per serving: Calories, 150; Protein, 1 g; Fat, 12 g (69% cal.); Cholesterol, 10 mg; Carbohydrates, 11 g; Fiber, 2 g; Sodium, 40 mg.

Note: Plain mayonnaise may be used instead of Chantilly dressing.

VARIATIONS

Any of the following ingredients may be added to the basic Waldorf mixture. If any of these changes is made, the item should no longer be called simply Waldorf Salad. Change the menu name to indicate the product contains other ingredients. For example: Pineapple Waldorf Salad or Apple Date Salad.

    8 oz (225 g) diced pineapple

    4 oz (100 g) chopped dates, *substituted for* the walnuts

    4 oz (100 g) raisins, plumped in hot water and drained

    1 lb (450 g) shredded cabbage or Chinese cabbage, *substituted for* the celery

Arugula, Citrus, and Fennel Salad

PORTIONS: 12   PORTION SIZE: 4 OZ (125 G)

U.S.	METRIC	INGREDIENTS	PROCEDURE
1 fl oz	30 mL	Lime juice	1. Mix the lime juice, orange juice, shallots, ginger, and zest.
2 fl oz	60 mL	Orange juice	2. Whip in the olive oil to make a vinaigrette.
½ oz	15 g	Shallots, chopped fine	3. Add salt to taste.
1 tsp	5 mL	Grated fresh ginger root	
2 tsp	10 mL	Grated lime zest	
3 fl oz	90 mL	Olive oil	
to taste	to taste	Salt	
2 lb	1 kg	Grapefruit	4. Peel and section the grapefruit according to the procedure illustrated on page 124. You should have about 1 lb (500 g) grapefruit sections.
1 lb	500 g	Fennel, trimmed	5. Cut the fennel bulb in half vertically. Lay the halves on the cutting board, cut side down, and cut vertically into thin slices.
6 oz	180 g	Arugula	6. Trim the stems from the arugula. Tear into pieces.
			7. Just before serving, toss together the grapefruit, fennel, and arugula.
			8. Mound on cold salad plates.
			9. Drizzle 1 tbsp (15 mL) vinaigrette over each portion.

Per serving: Calories, 90; Protein, 1 g; Fat, 7 g (66% cal.); Cholesterol, 0 mg; Carbohydrates, 7 g; Fiber, 2 g; Sodium, 25 mg.

Arugula, Citrus, and Fennel Salad

Composed Salads

PRINCIPLES

Composed salads are salads made by arranging two or more elements attractively on a plate. They are called composed because the components are arranged on the plate rather than being mixed together. One or more of the elements may be mixed or tossed salads, but the individual mixed salads are arranged on the plate with other components for the final presentation.

Because they are more elaborate and can be substantial in size, composed salads are usually served as main courses or first courses rather than as accompaniments or side dishes.

There are so many kinds of composed salad that guidelines for preparing this category of salad are very general.

Guidelines for Preparing Composed Salads

1. Observe the guidelines for preparing each of the salad components. For example, if one of the components is a mixed green salad, observe the guidelines for preparing green salads.

2. Prepare and season each component separately, and evaluate it for flavor and quality. If one or more of the components is a salad, dressing may be added to each salad component separately, or in some cases dressing may be added to the entire salad just before serving.

3. Arrangements may be plated ahead of time only if the components will hold well. Add delicate items just before serving.

4. If any of the components is to be served hot or warm, prepare and add that item just before serving.

5. Flavors and textures of all components should harmonize or provide pleasing contrast. See the discussion of flavor building in Chapter 4.

6. Observe the general concepts of plating and presentation discussed in Chapter 15.

Chef's Salad

PORTIONS: 25

U.S.	METRIC	INGREDIENTS
6 lb	3 kg	Mixed salad greens, washed, trimmed, and crisped
1½ lb	700 g	Turkey breast, cut into thin strips
1½ lb	700 g	Pullman ham, cut into thin strips
1½ lb	700 g	Swiss cheese, cut into thin strips
50	50	Tomato wedges or cherry tomatoes
50	50	Hard-cooked egg quarters
25	25	Radishes
8 oz	225 g	Carrots, cut bâtonnet
25	25	Green bell pepper rings

PROCEDURE

1. Place the greens in cold salad bowls, approximately 4 oz (125 g) per portion.
2. Arrange the turkey, ham, and cheese strips neatly on top of the greens. Keep the items separate—do not mix them all together.
3. Arrange the remaining items attractively on the salad.
4. Hold for service. If salads must be held for over 1 hour, they should be covered so the meats and cheese don't dry out.
5. Serve with any appropriate salad dressing on the side in a separate container.

Per serving: Calories, 400; Protein, 37 g; Fat, 25 g (54% cal.); Cholesterol, 485 mg; Carbohydrates, 10 g; Fiber, 3 g; Sodium, 570 mg.

VARIATIONS

Other vegetable garnish may be used in addition to or in place of the items in the basic recipe. See lists on pages 396–397.

Roasted Beet Salad with Gorgonzola

PORTIONS: 12   PORTION SIZE: 5 OZ (150 G)

U.S.	METRIC	INGREDIENTS
1 lb 8 oz	750 g	Red beets, medium to large
1 lb 8 oz	750 g	Yellow beets, small
12 oz	375 g	Mesclun
12 fl oz	375 mL	Mustard Vinaigrette (p. 387)
6 oz	180 g	Gorgonzola cheese, crumbled

PROCEDURE

1. Wrap the red beets in foil. Wrap the yellow beets in a separate foil package.
2. Bake at 400°F (200 °C) until the beets are tender, about 1 hour.
3. Cool the beets slightly. Trim the root and stem ends, and pull off the peels.
4. Cut the red beets crosswise into thin slices.
5. Cut the yellow beets vertically into quarters.
6. Arrange the sliced red beets in circles on cold salad plates.
7. Toss the mesclun with half the vinaigrette.
8. Drizzle the remaining vinaigrette over the sliced beets.
9. Place a small mound of greens in the center of each plate.
10. Arrange the quartered yellow beets around the greens.
11. Sprinkle the tops of the salads with the crumbled gorgonzola.

Per serving: Calories, 290; Protein, 6 g; Fat, 26 g (76% cal.); Cholesterol, 15 mg; Carbohydrates, 12 g; Fiber, 3 g; Sodium, 590 mg.

Roasted Beet Salad with Gorgonzola

Salade Niçoise

PORTIONS: 25

U.S.	METRIC	INGREDIENTS
3 lb	1.4 kg	Waxy potatoes, scrubbed
3 lb	1.4 kg	Green beans, washed and trimmed
2 lbs	900 g	Mixed salad greens, washed, trimmed, and crisped
1 60-oz can	1 1700-g can	Tuna, solid pack or chunk
25	25	Anchovy fillets
50	50	Olives, black or green
50	50	Hard-cooked egg quarters
100	100	Tomato wedges
½ cup	60 mL	Chopped parsley
		Vinaigrette:
1 qt	1 L	Olive oil
1 cup	250 mL	Wine vinegar
1 tsp	5 mL	Garlic, chopped fine
1 tbsp	15 mL	Salt
½ tsp	2 mL	Pepper

Per serving: Calories, 710; Protein, 37 g; Fat, 53 g (67% cal.); Cholesterol, 440 mg; Carbohydrates, 22 g; Fiber, 5 g; Sodium, 890 mg.

Note: Salade Niçoise (nee-swahz) may be plated on large platters or in bowls to serve 2–6 portions each.

PROCEDURE

1. Cook the potatoes in boiling salted water until just tender. Drain and let cool. Peel. Cut into thin slices. Hold in refrigerator, covered.

2. Cook the beans in boiling salted water. Drain and cool under cold running water. Cut into 2-in. (5-cm) pieces. Hold in refrigerator.

3. Line cold salad bowls or plates with the lettuce leaves (see Note).

4. Combine the potatoes and green beans. Divide the mixture among the salad bowls, about 3 oz (90 g) per portion.

5. Drain the tuna and break it into chunks. Place a 1½-oz (50-g) portion in the center of each salad.

6. Arrange the anchovy fillets, olives, egg quarters, and tomato wedges attractively on the salads.

7. Sprinkle the salads with chopped parsley.

8. Hold for service in refrigerator.

9. Combine the dressing ingredients and mix well. Just before service, mix again and dress each salad with 1½ fl oz (50 mL) dressing.

Salade Niçoise

Cobb Salad

PORTIONS: 12 LUNCH ENTRÉES

U.S.	METRIC	INGREDIENTS
1 lb 8 oz	720 g	Tomatoes, peeled and seeded
1 lb 8 oz	720 g	Chicken breast, cooked
6	6	Hard-cooked eggs
1 lb 2 oz	540 g	Roquefort or other blue cheese
24 strips	24 strips	Bacon, crisp
4	4	Avocados
12 oz	360 g	Romaine
12 oz	360 g	Iceberg lettuce
6 oz	180 g	Watercress
6 oz	180 g	Frisée
1½ pt	720 mL	Mustard Vinaigrette (p. 387)

PROCEDURE

1. Cut the tomatoes into small dice.
2. Cut the chicken into small dice.
3. Chop the hard-cooked eggs.
4. Crumble the blue cheese.
5. Crumble the bacon.
6. Cut the avocados into small dice. Do not do this until just before serving, so it does not discolor before it is served.
7. Cut the salad greens into bite-size pieces and place in a bowl.
8. Add half the vinaigrette to the greens and toss.
9. Place the greens in individual salad bowls.
10. Arrange the tomatoes, chicken, eggs, cheese, bacon, and avocado on top of the greens.
11. Drizzle the remaining vinaigrette over the salads. Serve immediately.

Per serving: Calories, 880; Protein, 39 g; Fat, 78 g (77% cal.); Cholesterol, 210 mg; Carbohydrates, 12 g; Fiber, 6 g; Sodium, 1760 mg.

Cobb Salad

COBB SALAD

The first Cobb salad was made by Robert Cobb, owner of the Brown Derby restaurant in Hollywood, California. According to the story, late one night in 1938, Mr. Cobb was hungry for a snack and found a variety of ingredients in the refrigerator, including avocado, hard-cooked egg, tomato, and Roquefort cheese. He chopped them up, put them in a salad, and a legendary dish was born. After he put it on the restaurant's menu, it quickly became popular, and other restaurants picked up the idea.

Goat Cheese and Walnut Salad

PORTIONS: 12

U.S.	METRIC	INGREDIENTS	PROCEDURE
6 oz	180 g	Belgian endive or radicchio	1. Trim, wash, and drain the salad greens.
9 oz	270 g	Arugula	2. Tear into bite-size pieces. Toss together.
6 oz	180 g	Bibb lettuce	
9 oz	270 g	Romaine lettuce	
1 cup	240 mL	Bread crumbs, dry	3. Mix the crumbs, herbs, and pepper.
1 tbsp	15 mL	Dried thyme	4. Slice the cheese into 1-oz (30-g) pieces. Roll the pieces in the seasoned crumbs to coat
1 tbsp	15 mL	Dried basil	them.
1½ tsp	7 mL	Black pepper	
1 lb 8 oz	720 g	Fresh goat's milk cheese, preferably in log shape	
4½ oz	135 g	Walnut pieces	5. At service time, arrange the cheese pieces on a sheet pan. Bake at 425°F (220°C) for
8 fl oz	240 mL	Vinaigrette (p. 387) made with red wine vinegar and olive oil	10 minutes.
			6. At the same time, toast the walnuts in a dry sauté pan or in the oven with the cheese.
			7. Toss the greens with the vinaigrette and arrange on cold plates. Top each plate of greens with 2 pieces of cheese and sprinkle with walnuts.

Per serving: Calories, 460; Protein, 17 g; Fat, 40 g (75% cal.); Cholesterol, 50 mg; Carbohydrates, 13 g; Fiber, 3 g; Sodium, 530 mg.

VARIATIONS

Mixed Green Salad with Blue Cheese and Walnuts

Omit the goat cheese and herbed crumbs from the basic recipe. Instead, sprinkle the salads with crumbled gorgonzola, stilton, Roquefort, or other blue cheese.

Goat Cheese and Walnut Salad

Gelatin Salads

PRINCIPLES

Gelatin salads have a distinguished history. Their ancestors are aspics, the highly ornamented appetizers and elaborate buffet pieces made with meat and fish stocks rich in natural gelatin extracted from bones and connective tissue. Aspics are part of the glory of classical cuisine and still an important part of modern buffet work.

It's no longer necessary to extract gelatin from bones in your kitchen. Purified, granular gelatin and gelatin sheets have long been available for use in the pantry. Many excellent gelatin-based salads can be made with little labor using these products. However, most gelatin products today are made with sweetened prepared mixes whose high sugar content and heavy reliance on artificial color and flavor make their appropriateness as salads somewhat questionable. (Often, in a cafeteria line, you will see in the salad section little squares of gelatin with a lettuce leaf underneath and a dab of mayonnaise on top, and in the dessert section the identical product, without the lettuce leaf and with a dab of whipped cream in place of the mayo.)

Nevertheless, as a professional cook, you need to know how to prepare these products because many customers expect them. You should also know how to prepare salads using unflavored gelatin, relying on fruit juices and other ingredients for flavor. Unflavored gelatin is especially valuable for preparing molded vegetable salads because shredded cabbage and other vegetables make a poor combination with highly sweetened dessert gelatin.

Guidelines for Making Gelatin Salads

1. It is important to use the right amount of gelatin for the volume of liquid in the recipe. Too much gelatin makes a stiff, rubbery product. Too little makes a soft product that will not hold its shape.

   Basic proportions for unflavored gelatin are 2½ ounces dry gelatin per gallon (19 g per L) liquid, but you will almost always need more than this because of acids and other ingredients in the recipe. Basic proportions for sweetened, flavored gelatin are 24 ounces per gallon (180 g per L) liquid.

   Acids, such as fruit juices and vinegar, weaken the gelatin set, so a higher proportion of gelatin to liquid is needed, sometimes as much as 4 ounces or more per gallon (30 g per L). The setting power is also weakened by whipping the product into a foam and by adding a large quantity of chopped foods. It is impossible to give a formula for how much gelatin to use, as it varies with each recipe. Test each recipe before using it.

2. Gelatin dissolves at about 100°F (38°C), but higher temperatures will dissolve it faster.

   To dissolve unflavored gelatin, stir it into cold liquid to avoid lumping and let it stand 5 minutes to absorb water. Then heat it until dissolved, or add hot liquid and stir until dissolved.

   To dissolve sweetened, flavored gelatin, stir it into boiling water. It will not lump because the gelatin granules are held apart by sugar granules, much the way starch granules in flour are held separate by the fat in a roux.

3. To speed setting, dissolve the gelatin in up to half the liquid and add the remainder cold to lower the temperature. For even faster setting, add crushed ice in place of an equal weight of cold water. Stir until the ice is melted.

4. Do not add raw pineapple or papaya to gelatin salads. These fruits contain enzymes that dissolve the gelatin. If cooked or canned, however, these fruits may be included.

5. Add solid ingredients when the gelatin is partially set—that is, when thick and syrupy. This will help keep them evenly mixed rather than floating or settling.

6. Canned fruits and other juicy items must be well drained before being added, or they will dilute the gelatin and weaken it.

7. For service, pour into pans and cut into equal portions when set, or pour into individual molds.

8. To unmold gelatin:
   - Run a thin knife blade around the top edges of the mold to loosen.
   - Dip the mold into hot water 1 or 2 seconds.
   - Quickly wipe the bottom of the mold and turn it over onto the salad plate (or invert the salad plate over the mold and flip the plate and mold over together). Do not hold in the hot water for more than a few seconds, or the gelatin will begin to melt.
   - If the gelatin doesn't unmold after a gentle shake, repeat the procedure. You may also wrap a hot towel (dipped in hot water and wrung out) around the mold until it releases, but this is more time-consuming.

9. Refrigerate gelatin salads until service to keep them firm.

Basic Flavored Gelatin with Fruit

PORTIONS: 25   PORTION SIZE: 4 OZ (125 G)

U.S.	METRIC	INGREDIENTS	PROCEDURE
12 oz	375 g	Flavored gelatin mix	1. Place the gelatin in a bowl.
1 qt	1 L	Water, boiling	2. Pour in the boiling water. Stir until dissolved.
1 qt	1 L	Water or fruit juice, cold	3. Stir in the cold water or juice.
			4. Chill until thick and syrupy but not set.
2 lb	1 kg	Fruit, well drained	5. Fold the fruit into the gelatin mixture.
			6. Pour into molds or into a half-hotel pan.
			7. Chill until firm.
			8. Unmold. If using a hotel pan, cut 5 × 5 into portions.

Per serving: Calories, 70; Protein, 1 g; Fat, 0 g (0% cal.); Cholesterol, 0 mg; Carbohydrates, 18 g; Fiber, 0 g; Sodium, 40 mg.

VARIATIONS

The possible combinations of fruits and flavored gelatin is nearly limitless. The following suggestions are only a few possibilities. *Note:* When using canned fruits, use the syrup from the fruits as part of the liquid in step 3.

Black cherry-flavored gelatin; Bing cherries

Raspberry-flavored gelatin; peach slices or halves

Strawberry, raspberry, or cherry-flavored gelatin; canned fruit cocktail

Orange-flavored gelatin; equal parts sliced peaches and pears

Cherry-flavored gelatin; equal parts crushed pineapple and Bing cherries

Lime-flavored gelatin; grapefruit sections or pear halves or slices

Salad Bars and Buffet Service

Salad bars are frequent fixtures in restaurants and are popular with both customer and restaurateur. Diners enjoy customizing their own salads with selections from a large bowl of greens, smaller containers of assorted condiments, and a variety of dressings. The restaurateur likes salad bars because they take some pressure off the dining room staff during service. Many restaurants have designed unique salad bars that have become almost a trademark. Others may not have salad bars as part of their regular meal service but rely on them for efficiency at certain times, such as weekend brunch.

For successful salad bar service, it is important to keep several points in mind:

1. Keep the salad bar attractive and well stocked from the beginning until the end of service. Refill containers before they begin to look depleted, wipe the edges of dressing containers, and clean up debris scattered by customers.

2. Keep the components simple but attractive. Elaborately arranged salad bowls lose their effect as soon as two or three customers have dug into them.

3. Select a variety of condiments to appeal to a variety of tastes. Try both familiar and unusual items to make your salad bar stand out. There is no reason to restrict the choices to the same old stuff everyone else is serving.

   There are two basic kinds of salad bar condiments:

   • *Simple ingredients.* Nearly any item in the salad ingredient list on pages 396–397 might be selected. Your choice will depend on balance of flavors and colors, customer preference, and cost.

   • *Prepared salads.* Marinated vegetable salads, such as three-bean salad, and cooked salads, like macaroni salad, are especially suitable. The choice is large.

4. Arrange the salad bar in the following order (see Figure 14.3):

- Plates.

- Mixed greens.

- Condiments (put the expensive ones at the end).

- Dressings.

- Crackers, breads, etc., if desired.

Figure 14.3 Suggested arrangement of a salad bar. Key: (1) plates; (2) large bowl of salad greens; (3) condiments; (4) dressings; (5) crackers, breads, etc.

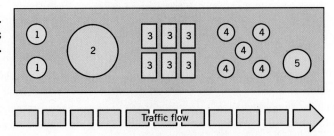

5. Make sure your setup conforms to your state health department regulations.

6. Some portion control can be achieved by selecting the right size plates, condiment servers, and dressing ladles.

KEY POINTS TO REVIEW

- What are the guidelines for making arranged or composed salads?

- What are the guidelines for making gelatin salads?

- What guidelines should be kept in mind when planning and setting up a salad bar?

TERMS FOR REVIEW

winterized oil
strength of acidity
Roquefort cheese
emulsion
temporary emulsion

vinaigrette
appetizer salad
accompaniment salad
main-course salad
separate-course salad

dessert salad
full slip
four parts of a salad
vegetable salad
bound salad

fruit salad
composed salad
gelatin salad

QUESTIONS FOR DISCUSSION

1. List three or four salads that may be served as appetizers, as accompaniments, as main dishes, as separate-course salads, and as desserts. Give reasons for your choices.
2. What is the effect of salad dressing on the crispness of salad greens, and what are some ways to solve this problem?
3. You are asked to prepare 250 Waldorf salads for a banquet. Explain the procedure you will use. List each step, from raw ingredients to plated salads. (You may refer to the recipe on p. 426.)
4. How can you ensure salad greens will be crisp?
5. You are making mixed green salads and have the following ingredients to choose from. Which would you toss together, and which would you add after plating or at service time? Why?

   Iceberg lettuce   Chicory

   Shredded red cabbage   Avocado slices

   Carrot strips or shreds   Tomato wedges

   Watercress   Romaine lettuce

   Sliced celery

6. You are preparing tossed green salads, potato salads, and avocado and grapefruit salads for luncheon service. How will you plan your preparation—that is, what will you do first, second, and so on?
7. You are trying a new recipe for a molded vegetable salad using unflavored gelatin. After evaluating the flavor, you decide it isn't tart enough and more vinegar should be added. Should you make any other adjustments?
8. When you are making mayonnaise, you should take a number of precautions to make sure a good emulsion is formed. Name as many as you can. If you forget one of these and your mayonnaise breaks, what can you do?

Chapter 15

Goat Cheese and Walnut Salad, page 431.

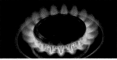
Food Presentation and Garnish

Until this point, most of the focus of this book has been on the preparation of food, from the selection of ingredients through mise en place and final cooking. We still have not reached our final goal, however. The point of learning and practicing procedures to prepare food of high quality is to ensure the food is eaten and enjoyed.

In other words, our work isn't done until the food we have prepared is arranged on plates or platters and ready to be presented to the diner.

In traditional classical cuisine, until well after the middle of the twentieth century, the normal practice in fine dining establishments was to send the food on platters and in casseroles and other serving dishes to the dining room, where it would be transferred to dinner plates by the serving staff, sometimes after carving or portioning. The chefs who developed nouvelle cuisine, however, wanted to control the appearance of the food down to the last detail and so began to arrange food on dinner plates in the kitchen. Since that time, many styles of plating have come and gone, as chefs have devoted much attention to the appearance and arrangement of food on dinner plates.

Throughout this book, we stress making food look good as well as taste good. We talk about accurate, neat cutting of vegetables and fruits, about proper trimming of meats, poultry, and fish, about grill-marking steaks, about preserving color in cooked vegetables, and about attractive plating of salads. In this chapter, we continue the discussion of making food attractive.

> **After reading this chapter, you should be able to**
>
> 1. Explain why attractive food presentation is important.
> 2. Serve food that is attractively arranged on the plate or platter, with proper balance of color, shape, and texture.
> 3. Identify common terms from classical garniture that are still in general use today

HOT FOOD PRESENTATION

We eat for enjoyment as well as for nutrition and sustenance. Cooking is not just a trade but an art that appeals to our senses of taste, smell, and sight.

"The eye eats first" is a well-known saying. Our first impressions of a plate of food set our expectations. The sight of food stimulates our appetite, starts our digestive juices flowing, and makes us eager to dig in. Our meal becomes exciting and stimulating.

On the other hand, if the food looks carelessly served, tossed onto the plate in a sloppy manner, we assume it was cooked with the same lack of care. If the colors are pale and washed out, with no color accent, we expect the flavors to be bland and monotonous. If the size of the plate makes the steak *look* small (even if it's not), we go away unsatisfied.

Your job as a cook and a chef, then, is to get your customers interested in your food or, better yet, excited about it. You can't afford to turn them off before they even taste it. Your success depends on making your customers happy.

Fundamentals of Plating

When a chef plans a new dish, appearance as well as flavor must be considered. Turn back to page 70 and look once again at the section called "Building Flavor Profiles." Remember that the senses of sight, taste, smell, and touch all come into play when we evaluate and enjoy food. How a dish looks is part of the identity of the dish, just like how it tastes, smells, and feels in the mouth.

In other words, how a dish looks is not something you think about only after you have prepared it. It is something you have in mind from the beginning of preparation. Remembering this helps you create natural-looking presentations, so the food looks like what it is rather than like an artificial construction with a complicated design.

Most of us have had the experience in a restaurant of seeing another dish carried past our table by a server and immediately thinking, "I want whatever that is." Only rarely is this thought prompted by an over-elaborate, fussy arrangement. Rather, the dish appeals to us most likely because it simply has the appearance and the aroma of well-prepared food.

Three Essentials of Food Presentation

Making food look good requires careful attention to all kitchen tasks. The following three principles should be observed in order to create attractive food. Note that only one of them concerns arranging the food on the plate.

GOOD PREPARATION AND COOKING TECHNIQUES

If vegetables are improperly cut during prep, the plate presentation will look improper. If meat is badly trimmed before cooking, a fancy plating design won't correct it. If a fish is overcooked and dry or a green vegetable is drab and mushy, it won't look good no matter what you do with it. On the other hand, well-prepared and properly cooked food with a good aroma is usually appealing all by itself.

PROFESSIONAL WORK HABITS

Serving attractive food is largely a matter of being neat and careful and using common sense. This is an aspect of the professionalism we discussed in Chapter 1. Professionals take pride in their work and in the food they serve. They don't send a plate to the dining room with sauce accidentally dribbled across the rim and maybe a thumbprint or two for extra effect—not because their supervisors told them not to or because a rule in a textbook says so but because pride of workmanship prevents it.

VISUAL SENSE

Beyond just being neat, effective food presentation depends on developing an understanding of techniques involving balance, arrangement, and garniture. These are the subjects of our next sections.

Balance

Balance is a term we used when talking about menu planning in Chapter 5. The rules of good menu balance also apply to plating. Select foods and garnishes that offer variety and contrast while avoiding combinations that are awkward or jarring.

COLORS

Two or three colors on a plate are usually more interesting than just one. Visualize this combination: poached chicken breast with suprême sauce, mashed potatoes, and steamed cauliflower. Appetizing? Or how about fried chicken, French fries, and corn? Not quite as bad, but still a little monotonous.

Many hot foods, especially meats, poultry, and fish, have little color other than shades of brown, gold, or white. It helps to select vegetables or accompaniments that add color interest—one reason why green vegetables are so popular.

Garnish is often unnecessary, especially if the accompaniments have color, but it is very important in some cases. The classic combination of broiled steak (brown) and baked potato (brown and white) looks a little livelier with a few asparagus spears on the plate or even with the simple addition of a healthy sprig of watercress.

SHAPES

Plan for variety of shape and form as well as of color. For example, you probably do not want to serve Brussels sprouts with meatballs and new potatoes. Too many items of the same shape, in this case round, looks monotonous or even odd. Green beans and whipped potatoes might be better choices for accompaniment. Try for a variety of shapes that work together well.

Cutting vegetables into different shapes gives you great flexibility. Carrots, for example, which can be cut into dice, rounds, or sticks (bâtonnet, julienne, etc.), can be adapted to nearly any plate.

TEXTURES

Textures are not strictly visual considerations, but they are as important in plating as in menu planning (Chapter 5). Good balance requires a variety of textures on the plate. Perhaps the most common error is serving too many soft or puréed foods, such as baked salmon loaf with whipped potatoes and puréed squash.

FLAVORS

You can't see flavors, either, but this is one more factor you must consider when balancing colors, shapes, and textures on the plate. Consult the menu planning guidelines in Chapter 5.

Portion Size

Portion sizes are important for presentation as well as for costing.

MATCH PORTION SIZES AND PLATES

Select plates large enough to hold all the items without crowding. Too small a plate makes an overcrowded, jumbled, messy appearance.

On the other hand, too large a plate may make the portions look skimpy. If a plate does not look sufficiently full, customers may feel they are not getting good value.

BALANCE THE PORTION SIZES OF THE ITEMS ON THE PLATE

One item, generally a meat, poultry, or fish preparation, is usually considered the main item on the plate. It is the center of attention and is larger than the accompaniments. Don't let the main item get lost amid excessive garnish and huge portions of vegetable and starch items.

Where there is no main item, as in some vegetable plates, strive for a logical balance of portions.

Arrangement on the Plate

Until recent years, plated main courses followed a standard pattern: meat or fish item at the front of the plate (closest to the diner), vegetable and starch items at the rear.

This arrangement is still the most commonly used because it is one of the simplest and most convenient. Nevertheless, many chefs are eager to display their creativity with imaginative plating presentations.

In high-end restaurants in both Europe and North America, for most of the twentieth century, food was not plated in the kitchen. Instead, items were arranged on platters and presented to the diner by the serving staff. After performing various finishing tasks, such as carving small roasts, the dining room staff then plated the main items, side dishes, and sauces and set them before the customers. All this changed in the 1970s, when chefs practicing Nouvelle Cuisine decided they wanted more control over plate appearance and began plating in the kitchen. Since then, plating styles have been changing constantly, and what is considered fashionable one year may be out of style the next.

A style popular with today's chefs is to stack everything in one multilayered tower in the center of the plate. When used with restraint, this can make an effective and impressive plating. Often, however, it is carried to extremes, and customers are faced with the job of carefully deconstructing a tower of food and rearranging the items on the plate so they can begin eating. Some chefs like this style so much they use it for nearly everything on the menu. Perhaps it works best for small dishes, such as some appetizers and the small portions of a tasting menu. It is important to keep the convenience and comfort of the diner in mind when plating.

A plate arrangement consists of some or all of the following four components. The first one is almost always present. The others may or may not be included on the same plate.

Main item. This is usually a meat, poultry, or fish item, although it may also be a pasta dish or a vegetarian item.

Side dishes or accompaniments. These are usually vegetable and starch preparations that are appropriate to serve with the main item. The term *side dish*, usually abbreviated to *side*, was originally used for separate dishes of vegetables or other items served on the side of the main plate. Today we use the term for any substantial vegetable or starch accompaniment.

Sauce or sauces. Sauces, if used, may be served around, under, or over other items on the plate.

Other garnish. In classical cuisine, the term *garnish* was used for any item served with the main item. It included side dishes as well as purely decorative items. Today, we use the term primarily for small edible items (smaller than side dishes) intended to enhance the visual appeal of the dish. Flavors and textures of garnishes should serve as an appropriate complement or contrast to the main item.

Today's plating styles are many and varied. The following descriptions are examples of popular plating styles, and they serve as starting points for countless variations. The accompanying photos, as well as the remaining photos accompanying recipes throughout the text, show additional style variations and interpretations.

- The classic arrangement: main item in front, vegetables, starch items, and garnish at the rear.

- The main item alone in the center of the plate, sometimes with a sauce or simple garnish.

- The main item in the center, with vegetables distributed randomly around it, sometimes with a sauce underneath.

- The main item in the center, with neat piles of vegetables carefully arranged around it in a pattern.

- A starch or vegetable item heaped in the center; the main item sliced and leaning up against it; additional vegetables, garnish, and/or sauce on the plate around the center items.

- Main item, vegetable and starch accompaniments, and other garnish stacked neatly one atop the other in the center of the plate. Sauces or additional garnish may be placed around the outside.

- Vegetable in center of plate, sometimes with sauce; main item (in slices, medallions, small pieces, etc.) arranged around it toward the outside of the plate.

- Slices of the main item shingled on a bed of vegetables or a purée of vegetables or starch, with, perhaps, additional garnish to one side or around.

- Asymmetrical or random-looking arrangements that don't seem to follow any pattern. These often create the impression that the food was rushed to the dining room the instant it was cooked, without thought to the design. Of course, to be effective, these arrangements must be carefully thought out in advance.

- Arrangements resembling abstract art. Carefully cut portions of foods are arranged in an asymmetrical pattern, perhaps on a rectangular or other nonstandard plate, with streaks or ribbons of sauce to unite the various elements. Such arrangements are more appropriate to first courses or to the many small courses that might make up a tasting menu.

The following guidelines will help you plate attractive, appealing food, no matter what plating style you are using.

1. **Keep food off the rim of the plate.**

   This guideline means, in part, selecting a plate large enough to hold the food without it hanging off the edge. In general, the rim should be thought of as the frame for the food presentation.

   Some chefs like to decorate this frame with a sprinkling of spice or chopped herbs or dots of a sauce. When tastefully done, this can enhance the appeal of the plate, but, if overdone, it can make the plate look unattractive. Some restaurants got into the habit of throwing some badly chopped parsley over every plate that left the kitchen. Over the years, this practice has been so carelessly done, and—worse—so many customers have soiled their sleeves on sauced rims, that decorating the rim is falling out of fashion.

2. **Arrange the items for the convenience of the customer.**

   Put the best side of the meat forward. The customer should not have to turn the item around to start on it. The bony or fatty edge of the steak, the back side of the half-duckling, the boniest parts of the chicken pieces, and so on, should face away from the customer.

   Often the most imaginative platings are the most inconvenient. Tall, precarious towers of food are difficult to eat, and the customer may have to rearrange the food before eating.

3. **Keep space between items, unless, of course, they are stacked on one another.**

   Don't pile everything together in a jumbled heap. Each item should have its own identity. This is, of course, related also to selecting the right plate size.

   Even when items are stacked, this should be done neatly so that each item is identifiable.

4. **Maintain unity.**

   Basically, there is unity when the plate looks like one meal that happens to be made up of several items rather than like several unrelated items that just happen to be on the same plate.

   Create a center of attention and relate everything to it. The meat is generally the center of attention and is often placed front and center. Other items are placed around and behind it so as to balance it and keep the customer's eyes centered rather than pulled off the edge of the plate.

   Visual balance is similar to the balance of flavors. In that discussion, we introduced the concept of primary flavors and supporting flavors. The primary flavors, you recall, are those of the main ingredients, and the supporting or secondary flavors are those of additional ingredients selected to enhance, harmonize with, or contrast with the primary flavors. Visual design works in a similar way. The main item on the plate is the primary design element. Other items, including side dishes and garnishes, are supporting design elements. Each item should enhance, harmonize with, or contrast with the main element and each other in a pleasing way.

5. **Make every component count.**

Garnishes are not added just for color. Sometimes they are needed to balance a plate by providing an additional element. Two items on a plate often look unbalanced, but adding a simple sprig of parsley completes the picture.

On the other hand, don't add unnecessary elements, especially unnecessary inedible garnishes. In many or even most cases, the food is attractive and colorful without garnish, and adding it clutters the plate and increases your food cost as well.

In any case, it is usually best to add nothing to the plate that is not intended to be eaten. Before you place the parsley alongside the fish fillet or plant a bushy sprig of rosemary in the mashed potatoes, first consider if the plate needs an extra item. If it does, then consider whether or not it wouldn't be better to add something edible to enhance the other foods with its taste and texture as well as its appearance.

6. **When using a sauce or gravy, add it attractively.**

Sauces are essential parts of many dishes, but sometimes ladling sauce all over an item hides colors and shapes. If the item is attractive by itself, let the customer see it. Ladle the sauce around or under it, or possibly covering only part of it, as with a band of sauce across the center. Always think of the sauce as part of the overall design of the plate.

7. **Keep it simple.**

As you have heard before, simplicity is more attractive than overworked, contrived arrangements and complicated designs. Unusual patterns are occasionally effective, but avoid making the food look too cute or too elaborate.

One of the simplest plating styles can also be one of the most attractive if it is carefully done—that is, placing only the meat or fish item and its sauce, if any, in the center of the plate, and serving vegetable accompaniments in separate dishes. This method is often used in restaurants to simplify service in the kitchen. However, it is usually best to use this method for only some of the menu items in order to avoid monotony.

Temperature

Serve hot foods hot, on hot plates.

Serve cold foods cold, on cold plates.

Your arrangement of beautiful food will not make much of a final impression if you forget this rule.

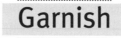

Garnish

What Is Garnish?

The word *garnish* is derived from a French word meaning "to adorn" or "to furnish." In English, we use the word to mean "to decorate or embellish a food item by the addition of other items." The word is used also for the decorative items themselves.

This definition, at first, seems vague because it could include just about anything. To many people, the word *garnish* means a sprig of parsley haphazardly placed on the plate. Just as common is the practice in some restaurants of adopting a single garnish and using it routinely on every plate, from prime rib to batter-fried shrimp. No one garnish is appropriate for every plate, just as no one side dish is appropriate for every plate.

In fact, the term *garnish* has been used for a great variety of preparations and techniques in the history of classical and modern cuisines. Today, the use of parsley sprigs on every plate has become rare, and we are again using the word *garnish* in a more traditional way.

Classical Garnish

In classical cooking, the terms *garnish* and *garniture* have been used the way we use the term *accompaniments*. In other words, garnishes are any items placed on the platter or plate or in the soup bowl in addition to the main item. It happens that these accompaniments also make the food look more attractive, but that is not the emphasis.

The classical French chef had a tremendous repertoire of simple and elaborate garnishes, and they all had specific names. A trained chef, or a well-informed diner, for that matter, knew the word *Rachel* on the menu meant the dish was served with artichoke bottoms filled with poached marrow, and *Portugaise* meant a garnish of stuffed tomatoes.

There were so many of these names, however, that no one could remember them all. So they were cataloged in handbooks to be used by chefs. *Le Répertoire de la Cuisine*, first published in 1914 and one of these handbooks, has 209 listings in the garnish section alone, not to mention nearly 7,000 other preparations, all with their own names. The garnishes may be as simple as the one called *Concorde* or as complex as the one called *Tortue*, quoted here to give you an idea of the complexity and elaborateness of *classical garnish*.

Concorde *(for large joints)*—Peas, glazed carrots, mashed potatoes.

Tortue *(for Entrées)*—Quenelles, mushroom heads, gherkins, garlic, collops of tongue and calves' brains, small fried eggs, heart-shaped croutons, crayfish, slices of truffles. Tortue sauce.

CLASSICAL TERMS IN THE MODERN KITCHEN

Many of the classical names for garnishes are still used in modern kitchens, although they have lost the precise meanings they once had. You will encounter some of these terms in your career, so it is worthwhile learning them.

Remember that the following definitions are not the classical ones but simply the garnish or accompaniment generally indicated by the terms in today's kitchens.

Bouquetière: bouquet of vegetables	**Jardinière:** garden vegetables
Printanière: spring vegetables	**Primeurs:** first spring vegetables

These four terms refer to assortments of fresh vegetables, including carrots, turnips, peas, pearl onions, green beans, cauliflower, sometimes asparagus, and artichokes.

Clamart: peas	**Lyonnaise:** onions
Crécy: carrots	**Niçoise:** tomatoes concassé cooked with garlic
Doria: cucumbers (cooked in butter)	
Dubarry: cauliflower	**Parmentier:** potatoes
Fermière: carrots, turnips, onions, and celery, cut into uniform slices	**Princesse:** asparagus
	Provençale: tomatoes with garlic, parsley, and, sometimes, mushrooms and/or olives
Florentine: spinach	
Forestière: mushrooms	**Vichy:** carrots (especially Carrots Vichy, p. 288)
Judic: braised lettuce	

KEY POINTS TO REVIEW

- Why is it important to plate food attractively?

- What is meant by when applied to plate arrangements? What elements should be balanced?

- What are some examples of different plating styles?

- What guidelines should be observed when plating food or planning plate arrangements?

- What garnish terms from classical cuisine are still used today? What do they mean?

TERMS FOR REVIEW

garnish   garniture

QUESTIONS FOR DISCUSSION

1. Discuss the idea of professionalism and how it applies to the presentation of food.

2. Following are several popular food combinations. Describe what plating problems they present, if any, and how you might efficiently and economically solve them.

   Fish and chips (deep-fried fillets and French fries)

   Prime rib of beef and baked potato

   Meat loaf, mashed potatoes, and gravy

   Open-faced hot turkey sandwich

   Beef stroganoff and egg noodles

   Chicken à la king in a patty shell

3. What is meant by plating food for the convenience of the customer, and how does this affect other rules of plating?

Metric Conversion Factors

WEIGHT

1 ounce = 28.35 grams
1 gram = 0.035 ounce
1 pound = 454 grams
1 kilogram = 2.2 pounds

VOLUME

1 fluid ounce = 29.57 milliliters
1 milliliter = 0.034 ounce
1 cup = 237 milliliters
1 quart = 946 milliliters
1 liter = 33.8 fluid ounces

LENGTH

1 inch = 25.4 millimeters
1 centimeter = 0.39 inch
1 meter = 39.4 inches

TEMPERATURE

To convert Fahrenheit to Celsius:

Subtract 32. Then multiply by $\frac{5}{9}$.

Example: Convert 140°F to Celsius.

$$140 - 32 = 108$$
$$108 \times \tfrac{5}{9} = 60°C$$

To convert Celsius to Fahrenheit:

Multiply by $\frac{9}{5}$. Then add 32.

Example: Convert 150°C to Fahrenheit.

$$150 \times \tfrac{9}{5} = 270$$
$$270 + 32 = 302°F$$

Note: The metric equivalents in the recipes in this book are rounded off. See pages 107–108 for complete explanation.

Standard Can Sizes

Can Name	Volume U.S	Volume Metric	Approximate Weight[a] U.S.	Approximate Weight[a] Metric
6 oz	5.75 fl oz	170 mL	6 oz	170 g
8 oz	8.3 fl oz	245 mL	8 oz	227 g
No. 1 picnic	10.5 fl oz	311 mL	10.5 oz	298 g
No. 211 cylinder	12 fl oz	355 mL	12 oz	340 g
No. 300	13.5 fl oz	399 mL	14 oz	397 g
No. 303	15.6 fl oz	461 mL	16–17 oz	454–482 g
No. 2	20 fl oz	591 mL	1 lb 4 oz	567 g
No. 2½	28.5 fl oz	843 mL	1 lb 13 oz	822 g
No. 3 cylinder	46 fl oz	1360 mL	3 lb	1360 g
No. 5	56 fl oz	1656 mL	3 lb 8 oz	1588 g
No. 10	103.7 fl oz	3067 mL	6½–7 lb	2722–2948 g

[a]Because the density of food varies, so does the net weight for any given can size.

Approximate Weight-Volume Equivalents of Dry Foods

The following equivalents are rough averages only. Actual weight per volume varies considerably. For accurate measurement, all ingredients should be weighed.

BREAD FLOUR, SIFTED

1 pound = 4 cups
1 cup = 4 ounces

BREAD FLOUR, UNSIFTED

1 pound = 3⅓ cups
1 cup = 4.75 ounces

CAKE FLOUR, SIFTED

1 pound = 4¼ cups
1 cup = 3.75 ounces

CAKE FLOUR, UNSIFTED

1 pound = 3½ cups
1 cup = 4.5 ounces

GRANULATED SUGAR

1 pound = 2¼ cups
1 cup = 7 ounces

CONFECTIONERS' SUGAR, SIFTED

1 pound = 4 cups
1 cup = 4 ounces

CONFECTIONERS' SUGAR, UNSIFTED

1 pound = 3½ cups
1 cup = 4.5 ounces

CORNSTARCH, SIFTED

1 pound = 4 cups
1 cup = 4 ounces
1 ounce = 4 tablespoons = ¼ cup
1 tablespoon = 0.25 ounce

CORNSTARCH, UNSIFTED

1 pound = 3½ cups
1 cup = 4.5 ounces
1 ounce = 3½ tablespoons
1 tablespoon = 0.29 ounce

COCOA, UNSIFTED

1 pound = 5 cups
1 cup = 3.2 ounces
1 ounce = 5 tablespoons
1 tablespoon = 0.2 ounce

GELATIN, UNFLAVORED

1 ounce = 3 tablespoons
¼ ounce = 2¼ teaspoons
1 tablespoon = 0.33 ounce
1 teaspoon = 0.11 ounce

BAKING SODA

1 ounce = 1 tablespoon + 2¼ teaspoons
0.25 ounce = 1⅓ teaspoons
1 tablespoon = 0.57 ounce
1 teaspoon = 0.19 ounce

BAKING POWDER (PHOSPHATE TYPE AND SODIUM ALUMINUM SULFATE TYPE)

1 ounce = 2 tablespoons
0.25 ounce = 1½ teaspoons
1 tablespoon = 0.5 ounce
1 teaspoon = 0.17 ounce

CREAM OF TARTAR

1 ounce = 4 tablespoons
0.25 ounce = 1 tablespoon
1 teaspoon = 0.08 ounce

SALT

1 ounce = 4¼ teaspoons
0.25 ounce = 1⅛ teaspoons
1 teaspoon = 0.22 ounce

PAPRIKA AND GROUND CHILES

1 ounce = 17 teaspoons
0.25 ounce = 4¼ teaspoons
1 teaspoon = 0.06 ounce

GROUND SPICES (EXCEPT PAPRIKA AND GROUND CHILES)

1 ounce = 14 teaspoons
0.25 ounce = 3½ teaspoons
1 teaspoon = 0.07 ounce

GRATED LEMON ZEST

1 ounce = 4 tablespoons
1 teaspoon = 0.08 ounce

DRIED BEANS

1 cup = 6.5 ounces
1 pound = 2½ cups
    (yields 6 cups cooked)

RICE, LONG-GRAIN

1 cup = 7 ounces
1 pound = 2¼ cups
    (yields 8 cups cooked)

Kitchen Math Exercises: Metric Versions

T his appendix includes metric sample calculations corresponding to the calculations in the text that use U.S. measures. Refer to the appropriate pages in the text for explanations.

Recipe Conversion, Pages 98–100

Beef Tenderloin Tips and Mushrooms à la Crème

PORTIONS: 8	PORTION SIZE: 250 G
Butter	60 g
Onions	125 g
Flour	15 mL
Mushrooms	250 g
Beef tenderloin	1250 g
White wine	125 mL
Prepared mustard	10 mL
Brown sauce	750 mL
Heavy cream	250 mL
Salt	to taste
Pepper	to taste

To determine quantities for 18 portions, divide the new yield by the old yield to find the conversion factor:

$$\frac{\text{new yield}}{\text{old yield}} = \frac{18}{8} = 2.25$$

Example 1

INGREDIENT	QUANTITY	TIMES	CONVERSION FACTOR	EQUALS	NEW QUANTITY (ROUNDED OFF)
Butter	60 g	×	2.25	=	135 g
Onions	125 g	×	2.25	=	275 g
Flour	15 mL	×	2.25	=	35 mL
Mushrooms	250 g	×	2.25	=	575 g
Beef tenderloin	1250 g	×	2.25	=	2800 g
White wine	125 mL	×	2.25	=	275 mL
Prepared mustard	10 mL	×	2.25	=	23 mL
Brown sauce	750 mL	×	2.25	=	1700 mL
Heavy cream	250 mL	×	2.25	=	575 mL

To determine quantities for 40 portions at 175 grams each, first find the total yield of the old recipe. Multiply the portions by the portion size:

$$8 \text{ (portions)} \times 250 \text{ g} = 2000 \text{ g}$$

Do the same calculation for the desired yield:

$$40 \text{ (portions)} \times 175 \text{ g} = 7000 \text{ g}$$

Divide the desired yield by the old yield to find the conversion factor:

$$7000 \div 2000 = 3.5$$

Example 2

INGREDIENT	QUANTITY	TIMES	CONVERSION FACTOR	EQUALS	NEW QUANTITY (ROUNDED OFF)
Butter	60 g	×	3.5	=	200 g
Onions	125 g	×	3.5	=	450 g
Flour	15 mL	×	3.5	=	50 mL
Mushrooms	250 g	×	3.5	=	875 g
Beef tenderloin	1250 g	×	3.5	=	4375 g
White wine	125 mL	×	3.5	=	450 mL
Prepared mustard	10 mL	×	3.5	=	35 mL
Brown sauce	750 mL	×	3.5	=	2625 mL
Heavy cream	250 mL	×	3.5	=	875 mL

Completed Raw Yield Test Form (Metric), Page 117

Item	veal leg to scaloppine	Test number	3	Date	6/5/2010
Purveyor	ABC Meats	Price per kilogram	$11.00	Total cost	$148.50
AP weight (1)	13.5 kg	Kg price (2)	$11.00	Total cost (3)	$148.50

Trim, salvage, and waste:

	ITEM	WEIGHT	VALUE/KG	TOTAL VALUE (KG X VALUE)
(4)	fat	1.14 kg	$0.25	$0.29
(5)	bone	1.5 kg	$0.88	$1.32
(6)	ground veal	0.95 kg	$9.75	$9.26
(7)	stew meat	1.4 kg	$10.95	$15.33
(8)	unusable trim	0.4 kg	0	0
(9)	cutting loss	0.09 kg	0	0
(10)				

Total weight (4–10) (11)   5.48 kg   Total value (4 thru 10) (12) $26.20

Total yield of item (13)   8.02 kg

Net cost (3 – 12) (14) $122.30

Cost per kg (14 ÷ 13) (15) $15.25

Percentage of increase (15 ÷ 2) (16)   1.39 (139%)

Completed Cooked Yield Test Form (Metric), Page 119

Item	roast fresh ham	Test number	2	Date	6/5/2010

AP price per kg	$7.75
Cooking temperature	165°C

Net raw weight (1)	5.5 kg	Net cost per kg (2)	$8.73
		Total net cost (3)	$48.02

Weight as served (4)   3.75 kg

Cooked cost per kg (3 ÷ 4) (5) $12.81

Shrinkage (1 – 4) (6)   1.75 kg

Percentage of shrinkage (6 ÷ 1) (7)   32%

Total percentage of cost increase (5 ÷ AP price per kg) (8)   165%

Metric Example: Costing a Recipe, Page 120
Item: Baked Rice

INGREDIENT	RECIPE QUANTITY	AP QUANTITY	PRICE	TOTAL
Rice, long-grain	2 kg	2 kg	$1.59/kg	$3.18
Butter	375 g	0.375 kg	4.25/kg	1.59
Onions	500 g	0.5 kg	0.79/kg	0.40
Chicken stock	4 L	4 L	0.30/L	1.20
Salt	30 g	0.03 kg	0.35/kg	0.01
			Total cost	$6.38
			Number of portions	50
			Cost per portion	$0.13

Bibliography

A

Achatz, Grant. *Alinea*. Berkeley, California: Ten Speed Press, 2008.

Amendola, Joseph. *The Baker's Manual for Quantity Baking and Pastry Making*, 5th ed. Hoboken, New Jersey: John Wiley & Sons, 2002.

American Culinary Federation. *Culinary Fundamentals*. Upper Saddle River, New Jersey: Prentice Hall, 2006.

Anderson, Jean. *The Food of Portugal*. New York: Morrow, 1986.

Anderson, Jean, and Hedy Wurz. *The New German Cookbook*. New York: HarperCollins, 1993.

Andoh, Elizabeth. *At Home with Japanese Cooking*. New York: Knopf, 1980.

B

Bayless, Rick. *Authentic Mexican*. New York: Morrow, 1987.

Bertolli, Paul, and Alice Waters. *Chez Panisse Cooking*. New York: Random House, 1988.

Bickel, Walter, ed. *Hering's Dictionary of Classical and Modern Cookery*. London: Virtue, 1991.

Bissel, Frances. *The Book of Food*. New York: Henry Holt, 1994.

Blocker, Linda, and Julia Hill. *Culinary Math*, 3rd ed. Hoboken, New Jersey: John Wiley & Sons, 2007.

Bocuse, Paul. *Paul Bocuse's French Cooking*. New York: Pantheon, 1977.

Boni, Ada. *Italian Regional Cooking*. New York: Bonanza, 1969.

Bugialli, Giuliano. *Classic Techniques of Italian Cooking*. New York: Simon & Schuster, 1982.

———. *The Fine Art of Italian Cooking*. New York: Times Books, 1977.

C

Casas, Penelope. *The Foods and Wines of Spain*. New York: Knopf, 1987.

Claiborne, Craig, and Virginia Lee. *The Chinese Cookbook*. Philadelphia: Lippincott, 1972.

Cordon Bleu, Le. *Kitchen Essentials*. Hoboken, New Jersey: John Wiley & Sons, 2001.

Cox, Beverly. *Cooking Techniques*. Boston: Little, Brown, 1981.

Culinary Institute of America. *Garde Manger: The Art and Craft of the Cold Kitchen*, 3rd ed. Hoboken, New Jersey: John Wiley & Sons, 2008.

———. *The Professional Chef*, 8th ed. Hoboken, New Jersey: John Wiley & Sons, 2006.

———. *The Professional Chef's Knife Kit*. New York: John Wiley & Sons, 2000.

———. *Techniques of Healthy Cooking*, 3rd ed. Hoboken, New Jersey: John Wiley & Sons, 2008.

D

David, Elizabeth. *French Provincial Cooking*. Harmondsworth, England: Penguin, 1960.

———. *Italian Food*. Harmondsworth, England: Penguin, 1954.

Davidson, Alan. *The Oxford Companion to Food*. Oxford: Oxford University Press, 1999.

D'Ermo, Dominique. *The Modern Pastry Chef's Guide to Professional Baking*. New York: Harper & Row, 1962.

Dornenberg, Andrew, and Karen Page. *Culinary Artistry*. New York: John Wiley & Sons, 1996.

E

Egan, Maureen, and Susan Davis Allen. *Healthful Quantity Baking*. New York: John Wiley & Sons, 1992.

Escoffier, A. *The Escoffier Cook Book*. New York: Crown, 1969.

F

Feinstein, Andrew Hale, and John M. Stefanelli. *Purchasing: Selection and Procurement for the Hospitality Industry*, 7th ed. Hoboken, New Jersey: John Wiley & Sons, 2008.

Friberg, Bo. *The Professional Pastry Chef*, 4th ed. Hoboken, New Jersey: John Wiley & Sons, 2002.

G

Gisslen, Wayne. *Advanced Professional Cooking*. New York: John Wiley & Sons, 1992.

———. *Professional Baking*, 5th ed. Hoboken, New Jersey: John Wiley & Sons, 2009.

Graham, Kevin. *Grains, Rice, and Beans*. New York: Artisan, 1995.

Grausman, Richard. *At Home with the French Classics*. New York: Workman, 1988.

H

Hazan, Marcella. *The Classic Italian Cookbook*. New York: Knopf, 1976.

———. *More Classic Italian Cooking*. New York: Knopf, 1978.

Hom, Ken. *Chinese Technique*. New York: Simon & Schuster, 1981.

K

Kapoor, Sandy. *Professional Healthy Cooking*. New York: John Wiley & Sons, 1995.

Katsigris, Costas, and Chris Thomas. *Design and Equipment for Restaurants and Foodservice*, 3rd ed. Hoboken, New Jersey: John Wiley & Sons, 2009.

Keller, Thomas. *Under Pressure: Cooking Sous Vide*. New York: Artisan, 2008.

Kennedy, Diana. *The Cuisines of Mexico*, 2nd ed. New York: Harper & Row, 1986.

———. *Mexican Regional Cooking*. New York: Harper & Row, 1978.

Kinsella, John, and David T. Harvey. *Professional Charcuterie*. New York: John Wiley & Sons, 1996.

Knight, John B., and Lendel H. Kotschevar. *Quantity Food Production, Planning, and Management*, 3rd ed. New York: John Wiley & Sons, 2000.

L

Labensky, Sarah, and Alan M. Hause. *On Cooking*. Upper Saddle River, New Jersey: Prentice Hall, 2007.

Lang, George. *The Cuisine of Hungary*. New York: Bonanza, 1971.

Larousse, David Paul. *The Professional Garde Manger*. New York: John Wiley & Sons, 1996.

———. *The Sauce Bible*. New York: John Wiley & Sons, 1993.

Librairie Larousse. *Larousse Gastronomique*. New York: Clarkson Potter, 2001.

Loken, Joan K. *The HACCP Food Safety Manual*. New York: John Wiley & Sons, 1995.

M

McClane, A.J. *The Encyclopedia of Fish*. New York: Holt, Rinehart & Winston, 1977.

McGee, Harold. *The Curious Cook*. San Francisco: North Point, 1990.

———. *On Food and Cooking: The Science and Lore of the Kitchen*, rev. ed. New York: Scribner, 2004.

Madison, Deborah. *The Greens Cookbook*. New York: Broadway Books, 1987.

———. *Vegetarian Cooking for Everyone*. New York: Broadway Books, 1997.

Miller, Gloria Bley. *The Thousand Recipe Chinese Cookbook*. New York: Grosset & Dunlap, 1970.

Mizer, David A., Mary Porter, Beth Sonnier, and Karen Eich Drummond. *Food Preparation for the Professional*, 3rd ed. New York: John Wiley & Sons, 2000.

Molt, Mary K. *Food for Fifty*, 12th ed. Upper Saddle River, New Jersey: Prentice Hall, 2005.

N

National Association of Meat Processors. *Meat Buyers Guide*. Reston, Virginia: National Association of Meat Processors, 1997.

National Restaurant Association Educational Foundation. *ServSafe Coursebook*, 5th ed. Chicago: National Restaurant Association Educational Foundation, 2008.

P

Pauli, Eugen. *Classical Cooking the Modern Way: Recipes*, 3rd ed. Arno Schmidt, trans., and Margaret Schmidt, ed. New York: John Wiley & Sons, 1997.

———. *Classical Cooking the Modern Way: Methods and Techniques*, 3rd ed. Arno Schmidt, trans., and Margaret Schmidt, ed. New York: John Wiley & Sons, 1999.

Pepin, Jacques. *The Art of Cooking*. New York: Knopf, 1987.

———. *La Technique: The Fundamental Techniques of Cooking: An Illustrated Guide*. New York: Quadrangle/Times Books, 1976.

Peterson, James. *Fish and Shellfish*. New York: Morrow, 1996.

———. *Sauces*, 3rd ed. Hoboken, New Jersey: John Wiley & Sons, 2008.

———. *Splendid Soups: Recipes and Master Techniques for Making the World's Best Soups*. New York: John Wiley & Sons, 2001.

R

Roca, Juan, and Salvador Brugués. *Sous Vide Cuisine*. Barcelona: Montagud Editores, 2005.

S

Saulnier, L. *La Répertoire de la Cuisine*. Woodbury, New York: Barron's, 1976.

Schmidt, Arno, and Inja Nam. *The Book of Hors d'Oeuvres and Canapés*. New York: John Wiley & Sons, 1996.

Schneider, Elizabeth. *Uncommon Fruits and Vegetables: A Commonsense Guide*. New York: Harper & Row, 1986.

———. *Vegetables from Amaranth to Zucchini*. New York: William Morrow, 2001.

Sheraton, Mimi. *The German Cookbook*. New York: Random House, 1965.

Somerville, Annie. *Field of Greens*. New York: Bantam, 1993.

Sonnenschmidt, Frederic H., and Jean F. Nicolas. *The Professional Chef's Art of Garde Manger*, 5th ed. New York: John Wiley & Sons, 1993.

Sultan, William J. *Practical Baking*, 5th ed. New York: John Wiley & Sons, 1990.

T

Torres, Marimar. *The Spanish Table*. Garden City, New York: Doubleday, 1986.

Tsuji, Shizuo. *Japanese Cooking: A Simple Art*. Tokyo: Kodansha, 1980.

W

Waters, Alice. *Chez Panisse Vegetables*. New York: HarperCollins, 1996.

Willan, Anne. *La Varenne Pratique*. New York: Crown, 1989.

Glossary and Cooking Vocabulary

Note: Phonetic guides are included for difficult French words, giving the approximate pronunciation using English sounds. Exact rendering is impossible in many cases because French has a number of sounds that don't exist in English.

A

Abaisser (ah bess say) To roll a dough to the desired thickness with the aid of a rolling pin.

Abats (ah bah) Offal; internal organs of butchered animals. Also called *variety meats*.

Aboyeur (ah bwah yer) Kitchen worker who accepts and transmits orders from waiters, calls for orders to be finished, inspects finished dishes, and passes them to the dining room staff.

Accompaniment Salad A salad served as a side dish—that is, at the same time as a main course.

Acidifier (ah si di fee ay) To add lemon juice or vinegar to fruits, vegetables, and fish to prevent oxidation.

Aciduler (ah see dyoo lay) To make a preparation slightly acidic, tart, or tangy by adding a little lemon juice or vinegar.

Active Dry Yeast A dry, granular form of yeast that must be re-hydrated in 4 times its weight of warm water before use.

Adductor Muscle The muscle with which a mollusk closes its shell. In the case of American and Canadian scallops, this is usually the only part that is eaten.

Aerobic Requiring oxygen to live and grow; said of bacteria.

Aging Holding meats in coolers under controlled conditions to allow natural tenderizing to take place.

Aiguillette (ay gwee yet) A long, narrow slice of meat cut from the breast of poultry (especially duck) and game birds.

À la Carte (1) Referring to a menu on which each individual item is listed with a separate price. (2) Referring to cooking to order, as opposed to cooking ahead in large batches.

Al Dente Firm, not soft or mushy, to the bite. Said of vegetables and pasta.

Allemande (1) German style. (2) A sauce made of velouté (usually veal), a liaison, and lemon juice.

Allergen A substance that causes an allergic reaction.

All-Purpose Potato An irregularly shaped potato suitable for most purposes, though not usually for baking due to its shape; not as dry, starchy, or expensive as a russet.

Allumette Cut into matchstick shapes; usually refers to potatoes.

Amaranth A tiny, yellow-brown seed high in good-quality protein and having a somewhat spicy, nutty flavor when cooked; often used in vegetarian diets.

Americano Espresso diluted with hot water.

Amino Acids Long chains of smaller compounds that, when joined in various combinations, make up over 100,000 proteins in the human body.

Amuse Bouche A tiny appetizer or hors d'oeuvre offered to guests seated at their tables, either before or after they have ordered from the menu, in order to welcome guests and showcase an aspect of the chef's cooking style and talent.

Anadromous Referring to fish that live in salt water but spawn in fresh water.

Anaerobic Requiring an absence of oxygen to live and grow; said of bacteria.

Angel Food Method Mixing method for angel food cakes, involving folding dry ingredients into an egg-white foam.

Anthocyanins Red or purple pigments in vegetables and fruits.

Anthoxanthin (an tho zan thin) A type of white or pale yellow pigment in vegetables.

Antipasto Italian hors d'oeuvre.

AP Weight As purchased; the weight of an item before trimming.

Appareil (ah pa ray) A mixture of the principal elements of a final recipe (usually egg-based).

Appetizer A generally small-portioned first course of a multicourse meal, used to whet the appetite, often to the accompaniment of drinks.

Appetizer Salad Salad used to stimulate appetite with fresh, crisp ingredients; tangy, flavorful dressing; and attractive appearance.

Arborio Rice A variety of short-grain rice from Italy.

Argenteuil (ar zhawn toy) Garnished with asparagus.

Aromate (ah row mat) A condiment or vegetable with a characteristic smell or taste. Often used in reference to a combination of flavoring vegetables, such as carrot, onion, leek, and celery.

Artisan(al) Cheese A cheese produced primarily by hand, in small batches, with particular attention to the tradition of the cheese maker's art and using as little mechanization as possible.

Aspic Jelly A clarified stock that contains enough gelatin to solidify when cold.

Aspic Powder Unflavored gelatin mixed with a powdered stock base.

As Purchased (AP) Term for the untrimmed quantity of a food item, in the form in which it is purchased.

AS Weight As served; the weight of an item as sold or served, after processing and/or cooking.

Au Gratin (oh gra tan) Having a browned or crusted top, often made by topping with bread crumbs, cheese, and/or a rich sauce and passing under the broiler or salamander.

Au Jus (oh zhoo) Served with its natural juices, usually unthickened pan drippings.

Au Sec (oh seck) Until dry.

Avgolemono Greek soup made of chicken stock, egg, and lemon juice.

B

Bacteria Microscopic organisms, some of which cause disease, including food-borne disease.

Bagged Cookies Cookies made from dough that is forced through a pastry bag into various shapes.

Bain-Marie A container of hot water used for keeping foods hot.

Bake To cook foods by surrounding them with hot, dry air. Similar to *roast*, but the term *bake* usually applies to breads, pastries, vegetables, and fish.

Baked Alaska A dessert consisting of ice cream on a sponge cake base, covered with meringue and browned in the oven.

Baked Egg Egg baked in an individual serving dish. Also called *shirred egg* and *egg en cocotte*.

Baked Pudding Custard that contains additional ingredients, usually starchy ingredients in large quantities, and is baked in the oven.

Baking Blind Baking a pie or tart shell without a filling.

Baking Powder, Single- and Double-Acting A mixture of baking soda and a reacting acid used to leaven baked goods. While single-acting baking powder requires only moisture to release gas, double-acting requires heat for a complete reaction.

Ballotine (ball oh teen) A piece of meat or poultry that is boned and stuffed.

Barbecue To cook with dry heat created by the burning of hardwood or by the hot coals of this wood.

Bar Cookies Cookies for which the dough is shaped into long bars, then baked and cut. They may be baked again after cutting.

Barding Tying thin slices of fat, such as pork fatback, over meats with no natural fat cover to protect them while roasting.

Barley Type of grain, usually purchased as pearled barley.

Barquette (bar ket) A small, long oval pastry mold, or an item baked in such a mold.

Basic Grind Referring to sausages made simply by grinding meats to various stages of coarseness or fineness.

Basmati Rice A variety of long-grain rice from India.

Basquaise (bas kez) In the Basque style; usually indicates the presence of red peppers in the dish.

Basted Style of fried egg cooked covered so the top is cooked by retained steam.

Batch Cooking Cooking method that involves dividing food into batches and cooking them one a time, as needed, in order to cook them as close as possible to serving time.

Bâtonnet (bah toh nay) Cut into sticks, $\frac{1}{4} \times \frac{1}{4} \times 2$–$2\frac{1}{2}$ inches (6 mm × 6 mm × 5–6 cm).

Batter Semiliquid mixture containing flour or other starch, used for the production of such products as cakes and breads and for coating products to be deep-fried.

Batterie (bat tree) Set; complete set of kitchen utensils.

Bavarian Cream A dessert made of custard sauce, gelatin, and whipped cream.

Bavarois (ba var wha) Bavarian cream.

Bean Curd See Tofu.

Bean Paste See Miso.

Bean Thread Thin noodle made with mung bean starch.

Béarnaise (bare nez) A sauce made of butter and egg yolks and flavored with a reduction of vinegar, shallots, tarragon, and peppercorns.

Béchamel A sauce made by thickening milk with a roux.

Beignet Fritter.

Bercy (bare see) A white or brown sauce flavored with a reduction of white wine and shallots.

Beurre (burr) Butter.

Beurre Blanc (burr blahn) Butter-based sauce consisting of an emulsion of butter with a reduction of dry white wine, vinegar, and shallots.

Beurre Clarifié (burr cla ri fee ay) Clarified butter; butter that is gently melted in order to remove the impurities that float to the top and the whey that sinks to the bottom.

Beurre Composé (burr com po zay) Butter mixed with one or more flavoring ingredients.

Beurre Manié (burr mahn yay) A mixture of equal parts raw butter and flour mixed into a smooth paste.

Beurre Noir (burr nwahr) Butter heated until it is dark brown, then flavored with vinegar.

Beurre Noisette (burr nwah zett) Whole butter heated until it is light brown.

Beurrer (burr ray) (1) To lightly coat a container with butter in order to prevent sticking. (2) To add butter to a sauce or dough.

Biscuit Method Mixing method involving rubbing solid fat into dry ingredients and then mixing with combined wet ingredients. Similar to Rubbed Method, but using more liquid.

Bisque A cream soup made from shellfish.

Bivalve A mollusk with a pair of hinged shells, such as clam and oyster.

Blanc (blahn) (1) White. (2) A mixture of flour and acidulated water (usually with lemon juice), used to prevent certain foods from discoloring during cooking.

Blanch To cook an item partially and briefly in boiling water or hot fat. Usually a pre-preparation technique, as to loosen peels from vegetables, fruits, and nuts, to partially cook French fries or other foods before service, to prepare for freezing, or to remove undesirable flavors.

Blanch-and-Chill To partially cook, chill, and finish-cook foods as needed in order to reduce the amount of time required to cook completely to order.

Blancmange (1) An English pudding thickened with cornstarch. (2) A French almond-flavored pudding containing gelatin and milk.

Blanquette A white stew made of white meat or poultry simmered without preliminary browning and served with a white sauce.

Blending Method See Two-Stage Method.

Blitz Puff Pastry A pastry similar to puff pastry but quickly made by a variation of the Rubbed Dough Method and then rolled and folded to increase flakiness.

Blond Roux Roux cooked until it begins to change to a slightly darker color; used for veloutés, or sauces based on white stocks.

Blue Corn Corn with a blue or purplish color, derived from early varieties of corn grown by Native Americans.

Boar Wild pig, or the meat from this animal.

Boeuf à la Mode A classic French dish of braised beef.

Boil To cook in water or other liquid that is bubbling rapidly, about 212°F (100°C) at sea level and at normal pressure.

Bolster A raised ridge of metal at the heel end of a knife blade.

Bombe A molded ice cream or sherbet dessert.

Bordelaise A brown sauce flavored with a reduction of red wine, shallots, pepper, and herbs and garnished with marrow.

Botulism A deadly food-borne intoxication usually associated with improperly canned foods.

Bouchée (boo shay) A small round of puff pastry that can be filled with different mixtures.

Bouillir (boo year) To boil; to bring a liquid to the boiling point.

Boulangère (boo lawn zhare) Cooked with stock, onions, and potatoes; a style of meat preparation.

Bound Salad A salad mixed with a heavy dressing in order to bind the ingredients together.

Bouquet Garni A combination of fresh herbs tied together, used for flavoring.

Bouquetière (book tyair) Garnished with an assortment or bouquet of fresh vegetables, such as artichokes, carrots, turnips, green beans, peas, cauliflower, and potatoes.

Braise (1) To cook covered in a small amount of liquid, usually after preliminary browning. (2) To cook (certain vegetables) slowly in a small amount of liquid without preliminary browning.

Bran The tough but edible layer that covers the endosperm of a grain.

Bread Flour A strong flour used for making breads, hard rolls, and any product requiring high gluten.

Breakfast Cook A type of short-order cook who is skilled in quickly and efficiently cooking egg dishes and other breakfast items to order.

Breakfast Sausage Fresh pork that has been ground and seasoned; in patty, link, or bulk form.

Breve (bray vay) A mixture of espresso and steamed half-and-half.

Brine A water-based solution of salt and other ingredients, used to cure meats and other foods.

Brine Cure A curing method in which the food is immersed in a solution (brine) made of the curing ingredients dissolved in water.

Brioche Rich yeast dough containing large amounts of eggs and butter, or the product made from this dough.

Brochette (broe shet) (1) A skewer made of wood or bamboo. (2) Small pieces of food stuck on a long piece of metal or wood and grilled.

Broil To cook with radiant heat from above.

Broth A flavorful liquid obtained from the simmering of meats and/or vegetables.

Brown Rice Rice with the bran layer left on, which gives it a light brown color, a slightly coarse, crunchy texture, and a nutty flavor.

Brown Roux Roux cooked until it takes on a light brown color and a nutty aroma. When heavily browned, it contributes flavor and color to brown sauces.

Brunoise (broon wahz) (1) Cut into very small (⅛ in./3 mm) dice. (2) Garnished with vegetables cut in this manner.

Bruschetta (broo sket ta) A slice of toasted Italian bread served as an appetizer, usually rubbed with garlic and moistened with olive oil, often served with additional toppings.

Buckwheat A type of seed used as a grain, either whole or ground into flour. Technically not a grain, it is the seed of a plant with branched stems and broad, arrow-shaped leaves.

Buffet-Style Hors d'Oeuvre Service Offering hors d'oeuvres arranged attractively on one or more tables for guests to help themselves.

Bulgur A type of cracked wheat that has been partially cooked.

Butcher To kill and dress a meat animal.

Butler-Style Service Offering hors d'oeuvres to guests by service staff carrying small trays as they pass among the assembled party.

Butter Fat derived from milk, usually consisting of about 80 percent fat, with the remainder being water and milk solids.

Buttercream An icing made of butter and/or shortening blended with confectioners' sugar or sugar syrup and, sometimes, other ingredients.

Butterfat Milk fat.

Butterflied Cut partially through and spread open to increase the surface area.

Buttermilk (1) Fresh, liquid milk, usually skim milk, that has been cultured or soured by bacteria. (2) The liquid that remains after butter is removed from churned cream.

C

Cacao (ka ka oh) Cocoa.

Café au Lait French term meaning "coffee with milk." It is similar to a latte, but may be made with strong regular dark roast coffee rather than espresso.

Cake Flour A weak or low-gluten flour made from soft wheat.

Calamari Italian for "squid" (plural).

Calorie The amount of heat needed to raise the temperature of 1 kg water by 1°C. Used as a measure of food energy. More correctly called a *kilocalorie*.

Calvados (cal vah dose) An alcoholic beverage distilled from cider, made exclusively in the Normandy region of France.

Canapé (can ah pay) Tiny open-faced sandwich, served as an hors d'oeuvre.

Canard (can arr) Duck.

Caneton (can e tone) Male duckling.

Canette (can net) Female duckling.

Capon A castrated male chicken.

Cappuccino Mixture of equal parts espresso and frothy, steamed milk.

Caraméliser (care a mel ee zay) To caramelize; to coat a mold with cooked sugar; to cook sugar until dark for use in other preparations (to coat or to make a sauce).

Caramelization The browning of sugars caused by heat.

Carbohydrate Any of a group of compounds, including starches and sugars, that supply energy to the body.

Carême, Marie-Antoine Famous nineteenth-century French chef, often considered the founder of classical cuisine.

Carotenoids Yellow or orange pigments in vegetables and fruits.

Carpaccio Very thin slices of meat or fish, served raw.

Carryover Cooking The rise in temperature inside roast meat after it is removed from the oven.

Carve To cut cooked meat for serving.

Catadromous Referring to fish that live in fresh water but spawn in the ocean.

Caul A fatty membrane that covers the stomach of a pig; used for wrapping meats for cooking and for lining terrines.

Caviar (1) The salted roe or eggs of sturgeon. (2) The salted roe of another fish, such as salmon or whitefish, if that fish is designated in the name, e.g., whitefish caviar.

Cellophane Noodle Another term for bean thread noodle.

Celsius Scale The metric system of temperature measurement, with 0°C set at the freezing point of water and 100°C set at the boiling point of water.

Centi- Prefix in the metric system meaning "one-hundredth."

Cêpe (sepp) Bolete or porcini mushroom.

Cephalopod A member of the class of mollusks that includes octopus and squid.

Certified Pork Pork that is guaranteed or certified to be free of trichinosis.

Chai A sweetened blend of spiced milk and tea.

Chamber Vacuum Packer Packaging equipment specifically designed to seal food in a plastic vacuum bag by pulling air from the bag at various pressures.

Champignon (shamp in yon) Mushroom.

Chantilly (shawn tee yee) Whipped cream to which sugar and vanilla have been added.

Chapelure (shap a lure) Dried bread crumbs made from both the crust and center of dried bread. Used for breading.

Charcuterie (shar koo tree) The art of preparing fresh and cured pork products, including sausages and pâtés.

Charcutier (shar koo tyay) One who prepares and sells pork products, including sausages and pâtés.

Charlotte (shar lott) (1) A dessert, often containing Bavarian cream, made in a special mold. (2) A savory preparation made in this mold.

Chasoba Buckwheat noodles made with powdered green tea in addition to the buckwheat.

Chasseur (sha sur) "Hunter style," usually referring to items served with a brown sauce containing mushrooms, tomato, and white wine.

Château Potato Potato tournéed to about 2 inches (5 cm) long.

Chaud-Froid Sauce An opaque sauce containing gelatin, used to coat certain cold foods.

Chef Person in charge of a kitchen or of a department of a kitchen.

Chef de Cuisine French term meaning "head of the kitchen." The cook who runs the stove department of the kitchen and to whom the meat chef and pastry chef report. Also known as the *cuisinier*.

Chemical Leavener Leavener that releases gases produced by chemical reactions.

Chèvre (1) Goat. (2) Goat cheese (short for *fromage de chèvre*).

Chiffon (1) A light, fluffy dessert or pie filling containing gelatin and beaten egg whites. (2) A type of cake made with an egg-white foam and with oil as a shortening.

Chiffonade Cut into fine shreds; usually said of leafy vegetables and herbs.

Chiffon Method A cake-mixing method involving folding an egg-white foam into a mixture of flour, egg yolks, flour, sugar, and liquids.

Chiffon Pie Pie made with filling lightened by the addition of beaten egg white.

China Cap A cone-shaped strainer.

Chinois (shee nwah) A fine conical strainer.

Chitterlings Pork intestines.

Chlorophyll Green pigment in vegetables and fruits.

Cholesterol A fatty substance found in foods derived from animal products and in the human body; it has been linked to heart disease.

Chop To cut into irregularly shaped pieces.

Choucroute (shoo kroot) Sauerkraut.

Choucroute Garni Sauerkraut cooked with sausage, pork, and, sometimes, poultry products. A specialty of Alsace, France.

Chowder A hearty American soup made from fish, shellfish, and/or vegetables, usually containing milk and potatoes.

Chukasoba Wheat noodles made with flour and water with an alkali additive to the water; typically used in ramen dishes.

Chutney Any of several types of spicy condiment or relish.

Cilantro The fresh coriander plant, used as an herb.

Clamart Garnished with or containing peas.

Clarification The mixture of ingredients used to clarify a stock.

Clarified Butter Purified butterfat, with water and milk solids removed.

Clarifier (clare re fee ay) (1) To clarify; to clear a cloudy liquid by straining, heating, and gently simmering with egg whites. (2) To separate butterfat from the milk solids and water in whole butter.

Class A, B, C, and K Fires The four classes of fire identified by the type of fuel involved. Class A: ordinary combustibles, such as wood, paper, and cloth; Class B: burning liquids, such as grease, oil, gasoline, and solvents; Class C: electrical equipment, such as switches and motors; Class K: combustible cooking appliances and products, such as vegetable or animal oils and fats.

Classical Garnish In classical cuisine, any food or combination of foods placed on a plate or platter to accompany the main item; each garnish combination is assigned a standard name.

Clearmeat A mixture of ground meat, egg whites, and flavoring ingredients, used to clarify consommés.

Clear Soup A soup based on a clear, unthickened broth or stock that may be served plain or garnished with a variety of vegetables and meats.

Club Sandwich A sandwich consisting of three slices of toast and filled with such ingredients as sliced chicken or turkey, lettuce, tomato, and bacon.

Coagulation The process by which proteins become firm, usually when heated.

Cockle A type of small bivalve mollusk from a different family than clam. It may be cooked like a clam, however, and is almost always served in the shell.

Cocktail A type of appetizer generally made of seafood or fruit and often served with a tart or tangy sauce.

Cocotte Potato Potato tournéed to about 1½ inches (4 cm) long.

Cold Smoking A smoking method in which foods are smoked at a low temperature, usually at or below 85°F (30°C), so they are not cooked in the process.

Collagen A type of connective tissue in meats that dissolves when cooked with moisture.

Collagen Casing An edible artificial sausage casing molded from animal materials.

Coller (cole lay) To thicken or set using gelatin, as in making jelly or fruit mousse.

Colloid A mixture in which one substance (the dispersed phase) is evenly mixed throughout another substance (the continuous phase).

Combi (Combination) Oven An oven that can operate in conventional, convection, and steamer modes.

Commercial Dried Pasta Pasta dough that has been shaped and dried; usually made of semolina flour and water.

Common Meringue Meringue made from egg whites at room temperature, beaten with sugar.

Complementary Proteins Proteins supplied by foods that, if eaten together, supply all the amino acids necessary in the human diet.

Complete Protein A protein that supplies all the amino acids necessary in the human diet.

Composed Salad A salad made by arranging two or more ingredients attractively on the plate rather than by mixing them.

Compound Butter A mixture of raw butter and various flavoring ingredients.

Concasser (cone cas say) To break up coarsely with a knife or mortar. To chop coarsely.

Concassé (de tomates) (cone cas say duh to maht) Peeled, seeded, and diced tomatoes.

Condensed Milk Whole milk heavily sweetened with sugar, with about 60 percent of the water removed.

Conduction The transfer of heat from one item to something touching it or to a cooler part of the first item.

Confectioners' Sugar Fine powdered sugar mixed with a small amount of starch to prevent caking.

Confit (cone fee) A food saturated with one of the following: vinegar (for vegetables); sugar (for fruits); alcohol (for fruits); fat (for poultry and meat). Literally, "preserved."

Connective Tissue Certain proteins in meat, poultry, and fish that contribute to toughness; some are broken down by heat and some are not.

Consommé A rich, flavorful seasoned stock or broth clarified to make it perfectly clear and transparent.

Contaminated Containing harmful substances not originally present in food.

Convection The transfer of heat by the movement of a liquid or gas.

Convection Oven An oven in which hot air is circulated by a fan.

Convenience Food Any food product that has been partially or completely prepared or processed by the manufacturer.

Conversion Factor The number used to increase or decrease the amount of each ingredient when converting a recipe to a different yield.

Cooked Juice Method Method for making fruit pie fillings, used when only the juice requires cooking.

Cooked Fruit Method Method for making pie fillings, used when the fruit requires cooking, or when there is not enough liquid for the cooked juice method.

Cooking The art or practice of preparing edible food by applying heat and/or combining select measured ingredients in an ordered process.

Coq au Vin (coke oh van) A French dish of chicken braised in wine.

Coquille (coe kee) Shell.

Coral The roe or eggs of certain shellfish.

Corn A grain with a set of husks covering the entire seed head, or ear. Unlike other grains, it may be eaten as a fresh vegetable.

Corne (corn) Plastic tool used for scraping the contents out of containers.

Corrective Action A procedure that must be followed whenever a critical limit is not met. Corrective actions should be identified in written procedures that clearly communicate to the worker what must be done in a particular situation.

Coucher (koo shay) (1) To lay; to place a rolled piece of dough on a baking sheet. (2) To spread; to spread a layer of cream or other garnish. (3) To pipe; to cover with a layer using a piping bag.

Coulis (koo lee) A vegetable or fruit purée, used as a sauce.

Coupe (koop) (1) Cup. (2) A dessert consisting of one or two scoops of ice cream or sherbet in a dish or glass, topped with syrups, fruits, toppings, and/or garnishes; a sundae.

Couper (koo pay) To cut.

Course A food or group of foods served at one time or intended to be eaten at the same time.

Court Bouillon (koor bwee yohn) Water containing seasonings, herbs, and, usually, an acid; used for cooking fish.

Couscous A type of granular pasta from North Africa that resembles a grain.

Cracked Wheat Whole wheat grain that has been cut into pieces.

Crayfish A freshwater crustacean resembling a small lobster; also called *crawfish*.

Creaming The process of beating fat and sugar together to incorporate air.

Creaming Method Cake-mixing method involving mixing flour and eggs into creamed sugar and fat; also used for some muffins and coffee cakes.

Cream Pie Pie made with pudding or boiled custard-type filling.

Cream Pudding Milk-based pudding thickened with starch and eggs; essentially pastry cream with various flavorings.

Cream Soup A soup thickened with roux or another thickening agent and containing milk and/or cream.

Crécy (kray see) Garnished with or containing carrots. Also, the name of an area known for its carrot production.

Crème Anglaise (krem awng lezz) A light vanilla-flavored custard sauce made of milk, sugar, and egg yolks.

Crème Fouettée (krem foo eh tay) Whipped cream; cream that has been whisked in order to incorporate air.

Crème Fraîche A thick, slightly aged heavy cream.

Crème Pâtissière (krem pa tis see air) Pastry cream; sweetened milk thickened with starch and eggs, used for pastry making.

Crémer (kray may) (1) To cream together sugar and butter. (2) To add cream.

Crêpe (krep) Very thin pancake.

Crépinette A sausage patty wrapped in caul.

Critical Control Point (CCP) An action that can be taken to eliminate or minimize a food safety hazard.

Croissant A crescent-shaped roll made from a rich, rolled-in yeast dough.

Croquette (crow kett) Food that has been puréed or bound with a thick sauce, made into small shapes, breaded, and fried.

Cross-Contamination The transfer of bacteria to food from another food or from equipment or work surfaces.

Croustade (krew stahd) (1) A crisp crust that is fried. (2) An empty pastry case.

Croûte (kroot) Crust; the brown outer covering of bread. A meat or fish en croûte is one that is wrapped in a crust.

Croûton (kroo tohn) A slice or piece of toasted bread.

Crudité (croo dee tay) A raw vegetable served as a relish.

Crumb Crust Pie crust made of cookie crumbs, butter, and sugar.

Crustacean A sea animal with a segmented shell and jointed legs, such as lobster and shrimp.

Cryovac Brand name of a machine used to vacuum-pack meats and other foods in plastic. The air- and moisture-proof packaging protects the contents from bacteria and mold and prevents weight loss due to drying.

Crystallize To form sugar crystals. May occur when sugar is cooked.

Cuisson (kwees sohn) (1) The liquid used for cooking a food. (2) The cooking; the action and manner of cooking a food.

Curdle The separation of protein solids, such as egg solids from liquids due to coagulation.

Custard A liquid that is thickened or set firm by the coagulation of egg protein.

Custard, baked A combination of beaten eggs and liquid, usually milk or cream, baked until it sets to a solid, due to the coagulation of egg protein.

Cutting Loss Loss of weight of meat due to drying or to particles of meat and fat sticking to the cutting board.

Cuttlefish A cephalopod similar to squid, but with a chalky interior bone and a squatter body shape.

Cycle Menu A menu that changes every day for a certain period, then repeats the same daily items in the same order.

D

Dal The generic term in India for dried legume.

Danish A rich, sweet, flaky yeast dough containing layers of rolled-in fat.

Dariole (dahr ree ole) A small, thimble-shaped mold.

Dark Meat Poultry meat with darker color and more fat and connective tissue, found in drumsticks and thighs.

Darne (darn) Thick slice, containing the central bone, cut from round fish.

Dashi (dah shee) Japanese soup stock.

Daube (dobe) Stew of meat braised in red wine.

Decaffeinated Coffee Coffee from which the caffeine has been removed by solvents.

Deci- Prefix in the metric system meaning "one-tenth."

Découper (day koo pay) To cut; to cut using scissors, a knife, or pastry cutter.

Deep-Fried Sandwich A sandwich dipped in beaten egg mixture and, sometimes, in bread crumbs, and then deep-fried.

Deep-Fry To cook submerged in hot fat.

Déglacer (day gla say) To deglaze.

Deglaze To swirl a liquid in a sauté pan or other pan to dissolve cooked particles or food remaining on the bottom.

Dégraisser (day gray say) To degrease; to remove excess fat from the surface of a food or sauce.

Degree Celsius Metric unit for measuring temperature; also called *degree centigrade*.

Demi-Glace A rich brown sauce that has been reduced by half.

Demitasse Literally, "half-cup." Strong, black coffee served in small cups after dinner.

Denature To change the structure of protein molecules by means of heat or chemicals.

Dessert Salad A salad containing sweet ingredients such as fruits, sweetened gelatin, nuts, and cream. It is best served as a dessert or as part of a buffet or party menu.

Dessert Syrup A flavored simple syrup, used to moisten and flavor some cakes.

Détrempe (day trompe) Dough made of flour and water; used for puff pastry.

Dice To cut into small cubes.

Dip Accompaniment to potato chips, crackers, and raw vegetables that is thick enough to stick to items used as dippers.

Doneness The degree of a meat's protein coagulation, as determined by internal temperature, or the degree to which its connective tissues have broken down, as determined by tenderness.

Doria Garnished with cucumbers cooked in butter.

Double-Crème Cheese A rich cheese containing at least 60 percent fat.

Dough Arm Agitator attachment for electric mixers, used for mixing and kneading yeast doughs.

Doughs, Young and Old Dough is considered young when underfermented and old when overfermented.

Drawn With entrails removed.

Dressed (1) Poultry market form: killed, bled, and plucked. (2) Fish market form: viscera, scales, head, tail, and fins removed.

Dresser (dres say) To arrange prepared food on a plate or platter before serving.

Dried Whole Milk Whole milk that has been dried to a powder.

Drop Batter A batter that is too thick to pour but that drops from a spoon in lumps.

Dropped Cookies Cookies made from soft dough or batter dropped on baking sheets with a spoon, scoop, or other measuring implement.

Dry Aging The process of storing meats, typically large cuts, under carefully controlled conditions of temperature, humidity, and air circulation in order to develop flavor and tenderness.

Dry Cure A curing method in which the curing ingredients are packed or rubbed over the food.

Dry-Heat Methods Cooking methods in which heat is conducted to foods without the use of moisture.

Dubarry Garnished with or containing cauliflower.

Duchesse Potatoes (doo shess) Potato purée mixed with butter and egg yolks.

Duck A bird with a thick layer of fat under the skin and low yield, compared with chicken or turkey. It is usually roasted whole, though its parts are sometimes cooked separately.

Dugléré (dew glay ray) A classic preparation for fish incorporating white wine and tomato; named for a nineteenth-century chef.

Dumpling Any of a variety of small starch products made from soft dough or batter and cooked by simmering or steaming.

Duxelles (duke sell) A coarse paste or hash made of finely chopped mushrooms sautéed with minced shallots; used as a garnish or filling.

E

E. coli A bacterium (*Escherichia coli*) that causes severe illness, either as an intoxication or an infection, typically due to consumption of raw or undercooked red meats, unpasteurized dairy products, or fish from contaminated water.

Edible Portion (EP) The quantity of a raw, uncooked food item after it is trimmed.

Egg Pasta Pasta containing at least 5 percent egg solids in addition to flour and water; usually in the form of flat noodles of various widths.

Elastin A type of connective tissue in meats that does not dissolve when cooked.

émincer (eh man say) To cut into very thin slices.

Empty Calorie A food that supplies few nutrients per calorie.

Emulsified Grind Referring to sausages made by processing meat and fat to a purée, usually with the addition of water or another liquid.

Emulsified Shortening An easy-spread shortening used when the weight of sugar in a cake batter is greater than the weight of flour.

Emulsion A uniform mixture of two unmixable substances—in the kitchen, usually liquids.

En Croûte (on kroot) Wrapped in pastry.

Endosperm The starchy mass that forms most of a grain kernel.

Enriched Rice Rice that has received a coating of vitamins to compensate for some of the nutrients lost during milling.

Enrober (on robe bay) To coat; to completely cover with various ingredients, such as chocolate or dough.

Entremet (on tre may) Literally, "between courses"; originally a course served between the roast and the dessert. Today the term is used for various desserts, usually containing cream.

Entremetier (awn truh met yay) The cook who prepares vegetables, starches, soups, and eggs.

Epazote (ep ah so tay) A pungent herb used in Mexican cooking.

EP Weight Edible portion; the weight of an item after all trimming and preparation is done.

Escaloper (eh scal oh pay) To cut scallops; to cut meat or fish on a bias.

Escoffier, Georges-Auguste Great chef of the early twentieth century and the father of modern cookery.

Essence (ess sahns) Essence; concentrated extract, used as a flavoring (e.g., coffee essence).

Essential Amino Acid Any of nine of the 20 amino acids, excluding those that can be made in the body, that must be included in the diet in order for the body to produce all the proteins it needs.

Essential Fatty Acid A fatty acid that must be consumed in the diet because it can't be made by the body.

Espagnole A sauce made of brown stock and flavoring ingredients and thickened with a brown roux.

Espresso, Expresso Strong, dark coffee made from beans roasted until almost black, ground very fine, and brewed under steam pressure.

Éclair Paste Dough used to make éclairs and cream puffs.

Étuver (eh too vay) To stew or cook slowly; to gently cook a food covered with fat and a little water without changing the color of the ingredients.

Evaporated Milk Sterilized and canned whole or skim milk with about 60 percent of the water removed.

Evaporation The process by which water turns from a liquid to a gas at any temperature.

Executive Chef The manager of a large kitchen or food production department.

Extended Meal Service Service of a meal at which customers eat at different times.

Expediter Kitchen worker who accepts and transmits orders from waiters, calls for orders to be finished, inspects finished dishes, and passes them to the dining room staff.

Extract Flavorful oil or other substance dissolved in alcohol; used for flavoring.

F

Fabricate To cut raw meat into pieces.

Fabricated Cuts Raw meat that is cut up into pieces and trimmed.

Facultative Able to live and grow with or without the presence of oxygen; said of bacteria.

Farce Forcemeat stuffing; a mixture of ground ingredients (meat, herbs, vegetables) used to fill poultry, fish, vegetables, etc.

Farci (far see) Stuffed.

Farmstead Cheese Cheese made entirely with milk from a farmer's own herd or flock on the farm where the animals are raised.

Farro A grain that is the ancestor of modern wheat.

Fat Fish Fish with high fat content.

Fermentation The process by which yeast acts on carbohydrates to change them into carbon dioxide gas and alcohol.

Fermière (fair myair) (1) Garnished with carrots, turnips, onions, and celery cut into uniform slices. (2) Farm-made or farm-raised.

Fettuccine Flat egg noodles.

Fiber A group of indigestible carbohydrates found in grains, fruits, and vegetables.

Filet Boneless tenderloin.

Fillet Boneless side of fish; to remove the fillet from the fish bone.

Fines Herbes (feen zairb) Mixture of edible aromatic plants used as seasoning (parsley, tarragon, chives).

Fin Fish Fish with fins and internal skeletons.

Fish Carpaccio Very thin slices of firm, meaty fish served with garnishes and typically with a piquant sauce.

Fish Tartare A mixture of chopped raw fish, condiments, and seasonings.

Flaking An indication of doneness of cooked fish, when the flesh breaks apart into its natural separations.

Flaky Pie Dough Dough made by cutting or rubbing but not entirely blending fat into flour, leaving pieces of fat that contribute to a flaky texture.

Flamber (flahm bay) To light alcohol in a preparation (e.g., crêpes Suzette); to flame.

Flan (flahn) (1) Open pastry case or shell. (2) A custard tart.

Flatfish A flat type of fish, such as flounder and sole, with both eyes on one side of the head.

Flat Icing A mixture of 10X sugar, water, and, sometimes, corn syrup and flavoring. Also called *water icing*.

Flavonoids White pigments in vegetables and fruits.

Flavored Milk Milk containing flavoring ingredients.

Flavoring Adding a new flavor to a food, therefore changing or modifying the original flavor.

Flavor Profile The combination of flavors and aromas that make up the total taste impression of a dish.

Flaxseed A type of seed containing beneficial fiber and omega-3 fatty acids, used mostly in small quantities in breads and commercial breakfast cereal preparations.

Fleuron (flur rohn) Puff pastry piece cut into a crescent shape; served as decoration with fish dishes.

Florentine Garnished with or containing spinach.

Flow of Food The path that food travels in a food-service operation from receiving to serving.

Foam Icing Meringue made with boiling syrup that may contain stabilizing ingredients like gelatin. Also called *boiled icing*.

Foaming The process of beating eggs, with or without sugar, to incorporate air.

Foaming Method A cake-mixing method that incorporates whipped eggs into a batter.

Foie Gras (fwah grah) Liver of specially fattened geese and ducks.

Fond (fohn) Stock.

Fondant A smooth, creamy white icing or candy consisting of very finely crystallized sugar syrup.

Fond Lié A sauce made by thickening brown stock with cornstarch or a similar starch.

Fondu (fone dew) Melted.

Fondue, Swiss A dish consisting of melted Gruyère and Emmentaler cheeses and white wine into which cubes of bread are dipped and eaten. From the French word meaning "melted."

Food Cost Percentage The raw food cost, or portion cost, divided by the menu price.

Food Danger Zone The temperature range of 41° to 135°F (5° to 57°C) in which bacteria grow rapidly.

Forcemeat A seasoned mixture of ground meats and other foods, used as a filling or stuffing or as a base for terrines and pâtés.

Forestière Garnished with mushrooms.

Four-Hour Rule The sanitary practice of permitting foods to remain in the food danger zone for a cumulative total of no more than four hours between receiving and serving.

Four Parts of a Salad The base or underliner, body, garnish, and dressing.

Free-Range Referring to animals, usually poultry, that are allowed to move relatively freely outdoors as they are raised for market.

French Dressing Salad dressing made of oil, vinegar, and seasonings.

French-Style Ice Cream Ice cream containing egg yolks.

Fresh Not frozen, canned, or dried.

Fresh Yeast Form of yeast that is moist and perishable; also called *compressed yeast*.

Fricassée A white stew in which the meat is cooked in fat without browning before liquid is added.

Frire (freer) To deep-fry.

Frisée A variety of curly endive or chicory that is more tender and lighter in color than curly endive.

Frittata A flat, unfolded omelet.

Friture (free tur) (1) Deep fryer. (2) Deep-fried foods.

Frozen Yogurt Ice cream that contains yogurt in addition to the usual ingredients.

Fruit Pie Pie that contains fruit filling; usually has a top crust.

Fruit Salad A salad containing fruits as its main ingredients.

Fry To cook in hot fat.

Fudge Icing Rich cooked icing that is heavy and thick; it may be flavored with a variety of ingredients, and it is often somewhat like candy.

Full Slip Describes melons picked ripe, with no portion of the stems attached.

Fumet (foo may) A flavorful stock, usually fish stock.

Fusion Cuisine The use of ingredients and techniques from more than one regional or international cuisine in a single dish.

G

Galantine (ga lawn teen) A forcemeat wrapped in the skin of the animal from which it is made, such as a chicken or duck, or rolled into a cylinder without the skin.

Game Meat from animals and birds normally found in the wild; many game animals are now farm-raised.

Garde Manger (gard mawn zhay) (1) The cook in charge of cold food production, including salads and buffet items. (2) The department of a kitchen in which these foods are prepared.

Garni Garnished; having had garnish added to it.

Garnish (1) Decorative edible item used to ornament or enhance the eye appeal of another food item. (2) To add such a decorative item to food.

Garniture (1) Garnish. (2) The act or process of garnishing.

Gastrique A mixture of caramelized sugar and vinegar, used to flavor sauces.

Gaufrette (go frett) Waffle.

Gazpacho A cold Spanish soup made of puréed raw vegetables.

Gelatinization The process by which starch granules absorb water and swell in size.

Gelatin Salad A salad made from flavored or unflavored gelatin, fruits, and, sometimes, vegetables.

Gelée Aspic jelly.

Genoise (zhen wahz) A French sponge cake.

Germ The portion of a whole grain consisting of a tiny embryo that forms the new plant once the seed sprouts.

Glaçage (glah sahj) Glaze; mixture of ingredients with a syrupy consistency, sweet or savory, used to coat pastries, candies, and certain savory foods.

Glace (glahss) (1) Ice cream. (2) Glaze; stock reduced until thick and syrupy.

Glacé (glah say) (1) Glazed (usually refers to vegetables). (2) Frozen. (3) Served with ice cream (e.g., meringue glacée).

Glace de Poisson Fish glaze; a reduction of fish stock.

Glace de Viande (glahss duh vee awnd) Meat glaze; a reduction of brown stock.

Glace de Volaille Chicken glaze; a reduction of chicken stock.

Glacer (glah say) To glaze; to cover or coat pastries with a glaze.

Glaze (1) A stock reduced until it coats the back of a spoon. (2) A shiny coating, such as a syrup, applied to a food. (3) To make a food shiny or glossy by coating it with a glaze or by browning it under a broiler or in a hot oven.

Gluten A substance made of proteins present in wheat flour that gives structure and strength to baked goods.

Glutinous or Sticky Rice A type of short-grain rice that becomes sticky and chewy when cooked.

Goujonnettes (goo zhone nett) Strips of fish, breaded and deep-fried.

Goulash A Hungarian stew flavored with paprika.

Grading Designation of the quality of a meat based on its texture, firmness, color, marbling, and the age or maturity of the animal.

Gram The basic unit of weight in the metric system; equal to about one-thirtieth of an ounce.

Grandmère (grahn mare) A classic garniture made from bacon, sautéed button mushrooms, and glazed pearl onions.

Granité (grah nee tay) A coarse, crystalline frozen dessert made of water, sugar, and fruit juice or other flavoring.

Gras-Double (grah doo bl') A type of beef tripe that is smooth rather than honeycombed.

Gratiner (gra tee nay) (1) To brown under the grill or salamander. (2) To glaze.

à la Grecque (ah la grek) Refers to a preparation of vegetables cooked in white wine.

Green Meat Meat that has not had enough time after slaughter to develop tenderness and flavor.

Green Wheat Wheat that is harvested while immature, then dried.

Griddle (1) To cook on a flat, solid cooking surface. (2) The surface itself.

Grill To cook on an open grid over a heat source.

Grillardin (gree ar dan) Broiler cook.

Grilled Sandwich A simple sandwich that is buttered on the outside and browned on the griddle, in a hot oven, or in a panini grill.

Griller (gree yay) To grill; to cook on a grill.

Grosse Pièce (gross pyess) Centerpiece of a buffet platter.

Guinea A domestically raised relative of the pheasant.

H

HACCP Hazard Analysis Critical Control Point; a food safety system of self-inspection designed to highlight hazardous foods and to control food handling with the goal of avoiding hazards.

Hacher (ah shay) To chop; to reduce to small pieces with a knife.

Half-and-Half Fresh cream that contains 10 to 18 percent fat, which is too low a proportion for the liquid to be called *cream*.

Hard Meringue Meringue made with up to twice as much sugar as egg whites.

Hare A game animal similar to rabbit, with dark red, lean meat.

Haricot (ahr ree co) Bean.

Haricot Bean A variety of green bean that is allowed to ripen until the seed is mature and dry.

Haricot Blanc (ahr ree co blahn) White bean.

Haricot Vert (ahr ree co vare) Green bean.

Hash (1) To chop. (2) A dish made of chopped foods.

Hazard A potentially dangerous food condition due to contamination, growth of pathogens, survival of pathogens, or presence of toxins.

HDL High-density lipoprotein, a compound that helps remove cholesterol from the bloodstream and eliminate it from the body, preventing heart disease.

Herbal Tea Beverage that is brewed like tea but made with herbs, spices, dried fruits, and other plant ingredients in place of or in addition to tea leaves.

Herb The leaves of certain plants, used in flavoring. These plants usually grow in temperate climates.

Hidden (Food) Cost The cost of supplementary ingredients, such as garnishes and condiments.

High-Fat Cakes Cakes with a relatively high fat content, best made by means of the creaming method or the two-stage method.

Holding Temperatures Temperatures at which certain products are kept for service or for storage.

Hollandaise A sauce made of butter, egg yolks, and flavorings (especially lemon juice).

Homard (oh mahr) Lobster.

Homemade Made on the premises.

Hominy Corn that has been treated with lye.

Homogenized Milk Milk that has been processed so the cream doesn't separate out.

Hongroise (ong grwahz) Hungarian style.

Hors d'oeuvre A small food item usually served before or separately from a meal; appetizer. French for "outside the work."

Hot Smoking A smoking method in which foods are smoked at a temperature high enough to cook or partially cook them.

Huile (weel) Oil.

Huile d'Olive (weel doe leave) Olive oil.

Huile d'Arachide (weel da rah sheed) Peanut oil.

Huile de Noix (weel de nwah) Walnut oil.

Hydrocolloid A colloid in which the continuous phase is water.

Hygroscopic Readily absorbing moisture.

I

Ice Frozen dessert made from fruit juices, water, sugar, and. sometimes, egg whites.

Icebox Cookies Cookies for which rolls of dough are made in advance, refrigerated, and then sliced and baked as needed.

Ice Cream Smooth, frozen mixture of milk, cream, sugar, flavorings, and, sometimes, eggs.

Iced Coffee Cold coffee made from double-strength brewed coffee to compensate for dilution by melting ice.

Ice Milk Frozen dessert similar to ice cream, but with a lower butterfat content.

Immersion Circulator A device for maintaining circulating water in a water bath at a precisely steady temperature.

Imported Coming from outside a country.

Incomplete Proteins Proteins that are missing or do not contain a high enough concentration of one or more of the essential amino acids.

Induction Cooktop A type of cooktop that works by using magnetic energy to make pots hot without getting hot itself.

Infection Disease, including much food-borne disease, caused by bacteria in the body.

Infrared A type of radiation used to cook food, such as when broiling.

Insoluble Fiber Fiber that absorbs less water than soluble fiber and forms bulk in the intestines. It is found in cell walls and other structural parts of plants.

Inspection Government-mandated examination of meat and other foods, intended to guarantee their wholesomeness and fitness for human consumption.

Instant Coffee A powdered, soluble extract from coffee beans made by brewing regular coffee and drying it.

Instant Dry Yeast A dry, granular form of yeast that does not have to be dissolved in water before use, as it absorbs water more quickly than regular dry yeast.

Instant Rice Rice that has been precooked and dried so it can be prepared quickly.

Instant Starch Starch that has already been cooked and dried. Also called *pregelatinized starch*.

Institution Meat Purchase Specifications (IMPS) A set of specifications followed by food-service suppliers that lists all meat and poultry cuts by number and describes them in detail for purchasers.

Integral Sauce A sauce based on the juices released during the cooking of a meat, poultry, fish, or vegetable.

Intoxication Disease caused by poisons that bacteria produce while they are growing in food.

Irradiation A process of exposing foods to radiation in order to kill bacteria, parasites, and other potentially harmful organisms.

Italian Meringue Meringue made by beating a hot sugar syrup into egg whites. It is the most stable meringue because the egg whites are cooked by the heat of the syrup.

J

Jambon (zhom bohn) Ham.

Jambonnette (zhom bo nett) Stuffed poultry leg made to resemble a small ham.

Jardinière (zhar din yair) Garnished with fresh garden vegetables, such as carrots, turnips, green beans, peas, and cauliflower.

Jasmine Rice A type of aromatic rice from Southeast Asia.

Jerk A traditional Jamaican cooking style in which meats are mari-×nated in a special spice mixture containing allspice and Scotch bonnet peppers before grilling.

Joue (zhoo) Cheek (beef, pork, or veal).

Judic Garnished with braised lettuce.

Julienne (zhoo lee yen) (1) Cut into small, thin strips, about ⅛ × ⅛ × 1–2 inches (3 mm × 3 mm × 25–50 mm). (2) Garnished with foods cut in this manner.

Jus (zhoo) (1) Juice. (2) Unthickened juices from a roast. (3) Liquid made from pressing a fruit or vegetable.

Jus Lié Thickened juices from a roast.

K

Kamut An ancient relative of wheat, similar to spelt in composition and flavor.

Kasha Whole buckwheat groats.

Katsuobushi (kaht soo oh boo shee) Japanese shaved, dried bonito. Used to make stock.

Ketone Body A toxic compound that can form in the blood if fats are burned with no carbohydrates present.

Ketosis A condition in which the blood becomes unable to carry oxygen, sometimes the result of consuming insufficient carbohydrates.

Kilo- Prefix in the metric system meaning "one thousand."

Kombu A type of seaweed used to make Japanese soup stock.

L

Lacto-Ovo-Vegetarian Referring to a vegetarian diet that includes dairy products and eggs.

Lacto-Vegetarian Referring to a vegetarian diet that includes milk and other dairy products.

Lag Phase The time needed for bacteria to adjust to a new environment before they start to multiply.

Lait (lay) Milk.

Langoustine (lawn goo steen)/Langostino (1) Prawn; a type of crustacean. (2) A smaller relative of the rock lobster, marketed as *rock shrimp*.

Lard (1) The rendered fat of hogs. (2) To insert strips of pork fat into lean meats, using a larding needle, to prevent the meat from drying out during cooking.

Larder (lahr day) To lard.

Lardon (lahr doan) A small piece or strip of slab bacon.

Lasagna Broad, flat egg noodle.

Lasagne A baked, layered casserole made with lasagna noodles. ("Lasagne" is the plural of "lasagna.")

Latte Short for *caffe latte*. A mixture of 1 part espresso and 2 or more parts steamed milk.

LDL Low-density lipoprotein, the most important carrier of cholesterol. If too much is present in the bloodstream, it may deposit excess cholesterol inside the arteries and block blood flow.

Leading Sauce A basic sauce used in the production of other sauces. The five leading hot sauces are béchamel, velouté, espagnole, tomato, and hollandaise. Mayonnaise and vinaigrette are often considered leading cold sauces.

Lean Dough Dough that is low in fat and sugar.

Lean Fish Fish with low fat content.

Leavening The production or incorporation of gases in a baked product to increase volume and to produce shape and texture.

Legume (leh gyoom) (1) A plant that bears seed pods that split along two opposite sides when ripe. (2) French word meaning "vegetable."

Lemongrass A tropical grass with the aroma of lemon, used for flavoring.

Lentil A small, lens-shaped legume.

Lentille (lawn teey) Lentil.

Levain (le vanh) Starter dough; a dough made from live yeast and flour, used to make breads.

Levure (le vure) Yeast.

Liaison A binding agent, usually made of cream and egg yolks, used to thicken sauces and soups.

Lier (lee ay) To thicken; to change the consistency of a liquid by adding a roux, starch, egg, flour, or beurre manié.

Light Cream Fresh cream that contains 18 to 30 percent fat. Also called *table cream* or *coffee cream*.

Light Meat Poultry meat with lighter color and less fat and connective tissue than dark meat; breast meat.

Limiting Amino Acid An amino acid that is in short supply, therefore limiting the usefulness of other amino acids in forming complete proteins.

Line Cook A cook responsible for preparing or finishing hot à la carte items during service in a restaurant.

Lipid Any of a group of compounds that includes fats and cholesterol.

Lipoprotein Combinations of protein and fat that carry cholesterol and fat through the bloodstream. There are two important types: low-density lipoprotein (LDL) and high-density lipoprotein (HDL).

Liter The basic unit of volume in the metric system; equal to slightly more than 1 quart.

London Broil Flank steak or other cut of beef broiled rare and cut in thin slices.

Long-Grain Rice Rice with long, slender grains that stay separate and fluffy when properly cooked.

Lotte (lot) Monkfish.

Low-Fat Cakes Cakes with low fat but high egg and sugar content, best mixed using the egg-foam method.

Low-Fat Milk Milk with a fat content of 0.5 to 2 percent.

Lozenge Diamond-shape cut.

Lyonnaise (lee oh nez) Containing or garnished with onions.

M

Macaroni Dried noodle product made of flour (usually semolina) and water.

Macchiato (mah kee ah toe) Espresso topped with frothed milk.

Mâche A small, tender leafy green with a delicate taste.

Macédoine (mass e dwan) A mixture of vegetables or fruit, cut into small cubes.

Macérer (mass e ray) To macerate; to soak an element in alcohol in order to flavor it (usually done for pastry).

Magret (mah gray)
The boneless breast of the moulard duck.

Maillard Reaction A complex chemical reaction that occurs when heated proteins react with carbohydrate molecules, resulting in browning and flavor changes.

Main-Course Salad A large salad, served as a full meal, containing a substantial portion of protein.

Maître d'Hôtel Butter (may truh doh tell) Compound butter containing parsley and lemon juice.

Major Mineral Mineral that must be consumed in relatively large amounts—greater than 100 milligrams daily—such as calcium chloride, magnesium, phosphorus, sulfur, sodium, and potassium.

Mandoline (man do leen) A slicer with several blades that allow for various cuts and thicknesses of fruits and vegetables.

Marbling The fat deposited within muscle tissue.

Margarine A manufactured product made of vegetable or animal fats and intended to resemble butter in taste, texture, and appearance.

Marinate To soak a food in a seasoned liquid.

Marsala A flavorful sweet to semidry wine from Sicily.

Matignon (mah teen yohn) A type of mirepoix containing ham in addition the vegetables and moistened with Madeira. A matignon is usually cooked in butter before being used.

Maturity The age of an animal, a major consideration when selecting among classes of poultry.

Mayonnaise A semisolid cold sauce or dressing consisting of oil and vinegar emulsified with egg yolks.

Mayonnaise Chaud-Froid A mixture of aspic jelly and mayonnaise, used like regular chaud-froid.

Mealy Pie Dough Dough for which the fat is blended into the flour until the mixture looks like coarse cornmeal.

Médaillon (may die yohn) Medallion; round slice of meat, fowl, fish, or crustacean, served hot or cold.

Medium-Grain Rice Rice with small, short kernels that become sticky when cooked.

Meringue A foam made of beaten egg whites and sugar.

Meringue Glacée Baked meringue shells served with ice cream.

Mesclun A mixture of tender baby lettuces.

Meter The basic unit of length in the metric system; slightly longer than 1 yard.

Metric System An international system of measurement used in most countries outside of the United States.

Meunière Referring to fish prepared by dredging in flour and sautéing, served with brown butter, lemon juice, and parsley.

Microorganism A tiny, usually single-celled organism visible only through a microscope. Some types can contaminate food and cause disease.

Microwave Radiation generated in special ovens and used to cook or heat foods.

Mie de Pain (mee de pan) Fresh bread crumbs.

Milk Fat Fat content of milk. Also known as *butterfat*.

Millet A small, round, yellow grain high in protein that is an important food source in much of Africa and Asia.

Milli- Prefix in the metric system meaning "one-thousandth."

Mince To chop into very fine pieces.

Minestrone Italian vegetable soup.

Minimum Internal Cooking Temperature The lowest temperature to which a food item must be heated and at which it must be held for a given time in order to be considered safe.

Minimum-Use Ingredient Ingredient used in very small quantities in the preparation of an operation's menu.

Mirepoix (meer pwah) A mixture of rough-cut or diced vegetables, herbs, and spices, used for flavoring.

Mise en Place (meez on plahss) French term meaning "put in place" or "everything in place." The setup for food production. All the preparation and organization that must be achieved before actual production can begin.

Miso A paste made of fermented soybeans, sometimes with the addition of other grains. Also called *bean paste*.

Mocha (moh kah) (1) A variety of Arabian coffee. (2) A mixture of espresso and hot chocolate or cocoa. (3) A flavoring made of coffee and chocolate.

Modified Straight Dough Method Mixing method used for rich sweet doughs to ensure even distribution of fat and sugar in the dough.

Moist-Heat Methods Cooking methods in which heat is conducted to foods by water or other liquid or by steam.

Molded Cookies Cookies for which the dough is divided into equal portions and then molded into the desired shape.

Molecular Gastronomy The study of the chemical and physical processes that occur in cooking and the application of this science to food preparation. In general, a range of techniques used by avant-garde chefs.

Mollusks Soft-bodied sea animals, usually inside a pair of hinged shells, such as clam and oyster.

Monounsaturated Fat A type of fat, liquid at room temperature, typically found in olive oil and canola oil.

Monter (mohn tay) (1) To whisk (egg whites, cream) in order to incorporate air and increase volume. (2) To add butter to a sauce in small pieces.

Monter au Beurre (mohn tay oh burr) To finish a sauce or soup by swirling in raw butter until it is melted.

Morille (moh reey) Morel mushroom.

Mornay A sauce made of béchamel and Gruyère cheese.

Moulard A breed of duck with a thick, meaty breast, raised for its large, fatty liver.

Mousse A soft, creamy food, either sweet or savory, made light by the addition of whipped cream, beaten egg whites, or both.

Mousseline Forcemeat A forcemeat made of puréed fish, poultry, or meat, heavy cream, and, usually, egg whites.

Mozzarella A mild unripened cheese, used in pizzas and many other Italian-style dishes.

Muffin Method Mixing method in which combined liquid ingredients are mixed with combined dry ingredients; used for many muffins, other quick breads, and pancakes.

Multidecker Sandwich Sandwich made with more than two slices of bread.

N

à la Nage Literally, "swimming." A style of cooking and serving poached seafood and other items in their poaching liquids.

Nappé Having the proper texture in a sauce to lightly coat foods.

Napper (nap pay) To coat; to cover a food, savory, or sweet with a light layer of sauce, aspic, or jelly.

Natural Casing A sausage casing made from the intestines of meat animals.

Navarin A brown lamb stew.

New England Boiled Dinner A dish consisting of simmered corned beef and simmered vegetables, served together.

New Potato Immature potato with tender, thin skin, harvested while the plant top is still green.

Niçoise (nee swahz) (1) Prepared in the style of Nice, France. (2) Garnished with or containing tomato concassé cooked with garlic.

Nitrosamine A cancer-causing compound formed when meats containing sodium nitrate are subjected to high heat.

Noisette (nwah set) (1) Hazelnut. (2) Small, nut-size cuts made with a ball cutter. See also Beurre Noisette.

Nonfat Dry Milk Skim milk that has been dried to a powder.

Nouvelle Cuisine A modern style of cooking that emphasizes lightness of sauces and seasonings, shortened cooking times, and new and sometimes startling combinations of foods.

Nutrient Density The amount of nutrients per calorie in a food.

O

Oats Type of cereal grain that is most familiar in North America as a breakfast food.

Oblique Cut Diagonal cut used for long, cylindrical vegetables. Also called the *roll cut*.

Oeuf (euf) Egg.

Offal Variety meats.

Oie (wah) Goose.

Graisse d'Oie (gress dwah) Goose fat.

Oignon Brûlé (awn yohn broo lay) French for "burnt onion." A halved onion whose cut surface has been caramelized. Used to color stocks.

Oignon Piqué (awn yohn pee kay) An onion to which a bay leaf is fastened by piercing with a whole clove. Used to flavor simmering liquids.

Oil A fat that is normally liquid at room temperature.

Omega-3 Fatty Acid One of a family of essential unsaturated fatty acids that play vital roles in growth, in the immune system, in proper eyesight, and in cell structure. The family consists of three major nutrients: alpha-linoleic acid (ALA), docosahexaenoic acid (DHA), and eicosapentaenoic acid (EPA).

One-Stage Cooling Method A method for cooling hot foods to a safe, cold temperature within a limited time (no more than 4 hours).

One-Stage Method Method of mixing for low-moisture cookies, combining all ingredients in one step.

Oolong A greenish-brown, partially fermented tea.

Open-Faced Sandwich (Hot or Cold) Sandwich made with a single slice of bread and either hot or cold toppings.

Organic Grown or raised without chemical growth enhancers or medications or, for plants, without artificial fertilizers or pesticides.

Os (ohss) Bone.

Oven Spring The rapid rise of yeast goods in the oven due to the production and expansion of trapped gases as a result of the oven heat.

Over Easy Style of fried egg that is fried, flipped over, and cooked just until the white is set but the yolk is still liquid.

Over Hard Style of fried egg that is fried, flipped over, and cooked until the yolk is completely set.

Overhead Broiler A broiler that generates heat from above, with food items placed on a grate beneath the heat source.

Over Medium Style of fried egg that is fried, flipped over, and cooked until the yolk is partially set.

Overrun The increase in volume of ice cream or frozen desserts due to the incorporation of air while freezing.

Ovo-Vegetarian Referring to a vegarian diet that includes eggs in addition to plant products.

P

Paddle A flat-bladed mixer attachment used for general mixing.

Paner (pan ay) To coat a food with fresh or dry bread crumbs after dipping in an egg wash.

Pan Gravy A type of sauce made with the pan drippings of the meat or poultry it is served with.

Pan-Broil To cook uncovered in a sauté pan or skillet without fat.

Pan-Fry To cook in a moderate amount of fat in an uncovered pan.

Panini Plural of *panino*.

Panino (1) Originally, a small Italian sandwich made with a dinner roll. (2) A grilled sandwich usually made in a device that grills both sides at once while compressing the sandwich.

Panko (pahn ko) Coarse Japanese-style bread crumbs.

Pan-Smoking See Rangetop Smoke-Roasting.

Pan-Steaming Cooking (vegetables) in a small amount of water in a covered pan.

Papillote (pa pee yote) (1) Buttered or oiled paper, used to wrap fruits, meats, fish, etc., for cooking. (2) Paper frill used to decorate the ends of bones of certain poultry and meats.

en Papillote (on poppy yote) Wrapped in paper or foil for cooking so the food steams in its own moisture.

Parasite An organism that survives by living on or inside another organism, the host. It passes from one host organism to another as it completes its life cycle.

Parboil To cook partially in a boiling or simmering liquid.

Parboiled or Converted Rice Long-grain rice that is specially processed to provide higher vitamin and mineral content than regular milled white rice.

Parcook To partially cook by any method.

Parfait (1) A dessert consisting of alternating layers of ice cream and fruit or syrup in a tall, narrow glass. (2) A frozen dessert made of a sweet egg-yolk foam and whipped cream.

Parisienne Large spherical cuts made with a ball cutter.

Parmentier (par mawn tyay) Garnished with or containing potatoes.

Par Stock The inventory of goods an operation must have on hand to continue operating between deliveries.

Pasta General term for any shape of macaroni product or egg noodle.

Pasteurized Heat-treated to kill bacteria that might cause disease or spoilage.

Pastry Cream A thick custard sauce containing eggs and starch.

Pastry Flour Flour that is lower in gluten than bread flour but higher than cake flour; used for making pie and pastry doughs, quick breads, and other tender items.

Partridge A game bird usually weighing about 1 pound (500 g).

Pâte (paht) (1) Dough or batter. (2) Pasta. (French for "paste.")

Pâté (pah tay) A dish made of a baked forcemeat, usually in a crust.

Pâté Choux (pot a shoo) A soft dough used for making éclairs and cream puffs. Also called *éclair paste*.

Pâté Pâté Dough or pastry used to make a crust for pâté.

Pâté de Campagne A pâté or terrine characterized by a coarse texture.

Pâté en Croûte A pâté in a pastry crust.

Pathogen A bacteria microorganism that causes disease.

Pâtissier (pat tee see ay) Pastry chef.

Paysanne (pie zahn) In thin slices, roughly ½ × ½ × ⅛ inches (12 mm × 12 mm × 3 mm), round, square, or rectangular.

Peach Melba A sundae consisting of vanilla ice cream, a peach half, and Melba (raspberry) sauce.

Pear Belle Hélène Vanilla ice cream dessert topped with a poached or canned pear half, napped with chocolate sauce, and garnished with toasted almond slices.

Pearled Barley Type of barley that has been milled to remove the outer bran layers.

Persillade (pear see yahd) A mixture of bread crumbs, parsley, and garlic, used to coat roast meat items, usually lamb.

Pesco-Vegetarian Referring to a vegetarian diet that includes fish.

Pheasant Game bird with delicate, light-colored meat and a subtle flavor similar to that of chicken.

Philadelphia-Style Ice Cream Ice cream containing no eggs.

Physical Contamination The contamination of food with objects that may be nontoxic but may cause injury or discomfort.

Pigment Any substance that gives color to an item.

Pilaf Rice or other grain product that is first cooked in fat, then simmered in a stock or other liquid, usually with onions, seasonings, or other ingredients.

Pintade (pan todd) Guinea fowl.

Piquer (pee kay) (1) To pick; to lard a piece of meat, using a larding needle, in order to keep the meat from drying out during cooking. (2) To make small holes in dough, using a fork, to prevent it from rising too much.

Pizza A thin sheet of lean bread dough baked with a topping.

Pluche (ploosh) Sprig; small leaves picked off their stems (e.g., sprig of chervil).

Poach To cook gently in water or another liquid that is hot but not actually bubbling, 160° to 180°F (71° to 82°C).

Poêlé (pwah lay) (1) In classical cuisine, a type of roast or pot roast in which the item, usually poultry or white meat, is baked on a bed of matignon and basted with butter during cooking. (1) In modern French terminology, pan-fried.

Poissonier (pwah so nyay) Fish cook.

Polenta Italian-style cornmeal.

Polyunsaturated Fat Fat typically found in vegetable oils, such as corn oil, safflower oil, sunflower oil, and cottonseed oil; liquid at room temperature.

Portion Control The measurement of portions to ensure the correct amount of an item is served.

Portion-Controlled Cuts Ready-to-cook meats cut according to a customer's specifications.

Portion Cost Total cost of all the ingredients in a recipe divided by the number of portions served. Also called *raw food cost*.

Potage A general term for soup, though it is sometimes associated specifically with thick, hearty soups.

Potentially Hazardous Food A food that provides a good environment for the growth of hazardous bacteria.

Pot Roast A large cut of meat cooked by braising.

Poulet (poo lay) Chicken.

Poulette Allemande sauce flavored with mushrooms, parsley, and lemon juice.

Pour Batter A batter that is liquid enough to pour.

Poussin A young chicken weighing 1 pound (500 g) or less.

Pozole (poh soh leh) Whole-grain hominy.

Prague Powder #1 A blend of 6 percent sodium nitrite and 94 percent sodium chloride (table salt), used to cure meats; also called *curing salt* and *tinted curing mix*.

Prague Powder #2 A curing mixture similar to Prague Powder #1 but containing sodium nitrate in addition to sodium nitrite.

Praline (prah leen) Caramelized sugar with almonds or hazelnuts, ground to a smooth paste; used to flavor and decorate pastries.

Prawn Large shrimp or langoustine.

Pressure-Fry To deep-fry in a special covered fryer that traps the steam given off by the foods being cooked, increasing the pressure inside the kettle.

Primal Cuts One of the primary divisions of meat quarters, foresaddles, hindsaddles, and carcasses as they are broken down into smaller cuts.

Primary Flavor The basic flavor of a main ingredient of a dish; one of the components of a flavor profile.

Primeur (pree mur) Garnished with fresh spring vegetables such as carrots, turnips, green beans, peas, cauliflower, and small potatoes.

Princesse Garnished with asparagus.

Printanière (pran tawn yair) Garnished with fresh spring vegetables such as carrots, turnips, pearl onions, peas, green beans, and asparagus.

Prix Fixe (pree feex) French term meaning "fixed price"; referring to a menu offering a complete meal, with a choice of courses, for one given price.

Process Cheese A product made by grinding and melting one or more cheeses, blending them with other ingredients, and pouring the mixture into molds to solidify.

Professionalism An unwritten code of behavior and set of attitudes followed by the successful food-service employee.

Profiterole A tiny round pastry made from éclair paste, filled with savory fillings and served as an hors d'oeuvre or filled with ice cream and served as a dessert.

Progressive Grinding Process of grinding meat, starting with the largest die and continuing with the next smaller die, until the desired texture is achieved.

Proofing The process during which the volume of shaped dough increases due to fermentation.

Provençale (pro vawn sal) Garnished with or containing tomatoes, garlic, parsley, and, sometimes, mushrooms and olives.

Puff Pastry A light, flaky pastry made from a rolled-in dough and leavened by steam.

Pullman Loaf A long, rectangular loaf of bread.

Pumpernickel (1) Coarsely ground rye flour. (2) Bread made with this flour.

Punching A method of deflating dough by pulling up the dough on all sides, folding over the center, pressing down, and turning the dough upside down in the bowl. Also called *folding*.

Purée (1) A food product that has been mashed or strained to a smooth pulp. (2) To make such a pulp by mashing or straining a food.

Q

Quail A small game bird, now domestically raised, usually weighing 6 ounces (175 g) or less.

Quatre épices (kaht ray peace)

A spice mixture commonly used to season sausages and forcemeats; French for "four spices."

Quenelle (kuh nel) (1) Dumpling made of meat, poultry, or fish purée, mixed with egg white and cream. Usually molded with two spoons into an egg shape. (2) Oval three-sided shape made using two large spoons.

Quiche A savory tart or pie consisting of a custard baked in a pastry shell.

Quick Bread A bread leavened by chemical leaveners or steam rather than yeast.

Quinoa (keen wah) A tiny, ivory-colored, round grain native to the South American Andes, high in good-quality protein and lower in carbohydrates than other grains.

R

Radiation The transfer of energy by waves, such as infrared or light waves.

Rafraîchir (rah fray sheer) To refresh, to cool, to chill; to quickly cool in cold water a food that has been blanched.

Raft The coagulated clearmeat that forms when stock is clarified.

Rangetop Smoke-Roasting Procedure using wood chips in a closed container to create smoke and cook small, tender, quick-cooking items. Also called *pan-smoking*.

Râpé (rah pay) Grated.

Ratatouille (ra ta twee) A Southern French vegetable stew of onions, tomatoes, zucchini, eggplant, and green bell peppers.

Ratite A category of farm-raised birds including ostrich and emu.

Ravier (rahv yay) Oval relish dish.

Ravioli Dumplings consisting of filled egg noodles.

Recipe A set of instructions for producing a certain dish.

Reduce To cook by simmering or boiling until quantity is decreased; often done to concentrate flavors.

Reduction (1) A liquid concentrated by cooking it to evaporate part of the water. (2) The process of making such a liquid.

Regular Shortening Shortening with good creaming ability, which allows a large quantity of air to be mixed into the batter to give it lightness and leavening power.

Relish (1) A type of appetizer consisting of raw or pickled vegetables. (2) A mixture of chopped vegetables and, sometimes, fruits, at least one of which has been pickled in vinegar or a salt solution.

Remonter (re moan tay) To remount; to repair a sauce or a cream that has separated by returning it to its proper appearance and texture.

Remouillage (ray mwee yahzh) A stock made from bones that were already used once to make stock.

Rice Noodle Noodle made from rice flour or starch.

Rice Stick Another term for rice noodle.

Rice Vermicelli Fine, hairlike rice noodles often cooked by deep-frying them dry.

Ricotta An Italian-style cheese similar to cottage cheese but smoother, moister, and sweeter in flavor.

Rillettes (ree yet) A seasoned mixture of meat, such as pork, and fat, mashed to a paste; served as an appetizer.

Ring-Top Range A type of flattop that has removable rings, allowing access to more intense heat from the flames underneath.

Ripening Process that converts freshly made curds into distinctive, flavorful cheeses.

Risotto A moist Italian dish of rice cooked in butter and stock.

Rissolé (riss oh lay) Browned. Often referring to potatoes cut in small shapes, parboiled, and browned in hot fat.

Roast To cook foods by surrounding them with hot, dry air in an oven or on a spit over an open fire.

Roaster A young chicken of either sex, usually 3½–5 pounds (1.6–2.3 kg).

Rock Shrimp Small crustacean resembling shrimp, also referred to as *langoustine* or *langostino*.

Roe Fish eggs.

Rösti Potatoes Boiled potatoes that are grated, formed into small cakes, and pan-fried until crisp.

Rolled Cookies Cookies cut from a stiff rolled-out dough.

Rolled-In or Laminated Dough Dough into which a fat was incorporated in many layers by means of a rolling and folding procedure.

Rolled Oats Whole grains that have been steamed until soft and then flattened between rollers, which reduces their cooking time considerably.

Rondeau A round, broad, shallow, heavy-duty pot with straight sides, used for browning, braising, and stewing meats. Also called a *brazier*.

Rondelle (ron dell) A round or bias-round cut that varies in diameter and thickness.

Roquefort A blue-veined cheese made in Roquefort, France, from sheep's milk.

Rotisserie An item of cooking equipment that slowly rotates meat or other foods in front of a heating element.

Rôtisseur (ro tee sur) Cook who prepares roasted, braised, and broiled meats.

Rough Prep The preliminary processing of ingredients to the point at which they can be used in cooking.

Round Fish A round-shaped fish, such as cod and trout; distinct from flat fish, such as flounder.

Roux A cooked mixture of equal parts flour and fat.

Royal Icing An icing made of confectioners' sugar and egg whites, used for decorating.

Rubbed Dough Method Mixing method for pie doughs that requires fat to be rubbed into the sifted dry ingredients.

Russet Starchy potato often used for baking and deep-frying.

Rye Blend A mixture of rye flour and hard wheat flour.

S

Sabayon (sa ba yohn) A thick, frothy sauce, either sweet or savory, made by whisking egg yolks and liquid over low heat.

Sachet d'épices (sa shay day peace) A mixture of herbs and spices tied in a cheesecloth bag. Often called simply *sachet*.

Salamander Small broiler used primarily for browning or glazing the tops of certain items.

Salmonella A food-borne disease spread by improper food handling and inadequate sanitation.

Salsa The Spanish and Italian term for "sauce." A mixture of raw or cooked chopped vegetables, herbs, and, occasionally, fruits.

Sanitize To kill disease-causing bacteria, usually by means of heat or chemical disinfectants.

Saturated Fat A fat that is normally solid at room temperature.

Sauce A flavorful liquid, usually thickened, used to season, flavor, and enhance other foods.

Saucier (so see ay) Sauce cook; prepares sauces and stews and sautés foods to order.

Sauerbraten A German dish consisting of beef marinated in and then cooked with vinegar and other ingredients.

Sausage A mixture of ground meat, usually pork, and seasonings, usually stuffed into casings.

Sausage, Cured A sausage that contains nitrites or nitrates.

Sausage, Fresh A sausage that contains no nitrites or nitrates.

Sausage, Smoked A cured sausage that is hot smoked or cold smoked.

Sauté To cook quickly in a small amount of fat.

Sauteuse A slope-sided sauté pan.

Sautoir A straight-sided sauté pan.

Scampi A kind of shellfish similar to large shrimp. In the United States, the term is often used for large shrimp, especially if broiled with garlic butter.

Scorching The burning of milk due to the coagulation of proteins on the bottom of the pan.

Sear To brown the surface of a food quickly at high temperature.

Seasoning (1) Enhancing the natural flavor of a food without significantly changing its flavor. (2) Any ingredient, such as salt, used for this purpose.

Semolina A hard, high-protein flour often used for the best-quality macaroni products.

Separate-Course Salad A light salad, usually with delicate greens and light dressing, served after the main course.

Set Meal Service Service of a meal at which all customers eat at one time.

Seviche A preparation of raw seafood marinated in an acid mixture, which coagulates the protein so the texture of the raw fish resembles that of cooked fish. Also called *ceviche*, it is native to Latin America.

Shallow Poaching Poaching an item only partially submerged in the liquid.

Sheet Cookies Cookies for which the dough is spread out and baked in sheet pans and then cut into individual shapes.

Shell (Egg) The hard but fragile outer covering of an egg. Because it is porous, odors and flavors can be absorbed by the egg, which also loses moisture over time even when intact.

Shellfish Fish with external shells but without internal bone structure.

Sherbet Frozen dessert made from fruit juice, water, and sugar. It also may contain milk, cream, or egg whites.

Shirred Egg Egg baked in a shallow buttered dish.

Short Having a high fat content, which makes the product (such as a cookie or pastry) crumbly and tender.

Short Dough A kind of pastry or cookie dough that is richer than regular pie pastry and contains butter, sugar, and eggs.

Shortening (1) Any fat used in baking to tenderize the product by shortening gluten strands. (2) A white, tasteless, solid fat formulated for baking or deep-frying.

Short-Grain Rice Rice with small, round kernels that become sticky when cooked. It is used for rice pudding and rice molds as well as for making sushi and daily eating in Japanese cuisine.

Short-Order Cook The cook responsible for the preparation of foods that are quickly prepared to order during service time. May handle the broiler, deep fryer, griddle, sandwich production, and sautéed items.

Shred To cut into thin but irregular strips, either with the coarse blade of a grater or with a knife.

Sieve Size Size of individual pieces, usually of canned vegetables.

Silverskin A thin layer or sheet of connective tissue covering parts of some muscles.

Simmer To cook in water or other liquid that is bubbling gently, 185° to 200°F (85° to 93°C).

Simple Sandwich (Hot or Cold) Sandwich made with two slices of bread and either hot or cold fillings.

Simple Syrup A solution of equal weights of sugar and water.

Singer (san jay) To sprinkle with flour at the start of cooking in order to eventually give a certain consistency to the sauce.

Sirniki Russian pan-fried cheesecakes.

Skim (Nonfat) Milk Milk that has had all or nearly all of the fat removed.

Slurry A mixture of raw starch and cold liquid, used for thickening.

Small Sauce A sauce made by adding one or more ingredients to a leading sauce.

Smoke Point The temperature at which fats begin to deteriorate rapidly and smoke when heated.

Smoker An enclosure used for making hot-smoked and cold-smoked foods.

Smoke-Roast To cook with dry heat in the presence of wood smoke.

Soba Thin Japanese noodles made with buckwheat and wheat flour.

Sodium Nitrate A compound, $NaNO_3$, used to cure certain meats, especially air-dried meats.

Sodium Nitrite A compound, $NaNO_2$, used to cure meats.

Soft Meringue Meringue with a lower sugar content than hard meringue, typically used for pie topping.

Soft Pie Pie with custard-type filling, usually baked with a single crust.

Soft-Shell Crab A just-molted crab whose new shell has not yet hardened.

Solanine A poisonous substance found in potatoes that have turned green.

Soluble Fiber Fiber that absorbs water and forms a kind of gel. It is found inside and between plant cells.

Somen Thin, white Japanese noodles made from wheat flour and water, usually packed in small bundles.

Sorbet (sor bay) Sherbet, usually made without milk products.

Soufflé A light, fluffy baked egg dish consisting of a base (such as a heavy white sauce) mixed with egg yolks and flavoring ingredients into which beaten egg whites are folded just before baking. May be sweet or savory.

Sour Cream Cream that has been fermented or cultured by added lactic acid bacteria, making it thick and slightly tangy.

Sous Chef (soo shef) Cook who supervises food production and who reports to the executive chef.

Sous Vide (soo veed) French for "under vacuum"; a technique for cooking vacuum-packed foods at precise temperatures.

Soy Milk A liquid milk substitute made by soaking dried soybeans, grinding them with water, and finally straining the mixture.

Spaetzle Small dumplings or noodles made from a thin egg and flour batter.

Specialty Cheese Cheese in limited production, made with particular attention to natural flavor and texture profiles.

Spelt A type of wheat grain similar to farro.

Spice Any part of a plant, other than the leaves, used in flavoring foods.

Sponge Method (1) Bread-mixing method involving fermenting part of the flour and water before adding the remaining ingredients. (2) Cake-mixing method involving folding flour and other ingredients into an egg foam.

Spread The capacity of cookie dough to expand during baking.

Squab Young domestically raised pigeon.

Staling The change in texture and aroma of baked goods due to the loss of moisture by its starch granules.

Standard Breading Procedure The procedure for coating a food product with bread crumbs (or other crumbs or meal) by passing it through flour, then egg wash, then crumbs.

Standardized Recipe A set of instructions describing the way a particular establishment prepares a particular dish.

Staphylococcus, Staph A bacterium that causes food-borne disease by producing a toxin or poison in improperly stored foods.

Static Menu A menu that offers the same dishes every day.

Station Chef Cook in charge of a particular department in a kitchen or food production facility.

Steam To cook by direct contact with steam.

Steel-Cut Oats Whole-grain oats cut into small pieces; usually cooked as porridge.

Stew (1) To simmer a food or foods in a small amount of liquid that is usually served with the food as a sauce. (2) A dish cooked by stewing, usually one whose main ingredients are cut in small pieces.

Stewing Cooking small pieces of meat by simmering or braising.

Still-Frozen Frozen without being churned in an ice-cream freezer.

Stock A clear, thin—that is, unthickened—liquid flavored with soluble substances extracted from meat, poultry, or fish, their bones, and vegetables and seasonings.

Straight Dough Method Bread-mixing method involving mixing all ingredients, including presoaked yeast, in one step.

Strength of Acidity The acetic acid content of vinegar, which determines the tartness of vinegar and of dressings made from it.

Streusel (stroy zel) A crumbly topping for baked goods, consisting of fat, sugar, and flour rubbed together.

Strong Flour   Flour with a high protein or gluten content.

Submersion Method   Method by which fish and other items are cooked completely submerged in court bouillon.

Sucrose   Chemical name for the sugar that constitutes table sugar.

Suer (soo ay)   To sweat; to gently cook vegetables in a little fat, without coloring them, in order to bring out their flavor.

Sundae   Dessert consisting of one or more scoops of ice cream or sherbet in a dish or glass, topped with syrups, fruits, toppings, and garnishes.

Sunny Side Up   Style of fried egg that is cooked slowly without flipping until the white is completely set but the yolk is still soft and yellow.

Supporting Flavor   Flavors of seasoning and flavoring ingredients and other secondary ingredients of a dish; flavors that support and enhance the primary flavors.

Suprême (soo prem)   (1) The breast part of the fowl. (2) A filet of fish.

Suprême Sauce   A sauce made of chicken velouté and heavy cream.

Surimi   A processed seafood product manufactured to resemble shellfish such as crab.

Sushi   A seasoned Japanese short-grain rice that is often, but not always, garnished with raw fish.

Sweat   To cook in a small amount of fat over low heat, sometimes covered.

Sweetbreads   The thymus glands of calves and young animals, used as food.

Sweet or Unsalted Butter   Butter that contains no salt. It has a fresher, sweeter taste than salted butter and is more perishable as well.

Swiss Meringue   Meringue made from egg whites and sugar warmed over a double boiler while beating.

Swiss Steak   Beef round steaks braised in brown sauce.

T

Table d'Hôte (tobble dote)   (1) Referring to a fixed-price menu with no choices. (2) Referring to a menu on which prices are listed for complete meals rather than for each separate item.

Tagine (tah zheen)   A spiced stew from North Africa, originally made in an earthenware dish with a conical lid; the dish is also called a *tagine*.

Tamis   A drum sieve, consisting of a screen mesh in a round metal or wood frame.

Tamiser (tah mee zay)   To sift; to press through a fine drum sieve.

Tang   The portion of a metal knife blade that is inside the handle.

Tapa   Any of a variety of Spanish-style appetizers, intended to be served with wine or other drinks.

Tapenade (ta peh nahd)   Purée of black olives, anchovies, and olive oil.

Tasting Menu   A type of fixed-price menu designed to showcase the chef's art by presenting a series of small courses.

Tatsoi   A leafy vegetable or salad green related to mustard and watercress.

Tea Sandwich   Any small, fancy sandwich generally made from light, delicate ingredients and bread trimmed of the crust.

Tempeh   A fermented soy product with a dense, meaty texture.

Temper   To raise the temperature of a cold liquid gradually by slowly stirring in a hot liquid.

Temporary Emulsion   An unstable emulsion whose components will eventually separate.

Teriyaki   A grilled or pan-broiled food finished with a soy sauce–based glaze.

Terrine (tare reen)   (1) A deep rectangular mold, traditionally made of white porcelain, used to cook seasoned ground meats, fish, or poultry. (2) The food cooked in such a mold.

Textured Vegetable Protein (TVP)   A high-protein product made from defatted soy flour, processed to give it a spongelike texture; it is available unflavored or flavored to resemble various meats.

Timbale (tam ball)   (1) A mold in the shape of a large thimble. (2) Type of dough shaped as a container, baked, and filled with various foods.

Tinted Curing Mix (TCM)   See Prague Powder #1.

Tofu   A bland, white food made by coagulating soy milk. Also called *bean curd*.

Tomalley   The liver of lobsters and some other shellfish.

Tournant (toor nawn)   Cook who replaces other station cooks; relief cook or swing cook.

Tourné   To cut a vegetable into a neat seven-sided oval shape.

Tournedos (toor nuh doe)   A small beef steak cut from the tenderloin.

Tourner (tour nay)   Literally, "to turn." (1) To give certain vegetables a regular long shape, using a knife (see Tourné). (2) To mix ingredients using a circular motion.

Toxin-Mediated Infection   An infection that occurs when pathogens enter the body and multiply, producing toxins in the body.

Trace Mineral   An essential mineral nutrient that must be consumed in small amounts—less than 100 milligrams daily—such as chromium, copper, fluoride, iodine, iron, manganese, molybdenum, selenium, and zinc.

Trans Fat   A solid fat, usually manufactured by hydrogenation, that limits the body's ability to rid itself of cholesterol.

Treviso   A red-leafed relative of radicchio and Belgian endive with elongated leaves.

Trichinosis   A food-borne disease caused by a parasite sometimes found in undercooked pork.

Tripe   The muscular stomach lining of beef or other meat animals.

Triple-Crème Cheese   A very rich cheese with at least 75 percent fat, dry weight.

Triticale   A high-protein hybrid of wheat and rye with a nutty, sweet flavor.

Truffer (troo fay)   (1) To add chopped truffles to a dish, stuffing, or foie gras. (2) To slide a thin slice of truffle under the skin of poultry.

Truite au Bleu   Poached trout that was alive until cooking time and that turns blue when cooked in court bouillon.

Trunnion Kettle   Steam-jacketed kettle that can be tilted for emptying.

Trussing   Tying poultry into a compact shape for cooking.

Tunneling   A condition of muffin products characterized by large, elongated holes; caused by overmixing.

Turban (toor bahn)   (1) A type of ring mold. (2) Food prepared in such a mold.

TVP   See Textured Vegetable Protein.

Two-Stage Cooling Method   A method for cooling hot foods to a safe, cold temperature within two consecutive periods totaling no more than 6 hours.

Two-Stage Method   Mixing method for high-fat, high-ratio cakes using emulsified shortening; it requires the addition of liquids in two stages.

U

Udon   Thick white Japanese noodles made from wheat flour.

Ultra-High-Temperature (UHT) Pasteurization
Process by which a product is heated at a temperature higher than for ultra-pasteurized products. The resulting product is packaged in shelf-stable, sterile cartons.

Ultra-Pasteurized   Describes a product whose shelf life has been expanded through heating at a much higher temperature than for normal pasteurization. This process destroys nearly all organisms that cause spoilage.

Umami Known as the *fifth taste*, often described as the perception of meatiness.

Univalve A mollusk with a single shell, such as abalone.

Unsalted Butter See Sweet or Unsalted Butter.

Unsaturated Fat A fat that is normally liquid at room temperature.

V

Vapeur (va purr) Steam.

Variety Meats Organs, glands, and other meats that don't form a part of the dressed carcass.

Vegan Referring to a vegetarian diet that omits all animal products, including dairy products and eggs.

Vegetable Salad A salad containing vegetables other than lettuce or other leafy greens as its main ingredients.

Vegetable Soup A clear, seasoned stock or broth with the addition of one or more vegetables. Meat or poultry products and starches are sometimes also added.

Vegetarian Referring to a diet consisting entirely or mostly of foods derived from plants.

Velouté A sauce made by thickening white stock with a roux.

Venison The meat of wild or farm-raised deer.

Venting Allowing circulation or escape of a liquid or gas, such as by setting a pot of hot stock on blocks in a cold-water bath so the cold water can circulate around the pot.

Viande (vee awnd) French for "meat."

Vichyssoise (vee she swahz) Cold purée of leek and potato soup with cream.

Vin Wine.

Vin Blanc White wine.

Vin Rouge Red wine.

Vinaigre (vee negre) Vinegar.

Vinaigrette Dressing or sauce made of oil, vinegar, and flavoring ingredients.

Vitamin Any of a group of compounds that are present in foods in very small quantities and that are necessary for regulating body functions.

Volaille (voe lye) Poultry.

Blanc de Volaille (blahn duh voe lye) Chicken breast.

Cuisse de Volaille (kweese duh voe lye) Chicken leg.

Volatile Evaporating quickly when heated.

W

Wash (1) To brush or coat a food item with a liquid such as egg wash or milk. (2) The liquid used in this procedure.

Water Activity (a_w) Measured by the availability of water to bacteria. The scale runs for 0 (no water available) to 1.0.

Water Ice See Ice.

Waxy Potato A young potato high in sugar and low in starch.

Weak Flour Flour with a low protein or gluten content.

Well-Mixing Method Mixing method wherein a well is made in the dry ingredients so the liquid ingredients, when poured into it, are confined.

Welsh Rabbit A dish made of melted cheddar cheese and, usually, ale or beer. Sometimes called *Welsh rarebit*.

Wheatberry The whole wheat grain without the hull.

Whipping Cream Fresh cream with a fat content of 30 percent or more that can be whipped into a foam.

White The part of an egg that is clear and soluble when raw but white and firm when coagulated. It consists primarily of albumin protein and also contains sulfur.

White Pekin The most common breed of domestic duck in the United States.

White Roux Roux cooked for a just few minutes, just enough to cook out the raw taste. It is made from butter and flour and is used for béchamel and other white sauces based on milk.

Whitewash A thin mixture or slurry of flour and cold water.

Whole Milk Fresh milk as it comes from the cow with nothing removed or added, usually containing about 3½ percent milk fat.

Whole Wheat Flour Flour made by grinding the entire wheat kernel, including the bran and germ.

Wild Rice Not a rice but rather the seed of an unrelated grass native to the northern United States and Canada. Scarce and expensive, it has long, slender, hard, dark brown grains with a distinctive nutty flavor.

Winterized Oil Vegetable oil that stays clear and liquid when refrigerated.

Wire Whip A hand tool or mixer attachment used for whipping tasks, such as beating cream and eggs and making mayonnaise.

Working Chef The cook in charge of operations of a kitchen not large enough to have an executive chef. May work one or more production stations.

Wrap A sandwich in which the filling is wrapped, like a Mexican burrito, in a large flour tortilla or similar flatbread.

Y

Yield (1) The amount of usable meat in proportion to fat. (2) The edible amount remaining after trimming any food. (3) The total quantity of food produced using a given recipe.

Yield Grade The designation of the quality of meat according to the amount of usable meat in proportion to fat.

Yield Test A test to determine the cost per unit of weight of meat after trimming and boning.

Yogurt Milk cultured by special bacteria and having a custardlike consistency.

Yolk The yellow part of the egg; it has a high fat and protein content and contains iron and several vitamins.

Z

Zest The colored part of the peel of citrus fruits.

Zester (zes tay) To zest; to remove the colored part of the skin of a citrus fruit (e.g., orange, lemon).

Subject Index

Recipe Index